EIGHTH EDITION

THE **THEORY OF CATERING**

Ronald Kinton BEd (Hons), FHCIMA
Formerly of Garnett College, College of Education
for Teachers in Further and Higher Education

Victor Ceserani MBE, CPA, MBA, FHCIMA
Formerly Head of The School of Hotelkeeping and Catering,
Ealing College of Higher Education(now Thames Valley University)

Professor David Foskett BEd (Hons), FHCIMA
Programmes Manager, School of Hospitality Studies,
Thames Valley University

Hodder & Stoughton

A MEMBER OF THE HODDER HEADLINE GROUP

British Library Cataloguing-in-Publication Data

Ceserani, V.
    The theory of catering – 8th ed.
    I. Title   II. Kinton, R.   III. Foskett, D.
    647.95
    ISBN 0–340–630744

First published 1964
Second edition 1970
Third edition 1973
Fourth edition 1978
Fifth edition 1984
Sixth edition 1989
Seventh edition 1992
Eighth edition 1995

Impression number   10   9   8   7   6   5   4   3   2   1
Year   1999   1998   1997   1996   1995

Typeset by Wearset, Boldon, Tyne and Wear.
Printed in Great Britain for Hodder & Stoughton Educational,
a division of Hodder Headline plc, 338 Euston Road,
London NW1 3BH by Butler & Tanner Ltd, Frome.

Contents

INTRODUCTION TO THE EIGHTH EDITION

This book is designed to meet the needs of all those involved in the catering industry, particularly students on the many catering courses. In it we emphasise the importance of understanding the relationship between theoretical knowledge and practical experience.

The eighth edition has been revised and updated to keep in line with the continuing changes both in the industry and in catering education. When using this book refer also to appropriate information which may be found in the different chapters, such as food commodities and nutrition and food science.

As in previous editions we have not attempted to write a completely comprehensive book, but rather have set out an outline as a basis for further study. In this way we hope to assist students at all levels and, for those who wish to study at greater depth, further references are suggested where appropriate. To assist students in their learning and to help them test their knowledge we recommend the use of the companion book *Questions and Answers on the Theory of Catering*.

ABOUT THE AUTHORS

Ronald Kinton trained at Westminster Technical College and was employed as a chef at the head offices of ICI Ltd and at the Waldorf Hotel and Claridges. He was formerly Senior Lecturer at the School of Hotelkeeping and Catering, Ealing College of Higher Education (now Thames Valley University), where he taught for fifteen years. He subsequently taught at Garnett College, the College of Education (Technical) concerned with the training of catering teachers (now part of Greenwich University). He obtained a BEd Honours degree, in which his special studies related to catering education.

Victor Ceserani was apprentice chef at the Ritz Hotel, commis chef at the Orleans Club and chef at Boodles, all rightly renowned for the excellence of their cuisine. He was formerly Head of Department, School of Hotelkeeping and Catering, at Ealing College of Higher Education (now Thames Valley University), and has been an examiner for City and Guilds Advanced Cookery (706/3). He is a well-known judge at national food and cookery competitions and is currently a Fellow of the HCIMA, Honorary Member of the City and Guilds of London Institute, Honorary Fellow of Thames Valley University, Honorary Member of the Restaurateurs' Association of Great Britain, Honorary Member of The Chefs and Cooks Circle, Honorary Member of the Association Culinaire Française and Honorary Member of the Académie Culinaire de France.

David Foskett is Programmes Manager, School of Hospitality Studies, Thames Valley University. He was Director of Hospitality, Education and Training at the Polytechnic of West London. He has worked at the Dorchester and Savoy hotels and in industry at the head office of BP, and has also been employed as a chef technologist in test kitchens for food manufacturers.

ACKNOWLEDGEMENTS

The authors and publishers gratefully acknowledge the contribution of the following people and organisations: Gardner Merchant; British Gas; Michael Harrison, Electricity Association; Sea Fish Industry Authority; Coffee Information Service; British Egg Information Service; National Dairy Council's Dairy Product Advisory Service; National Association of Catering Butchers; Energy Efficiency Office; Refrigeration and Unit Air-Conditioning Group; Mrs F. Cable, Principal Lecturer, TVU, for the chapters on Hygiene and Nutrition; Robert Wellman, Richmond-upon-Thames College, for the chapter on Water; Sutton District Water plc; Paul Hambleton, Teaching and Resources Manager, TVU, for his contribution on the use of computers in catering; and the Institute of Environmental Health Officers.

The publishers would also like to thank the following for permission to include copyright material and photographs:

For Copyright colour plates: Anthony Blake Photo Library, pl. 7, 8, 86, 91, 92, 94, 95; British Airways, pl. 130; British Gas, pl. 1, 2, 4; Caterer and Hotelkeeper, pl. 5; Chubb Fire Ltd, pl. 131–2; Comark Ltd, pl. 106–109; Cookshack, pl. 97; Ken Crook, pl. 89, 119; Drywite Ltd, pl. 127; Edwardian Hotels, pl. 110, 111, 126; Food From Spain, pl. 85; Forte Restaurants, pl. 98–9; Foster Refrigerator (UK) Ltd, pl. 114, 124; Gardner Merchant Ltd, pl. 3, 112; Health Education Authority, pl. 6; Hobart Still, pl. 123; Hospitality Magazine, pl. 118; Meat and Livestock Commission/National Association of Catering Butchers/Mr John Stone, pl. 10–57; Merrychef Ltd, pl. 121; Multivac UK Ltd, pl. 129; National Dairy Council, pl. 87; The Ritz Hotel, Picadilly, London, pl. 100; Robot Coupe (UK) Ltd, pl. 122; Val Sassoon/Burnett Associates, London, pl. 96; Showcard Systems, pl. 113, 116–7; Stacarac(UK) Ltd, pl. 105; Zanussi CLV Systems Ltd, pl. 115.

For Copyright black and white figures: The Automatic Vending Association of Britain, fig. 9.2; Braebourne Spring Ltd, fig. 10.7; Jennifer Brennan from 'Cuisine of Asia', fig. 3.2; British Gas, fig. 12.4–8; Buderus Kuchentechnik GmbH, fig. 11.2–3; Caterer and Hotelkeeper, fig. 1.4, 3.2, 10.2 (by Stuart Knight, sponsored by TICC), 10.7–8, 16.9, 16.11, 17.1; Catering Management and Dawsons, fig. 16.7; Chubb Fire Ltd, fig. 15.8; Cona Group, fig. 11.25; Corporation of London, fig. 4.1, 4.9; John Crocker, fig. 11.26–31; Crypto-Peerless Ltd, fig. 11.20; Dualit Ltd, fig. 11.25; Electricity Association, fig. 4.11, 11.4, 11.13, 11.19–20, 12.17; Excel Equipment Ltd, fig. 12.10; Falcon Catering Equipment Ltd, fig. 11.8a, 11.15–16, 12.9; Food (and other) Matters, fig. 4.10; Foster Refrigerator (UK) Ltd, fig. 13.4, 13.6–7, 13.11; Garland Catering Equipment Ltd, fig. 11.15; Highfield Publications, fig. 16.14; Hobart Still, p. 167, p. 349, 11.18; Insect-o-Cutor Ltd, fig. 16.22; Peter Jordan/Network, p. 507; Lcynse/Rea, Katz Pictures, p. 11; Macdonald and company (Publishers), fig. 16.1; Merrychef Ltd, fig. 11.5; The PKL Group (UK) Ltd, fig. 1.5a–b; Ted Poole, The College, Swindon, fig. 15.4; The Portman Intercontinental Hotel, fig. 5.10; Rentokil Ltd, fig. 16.19; Rotalux International Ltd, fig. 16.2; Simply Sausages, fig. 6.4; Stangard Induction, fig. 11.6; Stott Benham, fig. 11.6, 11.12;

Thomson Regional Newspapers, fig. 10.14; Tucker Burnguard, fig. 15.3; XI Data Systems, fig. 14.1–2; Zanussi CLV Systems Ltd, fig. 11.9–10, 11.13.

The authors and publishers would particularly like to thank Claridge's Hotel for the use of their facilities, and chef Marjan Lesnik and his team for producing the food. Also thanks to Roddy Paine for his photography.

Every effort has been made to trace copyright holders of material reproduced in this book. Any rights not acknowledged here will be acknowledged in subsequent printings if notice is given to the publisher.

Cover illustrations: the publishers thank the suppliers of copyright photographs: Chubb Fire Limited, Hobart Still, Robert Harding Picture Library, Derek Berwin/ The Image Bank.

Part
1

THE CATERING INDUSTRY

Introduction to the catering industry

DEFINITION OF THE CATERING INDUSTRY

The catering industry which is sometimes referred to as the hospitality industry provides food, drink and, in certain sections, accommodation for people at school, in hospital, at work and at leisure.

Economics

Because of a steady growth in the standard of living, an increasing number of people take more holidays and eat away from home. As a result the catering industry has grown steadily since the 1950s. It is one of the largest employers, one of the biggest industries in the country and makes a major contribution to the gross national product; in consequence, it is considered one of the country's most important industries.

Function

The function of the catering industry is to provide food, drink and accommodation at any time of the day or night for people of all ages, races, creeds and from all walks of life.

Consumer demand

Because it is a service industry, caterers must, at all times, be concerned and seek to identify and meet customer requirements. Business and leisure travel is continually increasing and more overseas visitors from a wide variety of countries spend time here. Different races and creeds may have social and religious requirements that are reflected in the request for certain foods or dishes.

One thing is common to all – **the need for food to be cooked and served well**. Certain groups of people, however, have special food requirements; for example, some old people, due to poor digestion and because they may have dentures, require foods that are easily digested and need little chewing. Likewise when young people are catered for, it is particularly important to consider the nutritional needs of those who are still growing. An adequate supply of protein and calcium is essential.

In a world of increased travel and better communications, it is increasingly important to be aware of the social and religious requirements of others. Social customs involving the use of certain foods or dishes often originated because of religious events such as fasts or feasts. Many of the traditional observances are declining and the origins forgotten. Fish on Friday and pancakes on Shrove Tuesday have less significance today. This is not only because of the changing influence of religion, social attitudes and customs, but also because of increased use of technology: perishable foods, for example, are now refrigerated and fish does not have to be dried and salted to meet religious demands.

The geographical situation dictates what constitutes a national diet. In certain areas of the world, rice will be commonplace, in other areas yams or sweet potatoes, and elsewhere wheat. Nationals from other countries should be considered so that the foods they require are available to them.

People restrict themselves to a vegetarian diet on religious grounds, for ethical reasons (because they consider eating meat morally wrong) or because they are concerned with their physical well-being. The provision of vegetarian foods should be available for those preferring them.

An awareness of people's food needs and how to meet them is the responsibility of those employed in the catering industry.

TYPES OF CATERING ESTABLISHMENTS

Students need to be aware of the scope for employment in the industry, and should realise both the social and economic importance of the industry. The economic health of a nation is reflected by the food served in the home and in the eating establishments of the country. With full employment, businesses boom; with the expansion of overseas tourism, the catering industry also expands. Initial employment is usually in one of four areas: food preparation, food services, housekeeping or reception.

The UK needs an industry capable of contributing to the stability of the national economy, therefore all aspects of the catering industry have an important part to play.

The various types of catering establishments are listed in the table below.

VARIOUS TYPES OF CATERING ESTABLISHMENTS

HOTELS AND RESTAURANTS	WELFARE AND INDUSTRIAL	TRANSPORT	OTHER ASPECTS
hotels/motels	hospitals	railways	contracts
restaurants	nursing homes	motorways	outdoor
cafés	residential establishments, e.g.	airlines	Services
clubs	schools and colleges	ferries, cruise	Navy
public houses	halls of residence	ships etc.	Army
wine bars	hostels		Air Force
speciality restaurants	old people's homes		police
fast foods	workers in industry and		prisons
take-aways	commerce		
departmental stores			
chainstore cafeterias			
ethnic			

Commercial catering

HOTELS AND RESTAURANTS

The great variety of hotels and restaurants can be demonstrated by comparing the palatial, first-class luxury hotel with the small hotel owned and run as a family concern. With restaurants, a similar comparison may be made between the exclusive top-class restaurant and the small one which may just serve a few lunches.

Hotels are residential and most of them will provide breakfasts, lunches, teas, dinners and snacks. In some hotels, conferences and banquets will be an important part of the business.

Restaurants will vary with the kind of meals they serve. Some will serve all types of meals whilst others will just serve lunch and dinner or lunch and tea. Again, banqueting may form an important part of the restaurant's service.

In some cases special types of meal service, such as grill rooms or speciality restaurants, may limit the type of foods served – e.g. smörgasbord or steaks will be provided.

WINE BARS, FAST FOODS, TAKE-AWAY

Customer demand has resulted in the rapid growth of a variety of establishments offering a limited choice of popular foods at a reasonable price, with little or no waiting time, to be consumed either on the premises or taken away.

CLUBS

These are usually administered by a secretary or manager appointed by a management committee formed from club members. Good food and drink with an informal service in the old English style are required in most clubs, particularly in the St James's area of London.

Night clubs and casinos usually have the type of service associated with the restaurant trade.

CHAIN-CATERING ORGANISATIONS

There are many establishments with chains spread over wide areas and in some cases overseas. Prospects for promotion and opportunities are often considerable, whether it is in a chain of hotels or restaurants. These are the well-known hotel companies, restaurant chains, the popular type of restaurant, chain stores and the shops with restaurants, which often serve lunches, teas and morning coffee, and have snack bars and cafeterias.

LICENSED-HOUSE (PUB) CATERING (see Figure 1.1)

There are approximately 70 000 licensed houses in England and Wales and almost all of them offer food in some form or another. To many people the food served in public houses is ideal for what they want, that is, often simple, moderate in price and quickly served in a congenial atmosphere.

There is great variety in public-house catering, from the ham and cheese roll operation to the exclusive à la carte restaurant. Public-house catering can be divided into four categories:

Fig. 1.1   Licensed house (pub) catering

- the luxury-type restaurant;
- the speciality restaurant, e.g. steak bar, fish restaurant; carvery, theme;
- fork dishes served from the bar counter where the food is consumed in the normal drinking areas;
- finger snacks, e.g. rolls, sandwiches.

Welfare catering

The fundamental difference between welfare catering and the catering of hotels and restaurants is that the hotel or restaurant is run to make a profit and provide a service. The aim of welfare catering is to minimise cost by achieving maximum efficiency. The standards of cooking should be equally good, though the types of menu may be different.

HOSPITAL CATERING (see Plates 1 to 3, pages 34, 35)

Hospital catering is classified as welfare catering, the object being to assist the nursing staff to get the patient well as soon as possible. To do this it is necessary to provide good quality food which has been carefully prepared and cooked to retain the maximum nutritional value, and presented to the patient in an appetising manner.

It is recognised that the provision of an adequate diet is just as much a part of the patient's treatment as careful nursing and skilled medical attention. Within the health service approximately two million meals are served every 24 hours and the number served in one establishment can vary from 20 to 2000 people. In nearly all hospitals patients are provided with a menu choice (see the following table on pages 16–17 and Figure 1.2). The staff in the hospital catering service are organised as follows:

- **Catering managers** plan menus, obtain supplies and supervise the preparation, cooking and service of the meals, and are also responsible for training and safety. They visit the wards to advise on the service of food to the patients, and control the provision of the catering facilities for the doctors, nurses and other hospital employees.
- **Assistant catering managers** assist and deputise for the catering managers with all or part of their duties, or they may be responsible for a small hospital.

HOSPITAL MENU FOR ONE WEEK: LUNCHES FOR PATIENTS AND STAFF (P/S)

TUESDAY	WEDNESDAY	THURSDAY	FRIDAY	SATURDAY	SUNDAY	MONDAY
Home-made vegetable soup	Home-made potato and leek soup	Home-made Scotch broth	Home-made spiced lentil soup	Minestrone soup	Scotch broth	Home-made carrot and onion soup
Chicken Maryland (S)	Cottage pie (P/S)	Roast leg of pork and apple sauce (P/S)	Fried haddock (S)	Shepherd's pie (P/S)	Roast beef, Yorkshire pudding and horseradish sauce (P/S)	Gammon and pineapple (P/S)
Roast chicken (P)	Wholemeal pizza (P/S)	Cauliflower cheese (P/S)	Grilled plaice (P)	Sweetcorn and mushroom vol-au-vent (P/S)	Macaroni cheese (P/S)	Mild vegetable curry and boiled rice
Courgette and mushroom pasta bake (P/S)	Toad in the hole (S)	Mild chicken curry and rice (S)	Home-made vegetable pie (P/S)	Scotch egg salad	Tuna fish salad	Lasagne (S)
Bacon roll and tomato sauce (S)	Ham and peach salad	Corned beef salad	Chilli con carne and boiled rice (S)	Parsley potatoes	Roast potatoes	Cold meat and salad
Edam cheese salad	Jacket potatoes	Roast potates	Sardine and egg salad	Creamed potatoes	Creamed potatoes	Sauté potatoes
Chipped potatoes	Creamed potatoes	Creamed potatoes	Chipped potatoes	Courgettes	Sprouts	Creamed potatoes
Creamed potatoes	Baby carrots	Diced swede	Creamed potatoes	Side salad	Peas	Diced carrots
Cabbage	Spinach	Broccoli	Peas	Steamed jam pudding and custard	Apple and blackberry pie and custard	Broad beans
Peas	Baked beans (S)	Wholemeal apple crumble and custard	Cauliflower	Fruit yoghurt	Ice-cream	Semolina and jam
Wholemeal raspberry and apple pie and custard	Bread pudding and custard	Strawberry whip	Spotted Dick and custard	Dessert banana	Dessert apple	Pear Condé
Ice-cream	Fruit yogurt	Dessert orange	Fruit jelly			Dessert orange
Dessert banana	Dessert apple		Dessert apple			

SUPPERS

TUESDAY	WEDNESDAY	THURSDAY	FRIDAY	SATURDAY	SUNDAY	MONDAY
Home-made vegetable soup	Home-made potato and leek soup	Home-made Scotch broth	Home-made spiced lentil soup	Minestrone soup	Scotch broth	Home-made carrot and onion soup
Home-made Cornish pasty (P/S)	Cod Portugaise (P/S)	London pie (P/S)	Sausage and egg pie and tomato sauce (P/S)	Breaded plaice fillet (P/S)	Chicken pilaff and curry sauce (P/S)	Quiche Lorraine (P/S)
Stuffed tomatoes (P/S)	Baked jacket potato with cheese (P/S)	Fish fingers (P/S)	Celery and ham au gratin (P/S)	Beef curry and boiled rice (P/S)	Fish cakes (P/S)	Savoury mince (P/S)
Liver sausage and lettuce sandwich	Corned beef and tomato sandwich	Cheese and chutney sandwich	Tuna fish and cucumber sandwich	Salad sandwich	Egg and cress sandwich	Cream cheese and cucumber sandwich
Jacket potatoes	Parsley potatoes	Creamed potatoes	Creamed potatoes	Chipped potatoes	Parsley potatoes	Jacket potatoes
Side salad	Side salad	Side salad	Side salad	Side salad	Side salad	Side salad
Courgettes	Mixed vegetables	Baked beans	Sweetcorn	Mixed vegetables	Runner beans	Spinach
Chocolate blancmange	Pineapple whip	Créme caramel	Milk jelly	Cheesecake	Fruit salad	Apricot fool
Ice-cream	Ice-cream	Ice-cream	Ice-cream	Ice-cream	Ice-cream	Ice-cream
Cheese and biscuits	Cheese and biscuits	Cheese and biscuits	Cheese and biscuits	Cheese and biscuits	Cheese and biscuits	Cheese and biscuits

- **Kitchen superintendents** are responsible to the catering manager or the assistant catering manager for the running of one or more hospital kitchens.
- **Cooks** are graded: 1. assistant cook, 2. assistant head cook, 3. head cook. The head cook would be in charge of a kitchen under the control of the kitchen superintendent or catering manager.
- **Dining room supervisors** are in charge of the staff during meal service and they are responsible to the catering manager.

Many hospitals are managed by Trust Boards, some of which have chosen to appoint a **Hotel Services Manager**, who has responsibility for the management of catering, domestic, portering and other services.

People interested in being of service to the community and gaining job satisfaction could find this aspect of catering rewarding. Conditions, hours of work and pay as well as promotion prospects are factors which contribute to making this a worthwhile career.

Dieticians

In many hospitals a qualified dietician is responsible for:

- collaborating with the catering manager on the planning of meals;
- drawing up and supervising special diets;
- instructing diet cooks on the preparation of special dishes;
- advising the catering manager and assisting in the training of cooks with regard to nutritional aspects;
- advising patients.

In some hospitals the food will be prepared in a diet bay by diet cooks.

Diets

Information about the type of meal or diet to be given to each patient is supplied daily to the kitchen. The information will give the number of full, light, fluid and special diets, and with each special diet will be given the name of the patient and the type of diet required.

The main hospital kitchen

All food, except diets and food cooked in the ward kitchens, is cooked in the main kitchen. In this kitchen all meals for patients, doctors, nurses, clerical and maintenance staff are prepared. In hospitals where a canteen is provided for out-patients and visitors this will come under the control of the catering officer.

Hospital routine

Hospital catering has its own problems, which often make it very difficult to provide correctly served meals. Wards are sometimes spread over a wide area, and, in a large hospital where there are long distances for the food to travel, provision of modern trolleys is essential to keep the food hot.

The routine of a hospital is strictly timed and meals have to fit in with the duties of the nursing staff.

The cost-effectiveness of hospital catering is tested by inviting tenders from commercial contractors who compete with the in-house catering team in each hospital. Most contracts have been awarded in-house.

The amount of money the catering manager has to spend on food, drink and labour is stated as so much per head. Good, wholesome varied meals can only be provided by careful buying and the elimination of waste.

Further information

Hospital Caterers Association, The Ridgewood Centre (DHQ), Old Bisley Road, Frimley, Camberley, Surrey GU1Q 5QE. Dietetic advice can be obtained from the British Dietetic Association, 7th Floor Elisabeth House, 22 Suffolk Street, Queensway, Birmingham B1 1LS.

SCHOOL MEALS SERVICE (see Plate 4, page 36)

The provision of a midday meal at school for children up to and including secondary school age has been a statutory duty of local education authorities since 1941, and the policy governing this provision is laid down by the Department of Education and Science.

Over the years, however, this policy has varied, generally due to the economic situation of the country at the time. At the present time local education authorities may decide for themselves:

- their own free school meals policy, subject to free meals being provided to pupils from families in need;
- the kind of meals service they wish to provide;
- the charge they wish to make for meals.

The school meals service is controlled by school meals organisers responsible for the catering service, including control of finance within the budget, menu planning, advice on food purchasing, kitchen planning and general administration. Supervision of the school meals kitchens is undertaken by catering officers or cook supervisors and in smaller units by a cook-in-charge. Many women are employed in this area; they find that working in the school meals service can be fitted in with their responsibilities at home. Some work only for two or two-and-a-half hours each day during the actual meal service. However, kitchen staff at all levels receive training.

Many schools now offer a multi-choice menu, with up to a dozen choices of both courses, which is operated on a cash cafeteria system such as exists in most departmental stores. In recent years cook-freeze and cook-chill systems have been introduced by some authorities to reduce labour costs.

School kitchens are well equipped. The highest standard of personal and kitchen hygiene is demanded.

Staff training 'in service' and by day and block release are the accepted methods of ensuring a high standard of efficiency in the kitchens.

There is continuing emphasis on healthy eating which is reflected in the menus and recipes used, and attention is paid to the special needs of children of various cultural and religious backgrounds.

Breakfast

DAY ......SATURDAY...... NAME......		WEEK ...2... WARD...
☐	1 Porridge	C = 10 DRFS
☐	2 Cornflakes	C = 10 DRFS
☐	3 Weetabix	C = 20 DRFS
☐	4 All Bran	C = 20 DRFS
☐	5 Butter	D S
☐	6 Honey	FS
☐	7 Jam	FS
☐	8 Marmalade	FS
☐	9 Cheese spread	DR
☐	10 Brown bread roll	C = 20 DRFS
☐	11 White bread roll	C = 25 DRFS
☐	12 Sliced bread	C = 15 DRFS
☐	13 Orange juice	C = 10 DRFS
☐	14 Pineapple	C = 10 DRFS
☐	15	

Lunch

DAY ......SATURDAY...... NAME......		WEEK ...2... WARD...
☐	1 Casserole of beef	10 DRFS
☐	2 Vegetable burger	C = 10 DRFS
☐	3 Ploughman's lunch	C = 30 D
☐	4 Cheese salad	DR
☐	5 Egg & cress sandwich	C = 30 DRFS
☐	6 Cabbage	DRFS
☐	7 Parsley potatoes	C = 10 DRFS
☐	8 Boiled rice	C = 30 DRFS
☐	9 Pear halves	C = 10 DRFS
☐	10 Cream	D S
☐	11 Ice-cream	C = 10 D S
☐	12 Brown bread	C = 15 DRFS
☐	13 Butter	D S
☐	14	
☐	15	

Supper

DAY ......SATURDAY...... NAME......		WEEK ...2... WARD...
☐	1 Leek soup	C = 10 D F
☐	2 Chicken curry	C = 10 DRFS
☐	3 Jacket potato with chives & cottage cheese	C = 30 DRFS
☐	4 Quiche salad	C = 20 D S
☐	5 Cheese & pickle sandwich	C = 30 DR
☐	6 Mixed vegetables	DRFS
☐	7 Creamed potatoes	C = 10 DRFS
☐	8 Boiled rice	C = 30 DRFS
☐	9 Strawberry mousse	FS
☐	10 Fresh fruit	C = 10 DRFS
☐	11 Ice-cream	C = 10 D S
☐	12 Brown bread	C = 15 DRFS
☐	13 Butter	D S
☐	14	
☐	15	

WE HOPE YOU ENJOY YOUR MEAL

THE CATERING STAFF WISH YOU A SPEEDY RECOVERY

DIET CODES: Dishes marked are suitable for:

D – Diabetic R – Reducing
F – Low fat S – Low salt

Fig. 1.2 Example of a hospital menu

Fig. 1.3
Schools meals
being served

The staff supervising the children at mealtimes, particularly in primary and junior schools, have the responsibility of ensuring good behaviour and table manners and also encouraging children to develop the right attitude to healthy eating (see Figure 1.3).

For up-to-date information on the School Meals Service obtain the current circulars issued by the Department of Education, Sanctuary Buildings, Great Smith Street, London SW1P 3BT, or contact the local education authority's school meals organiser.

An interpretation of a healthy sample menu cycle (as seen in table on page 22 and Figure 1.4 on page 23)

Main course items (no soya used)

- Spaghetti bolognese   Wholemeal spaghetti, low fat meat and beans
- Fried fish   Pure white cod, fried in unsaturated oil
- Sausages   Low fat, high pork content
- Meat pie   Wholemeal flour, low fat meat, pulses added
- Beefburgers   High beef content, reduced saturated fat content
- Cheese and egg flan   Wholemeal pastry, skimmed milk used
- Lancashire flan   Wholemeal pastry, low fat meat, pulses added
- Beef stew   Low fat meat, pulses added and pasta

FOUR-WEEKLY MENU FOR PRIMARY SCHOOLS

	MONDAY	TUESDAY	WEDNESDAY	THURSDAY	FRIDAY
Week beginning	Spaghetti bolognese Carrots, potatoes Pineapple shortbread Fresh fruit	Cod au gratin Peas, mashed potatoes Fruit sponge and custard Fresh fruit	Sausages Spaghetti rings, sauté potatoes Baked rice pudding Fresh fruit	Meat pie Cabbage, potatoes Yogurt Fresh fruit	Turkey grill Baked beans, chips Apple crumble with custard Fresh fruit
Week beginning	Cheese and egg flan Jacket potatoes, salad Fruit and custard Fresh fruit	Sausages Beans, chips Apple and raisin stir-up with custard Fresh fruit	Lancashire flan Carrots, potatoes Yogurt Fresh fruit	Beefburgers Jacket wedges, green beans Iced buns Fresh fruit	Wholemeal ham pizza Corn or peas, potatoes Chocolate chip sponge with chocolate sauce Fresh fruit
Week beginning	Beef stew with pasta Cabbage, potatoes Yogurt Fresh fruit	Fish fingers Beans, chips Apricot crumble with custard Fresh fruit	Ham salad Jacket potatoes Delaware pudding with custard Fresh fruit	Chicken pie Peas, potatoes Stewed fruit with custard Fresh fruit	Sausages Green beans, potatoes Peach shortbread Fresh fruit
Week beginning	Boiled ham with parsley sauce Carrots, potatoes Iced sponge with custard Fresh fruit	Wholemeal pasta with mince Peas or carrots Plum pie with custard Fresh fruit	Egg and cheese salad Jacket potatoes Milk pudding Fresh fruit	Beefburgers Beans, chips Stewed fruit with evaporated milk Fresh fruit	Cornish pasty Cabbage, potatoes Yogurt Fresh fruit

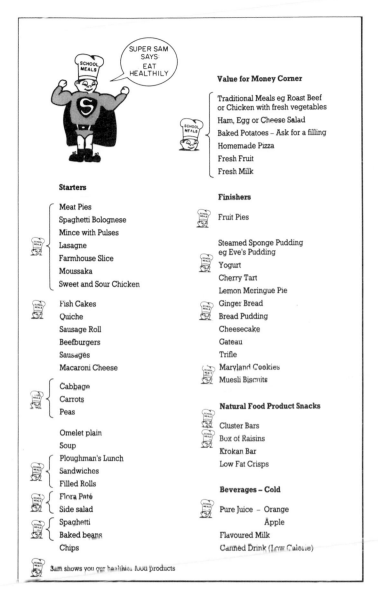

Fig. 1.4 School cafeteria menu

- Fish fingers   Additive-free crumbs, pure cod only used
- Ham salad   Best hocks of ham, boiled and sliced
- Chicken pie   Low fat meat, wholemeal pastry used, pulses
                      added to meat mix
- Cornish pasty   Low fat meat, wholemeal pastry, pulses added
- Egg and cheese salad Salad to include lettuce, cucumber, tomato,
                      carrot, beetroot, etc.

Vegetables
Only fresh or frozen vegetables are used with the exception being:
- Baked beans   With reduced sugar and fat contents

- Spaghetti   With reduced sugar and fat content and use of a wholemeal variety
- Chips   Only served once a week

Puddings
- Fresh fruit available for all school children.
- Majority of puddings do contain a fruit percentage, either solid pack or dried, e.g. plate pies and crumbles.
- Suet and other animal fats have been removed from puddings, e.g. Spotted Dick.
- Milk puddings are made with skimmed milk.
- Popular fruits with custard are available.
- Fruits will be served on biscuits, e.g. Pineapple Shortbread.
- Reduced sugar content, e.g. custard.
- Yogurt may be provided daily.

Additives
All additives considered by some medical experts to be harmful have been removed.

RESIDENTIAL ESTABLISHMENTS
Under this heading are included schools, colleges, halls of residence, nursing homes, homes for the elderly, hostels, where all the meals are provided. It is essential that in these establishments the nutritional balance of food is considered, and it should satisfy all the residents' nutritional needs, as in all probability the people eating here will have no other food. Since many of these establishments cater for students, and the age group which leads a very energetic life, these people usually have large appetites, and are growing fast. All the more reason that the food should be well cooked, plentiful, varied and attractive.

Catering for industry (industrial catering)

The provision of staff dining rooms for industrial workers has allowed many catering workers employment in first-class conditions. Apart from the main lunch meal, tea trolley rounds and/or vending machines may be part of the service. In some cases a 24-hour service is necessary and it is usual to cater for the social activities of the workers. Not only are lunches provided for the manual workers but the clerical staff and managerial staff will in most cases have their meals from the same kitchen and dining-room. There is ample scope for both men and women, and in this branch of the industry there are many top jobs for women.

Many industries have realised that output is related to the welfare of the employees. Well-fed workers produce more and better work and because of this a great deal of money is spent in providing first-class kitchens and dining-rooms and in subsidising the meals. This means that the workers receive their food at a price lower than its actual cost, the rest of the cost being borne by the company.

Further information can be obtained from: Industrial Catering Association, 1 Victoria Parade, 331 Sandycombe Road, Richmond, Surrey TW9 3NB.

LUNCHEON CLUBS

Clerical staffs in large offices are provided with lunching facilities, usually called a luncheon club or staff restaurant. These are often subsidised and in some instances the meal may be supplied without charge. The catering is frequently of a very high standard and the kitchen or kitchens will provide meals for the directors, which will be of the very best British fare or international cuisine.

Business lunches are served in small rooms so that there is privacy; the standard of food served will often be of the finest quality since the company will probably attach considerable importance to these functions. The senior clerical staff may have their own dining-room, whilst the rest of the staff will in some cases have a choice of an à la carte menu, a table d'hôte menu, waitress service or help-yourself and snack-bar facilities.

Luncheon clubs are provided by most large offices belonging to business firms, such as insurance head offices, petroleum companies, banks, etc. When luncheon facilities are not provided, many firms provide their employees with luncheon vouchers.

Large stores also provide lunching arrangements for their staff as well as the customers' restaurants.

Transport catering

AIRCRAFT (see page 487)

Aircraft catering is concerned with the provision of meals during flights and this form of catering presents certain problems. Owing to very limited space on the plane special ovens are provided to heat the food, which may be frozen or chilled. The food is prepared by the aircraft company or by an outside contract company.

RAILWAY

Meals on trains may be served in restaurant cars and snacks from buffet cars. The space in a restaurant car kitchen is very limited and there is considerable movement of the train, which causes difficulty for the staff.

Two train services run by separate companies are plying the route through the **Channel Tunnel**. One is Euro Tunnel's Le Shuttle train, which transports drivers and their vehicles between Folkestone and Calais in 35 minutes. Food and drink is limited to that bought on dry land before the train departs.

Foot passengers wishing to ride from Waterloo to Paris or Brussels travel on Eurostar Trains. Eurostar sees the airlines as its direct competition; therefore it provides airline catering standards on board the train. Meals are served by uniformed stewards and stewardesses in an environment similar to airline's club class. This food is included in the ticket price. (See sample menu below.)

Depending on the time of departure, a main meal of breakfast, lunch or dinner will be served, supplemented by a snack such as afternoon tea or mid-morning elevenses. Menu planning must take into account the combination of departure time, body clock and time difference between countries.

SAMPLE MENU FOR THE EUROSTAR FIRST-CLASS SERVICE

STARTERS	MAIN COURSES	DESSERT
Vegetable terrine	Blanquette lotte (monkfish)	Chocolate mousse
Goat's cheese salad	Tagliatelle thon (tuna)	Fruit tart
Smoked salmon and Lyon sausage	Suprême de volaille aux morilles (wild mushrooms)	Fruit terrine in a raspberry coulis
	Noisettes d'agneau, pommes de terre au thym, champignons sautés	Fruit dessert in custard
	Coeur de rumpsteak	
	Niçois et chouxfleurs au beurre	

Food will be cook-chill rather than freshly prepared on board. Food should and will reflect the mix of French, British and Belgian tastes.

MARINE

The large liner's catering is of similar standard to the big first-class hotels and many shipping companies are noted for the excellence of their cuisine. The kitchens on board ship are usually oil-fired and extra precautions have to be taken in the kitchen in rough weather. Catering at sea includes the smaller ship, which has both cargo and passengers, and the cargo vessels which include the giant tankers of up to 100 000 tonnes.

Other aspects of catering

THE SERVICES

Catering for the armed services is specialised and they have their own training centre; details of catering facilities and career opportunities can be obtained from career information offices.

CONTRACT CATERING

There are many catering concerns which are prepared to undertake the catering for businesses, schools or hospitals, leaving these establishments free to concentrate on the business of educating or nursing, etc. By employing contract caterers and using the services of people who have specialised in catering, organisations can thus relieve themselves of the worry of entering a field outside their province. Contract caterers are used by nearly every type of organisation, including the armed forces. The arrangements made will vary – the contractor may meet certain operating costs or receive a payment from the company employing the contractor. Often the cost of food, wages and light equipment is the responsibility of the contractor, whilst the cost of fuel and heavy equipment maintenance is borne by the company.

OUTSIDE CATERING (see Plate 5, page 37 and Figure 1.5, page 27)

When functions are held where there is no catering set-up or where the function is not within the scope of the normal catering routine, then certain firms will take over completely. Considerable variety is offered to people employed on these undertakings and often the standard will be of the very highest order. A certain

Fig. 1.5   A portable kitchen is delivered (left); within an hour of arrival, the kitchen is ready for action

amount of adaptability and ingenuity is required, especially for some outdoor jobs, but there is less chance of repetitive work. The types of function will include garden parties, agricultural and horticultural shows, the opening of new buildings, banquets, parties in private houses, etc.

TOPICS FOR DISCUSSION

1. Give your impressions of the food that was served at previous schools with suggestions for improvement.
2. Explain the importance of food for the hospital patient with suggestions for the types of food to be offered.
3. Industrial catering is an important aspect of the catering industry; discuss why this is so and give examples of menus for three different dining rooms.
4. Discuss what you think persons travelling on aircraft would like to eat and explain how it may, or may not, be feasible to provide.
5. How do you think changes in the industry will occur over the next 10 years? Explain why you think they will happen.

2

Food and society

—

Why do we eat what we eat, select one dish from the menu in preference to another, choose one particular kind of restaurant or use a take-away? Why are these dishes on the menu in the first place? Is it because the chef likes them, the customer or the consumer wants them or is this the only food available – what dictates what we eat?

Catering reflects the eating habits, history, customs and taboos of society but it also develops and creates them. You have only to compare the variety of eating facilities available on any major street today with those of a short while ago.

TASTE

Taste affects food choice, based on biological social and cultural perspectives. The perception of taste results from the stimulation of the taste cells which make up the taste buds. Taste is not specific to individual foods, but to the balance between four main types of chemical compound. These compounds correspond to four sensations of:

- Sour   hydrogen ion concentration
- Salt   ions of salt
- Sweet   organic compounds
- Bitter   a number of types of compound including alkaloids and glycosides

Some scientists say that there is a fifth flavour:

- Savouriness   glutamate and nucleotides

The difference in taste of different foods is based to some extent on the balance between these flavour aspects, but far more on the contribution of smell.

Taste cells are extremely sensitive, able to detect bitterness at a concentration of only 1 part in 2 000 000. Through our sense of taste we are able to identify flavours such as orange oil, which contains over 100 different chemicals and to distinguish between different types of coffee, which contain over 1000 different substances. There are approximately 50 taste cells in each taste bud; adults have about 10 000 taste buds, located mainly on the tongue, and organised roughly according to their sensitivity to salt, sour, sweet and bitter flavours. Sweetness is experienced mainly on the tip of the tongue, bitter flavours at the back, sour along the sides and salt mainly in the front but can be detected all over.

The sensitivity appears to be affected by a number of physiological factors including

- genetics;
- nutrition (zinc deficiency can reduce an individual's ability to pick up certain substances);
- pregnancy (foods previously enjoyed are often found repulsive, and cravings for other foods are experienced);
- age (beyond 45 the replacement of the taste buds slows down accompanied by decreasing sensitivity);
- acquisition and learning (the pattern of food intake in childhood appears to be extremely important in shaping future tastes and the power of the socially constructed meanings of food should not be underestimated).

SOME FACTORS WHICH AFFECT WHAT WE EAT

The individual

Everyone has needs and wants these to be met according to his or her own satisfaction.

- **Tastes** and **habits** in eating are influenced by three main factors: upbringing, peer group behaviour and social background. For example, children's tastes are developed at home according to the eating patterns of their family, as is their expectation of *when* to eat meals; teenagers may frequent hamburger or other fast-food outlets, and adults may eat out once a week at an ethnic or high-class restaurant, steakhouse or pub.
- Degree of **hunger** will affect what is to be eaten, when, and how much to eat – although some people in the Western world overeat, food shortages cause undernourishment in poorer countries. Everyone ought to eat enough to enable body and mind to function efficiently; if you are hungry or thirsty it is difficult to work or study effectively.
- **Health** considerations may influence choice of food, either because a special diet is required for medical reasons, or (as the current emphasis on healthy eating shows – see Plate 6, page 38) because everyone needs a nutritionally balanced diet. Many people nowadays feel it is more healthy not to eat meat or dairy products. Others are vegetarian or vegan on moral or religious grounds.

Relationships

Eating is a necessity, but it is also a means of developing social relationships. The needs and preferences of the people you eat with should be considered. This applies in the family or at the place of study or work. School meals can be a means of developing good eating habits, both by the provision of suitable foods and dishes and by creating an appropriate environment to foster social relationships. Canteens, dining rooms and restaurants for people at work can be places where relationships develop.

Often the purpose of eating, either in the home or outside it, is to be sociable and to meet people, or to renew or provide the opportunity for people to meet each other. Frequently there is a reason for the occasion (such as birthday, anniversary, wedding, awards ceremony), needing a special party or banquet menu – or it may just be for a few friends to have a meal at a restaurant.

Business is often conducted over a meal, usually at lunchtime but also at breakfast and dinner. Eating and drinking help to make work more enjoyable and effective.

Emotional needs

Sometimes we eat not because we need food but to meet an emotional requirement:

- for sadness or depression – eating a meal can give comfort to oneself or to someone else; after a funeral people eat together to comfort one another;
- for a reward or a treat, or to give encouragement to oneself or to someone else; an invitation to a meal is a good way of showing appreciation.

IDEAS ABOUT FOOD

People's ideas about food and meals, and about what is and what is not acceptable, vary according to where and how they were raised, the area in which they live and its social customs.

Different societies and cultures have had in the past, and still have, conflicting ideas about what constitutes good cooking and a good chef, and about the sort of food a good chef should provide. The French tradition of producing fine food and highly respected chefs continues to this day – whereas other countries may traditionally have less interest in the art of cooking, and less esteem for chefs.

What constitutes people's idea of a snack, a proper meal or a celebration will depend on their backgrounds, as will their interpretation of terms such as lunch or dinner. One person's idea of a snack may be another person's idea of a main meal; a celebration for some will be a visit to a hamburger bar; to others, a meal at a fashionable restaurant.

The idea of what is 'the right thing to do' regarding eating varies with age, social class and religion. To certain people it is right to eat with the fingers, others use only a fork; some will have cheese before the sweet course, others will have cheese after it; it is accepted that children and often elderly people need food to be cut up into small pieces, and that people of some religions do not eat certain foods. The ideas usually originate from practical and hygienic reasons although sometimes the origin is obscure.

IMAGES OF FOOD

Fashions, fads and fancies affect foods and it is not always clear if catering creates or copies these trends.

- Nutritionists inform us what foods are good and necessary in the diet, what the effect of particular foods will be on the figure and how much of each food we require. This helps to produce an 'image' of food. This image changes according to research, availability of food and what is considered to constitute healthy eating.
- What people choose to eat says something about them as a person – it creates an image. We are what we eat, but *why* do we choose to eat what we do when there is *choice*? One person will perhaps avoid trying snails because of ignorance of how to eat them, or because the idea is repulsive, whilst another will select them deliberately to show off to guests. One person will select a dish because it is a new experience, another will choose it because it was enjoyed when eaten before. The quantity eaten may indicate a glutton or a gourmand; the quality selected, a gourmet.

The food itself

Crop failure or distribution problems may make a food scarce or not available at all. Foods in season are now supplemented by imported foods, so that foods out of season at home are now available much of the time. It means that there is a wide choice of food for the caterer and the customer.

- Food is available through shops, supermarkets, cash and carry, wholesalers and direct suppliers. People at home and caterers are able to purchase, prepare, cook and present almost every food imaginable due to rapid air transport and food preservation. Food spoilage and wastage are minimised; variety and quality are maximised.
- It is essential that food looks attractive, has a pleasing smell and tastes good. Food which is nutritious but does not look, smell or taste nice is less likely to be eaten. With cooking, these points must be considered, but it should be remembered that people's views as to what is attractive and appealing will vary according to their background and experience.

RESOURCES

Money, time and facilities affect what people eat – the economics of eating affects everyone.

- **How much money** an individual is able, or decides to spend on food is crucial to what is eaten. Some people will not be able to afford to eat out, others will only be able to eat out occasionally, but for others eating out will be a frequent event. The money that individuals allocate for food will determine whether they cook and eat at home, use a take-away (e.g. fish and chips, Chinese), go to a pub, eat at a pancake house, or at an ethnic or other restaurant.
- The **amount of time** people have to eat at work will affect whether they use any facilities provided, go out for a snack or meal, or bring their own food to work.

- The **ease of obtaining food,** the use of convenience and frozen food and the facility for storing foods, has meant that in the home and in catering establishments the range of foods is wide. Foods in season can be frozen and used throughout the year, so if there is a glut then spoilage can be eliminated.

INFLUENCES

The media influences what we eat – television, radio, newspapers, magazines and literature of all kinds have an effect on our eating habits (see table on page 33).

- Healthy eating, nutrition, hygiene and outbreaks of food poisoning are publicised; experts in all aspects of health including those extolling exercise, diet and environmental health, state what should and should not be eaten.
- Information regarding the content of food packets and the advertising of food influences our choice. Knowledge about eating and foods is learnt from the family, through teachers, at school meals, at college, through the media and through the experience of eating at home and abroad.

The following examples illustrate how these factors can affect what people eat: A TV programme shows the effects of a drought in Africa, in a region where political factions are at war, thus preventing food distribution. Money is given by people morally concerned that others are starving, so air transport is used to deliver foods that have been preserved to provide adequate nutrition. The food should also be in keeping with the religious beliefs and cultural background of those in need.

Another example is related to planning a menu. The first thing to consider is who it is for; therefore it must not conflict with the consumer's religious beliefs or ethnic origin. The price must be affordable and the items on the menu obtainable. To illustrate further: let us say that a restaurant owner has advertised in the local paper, and a family decide to go to this restaurant to celebrate an anniversary. The food they select will be in keeping with their taste, and it may include dishes they are familiar with or new dishes on the menu (which, perhaps, are prepared off the premises and reheated in the owner's new technological equipment). Some of the items available on the menu may have been flown in from countries which have a climate that allows the production of foods not grown here. In addition, it might so happen that the restaurant is part of a pub which was, say, an original coaching inn named after Bonnie Prince Charlie – so perhaps Scottish dishes are always available, particularly on special occasions such as Burns night, when the local Scots celebrate and eat haggis which is traditional, nutritionally beneficial and flown down from Scotland. (Also, the host and his wife may have relations in Ireland and Wales, so perhaps national dishes of these countries feature on the menu as well.)

We are all creatures of habit conditioned by customs and restrictions, as much in what we do or do not eat, as in what we will or will not wear. Variety is not only the spice of life: it is the ingredient which makes catering and cooking so fascinating.

INFLUENCES ON WHAT PEOPLE EAT

MEDIA	TRANSPORT	RELIGIOUS
TV	transport of foods by:	
books	sea	taboos
newspapers	rail	festivals
journals	air	
	transport of people	

GEOGRAPHICAL	HISTORICAL	ECONOMIC
climate	explorations	money to purchase
indigenous:	invasions	goods to exchange
fish	establishment of	
birds	trade routes	
animals		
plant life		

SOCIOLOGICAL	POLITICAL	CULTURAL
family	tax on food	ethnic
school	policies on food 'mountains'	tribal
work place	export and import	celebrations
leisure	restrictions	
fashion and trends		

PSYCHOLOGICAL	PHYSIOLOGICAL	SCIENTIFIC
appearance of food	nutritional	preservation
smell	healthy eating	technology
taste	illness	
aesthetics	additives	
reaction to new foods		

These influences are separated for convenience but in reality overlap. Only when sufficient food is available for survival can pleasure from food develop.

FOOD CHANGES IN BRITISH SOCIETY

In the past, inns catered for people travelling by coach, with coffee houses in the towns. Later, with the development of railways, the hotel and catering industry expanded rapidly.

The twentieth century has brought sweeping changes in eating patterns and health. A hundred years ago, most people ate plenty of fibre from bread and potatoes, but they lacked an adequately varied diet. Diseases caused by a lack of vitamins and minerals were common. Today, the problems are different. Many people eat too much meat, dairy produce and sugar, and too little fibre for good health. New methods of farming and food processing, food selling and storage have helped to alter what we eat.

Plate I   Hospital kitchen

Plate 2   Staff restaurant in a hospital

Plate 3   Patient being served
in a hospital

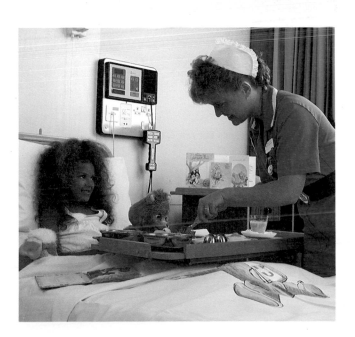

Plate 4   School meals service kitchen

Plate 5 An outdoor barbecue

Plate 6   Are you a healthy weight?

ARE YOU A HEALTHY WEIGHT?

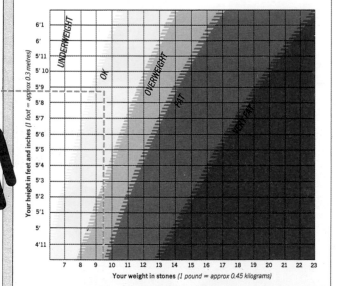

Take a straight line across from your height (without shoes) and a line up from your weight (without clothes). Put a mark where the two lines meet.

Your height in feet and inches (1 foot = approx 0.3 metres)

UNDERWEIGHT

OK

OVERWEIGHT

FAT

VERY FAT

6'1 · 6' · 5'11 · 5'10 · 5'9 · 5'8 · 5'7 · 5'6 · 5'5 · 5'4 · 5'3 · 5'2 · 5'1 · 5' · 4'11

7 8 9 10 11 12 13 14 15 16 17 18 19 20 21 22 23

Your weight in stones *(1 pound = approx 0.45 kilograms)*

UNDERWEIGHT   Maybe you need to eat a bit more. But go for well-balanced nutritious foods and don't just fill up on fatty and sugary foods. If you are *very* underweight, see your doctor about it.

OK   You're eating the right *quantity* of food but you need to be sure that you're getting a healthy *balance* in your diet.

OVERWEIGHT   You should try to lose weight.

FAT   You need to lose weight.

VERY FAT   You urgently need to lose weight. You would do well to see your doctor, who might refer you to a dietitian.

If you need to lose weight
Aim to lose 1 or 2 pounds a week until you get down to the 'OK' range. Go for fibre-rich foods and cut down on fat, sugar and alcohol. You'll need to take regular exercise too.

Plate 7   A Japanese cook at work

Plate 8   A selection of Japanese dishes

Plate 9 Meat cold room

1900s

As the population grew rapidly at the turn of the century, so food imports rose. By 1914 British farmers met less than a quarter of the country's food needs.

New manufacturing processes created new products; people began to eat less bread and potatoes as the new shops brought in cheap cod packed in ice. Flour, margarine and tinned condensed milk were cheap and popular; biscuits, jam, chocolate and cheese also began to be factory-made. Such products were often cleaner and purer than those previously available, but sometimes of less nutritional value. In towns the first grocery store chains appeared and new co-operative retail societies also flourished. Eating out was limited to fish and chip shops, chop houses and pubs.

Beneath the outward prosperity of Edwardian England were various social problems. One-third of the population was poor and undernourished, a situation that led eventually to school medical inspections and clinics.

1930s

The First World War had brought home just how dependent Britain was on imported food, and how unfit the nation was – thousands of men had been graded unfit for active service. Measures were taken to boost British food production such as subsidies and import restrictions. However, cheap meat, wheat and butter from abroad encouraged farmers to specialise in milk, eggs and vegetables.

More of almost every type of food was eaten, but even so researchers found that less than half the population could afford a healthy diet. Rickets, tuberculosis, anaemia and physical underdevelopment were common among the poor, leading eventually to the introduction of free school milk and infant welfare clinics to help combat these problems.

A number of companies started to dominate food processing and retailing during the 1930s, and shops increasingly sold preprepared brand-name goods. Eating out also became more popular with the introduction of milk bars and modestly priced Restaurants such as Lyons Tea Shops and ABC (Aerated Bread Company) Tea Shops.

1950s

The Second World War had created food shortages but rationing and other Government action meant that on average the nation's diet was better than before the war. When rationing ended, consumers splashed out on foods that had been in short supply. However, only half the population ate a cooked breakfast, and breakfast cereals became fashionable.

At the time, health experts were concerned to ensure that people were eating a balanced diet, with sufficient vitamins and protein. However, these years of plenty were laying down the foundations for increasing obesity and heart disease. Other changes were that shops began to convert to self-service due to rising labour costs. Chinese restaurants became popular for eating out due to their cheapness, because they offered a take-away service, and because people were becoming more adventurous in their choice of foods.

1970s

By now UK farmers produced two-thirds of the nation's food, due to increasing use of technology and pesticides, fertilisers and hormones. Joining the EC gave farmers new subsidies and guaranteed prices, which resulted in overproduction of some foods. Most people began the day with a cereal breakfast and approximately 18% ate nothing. Fewer midday meals were taken at home. Tea shops went out of fashion and were replaced by burger bars. There was growing interest in foreign food. Health experts' attention shifted from the problems of inadequate nutrition to the new health risks of eating too much of certain types of food.

1980s

Supermarkets continued to expand and, due to air-cargo transport, almost every type of food became available. The demand for ethnic dishes continued, leading to the opening of many ethnic restaurants. **Nouvelle cuisine** became fashionable, but it tended to give way to healthy eating which was popularised not only in **haute cuisine** but also in the home and school meals. British chefs and cooking were now earning respect. The microwave oven greatly affected people's eating habits at home, and supermarkets responded by popularising products which could be cooked or reheated in the microwave. The 1970s saw the expansion of the use of the freezer; in the 1980s it was the expansion of the use of the microwave.

1990s onwards

Increasing numbers of customers have become aware of and require healthy eating, demanding, for example, lighter dishes, less fat, sugar and salt. Food additives have also come under closer scrutiny. Severe cases of food contamination have made the national press, causing concern to the caterer and public alike. The majority of the cases have been caused by Salmonella, Listeria and staphyolococcal organisms. As a result, hygiene codes of practice have come under close examination and legislation has been passed in Parliament resulting in the Food Act of 1991.

Legislation from the EC has caused caterers to be increasingly aware of laws affecting the industry. These particularly affect safety at work and temperature of foods.

Considerable attention is being paid to 'green' issues, the production and use of organic foods and all environmental issues, in particular the control of waste. There is a trend towards more informal eating with bistros and theme restaurants (particularly US Theme restaurants such as Exchange Diner, TGI Friday) and also restaurant branding (such as Café Flo and Café Rouge); there has been a move away from French menu terminology. Travel lodges are increasing alongside motorway service stations and some hotels are subcontracting their restaurants.

Dishes on menus reflect the great variety of foodstuffs available and imaginative and attractive presentation results.

Certain foodstuffs are now giving rise for concern:

- beef (mad cow disease);
- nuts (causing allergy in a small number of people);
- sweetbreads.

There is an increasing demand for vegetarian dishes.

Topics for discussion

1. The food preferences of the group and how they have evolved.
2. Healthy eating: what is your opinion regarding this topic?
3. The value of conducting business during a meal such as breakfast or lunch.
4. The group's ideas about food.
5. Influences on what we eat.
6. Potential future changes in British society that could affect eating habits.

Further information can be obtained from the Vegetarian Society, Parkdale, Durham Road, Altrincham, Cheshire WA14 4OG.

3

Influences of ethnic cultures

—

The races and nations of the world represent a great variety of cultures each with their own ways of cooking. Knowledge of this is essential in catering because:

- There has been a rapid spread of tourism, creating a demand for a broader culinary experience.
- Many people from overseas have opened restaurants using their own foods and styles of cooking.
- The development of air-cargo means perishable foods from distant places are readily available.
- The media, particularly television, has stimulated an interest in worldwide cooking.

A few years ago it was necessary for a chef to be knowledgeable about traditional classical French cooking; today chefs must also be aware of the foods and dishes of many other races. It is not within the scope of this book to deal in depth with gastronomy, but it is hoped that this brief introduction will stimulate an interest in terms and food associated with ethnic cooking.

RELIGIOUS INFLUENCES

Throughout the world religion always has, and still does, affect what many people eat. Some people's diets are restricted daily by their religion; others are influenced by what they eat on special occasions. Fasts, feasts, celebrations and anniversaries are important happenings in many people's lives. It is necessary for those involved in catering to have some basic knowledge of the requirements and restrictions associated with religions.

Christian

For most Christians, eating habits are not affected – though some will be vegetarians, usually for moral reasons, and some will refrain from eating meat on Fridays. Some sects, for instance Mormons, have many rules and restrictions regarding eating and drinking, for example complete abstinence from tea, coffee and alcohol, and an emphasis on wholesome eating. Many Christians refrain from eating certain foods during Lent – usually something they like very much. Other religious days often observed are:

- Shrove Tuesday: the day before the start of Lent, when pancakes are on many menus, traditionally to use up ingredients prior to Lent.
- Good Friday: hot cross buns are often eaten as a reminder of Christ's crucifixion.
- Easter Sunday: simnel cakes are made with marzipan and chocolate, and Easter eggs (decorated boiled or chocolate eggs) are eaten as a symbol of new life and the Resurrection.
- Christmas (25 December): celebrated with feasting, with roast turkey today often replacing the traditional roast beef and boar's head, followed by Christmas pudding and mince pies.

Other predominantly Christian countries celebrate different saints days by special events. For example, St Nicholas, patron saint of children, is celebrated on 6 December in Holland by eating Dutch St Nicholas biscuits. In Spain the Three Kings are remembered with a special crown cake on 6 January. The fourth Thursday of November in the USA is Thanksgiving Day, when traditionally turkey and pumpkin pie are served.

Muslim

Muslims celebrate the birth of Mohammed at the end of February or early in March. Alcohol and pork are traditionally forbidden in their diet. Only meat that has been prepared according to Muslim custom by a *halal* butcher is permitted. During *Ramadan*, which lasts for one month and is the ninth month of the Muslim calendar, Muslims do not eat or drink anything from dawn to sunset. The end of the fast is celebrated with a feast called *Idd-ul-Fitar*, with special foods. Muslims from Middle Eastern countries would favour a dish like lamb stew with okra; those from the Far East, curry and rice.

Hindu

Most Hindus do not eat meat (strict Hindus are vegetarians) and none eat beef since the cow is sacred to them. *Holi* is the festival which celebrates the end of winter and the arrival of spring. *Raksha Bandha* celebrates the ties between brothers and sisters at the end of July or in August, and *Janam Ashtami* celebrates the birth of Krishna, also in August. *Dussehra* is the festival of good over evil; *Divali* is the festival of light, celebrating light over darkness, held in October or November. Samosas (triangles of pastry containing vegetables), banana fudge and vegetable dishes of all kinds, as well as favourite foods, are eaten to celebrate.

Sikh

The Sikhs do not have strict rules regarding food but many are vegetarians. *Baisakhi* day in April celebrates the new year and is the day Sikhs are baptised into their faith.

Buddhist

Strict Buddhists are vegetarians and their dishes vary since most live in India and China, where available foods will be different. *Vesak* in May is the festival to celebrate the life of the Buddha.

Judaism

The religion of the Jews has strict dietary laws. Shellfish, pork and birds of prey are forbidden. Acceptable foods are fish with scales and fins, animals that have 'cloven hoof' and birds killed according to the law. Strict Jews eat only meat that has been specially slaughtered known as *kosher* meat.

Milk and meat must neither be used together in cooking nor served at the same meal, and three hours should elapse between eating food containing milk and food containing meat.

The Jewish Sabbath, from sunset on Friday to sunset on Saturday, is traditionally a day of rest. In the evening, plaited bread called *chollah* is broken into pieces and eaten. *Matzo*, an unleavened crispbread, is served at Passover as a reminder of the exodus of the Jews from Egypt. *Pentecost* celebrates the giving of the Ten Commandments to Moses on Mount Sinai; cheesecake is now a traditional dish served at this celebration. *Hanukkah*, the Jewish Festival of Lights in December, is a time of dedication when pancakes and a potato dish, potato *latkes*, are usually eaten.

EUROPEAN COOKERY

British

Due to the climate, British cooking tends to be warming and filling. Breakfast, afternoon tea and high tea are examples of meals peculiar to Britain. Selections of some British foods and dishes are given below.

ENGLISH
- Potted shrimps
- Fried cod and chips
- Fish cakes
- Roast beef and Yorkshire pudding with horseradish sauce
- Roast lamb with mint sauce
- Steak and kidney pie (a pie covering of short or puff pastry)
- Steak and kidney pudding (a suet paste meat pudding)
- Cornish pasty (a pastry containing potatoes, vegetables and meat)
- Apple pie (apples covered with short paste)
- Trifle (layers of fruit, sponge, custard and cream)
- Treacle pudding (a steamed sponge pudding)
- Fool (a purée of mixed fruit with whipped cream)
- Chelsea buns (a yeast bun containing dried fruit)
- Worcestershire sauce (a bottled spicy sauce used in meat dishes)

WELSH
- Welsh lamb pie
- Welsh rarebit (a cheese savoury dish)
- Welsh cake (a flat scone-like griddle cake)
- Lava bread
- Leek pie

SCOTTISH
- Haggis (chopped sheep's liver, lights (lungs) and heart with oatmeal and seasoning, cooked inside a sheep's stomach which has been thoroughly cleaned and turned inside out)
- Finnan haddie (smoked haddock)
- Cock-a-leekie (a soup of leek and chicken garnished with prunes)
- Venison (the flesh of deer)
- Scotch eggs (hard-boiled eggs covered in sausage meat, crumbed and deep fried)

IRISH
- Irish stew (a stew of many vegetables and potatoes and lamb)
- Colcannon (mashed potatoes and cabbage with butter and milk)
- Irish herring soup
- Bacon and cabbage
- Carageen moss pudding (a sweet made from milk, eggs, sugar and dried seaweed)

French

Many famous dishes have been created in France, the home of classical cooking, but only a few examples are given here. Each region of France has its specialities and styles of cooking.

- Choucroûte (a dish from Alsace of white cabbage, bacon, and frankfurter sausage)
- Bouillabaisse (a stew or soup of assorted fish and shellfish of many varieties with vegetables)
- Tournedos Rossini (a cut from a fillet of beef, shallow fried and garnished with *foie gras* (fat goose liver) and a slice of truffle and Madeira sauce)
- Snails (escargots) (snails served in their shells with garlic butter)
- Coq au vin (chicken in red wine sauce)
- Fricassée (white stew of meat or poultry)

Italian

The Italians brought their culinary skills to France in 1533 and justifiably claim to have influenced French cooking. Italy is noted for its pastas, risottos, cheeses, pizzas and much more. Examples of some food and dishes are:

- Gnocchi (there are several kinds made from choux paste, potatoes or semolina)
- Minestrone (a vegetable soup containing pasta and served with cheese)
- Parma ham (*prosciutto*) (this ham is cut into thin slices and eaten raw)

- Salami (a cured pork sausage which is cut into very thin slices)
- Parmesan cheese (a very hard cheese which is grated and used for cooking)
- Osso buco (a stew of the shin of veal cut across, with the bone)
- Risotto (a moist rice dish cooked in stock and finished with cheese)

German and Austrian

German and Austrian dishes are filling, meat being used extensively. Sausages (*wursts*) are produced in a great many varieties and braised red and green cabbage is popular, whilst Austrian pastries are renowned:

- Apfelstrudel (a special thin pastry with applies, dried fruit and spice)
- Sauerkraut (a pickled white cabbage served hot)
- Wiener schnitzel (a thin slice of veal, crumbed and shallow fried Vienna style)
- Sachertorte (a chocolate cake with bitter sweet chocolate filling)

Russian

Russian cooking has provided one of the most popular classical dishes, namely, Chicken à la Kiev. Bortsch, a famous Russian beetroot soup, originated in the sixteenth century. Foods and terms associated with Russia include:

- Blinis (thin pancakes served with caviar, roe, etc.)
- Coulibiac (puff or brioche pastry with layers of flaked fish, sturgeon or salmon, pancakes cut in strips, and hard-boiled eggs)
- Chicken à la Kiev (supreme of chicken stuffed with butter, crumbed and deep fried)
- Caviar (raw, slightly salted sturgeon's roe from the Baltic and Caspian seas)
- Stroganoff (a sauté of prime beef with a sauce of soured cream)

Eastern European

Hungary and Poland have given us respectively:
- *Goulash* (*gulyas*) (a meat stew using paprika)
- *Baba* (yeast savarin paste soaked in syrup containing rum)

Swiss

French, Italian and German cookery influences the cooking of Switzerland, a country famous for its cheeses:

- Rösti potatoes (shredded potatoes cooked to a golden brown cake)
- Raclette (a melted cheese dish taken from the name of the dish in which the cheese is melted)
- Fondue (cheese melted with white wine, eaten off chunks of bread)
- Emmental and Gruyère (two of the best known cheeses)

Spanish

The dishes in this country are varied because of its geographical situation, each area having its own specialities. Some of them are well known:

- Paella (rice with shellfish, chicken, vegetables and saffron simmered in stock and olive oil in a paella pan)
- Gazpacho (a cold soup of tomatoes, peppers, cucumber, garlic, etc.)
- Tortilla (a flat omelet of potatoes, onions and garlic served hot or cold)
- Tapas (snacks, usually served at bars, of omelet, squid, shellfish, etc.)

Scandinavian

Denmark, Norway and Sweden, due to their proximity to the sea, eat a large amount of fish particularly herrings. Butter, blue cheese and bacon are imported into Britain in considerable quantities. Rye which grows in northern climates is used for crispbreads which are popular, particularly for low-calorie diets:

- Smörgäsbord (term for 'buffet', including many dishes particularly those using fresh, smoked and pickled herrings and other fish, shrimps and prawns)
- Smørrëbrod (Danish open sandwiches)
- Gravlax (gravad lax) (Swedish dish of marinated, filleted salmon coated with dill)

MEDITERRANEAN AND MIDDLE EASTERN COOKERY

(see Figure 3.1, page 50)

Cooking in this area is affected by religious, as well as by geographical and historical influences, sometimes making it unclear where certain dishes originated. Foods from the Mediterranean area include olives, aubergines, lemons, squid, octopus, yogurt and lamb; from the Middle East, wheat, rice, beans, chick peas, lentils, figs, dates and citrus fruits. Burghul, known as 'cracked wheat', is whole wheat grains partially cooked, dried and cracked, and used in many soups, stews and salads.

- Feta (a semi-soft, crumbly, salted white goat or sheep's milk cheese)
- Avgolemono (egg, lemon and chicken soup or sauce)
- Dolmades (dolmas) (vine leaves stuffed with rice)
- Filo (phyllo) (a very thin paste used for sweet and savoury dishes)
- Baklava (layers of filo paste with nuts, sugar and spice baked and finished with sugar and lemon syrup)
- Moussaka (a dish of minced meat, aubergines, tomatoes and cheese sauce)
- Taramasalata (a first course dish or dip of fish roes blended with bread, olive oil and lemon sauce)
- Pitta bread (small, flat, round yeast breads)
- Couscous (North African dish of cracked wheat, resembling semolina, cooked by steaming over stews); it can have nuts and dried fruit added and used as a base for stuffings

- Kebabs (skewered lamb with peppers, tomatoes, mushrooms and onions grilled and served on rice pilaff)
- Börek (Turkish dish of filo pastry wrapped around garlic-flavoured goat cheese, lamb or vegetables)
- Keftedes (fried minced meat balls with onion, oregano, mint and parsley)
- Hummus (a purée of chick peas)

Fig. 3.1   Greek pastry cooks

AMERICAN COOKERY

Although English is spoken in the USA some culinary terms are not the same as in the UK; for example:

- cornstarch = cornflour
- granulated sugar = caster sugar
- confectioner's sugar = icing sugar
- superfine = caster sugar
- cookies = biscuits
- heavy cream = double cream
- molasses = treacle
- powdered sugar = icing sugar

Another difference is that many American recipes are given using cupfuls as a means of measuring. The fast-food industry is immense; but in a country as cosmopolitan as the USA, cooking is influenced by many European and Asian cookery traditions:

- Gumbo (a soup or stew of okra with smoked meat, shellfish and vegetables from Louisiana)
- Chowder (a fish soup usually with a shellfish base)
- Cheesecake (a biscuit base with a cream cheese filling, usually topped with blueberries or other fruits)
- Baked Alaska (ice-cream coated with meringue and baked)
- Strawberry shortcake (shortbread or scone base topped with strawberries, with whipped cream between)
- Corned beef hash (corned beef and potato)

- Chicken Maryland (deep fried battered or crumbed chicken pieces with corn fritters and bacon)
- Jambalaya (Creole dish of rice, wine, chicken, shellfish etc.; the consistency of thick soup)

MEXICAN AND SOUTH AMERICAN COOKERY

Mexican cookery shows the country's Aztec roots and Spanish influence. It is noted for the hot flavour of its dishes which contain chillies, and for the use of unsweetened chocolate.

- Tortilla (unleavened cornmeal dough, flattened to a pancake shape, and griddled)
- Tacos (a tortilla with minced meat or chicken filling; a crisp version is deep fried)
- Enchiladas (tortilla dipped in chilli sauce, fried and filled with cheese, turkey or chicken, topped with chilli sauce and cheese)
- Guacamole (a purée of avocado, chillies, onion and lemon juice used as a dip or garnish)
- Mole (a chilli sauce enriched with unsweetened chocolate)

South American cooking is influenced by Spanish and Portuguese cookery:

- Ceviche (Peruvian dish of raw fish 'cooked' by the acid of citrus fruit)

CARIBBEAN COOKERY

African and European settlers on the Caribbean Islands have greatly influenced the cooking of this area. Yams, coconuts, guavas, mango and paw paw are ingredients readily available.

- Calaloo (soup made of the vegetable called 'calaloo', originating in Africa, with okra, garlic, onions, cloves, herbs, chillies and coconut milk)
- Blaff (white fish poached in wine and water with hot chillies, allspice, garlic and peppercorns)

INDIAN, PAKISTANI AND BANGLADESHI COOKERY

Indian cookery is noted for its use of spices, herbs and flavourings but the subcontinent should not be associated only with curry. Northern India's speciality, tandoori cooking, is named after the unusual oven called the *tandoor* (see Figure 3.2) which produces slightly charred spiced chicken and lamb dishes. Southern India features vegetarian dishes and *vindaloo*. Bangladesh favours seafood. Pakistan uses yogurt extensively, and kebabs are common.

Examples of some terms and dishes are:

- Chapati (a wholewheat unleavened bread-like pancake)
- Ghee (clarified butter)

Fig. 3.2 A traditional tandoor oven

- Poppadums (a very thin round biscuit made from dhal, deep fried or grilled and served with curry, etc.)
- Bombay duck (a salted dried fish)
- Vindaloo (very hot curry)
- Tandoor (a clay oven heated by wood or charcoal)
- Samosas (small deep-fried pastries containing vegetables and meat)
- Pakoras (deep-fried dumplings)
- Garam masala (literally a mixture of spices: hot spices, black cardamom, cinnamon, cloves, peppercorns and nutmeg)

CHINESE COOKERY

China is a vast country with a wide climatic variation, and therefore many kinds of foods are available. Because of its size, four major styles of cooking have developed over the centuries, and foods produced in these areas predominate. The areas are divided into:

- Eastern: Shanghai (wide variety of fruit, vegetables and fish; light and delicate seasoning; stir fry and steaming are favoured cooking methods; soy sauce from this area is considered the best in China)
- Northern: Beijing or Peking (wheat and corn are produced in this area, not rice, so noodles, pancakes and dumplings are served; due to the climate many foods are preserved; less meat is available; garlic, leeks, onions and sesame seeds are used extensively)
- Western: Sichuam or Szechuan (strong flavourings and hot spices predominate, e.g. red chillies, peppercorns, ginger, fruit, vegetables, meat and fish are plentiful)
- Southern: Guangdong or Canton (foods are not overcooked, and less use is made of garlic; rice is the staple food; sweet and sour dishes and dim sums are renowned; stir fry and steaming are the most common methods of cooking.

Chinese cooking is based on five flavours which affect parts of the body:

FLAVOUR	ORGAN
sweet	spleen
acid	liver
sour	kidneys
bitter	heart
sharp	lungs

The Chinese diet is characterised by cooking methods which preserve vitamins, the absence of dairy produce, and little meat. Foods are divided into: *yin*, cooling food; *yang*, heating foods; *yin yang*, neutral foods. Yin foods include crab and duck, and yang foods beef, coffee and smoked fish; yin yang foods include rice, fruit and vegetables.

All parts of animals and birds, other than the fur and feathers, are used for food. Some of the following are items and dishes associated with Chinese cooking:

- Soy sauce (made from soya beans, flour and water; light soy sauce is best and is known as *superior soy*; dark soy sauce is suitable for stews and is known as *soy superior sauce*)
- Bean curd (doufu; bland nutritious curd made from soya beans, used extensively in soup, meat and vegetable dishes)
- Water chestnuts (sweet root vegetable which is white and crunchy, and used particularly in southern Chinese dishes)
- Bamboo shoots (edible shoots, pale yellow, used in vegetable dishes)
- Fresh coriander or Chinese parsley (flat, feathery leaves have a citrus-like flavour used in sauces, etc.)
- Root ginger (fresh root ginger used in soups and meat and vegetable dishes)
- Peking duck (specially raised ducks, firstly basted with a honey mixture then roasted and served with Chinese pancakes)
- Dim sum (savoury and sweet, steamed, baked or fried tea delicacies, such as spring roll filled with bean sprouts on pork, and small sweet egg custard tartlets)

JAPANESE COOKERY (see Plate 7 and 8, page 39)

Japanese cookery is unique in its artistic presentation and the wide variety of small amounts of different dishes served to please the eye as well as the appetite. Fish, rice, noodles and vegetables as well as soy sauce predominate. Raw fish which is exceptionally fresh is used extensively.

- Sushi (cooked cold rice seasoned with rice vinegar, with raw or cooked fish)
- Teriyaki (a cooking technique of glaze grilling, using the marinade)
- Yakitori (grilled chicken kebabs basted with soy sauce containing sake and mirin)
- Mirin (a type of sweet cooking wine)

- Tofu (soya bean curd used extensively)
- Sukiyaki (sautéed sliced beef with vegetables, tofu, noodles and soy sauce)
- Sake (an alcoholic beverage made from rice)

SOUTH EAST ASIAN COOKERY

South East Asia is influenced by both Chinese and Indian cooking. Singapore, Indonesia, Burma and Thailand use rice extensively as well as pineapples, pomelos, mandarins, bananas, coconut, mangoes and paw paws.

- Gado gado (vegetables with peanut sauce; salad of vegetables, beans, carrots and cauliflowers, cooked *al dente* with salad vegetables; hard-boiled eggs with hot dressing of peanut butter, sugar, chillies and coconut milk)
- Satay (Indonesian kebabs; skewered, grilled meat served with spicy peanut sauce)

This area produces many spices such as nutmeg, cloves, and ginger. Coconuts, rice and other tropical fruits including pineapples and bananas are common.

AFRICAN COOKERY

The climate of Africa enables bananas, paw paws, mangoes, grapes, citrus fruits and sugar cane to grow well. From North Africa comes couscous, the national dish of Morocco, Tunisia and Algeria, which is a fine semolina made from wheat steamed over soup, stew or fish. East Africa, which includes Ethiopia, is where coffee originated. Both coffee and tea are grown here and maize is an important crop. In West Africa *cassava* is the staple food, and Ghana is the main cocoa-producing country in the world. Groundnut is grown in Nigeria. South Africa produces sugar cane and maize and cattle and sheep are raised.

- Bobotie (a South African dish of curried minced meat with nuts and raisins covered with a savoury custard)
- Groundnut stew (a chicken stew enriched with peanut butter)
- Ugali (maize porridge served with soups and stews)

TOPICS FOR DISCUSSION

1. The effects of religion on the eating habits of certain cultures.
2. The most popular British foods; why they are the most popular.
3. The benefits of having a wide variety of ethnic restaurants in the country.
4. The effects of people's eating habits other than cultural or religious.

Part

2

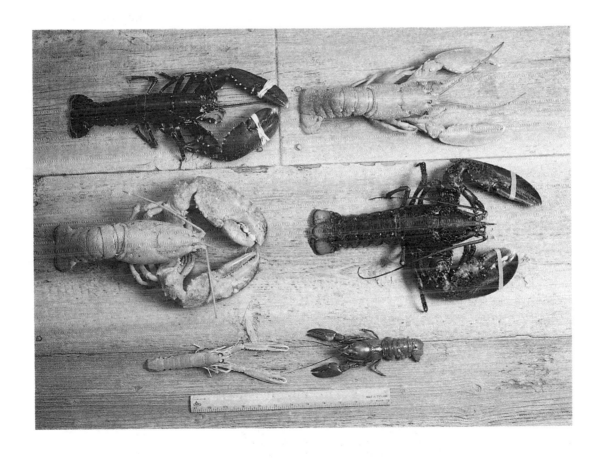

*F*OOD AND THE CATERER

4
Food commodities

—

When studying commodities, students are recommended to explore the markets to get to know both fresh foods and all possible substitutes such as convenience or ready-prepared foods. Comparison should be made between various brands of foods, and between convenience and fresh unprepared foods. Factors to be considered when comparing should include quality, price, hygiene, labour, cost, time, space required and disposal of waste.

Students are advised to be cost conscious from the outset in all their studies and to form the habit of keeping up to date with current prices of all commodities, equipment, labour and overheads. An in-built awareness of costs is an important asset to any successful caterer. A list of food prices is printed weekly in the *Caterer and Hotelkeeper*. A list of other commodities is given on pages 194 and 195, so students can keep up to date by marking prices in pencil.

The catering student should begin to form opinions as to when and in what circumstances fresh, convenience or possibly a combination of both foods should be used. Convenience or ready-prepared foods are not new and have been in use for many years. However, there are many more products on the market today, and the wise caterer will make a thorough study of all types available and, if and when they are suitable, incorporate them into the organisation.

The most important factor when considering the use of convenience (ready-made) foods is the same as for traditional foods: who is the food intended for? What price are they able to pay? Having considered these points, it is possible to predict whether the customer will accept, reject or possibly even prefer convenience foods.

Organic foods

Consumers are gradually becoming more organic and environmentally friendly. There are no nutritional reasons for using organic produce. Organic foods are said to contain fewer contaminants. They have a lower content of pesticides, or none at all, but global sources of contamination cannot be avoided by the organic farmer.

Food inspection particularly by the Ministry of Agriculture Fisheries and Food keep a good check on the content of undesirable substances in conventional produce. The aspect of contamination, therefore, is not a good reason for using organically grown produce either. The main argument for using organic produce is that they support an environmentally sensible development in farming. Caterers may thus consider using organic produce as a social priority. Some caterers have started using organic produce as they become environmentally conscious.

Today's consumers, whether guests in a restaurant or staff in firms' restaurants or hospital patients, have a national expectation that insensitive use of the environment or resources should be avoided. Staff in catering have a natural expectation with regard to a sensible working environment.

One of the problems for the organic market is a lack of a good distribution network. It is difficult to establish a distribution network as long as there are only a few catering kitchens which use organic vegetables. The solution to the problem is to distribute organic produce through traditional distribution channels. The quality of organic produce is variable. The majority of caterers and food manufacturers at present take organic produce seriously. The trend for the future is likely to be towards environmentally friendly food products rather than organic food products.

ENVIRONMENTALLY FRIENDLY FOOD PRODUCTS

These are foods which are produced under conditions which save on electricity and water as well as other environmental factors, or they can be products made with environmentally friendly technology. Products may be packed in environmentally friendly packaging and produce is grown with a limited use of fertilisers and crop sprays, but is not necessarily totally organic. In this way a trend may be expected in which industry slowly takes on the idea of organic production and increasingly begins to market environmentally friendly food products to the catering industry.

MEAT (Figure 4.1)

Meat is probably our most important food, accounting as it does for a major share of our total expenditure on food.

Cattle, sheep and pigs are reared for fresh meat and certain pigs are specifically produced for bacon. The animals are humanely killed and the meat prepared in hygienic conditions. The skins or hides are removed, the innards are taken out of the carcass and the offal is put aside.

Fig. 4.1
Wholesale purchasing of meat

Carcasses of beef are split into two sides and those of lambs, sheep, pigs and calves are left whole; they are then chilled in a cold room before being sent to market.

To cook meat properly it is necessary to know and understand the structure of meat. Lean flesh is composed of muscles, which are numerous bundles of fibres held together by connective tissue. The size of these fibres is extremely small, especially in tender cuts or cuts from young animals, and only the coarsest fibres may be distinguished by the naked eye. The size of the fibres varies in length, depth and thickness and this variation will affect the grain and the texture of the meat.

The quantity of connective tissue binding the fibres together will have much to do with the tenderness and eating quality. There are two kinds of connective tissue, the yellow (*elastin*) and the white (*collagen*). The thick yellow strip that runs along the neck and back of animals is an example of elastin. Elastin is found in the muscles, especially in older animals or those muscles receiving considerable exercise. Elastin will not cook, and it must be broken up mechanically by pounding or mincing. The white connective tissue (collagen) can be cooked, as it changes in moist heat to form gelatine.

The quantity of fat and its condition are important factors in determining eating quality. Fat is found on the exterior and interior of the carcass and in the flesh itself. Fat deposited between muscles or between the bundles of fibres is called marbling. If marbling is present, the meat is likely to be tender, of better flavour and moist. Much of the flavour of meat is given by fats found in lean or fatty tissues of the meat. Animals absorb flavour from the food they are given, therefore the type of feed is important in the final eating quality of the meat.

Extractives in meats are also responsible for flavour. Muscles that receive a good deal of exercise have a higher proportion of flavour extractives than those receiving less exercise. Shin, shank, neck and other parts receiving exercise will give richer stock and gravies, and meat with more flavour than the tender cuts.

Tenderness, flavour and moistness are increased if beef is hung after slaughter. Pork and veal are hung for 3–7 days according to the temperature. Meat is generally hung at a temperature of 1°C (34°F).

Supply sources

- Lamb and mutton – England, Scotland, New Zealand and Australia.
- Beef – England, Ireland and Scotland.
- Veal – England, Scotland and Holland.
- Pork – England.
- Bacon – England and Denmark.
- Farmed venison – Scotland.

Storage (see Plate 9, page 40)

Meat should be stored at its appropriate temperature, usually between 1° and 5°C (34–41°F). Raw meat should be stored separately from cooked meat or meat products. Chilled meat must be used by the 'use-by date' unless written permission to use it later has been given by the supplier.

Temperatures of chillers and freezers should be measured regularly. Chilled cooked meat must generally be stored below 8°C (46.4°F) but if it has been prepared for consumption without further cooking or reheating the temperature must be at or below 5°C (41°F). Cut or sliced, smoked or cured meats must be stored at or below 5°C (41°F).

Preparation

During preparation, storage temperatures should be maintained for safe cooking. A joint of meat should be no larger that 2.5 kg (5 lb). Larger joints should be divided into smaller portions.

Cutting boards and utensils should be colour coded to separate raw from cooked meats, thus reducing the risk of cross contamination.

Frozen meats should be thawed in refrigerators.

Cooking (see table overleaf)

Heat should reach a minimum core 2 temperature of 70°C (158°F) for at least two minutes. If a joint is not to be used immediately, it should be cooled as quickly as possible to or below 5°C (41°F).

APPROXIMATE COOKING TIMES FOR MEAT

ROASTING

Degree required	Allow: minutes per 450 g (1 lb)	Meat thermometer/ probe readings
Beef		
rare	20 minutes per 450 g (1 lb) plus 20 minutes	60°C (140°F)
medium	25 minutes per 450 g (1 lb) plus 25 minutes	70°C (160°F)
well done	30 minutes per 450 g (1 lb) plus 30 minutes	80°C (175°F)
Pork		
medium	30 minutes per 450 g (1 lb) plus 30 minutes	75–80°C (170–175°F)
well done	35 minutes per 450 g (1 lb) plus 35 minutes	80–85°C (175–185°F)
Lamb		
medium	25 minutes per 450 g (1 lb) plus 25 minutes	70–75°C (160–170°F)
well done	30 minutes per 450 g (1 lb) plus 30 minutes	75–80°C (170–175°F)

NB: Smaller joints weighing less than 1.25 kg (2½ lb) may need 5 minutes per 450 g (1 lb) extra cooking time.

GRILLING

These vary considerably according to the thickness of the meat and degree of cooking preferred.

Type of meat	Thickness	Time for each side	
Beef			
steak (sirloin and rump)	2 cm (1 in)	rare:	2½ minutes
		medium:	4 minutes
		well done:	6 minutes
steaks (fillet)	2–3 cm (1–1½ in)	rare:	3–4 minutes
		medium:	4–5 minutes
		well done:	6–7 minutes
minute steak	1 cm (½ in)	1 minute	
burgers	1–2 cm (½–1 in)	4–6 minutes	
Pork			
chops (loin, chump, spare rib)	2–3 cm (1–1½ in)	8–10 minutes	
steaks (double loin, leg, shoulder)	1½–2 cm (1 in)	6–8 minutes	
	2 cm+ (1 in+)	8–10 minutes	
fillet/tenderloin, sliced	1–1½ cm (½–¾ in)	3–5 minutes	
escalope	½ cm (¼ in)	3–4 minutes	
spare ribs	approx. 15 cm (6 in) in length	10–15 minutes in total; turn occasionally	
belly slices	1–2 cm (½–1 in)	8–10 minutes depending on degree of crispness preferred	
Lamb			
chops (loin, leg)	2–3 cm (1–1½ in)	6–8 minutes	
steaks (leg)	1–2 cm (½–1 in)	4–6 minutes	
	2 cm+ (1 in+)	6–8 minutes	
cutlets	2–3 cm (1–1½ in)	4–6 minutes	
butterfly chop	2–3 cm (1–1½ un)	8–10 minutes	
valentine steak	1½–2 cm (¾–1 in)	4–6 minutes	

Cuts and joints

For economic reasons of saving on both labour and storage space, very many caterers purchase meat by joints or cuts rather than by the carcass.

The Meat Buyer's Guide to Caterers is a manual which has been designed to assist caterers who wish to simplify and facilitate their meat purchasing.

The lists (and plates) (but not the tables) illustrating the various ways in which meat can be ordered are taken from the manual. Some of the terminology varies slightly from that in more general use by many caterers, but this should not be a major problem.

Food value

Meat, having a high protein content, is valuable for the growth and repair of the body and as a source of energy.

Preservation

- Salting. Meat can be pickled in brine, and this method of preservation may be applied to silverside, brisket and ox-tongues. Salting is also used in the production of bacon, before the sides of pork are smoked. This also applies to hams.
- Chilling. This means that meat is kept at a temperature just above freezing point in a controlled atmosphere. Chilled meat cannot be kept in the usual type of cold room for more than a few days, and this is sufficient time for the meat to hang, enabling it to become tender.
- Freezing. Small carcasses, such as lamb and mutton, can be frozen and the quality is not affected by freezing. They can be kept frozen until required and then thawed out before being used. Some beef is frozen, but it is inferior in quality to chilled beef.
- Canning. Large quantities of meat are canned and corned beef is of importance since it has a very high protein content. Pork is used for tinned luncheon meat.

Further information

Institute of Meat, Third Floor, 50–60 St John St, London EC1M 4DT; Meat and Livestock Commission, PO Box 44, Winterhill House, Snowdon Drive, Milton Keynes, MK6 1AX.

Beef

Approximately 80% of beef used in Britain is home produced.

The hanging or maturing of beef at a chill temperature of 1°C (34°F) for up to 14 days has the effect of increasing tenderness and flavour. This hanging process is essential as animals are generally slaughtered around the age of 18–21 months, and the beef can be tough. Also a short time after death an animal's muscles stiffen, a condition known as *rigor mortis*. After a time chemical actions caused by enzymes and increasing acidity relax the muscles and the meat becomes soft and pliable. As meat continues to hang in storage rigor mortis is lost and tenderness, flavour and moistness increase. (Pork, lamb and veal are obtained from young animals so that toughness is not a significant factor.)

Large quantities of beef are prepared as chilled boneless prime cuts, vacuum packed in film. This process has the following advantages: it extends the storage life of the cuts. The cuts are boned and fully trimmed thus reducing labour cost and storage space.

It is essential to store and handle vacuum packed meat correctly. Storage temperature should be 0°C (32°F) with the cartons the correct way up so that the drips cannot stain the fatty surface. A good circulation of air should be allowed between cartons.

When required for use, the vacuum film should be punctured in order to drain away any blood before the film is removed. On opening the film a slight odour is usually discernible, but this should quickly disappear on exposure to the air. The vacuum packed beef has a deep red colour, but when the film is broken the colour should change to its normal characteristic red within 20–30 minutes. Once the film is punctured the meat should be used as soon as possible.

QUALITY
- Lean meat should be bright red, with small flecks of white fat (marbled).
- The fat should be firm, brittle in texture, creamy white in colour and odourless.
- Home-killed beef is best.

BEEF JOINTS (see Plates 10–16 page 73; Figures 4.2–4.4)
- Topside and silverside – whole or rolled.
- Rump – whole or boneless.
- Sirloin – with rump, fillet and wing rib.
- Sirloin – short cut, thin flank removed.
- Sirloin – boned and rolled, fillet removed.
- Sirloin – boneless.
- Sirloin – with rump and fillet (known as chump end).
- Sirloin – chump end, boned and rolled.
- Wing rib – on the bone or boned and rolled.
- Striploin – boned, fillet and thin flank removed.
- Striploin – special trim boned; fillet, thin flank removed and trimmed.
- Fillet, standard – untrimmed.
- Fillet, larder trim – all skin, fat and muscle removed.
- Fillet, special – trimmed.
- Fore rib – untrimmed, oven prepared, carvery prepared or boned and rolled.
- Rib-eye roll – prepared from the fore-rib; the main eye of meat with cartilage, muscle, fat and gristle removed.
- Brisket – boneless and rolled.
- Pony – prepared from fore-rib after brisket, shank and sticking piece are removed.

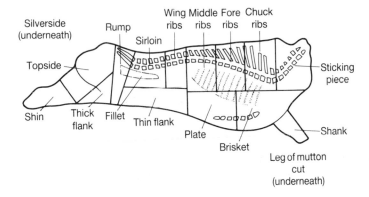

Fig. 4.2 Side of beef

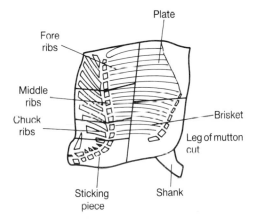

Fig. 4.3 Forequarter of beef

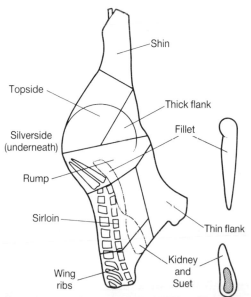

Fig. 4.4 Hindquarter of beef

- Back, top or middle ribs – prepared joints.
- Chuck steak – boneless.
- Shin – boneless.
- Full baron – consists of a pair of rumps, loins and wing ribs.
- Short baron – consists of a pair of rumps and loins.
- Baron (double sirloin) – consists of a pair of sirloins.
- Roastings – consists of half a full baron cut lengthwise.
- Loin and rib – consists of half a full baron cut lengthwise with rumps removed.

BEEF CUTS (see Plates 17–23, pages 73 and 74)
- Beef olives, braising steaks, rump steaks.
- 'T' bone steaks, standard.
- 'T' bone steaks, short-cut – flank removed.
- Club steaks – prepared from the sirloin and wing rib.
- Sirloin steaks, standard.
- Sirloin steaks, short cut – flank removed.
- Sirloin steaks, special trim – flank removed and trimmed.
- Sirloin steaks, larder trim – flank removed.
- Minute steaks.
- Fillet steaks, standard.
- Fillet steaks, special trim.
- Fillet steaks, larder trim.
- Fillet tails.
- Rib steaks – bone in, prepared from fore rib.
- Rib-eye steaks – bone removed.
- Braising steaks.
- Beefburgers – pure.
- Beefburgers – seasoned.
- Beefburgers – economy.

Veal

Originally most top quality veal came from Holland, but as the Dutch methods of production are now used extensively in Britain, supplies of home-produced veal are available all the year round. Good quality carcasses weighing around 100 kg (220 lb) can be produced from calves slaughtered at 12–24 weeks. This quality of veal is necessary for first-class cookery. Calves which are not considered by the producer to be suitable for quality veal or beef are, however, slaughtered within 10 days after birth and are known as 'Bobby' calves. The meat obtained is suitable for stewing, pies, casseroles, etc.

- The flesh of veal should be pale pink, firm, not soft or flabby.
- Cut surfaces must not be dry, but moist.
- Bones in young animals should be pinkish white, porous and with a small amount of blood in their structure.
- The fat should be firm and pinkish white.
- The kidney ought to be firm and well covered with fat.

BEEF: USES AND MENU EXAMPLES

JOINT	USE	MENU EXAMPLE
Hindquarter		
shin	consommé, beef tea, stewing	Consommé royale
topside	braising, stewing, second-class roasting	Braised beef with noodles, Bitok
silverside	pickled and boiled	Boiled silverside, carrots and dumplings
thick flank	braising and stewing	Beef and vegetable stew
rump	grilling and frying as steaks	Grilled rump steak
sirloin	roasting, grilling and frying as steaks	Roast sirloin or beef, grilled entrecôte steak
wing ribs	roasting, grilling and frying as steaks	Roast beef, Yorkshire pudding
thin flank	stewing, boiling, sausages	Boiled beef French style
fillet	roasting, grilling, frying	Tournedos chasseur
Forequarter		
fore-ribs	roasting, braising	Roast beef and Yorkshire pudding
middle ribs		
chuck ribs	stewing, braising	Beef steak pie
sticking piece	stewing, sausages	Sausage toad in the hole
plate and brisket	pickled and boiled	Pressed beef, Hamburgers
leg of mutton cut	braising and stewing	Savoury minced beef
shank	consommé, beef tea	Clear soup with vegetables

1 Hock/knuckle

2a Topside

2b Silverside

2c Thick flank

3 Chump

4a Loin end

4b Best end

5 Thin flank

6 Breast

7 Oyster

8 Middle neck

9 Scrag

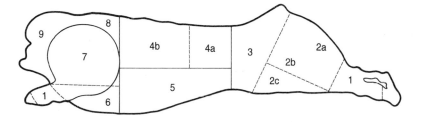

Fig. 4.5 Side of veal

Veal joints (see Plates 24–26, page 74; Figure 4.5)

- Hind and end – as a pair, the remaining portion of the carcass after removing the breasts; can be supplied singly.
- Hind – as above with the best ends removed, singly or as a pair.
- Haunch – as above with the loins removed, singly.
- Haunch – boned and rolled.
- Leg – the haunch with the chump-end removed.
- Leg – boned and rolled.
- Topside – prepared from the leg after removing the knuckle.
- Cushion – a prepared muscle block of meat cleared of fat and sinew.
- Top rump – thick flank.
- Silverside – under cushion.
- Whole rump.
- Chine and end – remaining portion of the hind and end after removing the haunches.
- Long striploin – prepared from the single chine and end.
- Long striploin – special trim.
- Long striploin – larder trim (further trimmed).
- Saddle.
- Loin – boneless or with bone in.
- Short striploin – prepared from the loin.
- Short striploin – special trim.
- Short striploin – larder trim (further trimmed).
- Fillet.
- Knuckle.
- Best end.
- Rack – a prepared single best-end.
- Breast.
- Shoulder – bone-in, or boned and rolled.
- Diced veal.
- Minced veal.

Veal cuts (see Plate 27, page 74)

- Escalopes, ex cushion – prepared from the cushion.
- Escalopes – prepared from topside, top rump and silverside.
- Chops, standard – prepared from the loin.
- Chops, short cut – as above with the flank removed.
- Steaks, larder trim – prepared from short striploin.
- Osso buco – cuts across the shin including bone approximately 2 cm (1 in).
- Cutlets – prepared from the best-end.
- Cutlets, larder trim.

VEAL: USES AND MENU EXAMPLES

JOINT	USE	MENU EXAMPLE
leg	escalopes, roasting, sauté, braising	Roast leg of veal
loin	roasting, frying, grilling	Veal chops with spaghetti
best-end	roasting, frying, grilling	Veal cutlet Milanaise style
shoulder	braising, stewing	Goulash of veal
neck-end	stewing	Fricassée of veal with onions and button mushrooms
scrag	stock, stewing	Veal stock
breast	stewing, roasting	White stew of veal with noodles
Leg of veal		
knuckle	stewing	Osso buco
cushion	escalopes, roasting, sauté, braising	Braised veal with vegetable garnish
under cushion	escalopes, roasting, sauté, braising	Escalope of veal viennoise
thick flank	escalopes, roasting, sauté, braising	Sauté of veal Marengo

Pork

Approximately 95% of pork used in Britain is home produced.

- Lean flesh of pork should be pale pink.
- The fat should be white, firm, smooth and not excessive.
- Bones must be small, fine and pinkish.
- The skin, or rind, ought to be smooth.

Suckling pigs weigh 5–9 kg (10–20 lb) dressed and are usually roasted whole. Boars are wild or uncastrated male pigs. The meat of boars is available from special farms.

PORK JOINTS (see Plates 28–37, page 70; Figure 4.6)
- Side – half a carcass split down the middle lengthwise, available with or without the head.
- Leg and long loin – a side with head, hand and belly removed.
- Leg and short loin – as above with the neck-end removed between fourth and fifth ribs.

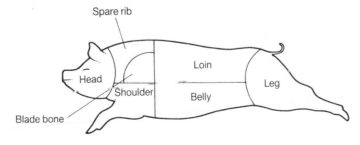

Fig. 4.6   Side of pork

- Leg – available with bone-in, boned, boned and rolled and carvery cut.
- Long loin – the portion remaining after removing the leg.
- Long loin – available boneless or boned and rolled.
- Short loin – the portion remaining after removing the leg.
- Short loin – available boneless or boned and rolled.
- Middle loin – short loin with chump end removed, available with bone-in or boned and rolled.
- Long hogmeat – long loin with skin and excess fat removed, available with bone-in or boned and rolled.
- Short hogmeat – short loin with skin and excess fat removed, available with bone-in or boned and rolled.
- Middle hogmeat – middle loin prepared and available as above.
- Neck-end – the remaining portion of long loin after removing short loin, available as above.
- Fillet – also known as tenderloin.
- Belly.
- Hand – the remaining portion of a side when the leg and long loin are removed. Available bone-in, boned and boned and rolled.
- Shoulder – the shoulder is removed from a side by a perpendicular cut between fourth and fifth ribs; available as above.
- Spare rib – the remaining portion of the neck-end after removing the blade-bone.
- Boneless neck – spare rib with bones removed.
- Blade-bone – the remaining portion of the neck-end after removing the spare rib; available boneless.
- Barbecue spare ribs – the rib bones and related meat removed from the belly.
- Diced pork – produced from any combination of cuts.
- Minced pork – fat content should not exceed 25%.
- Suckling pig – young piglet which is slaughtered prior to weaning which normally takes place 5–7 weeks after birth; supplied as a carcass with head weighing between 5–10 kg (10–22 lb).

PORK CUTS
- Escalopes – cut from the leg or chump end, trimmed and battened out.

PORK: USES AND MENU EXAMPLES

JOINT	USE	MENU EXAMPLE
leg	roasting, boiling	Roast leg of pork, apple sauce
loin	roasting, frying, grilling	Roast loin of pork
spare rib	roasting, pies	Pork pie
blade-bone	roasting, pies	Boiled belly of pork and pease pudding
shoulder	roasting, sausages, pies	Grilled pork sausage, Charcutier sauce
head	brawn	Pork brawn and salad

- Chops, rind-on – prepared from the short loin.
- Chops, trimmed – prepared from short hogmeat.
- Steaks – prepared from middle hogmeat.
- Neck-end chops – prepared from the neck-end, supplied rind-on or trimmed.
- Sliced belly – cut from the prepared belly.
- Spare ribs chops – cut from the spare rib.

Bacon (Figure 4.7)

Bacon is the cured flesh of a pig (60–75 kg (120–150 lb) dead weight) specifically reared for bacon because its shape and size yield economic bacon joints.

The curing process consists of salting either by a dry method and smoking, or by soaking in brine followed by smoking.

Green bacon is brine cured but not smoked; it has a milder flavour and does not keep as long as smoked bacon.

- There should be no sign of stickiness.
- There must be no unpleasant smell.
- The rind should be thin, smooth and free from wrinkles.
- The fat ought to be white, smooth and not excessive in proportion to the lean.
- The lean meat of bacon should be deep pink in colour and firm.

Bacon should be kept in a well-ventilated cold room. Joints of bacon should be wrapped in muslin and hung, preferably in a cold room. Sides of bacon are also hung on hooks. Cut bacon is kept on trays in the refrigerator or cold room.

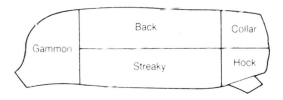

Fig. 4.7 Side of bacon

BACON: USES AND MENU EXAMPLES

JOINT	USE	MENU EXAMPLE
collar and hock	boiling, grilling	Boiled bacon, pease pudding and parsley sauce
back	grilling, frying	Egg and bacon
streaky	grilling, frying	Chicken liver and bacon on roast
gammon	boiling, grilling, frying	Braised gammon, Madeira sauce Grilled gammon and pineapple
trotters	boiling, grilling	Split and grilled devilled pig's trotters

Ham

Ham is the hind leg of a pig cut round from the side of pork with the aitch bone; it is preserved by curing or pickling in brine and then dried and smoked. York, Bradenham (Wiltshire) and Suffolk are three of the most popular English hams.

Bradenham is easily distinguished by its black skin. The Bradenham and Suffolk hams are sweet and mildly cured. Imported hams include the Parma, Serrano, Bayonne and Westphalian, all of which are carved paper thin and eaten raw as hors-d'œuvre.

Lamb and mutton

In Britain, five times as much lamb and mutton is eaten than in any other European country. Approximately two thirds of all lamb consumed is home produced and the balance comes from Australia and New Zealand. As the seasons in Australia and New Zealand are opposite to those in Britain these supplies can be integrated with our own. Most lamb carcasses imported are from animals aged between 4–6 months.

- Lamb is under one year old – after one year it is termed mutton.
- The carcass should be compact and evenly fleshed.
- The lean flesh of lamb and mutton ought to be firm and of a pleasing dull red colour and of a fine texture or grain.
- The fat should be evenly distributed, hard, brittle, flaky and clear white in colour.
- The bones should be porous in young animals.

The factors influencing lamb and mutton composition, quality and value are essentially similar to those previously described for beef.

THE DIFFERENCE BETWEEN LAMB AND MUTTON

Lamb refers to a young sheep slaughtered for meat in the year of birth either at weaning time or a few months afterwards. Slaughter lambs are generally either wethers (castrates) or ewes (female). Young male lambs up to six or seven months of age may be slaughtered entire (uncastrated), but they are in the minority, even in flocks from which lambs are slaughtered at weaning (milk-fed lambs). From the first day of each year it is customary to refer to lambs born the previous year, or their carcasses, as 'hoggetts'. The distinction has no bearing on meat quality as lambs slaughtered in the last week of December are indistinguishable from lambs slaughtered from the same flock in January. The retail meat trade, catering butchers and consumers generally accept, therefore, that carcass meat from lambs and hoggetts is termed lamb until the supply of 'new season lamb' from lambs born early in the following year becomes generally available. From March to the end of April 'lamb' from hoggetts which are then young sheep slaughtered at about twelve months of age is available simultaneously with small quantities of new season lamb, most of which is taken up by the luxury end of the catering trade, as long as it is in short supply.

HOME-PRODUCED MUTTON

The supply of hoggetts declines rapidly in March and April and by May when those remaining are well over a year old they are referred to as 'clean sheep' which when slaughtered will be described as mutton instead of lamb. The term 'clean sheep' is applied to ewes which have not borne or carried lambs and to castrated males. The term breeding sheep is used to describe ewes which have carried lambs, or rams with the exception of those slaughtered at an early age before the development of masculine characteristics which affect carcass quality.

Meat from a breeding sheep is always described as mutton although generally there is a clear distinction between mutton from 'clean sheep' and that from breeding sheep which may be described as ewe mutton.

LAMB JOINTS (see Plates 38–44, page 75; Figure 4.8 page 72)

- Hind and end, long – the remainder of the carcass after the breast, neck and shoulders are removed.
- Hind and end, short – as above with the middle neck also removed.
- Hind – consists of two legs and loins, uncut.
- Haunch – a leg with the chump end.
- Haunch – boneless.
- Leg – a leg with the chump end removed.
- Leg – boneless or boned and rolled.
- Leg, carvery cut – prepared from the leg or haunch with the aitch bone, cod fat and tail removed, excess fat and shank end removed, the knuckle bone cleaned and the joint tied.
- Chine and end, long – the remainder of the carcass after removing the breasts, neck, shoulders and legs.
- Chine and end, short – the remainder of the carcass after removing the breasts, neck, shoulders, legs and middle neck.
- Saddle – an uncut pair of loins and chump ends.
- Saddle, oven-prepared – the flanks, kidney knobs, bark and all internal fat removed.
- Saddle, boned and rolled – oven-prepared, boned and tied or netted.
- Short saddle – an uncut pair of loins without chump ends; also available oven-prepared or boned and rolled.
- Best-end, long – a pair of uncut ends with 11 rib bones each side.
- Best-end, short – a pair of uncut ends with seven rib bones each side.
- Best-end, split and chined – prepared from short best-ends.
- Rack – best-end split and chined and trimmed ready for cooking.
- Rack, larder-trimmed – a rack further trimmed with $1\frac{1}{2}$ cm ($\frac{3}{4}$ in) of the ends of the rib bones cleaned.
- Fore – the remaining portion of the carcass after removing the hind.
- Short fore – a fore with the breasts and short best-ends removed, can be boned and rolled.
- Shoulder – also available boneless or boned and rolled.

LAMB AND MUTTON: USES AND MENU EXAMPLES

JOINT	USE	MENU EXAMPLE
shoulder	roasting, stewing	Roast, stuffed shoulder of lamb
leg	roasting (mutton – boiled)	Roast leg of lamb, mint sauce Boiled leg of mutton, caper sauce
breast	stewing, roasting	Irish stew
middle neck	stewing	Navarin of lamb
scrag-end	broth	Mutton broth
best-end	roasting, grilling, frying	Roast rack of lamb with a breadcrumb, herb and garlic topping
loin	roasting, grilling, frying	Roast stuffed loin of lamb
chop	grilling, frying	Grilled loin chop
cutlet	grilling, frying	Lamb cutlets reform
fillet	grilling, frying	Shish kebab

- Neck and middle – short fore with the shoulders removed, five rib bones each side.
- Middle neck – neck and middle with the neck removed between the first and second ribs, leaving four rib bones each side.
- Breast.

LAMB CUTS (see Plates 45–47, pages 75 and 76)
- Diced lamb, stewing – prepared from any combination of cuts.
- Diced lamb – kebabs, prepared from the legs.
- Minced lamb – the fat content should not exceed 25%.
- Economy chops – prepared from the chine and short-end from which the flank has been removed.
- Loin chops, trimmed – prepared from the saddle (two loins).
- Noisettes – prepared from boned loins, rolled, tied and cut into pieces.
- Valentine of lamb – prepared from the boned short saddle, partially sliced to give a butterfly cut.

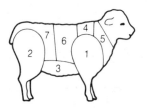

1. Shoulders (2)
2. Legs (2)
3. Breasts (2)
4. Middle neck
5. Scrag-end
6. Best-end
7. Saddle

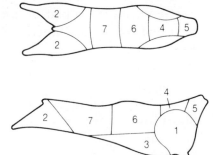

Fig. 4.8 Carcass of lamb

Plate 10   Beef, silverside (rolled)

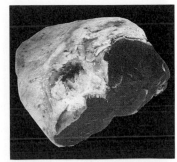

Plate 11   Beef, topside

Plate 12   Beef, striploin (larder trim)

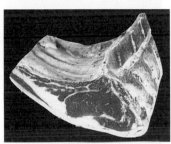

Plate 13   Beef, 'Scotch cut' forerib (carvery cut)

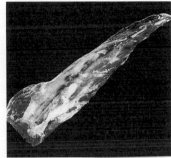

Plate 14   Beef, long fillet (special trim)

Plate 15   Beef, boneless shin

Plate 16   Beef, chuck steak

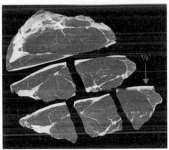

Plate 17   Beef, rump steaks

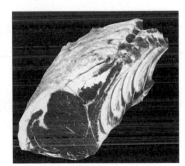

Plate 18   Beef, sirloin (using rib)

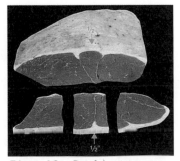

Plate 19   Beef, braising steaks (ex-silverside)

Plate 20   Beef, sirloin steaks (short cut)

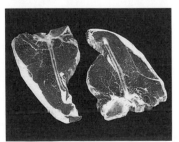

Plate 21   Beef, 'T' bone steaks (short cut)

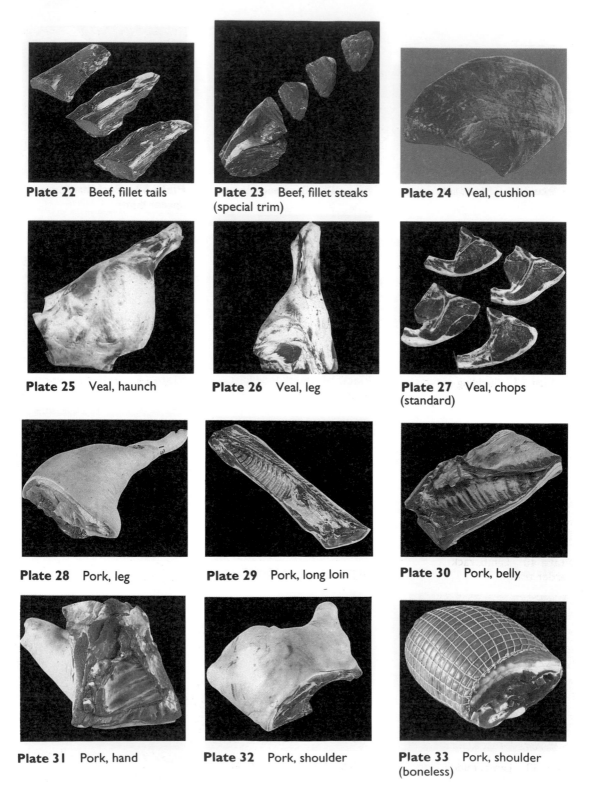

Plate 22   Beef, fillet tails

Plate 23   Beef, fillet steaks (special trim)

Plate 24   Veal, cushion

Plate 25   Veal, haunch

Plate 26   Veal, leg

Plate 27   Veal, chops (standard)

Plate 28   Pork, leg

Plate 29   Pork, long loin

Plate 30   Pork, belly

Plate 31   Pork, hand

Plate 32   Pork, shoulder

Plate 33   Pork, shoulder (boneless)

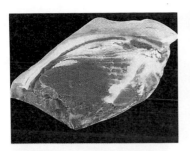

Plate 34   Pork, spare rib

Plate 35   Pork, blade-bone

Plate 36   Pork, barbecue spare ribs

Plate 37   Suckling pig

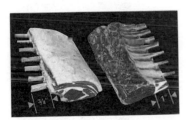

Plate 38   Lamb, short saddle

Plate 39   Lamb, best-end (short)

Plate 40   Lamb, rack (larder trim)

Plate 41   Lamb, shoulder

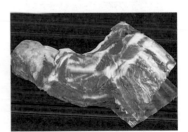

Plate 42   Lamb, neck and middle

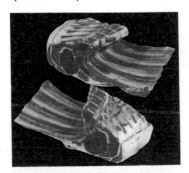

Plate 43   Lamb, middle neck

Plate 44   Lamb, breast

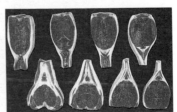

Plate 45   Lamb, valentine steaks

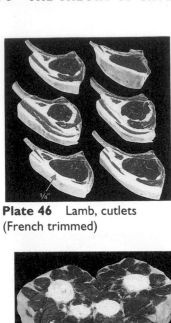

Plate 46   Lamb, cutlets (French trimmed)

Plate 47   Lamb, crown of

Plate 48   Tripe

Plate 49   Oxtail

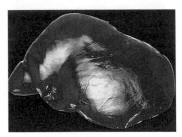

Plate 50   Calf liver

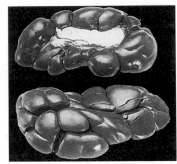

Plate 51   Ox kidney

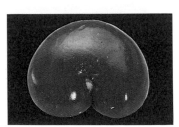

Plate 52   Lamb kidney

Plate 53   Ox heart

Plate 54   Lamb heart

Plate 55   Lamb tongue

Plate 56   Calf sweetbread

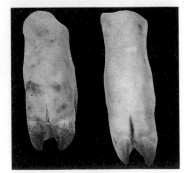

Plate 57   Pig trotters

Plate 58   Poultry (left to right, top to bottom): boiling fowl 2 kg (4 lb), turkey 5 kg (10 lb), chicken 1 kg (2 lb), French chicken (Bresse) 1 kg (2 lb), corn-fed chicken 1 kg (2 lb), chicken fermier 1 kg (2 lb), Poussin 400 g (1 lb)

Plate 59   Poultry (left to right, top row first): croise duck 1 kg (2 lb), duck 2 kg (4 lb), guinea fowl 1 kg (2 lb), squab 32 g, quail 13 g, woodpigeon 28 g

Plate 60   Haunch of venison 23 kg (46 lb) (top), and saddle of venison 13 kg (26 lb)

Plate 61   Hare $2\frac{1}{2}$ kg (5 lb) (top), skinned hare and fillets of hare; tame rabbit 750 g ($1\frac{1}{2}$ lb), saddle of rabbit and skinned rabbit

Plate 62   Cock pheasant 1 kg (2 lb), prepared hen pheasant, prepared cock pheasant

Plate 63 Prepared grouse (top), grouse 750 g (1½ lb), prepared partridge, partridge 750 g (1½ lb), prepared red legged partridge, snipe 300 g (12 oz) and prepared snipe (note trussed with beak)

Plate 64 Capercaillie 1 kg (2 lb) (top), wild duck 750 g (1½ lb), oven-ready wild duck, wild duck 750 g (1½ lb)

- Crown or Barnsley chops – cut across the short saddle giving an uncut pair of loin chops.
- Cutlets, trimmed – cut from the best-end.
- Butterfly cutlets – cut across an uncut pair of best-ends, producing double cutlets.
- Cutlets, French trimmed – prepared from the rack (larder-trimmed).
- Band saw chops – prepared from the unacceptable chump ends from loin chops and the unacceptable blade-bone cutlets from the best-end.
- Pauillac lamb – young milk-fed lambs supplied with head and liver weighing between 7–10 kg (15–22 lb).
- Dressed saddle – an oven-prepared saddle, decorated and embellished for buffet presentation.
- Crown of lamb – prepared from two best-ends tied in a round shape with the rib bones slanting outwards.

OFFAL AND OTHER EDIBLE PARTS OF THE CARCASS

Offal is the name given to the edible parts taken from the inside of the carcass: liver, kidney, heart and sweetbread. Tripe, brains, oxtail, tongue and head are sometimes included under this term. Fresh offal (unfrozen) should be purchased as required and can be refrigerated under hygienic conditions at a temperature of 1°C (30°F), at relative humidity of 90% for up to seven days. Frozen offal should be kept frozen until required.

Tripe (see Plate 48, page 76)

Tripe is the stomach lining or white muscle of beef cattle. Honeycomb tripe is the second compartment of the stomach and considered the best. Smooth tripe is the first compartment of the stomach, and is not considered to be as good as honeycomb tripe. Sheep tripe, darker in colour, is obtainable in some areas. It may be boiled or braised. A menu example would be Tripe and onions.

Oxtail (see Plate 49, page 76)

Oxtails should be 1½–1¾ kg) (3–5 lb), lean and with no signs of stickiness. They are usually braised or used for soup. Menu examples are Oxtail soup or Braised oxtail.

Head

Sheep's heads can be used for stock, and pigs' heads for brawn. The calf's head is used for soup and certain dishes such as calf's head vinaigrette.

Sheep's and calves' heads should not be sticky; they should be well fleshed and odourless.

Suet

Beef suet should be creamy white, brittle and dry. It is used for suet paste. Other fat should be fresh and not sticky. Suet and fat may be rendered down for dripping.

Marrow

Beef marrow is obtained from the bones of the leg of beef. It should be of good size, firm, creamy white and odourless. It may be used as a garnish for steaks and for savouries. A menu example would be Toast baron.

Brains

Calf's brains are those usually used; they must be fresh. A menu example is Calf's brain with black butter sauce.

Bones

Bones must be fresh, not sticky; they are used for stock.

Liver (see Plate 50, page 76)

Calf's liver is the most expensive and is considered the best in terms of tenderness and delicacy of flavour and colour.

Lamb's liver is mild in flavour, tender and light in colour.

Sheep's liver, being from an older animal, is firmer in substance, darker in colour and has a stronger flavour than lamb's or calf's liver.

Ox or beef liver is the cheapest and if taken from an older animal can be coarse in texture and strong in flavour.

Pig's liver is full flavoured and used in many pâté recipes.

QUALITY

- Liver should appear fresh and have an attractive colour.
- It must not be dry or contain tubers.
- It should be smooth in texture.

FOOD VALUE

Liver is valuable as a protective food; it consists chiefly of protein and contains useful amounts of vitamin A and iron.

Kidney (see Plates 51–52, page 76)

Lamb's kidney is light in colour, delicate in flavour and is ideal for grilling and frying.

Sheep's kidney is darker in colour and has a stronger flavour than lamb's kidney.

Calf's kidney is light in colour, delicate in flavour and can be used in a wide variety of dishes.

Ox kidney is dark in colour, strong in flavour and is generally used mixed with beef, for steak and kidney pie or pudding.

Pig's kidney is smooth, long and flat by comparison with sheep's kidney; it has a strong flavour.

QUALITY
- Ox kidney should be fresh and deep red in colour.
- Lamb's kidney should be covered in fat which is removed just before use; the fat should be crisp and the kidney moist.

FOOD VALUE
The food value of kidney is similar to liver, i.e. a protective food containing vitamin A and iron.

Hearts (see Plates 53–54, page 76)

Ox or beef hearts are the largest used for cooking. They are dark coloured, solid and tend to be dry and tough.

Calf's heart, coming from a younger animal, is lighter in colour and more tender.

Sheep's heart is dark and solid and can be dry and tough unless cooked carefully.

Lamb's heart is smaller and lighter and is normally served whole. Larger hearts are normally sliced before serving.

QUALITY
Hearts should not be too fatty and should not contain too many tubes. When cut they should be moist.

FOOD VALUE
They have a high protein content and are valuable for growth and repair of the body.

Tongue (see Plate 55, page 76)

- Tongues must be fresh.
- They should not have an excessive amount of waste at the root end.
- Ox tongues may be used fresh or salted.
- Sheep's tongues are used unsalted.

Sweetbreads (see Plate 56, page 76)

There are two kinds of sweetbread, unequal in shape and quality. The heart bread (thymus) is round and plump and of much better quality than the throat or neck breads (pancreas), which are longer and uneven in shape. Calf's heart bread weighs up to $\frac{3}{4}$ kg ($1\frac{1}{2}$ lb); lamb's heart bread up to 100 g (4 oz).

QUALITY
- Heart and neck breads should be fleshy and large.
- They ought to be creamy white in colour.
- Heart breads are of better quality than neck breads.

FOOD VALUE
Sweetbreads are valuable foods, particularly for hospital diets. They are very easily digested and useful for building body tissues.

DIFFERENT KINDS OF OFFAL: USES AND MENU EXAMPLES

JOINT	USE	MENU EXAMPLE
Liver		
calf's liver	frying	Calf's liver and bacon
lamb's liver	frying	Shish kebab
pig's liver	frying, pâté	Liver pâté
ox liver	braising, frying	Braised liver and onions
Kidney		
calf's kidney	grilling, sauté	Mixed grill
lamb's kidney	grilling, sauté	Fried kidneys with mushrooms and chipolatas
pig's kidney	grilling, sauté	Grilled kidneys and bacon
ox kidney	stewing, soup	Kidney soup
Heart		
sheep's heart	braising	Stuffed braised sheep's heart
ox heart		Braised ox heart
Tongue		
lamb's tongue	boiling, braising	Lamb's tongue in cream sauce
ox tongue	boiling, braising	Braised tongue with Madeira sauce
Sweetbreads		
lamb's sweetbreads	braising, frying	Breadcrumbed lamb's sweetbreads with artichoke and peas
calf's sweetbreads	braising, frying	Braised veal sweetbreads with vegetable julienne

MEAT SUBSTITUTES

Textured vegetable protein (TVP)

This is a meat substitute manufactured from protein derived from wheat, oats, cotton-seed, soya bean and other sources. The main source of TVP is the soya bean, due to its high protein content.

TVP is used chiefly as a meat extender, varying from 10–60% replacement of fresh meat. Some caterers on very tight budgets make use of it, but is main use is in food manufacturing.

By partially replacing the meat in certain dishes, such as casseroles, stews, pies, pasties, sausage rolls, hamburgers, meat loaf and pâté, it is possible to reduce costs, provide nutrition and serve food acceptable in appearance.

Myco-protein

A meat substitute is being produced from a plant which is a distant relative of the mushroom. This myco-protein contains protein and fibre and is the result of a fermentation process similar to the way yogurt is made. It may be used as an alternative to chicken or beef or in vegetarian dishes.

QUORN

Quorn is the brand name of Rank Hovis McDougall's myco-protein, produced by fermentation process from a plant which is a distant relative of the mushroom. In late 1984 RHM and ICI formed a joint company Marlow foods, which built and now operates a plant at Billingham with a nominal capacity of 1500 tonnes per year.

Quorn's big advantage is its texture. It has a fibrosity of its own which results from the natural fibrosity of the myco-protein, aided by the method of processing. From the fermentation the myco-protein is filtered through a vacuum filter and it comes out as a mat of fibres. Two processing stages follow. In the first it is mixed with a little egg albumen and water in a mixer, together with natural flavours and colours according to the final product being made. The resulting soft dough has the fibres randomly aligned and is further processed to align the fibres.

To make Quorn with a soft, short texture the material is simply extruded. The other type has a coarser fibrosity and a firmer texture; this is produced by rolling and folding the material in a manner similar to the production of flaky pastry. This, causes individual fibres to form bundles which resemble the micro-structure of meat. In both cases the final product is heated to set the albumen, which acts as a binder and then cut to size and frozen.

Quorn can be subjected to all kinds of coating and forming techniques, it can be oven heated, grilled or fried. Quorn contains no animal fat (so it is suitable for vegetarians), is low in fat and high in dietary fibre.

Further information can be obtained from The Quorn Catering Information Service, PO Box 7, Brentford, London TW8 9BR.

POULTRY (see Plates 58 and 59, pages 77 and 78; Figure 4.9)

Poultry is the name given to domestic birds specially bred to be eaten and for their eggs.

Season

Owing to present-day methods of poultry production in batteries, and to deep freezing, poultry is available all the year round.

Food value

The flesh of poultry is more easily digested than that of butchers' meat. It contains protein and is therefore useful for building and repairing body tissues and providing

Fig. 4.9 Wholesale purchasing of poultry and game

heat and energy. Fat content is low and contains a high percentage of unsaturated acids.

Storage

Fresh poultry must be hung by the legs in a well-ventilated room for at least 24 hours, otherwise it will not be tender; the innards are not removed until the bird is required.

Frozen birds must be kept in a deep-freeze cabinet until required. To reduce the risk of food poisoning, it is essential that frozen birds be completely thawed, preferably in a refrigerator before being cooked.

Chicken (see Plate 58, page 77)

QUALITY
- The breast of the bird should be plump.
- The vent-end of the breast-bone must be pliable.
- The flesh should be firm.
- The skin ought to be white and unbroken, with a faint bluish tinge.
- The legs should be smooth, with small scales and small spurs.
- Old birds have large scales and large spurs on the legs.

TYPES OF CHICKENS

- **Free-range birds** live a reasonable natural life in a large pen; traditional free-range means that the bird is a traditional slow growing breed allowed to roam and forage outdoors and fed with a cereal/vegetable diet.
- **Bresse chickens** are reared in France; when young they are free range but when older they are penned and fed a special diet including milk and maize; Bresse chickens are highly esteemed for their quality and flavour.
- **Broiler** chickens, so called after the American word for roasting, are reared until they reach the required weight – averaging between $1\frac{1}{2}$–2 kg (3–$4\frac{1}{2}$ lb) – which takes approximately six or seven weeks.
- **Whole** chickens weighing up to 3 kg (6 lb) are also available.
- **Oven-ready fresh** chickens are sold completely eviscerated, normally chilled, with or without giblets.
- **Frozen** chickens are first cleaned and then quickly frozen.
- **Poussins**, or spring chickens as they used to be known, are four to six weeks old, weighing about $\frac{1}{2}$ kg (1 lb) and are available fresh or frozen.
- **Corn-fed** chickens are reared on a diet of maize which gives them their distinctive yellow hue; mostly available fresh, but some are frozen.
- **Chicken portions**, both fresh and frozen, are available in a wide variety of packs including breasts, drumsticks, thighs or packs of mixed portions.
- **Boiling** fowl are either smaller, less meaty birds weighing 1–2 kg (2–4 lb) or large tough old hens which have finished laying. They are chiefly used for stocks, soups and sauces.

USE

Chickens are suitable for cooking whole by roasting, grilling (split open), pot-roasting and braising. They can also be cooked in pieces as suprêmes, ballottines, sautés, pies, galantines, and in vol-au-vents, salads and sandwiches; also stocks, soups and sauces.

FURTHER INFORMATION

British Chicken Information Service, Bury House, 126–128 Cromwell Road, London SW7 4ET.

Duck/duckling and Goose/gosling (see Plate 59, page 78)

Goose is traditionally in season from Michaelmas, September 29 until Christmas.

QUALITY

- The feet and bills should be bright yellow.
- The upper bill should break easily.
- The web feet must be easy to tear.

Ducks and geese may be roasted or braised. Menu examples include Roast Aylesbury duckling; Duck with apple sauce and sage and onion stuffing; Braised duck with peas; Roast goose with sage and onion stuffing and apple sauce; Braised goose with turnips.

Turkey

QUALITY
- The breast should be large, the skin undamaged and with no signs of stickiness.
- The legs of young birds are black and smooth, the feet supple with a short spur.
- As the bird ages the legs turn reddish grey and become scaly. The feet become hard.

Turkeys are usually roasted. Menu examples include Roast Norfolk turkey and chestnut stuffing; Sliced turkey in sherry flavoured cream sauce with pimento.

Guinea fowl (see Plate 59, page 78)

When plucked these grey-and-white feathered birds resemble a chicken with darker flesh. The young birds are known as squabs.

The quality points relating to chicken apply to guinea fowl.

Menu examples include Braised guinea fowl with wild mushrooms; Breast of guinea fowl with noodles and pepper sauce.

Pigeon (see Plate 59, page 78)

Pigeon should be plump, the flesh mauve-red in colour and the claws pinkish. Tame pigeons are smaller than wood pigeons. Squabs are young specially reared pigeons.

Menu examples include Pigeon pie; Breast of pigeon with herb ravioli.

POULTRY: WEIGHTS AND PORTIONS

ENGLISH	UNDRAWN WEIGHT (approx.)	NUMBER OF PORTIONS (approx.)
single baby chicken (spring chicken)	360 g–$\frac{1}{2}$ kg (12 oz–1 lb)	1
double baby chicken	$\frac{1}{2}$–$\frac{3}{4}$ kg (1–1$\frac{1}{2}$ lb)	2
small roasting chicken	$\frac{3}{4}$–1 kg (1$\frac{1}{2}$–2 lb)	3–4
medium roasting chicken	1–2 kg (2–4 lb)	4–6
large roasting or boiling chicken	2–3 kg (4–8 lb)	6–8
boiling fowl	2$\frac{1}{2}$–4 kg (5–8 lb)	8–12
young turkey	3$\frac{1}{2}$ kg (7 lb)	*
turkey	3$\frac{1}{2}$–20 kg (7–40 lb)	*
duckling	1–1$\frac{1}{2}$ kg (2–3 lb)	3–4
duck	1$\frac{1}{2}$–2$\frac{1}{2}$ kg (3–5 lb)	4–6
gosling	2–3$\frac{1}{2}$ kg (4–7 lb)	*
goose	3$\frac{1}{2}$–7 kg (7–14 lb)	*
guinea fowl	1–1$\frac{1}{2}$ kg (2–3 lb)	3–4
pigeon	300–400 g (12 oz–1 lb)	1–2

Drawn poultry loses approximately 25% of its original weight. All poultry is bought by number and weight.
* For turkey and goose allow $\frac{1}{2}$ kg (1 lb) undrawn weight per portion.

GAME (Figure 4.9, page 86)

Game is the name given to certain wild birds and animals which are eaten; there are two kinds of game:

- feathered;
- furred.

Food value

As it is less fatty than poultry or meat, game is easily digested, with the exception of water fowl, which has oily flesh. Game is useful for building and repairing body tissues and for energy.

Storage

- Hanging is essential for all game. It drains the flesh of blood and begins the process of disintegration which is vital to make the flesh soft and edible, and also to develop flavour.
- The hanging time is determined by the type, condition and age of the game and the storage temperature.
- Old birds need to hang for a longer time than young birds.
- Game birds are not plucked or drawn before hanging.
- Venison and hare are hung with the skin on.
- Game must be hung in a well-ventilated, dry, cold storeroom; this need not be refrigerated.
- Game birds should be hung by the neck with the feet down.

Game availability

Game is available fresh in season between the following dates and frozen for the remainder of the year:

- Grouse   August 12–December 10
- Snipe   August 12–January 31
- Partridge   September 1–February 1
- Wild duck   September 1–January 31
- Pheasant   October 1–February 1
- Woodcock   October 31–February 1
- Venison, hares, rabbits and pigeons are available throughout the year.

Venison (see Plate 60, page 79)

Venison is the flesh from any member of the deer family which includes elk, moose, reindeer, caribou and antelope. Red deer meat is a dark, blood-red colour; the flesh of the roe deer is paler and the fallow deer is considered to have the best flavour.

Meat from animals over 18 months in age tends to be tough and dry and is usually marinated to counteract this. Young animals up to 18 months produce delicate, tender meat which does not require marinating. Nowadays, venison is extensively farmed in the UK.

Venison contains 207 calories per 100 g and young venison has only about 6% fat (compared to beef, lamb and pork around 20% fat). It has the highest protein content of the major meats. Venison is very suitable for a low-cholesterol diet because the fat is mainly polyunsaturated. The carcass has little intramuscular fat; the lean meat contains only low levels of marbling fat.

Farmed and wild venison is available. Joints should be well fleshed and a dark brownish red colour. Venison is usually roasted or braised in joints, served hot or cold with a peppery/sweet type sauce. Small cuts may be fried and served in a variety of ways. Venison is available as shoulder, boned and rolled; haunch, boned and rolled; prepared saddles and steaks; also as pâté, in sausages, burgers; and smoked.

Menu examples include Roast haunch of venison with Cumberland sauce; Fillet of venison with beetroot.

Hare and rabbit (see Plate 61, page 79)

The ears of hares and rabbits should tear easily. Old hares the lip is more pronounced than in young animals. The rabbit is distinguished from the hare by shorter ears, feet and body.

Hare may be cooked as a red wine stew called jugged hare and the saddle can be roasted.

Menu examples include Jugged hare; Roast saddle of hare with port-wine sauce.

Birds

- The beak should break easily.
- The breast plumage should be soft.
- The breast should be plump.
- Quill feathers should be pointed, not rounded.
- The legs should be smooth.

PHEASANT (see Plate 62, page 79)
This is one of the most common game birds. Average weight is $1\frac{1}{2}$–2 kg (2–4 lb). Young birds have a pliable breast bone and soft pliable feet. Hang for five to eight days. Used for roasting, braising or pot roasting.

Menu examples include Salmis of pheasant; Pot roasted pheasant with celery.

PARTRIDGE (see Plate 63, page 80)
The most common varieties are the grey legged and the red legged. Average weight is 200–400 g ($\frac{1}{2}$–1 lb). Hang for three to five days. Used for roasting or braising.

Menu examples include Braised partridge with cabbage; Roast partridge.

GROUSE (see Plate 63, page 80)
A famous and popular game bird is the red grouse which is shot in Scotland and Yorkshire. Average weight is 300 g (12 oz). Young birds have pointed wings and rounded soft spurs. Hang for five to seven days. Used for roasting.

Menu example includes Roast grouse.

GAME: WEIGHTS AND PORTIONS

ENGLISH	UNDRAWN WEIGHT (approx.)	NUMBER OF PORTIONS (approx.)
Furred		
venison	15 kg (33 lb)	15–20
hare	$2\frac{1}{2}$–$3\frac{1}{2}$ kg (5–7 lb)	6–8
rabbit	1 kg (2 lb)	4
Feathered		
pheasant	$1\frac{1}{2}$–2 kg (3–4 lb)	2–4
partridge	$\frac{1}{4}$–$\frac{1}{2}$ kg (8 oz–1 lb)	1–2
grouse	360 g (12 oz)	1–2
woodcock	$\frac{1}{4}$ kg–360 g (8–12 oz)	1
snipe	120 g (4 oz)	1
quail	150 g (5 oz)	1
wild duck	1–$1\frac{1}{2}$ kg (2–3 lb)	2–4
teal	$\frac{1}{2}$–$\frac{3}{4}$ kg (1–$1\frac{1}{2}$ lb)	1–2
woodpigeon	360 g (12 oz)	1

SNIPE (see Plate 63, page 80)
Weight is about 100 g (4 oz). Hang for three to four days. The heads and neck are skinned, the eyes removed; birds are then trussed with their own beaks. When drawing the birds only the gizzard, gallbladder and intestines are removed. The birds are then roasted with the liver and heart left inside.

Menu example includes Roast snipe.

WOODCOCK
Small birds with long thin beaks. Average weight is 200–300 g (8–12 oz). Prepare as for snipe. Usually roasted.

QUAIL (see Plate 59, page 78)
Small birds weighing 50–75 g (2–3 oz) produced on farms, usually packed in boxes of 12. Quails are not hung. They are usually roasted or braised.

Menu examples include Roast quail with grapes; Boned and stuffed quail and salad.

WILD DUCK (see Plate 64, page 80)
Wild duck include mallard and widgeon. Average weight is 1–$1\frac{1}{2}$ kg (2–3 lb). Hang for one or two days. Usually roasted or braised.

Menu example includes Wild duck with orange sauce.

TEAL
The smallest duck, weighing 400–600 g (1–$1\frac{1}{2}$ lb). Hang for one to two days. Usually roasted or braised. Young birds have small pinkish legs and soft down under the

wings. Teal and wild duck must be eaten in season otherwise the flesh is coarse and has a fishy flavour.

Menu example includes Roast teal.

FISH (see Plates 65–74, pages 113–116)

Fish have formed a large proportion of our food because of their abundance and relative ease of harvesting. It is interesting to note that fish consume the smaller organisms in the sea and are themselves the food of the larger organisms. In addition to providing fresh and processed food for human consumption, other valuable products such as oil and isinglass, as well as fertiliser, come from fish.

Unfortunately the fish supply is not unlimited due to overfishing, so it is now necessary to have fish farms (e.g. for trout and salmon) to supplement the natural sources. This is not the only problem: due to contamination by man, the seas and rivers are increasingly polluted, thus affecting both the supply and the suitability of fish, particularly shellfish, for human consumption.

Fish are valuable, not only because they are a good source of protein, but because they are suitable for all types of menus and can be cooked and presented in a wide variety of ways. The range of different types of fish of varying textures, taste and appearance is indispensable to the creative chef.

Types or varieties (see tables on pages 94–95)

- Oily fish – round in shape (herring, mackerel, salmon).
- White fish – round (cod, whiting, hake) or flat (plaice, sole, turbot).
- Shellfish and cephalopods are discussed on pages 108–12.

Purchasing unit

Fresh fish is bought by the kilogram, by the number of fillets or whole fish of the weight that is required. For example, 30 kg (66 lb) of salmon could be ordered as 2 × 15 kg (33 lb), 3 × 10 kg (22 lb) or 6 × 5 kg (11 lb). Frozen fish can be purchased in 15 kg (33 lb) blocks. Fish may be bought on the bone or filleted. (The approximate loss from boning and waste is 50% for flat fish, 60% for round fish.) Fillets of plaice and sole can be purchased according to weight. They are graded from 45 g ($1\frac{1}{2}$ oz) to 180 g (6 oz) per fillet and go up in weight by 15 g ($\frac{1}{2}$ oz).

Source

Fish is plentiful in the UK, because we are surrounded by water, although overfishing and pollution are having a detrimental effect on the supplies of certain fish. Most catches are made off Iceland, Scotland, the North Sea, Irish Sea and the English Channel. Salmon are caught in certain English and Scottish rivers, and are extensively farmed. Frozen fish is imported from Scandinavia, Canada and Japan; the last two countries export frozen salmon to Britain.

Storage

- Fresh fish are stored in a fish-box containing ice, in a separate refrigerator or part of a refrigerator used only for fish at a temperature of 1–2°C (34–36°F).
- The temperature must be maintained just above freezing point.
- Frozen fish must be stored in a deep-freeze cabinet or compartment at −18°C (0°F).
- Smoked fish should be kept in a refrigerator.

Quality points for buying (see Figure 4.10, page 100)

When buying whole fish the following points should be looked for to ensure freshness.

- Eyes: bright, full and not sunken; no slime or cloudiness.
- Gills: bright red in colour; no bacterial slime.
- Flesh: translucent and resilient so that when pressed the impression goes quickly; the fish must not be limp.
- Scales: these should lie flat, and be moist and plentiful.
- Skin: this should be covered with a fresh sea slime, or be smooth and moist, with a good sheen and no abrasions.
- Smell: this must be pleasant, with no smell of ammonia or sourness.
- There must be no bruising or blood clots.
- There should not be areas of discoloration.
- Fish should be purchased daily, preferably direct from the market or supplier.
- The fish should be well iced so that it arrives in good condition.
- Medium-sized fish are usually better than large fish, which may be coarse; small fish often lack flavour.

Food value

Fish is as useful a source of animal protein as meat. The oily fish, such as sardines, mackerel, herrings and salmon contain vitamins A and D in their flesh; in white fish, such as halibut and cod, these vitamins are present in the liver. Since all fish contains protein it is a good body-building food and oily fish is useful for energy and as a protective food because of its vitamins.

The bones of sardines, whitebait and tinned salmon, which can be eaten, provide calcium and phosphorus.

Owing to its fat content oily fish is not so digestible as white fish and is not suitable in cookery for invalids.

Preservation (see also Chapter 5, page 222)

FREEZING

Fish is either frozen at sea or as soon as possible after reaching port. It should be thawed out before being cooked. Plaice, halibut, turbot, haddock, sole, cod, trout, salmon, herring, whiting, scampi, smoked haddock and kippers are available frozen.

KINDS OF FISH: SEASONS AND PURCHASING UNITS

FISH	SEASON	PURCHASING UNIT
Oily		
anchovy	imported occasionally June to December (home waters)	number and weight
common eel	all year, best in autumn	number and weight
conger eel	March to October	weight
herring	all year except spring	number and weight
mackerel	September to July	number and weight or fillets
pilchard (mature sardines)	all year	number and weight
salmon (farmed)	all year	number and weight
salmon (wild)	February to August	number and weight
salmon trout	February to August	number and weight
salmon (Pacific)	July to November	number and weight
sprat	September to March	number and weight
sardines	all year	number and weight
trout	February to September	number and weight
trout (farmed)	all year	number and weight
tuna	all year	steaks or pieces
whitebait	when available	weight
White flat		
brill	June to February	number and weight
dab	March to December	number and weight
flounder	May to February, best in winter	number and weight
halibut	June to March	number and weight or steaks
megrim	April to February	number and weight
plaice	May to February	number and weight or fillets
skate	May to February	wings, number and weight
sole, Dover	May to March	number and weight or fillets
sole, lemon	all year, best in spring	number and weight or fillets
turbot	all year	number and weight or fillets
turbot (farmed)	when available	number and weight
witch	all year, best in spring	number and weight or fillets
Round		
bass	June to March	number and weight or fillets
bream, fresh water	August to April	number and weight or fillets
bream, sea	June to December	number and weight or fillets
carp (mostly farmed)	fluctuates throughout year	number and weight or fillets

FISH	SEASON	PURCHASING UNIT
Round		
cod	all year, not at best in spring	number and weight or fillets
dogfish (huss, flake, rigg)	all year, best autumn	steaks or fillets
grey mullet	May to February, best autumn and winter	number and weight
haddock	all year, best autumn and winter	number and weight or fillets
hake	June to February	number and weight or fillets
John Dory	September to May	number and weight or fillets
ling	September to July	number and weight or fillets
monkfish (angler-fish)	all year, best in winter	number and weight or tails
pike	all year	number and weight
perch	May to February	number and weight
pollack (yellow, green)	May to December	number and weight
redfish	all year	number and weight or fillets
red gurnard	all year, best from July to April	number or weight
red mullet	imported best in summer, UK autumn	number and weight and fillets
sea bream	June to February	number and weight
smelt	occasionally	number and weight
shark (porbeagle)	occasionally	steaks or pieces
snapper, red snapper	check with supplier	
whiting	all year, best in winter	number and weight or fillets

CANNING

The oily fish are usually canned. Sardines, salmon, anchovies, pilchards, tuna, herring and herring roe are canned in their own juice (as with salmon) or in oil or tomato sauce.

SALTING

In this country salting of fish is usually accompanied by a smoking process.

- Cured herrings – are packed in salt.
- Caviar – the slightly salted roe of the sturgeon which is sieved, tinned and refrigerated; imitation caviar is also obtainable (see page 187).

SMOKING (see also page 228)

Fish to be smoked may be gutted or left whole. It is then soaked in a strong salt solution (brine), and in some cases a dye is added to improve colour. After this it is drained and hung on racks in a kiln and exposed to smoke for 5 or 6 hours.

Cold smoking takes place at a temperature of no more than 33°C (91°F) (to avoid cooking the flesh). Therefore all cold smoked fish is raw and is usually cooked before being eaten, the exception being smoked salmon.

Fig. 4.10 A wholesale fish market

Hot smoking fish is cured at a temperature between 70–80°C (158–176°F) in order to cook the flesh, so does not require further cooking.

Choose fish with a pleasant smoky smell and a bright glossy surface. The flesh should be firm; sticky or soggy flesh means that the fish may have been of low quality or under smoked.

Refrigerate before use as the preservative quality of the smoke is only slight. Smoked fish products keep in good condition for a little longer than fresh fish.

Types of smoked fish

- Arbroath smokies (see Plate 78, page 118) – small haddocks smoked in Arbroath, Scotland; the fish is hot smoked and can be eaten uncooked or may be brushed with melted butter and grilled.
- Finnan haddock (see Plate 78, page 118) – name derives from Findon, South of Aberdeen; the haddocks are split, left on the bone, with the head removed. Salting takes 2 hours. The fish are then dried for 2–3 hours and finally smoked over peat, hardwood, sawdust or fir cones for 12 hours. Usually cooked by poaching in milk.
- Yellow smoked haddock (see Plate 78, page 118) – fish is split or filleted, cold smoked and dyed to give a bright yellow colour.
- Bloaters – whole herrings, lightly salted and cold smoked; they are traditionally smoked in Yarmouth and on the east coast; they only keep for a few days as they are mildly salted and the gut is not removed so that the body swells and has a gamey flavour; bloaters are usually gutted and grilled.
- Buckling – small, whole, lightly hot-smoked herring served either cold or warmed through.
- Kippers (see Plate 78, page 118) – gutted and flattened herring, salted and cold-smoked; high quality kippers come from Loch Fyne, Craister and the Isle of Man; mass produced varieties are available filleted and vacuum packed; kippers are at their best between August and April and are cooked by grilling or simmering in water.

- Red or hard smoked herrings – whole, heavily brined and smoked until very firm.
- Smoked cod – filleted, briefly soaked in brine with bright yellow colouring or dipped into a chemical solution to give colour and a slight smoky flavour; should be cooked before eating by poaching, grilling or baking.
- Smoked eel – smoked whole or in small fillets; usually served cold as a first course.

SMOKED HALIBUT (see Plate 78, page 118)
Smoked halibut is usually hot smoked and cut into thin slices for smoked salmon.
- Smoked mackerel – usually hot-smoked so does not require cooking; Cold-smoked mackerel is also available which needs to be cooked, usually by grilling.
- Smoked salmon (see Plate 78, page 118) – regarded as the best of the smoked fish, cured in two ways: the London cure involves light smoking and salting to give the salmon a delicate flavour and moist texture; the Scottish cure is a stronger smoking process giving the fish a more pronounced flavour; traditionally served thinly sliced as a first course.
- Smoked sprats – fish are hot-smoked and may be eaten cold or grilled.
- Smoked trout (see Plate 78, page 118) – fish are hot-smoked whole or in fillets and are usually served cold as a first course.
- Cod's roe (see Plate 78, page 118) – also smoked and usually served as first course.

PICKLING
Herrings pickled in vinegar are filleted, rolled and skewered and known as rollmops.

Oily fish

ANCHOVIES
Anchovies are small round fish used tinned in this country; they are supplied in 60 g and 390 g tins. They are filleted and packed in oil.

They are used for making anchovy butter and anchovy sauce, for garnishing dishes such as Scotch woodcock and Veal escalope viennoise. They may be used as a dish in a selection of hors-d'œuvre, as a savoury, and they can be used in puff pastry and served at cocktail parties.

COMMON EEL
Eels live in fresh water and are also farmed and can grow up to 1 m (39 in) in length. They are found in many British rivers and considerable quantities are imported from Holland. Eels must be kept alive until the last minute before cooking and they are generally used in fish stews. Menu examples include Bouillebaisse; Jellied eels.

CONGER EEL (see Plate 65, page 113)
The conger eel is a dark grey sea-fish with white flesh which grows up to 3 m (10 ft) in length. It may be used in the same way as eels, or it may be smoked. Menu example includes Smoked eel with horseradish sauce.

HERRING (see Plate 68, page 114)
Fresh herrings are used for breakfast and lunch menus; they may be grilled, fried or soused. Kippers (which are split, salted, dried) and smoked herrings are served for breakfast and also as a savoury. Average weight is 250 g (9 oz). Menu example includes Grilled herrings with mustard sauce.

MACKEREL (see Plate 68, page 114)
Mackerel are grilled, shallow fried or soused, and may be used on breakfast and lunch menus. They must be used fresh because the flesh deteriorates very quickly. Average weight, 360 g (12 oz). Menu example includes Grilled mackerel with anchovy butter.

PILCHARDS
These are mature sardines and can grow up to 24 cm (10 in). They have a good distinctive flavour and are best grilled or baked.

SALMON (see Plate 68, page 114)
Salmon is perhaps the most famous river fish and is caught in British rivers like the Dee, Tay, Severn, Avon, Wye and Spey. It is also extensively farmed. A considerable number are imported from Scandinavia, Canada, Germany and Japan. Apart from using it fresh, salmon is tinned or smoked. When fresh, it is usually boiled or grilled. When boiled it is cooked in a court-bouillon. Frequently, whole salmon are cooked and when cold decorated and served on buffets. Weight varies from $3\frac{1}{2}$–15 kg (8–33 lb). Salmon under $3\frac{1}{2}$ kg (8 lb) are known as grilse. Menu examples include Poached salmon with hollandaise sauce; Salmon mayonnaise.

SALMON TROUT (SEA TROUT) (see Plate 68, page 114)
Salmon trout are a sea fish similar in appearance to salmon, but smaller, and they are used in a similar way. Average weight, $1\frac{1}{2}$–2 kg (3–4 lb). Menu example includes Cold salmon trout with mayonnaise sauce.

SARDINES
Sardines are small fish of the pilchard family which are usually tinned and used for hors-d'œuvre, sandwiches and as a savoury. Fresh sardines are also available and may be cooked by grilling or frying.

SPRATS
Sprats are small fish fried whole and are also smoked and served as an hors-d'œuvre.

TROUT (see Plate 68, page 114)
Trout live in rivers and lakes and in the UK they are cultivated on trout farms. When served *au bleu*, they must be alive just before cooking; they are then killed, cleaned, sprinkled with vinegar and cooked in a court-bouillon. Trout are also served grilled or shallow fried, and may also be smoked and served as an hors d'œuvre. Average weight, 200 g (7 oz). Menu examples include Smoked trout with horseradish sauce; Pan-fried river trout.

TUNNY (TUNA) (see Plate 70, page 115)

Tunny is a very large fish cut into sections, used fresh or tinned in oil and is used mainly in hors d'œuvre and salads.

WHITEBAIT (see Plate 68, page 114)

Whitebait are the fry or young of herring, 2–4 cm ($\frac{3}{4}$–$1\frac{1}{2}$ in) long, and they are deep fried. Menu example includes Devilled whitebait.

White flat fish

BRILL (see Plate 66, page 113)

Brill is a large flat fish which is sometimes confused with turbot. Brill is oval in shape; the mottled brown skin is smooth with small scales. It can be distinguished from turbot by its lesser breadth in proportion to length; average weight, 3–4 kg (7–9 lb). It is usually served in the same way as turbot. Menu examples include Grilled brill steak with anchovy sauce; Poached supreme of brill with cheese sauce.

DAB

Dab is an oval-bodied fish with sandy brown upper skin and green freckles. Usual size is 20–30 cm (8–10 in). It has a pleasant flavour when fresh, and may be cooked by all methods.

FLOUNDER

This is oval, with dull brown upper skin (or sometimes dull green with orange freckles). Usual size is 30 cm (12 in). Flesh is rather watery and lacks flavour, needing good seasoning. It can be cooked by all methods.

HALIBUT (see Plate 67, page 113)

Halibut is a long and narrow fish, brown, with some darker mottling on the upper side; it can be 3 m (10 ft) in length and weigh 150 kg (330 lb). Halibut is served on higher class menus as it is much valued for its flavour. It is poached, boiled, grilled or shallow fried. Menu example includes Shallow fried fillet of halibut garnished with soft roes, mushroom and tomato.

MEGRIM

Megrim has a very long slender body, sandy-brown coloured with dark blotches. Usual size is 20–30 cm (8–12 in). It has a softish flesh and an unexceptional flavour, so needs good flavouring. It is best breadcrumbed and shallow-fried.

PLAICE (see Plate 73, page 116)

Plaice are oval in shape, with dark brown colouring and orange spots on the upper side, used on all types of menus; they are usually deep fried or grilled. Average weight, 360–450 g (12 oz–1 lb). Menu example includes Grilled plaice with lemon and parsley butter.

SKATE (see Plate 69, page 114)

Skate, a member of the ray family, is a very large fish and only the wings are used. It is always served on the bone and either shallow or deep fried or cooked in a court-bouillon and served with black butter. Menu examples include Skate with black butter; Fried skate.

SOLE (see Plate 73, page 116)

Sole is considered to be the best of the flat fish. The quality of the Dover sole is well known to be excellent. Soles are cooked by poaching, grilling or frying, both shallow and deep. They are served whole or filleted and garnished in a great many ways.

The usual size is 180–750 g (6 oz–1 lb 10 oz); fillets are taken from sole of 500 g (1 lb 2 oz) and over. A 180–250 g (6–9 oz) fish is referred to as a slip sole. When serving a whole fish, a 250–500 g (9 oz–1 lb 2 oz) sole may be used, the size depending on the type of establishment and the meal for which it is required. Menu examples include Sole colbert; Sole dieppoise; Fillets of sole Waleska; Paupiette of sole Newburg.

LEMON SOLE (see Plate 73, page 116)

This is related to Dover sole, but is broader in shape, and its upper skin is warm, yellowy brown and mottled with darker brown. It can weigh up to 600 g (1 lb 5 oz), and may be cooked by all methods.

TURBOT (see Plate 74, page 116)

Turbot has no scales and is roughly diamond in shape; it has knobs known as tubercules on the dark skin. In proportion to its length it is wider than brill; $3\frac{1}{2}$–4 kg (8–9 lb) is the average weight.

Turbot may be cooked whole, filleted or cut into portions on the bone. It may be boiled, poached, grilled or shallow fried. Menu examples include Poached turbot with Hollandaise sauce; Fillet of turbot on spinach with cheese sauce; Grilled turbot steak with parsley butter.

WITCH

This is similar in appearance and weight to lemon sole, with sandy-brown upper skin. It is best fried, poached, grilled or steamed.

White round fish

BASS

Bass have silvery grey backs and white bellies; small ones may have black spots. They have an excellent flavour, with white, lean, softish flesh (which must be very fresh). Bass can be steamed, poached, stuffed and baked, or grilled in steaks. Usual length is 30 cm (1 ft) but they can grow to 60 cm (2 ft).

BREAM (see Plate 70, page 115)

Sea bream is a short, oval-bodied, plump, reddish fish, with large scales and a dark patch behind the head. It is used on many less expensive menus; it is usually filleted and deep fried, or stuffed and baked, but other methods of cooking are employed. Average weight, $\frac{1}{2}$–1 kg (1–2 lb); size 28–30 cm (11–12 in). Menu examples include Fillet of bream with tartare sauce; Shallow fried fillets of bream.

CARP

This is a freshwater fish, usually farmed. The flesh is white with a good flavour, and is best poached in fillets or stuffed and baked. The usual size is 1–2 kg (2–4 lb).

COD (see Plate 71, page 115)

Cod varies in colour but is mostly greenish, brownish or olive grey. It can measure up to $1\frac{1}{2}$ m (5 ft) in length. Cod is cut into steaks or filleted and cut into portions; it can be deep or shallow fried or boiled. Small cod are known as codling. Average weight of cod, $2\frac{1}{2}$–$3\frac{1}{2}$ kg (6–8 lb). Menu examples include Fried cod and chips; Grilled cod steak.

COLEY (saith, coalfish, blackjack)

Coley is dark greenish-brown or blackish in colour, but the flesh turns white when cooked. It has a coarse texture and a dry undistinctive flavour, so is best for mixed fish stews, soups or pies. Size is 40–80 cm (16–31 in).

DOGFISH (huss, flake, rigg) (see Plate 72, page 116)

These are slender, elongated small sharks. The non-bony white or pink flesh is versatile, and is usually shallow or deep fried. It has a good flavour when very fresh. Length is usually 60 cm (24 in) and weight is $1\frac{1}{4}$ kg ($2\frac{1}{2}$ lb).

GREY MULLET (see Plate 70, page 115)

This has a scaly streamlined body, which is grey-silver or blue-green. Deep-sea or off-shore mullet has a fine flavour, with firm, moist flesh. It may be stuffed and baked or grilled in steaks. Some people believe that flavour is improved if the fish is kept in a refrigerator for two to three days, without being cleaned. Length is usually about 30 cm (1 ft); weight 500 g (1 lb 2 oz).

GUDGEON

Gudgeon are small fish found in Continental lakes and rivers. They may be deep fried whole. On menus in this country the French term *en goujon* refers to other fish such as sole or turbot, cut into pieces the size of gudgeon. Menu example includes Goujons of sole with tartar sauce.

GURNARD (see Plate 70, page 115)

A large family of tasty fish with many culinary uses.

HADDOCK (see Plate 71, page 115)

Haddock is distinguished from cod by the thumb mark on the side and by the lighter colour. Every method of cooking is suitable for haddock, and it appears on all kinds of menus. Apart from fresh haddock, smoked haddock is used a great deal for breakfast; it may also be served for lunch and as a savoury. Average weight, $\frac{1}{2}$–2 kg (1–4 lb). Finnan haddock is the most popular smoked haddock (see page 101. Menu examples include Haddock Monte Carlo; Fried fillet of haddock with tomato sauce.

HAKE (see Plate 71, page 115)

Owing to overfishing, hake is not plentiful. It is usually boiled and is easy to digest. The flesh is very white and of a delicate flavour. Menu example includes Boiled hake and egg sauce.

JOHN DORY (see Plate 70, page 115)

John Dory has a thin distinctive body, flattened from side to side, which is sandy beige in colour and tinged with yellow, with a blue silver grey belly. There is a blotch on each side referred to as 'thumbprint of St Peter'. It has very tough sharp spikes. The flavour is considered superb, and the fish may be cooked by all methods but is best poached, baked or steamed. The large bony head accounts for two-thirds of the weight. Usual size 36 cm (14 in).

LING

This is the largest member of the cod family, and is mottled brown or green with a bronze sheen; the fins have white edges. Size can be up to 90 cm (3 ft). Ling has a good flavour and texture and is generally used in fillets or cutlets, as for cod.

MONKFISH (see Plate 72, page 116)

Monkfish has a huge flattened head, with a normal fish-shaped tail. It is brown with dark blotches. The tail can be up to 180 cm (6 ft); weight 1–10 kg (2–22 lb). It may be cooked by all methods, and is a firm, close textured white fish with excellent flavour.

PIKE

Pike has a long body usually 60 cm (2 ft) which is greeny-brown, flecked with lighter green, with long toothy jaws. The traditional fish for quenelles, it may also be braised or steamed.

PERCH

Perch has a deep body, marked with about five shadowy vertical bars, and the fins are vivid orange or red. Usual size 15–30 cm (6–12 in). It is generally considered to have an excellent flavour, and may be shallow-fried, grilled, baked, braised or steamed.

POLLACK

This is a member of the cod family, and has a similar shape and variable colours. Its usual size is 45 cm (18 in). It is drier than cod, and is used for soups and stews.

REDFISH

This is bright red or orange-red, with a rosy belly and dusky gills. Usual size is 45 cm (18 in). It may be poached, baked or used in soups.

RED GURNARD (grey and yellow gurnard may also be available) (see Plate 70, page 115)

This has a large 'mail-checked', tapering body with very spiky fins. Usual size is 20–30 cm (8–12 in). It is good for stews, braising and baking.

RED MULLET (see Plate 70, page 115)

Red mullet is on occasion cooked with the liver left in, as it is thought that they help to impart a better flavour to the fish. Mullet are usually cooked whole, and the average weight is 360 g (12 oz). Menu examples include Shallowfried fillets of red mullet with lemon and capers; Red mullet en papillote.

ROCKFISH

Rockfish is the fishmonger's term applied to catfish (see Plate 72, page 116), coalfish, dogfish, conger eel, etc., after cleaning and skinning. It is usually deep fried in batter.

SHARK

The porbeagle shark, mako or hammerhead, fished off the British coast, gives the best quality food. It is bluish-grey above with a white belly and matt skin. Size is up to 3 m (10 ft). It may be cooked by all methods, but grilling in steaks or as kebabs are particularly suitable.

SMELT

Smelts are small fish found in river estuaries and imported from Holland; they are usually deep fried or grilled. When grilled they are split open. The weight of a smelt is from 60 to 90 g (2–3 oz). Menu example includes Fried breadcrumbed smelts.

SNAPPER

There are several kinds of snapper all of which are brightly coloured. Deep red or medium sized ones give the best flavour. Snapper may be steamed, fried, grilled, baked or smoked.

WHITING (see Plate 71, page 115)

Whiting are very easy to digest and they are therefore suitable for cookery for invalids. They may be poached, grilled or deep fried and used in the making of fish stuffing. Average weight, 360 g (12 oz). Menu examples include Fried whiting, tail in mouth.

WRASSE (see Plate 70, page 115)

Fish of variable colours but usually tinged with red and blue, covered white and SHELLgreen spots. Wrasse has a variety of culinary uses and can be baked and steamed.

Further information

Further information can be obtained from Seafish Industry Authority, 18 Logie Mill, Logie Green Road, Edinburgh EH7 4HG.

SHELLFISH (see table, page 104; Plates 75–77, pages 117–118)

Shellfish are of two types:

- Crustaceans (lobster, crabs)
- Molluscs (oysters, mussels)

Food value

Shellfish is a good body-building food. As the flesh is coarse and therefore indigestible a little vinegar may be used in cooking to soften the fibres.

SHELLFISH: SEASONS AND PURCHASING UNITS

SHELLFISH	SEASON	PURCHASING UNIT
clams	all year	number and weight
cockles	all year, best in summer	weight
common crab	all year, best April to December	number and weight
spider crab	all year	number and weight
swimming crab	all year	number and weight
king crab, red crab	check with supplier	imported frozen, shelled, prepared
soft-shelled crab	check with supplier	number and weight
crawfish	April to October	number and weight
Dublin Bay prawn	all year	number and weight
freshwater crayfish	mainly imported, some farmed in UK, wild have short season	number, weight and by case
lobster	April to November	number and weight
mussels	September to March	weight
oysters	May to August	by the dozen
prawn and shrimp	all year	number and weight
scallop	best December to March	number and weight
sea urchin	all year	number and by case

Purchasing points and storage

- With the exception of shrimps and prawns all shellfish, if possible, should be purchased alive, so as to ensure freshness.
- They should be stored in a cold room or refrigerator.
- Shellfish are kept in boxes and covered with damp sacks.
- Shellfish should be cooked as soon as possible after purchasing.
- Shrimps and prawns are usually bought cooked and may be obtained in their shell or peeled. They should be freshly boiled, of an even size and not too small. Frozen shrimps and prawns are obtainable in packs ready for use.

Crustaceans

CRAB (see Plate 76, page 117)
- Crab should be alive when bought to ensure freshness and both claws should be attached to the body.
- The claws should be large and fairly heavy.
- The hen crab has a broader tail, which is pink. The tail of the cock is narrow and whiter.
- There is usually more flesh on the hen crab, but it is considered to be of inferior quality to that of the cock.

Crabs are used for hors-d'œuvre, cocktails, salads, dressed crab, sandwiches and bouchées. Soft-shelled crabs are eaten in their entirety. They are considered to have an excellent flavour and may be deep or shallow fried or grilled.

CRAWFISH (see Plate 76, page 117)

Crawfish are like large lobsters without claws, but with long antennae. They are brick red in colour when cooked. Owing to their size and appearance they are used mostly on cold buffets but they can be served hot. The best size is $1\frac{1}{2}$–2 kg (3–4 lb). Menu example includes Langouste parisienne (Dressed crawfish Paris-style).

CRAYFISH (see Plate 75, page 117)

Crayfish are a type of small fresh-water lobster used for salads, garnishing cold buffet dishes and for recipes using lobster. They are dark brown or grey, turning pink when cooked. Average size is 8 cm (3 in).

LOBSTER (see Plate 75, page 117)

- Live lobsters are bluish black in colour and when cooked they turn bright red.
- They should be alive when bought in order to ensure freshness.
- Lobsters should have both claws attached.
- They ought to be fairly heavy in proportion to their size.
- Price varies considerably with size. For example, small $\frac{1}{2}$ kg (1 lb) lobsters are more expensive per kilogram than large lobsters.
- Lobster prices fluctuate considerably during the season.
- Hen lobsters are distinguished from the cock lobsters by a broader tail.
- There is usually more flesh on the hen, but it is considered inferior to that of the cock.
- The coral of the hen lobster is necessary to give the required colour for certain soups, sauces and lobster dishes. For these, 1 kg (2 lb) hen lobster should be ordered.
- When required for individual portions, cock lobsters of $\frac{1}{4}$–$\frac{1}{2}$ kg ($\frac{1}{2}$–1 lb) are used to give two portions.

Lobsters are served cold in cocktails, hors-d'œuvre, salads, sandwiches and on buffets. They are used hot for soup, grilled and served in numerous dishes with various sauces. They are also used as a garnish to fish dishes. Menu examples include Lobster mayonnaise; Lobster Mornay; Lobster soup.

PRAWNS

Prawns are larger than shrimps; they may be used for garnishing and decorating fish dishes, for cocktails, canapé, salad, hors-d'œuvre and for hot dishes, such as curried prawns. Prawns are also popular served cold with a mayonnaise type sauce. Menu examples include Prawn risotto, Stir-fried prawns; Curried prawns.

SCAMPI, DUBLIN BAY PRAWN

Scampi are found in the Mediterranean. The Dublin Bay prawn, which is the same family, is caught around the Scottish coast. These shellfish resemble small lobster about 20 cm (8 in) long and only the tail flesh is used for a variety of fish dishes, garnishing and salads. Menu examples include Fried scampi; Scampi provençale.

SHRIMPS

Shrimps are used for garnishes, decorating fish dishes, cocktails, sauces, salads, hors-d'œuvre, potted shrimps, omelets and savouries. Menu examples include Shrimp cocktail; Shrimp omelet.

Molluscs

CLAMS (see Plate 77, page 118)

There are many varieties; the soft or long neck clams such as razor, Ipswich and small hard-shell clams such as cherrystones, can be eaten raw. Large clams can be steamed, fried or grilled and used for soups (chowders) and sauces.

COCKLES

These are enclosed in pretty cream-coloured shells of 2–3 cm ($1–1\frac{1}{2}$ in). Cockles are soaked in salt water to purge and then steamed or boiled. They may be used in soups, salads and fish dishes, or served as a dish by themselves.

MUSSELS (see Plate 77, page 118)

Mussels are extensively cultivated on wooden hurdles in the sea, producing tender, delicately flavoured, plump fish. British mussels are considered good; French mussels are smaller; Dutch and Belgian mussels are plumper. All vary in quality from season to season.

- The shells must be tightly closed; this indicates they are alive.
- The mussels should be large.
- There should not be an excessive number of barnacles attached.
- Mussels should smell fresh.

Mussels are kept in boxes, covered with a damp sack and stored in a cold room. They may be served hot or cold or as a garnish. Menu examples include Mussels marinière; Mussels vinaigrette.

OYSTERS

Oysters are produced from centres in England, Scotland, Ireland and Wales. Since the majority of oysters are eaten raw it is essential that they are thoroughly cleansed before the hotels and restaurants receive them.

- Oysters must be alive; this is indicated by the firmly closed shells.
- They are graded in sizes and the price varies accordingly.
- Oysters should smell fresh.
- They should be purchased daily.
- Oysters are in season from September to April (when there is an r in the month).
- During the summer months oysters are imported from France, Holland and Portugal.

Oysters are stored in barrels or boxes, covered with damp sacks and kept in a cold room to keep them moist and alive. The shells should be tightly closed; if they are open, tap them sharply, and if they do not shut at once, discard them.

The popular way of eating oysters is in the raw state. They may also be served in soups, hot cocktail savouries, fish garnishes, as a fish dish, in meat puddings and savouries. Menu examples include Oysters Florentine; Oysters in Champagne sauce; Steak, kidney and oyster pudding.

SCALLOPS (see Plate 77, page 118)

Great scallops are up to 15 cm (6 in) in size; Bay scallops up to 8 cm (3 in); Queen scallops are small-cockle-sized, and are also known as 'Queenies'. Scallops may be steamed, poached, fried or grilled.

- Scallops are found on the sea-bed, and are therefore dirty, so it is advisable to purchase them ready cleaned.
- If scallops are not bought cleaned, the shells should be tightly closed.
- The orange part, roe, should be bright in colour and moist.
- If they have to be kept, they should be stored in an ice-box or refrigerator.

Scallops are usually poached or fried. Menu examples include Fried scallops; Scallops in white wine sauce.

SEA-URCHIN OR SEA HEDGEHOG

They have spine-covered spherical shells. Only the orange and yellow roe is eaten, either raw out of the shell or removed with a teaspoon and used in soups, sauces, scrambled eggs, etc.: 10 to 20 urchins provide approximately 200 g (7 oz) roe.

WINKLES

Winkles are small sea snails with a delicious flavour. They may be boiled for 3 minutes and served with garlic butter or on a dish of assorted shellfish.

CEPHALOPODS AND FISH OFFAL

Cuttlefish

They are usually dark with attractive pale stripes and the size can be up to 24 cm (10 in). They are available all year by number and weight. Cuttlefish are prepared like squid and may be stewed or gently grilled.

Octopus (see Plate 65, page 113)

Octopus are available all year by number and weight. Large species are tough and need to be tenderised; they are then prepared as for squid. Small octopus can be boiled, then cut up for grilling or frying. When stewing, a long cooking time is needed.

Squid (see Plate 65, page 113)

The common squid has mottled skin and white flesh, two tentacles, eight arms and flap-like fins. Usual size is 15–30 cm (6–12 in). Careful, correct preparation is important if the fish is to be tender. It may be stir-fried, fried, baked, grilled or braised.

Liver

An oil rich in vitamins A and D is obtained from the liver of cod and halibut. This is used medicinally.

Roe (see Plate 78, page 118)

Those used are the soft and hard roes of herring, cod, sturgeon and the coral from lobster. Soft herring roes are used to garnish fish dishes and as a savoury. Cod's roe is smoked and served as hors-d'œuvre. The roe of the sturgeon is salted and served raw as caviar and the coral of lobster is used for colouring lobster butter and lobster dishes, and also as a decoration for fish dishes.

VEGETABLES

Fresh vegetables and fruits are important foods both from an economic and nutritional point of view. On average, each person consumes 125–150 kg (275–330 lb) per year of fruit and vegetables.

The purchasing of these commodities is difficult because the products are highly perishable and supply and demand varies. The high perishability of fresh vegetables and fruits causes problems not encountered in other markets. Fresh vegetables and fruits are living organisms and will lose quality quickly if not properly stored and handled. Improved transportation and storage facilities can help prevent loss of quality.

Automation in harvesting and packaging speeds the handling process and helps retain quality.

Vacuum cooling, which is a process whereby fresh produce is moved into huge chambers, where, for about half an hour, a low vacuum is maintained, inducing rapid evaporation which quickly reduces field heat, has been highly successful in improving quality.

Experience and sound judgement are essential for the efficient buying and storage of all commodities, but none probably more so than fresh vegetables and fruit.

The grading of fresh fruit and vegetables within the EU

There are four main quality classes for produce:

- Extra Class – for produce of top quality,
- Class I – for produce of good quality,
- Class II – for produce of reasonably good quality,
- Class III – for produce of low marketable quality.

Food value

- Root vegetables – useful in the diet because they contain starch or sugar for energy, a small but valuable amount of protein, some mineral salts and vitamins; also useful sources of cellulose and water.
- Green vegetables – no food is stored in the leaves, it is only produced there;

SEASONS FOR HOME-GROWN VEGETABLES

SPRING

asparagus	cauliflower	broccoli – white and purple
new carrots	new turnips	new potatoes
greens		

SUMMER

artichokes, globe	turnips	asparagus
cauliflower	aubergine	cos lettuce
beans, broad	peas	radishes
beans, French	carrots	sea-kale
sweetcorn		

AUTUMN

artichokes, globe	parsnips	field mushrooms
artichokes, Jerusalem	aubergine	peppers
beans, runner	cauliflower	red cabbage
broccoli	celery	shallots
salsify	swedes	marrow
celeriac	turnips	

WINTER

Brussels sprouts	chicory	cabbage
kale	celery	parsnips
cauliflower	broccoli	red cabbage
Savoy cabbage	celeriac	swedes
turnips		

ALL THE YEAR ROUND

Although the following vegetables are available all the year round, nevertheless at certain times, owing to bad weather, a heavy demand or other circumstances, supplies may be temporarily curtailed. However, owing to air transport, most vegetables are available all year round.

beetroot	tomatoes	spinach	onions
mushrooms	leeks	watercress	lettuce
cucumber	carrots	cabbage	potatoes

therefore little protein or carbohydrate is found in green vegetables; they are rich in mineral salts and vitamins, particularly vitamin C and carotene; the greener the leaf the larger the quantity of vitamin present; chief mineral salts are calcium and iron.

Quality and purchasing points

Root vegetables must be:

- clean;
- firm;
- sound;
- unblemished;
- even size;
- even shape.

Green vegetables must be

- absolutely fresh;
- bright in colour, crisp and not wilted.

Cabbage and **brussels sprouts** should have tightly growing leaves and be compact. **Cauliflowers** should have closely grown flowers and a firm, white head; not too much stalk or too many outer leaves. **Peas** and **beans** should be crisp and of medium size. Peapods should be full, beans not stringy. **Blanched stems** must be firm, white, crisp and free from soil.

Storage

- Root vegetables should be emptied from sacks and stored in bins or racks.
- Green vegetables should be stored on well-ventilated racks.
- Salad vegetables can be left in their containers and stored in a cool place.

Preservation

- Canning – certain vegetables are preserved in tins: artichokes, asparagus, carrots, celery, beans, peas (fins, garden, processed), tomatoes (whole, purée), mushrooms, truffles.
- Dehydration – onions, carrots, potatoes and cabbage are shredded and quickly dried until they contain only 5% water.
- Drying – the seeds of legumes (peas and beans) have the moisture content reduced to 10%.
- Pickling – onions and red cabbage are examples of vegetables preserved in spiced vinegar.
- Salting – French and runner beans may be sliced and preserved in dry salt.
- Freezing – many vegetables such as peas, beans, sprouts, spinach and cauliflower are deep frozen.

―――

Types of vegetables

Roots

- Beetroot – two main types, round and long; used for soups, salads and as a vegetable.
- Carrots – grown in numerous varieties and sizes; used extensively for soups, sauces, stocks, stews, salads, and as a vegetable.
- Celeriac – large, light-brown, celery-flavoured root, used in soups, salads and as a vegetable.
- Horseradish – long, light-brown, narrow root, grated and used for horseradish sauce.
- Mooli – long, white, thick member of radish family, used for soups, salads or as a vegetable.
- Parsnips – long, white root tapering to a point; unique nut-like flavour; used in soups, added to casseroles and as a vegetable (roasted, purée, etc.).

- Radishes – small summer variety, round or oval, served with dips, in salads or as a vegetable in white or cheese sauce.
- Salsify – also called oyster plant because of similarity of taste; long, narrow root used in soups, salads and as a vegetable.
- Scorzonera – long, narrow root, slightly astringent in flavour; used in soups, salads and as a vegetable.
- Swede – large root with yellow flesh; generally used as a vegetable, mashed or parboiled and roasted; may be added to stews.
- Turnip – two main varieties, long and round; used in soups, stews and as a vegetable.

Tubers

- Artichokes, Jerusalem – potato-like tuber with a bitter-sweet flavour; used in soups, salads and as a vegetable.
- Potatoes – many varieties are grown but all potatoes should be sold by name (King Edward, Desirée, Maris Piper); this is important as the caterer needs to know which varieties are best suited for specific cooking purposes. The various varieties fall into four categories: floury, firm, waxy or salad potatoes; Jersey Royals are specially grown, highly regarded new potatoes. Further information can be obtained from the Potato Marketing Board, 50 Hans Crescent, Knightsbridge, London SW1X 0NB.
- Sweet potatoes – long tubers with purple or sand-coloured skins and orange flesh; flavour is sweet and aromatic; used as a vegetable (fried, puréed, creamed, candied) or made into a sweet pudding.
- Yams – similar to sweet potatoes, usually cylindrical, often knobbly in shape; can be used in the same way as sweet potatoes.

Bulbs (see Plate 79, page 119)

- Garlic – an onion-like bulb with a papery skin inside of which are small individually wrapped cloves; used extensively in many forms of cookery; garlic has a pungent distinctive flavour and should be used sparingly.
- Leeks – summer leeks have long white stems, bright green leaves and a milder flavour than winter leeks; these have a stockier stem and a stronger flavour; used extensively in stocks, soups, sauces, stews, hors-d'œuvre and as a vegetable.
- Onions – there are numerous varieties with different coloured skins and varying strengths; after salt, the onion is probably the most-used flavouring in cookery; can be used in almost every type of food except sweet dishes.
- Shallots – have a similar but more refined flavour than the onion and are therefore more often used in top class cookery.
- Spring onions – are slim and tiny like miniature leeks; used in soups, salads and Chinese and Japanese cookery.

Leafy (see Plates 79 and 80, page 119)

- Chicory – a lettuce with coarse, crisp leaves and a sharp, bitter taste in the outside leaves; inner leaves are milder.

TYPES OF VEGETABLES

ROOTS	TUBERS	BULBS	LEAFY
beetroot	Jerusalem	garlic	chicory
carrots	artichokes	leeks	Chinese leaves
celeriac	potatoes	onions	corn salad
horseradish	sweet potatoes	shallots	lettuce
mooli	yams	spring onions	mustard and cress
parsnips			radiccio
radish			sorrel
salsify			spinach
scorzonera			Swiss chard
swedes			watercress
turnips			

BRASSICAS	PODS AND SEEDS	FRUITING	STEMS AND SHOOTS	MUSHROOMS AND FUNGI
broccoli	broad beans	aubergine	asparagus	ceps
Brussels sprouts	butter or lima	avocado	beans	chanterelles
cabbage	beans	courgette	cardoon	horn of plenty
calabrese	runner beans	cucumber	celery	morels
cauliflower	mange-tout	marrow	endive	mushrooms
curly kale	okra	peppers	globe artichokes	
spring greens	peas	pumpkin	kohlrabi	
	sweetcorn	squash	sea kale	
		tomatoes		

- Chinese leaves – long white, densely packed leaves with a mild flavour resembling celery; makes a good substitute for lettuce and can be boiled, braised or stir-fried as a vegetable.
- Corn salad – sometimes called lamb's lettuce; small, tender, dark leaves with a tangy nutty taste.
- Lettuce - many varieties: cabbage, cos, little gem, iceberg, oakleaf, Webbs; used chiefly for salads, but can be cooked as a vegetable or used as a wrapping for other foods, e.g. fish fillets.
- Mustard and cress – embryonic leaves of mustard and garden cress with a sharp warm flavour; used mainly in, or as a garnish to, sandwiches and salads.
- Radiccio – round, deep red variety of chicory with white ribs and a distinctive bitter taste.
- Rocket – a type of cress with larger leaves and a peppery taste.
- Sorrel – bright-green sour leaves which can be overpowering if used on their own; best when tender and young; used in salad and soups.
- Spinach – tender dark green leaves with a mild musky flavour; used for soups, garnishing egg and fish dishes, as a vegetable and raw in salads.
- Swiss chard – has large, ribbed, slightly curly leaves with a flavour similar to but milder than spinach; used as for spinach.

Plate 65 Conger eel 1 kg (2 lb), octopus, squid

Plate 66 Brill 4 kg (9 lb) on the left
Plate 67 Halibut 2.5 kg (5 lb)

Plate 68 Top to bottom: salmon trout 2 kg (4 lb), salmon 5 kg (10 lb), mackerel 400 g (1 lb), sardine 300 g (12 oz), trout 1 kg (2 lb), herring 400 g (1 lb), whitebait

Plate 69 Skate 5.5 kg (12 lb)

Plate 70   Sea bream
2 kg (4 lb) (top), red
mullet 200 g (8 oz),
tuna steaks, John Dory
2 kg (4 lb), gurnard
550 g (1¼ lb), wrasse
1 kg (2 lb), grey mullet
1 kg (2 lb)

Plate 71
Haddock 3 kg
(6 lb) (top), cod 3 kg
(6 lb), hake 1 kg 400 g
1 lb, (2 lb) (left),
codling 500 g (1¼ lb),
whiting 300 g 400 g
1 lb (12 oz)

Plate 72   Dogfish 4 kg (9 lb) (top), monkfish 4 kg (9 lb), catfish 2.5 kg (5 lb)

Plate 73   Lemon sole 500 g (1 lb) (top), plaice 1 kg (2 lb), Dover sole 500 g (1 lb)

Plate 74   Turbot 5 kg (10 lb)

Plate 75
Scottish lobster, raw
and cooked (top),
Canadian lobster,
cooked and raw,
crayfish, langoustine

Plate 76
Spidercrab (top
left), crab, crawfish

Plate 77 Scallops (top), large clams, small clams, mussels

Plate 78 Smoked salmon (top), smoked haddock (natural), smoked haddock (coloured), kipper, cod's roe, smoked halibut, smoked trout, Arbroath smoky

Plate 79   Bulbs, leafy vegetables and pods (from top left), sorrel, asparagus, grelots, globe artichoke, red cabbage, fennel, mange-tout, red onion, onion, kohlrabi, celeriac, ginger, garlic, broccoli, haricots verts

Plate 80   Salad vegetables, (from top left), oakleaf, radishes, frisé endive, lettuce, spring onions, Belgian endive, radiccio, little gem, iceberg, watercress, lollo rosso, cos

Plate 81 Various vegetables (from top left), beef tomato, green pepper, red pepper, squash, aubergine, courgette flowers, yellow courgette, green courgette, baby cauliflower, yellow pepper, mooli, baby corn, squash

Plate 82 Mushrooms, wild and cultivated

- Watercress – long stems with round, dark, tender green leaves and a pungent peppery flavour; used for soups, salads, and for garnishing roasts and grills of meat and poultry.

BRASSICAS (see Plate 79, page 119)
- Broccoli – various types: white, green, purple-sprouting; delicate vegetable with a gentle flavour used in soups, salads, stir-fry dishes and cooked and served in many ways as a vegetable.
- Brussels sprouts – small green buds growing on thick stems; can be used for soup but are mainly used as a vegetable, and can be cooked and served in a variety of ways.
- Cabbage – three main types: green, white and red; many varieties of green cabbage available at different seasons of the year; early green cabbage is deep green and loosely formed; later in the season they firm up with solid hearts; Savoy is considered the best of the winter green cabbage; white cabbage is used for coleslaw; green and red as a vegetable, boiled, braised or stir-fried.
- Cauliflower – heads of creamy-white florets with a distinctive flavour; used for soup and cooked and served in various ways as a vegetable.

PODS AND SEEDS (see Plate 79, page 119)
- Broad beans – pale-green, oval-shaped beans contained in a thick fleshy pod; young broad beans can be removed from the pods and cooked in their shells and served as a vegetable in various ways; old broad beans will toughen and when removed from the pods will have to be shelled before being served.
- Butter or lima beans – butter beans are white, large, flattish and oval-shaped; lima beans are smaller; both used as a vegetable or salad, stew or casserole ingredient.
- Runner beans – popular vegetable that must be used when young; bright green colour and a pliable velvety feel; if coarse, wilted, or older beans are used they will be stringy and tough.
- Mange-tout – also called snow-peas or sugar peas; flat peapod with immature seeds which after topping, tailing and stringing, may be eaten in their entirety; used as a vegetable, in salads and for stir-fry dishes.
- Okra – curved and pointed seed pods with a flavour similar to aubergines; cooked as a vegetable or in creole-type stews.
- Peas – garden peas are normal size, petits pois are a dwarf variety; marrow fat peas are dried; popular as a vegetable, peas are also used for soups, salads, stews and stir-fry dishes.
- Sweetcorn – also known as maize or Sudan corn; available 'on the cob' fresh or frozen or in kernels, canned or frozen; a versatile commodity and used as a first course, in soups, salads, casseroles and as a vegetable.

FRUITING (see Plate 81, page 120)
- Aubergine – firm, elongated, varying in size with smooth shiny skins ranging in colour from purple-red to purple-black; inner flesh is white with tiny soft seeds;

almost without flavour, it requires other seasonings, e.g. garlic, lemon juice, herbs, to enhance its taste; may be sliced and fried or baked, steamed, stuffed and used in ratatouille.

- Avocado – fruit that is mainly used as a vegetable because of its bland, mild, nutty flavour; two main types: summer variety that is green when unripe and purple-black when ripe with golden-yellow flesh; winter ones are more pear-shaped with smooth green skin and pale green to yellow flesh; eaten as first courses and used in soups, salads, dips and garnishes to other dishes.
- Courgette – baby marrow, light to dark green in colour, with a delicate flavour becoming stronger when cooked with other ingredients, e.g. herbs, garlic, spices; may be boiled, steamed, fried, baked, stuffed and stir-fried.
- Cucumber – a long, smooth-skinned fruiting vegetable, ridged and dark green in colour; used in salads, soups, sandwiches, garnishes and as a vegetable.
- Marrow – long, oval-shaped edible gourds with ridged green skins and a bland flavour; may be cooked as for courgettes.
- Peppers – available in three colours: green peppers are unripened and they turn yellow to orange and then red (they must remain on the plant to do this); used raw and cooked in salads, vegetable dishes, stuffed and baked, casseroles and stir-fried dishes.
- Pumpkins – vary in size and can weigh up to 50 kg (110 lb); associated with Hallowe'en as a decoration but may be used in soups or pumpkin pie.
- Squash – there are many varieties; bright, golden-brown or green skins have flesh that is firm and floury; they can be boiled, steamed, puréed or baked.
- Tomatoes – along with onions, probably the most-used vegetable in cookery; several varieties including cherry, yellow, globe, large ridged (beef) and plum; used in soups, sauces, stews, salads, sandwiches and as a vegetable.

STEMS AND SHOOTS (see Plate 79, page 119)
- Asparagus – three main types: white, with creamy white stems and a mild flavour; French, with violet or bluish tips and a stronger more astringent flavour; and green, with what is considered a delicious aromatic flavour; used on every course of the menu, except the sweet course.
- Bean sprouts – slender young sprouts of the germinating soya or mung bean, used as a vegetable accompaniment, in stir-fry dishes and salads.
- Cardoon – longish plant with root and fleshy ribbed stalk similar to celery, but leaves are grey-green in colour; used cooked as a vegetable or raw in salads and dips.
- Celery – long-stemmed bundles of fleshy, ribbed stalks, white to light green in colour; used in soups, stocks, sauces, cooked as a vegetable and raw in salads and dips.
- Chicory – also known as Belgian endive; conical heads of crisp white, faintly bitter leaves approximately 15 cm (6 in) long; used cooked as a vegetable and raw in salads and dips.
- Globe artichokes – resemble fat pine cones with overlapping fleshy, green, inedible leaves, all connected to an edible fleshy base or bottom; used as a first

course, hot or cold; as a vegetable, boiled, stuffed, baked, fried or in casseroles.

- Kohlrabi – stem which swells to turnip shape above the ground; those about the size of a large egg are best for cookery purposes (other than soup or purées); may be cooked as a vegetable, stuffed and baked and added to stews and casseroles.
- Sea-kale – delicate white leaves with yellow frills edged with purple; can be boiled or braised or served raw like celery.

MUSHROOMS AND FUNGI (see Plate 82, page 120)
- Ceps – wild mushrooms with short, stout stalks with slightly raised veins and tubes underneath the cap in which the brown spores are produced.
- Chanterelles or Girolles – wild, funnel-shaped, yellow-capped mushrooms with a slightly ribbed stalk which runs up under the edge of the cap.
- Horns of plenty - trumpet-shaped, shaggy, almost black wild mushrooms.
- Morels – delicate, wild mushrooms varying in colour from pale beige to dark brown-black with a flavour that suggests meat.
- Oyster mushrooms – creamy gills and firm flesh; delicate with shorter storage life than regular mushrooms.
- Shitake mushrooms – solid texture with a strong, slightly meaty flavour.
- Mushrooms – field mushrooms found in meadows from late summer to autumn; creamy white cap and stalk and a strong earthy flavour.
- Cultivated mushrooms – available in three types: button (small, succulent, weak in flavour); cap and open or flat mushrooms.

All mushrooms both wild and cultivated have a great many uses in cookery, in soups, stocks, salads, vegetables, savouries and garnishes.

Further information

Fresh Fruit and Vegetable Information Bureau, Bury House, 126–128 Cromwell Road, London SW7 4EJ.

FRUITS

For culinary purposes fruit can be divided into various groups (see table below).

Seasons

The chief citrus fruits (oranges, lemons and grapefruit) are available all the year round. Mandarins, clementines, satsumas and tangerines are available in the winter.

Rhubarb is in season in the spring, and the soft and stone fruits become available from June in the following order: gooseberries, strawberries, raspberries, cherries, currants, damsons, plums.

Imported apples and pears are available all the year round; home-grown mainly from August to April. Many varieties of fruits are imported from all over the world and speedy air transport cargo services enable some fruits (e.g. strawberries) to be in season virtually the whole year round.

DIFFERENT KINDS OF FRUITS

STONE FRUITS	HARD FRUITS	SOFT FRUITS	CITRUS FRUITS	TROPICAL/ MEDITERRANEAN FRUITS	OTHER FRUITS
apricots	apples	bilberries	clementines	bananas	cranberries
cherries	crab apples	blackberries	grapefruit	Cape gooseberries	grapes
damsons	pears	blackcurrants	kumquats	carambola	melons
greengages		blueberries	lemons	dates	rhubarb
nectarines		gooseberries	limes	figs	
peaches		loganberries	mandarins	granadillas	
plums		raspberries	oranges	guavas	
		redcurrants	pomeloes	kiwi fruit	
		strawberries	tangerines	lychees	
			tangelos	mangosteens	
			(uglis)	mangoes	
				passion fruit	
				papayas	
				paw paws	
				persimmons	
				pineapples	
				sharon fruits	

Food value

The nutritive value of fruit depends on its vitamin content, especially vitamin C; it is therefore valuable as a protective food. The cellulose in fruit is useful as roughage.

Storage

*   Hard fruits, such as apples, are left in boxes and kept in a cool store.
*   Soft fruits, such as raspberries and strawberries, should be left in their punnets or baskets in a cold room.
*   Stone fruits are best placed in trays so that any damaged fruit can be seen and discarded.
*   Peaches and citrus fruits are left in their delivery trays or boxes.
*   Bananas should not be stored in too cold a place because the skins turn black.

Quality and purchasing points

*   Soft fruits deteriorate quickly, especially if not sound. Care must be taken to see that they are not damaged or too ripe when bought.
*   Soft fruits should appear fresh; there should be no shrinking, wilting or signs of mould.
*   The colour of certain soft fruits is an indication of ripeness (strawberries, dessert gooseberries).
*   Hard fruits should not be bruised. Pears should not be over-ripe.

DIFFERENT FRUITS AND THEIR SEASONS

FRUIT	SEASON	FRUIT	SEASON
apple	all year round	greengage	August
apricot	May to September	lemon	all year round
avocado pear	all year round	mandarin	November to June
banana	all year round	melon	all year round
blackberry	September to October	orange	all year round
blackcurrants	July to September	peach	September
cherry	June to August	pear	September to March
clementine	winter	pineapple	all year round
cranberries	November to January	plum	July to October
damson	September to October	raspberry	June to August
date	winter	red currants	July to September
fig	July to September	rhubarb	December to June
gooseberry	July to September	strawberry	June to August
grapefruit	all year round	tangerine	winter
grapes	all year round		

Because of modern storage methods and air transport the majority of these fruits may be available all year round.

Preservation

- Drying – apples, pears, apricots, peaches, bananas and figs are dried; plums when dried are called prunes, and currants, sultanas and raisins are produced by drying grapes.
- Canning – almost all fruits may be canned; apples are packed in water and known as solid packed apples; other fruits are canned in syrup.
- Bottling – bottling is used domestically, but very little fruit is commercially preserved in this way; cherries are bottled in maraschino.
- Candied – orange and lemon peel are candied; other fruits with a strong flavour, such as pineapple, are preserved in this way; the fruit is covered in hot syrup which is increased in sugar content from day to day until the fruit is saturated in a very heavy syrup. It is then allowed to dry slowly until it is no longer sticky.
- Glacé – the fruit is first candied and then dipped in fresh syrup to give a clear finish; this method is applied to cherries.
- Crystallised – after the fruit has been candied it is left in fresh syrup for 24 hours and then allowed to dry very slowly until crystals form on the surface of the fruit.
- Candied, glacé and crystallised fruits are mainly imported from France.
- Jam – some stone and all soft fruits can be used.
- Jelly – jellies are produced from fruit juice.
- Quick freezing – strawberries, raspberries, loganberries, apples, blackberries, gooseberries, grapefruit and plums are frozen and they must be kept below 0°C/32°F.

- Cold storage – apples are stored at temperatures between 1–4°C (34–39°F), depending on the variety of apple.
- Gas storage – fruit can be kept in a sealed store room where the atmosphere is controlled; the amount of air is limited, the oxygen content of the air is decreased and the carbon dioxide increased, which controls the respiration rate of the fruit.

Fruit juices, syrups and drinks

Fruit juices such as orange, lemon, blackcurrant are canned. Syrups such as rose hip and orange are bottled. Fruit drinks are also bottled; they include orange, lime and lemon.

Uses

With the exception of certain fruits (lemon, rhubarb, cranberries) fruit can be eaten as a dessert or in its raw state. Some fruits have dessert and cooking varieties, e.g. apples, pears, cherries and gooseberries.

STONE FRUITS (see Plate 83, page 153)

Damsons, plums, greengages, cherries, apricots, peaches and nectarines are used as a dessert; stewed (compote) for jam, pies, puddings and in various sweet dishes. Peaches are also used to garnish certain meat dishes.

Menu examples include Damson pie; Peach Melba; Braised ham with peaches; Braised duck with cherries.

HARD FRUITS

The popular English dessert apple varieties include Beauty of Bath, Discovery, Spartan, Worcester Pearmain, Cox's Orange Pippin, Blenheim Orange, Laxton's Superb and James Grieve; imported apples include Golden Delicious, Granny Smith and Sturmers. The Bramley is the most popular cooking apple. The William, Conference and Doyenne du Comice are among the best known pears.

Apples and pears are used in many pastry dishes. Apples are also used for garnishing meat dishes and for sauce which is served with roast pork and duck.

Menu examples include Apple pie; Apple fritters; Pear flan; Pear Belle Hélène; Apple charlotte; Apfelstrudel; Apple and red cabbage salad.

SOFT FRUITS (see Plate 84, page 153)

Raspberries, strawberries, loganberries and gooseberries are used as a dessert. Gooseberries, black and red currants and blackberries are stewed, used in pies and puddings. They are used for jam and flavourings. Menu examples include Gooseberry fool; Raspberry trifle; Strawberry tartlets; Blackcurrant tart.

CITRUS FRUITS (see Plate 83, page 153)

Oranges, lemons and grapefruit are not usually cooked, except for marmalade. Lemons and limes are used for flavouring and garnishing, particularly fish dishes. Oranges are used mainly for flavouring, and in fruit salads, also to garnish certain poultry dishes. Grapefruit are served at breakfast and as a first course generally for luncheon. Mandarins, clementines and satsumas are eaten as a dessert or used in sweet dishes. Kumquats look and taste like tiny oranges and are eaten with the skin on. Tangelos are a cross between tangerines and grapefruit, and are sometimes called uglis. Pomelos are the largest of the citrus fruits, predominantly round but with a slightly flattened base and pointed top.

Menu examples include Lime soufflé; Florida cocktail; Lemon pancakes; Orange bavarois; Duck with orange salad.

TROPICAL AND OTHER FRUITS (see Plate 83, page 153)

- Bananas – as well as being used as a dessert, bananas are grilled for a fish garnish, fried as fritters and served as a garnish to poultry (Maryland); they are used in fruit salad and other sweet dishes. Menu examples include Banana fritters; Fillets of sole caprice; Banana flan; Chicken Maryland.
- Cape gooseberries – a sharp, pleasant-flavoured small round fruit dipped in fondant and served as a type of petit four.
- Carambola – also known as starfruit, it has a yellowish-green skin with a waxy sheen. The fruit is long and narrow and has a delicate lemon flavour.
- Cranberries – these hard red berries are used for cranberry sauce, which is served with roast turkey.
- Dates – whole dates are served as a dessert; stoned dates are used in various sweet dishes and petits fours.
- Figs – fresh figs may be served as a first course or dessert. Dried figs may be used for fig puddings, and other sweet dishes.
- Granadillos – these are like an orange in shape and colour, are light in weight and similar to a passion fruit in flavour.
- Grapes – black and white grapes are used as a dessert, in fruit salad, as a sweet meat and also as a fish garnish.
- Guavas – size varies between that of a walnut to an apple; ripe guavas have a sweet pink flesh; they can be eaten with cream or mixed with other fruits.
- Kiwi fruit – have a brown furry skin; the flesh is green with edible black seeds which when thinly sliced gives a pleasant decorative appearance.
- Kiwanos – have a spiky or orange skin, the flesh is emerald green with jelly like texture and delicate flavour.
- Lychees – a Chinese fruit with a delicate flavour, obtainable tinned in syrup and also fresh.
- Mangoes – can be as large as a melon or as small as an apple; ripe mangoes have smooth pinky-golden flesh with a pleasing flavour; they may be served in halves sprinkled with lemon juice, sugar, rum or ginger; mangoes can also be used in fruit salads and for sorbets.
- Mangostines – are apple-shaped with tough reddish-brown skin which turns purple as the fruit ripens; they have juicy creamy flesh.
- Passion fruit – the name comes from the flower of the plant which is meant to represent the Passion of Christ; size and shape of an egg with crinkled purple-brown skin when ripe; flesh and seeds are all edible.
- Paw paw (papaya) – green to golden skin, orangey flesh with a sweet subtle flavour and black seeds; eaten raw sprinkled with lime or lemon juice.

- Persimmon – a round orange-red fruit with a tough skin which can be cut when the fruit is ripe; when under-ripe they have an unpleasant acid-like taste of tannin.
- Pineapple – served as a dessert; it is also used in many sweet dishes and as a garnish to certain meat dishes. Menu examples include Grilled gammon and pineapple; Pineapple fritters in apricot sauce.
- Sharon fruit – a seedless persimmon tasting like a sweet exotic peach.
- Rhubarb – forced or early rhubarb is obtainable from January; natural rhubarb from April–June; used for pies, puddings, fool and compote.

MELONS (see Plate 85, page 154)
There are several types of melon. The most popular are:

- Honeydew – these are long, oval-shaped melons with dark green skins; the flesh is white with a greenish tinge.
- Charentais – charentais melons are small and round with a mottled green and yellow skin; the flesh is orange coloured.
- Cantaloup – cantaloup are large round melons with regular indentations; the rough skin is mottled orange and yellow and the flesh is light orange in colour.
- Ogen – small round mottled green skins suitable for one portion (depending on size); mainly used as a dessert, hors-d'œuvre and sweet dishes.

Care must be taken when buying as melons should not be over- or under-ripe. This can be assessed by carefully pressing the top or bottom of the fruit. There should be a slight degree of softness to the cantaloup and charentais melons. The stalk should be attached, otherwise the melon deteriorates quickly.

Further information

Fruit and Vegetable Information, Bury House, 126–128 Cromwell Road, London SW7 4ET.

NUTS (see Plate 86, page 154)

Nuts are the reproductive kernel (seed) of the plant or tree from which they come. Nuts are perishable and may easily become rancid or infested with insects.

Season

Dessert nuts are in season during the autumn and winter.

Food value

Nuts are highly nutritious because of their protein, fat and mineral salts. They are of considerable importance to vegetarians, who may use nuts in place of meat; they are therefore a food which builds, repairs and provides energy. Nuts are difficult to digest.

Storage

Dessert nuts, those with the shell on, are kept in a dry, ventilated store. Nuts without shells, whether ground, nibbed, flaked or whole, are kept in airtight containers.

Quality and purchasing points

- Nuts should be of good size.
- They should be heavy for their size.
- There must be no sign of mildew.

Use

Nuts are used extensively in pastry and confectionery work and vegetarian cookery, and also for decorating and flavouring. They are used whole, or halves, and almonds are used ground, nibbed and flaked.

Almonds

Salted almonds are served at cocktail parties and bars. Ground, flaked, nibbed, are used in sweet dishes and for decorating cakes; they are used for cake mixtures, large and small, such as Dundee cake, Congress tarts, macaroons, for sweetmeats and large cakes.

Marzipan (almond paste) is used for covering fruit cakes; frangipane is an almond filling used in Bakewell tarts; praline (almond brittle) is used for ice cream and gâteaux; Berny potatoes are coated with chopped almonds.

Brazil nuts

Brazil nuts are served with fresh fruit as dessert and are also used in confectionery.

Chestnuts

Chestnuts are used as stuffing for turkeys; chestnut flour is used for soup, and as a garnish for ice cream. Chestnut purée is used in pastries and gâteaux.

Coconut

Coconut is used in desiccated form for curry preparations, and in all sizes of cakes and confectionery.

Hazel nuts

These nuts are used as a dessert and for praline.

Macadamia nuts

These expensive nuts have a rich, delicate, sweetish flavour. They can be used in pasta dishes, savoury sauces for meat, game and poultry and in ice-cream, sorbets and puddings.

Pecans

Pecan nuts are used salted for dessert, various sweets and ice-cream.

Peanuts and cashew nuts

These are salted and used in cocktail bars as bar snacks.

Pistachio nuts

These small green nuts, grown mainly in France and Italy, are used for decorating galantines, small and large cakes and petits fours. They are also used in ice-cream.

Walnuts

Walnuts, imported mainly from France and Italy, are used as a dessert, in salads and for decorating cakes and sweet dishes. They are also pickled, while green and unripe.

EGGS

The term egg applies not only to those of the hen, but also to the edible eggs of other birds, such as turkeys, geese, ducks, guinea fowl, quails and gulls. Around 28 million hens eggs are consumed each day in the UK and approximately 95% of these are produced in the UK.

The British Egg Products Association (BEPA) introduced a strict Code of Practice in 1993 which covers all stages of production, from sourcing of raw materials to packaging and finished production standards. Members of BEPA can qualify to show a Lion mark on their products which signifies that the products have been produced to standards higher than those demanded by UK and European law. The aim of the Lion Code of Practice is to reduce the risk of infection in hens, to monitor and take remedial action where necessary and to ensure that eggs are held and distributed under the best conditions.

Quality points for buying

- The eggshell should be clean, well-shaped, strong and slightly rough.
- When the egg is broken, there ought to be a high proportion of thick white to thin white.
- The yolk should be firm, round and of a good even colour.

If an egg is kept, the thick white gradually changes into thin white and water passes from the white into the yolk. The yolk loses strength and begins to flatten, water evaporates from the egg and is replaced by air, and as water is heavier than air fresh eggs are heavier than stale ones.

It is possible to determine the freshness of an egg by placing it in a 10% solution of salt (60 g salt to $\frac{1}{2}$ litre of water). A 2-day-old egg will float near the bottom of the

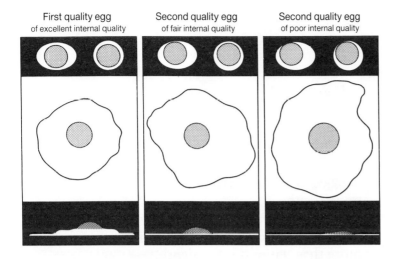

First quality egg
of excellent internal quality

Second quality egg
of fair internal quality

Second quality egg
of poor internal quality

Fig. 4.11 Quality of eggs

solution with its broad end upward. As the egg ages it becomes lighter and floats closer to the surface of the solution.

Storage and handling

The DHSS endorses the Code of Practice recommended by the egg industry itself in handling its product:

- Eggs must be stored in their packing trays blunt end upwards, in a cool but not too dry place; a refrigerator of 0–5°C (32–41°F) is ideal.
- No strongly smelling foods such as cheese, onions and fish should be stored near the eggs because the eggshells are porous and the egg will absorb strong odours.
- Eggs should be stored away from possible contaminants like raw meat.
- Eggs should not be washed before being stored as washing would remove the natural protective coating.
- Stocks should be rotated: first in, first out.
- Hands should be washed before and after handling eggs.
- Cracked eggs should *not* be used.
- Preparation surfaces, utensils and containers should be regularly cleaned and always cleaned between preparation of different dishes.
- Egg dishes should be *consumed as soon as possible* after preparation or, if not for immediate use, refrigerated.

Food value

Eggs contain most nutrients and are low in calories: two eggs contain 180 calories. Egg protein is complete and easily digestible, therefore it is useful for balancing meals. Eggs may also be used as the main dish; they are a protective food and provide energy and material for growth and repair of the body.

Production

Hens' eggs are graded in seven sizes:

Size 1	70 g	Size 3	60 g	Size 5	50 g
2	65 g	4	55 g	6	45 g
				7	under 45 g

The size of an egg does not affect the quality but does affect the price. The eggs are tested for quality, then weighed and graded.

- Grade A – naturally clean, fresh eggs, internally perfect with intact shells and an air cell not exceeding 6 mm ($\frac{1}{4}$ in) in depth.
- Grade B – eggs which have been down-graded because they have been cleaned or preserved, or because they are internally imperfect, cracked or have an air cell exceeding 6 mm ($\frac{1}{4}$ in) but not more than 9 mm ($\frac{3}{8}$ in) in depth.
- Grade C – are eggs which are fit for breaking for manufacturing purposes but cannot be sold in their shells to the public.

They are then packed into boxes containing 30 dozen, 360 (3 long hundreds). The wholesale price of eggs is quoted per long hundred (120). All egg-boxes leaving the packing station are dated.

Raw eggs and salmonella

Hens can pass salmonella bacteria into eggs and thus cause food poisoning. However in terms of the millions of eggs consumed daily in the UK the incidence of known infection is very small. Moreover, most infections cause only a mild stomach upset but the effects can be more serious in the very young, old or people weakened by other disease. Lightly cooked eggs should not be served to infants, the elderly or debilitated people, or pregnant women.

In September 1988, the Department of Health issued the following advice to all Chief Environmental Health Officers:

To advise food manufacturers and caterers that for all recipes currently needing raw shell eggs, which involve no cooking, pasteurised egg (frozen, liquid or dried) should be used instead.

Preservation

- Cold storage – eggs are kept a little above freezing point; the humidity of the air and the amount of carbon dioxide in the air are controlled; eggs will keep about nine months under these conditions.
- Frozen eggs – these are mainly used by bakers and confectioners and are sold in large tins of various sizes; eggs are washed, sanitised and then broken into sterilised containers; after the yolks and whites have been combined, they are strained, pasteurised, packed and quick-frozen. Egg yolks and whites are also frozen separately.

- Dried eggs – eggs are broken, well mixed and then spray-dried at a temperature of approximately 71°C (160°F); mainly used by bakers and confectioners.
- Grease method – a pure grease free from salt, water and other impurities must be used, such as Oteg, paraffin wax or lard; eggs are dipped into the liquid grease and then allowed to dry; the grease fills up the porous shell, forms a skin and so excludes air; eggs may then be stored in the same way as fresh eggs.
- Waterglass (sodium silicate) – a solution is made up with sodium silicate and boiling water; when used it must be quite cold; the newlaid eggs are packed point downwards in an earthenware bowl or galvanised pail and covered with the solution; a lid is placed on the container to prevent evaporation.
- Pasteurised eggs – the same procedure is followed as for frozen eggs; liquid eggs are heated to 63°C (145°F) for one minute, then rapidly cooled (this does not affect their culinary quality).
- Dried egg white – suitable for meringues, royal icing, etc.
- Dried egg white substitute – used for meringues, royal icing and similar albumen-based confections; dried egg white and dried egg white substitute must be stored in cool, dry conditions.

Uses of eggs

- Hors-d'œuvre – hard-boiled egg for egg mayonnaise and for salads.
- Soups – for the clarifying of consommé, in the preparation of royales for garnishing consommé, for thickening certain soups and veloutés.
- Egg dishes – scrambled, poached, soft-boiled, hard-boiled, en cocotte, sur le plat and omelets, etc.
- Fish – in the preparation of frying batters and for coating fish prior to crumbing.
- Sauces – mayonnaise, hollandaise, béarnaise, sabayon, etc.
- Meat and poultry – for binding mixtures such as Vienna steaks and coating cuts of meat and poultry prior to cooking.
- Pasta – eggs are used in the making of various pastas, e.g. ravioli, canneloni and noodles.
- Salads – usually hard boiled and included in many composed salads.
- Sweets and pastries – eggs are used in many ways for these items.
- Savouries – Scotch woodcock, cheese soufflé, savoury flans, etc.

Other types of eggs

- Turkeys' and guinea fowls' eggs may be used in place of hens' eggs.
- The eggs of the goose or duck may be used only if they are thoroughly cooked.
- Quails eggs are used in some establishments as a garnish, or as an hors-d'œuvre.

Availability

The table below shows the many egg products carrying the Lion mark that are currently available. If you would like something a little different, it's worth talking to your supplier as he may be able to tailor the product to meet your specific needs.

pasteurised whole egg *†‡	hard-boiled eggs *
salted whole egg *†	pickled eggs
sugared whole egg *†‡	chopped hard-boiled egg with mayonnaise *
pasteurised yolk *†‡	scrambled egg *†
salted yolk *†	omelettes †
sugared yolk *†‡	egg custard blend *†
pasteurised albumen *†‡	quiche blend *†
sugared albumen *	egg/milk blends *†‡
egg granules†	

* Chilled   † Frozen   ‡ Dried

Further information

British Egg Information, Bury House, 126–128 Cromwell Road, London SW7 4ET.

MILK (see Plate 87, page 155)

Milk is a white nutritious liquid produced by female mammals for feeding their young. The milk most used in this country is that obtained from cows. Goats' milk and ewes' milk can also be used.

Food value

Milk can make a valuable contribution to our daily eating pattern and can help to meet our nutritional needs as part of a balanced, varied diet. Milk is one of the most nutritionally complete foods available, containing a wide range of nutrients which are essential for the proper functioning of the body. In particular, milk is a good source of protein, calcium and B group vitamins, and whole milk is a good source of vitamin A.

Storage

Milk is a perishable product and therefore must be stored with care. It will keep for 4–5 days in refrigerated conditions. Milk can be easily contaminated and therefore stringent precautions are taken to ensure a safe and good quality product for the consumer. On the farm, cows are regularly checked for disease; both animals and premises are washed down before and after milking; handlers wear clean clothing and operate good hygienic practice; during transit and at the dairy strict hygiene guidelines are followed.

- Fresh milk should be kept in the container in which it is delivered.
- Milk must be stored in the refrigerator (4–5 days).
- Milk should be kept covered as it easily absorbs smells from other foods, such as onion and fish.
- Fresh milk should be ordered daily.
- Tinned milk should be stored in cool, dry ventilated rooms.

- Dried milk is packaged in airtight tins and should be kept in a dry store.
- Sterilised milk will keep for 2–3 months if *unopened*, but once opened must be treated in the same way as pasteurised milk.
- UHT (ultra-heat-treated) milk will keep unrefrigerated for several months. Before using, always check the date stamp which expires 6 months after processing and make sure to rotate stocks. Once opened it must be refrigerated and will keep for 4–5 days.

Packaging

Bulk fresh milk can be supplied in a variety of types of packaging. These come in the form of a plastic bag-in-box which holds a capacity of between 3–5 gallons. They should be placed in the appropriate refrigerated unit and the contents can be drawn off as required by fitting the correct tap device.

All packs contain fresh pasteurised homogenised milk and can be obtained in either whole, semiskimmed or skimmed varieties.

Other types of packaging include

- Polybottles (large plastic bottles) of fresh milk available in 2 pint, 4 pint and 6 pint size.
- Bottles of fresh milk available in 1 pint size.
- Cartons of fresh milk available in half pint, 1 pint and 2 pint sizes.

All the above milks are pasteurised and come in whole, homogenised whole, semiskimmed, and skimmed varieties; in addition milk in cartons is available as UHT (ultra-heat-treated) and milk in bottles is available in UHT and sterilised varieties.

Milk heat treatment and types of milk

Milk is heat treated in one of several ways to kill any harmful bacteria that may be present:

- Pasteurised milk – the milk is heated to a temperature of at least 71.7°C (161°F) for 15 seconds and then cooled quickly to less than 10°C (50°F).
- UHT (ultra-heat-treated) milk – milk is homogenised (see below) and then heated to a temperature of at least 132.2°C (270°F) for at least 1 second, the milk is then packed under sterile conditions.
- Sterilised milk – milk is preheated to 43°C (109.4°F) and homogenised. It is then heated to between 115° and 130°C (239°–266°F) for approximately 10–30 minutes and cooled.
- Homogenised milk – milk is forced through a fine aperture which breaks up the fat globules to an even size so that they stay evenly distributed throughout the milk and therefore do not form a cream line.
- Whole milk – comes as pasteurised or pasteurised homogenised and has a fat content of an average 3.9%.
- Semi-skimmed milk – comes as pasteurised and has a fat content of between 1.5 and 1.8%.

- Skimmed milk – comes as pasteurised and UHT and contains just 0.1% fat.
- Channel Islands milk – milk which comes from the Jersey and Guernsey breeds of cow and has a particularly rich and creamy taste and distinct cream line; it contains, on average 5.1% fat.
- Evaporated milk – a concentrated sterilised product with a final concentration about twice that of the original milk.
- Condensed milk – concentrated in the same way as evaporated milk but with addition of sugar; this product is not sterilised but is preserved by the high concentration of sugar it contains.
- Dried milk powder – milk produced by the evaporation of water from the milk by heat, or other means, to produce solids containing 5% or less moisture; available as a whole, or skimmed product; dried filled milk powder is skimmed milk powder to which vegetable fat has been added.

Uses of milk

Milk is used in:

- soups and sauces;
- cooking of fish, vegetables;
- making of puddings, cakes, sweet dishes;
- cold drinks (glass of milk, milkshakes, milk cocktails);
- hot drinks (tea, coffee, cocoa, hot chocolate).

Cream (see Plate 87, page 155, and table on pages 138–140)

Cream is the lighter weight portion of milk which still contains all the main constituents of milk but in different proportions. The fat content of cream is higher than that of milk and the water content and other constituents are lower. Cream is separated from the milk and heat treated.

STORAGE POINTS
- Fresh cream should be kept in the container in which it is delivered.
- Fresh cream must be stored in the refrigeration until required.
- Cream should be kept covered as it easily absorbs smells from other foods, such as onion and fish.
- Fresh cream should be ordered daily.
- Tinned cream should be stored in cool, dry ventilated rooms.
- Frozen cream should only be thawed as required and not refrozen.
- Artificial cream should be kept in the refrigerator

USING CREAM
- When whipping fresh cream, ensure the bowl and utensils are chilled before use. Pour cream into chilled bowl and whip until a matt finish is reached, continue slowly until cream stands in soft peaks.
- Fresh cream when overwhipped forms a granular, buttery texture. To thin

slightly overwhipped cream, carefully fold in 2 tablespoons of liquid cream or milk to 150 ml of the fresh whipped cream.

- Use fresh double cream for flambé dishes as it withstands higher temperatures.
- When adding fresh cream to hot liquids, dilute the cream with some of the liquid before adding to the main bulk; this helps to prevent the cream from separating.

Yogurt (see Plate 87, page 155, and table on page 141)

Yogurt is a cultured milk product made from cows, ewes', goats' or buffaloes' milk. Differences in the taste and texture of the product depends on the type of milk used and the activity of the micro-organisms involved. A bacterial 'starter culture' is added to the milk which causes the natural sugar 'lactose' to ferment and produce lactic acid. There are two types of yogurt:

- stirred yogurt, which has a smooth fluid consistency;
- set yogurt, which is more solid and has a firmer texture.

All yogurt is 'live' and contains live bacteria which remain dormant when kept at low temperatures, unless it clearly states on the packaging that it has been 'pasteurised, sterilised or ultra-heat-treated'. If stored at room temperature or above, the dormant bacteria become active again and produce more acid. Too high an acidity kills the bacteria, impairs the flavour and causes the yogurt to separate.

Other fermented milk products

- **Cultured buttermilk** – this product is made from skimmed milk with a culture added to give it a slightly thickened consistency and a sharp taste; it contains less than 0.5% fat and should be kept refrigerated.
- **Smetana** – this is a cultured product containing 10% fat; it has a slightly sharp flavour and can be served chilled as a drink or used as an alternative to soured cream in recipes.

Further information

National Dairy Council, 5–7 John Princes Street, London W1M 0AP.

FATS AND OILS

Storage of all fats

Fats should be kept in a cold store, and in a refrigerator in warm weather.

Butter

Butter is a natural dairy product made by churning fresh cream. During the churning process, the butterfat globules in the cream coalesce to form butter, and the excess liquid – known as buttermilk – is drained off. A little salt is added, between 1 and 2.5% depending on the type of butter, to enhance its flavour and keeping qualities.

CREAM: TYPES, PACKAGING, STORAGE AND USES

TYPE OF CREAM	% LEGAL MIN. FAT CONTENT	PROCESSING AND PACKAGING	STORAGE	CHARACTERISTICS AND USES
half cream	12	homogenised to prevent separation during storage and may be pasteurised* but usually ultra-heat-treated*; available in: (UHT) jiggers (portion sizes)	3 months unopened (UHT) 2–3 days once opened kept refrigerated	cannot be whipped or frozen; suitable for pouring, using in coffee and sauces
single cream	18	homogenised to prevent separation during storage, may be pasteurised* or ultra-heat-treated*, available in: (UHT) jiggers (portion sizes), I litre Tetra Brik; (pasteurised) 150 and 300 g cartons/pots; half gallon, one gallon Polybottles	2–3 days (pasteurised); keep refrigerated	cannot be whipped or frozen; suitable for pouring and in cooked dishes, sauces
soured cream	18	pasteurised*/homogenised single cream to which a 'starter culture' of harmless bacteria is added which converts the natural sugar, lactose, to lactic acid; produces a piquant slightly acid flavour; available in: 150 g cartons/pots, half gallon, one gallon Polybottles	2–3 days; keep refrigerated	cannot be whipped or frozen; suitable in sweet and savoury dishes, salad dressings and dips
whipping cream	35	not usually homogenised, but may be pasteurised* or ultra-heat-treated*; available in: (UHT) I litre Tetra Brik; (pasteurised) 150 and 300 g cartons/pots; half gallon, one gallon Polybottles	2–3 days (pasteurised); keep refrigerated	whips up to double its original volume; ideal for piping onto cakes, desserts and filling pastry; can be used for pouring; can be frozen for 2 months lightly whipped
double cream	48	sometimes homogenised and may be pasteurised* or ultra-heat-treated*, available in (UHT) I litre Tetra Brik; (pasteurised) 150 and 300 g cartons/pots; half gallon, one gallon Polybottles	2–3 days (pasteurised); keep refrigerated	whips up to $1\frac{1}{2}$ times its volume; suitable for pouring and cooking; ideal for piping on cakes, desserts; floats on coffee or soup; can be frozen (lightly whipped) for 2 months

	Fat content (%)	Production/packaging	Storage life	Uses/notes
clotted cream	55	in modern creamery production cream leaves the separator at a butterfat content of around 55%; it is then transferred to shallow pans and a water jacket heats the cream to about 90°C (194°F) for 30 minutes or longer. It is then quickly cooled and packed; available in 50, 100 and 225 g tubs	4–6 days; keep refrigerated	may be frozen and will keep up to 1 month; suitable for use with scones and on fruit and fruit pies; not recommended for cooking
sterilised half cream	12	homogenised/sterilised;* usually packaged in cans	2 years unopened; opened 2–3 days refrigerated	a pouring cream; has a distinct caramelised flavour
sterilised cream	23	homogenised/sterilised;* usually packaged in cans	2 years unopened; opened 2–3 days refrigerated	will not whip; the thicker consistency of this cream allows it to be spooned easily
ultra-heat-treated cream	12 (as half cream); 18 (as single cream); 35 (as whipping cream)	ultra-heat-treated homogenised,* and aseptically packed into Tetra Brik (cartons)	3 months unopened; once opened 2–3 days kept refrigerated	see half cream, single cream and whipping cream above
extra thick cream	18 (as single cream); 35–48 (as double cream)	homogenised/pasteurised,* and packed into plastic tubs	2–3 days; keep refrigerated	cannot be whipped or frozen; ideal spoonable cream on fruit and desserts
crème fraîche	30–40	pasteurised/homogenised cream to which a harmless bacterial culture (different from that used for soured cream) has been added which converts the natural sugar, lactose, to lactic acid producing a slightly soured flavour and thick consistency; available in tubs	3 weeks; keep refrigerated	cannot be whipped or frozen; suitable for use in sweet and savoury dishes
aerosol cream	18–38	ultra-heat-treated* and filled into aerosol cans under sterile conditions; nitrous oxide is used as a propellant to release the whipped cream from the can and aid aeration; cans fitted with finger-tip valve dispenser; available in 250, 500 and 750 g cans	18 weeks	suitable for instant dispensing of whipped cream onto coffee, milkshakes, and desserts; will collapse extremely quickly after use

CREAM: TYPES, PACKAGING, STORAGE AND USES

TYPE OF CREAM	% LEGAL MIN. FAT CONTENT	PROCESSING AND PACKAGING	STORAGE	CHARACTERISTICS AND USES
frozen cream	18 (as single cream); 35 (as whipping cream); 48 (as double cream); 55 (as clotted cream)	pasteurised,* cooled and frozen either by blast freezing for about 45 minutes or by passing the cream sandwiched between two belts, through a zone where it is frozen to − 18°C (0°F) in 2–4 minutes; available in cube or stick form to facilitate easy handling in premeasured amounts of 25 ml sticks or 50 ml cubes; larger quantities are available for catering purposes	1 year in a deep freeze; will be date stamped; thaw 2 hours before use; once thawed will keep for 2–3 days under refrigeration	see single, whipping, double and clotted cream above
non-dairy cream; imitation cream	varies from one product to another	cream substitutes which are based mainly on vegetable fats and oils which are emulsified in water and other permitted substances	varies from one product to another but should be kept refrigerated	suitable for pouring, spooning; some may be whipped; some perform better in cooked dishes than others

* See milk section for description of heat treatment processes and homogenisation (page 135).

YOGURT: TYPES, PROCESSING AND STORAGE

TYPE OF YOGURT	PROCESSING	% FAT CONTENT PER 150 g POT	STORAGE AND CHARACTERISTICS
very low fat yogurt – plain (natural)/fruit	pasteurised/homogenised skimmed milk to which Streptococcus thermophilus and Lactobacillus bulgaricus bacterial cultures are added and allowed to incubate; may be artificially sweetened; fruit and/or flavouring may be added	0.3	14 days if kept refrigerated; will not freeze
low fat yogurt – plain (natural)/fruit	pasteurised/homogenised semiskimmed milk to which Streptococcus thermophilus and Lactobacillus bulgaricus bacterial cultures are added and allowed to incubate; may be artificially sweetened; fruit and/or flavouring may be added	1.1–1.2	14 days if kept refrigerated; will not freeze
whole milk/creamy yogurt	pasteurised/homogenised whole milk to which Streptococcus thermophilus and Lactobacillus bulgaricus bacterial cultures are added and allowed to incubate; cream may be added to the milk also; may be artificially sweetened; fruit and/or flavouring may be added	4.2	14 days if kept refrigerated; will not freeze
Greek/Greek-style yogurt	pasteurised/homogenised cows' or ewes' whole milk to which Streptococcus thermophilus and Lactobacillus bulgaricus bacterial cultures are added and allowed to incubate; produced by a commercial process which involves centrifugal separation of skim milk yogurt which is then recombined with butter oil or cream to the desired fat content	13.7	14 days if kept refrigerated; will not freeze; it has a thick creamy consistency
bio or BA yogurt	pasteurised/homogenised milk to which the bacterial cultures Lactobacillus bulgaricus and Streptococcus thermophilus are added; two other cultures are also added (Bifido bacterium bifidum and Lactobacillus acidophilus); all are allowed to incubate; cream may be added also	as above for very low fat/ low fat/whole milk yogurts	14 days if kept refrigerated; will not freeze; it has a less tart flavour and is said to aid digestion

FOOD VALUE

Butter contains 80–82% fat and is therefore a high energy food. The remaining constituents are water (approximately 16%) and milk proteins. The fat soluble vitamins A and D are present in butter, and there is a small amount of calcium. Each 100 g of butter supplies 733 kilocalories (3014 kilojoules).

QUALITY

- The flavour of butter is rich, creamy and mellow.
- The colour of butter varies from a delicate pale yellow to a rich, bright colour; both are entirely natural, as explained below.
- Butter's texture is smooth and creamy, and remains firm when chilled. It should be kept refrigerated, below 5°C (41°F) for optimum quality, where it can be kept for up to 6 weeks. Butter kept at room temperature soon deteriorates and exposure to light causes rancidity. As a recommendation, butter should be kept covered in a cool, dark place, away from strong flavours or smells which could taint its delicate taste.

PRODUCTION

Essentially, there are two types of butter: lactic and sweetcream.

In lactic or 'continental taste' butter, the pasteurised cream is ripened before churning with a lactobacillus culture to produce a mildly acidic flavour. This mild acidity enhances the keeping properties, meaning that this type of butter can be purchased as unsalted or slightly salted, where 1–1.5% salt is added. These varieties of butter are mainly imported from Denmark, France and The Netherlands, although some is produced in the UK.

In sweetcream butter – traditionally produced in the UK and the Republic of Ireland, and imported from New Zealand – the cream is not ripened before churning and therefore the salt content needs to be a little higher to assist keeping qualities, between 1.5 and 2.5%.

Apart from the salt, there are no additives in butter. The colour of butter is entirely natural, and varies slightly according to the type of butter, the breed of cow and the pastures on which they feed. Seasonal variations affect the colour of the butter slightly, as the cow's diet changes during the year.

USE

The unique taste and texture of butter means that it is ideal for spreading and using in all types of cooking, both professionally and in the domestic kitchen. It is the foundation of many classic recipes, as it improves the flavour and appearance of a great many foods.

Butter is used as a base for making soups and sauces such as hollandaise and beurre blanc, for making compound butters to serve with grilled meats and fish (parsley butter, garlic butter, maître d'hôtel butter) and for making hard butter sauces like brandy butter to serve with Christmas pudding and mince pies.

It can be used for making cakes and pastries, where its taste and texture help to produce a fine flavour and melt-in-the mouth texture. For making butter icings and frostings, the flavour of butter produces excellent results. Sometimes unsalted butter is chosen for these recipes.

Butter is ideal for shallow frying foods, but it is not suitable for stir-frying or deep frying where higher temperatures would cause the butter to burn. Melted butter makes an ideal baste for brushing grilled foods, and can be combined with chopped fresh herbs, spices, grated citrus rind, etc., to vary the flavour.

For finishing cooked foods, butter can be used as a glaze. It is the perfect complement to a tureen of cooked fresh vegetables, where it adds an attractive sheen and enhances the flavour.

In sandwiches, butter acts as a protective layer, preventing moist foods from permeating the bread. The butter also gives the finished sandwich a delicious flavour.

Clarified butter can be made by gently heating butter until it has melted and separated. The milk solids can then be strained off. The resultant clarified butter can be used at higher temperatures. **Ghee** is a type of clarified butter, widely used as the basis of Indian cooking. A type of clarified butter known as **concentrated butter** is made by removing most of the water and milk solids. It is suitable for cooking and baking, but not for spreading or finishing foods.

FURTHER INFORMATION
The Butter Council, Tubs Hill House, London Road, Sevenoaks, Kent TN13 1BL.

Margarine

Margarine is produced from milk and a blend of vegetable oils emulsified with lecithin, flavouring, salt, colouring and vitamins A and D.

FOOD VALUE
Margarine is an energy and protective food. With the exception of palm oil, the oils used in the manufacture of margarine do not contain vitamins A and D, these are added during production. Margarine is not inferior to butter from the nutritional point of view.

QUALITY
There are several grades of margarine: block (hard or semi-hard); soft (butter substitute); semi-hard for making pastry; and cake margarine which creams easily and absorbs egg. Some margarines are blended with butter. Taste is the best guide to quality.

PRODUCTION
The vegetable oils are mainly obtained from Commonwealth countries, West Africa and South-east Asia. Margarine is made first by extracting the oils and fats from the raw materials, and these are next refined, blended, flavoured and coloured, then mixed with fat-free pasteurised milk. The emulsion is then churned, cooled and packed. Cake and pastry margarines are blended in a different manner to table margarine to produce the texture suitable for mixing.

USE
Margarine can be used in place of butter, the difference being that the smell is not so

pleasant, and nut brown (beurre noisette) or black butter (beurre noir) cannot satisfactorily be produced from margarine. The flavour of margarine when used in the kitchen is inferior to butter – it is therefore not so suitable for finishing sauces and dishes.

It should be remembered that it is equally nutritious and may be cheaper than butter.

Vegetable shortening and high-ratio fat are available. They are used extensively in bakery products.

Animal fats

LARD
Lard is the rendered fat from the pig. Lard has almost 100% fat content. It may be used in hot water paste and with margarine to make short paste. It can also be used for deep or shallow frying.

SUET
Suet is the hard solid fat deposits in the kidney region of animals. Beef suet is the best and it is used for suet paste and mincemeat.

DRIPPING
Dripping is obtained from clarified animal fats and it is used for deep or shallow frying.

FURTHER INFORMATION
Unilever Ltd, Unilever House, Blackfriars, London EC4.

Oils

Oils are fats which are liquid at room temperature. Oil is obtained from sunflower seed, soya bean, walnut, grape seed, sesame, almond, wheatgerm, olives, maize, groundnuts (peanuts), hazelnuts, pine kernels, palm and coleseed (rape).

FOOD VALUE
As oil has a very high fat content it is useful as an energy food.

STORAGE
- Oil should be kept in a cool place.
- If refrigerated some oils congeal; they return to a fluid state in a warm temperature.
- Oils keep for a fairly long time, but they do go rancid if not kept cool.

QUALITY
Olive oil is considered one of the best, owing to its flavour. Better grade oils are almost without flavour, odour and colour.

Herbal oils are available or can be made by adding chopped herbs (tarragon, thyme, marjoram, basil, etc.) to olive oil, pouring into screw top jars and leaving refrigerated for about three weeks. The oil can then be strained and rebottled. If fresh green herbs are being used, blanche and refresh them before chopping – this can enhance the colour of the oil.

OIL TEMPERATURES

TYPE	APPROX. FLASH-POINT (°C)	SMOKE POINT (°C)	RECOMMENDED FRYING TEMP. (°C)
finest quality vegetable oils	324	220	180
finest vegetable fat	321	220	180
high-class vegetable oil	324	204	180
pure vegetable fat	318	215	170–182
pure vegetable oil	330	220	
finest quality maize oil	224	215	180
finest fat	321	202	180
finest quality dripping	300	165	170–180
finest natural olive oil	270–273	148–165	175

PRODUCTION
- Olive oil is extracted from olives grown in Mediterranean countries, particularly Spain, Italy, Greece and France.
- Ground-nut oil is obtained from groundnuts grown in West Africa.
- Maize oil is obtained from maize grown in Europe and the USA. The oil is extracted from the raw material, refined and stored in drums.

USE
Olive oil is used for making vinaigrette and mayonnaise and in the preparation of hors-d'œuvre dishes. Walnut, hazelnut and groundnut oils may also be used. Olive oil is also used in making farinaceous pastes and for shallow frying.

Other oils are used for deep frying. Oil is used for lubricating utensils, trays and also marble slabs to prevent cooked sugar from sticking.

Oil may also be used to preserve foods by excluding air.

Points on the use of all fats and oils

For frying purposes a fat or oil must, when heated, reach a high temperature without smoking. The food being fried will absorb the fat if the fat smokes at a low temperature.

Fats and oils should be free from moisture, otherwise they splutter.

As they are combustible, fats and oils can catch fire. In some fats the margin between smoking and flash point may be narrow. A good frying temperature is 75–180°C (167–356°F).

Further information

British Edible Oils Ltd, Knights Road, London, E16; Proctor and Gamble, Hedley House, St Nicholas Avenue, Gosforth, Newcastle upon Tyne NE99 1EE.

CHEESE (see Plates 87–89, pages 155–156)

Cheese is made worldwide from cows', ewes' or goats' milk and it takes approximately 5 litres (9 pints) of milk to produce $\frac{1}{2}$ kg (1 lb) of cheese.

There are many hundreds of varieties; most countries manufacture their own special cheeses.

Quality

- The skin or rind of cheese should not show spots of mildew, as this is a sign of damp storage.
- Cheese when cut should not give off an overstrong smell or any indication of ammonia.
- Hard, semi-hard and blue-vein cheese when cut should not be dry.
- Soft cheese when cut should not appear runny, but should have a delicate creamy consistency.

Production

Rennet is the chief fermenting agent used in cheese-making and is a chemical substance found in the gastric juice of a calf or lamb.

A typical cheese-making process, briefly, is as follows:

1. 5 litres (9 pints) of milk makes approximately $\frac{1}{2}$ kg (1 lb) of cheese.
2. The milk is tested for acidity and then made sour by using a starter (bacteria which produce lactic acid).
3. Rennet is added, which causes the milk to curdle.
4. The curds are stirred, warmed and then allowed to settle.
5. The liquid (whey) is run off.
6. The curds are ground, salted and put into moulds. If a hard cheese is being made, then pressure is applied in order to squeeze out more of the whey.
7. The curds are now put into the special mould and a skin or rind is allowed to form.
8. When set, the cheese is removed from the mould and is then kept in special storage in order to mature and develop flavour.

Hygiene

Cheese is a living product and should be handled carefully. It should always be wrapped in film or foil, or put in a closed container. Cheese stored in a refrigerator should have plenty of air circulating around it.

Natural rind can be exposed to air, so it can breathe, but cut surfaces should be covered with film to prevent drying out. Mould ripened cheeses should be separated from other cheeses. Remove cheese from the refrigerator about one hour before serving to allow it to return to room temperature.

For storage and distribution the Food Safety Act 1990 requires all chilled food, such as cheese, to be kept at a temperature of 5°C (41°F). However, cheeses displayed on a cheese board or trolley can be exempted for up to four hours.

Recent scares about food poisoning included soft unpasteurised cheeses – this is because listeria can grow and multiply at a lower temperature than most bacteria; at 10°C (50°F) or warmer, growth is rapid.

Storage

All cheese should be kept in a cool, dry, well-ventilated store and whole cheeses should be turned occasionally if being kept for any length of time. Cheese should be kept away from other foods which may be spoilt by the smell.

Food value

Cheese is a highly concentrated form of food. Fat, protein, mineral salts and vitamins are all present. Therefore it is an excellent body-building, energy-producing, protective food.

Preservation

Certain cheeses may be further preserved by processing. A hard cheese is usually employed, ground to a fine powder, melted, mixed with pasteurised milk, poured into moulds then wrapped in lacquered tinfoil, e.g. processed Gruyère, Kraft, Primula.

Uses

SOUPS

Grated Parmesan cheese is served as an accompaniment to many soups, e.g. minestrone. It is also used to form a crust on top of brown onion soup.

PASTA

A grated hard cheese, usually Parmesan, is mixed in with or is also served as an accompaniment to most pasta dishes, e.g. spaghetti italienne, ravioli.

EGG DISHES

- Cheese omelet
- Poached eggs Florentine

FISH DISHES

- Scallops Mornay
- Fish pie

VEGETABLES

- Cauliflower cheese
- Sea kale Mornay

SAVOURIES

- Welsh rarebit
- Quiche lorraine

A well-ordered restaurant should always be able to offer a good selection of assorted cheeses on a 'cheese board', and this should be available after lunch or dinner (see Plate 88, page 155). At least six varieties should be presented, always in prime condition, e.g.:

- Cheddar
- Gruyère
- Camembert

- Gorgonzola
- Edam
- Caerphilly

If demand for cheese is low, then it may be a good policy to offer one or two cheeses only, provided they are in excellent condition, e.g. Stilton, Brie.

Types

ENGLISH AND WELSH CHEESE (see Plate 89, page 156)

- Cheddar – golden colour with a close texture and a fresh mellow, nutty flavour, available in mild, medium mature and mature versions.
- Cheshire – orange-red or white, loose crumbly texture and a mild mellow slightly salty flavour.
- Double Gloucester – orange-red, a buttery open texture with a delicate creamy flavour.
- Leicester – red in colour with a buttery open texture; a mellow medium-strength cheese famous for its use in Welsh rarebit.
- Derby – honey-coloured, close and buttery texture with a mild fresh flavour which goes well with fruit.
- Caerphilly – white in colour and flaky, with a fresh, mild, slightly salty flavour.
- Lancashire – white in colour, soft and crumbly with a fresh mild flavour; excellent for toasted cheese.
- Teifi – made with unpasteurised milk and based on a traditional Gouda recipe; well developed mild flavour.
- Wensleydale – white in colour, moderately close texture with a fresh, mild, slightly salty flavour; excellent with crisp apples or apple pie.
- Stilton – white with blue veins, soft and close texture and a strong flavour; 'The King of Cheeses' traditionally accompanied by port.

SCOTTISH CHEESE

- Baby Dunsyre – semisoft blue cheese made from unpasteurised Ayrshire milk from the Strabogie herd.
- Bonchester – raw milk version of Coulommiers made at Hawick from Jersey milk; mellow flavour, golden body.
- Caboc – small, full-cream cheese coated in oatmeal; slightly sharp nutty taste.
- Dunlop – similar to Cheddar and Double Gloucester, but paler, blander and more moist.

FRENCH CHEESE

- Brie – white, round cheese with close, soft, creamy texture and delicate flavour.
- Camembert – white, round (approximately 10 cm (4 in)) with soft, close, creamy texture and full flavour.
- Chèvre – a generic name for a wide range of goats' cheeses; easily digestible with a sharp sweetness and crumbly texture.
- Fourme d'Ambert – sometimes called a French stilton; salty, full flavour.
- Port Salut – round, cream-coloured, mild, almost bland, semihard.
- Roquefort – blue cheese made from ewe's milk; rich, sharp flavour with salty aftertaste.

ITALIAN CHEESE
- Bel Paese – round, firm, pearly-white texture and a fresh, creamy taste.
- Gorgonzola – blue vein with a rich, sharp flavour; Dolcelatte is a milder version.
- Mozzarella – originally made from buffalo milk; pale and plastic looking, sweet flavour with a little bite.
- Parmesan – hard, low-fat cheese with a rich pithy flavour; grated and used extensively in cooking.
- Ricotta – fresh, white, crumbly and slightly sweet, similar to cottage cheese.

OTHER CHEESES
- Germany – Cambazola: creamy-white round cheese with blue veins and what is considered a good flavour.
- Netherlands – Edam: round, full-flavoured with low-fat content; covered in red skin.
- Switzerland – Gruyère: firm, creamy-white with a full fruity flavour.
- Greece – Fetta: white, moist, crumbly with a refreshing salty-sour taste.

SOFT CURD CHEESES
- Curd cheese – made from pasteurised milk soured by the addition of a milk-souring culture and rennet; the milk separates into curds and whey; the whey is drained off, the curds are blended with a little salt and skimmed milk powder to produce a soft, milk-flavoured, low fat (11%) cheese; made from either skimmed or medium-fat milk.
- Cottage cheese – a low-fat, high protein product made from pasteurised skimmed milk; also available are very low-fat, sweet and savoury varieties.
- Fromage frais – (fresh cheese) or fromage blanc is a fat-free soft curd cheese to which cream can be added to give richer varieties; also available, low-fat, medium-fat, savoury and fruit flavours.
- Quark – a salt-free, fat-free soft cheese made from skimmed milk.

LOW-FAT HARD CHEESE
There is a range of hard cheese with half the fat of traditional cheese. These include 'Tendale' (available as Cheshire or Cheddar), 'Shape' (available as Cheshire or Cheddar) and 'Bodyline' available in $2\frac{1}{2}$ kg (5 lb) packs.

VEGETARIAN CHEESE
Traditional hard cheeses made using a non-animal rennet of microbial origin are available.

Further information
English Country Cheese Council, 5–7 John Prince's Street, London W1M 0AP.

CEREALS

Cereals are cultivated grasses, but the term is broadened to include sago, rice and arrowroot. All cereal products contain starch. The following are the important cereals used in catering: wheat, oats, rye, barley, maize, rice, tapioca, sago and arrowroot. A wide variety of cereals is processed into breakfast foods (barley, wheat, rice, bran and corn.

Wheat

SOURCE
Wheat is the most common cereal produced in the Western world and is grown in most temperate regions. Large quantities are home-grown and a great deal, particularly in the form of strong flour, is imported from Canada.

FOOD VALUE
Cereals are one of the best energy foods. Whole grain cereals provide vitamin B and are therefore protective foods.

STORAGE
- The store room must be dry and well ventilated.
- Flour should be removed from the sacks and kept in wheeled bins with lids.
- Flour bins should be of a type that can be easily cleaned.

Flour is probably the most common commodity in daily use. It forms the foundation of bread, pastry and cakes and is also used in soups, sauces, batters and other foods.

PRODUCTION OF FLOUR
The endosperm of the wheat grain contains all the material used by the baker. It consists of numerous large cells of net-like form in which starch grains are tightly packed. In addition, the cells contain an insoluble gluten protein. When flour is mixed with water it is converted into a sticky dough. This characteristic is due to the gluten which becomes sticky when moistened. The relative proportion of starch and gluten varies in different wheats, and those with a low percentage of gluten are not suitable for bread-making, i.e. soft flour. For this reason, wheat is blended.

In milling, the whole grain is broken up, the parts separated, sifted, blended and ground into flour. Some of the outer coating of bran is removed as is also the wheatgerm which contains oil and is therefore likely to become rancid and so spoil the flour. For this reason wholemeal flour should not be stored for more than 14 days.
- White flour contains 72 to 85% of the whole grain (the endosperm only).
- Wholemeal flour contains 100% of the whole grain.
- Wheatmeal flour contains 85–95% of the whole grain.
- High ratio or patent flour contains 40% of the whole grain.
- 'Self-raising flour' is white flour with the addition of cream of tartar and bicarbonate of soda.
- Semolina is granulated hard flour prepared from the central part of the wheat grain. White or wholemeal semolina is available.

USES OF WHEAT PRODUCTS (see Plates 90 and 91, page 156)
- Soft flour – large and small cakes, biscuits, all pastes except puff and flaky, thickening soups and sauces, batters and coating various foods.
- Strong flour – bread, puff and flaky pastry, and Italian pastes (pasta).
- Wholemeal flour – wholemeal bread and rolls.
- Gnocchi, milk puddings, moulds and as a dusting for certain pastes such as noodle and ravioli. Menu example includes Gnocchi Romaine.
- Macaroni and spaghetti – soups, pasta dishes, garnishes. Menu examples include Minestrone, Macaroni cheese.
- Noodles – garnishing soups, pasta dishes, meat dishes. Menu example includes Braised beef with noodles.

FURTHER INFORMATION
Flour Advisory Bureau, 21 Arlington Street, London SW1 1RN.

Oats

Oats are either rolled into flakes or ground into three grades of oatmeal: coarse, medium and fine.

SOURCE
Oats are one of the hardiest cereals, and are grown in large quantities in Scotland and the north of England.

FOOD VALUE
Oats have the highest food value of any of the cereals. They contain a good proportion of protein and fat.

STORAGE
Because of the fat content, the keeping quality of oat products needs extra care. They should be kept in containers with tight-fitting lids, and stored in a cool, well-ventilated store room.

USES
- Rolled oats – porridge.
- Oatmeal – porridge, thickening soups, coating foods, cakes and biscuits, haggis.
- Patent rolled oats nowadays largely displace oatmeal and have the advantage of being already heat treated and consequently more quickly and easily cooked.

Barley

The whole grain of barley is known as pot or Scotch barley and requires soaking overnight. Pearl barley has most of the bran and germ removed, and it is then polished. These products are used for making barley water for thickening soups and certain stews.

Barley when roasted, is changed into malt and as such is used extensively in the brewing and distilling of vinegar.

Barley needs the same care in storage as oats.

Buckwheat is the seed of the plant 'bran buckwheat'. The grain is usually roasted before cooking, and is also ground into a strong savoury flour for pancakes and baking.

Rye is a grain producing a dark flour used for rye bread and biscuits.

Maize

Maize is also known as corn, sweetcorn or corn-on-the-cob, and besides being served as a vegetable it is processed into cornflakes and cornflour. Maize yields a good oil suitable for cooking.

CORNFLOUR

Cornflour is produced from maize and is the crushed endosperm of the grain which has the fat and protein washed out so that it is practically pure starch.

Cornflour is used for making custard and blancmange powders, because it thickens very easily with a liquid, and sets when cold into a smooth paste that cannot be made from other starches.

Custard powder consists of cornflour, colouring and flavouring.

Cornflour is used for thickening soups, sauces, custards and also in the making of certain small and large cakes.

Rice (see Plate 92, page 157)

Rice needs a hot, wet atmosphere and is grown chiefly in India, the Far East, South America, Italy and the USA.

There are three main types used in this country:

- Long grain – a narrow, pointed grain, best suited for savoury dishes and plain boiled rice because of its firm structure, which helps to keep the rice grains separate, e.g. basmati, patna. Menu examples include Curried beef and rice; Kedgeree.
- Medium grain – an all-purpose rice suitable for sweet and savoury dishes, e.g. carolina, arborio.
- Short grain – a short, rounded grain, best suited for milk puddings and sweet dishes because of its soft texture, e.g. arborio. Menu examples include Baked rice pudding; Pear Condé.

TYPES

- Brown rice – any rice that has had the outer covering removed but retains its bran and as a result is more nutritious.
- Whole grain rice – whole and unprocessed rice.
- Wild rice – seed of an aquatic plant related to the rice family.
- Ground rice – used for milk puddings.
- Rice flour – used for thickening certain soups, e.g. cream soups.
- Rice paper – a thin edible paper produced from rice, used in the preparations of macaroons and nougat.
- Precooked instant rice, par-boiled, ready cooked and boil in the bag are also available.

Plate 83 Fruits: figs, peach, pineapple, pineapple flowers, pomegranate, granadillo, limes, paw-paw, charentis melon, prickly pear, rambukin, mango, ogen melon, mangostines, almonds, apricots, lychees, kumquat, blood orange, persimmon

Plate 84 Soft fruits: wild strawberries, white currants, blueberries, blackberries, blackcurrants, loganberries, strawberries, pink currants, raspberries, red currants, red gooseberries, golden raspberries, gooseberries

Plate 85   Variety of melons and a watermelon

Plate 86   Nuts, including almonds, cashew nuts, pistachio nuts, hazel nuts, walnuts, chestnuts and peanuts

Plate 87   A range of milk and cheese products

Plate 88   Cheese for the cheese board taken from the special refrigerator

Plate 89   Selection of English and Welsh cheeses

Plate 90   Making pasta – traditional method

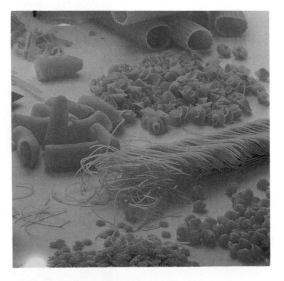

Plate 91   Types of pasta

Plate 92   A selection of pulses and rice

Plate 93   Herbs (left to right, top to bottom) thyme, dill, sage, mint, tarragon, fennel, chives, coriander leaves, rosemary, basil, flat leaf parsley

Plate 94   Herbs and spices

Plate 95   Delicatessen meat counter

YOU ARE WHAT YOU EAT

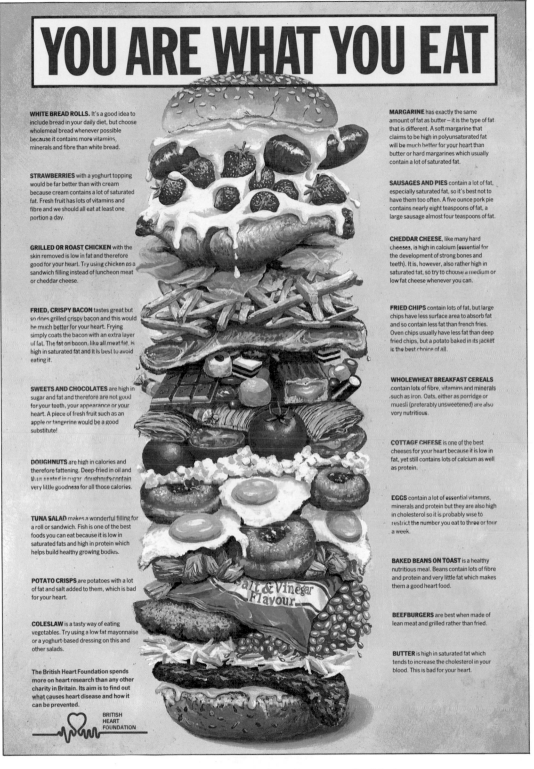

WHITE BREAD ROLLS. It's a good idea to include bread in your daily diet, but choose wholemeal bread whenever possible because it contains more vitamins, minerals and fibre than white bread.

STRAWBERRIES with a yoghurt topping would be far better than with cream because cream contains a lot of saturated fat. Fresh fruit has lots of vitamins and fibre and we should all eat at least one portion a day.

GRILLED OR ROAST CHICKEN with the skin removed is low in fat and therefore good for your heart. Try using chicken as a sandwich filling instead of luncheon meat or cheddar cheese.

FRIED, CRISPY BACON tastes great but so does grilled crispy bacon and this would be much better for your heart. Frying simply coats the bacon with an extra layer of fat. The fat on bacon, like all meat fat, is high in saturated fat and it is best to avoid eating it.

SWEETS AND CHOCOLATES are high in sugar and fat and therefore are not good for your tooth, your appearance or your heart. A piece of fresh fruit such as an apple or tangerine would be a good substitute!

DOUGHNUTS are high in calories and therefore fattening. Deep-fried in oil and then coated in sugar, doughnuts contain very little goodness for all those calories.

TUNA SALAD makes a wonderful filling for a roll or sandwich. Fish is one of the best foods you can eat because it is low in saturated fats and high in protein which helps build healthy growing bodies.

POTATO CRISPS are potatoes with a lot of fat and salt added to them, which is bad for your heart.

COLESLAW is a tasty way of eating vegetables. Try using a low fat mayonnaise or a yoghurt-based dressing on this and other salads.

The British Heart Foundation spends more on heart research than any other charity in Britain. Its aim is to find out what causes heart disease and how it can be prevented.

BRITISH
HEART
FOUNDATION

MARGARINE has exactly the same amount of fat as butter – it is the type of fat that is different. A soft margarine that claims to be high in polyunsaturated fat will be much better for your heart than butter or hard margarines which usually contain a lot of saturated fat.

SAUSAGES AND PIES contain a lot of fat, especially saturated fat, so it's best not to have them too often. A five ounce pork pie contains nearly eight teaspoons of fat, a large sausage almost four teaspoons of fat.

CHEDDAR CHEESE, like many hard cheeses, is high in calcium (essential for the development of strong bones and teeth). It is, however, also rather high in saturated fat, so try to choose a medium or low fat cheese whenever you can.

FRIED CHIPS contain lots of fat, but large chips have less surface area to absorb fat and so contain less fat than french fries. Oven chips usually have less fat than deep fried chips, but a potato baked in its jacket is the best choice of all.

WHOLEWHEAT BREAKFAST CEREALS contain lots of fibre, vitamins and minerals such as iron. Oats, either as porridge or muesli (preferably unsweetened) are also very nutritious.

COTTAGE CHEESE is one of the best cheeses for your heart because it is low in fat, yet still contains lots of calcium as well as protein.

EGGS contain a lot of essential vitamins, minerals and protein but they are also high in cholesterol so it is probably wise to restrict the number you eat to three or four a week.

BAKED BEANS ON TOAST is a healthy nutritious meal. Beans contain lots of fibre and protein and very little fat which makes them a good heart food.

BEEFBURGERS are best when made of lean meat and grilled rather than fried.

BUTTER is high in saturated fat which tends to increase the cholesterol in your blood. This is bad for your heart.

Plate 96   Which foods in this bun are healthy and which are unhealthy?

Plate 97   A smoke oven

STORAGE
Rice should be kept in tight-fitting containers in a cool, well-ventilated store.

Tapioca

Tapioca is obtained from the roots of a tropical plant called cassava. Flake (rough) and seed (fine) are available. Tapioca is used for garnishing soups and milk puddings. Menu examples include Tapioca pudding; Green pea soup with tapioca. Tapioca should be stored as for rice.

Sago

Sago is produced in small pellets from the pith of the sago palm. It is used for garnishing soups and for making milk puddings. A menu example includes Clear soup with sago. Sago should be stored as for rice.

Arrowroot

Arrowroot is obtained from the roots of a West Indian plant called maranta.

It is used for thickening sauces and is particularly suitable when a clear sauce is required as it becomes transparent when boiled. Arrowroot is also used in certain cakes and puddings, and is particularly useful for invalids as it is easily digested.

Arrowroot is easily contaminated by strong-smelling foods; therefore it must be stored in air-tight tins.

Potato flour

Potato flour is a preparation from potatoes, suitable for thickening certain soups and sauces.

RAISING AGENTS

The method of making mixtures light or aerated may be effected in several ways:

- sifting the flour (air is incorporated);
- rubbing fat into flour (air can be incorporated);
- whisking or beating with:
  - eggs, for sponges, genoise, Swiss rolls;
  - egg whites, for meringue;
  - butter or margarine, for puff or rough puff pastry;
  - sugar and fat, for creaming method of sponge puddings and rich cakes
  (In all cases the whisking, beating or rolling (as with puff pastry) encloses air in the mixture);
- using baking powder;
- using yeast;
- layering of fat in a puff paste (known as lamination) (during cooking, steam develops in between the layers of fat and paste in puff and flaky pastry, thus causing the pastry to rise).

Baking powder

Baking powder may be made from one part sodium bicarbonate to two parts of cream of tartar. In commercial baking the powdered cream of tartar may be replaced by another acid product, e.g. acidulated calcium phosphate.

When used under the right conditions it produces carbon dioxide gas; to produce gas, a liquid and heat are needed. As the acid has a delayed action, only a small amount being given off when the liquid is added, the majority of the gas is released when the mixture is heated. Therefore cakes and puddings when mixed do not lose the property of the baking powder if they are not cooked right away.

HINTS ON USING BAKING POWDER
- Mix the baking powder thoroughly with the flour.
- Replace the lid tightly on the tin.
- Measure accurately.
- Do not slam oven doors in early stages of cooking.
- Excess baking powder causes a cake to collapse in the middle and dumplings to break up.
- Insufficient baking powder results in a close, heavy texture.
- Use within one month of purchase.

USE
Baking powder is used in sponge puddings, cakes and scones and in suet puddings and dumplings.

Yeast

Yeast is a fungus form of plant life available as a fresh or dried product.

STORAGE AND QUALITY POINTS
- Yeast should be wrapped and stored in a cold place.
- It is ordered only as required.
- It must be perfectly fresh and moist.
- It should have a pleasant smell.
- Yeast should crumble easily.
- It is pale grey in colour.

FOOD VALUE
Yeast is rich in protein and vitamin B. It is therefore a help towards building and repairing the body and provides protection.

PRODUCTION
Yeast's minute cells grow and multiply at blood heat provided they are fed with sugar and liquid. The sugar causes fermentation – this is the production of gas (carbon dioxide) and alcohol in the form of small bubbles in the mixture or dough. When heat is applied to the mixture or dough it causes it to rise.

Dried yeast has been dehydrated and requires creaming with a little water before use. Its main advantage is that it will keep for several months in its dry state.

USE

To use yeast these points should be remembered:

- The yeast should be removed from the refrigerator and used at room temperature.
- Salt retards the working of yeast.
- The more salt used the slower the action of yeast.
- Best temperature for yeast action is 21–27°C (40–51°F).
- The liquid for mixing the dough should be 36–37°C (97–99°F).
- Temperatures over 52°C (126°F) destroy yeast.
- Yeast can withstand low temperatures without damage.
- The flour, bowl and liquid should be warm.
- Yeast doughs must be kneaded (worked) to make an elastic dough and to distribute the yeast evenly. An elastic dough is required to allow the gases to expand.
- Proving means that the dough is allowed to double its size. This should occur in a warm place, free from draughts. The dough must be covered. The quality of the dough is improved by 'knocking back'. This means the dough is pressed down to its original size and allowed to prove again. The dough is then lightly kneaded, moulded and proved again before baking. The dough should not overprove, either in the bowl or in the moulded state. Excess or uneven heat or too long a proving time can cause overproving, which spoils the dough.

USES

Yeast is used in:

- bread doughs: rolls, white, brown, wholemeal loaves, etc.;
- bun doughs: currant, Chelsea, Swiss, Bath, doughnuts;
- baba, savarin and marignans;
- croissants and brioche;
- Danish pastry;
- frying batter.

SUGAR

Sugar is produced from sugar cane grown in a number of tropical and subtropical countries and from sugar beet which is grown in parts of Europe, including the UK.

Food value

As sugar contains 99.9% pure sugar, it is invaluable for producing energy.

Types

- Refined white sugars: granulated, castor; cube; icing.
- Unrefined sugar: brown sugar.
- Partially refined sugar: demerara.

Storage

Sugar should be stored in a dry, cool place. When purchased by the sack, the sugar is stored in covered bins.

Production

The sugar is extracted from cane or beet, crystallised, refined and then sieved. The largest holed sieve produces granulated, the next size castor and fine linen sieves are used for icing sugar. Loaf or cube sugar is obtained by pressing the crystals while slightly wet, drying them in blocks and then cutting the blocks into squares.

Syrup and treacle are produced during the production of sugar. They are filtered and evaporated to the required colour and thickness.

Use

Sugar is chiefly used for pastry, confectionery and bakery work.

- Pastry uses – for pies, puddings, sweet dishes, ice-creams and pastries.
- Confectionery uses – decorating gâteaux and celebration cakes (birthday, christening, wedding), sweets and petits fours. Sugar work (pulled, blown and spun).
- Bakery uses – yeast doughs, large and small cakes.
- In the kitchen it is used in certain sauces, such as mint and Robert. Sugar may be added to peas and carrots. It is used in some meat dishes, e.g. Beef carbonnade; Baked sugar ham. Sugar is also added to the brine solution.
- Sugar is also used to give colour, e.g. Crème caramel and the production of blackjack.
- Glucose is a syrup made from potatoes, cane sugar and fruit, treated and refined to a liquid or powder form. Glucose is not as sweet as sugar, but it is an important energy producer. Glucose is used extensively in confectionery work.

Further information

British Sugar Refiners Association, Plantation House, Mincing Lane, London EC3.

BEVERAGES (DRINKS)

The simplest, cheapest drink of all is water which varies from place to place in taste and character according to the substances dissolved or suspended in it. Soft water has a low content of lime. Hard water has an abundance of lime (if the flavour of lime is too strong, the water may have to be softened to remove the excess of lime).

Water which has been artificially softened should not be used for coffee or tea making. The mineral content of water used for brewing can significantly affect the final taste of the coffee or tea. A blend of coffee or tea brewed in the very hard water of London has a completely different taste to the same blend brewed in Edinburgh, where the water is very soft. Water can also have varying degrees of other substances, e.g. iron and sulphur, which in some instances are considered to be beneficial to health and are known as mineral waters (see page 160).

Drink can be broadly classified into two categories, alcoholic and non-alcoholic (beverage or soft drink). Although the word beverage means a drink the generally accepted definition is a non-alcoholic liquid, e.g. chocolate, coffee, tea, cocoa, fruit drinks, mineral waters, milk.

Alcoholic drinks include cocktails, aperitifs, fancy drinks, wines, fortified wines, spirits, beers, cider, perry.

Non-alcoholic drinks

COFFEE

Coffee is produced from the beans of the coffee tree, and is grown and exported by 14 countries including Brazil, Columbia, Kenya, Indonesia and the Ivory Coast. The varieties of coffee are named after the areas where they are grown, such as Mysore, Kenya, Brazil, Mocha and Java.

Purchasing unit

Coffee beans either unroasted, roasted or ground, are sold by the pound (500 g) and in 7 lb (3 kg) or 28 lb (11 kg) parcels or tins. Coffee essence is obtained in $5\frac{1}{2}$ fl oz (125 ml), 10 fl oz (250 ml), 25 fl oz (625 ml) and 1 gal ($4\frac{1}{2}$ l) bottles.

Food value

It is the milk and sugar served with coffee that have food value. Coffee has no value as a food by itself.

Production

The coffee tree or bush produces fruit called a cherry which contains seeds. The outer-side pulp is removed and the seeds or beans are cleaned, graded and packed into sacks. When required, the beans are blended and roasted to bring out the flavour and aroma.

- French coffee usually contains chicory; the root is washed, dried, roasted and ground. The addition of chicory gives a particular flavour and appearance to the coffee.
- Coffee essence is a concentrated form of liquid coffee which may contain chicory.
- Instant coffee is liquid coffee which has been dried into powder form.
- Decaffeinated coffee has most of the caffeine removed, and is, therefore, less of a stimulant.

Composition

The composition of coffee is complex with a large range of compounds including flavanoids, chlorogenic acids, nicotinic acids and caffeine.

Uses

Coffee is mainly used as a beverage which may be served with milk, cream or as a flavouring for cakes, icings, bavarois and ice-cream.

It can be brewed to suit individual tastes. The many different pure blended and instant (soluble) coffees which can be brewed in a wide selection of different coffee makers, or by various special brewing methods, make it possible to provide a brew to suit everyone. Whatever type of coffee is drunk, and regardless of roasting time, fineness of grind or brewing method, there are basic rules to observe for making a good cup of coffee.

Rules for making coffee

- Use good coffee which is freshly roasted and ground.
- Use ground or vacuum-packed coffee within 10 days or the quality will deteriorate. Store in airtight containers in a cool place.
- Use freshly drawn, freshly boiled water cooled to 92–96°C (198–205°F) (to preserve the flavour and aroma of the coffee). Do not use boiling water.
- Measure the quantity of coffee carefully, 300–360 g (11–13 oz) per 5 litres (9 pints).
- After the coffee has been made it should be strained off, otherwise it will acquire a bitter taste if kept hot for more than 30 minutes. Do not reheat brewed coffee.
- Milk, if served with coffee, should be hot but not boiled.
- All coffee-making equipment must be kept scrupulously clean, washed thoroughly after each use and rinsed with clean hot water (never use soda).
- Make coffee in pots which have been thoroughly dried and warmed.

Instant coffee

The majority of people in the United Kingdom drink 'instant' coffee. After the seal is broken on the container of instant or soluble coffee it should be stored in an airtight container and kept in a cool place.

The flavour of instant coffee is improved if it is made in a pot using approximately one heaped teaspoon for each cup, and according to taste. Fresh water which is just off the boil should be added.

Instant coffee is convenient because it can be made into individual cups by adding water to the coffee and stirring.

Jug method

Although most people prefer to use china or earthenware jugs for making coffee, the old-fashioned enamel pot (such as cowboys used) is quite suitable. Before making the coffee, the pot should be scalded with boiling water and dried. This heats the pot. Medium ground coffee should then be added with just enough water to make the grounds wet.

After about a minute the remaining water should be added and the mixture stirred. The jug should be kept warm while it stands for about 10 minutes before the coffee is poured.

The cafetière (French for coffee-maker) or plunger pot method

The advantages of this system are:

- speed, space saving, ability to use a range of coffees;
- ease of operation, minimal staff training, labour saving;
- economy; no filter papers required and no waste;
- availability in two, three, four, six, eight and 12-cup pots.

To make coffee by this method

1. Remove the complete plunger unit, preheat the beaker with boiling water and empty.
2. Put fresh **medium ground** coffee into the beaker.
3. Fill the beaker up to the bottom of the spout with water just below boiling point, then stir. Water at this heat gives a better flavour.
4. Replace the plunger unit and lid on the beaker and leave to infuse for a few minutes.
5. Push the plunger down slowly, the grounds are then trapped under the filter and the coffee is ready to be served.

The automatic drip machine method

These machines are becoming more popular and when properly used they can make an excellent cup of coffee. They usually require a special disposable filter paper which can be thrown away with the grounds after brewing.

Although the manufacturers' instructions should be observed it is usual to add a measured quantity of fresh, cold water into the flask.

Finely ground coffee is placed into the filter, and once it is switched on, the machine will brew the coffee and keep it hot for serving. Coffee should not be allowed to stand in these machines for more than an hour or so.

Pour over coffee brewer method

These machines give total flexibility; they are more convenient, have reduced spillage and are safe to operate. They give maximum extraction from the coffee grounds, are easy to clean, give a consistent coffee flavour and maintain the coffee at the ideal holding temperature.

The drip pot method

These 'filter coffee makers' use the same principle as the automatic drip pot. Water which is just off the boil should be poured over the grounds to wet them. After a minute or so the remaining water is added and coffee drips through into a cup or pot.

Expresso coffee machine

Expresso coffee is produced by a pressure boiler providing hot water and steam being 'expressed' through a small amount of coffee to produce one or two cups at a time. Large models are available which produce up to 600 cups per hour. Expresso machines also have a steam jet and hot water supply to ensure that teas and other hot drinks can be provided. Some models have a coffee bean grinder and automotive controls which measure and grind the coffee, infuse the drink and dispose the waste grouts and filter paper into a container within the machine.

Expresso coffee has a strong slightly bitter flavour and if milk is required, the milk is heated by the steam jet which also aerates and makes it frothy. The frothy milk is poured onto the expresso; it is now known as **cappuccino**, which may be finally sprinkled with powdered chocolate.

The glass cone machine

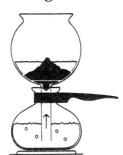

This vacuum method is sometimes abused in restaurants when coffee is left too long to 'stew'.

Cold water is poured into the lower bowl which is then twisted into the upper bowl containing the filter and a quantity of medium ground coffee.

This will make a seal and when the water boils it will rise up the funnel to make a coffee and water mixture in the upper bowl. This mixture is stirred as soon as the head is removed and the coffee will drip into the lower bowl, ready to serve.

Turkish or Greek coffee method

Ideally, Turkish coffee should be made in a traditional long-handled copper container called an *ibrik*, but a small, narrow and high-sided saucepan can be used.

Dark or continental roast coffee, ground as finely as possible will be required. This should be added at a rate of one heaped teaspoon of coffee to each demi-tasse of water.

Turkish or Greek coffee can be drunk without sugar but it is usual to add one heaped teaspoon of sugar for each spoon of coffee. This produces a sweet brew.

The sugar should be stirred into the water and brought to the boil. When it boils the heat should be removed and the process repeated about four times.

If the coffee is left to stand for a minute or so the grounds will settle, or can be precipitated by adding a drop of cold water.

This coffee should be poured without straining into very small cups. It is often served with a glass of iced water. Milk should never be used.

Coffee al fresco

Coffee can be made in a saucepan on a stove. This is the ideal method for campers or student bedsits.

Four tablespoons of medium or coarse ground coffee should be added to $\frac{1}{2}$ litre (1 pint) of water and brought to the boil in a covered saucepan. As soon as it boils, the coffee should be removed from the heat and left to stand for about five minutes before being strained into cups or mugs.

Iced coffee and coffee shakes

The ideal standby for making quick, refreshing, iced coffee, is home-made coffee syrup, to which can be added water and ice cubes, or creamy milk. It is also useful for milk shakes or cakes and desserts. Made and stored properly it keeps for a long time and has a better flavour than the instant or bottled varieties.

Using 227 g (8 oz) of ground coffee and 1 litre (1$\frac{3}{4}$ pints) of water, make the coffee in any of the ways described previously, and strain it, if necessary, into a saucepan. Add 680 g (1$\frac{1}{2}$ lb) of sugar, stir and bring to the boil. Leave to cool slightly, then pour into sterilised bottles. Store in a cool larder or refrigerator.

Further information

Coffee Information Centre, 22 Berners Street, London W1P 4DD.

TEA

Tea is the name given to the young leaves and leaf buds of the tea plant after they have been specially treated and dried.

Tea is produced in India, Pakistan, Assam, Darjeeling, Sri Lanka, Java, Sumatra, China, East Africa, Uganda, Kenya, Tanzania and Malawi.

Teas show marked differences according to the country and district in which they are produced and it is usual to blend several types.

China teas have the most delicate flavour of any, but lack 'body'.

Types

There are a large number of teas on the market, and as water in different districts affects the flavour, the only sure way to select a tea for continual use is by trying out several blends, tasting them and then assessing the one that gives the most satisfactory flavour.

Fruit and herb teas are increasingly popular because they do not contain caffeine and are available in a wide variety of flavours (camomile, peppermint, rosehip and hibiscus, lemon grass, lemon, blackcurrant, raspberry, strawberry, apple, peach, passion fruit, etc.).

Buying

Tea may be obtained in packs from $\frac{1}{2}$ oz (14 g) to 100 lb (220 kg) so that obviously many factors concerned with the type of business must be considered when deciding how to buy. The cheapest way of purchasing tea is in 100 lb (220 kg) chests which are lined with lead or aluminium paper. This is to prevent the tea from absorbing moisture and odours.

Storage

Tea should always be stored in dry, clean, airtight containers in a well-ventilated store room.

Food value

Tea alone has no nutritional properties, but it is a most refreshing drink. Nutritional value is only supplied by the milk and sugar in the tea.

Tannins are an important constituent of tea as they provide colour, astringency and body. Some essential oils provide the aroma.

The stimulating effect of tea comes from caffeine – the world's most common drug. In small quantities, its stimulating effects improve concentration, gastric secretions and coordination. It may also stimulate muscles making them less susceptible to fatigue. However, excessive consumption of tea may cause heartbeat irregularities, lack of sleep and nervous problems.

Use

1. Use a good tea – the ideal recipe is 60 g (2 oz) to 5 litres (9 pints) of boiling water; there should be no guess-work, and the tea should be weighed or measured for each brew.
2. Always use freshly drawn, freshly boiled water.
3. Heat the pot – unless this is done the water goes off the boil rapidly, thus preventing the correct infusion of the tea.
4. Take the pot to the boiling water – the water must be as near boiling point as possible to enable the leaves to infuse properly.
5. Allow the tea to brew for 4–5 minutes, and stir well before pouring.

Further information

The Tea Council, Sir John Lyon House, 5 High Timber Street, London EC4V 3NJ.

COCOA

Cocoa is a powder produced from the beans of the cacao tree. It is imported mainly from West Africa.

Food value
As cocoa contains some protein and a large proportion of starch it helps to provide the body with energy. Iron is also present in cocoa.

Storage
Cocoa should be kept in airtight containers in a well-ventilated store.

Production
The cocoa beans grow in the pods of the cacao tree. The beans are dried, fermented, redried and roasted. The shells are cracked and removed; the nibs which are left are ground to a thick brown liquid called cocoa mass. The mass is compressed, then crushed, ground and sifted, making cocoa. The cocoa butter is removed, because it would make the drink greasy.

Uses
For hot drinks, cocoa is mixed with milk, milk and water, or water. Hot liquid is needed to cook the starch and make it more digestible. Cocoa can be used to flavour puddings, cakes, sauces, icing and ice-cream. To make cocoa:
1. Measure the amount of cocoa and liquid carefully (30 g (1 oz) cocoa; 60 g (2 oz) sugar; 1 litre (1¾ pints) milk or milk and water).
2. Mix the cocoa with a little of the cold liquid.
3. Bring the remaining liquid to the boil, add the cocoa, stirring all the time.
4. Return to the pan and bring to the boil, stirring until it boils, then add the sugar.

CHOCOLATE
Cocoa beans are used to produce chocolate, and over half of the cocoa bean consists of cocoa butter. To produce chocolate, cocoa butter is mixed with crushed cocoa beans and syrup. With baker's chocolate, the cocoa fat (butter) is replaced by vegetable fat thus giving a cheaper product which does not need tempering. For commercial purposes, chocolate is sold in blocks known as *couverture*. Pure chocolate couverture is made from cocoa mass, highly refined sugar and extracted cocoa butter. It is the additional cocoa butter which gives couverture its qualities for moulding, its flavour and therefore its higher price.

Uses
Chocolate or couverture is used for icings, butter creams, sauces, dipping chocolates and moulding into shapes.

Drinking chocolate
This is ground cocoa from which less fat has been extracted and to which sugar has been added. It can be obtained in flake or powder form.
1. Measure the chocolate powder and liquid.
2. Place the chocolate in a pot, mug or cup, pour on the boiling liquid and mix thoroughly.

MINERAL WATERS
A wide range of mineral waters are available, both home produced and from

overseas, and either natural (still) in character or treated with gas (carbon dioxide) to give a light sparkle or fizz. Examples of natural mineral waters are Buxton and Malvern. Manufactured types include grapefruit, lime juice (still) and tonic water, Coca-Cola, ginger beer (sparkling).

Squashes and cordials are all concentrated fruit extracts, meant to be broken down with fresh or aerated water into a long drink, and to be served hot or iced. Fruit juices are the unfermented juice of fresh fruits such as apple, grape, orange, tomato.

Fruit syrups are concentrated fruit juices preserved with sugar or manufactured from compound colourings and flavours (orange, lime, cherry). A large range of compound flavourings is available.

MILK DRINKS
Milk can be offered plain either hot or cold. Other milk drinks include:

- Milkshakes – a mixture of fresh milk, ice-cream and a flavouring syrup, rapidly whisked and served in a tall glass.
- Ice-cream sodas – combination of fruit syrup and fresh cream in a long glass filled with soda water and topped with ice-cream.
- Egg noggs – beaten eggs (preferably pasteurised) with fruit syrup and sugar added, mixed with hot or cold milk in a tall glass and topped with grated nutmeg.
- Other products from which beverages are made either by the addition of hot water or milk include Bournvita, Bovril, Horlicks, Ovaltine.

SOFT DRINKS
Drinks are acidified, sweetened, coloured artificially, carbonated and very often chemically preserved. The formulation and flavouring of many well-known brands are a guarded secret. The water used for soft drinks must be well purified, free of micro-organisms, dissolved metals and organic compounds.

Sweetening has always been carried out by using syrups to give a sugar content of approximately 12%. For diet drinks sugar is replaced with saccharin or aspartame. The loss of body produced by sugar is rectified by the addition of pectin or carboxy-methylcellulose.

Natural flavours added to drinks are difficult to use in order to produce a standard product. Natural flavour extracts undergo changes in the presence of light, acid and storage. They do not often transport pigment of sufficient depth and are usually unstable in acid conditions. Synthetic products are developed to overcome all the problems encountered using natural materials.

Acids used in the manufacture of soft drinks are citric, malic, tartaric and phosphoric. Dissolved carbon dioxide also produces some acidity. Sodium benzoate is a common preservative used in soft drink manufacture.

Alcoholic drinks

WINE
Wine has been made for over 6000 years and is produced in most parts of the world. It is the fermented juice of the grape and is available in many styles: red, white, rosé, sparkling, organic, alcohol-free, de-alcoholised and low alcohol. Wines may be dry,

medium dry or sweet in character and according to the type and character they may be drunk while young (within a short time of bottling) or allowed to age (in some cases for many years).

Bottled wines should always be stored on their sides so that the wine remains in contact with the cork. This keeps the cork expanded and prevents air from entering the wine which, if allowed to happen, will turn the wine to vinegar.

Fortified wines

Fortified wines are those which have been strengthened by the addition of alcohol usually produced from grape juice; the best known are port, sherry and Madeira.

Aromatised wines

Aromatised wines are produced by flavouring a simple basic wine with a blend of ingredients (fruit, roots, bark, peel, flowers, quinine, herbs). Vermouth and Dubonnet are two examples of aromatised wines popular as aperitifs.

Composition

The composition quality and drinking characteristics of wine depend on:

- the variety of the grape;
- the soil;
- the climate;
- the method of production.

White wines are produced from the juice of any variety of grape, not just white grapes. Red wines can only be produced from black grapes, which are pulped and fermented with the skins. The skin pigments, known as anthocyanins, are extracted during the initial fermentation process. The alcohol produced by the fermentation assists this process. Tannins are also extracted which gives astringency to the wine.

Rosé wines are only allowed to ferment in the presence of the skins for a short time.

Grape juice contains sugar which is fermented by the yeast, *Saccharomyces ellipsoidens*. If all the sugars are fermented a dry wine is produced. Fully ripened grapes contain a high proportion of sugar, some of which may remain to produce a sweeter wine. In very sweet wines, such as sauternes, the grapes become shrivelled and raisin-like on the vines due to mould acid called 'noble rot'. The mould concentrates the sugars and produces glycerol which increases the sweetness of the finished wine.

Ripe grapes contain tartaric acid, which may crystallise out of the wines, on standing, to form cream of tartar. Red wines and white wines, such as hock and Moselle (from unripe grapes), contain more malic acid. In semisparkling wines the malic acid is converted by bacteria into lactic acid and carbon dioxide which gives the effervescent effect. Full sparkling wines like champagne require special alcohol-tolerant strains of yeasts, and fermentation is completed in the bottle.

Winemaking

Winemaking is carried out using the yeast, naturally present on the grapes, and known as a bloom.

The process is as follows:

1. The grapes are crushed and treated with sulphite to kill the wild yeasts and any bacteria present.
2. An active starter culture of yeast is added and fermentation starts at 22–25°C (42–47°F).
3. Fermentation finishes when all the sugar is exhausted and the yeast is inactivated by high alcohol levels.
4. The yeast falls to the bottom of the wine vessel.
5. Racking removes the yeast and any other foreign bodies.
6. Several rackings may be necessary as the wine is aged. Ageing is carried out in tanks or oak casks.
7. Red wines because of their tannin content, require more ageing to produce a more mellow, full-flavoured bouquet.
8. After maturation the wines are filtered and stabilised by adding sulphate or benzoate.
9. Further ageing is carried out after bottling.

SPIRITS
Spirits are distillations of fermented liquids which are converted into liquid spirit; they include whisky, gin, vodka, brandy and rum.

LIQUEURS
Liqueurs are flavoured and sweetened spirits. A wide range of flavouring agents are employed (aniseed, caraway, peaches, raspberries, violets, rose petals, cinnamon, sage, honey, coffee beans). Many different liqueurs are available (Cointreau, cherry brandy).

COCKTAILS AND MIXED DRINKS
Cocktails are usually a mixture of a spirit with one or more ingredients from liqueurs, fruit juices, fortified wines, eggs, cream, etc. Cocktails may be garnished with mint, borage, fresh fruit, olives, etc.

Mixed drinks have an assortment of names that include flips, fizzes, noggs, sours, cups.

Cocktails and mixed drinks can also be made from non-alcoholic ingredients.

BEER
Beer is a term that covers all beer-like drinks such as ale, stouts and lagers. It is made from a combination of water, grain (e.g. barley), hops, sugar and yeast. Types of beer include: bitter, mild, Burton, strong ale, barley wine, porter, lager.

Reduced alcohol beers are also available.

Beer is made from grain, particularly barley. The barley is first germinated in the malting process so that amylases can break down some of the starch to maltose. It is maltose which is fermented by the yeast.

Hops are used to preserve and flavour the beer with the bitter humulones they contain.

Beers are good sources of energy, they contain high levels of carbohydrates and protein. Beers are richer in minerals than wines, but lower in alcohol at only 2–5%.

Beer making

1. Malt and cereal grains are mixed and hot water added. The temperature is controlled at approximately 65°C (149°F) to encourage rapid amylase activity. This process is called mashing.
2. After about three hours the liquid is drained off. The liquid, known as wort, is rich in sugars. The wort is boiled and the hops are added. It is then filtered, cooled and the yeast added.
3. Fermentation is carried out at about 15°C (59°F). In traditional beers the production of carbon dioxide during fermentation carries the yeast to the top of the vessel. In lager the yeast ferments at the bottom and as a result is easier to separate after fermentation.
4. After fermentation, finings are added and filtration is carried out to remove yeast cells.
5. The beer is stored in bulk before bottling or loading into kegs. Traditionally some sugar was added in the bottle or keg to achieve carbonation of the beer. Modern breweries have carbon dioxide injection systems to achieve a consistent level of carbonation.

CIDER

Cider is fermented apple juice. Also in this category are:
*   Pomagne – a sparkling cider.
*   Scrumpy – strong, homemade, rough cider.

PERRY

Perry is fermented pear juice.

Further information

The Beverage Book, Durkans and Cousins, Hodder and Stoughton, 1995.

PULSES

Pulses are the dried seeds of plants which form pods.

Types (see Plate 92, page 157)

*   Aduki beans – small, round, deep red, shiny beans.
*   Black beans – glistening black skins and creamy flesh.
*   Black-eyed beans – white beans with a black blotch.
*   Borlotti beans – pink blotched mottled colour.
*   Broad beans – strongly flavoured beans, sometimes known as fava beans.
*   Butter beans – available large or small, also known as Lima beans.
*   Cannellini – Italian haricots, slightly fatter than the English.
*   Chick-peas – look like the kernel of a small hazel-nut.

- Dhal – is the Hindi word for dried peas and beans.
- Dutch brown beans – light brown in colour.
- Flageolets – pale-green, kidney-shaped beans.
- Ful medames or Egyptian brown beans – small, brown, knobbly beans, also known as the field bean in England.
- Haricot beans – white, smooth oval beans.
- Lentils – available in bright orange, brown or green.
- Mung beans – chiefly used for bean sprouts.
- Pinto beans – pink blotched mottled colour.
- Puy lentils – grey coloured beans; do not require soaking and they hold their shape when cooked.
- Red kidney beans – used in Chilli con carne.
- Soissons – the finest haricot beans.
- Soya beans – the most nutritious of all beans.
- Split peas – available in bright green or golden yellow.

Food value

Pulses are good sources of protein and carbohydrate and therefore help to provide the body with energy. With the exception of the soya bean, they are completely deficient in fat.

Storage

All pulses should be kept in clean containers in a dry, well-ventilated store.

Use

Pulses are used extensively for soups, stews, vegetables, salads and accompaniments to meat dishes and vegetarian cookery. Menu examples include Haricot oxtail; Boiled belly of pork; Pease pudding; Lentil soup; Lentil and courgette flan; Yellow-pea soup; Green-pea soup; Black-eyed peas with bacon.

HERBS (see Plates 93 and 94, pages 157 and 158)

Of the thirty well known types of herbs, approximately twelve are generally used in cookery. Herbs may be used fresh, but the majority are dried, so as to ensure a continuous supply throughout the year. The leaves of herbs contain an oil which gives the characteristic smell and flavour. They are simple to grow and where possible any well-ordered kitchen should endeavour to have its own fresh herb patch. Tubs or window-boxes can be used if no garden is available.

Herbs have no food value but are important from a nutritive point of view in aiding digestion because they stimulate the flow of gastric juices. These are the most commonly used herbs:

Basil

Basil is a small leaf with a pungent flavour and sweet aroma. Used in raw or cooked tomato dishes or sauces, salads and lamb dishes.

Bay leaves

Bay leaves are the leaves of the bay laurel or sweet bay trees or shrubs. They may be fresh or dried and are used for flavouring many soups, sauces, stews, fish and vegetable dishes, in which case they are usually included in a faggot of herbs (bouquet garni).

Borage

This is a plant with furry leaves and blue flowers that produces a flavour similar to cucumber when added to vegetables and salads.

Celery seed

Celery seed is dried and used for flavouring soups, sauces, stews, eggs, fish and cheese dishes, when fresh celery is unobtainable. If used in a white soup or sauce it should be tied in a piece of muslin, otherwise it can cause discoloration. When celery seed and salt are ground together it is known as celery salt (see page 183).

Chervil

Chervil has small, neatly shaped leaves with a delicate aromatic flavour. It is best used fresh, but may also be obtained in dried form. Because of its neat shape it is employed a great deal for decorating chaud-froid work. It is also one of the *fines herbes*, the mixture of herbs used in many culinary preparations.

Chive

Chive is a bright green member of the onion family resembling a coarse grass. It has a delicate onion flavour. It is invaluable for flavouring salads, hors-d'œuvre, fish, poultry and meat dishes, and chopped as a garnish for soups and cooked vegetables. It should be used fresh.

Coriander

A member of the parsley family, coriander is one of the oldest flavourings used by man. It is both a herb and a spice. The leaves have a distinctive pungent flavour.

Dill

Dill has feathery green-grey leaves and is used in fish recipes and pickles.

Fennel

Fennel has feathery bright green leaves, and a slight aniseed flavour and is used for fish sauces, meat dishes and salads.

Lemon grass

Lemon grass is a tall plant with long spear-shaped grass-like leaves with a strong lemon flavour.

Lovage

Lovage leaves have a strong celery-like flavour; when finely chopped they can be used in soups, stews, sauces and salads.

Marjoram

Marjoram is a sweet herb which may be used fresh in salads and pork, fish, poultry, cheese, egg and vegetable dishes, and when dried can be used for flavouring soups, sauces, stews and certain stuffings.

Mint

There are many varieties of mint. Fresh sprigs of mint are used to flavour peas and new potatoes. Fresh or dried mint may be used to make mint sauce or mint jelly for serving with roast lamb. Another lesser known but excellent mint for the kitchen is apple mint. Chopped mint can be used in salads.

Oregano

Oregano has a flavour and aroma similar to marjoram but stronger. It is used in Italian and Greek-style cooking in meats, salads, soups, stuffings, pasta, sauces, vegetable and egg dishes.

Parsley

Parsley is probably the most common herb in Britain and has numerous uses for flavouring, garnishing and decorating a large variety of dishes. When garnishing deep fried fish, fry whole heads of fresh parsley till crisp.

Rosemary

Rosemary is a strong fragrant herb which should be used sparingly and may be used fresh or dried for flavouring sauces, stews, salads and for stuffings. Rosemary can also be sprinkled on roasts or grills of meat, poultry and fish during cooking and on roast potatoes.

Sage

Sage is a strong, bitter, pungent herb which aids the stomach to digest rich fatty meat and is therefore used in stuffings for duck, goose and pork.

Tarragon

This plant has a bright green attractive leaf. It is best used fresh, particularly when decorating chaud-froid dishes. Tarragon has a pleasant flavour and is used in sauces, one well-known example being sauce béarnaise. It is one of the *fines herbes* and as such is used for omelets, salads, fish and meat dishes.

Thyme

Thyme is a popular herb in the UK and is used fresh or dried for flavouring soups, sauces, stews, stuffings, salads and vegetables.

Fine herbs (*fines herbes*)

This is a mixture of fresh herbs, usually chervil, tarragon and parsley, which is referred to in many classical cookery recipes.

Balm, bergamot, fennel, savory, sorrel, tansy, lemon thyme

These and other herbs are used in cookery, but on a much smaller scale.

Harvesting and drying of herbs

1. The shoots and leaves should be collected from the plants just before they bloom.
2. They should be inspected to see that they are sound.
3. They are then tied in small bundles and hung up to dry in a warm but not sunny place.
4. After 24 hours paper bags should be tied over them to keep out dust and to help retain colour in the leaves.
5. When sufficiently dry they should break up easily if rubbed between forefinger and thumb.
6. The leaves have the middle vein removed and they are then passed through a sieve.
7. The sieved herbs must be kept in airtight bottles or tins in order to conserve flavour.

SPICES (see Plate 94, page 158)

Spices are natural products obtained from the fruits, seeds, roots, flowers or the bark of a number of different trees or shrubs. They contain oils which aid digestion by stimulating the gastric juices. They also enhance the appearance of food and add a variety of flavours. As spices are concentrated in flavour, they should be used sparingly, otherwise they can make foods unpalatable. Most spices are grown in India, Africa, the West Indies and the Far East.

Allspice or pimento

This is so called because the flavour is like a blend of cloves, cinnamon and nutmeg. It is the unripe fruit of the pimento tree which grows in the West Indies. Allspice is picked when still green, and dried when the colour turns to reddish brown. Allspice is ground and used as a flavouring in sauces, sausages, cakes, fruit pies and milk puddings. It is one of the spices blended for mixed spice.

Anise

This is also known as sweet cumin, and has a sweet aniseed flavour. It is used for fish, sweets, creams and cakes.

Anise (pepper)

A strong, hot-flavoured red pepper.

Anise (star)

Stronger than anise, this has a slight liquorice flavour. Used in Chinese cookery with pork and duck.

Asafoetida

This is used in Indian cookery to add flavour to vegetarian dishes. Available in block or powder form.

Cardamom

Cardamom is frequently used in curry, and has a warm, oily sharp taste.

Caraway

Caraway seeds come from a plant grown in Holland. The seeds are about $\frac{1}{2}$ cm ($\frac{1}{4}$ in) long, shaped like a new moon and brown in colour. Caraway seeds are used in seed-cake and certain breads, sauerkraut, cheese and confectionery. Also for flavouring certain liqueurs such as Kümmel.

Cassia

This comes in thicker sticks than cinnamon, and is less delicate and more expensive. Used in spiced meats and curries.

Celery seed

Slightly bitter, this should be used sparingly if celery or celery salt is not available.

Chillies and capsicums

These are both from the same family and grow on shrubs. The large bright red type are capsicums and these are ground and known as paprika (used in Hungarian goulash). There are many types of chillies and they vary in taste, colour, piquancy and heat (always test the heat by cutting of a small piece and taste with the tip of the tongue). The seeds are one of the hottest parts of the chilli and they can be removed by splitting the chilli in half then scooping them out with the point of the knife. Hands should always be thoroughly washed after preparing chillies because the oils are exceptionally strong and will burn the eyes, mouth and other delicate areas of the body. Chillies are used in many dishes: pizzas, pasta and in Indian, Thai and Mexican cookery.

Chinese five spice powder

Usually consists of: powdered anise, fennel, cloves, cinnamon and anise pepper. Used extensively in Chinese cookery.

Cinnamon

Cinnamon is the bark of the small branches of the cinnamon shrub which grows in China and Sri Lanka. The inner pulp and the outer layer of the bark are removed and the remaining pieces dried. It is a pale brown colour and is obtained and used in stick or powdered form, mainly by bakeries and for pastry work. When stewing pears, a stick of cinnamon improves the flavour. Doughnuts may be passed through a mixture of sugar and ground cinnamon, and slices of apple for fritters may be sprinkled with cinnamon before being passed through the frying batter. It is another of the spices blended for mixed spice.

Cloves

Cloves are the unopened flower-buds of a tree which grows in Zanzibar, Penang and Madagascar. The buds are picked when green, and dried in the sun until they turn to a rich brown colour. They are used for flavouring stocks, sauces, studding roast ham joints and in mulled wine.

The studded onion (oignon piqué or clouté) is an onion and a bay leaf studded with a clove.

When apples are cooked, cloves are, in most cases, used as a flavouring. Cloves may be obtained in ground form and as such they are used in mixed spice.

Coriander

Coriander is a pleasant spice obtained from the seed of an annual plant grown chiefly in Morocco. It is a yellowish brown colour and tastes like a mixture of sage and lemon peel. It is used in sauces, curry powder and mixed spice.

Cumin

This is frequently used in curry and is powerful, warm, sweet and has a slightly oily taste.

Dill seeds

These are used for flavouring fish soups, stews and cakes.

Fennel seeds

Fennel seeds have a sweet aniseed flavour, used in fish dishes and soups.

Fenugreek

Fenugreek is roasted, ground and frequently used in curry; slightly bitter, with a smell of fresh hay.

Garam masala

This literally means 'hot spices' and is not a standardised recipe, but a typical mixture which could include: cardamom seeds, stick cinnamon, cumin seeds, cloves, black peppercorns, nutmeg.

Ginger

Ginger is the rhizome or root of a reed-like plant grown in the Far East. The root is boiled in water and sugar syrup until soft. Ground ginger is used mainly for pastry and bakery work and for mixed spice. Whole root is used for curries, pickles, stir-fry dishes and sauces.

Juniper berries

If these are added to game, red cabbage, pork, rabbit and beef dishes, they give an unusual background flavour.

Nutmegs and mace

The tropical nutmeg bears a large fruit like an apricot which, when ripe, splits. Inside is a dark brown nut with a bright red net-like covering which is the part that becomes mace. Inside the nut is the kernel or seed which is the nutmeg. Although the two spices come from the same fruit, the flavour is different. Mace is more delicate and is used for flavouring sauces and certain meat and fish dishes. Nutmeg is used in sweet dishes (particularly milk puddings), sauces, soups, vegetable and cheese dishes. It is also used for mixed spice.

Poppy seeds

Poppy seeds are used as a topping for bread and cakes, etc.

Saffron

The stigmas from a crocus known as the saffron crocus (grown chiefly in Spain) are dried and form saffron, which is a flavouring and colouring spice. It is used in soups, sauces and particularly in rice dishes, giving them a bright yellow colour and distinctive flavour. Saffron is very expensive as it takes the stigmas from approximately 4000 crocus flowers to yield 30 g (1 oz).

Sesame seeds

These are used as a topping for bread, cakes and in Chinese and vegetarian cookery.

Surmac seeds

These are used in Middle Eastern cooking for their acidic lemon peppery flavour. Deep red-maroon colour.

Turmeric

Turmeric grows in the same way as ginger and it is the rhizome which is used. It is without any pronounced flavour and its main use is for colouring curry powder. It is ground into a fine powder, which turns it yellow. Tumeric is also used in pickles, relishes and as a colouring in cakes and rice.

Ingredients for a typical curry powder

2 parts bay-leaves	2 parts garlic	4 parts cinnamon
3 parts ginger	3 parts caraway	4 parts mace
3 parts chillies	40 parts coriander	4 parts mustard
2 parts nutmeg	3 parts clove	4 parts pepper
3 parts saffron	3 parts allspice	20 parts turmeric

Ingredients for mixed spice

4 parts allspice	4 parts cloves	4 parts cinnamon
4 parts coriander	1 part nutmeg	1 part ginger

Further information

National Herb and Spice Information Bureau, Cavendish House, 51–55 Mortimer Street, London W1N 7TD.

CONDIMENTS

Salt

FOOD VALUE
Salt (sodium chloride) is essential for stabilising body fluids and preventing muscular cramp.

STORAGE
Salt must be stored in a cool, dry store as it readily absorbs moisture. It should be kept in airtight packets, drums or bins.

PRODUCTION
Salt occurs naturally in the form of rock salt in underground deposits, mainly in Cheshire. It may be mined or pumped out of the earth after water has been introduced into the rock salt. The salt is extracted from the brine by evaporation and it is then purified.

Flavoured salts (celery, herb) are available.

USE
Salt is used for curing fish such as herrings and haddocks and for cheese and butter making. Salt is also used for the pickling of foods, in the cooking of many dishes and as a condiment on the table.

Pepper

Pepper is obtained from black peppercorns, which are the berries of a tropical shrub.

White peppercorns are obtained by removing the skin from the black peppercorn. White pepper is less pungent than black, and both may be obtained in ground form.

Peppercorns are used whole in stocks, court-bouillons, sauces and dishes where the liquid is passed. They are crushed for reductions for sauces and used in a pepper-mill for seasoning meats before frying or grilling. Green peppercorns are fresh unripe pepper berries, milder than dried peppercorns, available frozen or in tins. Pink peppercorns are softer and milder than green peppercorns, available preserved in vinegar.

Ground pepper is used for seasoning many dishes and as a condiment at the table.

Cayenne pepper

Cayenne is a red pepper used on savoury dishes and cheese straws. It is a hot pepper which is obtained from grinding chillies and capsicums, both of which are tropical plants related to the tomato.

Paprika

Paprika is a bright red mild pepper used in goulash and for decorating hors-d'œuvre dishes such as egg mayonnaise.

It is produced from capsicums grown in Hungary.

Mustard

Mustard is obtained from the seed of the mustard plant, which is grown mainly in East Anglia. It is sold in powder form and is diluted with water, milk or vinegar for table use.

Mustard is used in the kitchen for sauces (mustard, mayonnaise, vinaigrette) for devilled dishes such as grilled leg of chicken, and in Welsh rarebit.

A large variety of continental mustards are sold as a paste in jars, having been mixed with herbs and wine vinegar.

Vinegar

Malt vinegar is made from malt, which is produced from barley. Yeast is added, which converts it to alcohol, and bacteria are then added to convert the alcohol into acetic acid. The resulting vinegar is stored for several months before being bottled or casked.

Artificial, non-brewed, pure or imitation vinegars are chemically produced solutions of acetic acid in water. They are cheaper and inferior to malt vinegar, having a pungent odour and a sharp flavour.

Spirit vinegars are produced from potatoes, grain or starchy vegetables, but they do not have the same flavour as malt vinegar.

Red or white vinegars are made from grapes and are more expensive and have a more delicate flavour than the other vinegars.

All vinegars can be distilled; this removes the colour. The colour of vinegar is no indication of its strength as burnt sugar is added to give colour.

Balsamic vinegar is a specially matured vinegar from Italy with a distinctive flavour which varies in strength according to the age of the vinegar.

Other vinegars include chilli, sherry, cider, rice, herb (especially tarragon) and fruit such as raspberry and strawberry.

To produce flavoured vinegar the required herbs are stored in a jar, covered with good quality vinegar and then stored for at least two weeks and used as required (sauce béarnaise).

Uses

Vinegar is used as a preservative for pickles, rollmops and cocktail onions; and as a condiment on its own or with oil as a salad dressing; it is used for flavouring sauces such as mayonnaise and in reductions for sharp sauces (sauce piquante, sauce diable).

Colourings, flavourings, essences

Colourings

A number of food colourings are obtained in either powder or liquid form. Natural colours include:

Cochineal

Cochineal is a red colour, produced from the cochineal beetle, used in pastry and confectionery work.

Green colouring

This can be made by mixing indigo and saffron, but chlorophyll, the natural green colouring of plants, such as in spinach, may also be used. This is used in pastry, confectionery and in green sauce which is sometimes served with salmon.

Indigo

Indigo is the blue colour seldom used on its own, but which, when mixed with red, produces shades of mauve.

Yellow colouring

A deep yellow colour can be obtained from turmeric roots and is prepared in the form of a powder mainly used in curry and mustard pickles.

Yellow is also obtained by using egg yolks or saffron.

Brown

Brown sugar is used to give a deep brown colour in rich fruit cakes; it also adds to the flavour.

Blackjack or browning

Blackjack or commercial caramel is a dark brown, almost black liquid, and is used for colouring soups, sauces, gravies, aspics and in pastry and confectionery.

Chocolate colour

This can be obtained in liquid or powder form, and is used in pastry and confectionery.

Coffee colour

This is usually made from coffee beans with the addition of chicory.

A large range of artificial colours are also obtainable; they are produced from coal tar and are harmless. Some mineral colours are also used in foodstuffs. All colourings must be pure and there is a list of those permitted for cookery and confectionery use.

Essences

Essences are generally produced from a solution of essential oils with alcohol, and are prepared for the use of cooks, bakers and confectioners.

Among the many types of essence obtainable are:

- Almond
- Pineapple
- Lemon
- Raspberry
- Orange
- Strawberry
- Peppermint
- Vanilla

Essences are available in many sized bottles and fall into three categories: natural, artificial and compound.

NATURAL ESSENCES
- Fruit juices pressed out of soft fruits (raspberries or strawberries).
- Citrus fruit peel (lemon, orange).
- Spices, beans, herbs, roots, nuts (caraway seeds, cinnamon, celery, mint, sage, thyme, clove, ginger, coffee beans, nutmeg and vanilla pod).

ARTIFICIAL ESSENCES
Artificial essences such as vanilla, pineapple, rum, banana, coconut, are produced from various chemicals blended to give a close imitation of the natural flavour.

COMPOUND ESSENCES
Compound essences are made by blending natural products with artificial products.

The relative costs vary considerably and it is advisable to try all types of flavouring essence before deciding on which to use for specific purposes.

GROCERY, DELICATESSEN

Delicatessen literally means 'provision store', but the name is commonly used to cover the place where a wide range of table delicacies may be bought.

Agar agar

This is obtained from the dried purified stems of a seaweed; also known as vegetable gelatine, and is used in vegetarian cookery.

Anchovy essence

This is a strong, highly seasoned commodity used for flavouring certain fish sauces and fish preparations such as anchovy sauce or fish cakes.

Angelica

This is not a herb, but can be found growing in herb gardens. It has a long bamboo-like stem, and grows to a height of about 1.5 m (5 ft). The stems are bleached, cut into 36 cm (14 in) pieces, boiled in green syrup, cooled, then reboiled daily in syrup for 5 days.

Aspic

Aspic jelly is a clear savoury jelly which may be the flavour of meat, game or fish. It may be produced from fresh ingredients (see *Practical Cookery*, page 165) or obtained in a dried form.

It is used for cold larder work, mainly for coating chaud-froid dishes, and may also be chopped or cut into neat shapes to decorate finished dishes.

Bombay duck

These are dried fillets of a fish found in southern Asia. They are lightly cooked, usually by grilling and served as an accompaniment to curry dishes of meat and poultry. Bombay duck are purchased in packets of 12 fillets.

Brawn

This is a preparation from the boiled, well-seasoned head of a pig. After being cooked the meat is picked off the bones, roughly chopped or minced, then set in a mould with some of the cooking liquor. When cold and set it is carved in thick slices and served as a cold meat.

Caviar

Caviar is the uncooked roe of the sturgeon which is prepared by carefully separating the eggs from the membranes of the roe and gently rubbing them through sieves of coarse hemp. It is then soaked in a brine solution, sieved and packed.

Sturgeon fishing takes place in the estuaries of rivers which run into the Caspian or Black Sea, therefore caviar is Russian or Iranian in origin. The types normally obtainable in Britain are Beluga, Osetrova and Sevruga. These names refer to the type of sturgeons from which the caviar is taken.

Caviar is extremely expensive and needs to be handled with great care and understanding. Caviar should be kept at a temperature of 0°C (32°F) but no lower otherwise the extreme cold will break the eggs down. Caviar must never be deep frozen.

A red caviar (keta) is obtained from the roe of salmon. From the lumpfish a mock caviar is obtained. These are considerably cheaper than genuine caviar.

Ceps

A species of French mushroom obtainable as cèpes au naturel or cèpes à l'huile.

They are sold fresh in season or in tins or bottles or in dried form and are used in many French-style dishes.

Chow-chow

- A Chinese or pidgin English word for a mixture. It is the name given to oriental fruits preserved in syrup which is served with curry.
- The name also of a fleshy fruit obtainable at Christmas time.

Continental sausages (see Plate 95, page 158)

A large variety of these are imported from European countries.

- Salami – this is a popular sausage imported chiefly from Italy and Hungary. It is usually made from pork, beef and bacon; highly seasoned and coloured with red wine; it is then well dried and cured so as to keep for years. It is thinly sliced and eaten cold; usually as part of an hors-d'œuvre.
- Cervelat beef or pork sausage – these sausages are chiefly imported from Germany; they are dried, smoked and eaten without further cooking.
- Frankfurt or Vienna sausage – there are several varieties of these small sausages which are made from ham or pork. They are dried, then smoked, and are boiled before being used. Frankfurters are obtained in tins. They should be served as part of the garnish to sauerkraut (choucroûte garni).
- Liver sausage – liver sausage is usually made from pigs' or calves' liver mixed with lean and fat pork and highly seasoned. It is sliced and served cold, usually as part of an hors-d'œuvre. Liver sausage is also used in sandwiches, and it may be served with other cold meats. This needs to be kept in a refrigerator.

Extracts (meat and vegetable)

Extracts are highly concentrated forms of flavouring used in some kitchens to strengthen stocks and sauces (Bovril, Marmite, Maggi, Jardox).

Foie gras

This expensive delicacy is obtained from the livers of specially fattened geese and is produced mainly in Strasbourg. It is obtainable either plain or with truffles in tins of various sizes, and at certain times of the year is also obtained in round pastry cases (foie gras en croûte) and in earthenware terrines. Foie gras is a classic first course for any lunch, dinner or supper menu. It is also used as a garnish (Tournedos Rossini) and is included in the rice stuffing for certain chicken dishes. A purée or mousse of foie gras is obtainable and is suitable for sandwiches and to help the flavour of certain stuffings.

Frogs' legs

The flesh of the hindquarters of a certain species of green frog are esteemed as a delicacy in certain continental restaurants. They are cooked in various ways (fried, braised, grilled).

Galantine

This is a cooked meat preparation made from well-seasoned finely minced chicken, veal or other white meat. A first-class galantine is stuffed with strips of fat pork, tongue, chicken or veal, truffles and pistachio nuts, then rolled in thin fat pork, tied in a cloth and boiled. When cold, galantines are coated with chaud-froid and masked with aspic and served on cold buffets (see *Advanced Practical Cookery*, page 54).

Gelatine

Gelatine is obtained from the bones and connective tissue, collagen, of certain animals; it is manufactured in leaf or powdered form and used in varying sweets such as bavarois. (See also 'Agar agar' on page 186.)

Haggis

This traditional Scottish dish is made from the heart, lungs (lights) and liver of the sheep, mixed with suet, onion and oatmeal and sewn up in a stomach bag. It is boiled and served with mashed potatoes.

Hams

A ham is the hind leg of a pig cured by a special process which varies according to the type of ham. One of the most famous English hams is the York ham weighing 6–7 kg (13–15 lb) which is cured by salting, drying and sometimes smoking. The Bradenham ham is of coal-black colour and is a sweet-cured ham from Chippenham in Wiltshire. Hams are also imported from Northern Ireland and Denmark.

All the above hams should be soaked in cold water for several hours before being boiled or braised. Ham may be eaten hot or cold in a variety of ways. Continental raw hams, Bayonne and Ardenne from France and Parma from Italy, are cut in thin slices and served raw, usually as an hors-d'œuvre.

Horseradish

Horseradish is a plant of which only the root is used. The root is washed, peeled, grated and used for horseradish sauce and horseradish cream. It is obtainable in sauce or cream form in jars or bottles; either may be served with hot or cold roast beef and smoked eel.

Pâté maison

Pâté is a well seasoned cooked mixture of various combinations of meat, poultry, game, fish or vegetables, usually served cold as a first course. There are numerous recipes, some of which can be found in *Advanced Practical Cookery* by Ceserani, Kinton and Foskett.

Pickles

These are vegetables and/or fruits preserved in vinegar or sauce and include:

- Red cabbage, which can be served as part of hors-d'œuvre and may also be offered as an accompaniment to Irish stew.

- Gherkins which are a small, rough-skinned variety of cucumber, the size of which should not exceed that of the small finger. Gherkins are used for hors-d'œuvre, tartare sauce, charcutière sauce, certain salads and for garnishing some cold dishes, and as an accompaniment to Boiled beef French-style.
- Olives are the fruit of the olive tree and there are three main varieties:
  - Manzanilla – the small green olive used for cocktail savouries, hors-d'œuvre and garnishing many dishes such as Veal escalope Viennese-style. These olives may also be obtained stuffed with pimento.
  - Spanish queens – the large green olives used for hors-d'œuvre and cocktail savouries.
  - Black olives – used for hors-d'œuvre and certain salads.
- Cocktail onions are the small queen or silver-skin onions used for cocktail savouries and hors-d'œuvre.
- Walnuts are pickled when green and tender before the shell hardens. They are used for hors-d'œuvre, salads and garnishing certain dishes such as Canapé Ivanhoe.
- Capers are the pickled flower buds of the caper plant. They are used in caper sauce, tartare sauce, piquant sauce and for garnishing many hot and cold dishes such as Trout grenobloise, Mayonnaise of lobster.
- Mango chutney is a sweet chutney which is served as an accompaniment to curried dishes.

Poppadums

These are thin round biscuits of Asian origin made from a mixture of finely ground pigeon peas (dhal) and other ingredients. When lightly cooked, either by frying or grilling, they are served as an accompaniment to curry dishes. Poppadums are obtainable in tins of 50 pieces.

Potted shrimps

These are the peeled tails of cooked shrimps, which are preserved in butter and are usually served as an hors-d'œuvre. They must be refrigerated but served warm.

Rollmops – Bismarck herrings

These are fillets of herring which are rolled, well spiced and pickled, then served cold, usually as an hors-d'œuvre.

Saltpetre

This is a natural product which may also be produced artificially. It is used for pickling, and is one of the chief ingredients in a brine-tub for pickling meats, such as silverside of beef and ox tongue.

Sauerkraut

Sauerkraut is a pickled product made by finely cutting white cabbage. Salt is added in a ratio of 1 kg (2 lb) salt to 40 kg (88 lb) cabbage, the mixture is packed tightly in containers and heavy weights placed on top. A liquid soon forms to cover the cabbage and fermentation begins. Sauerkraut can be kept in a cool place for 4–6 months.

Smoked herring fillets

These are preserved in oil and used as hors-d'œuvre.

Smoked salmon

London is a world-famous centre for this popular food. British, Scandinavian or Canadian salmon weighing between 6–8 kg (13–18 lb) are used for smoking. The salmon are cleaned, split into two sides, salted, rinsed, dried, then smoked. A good quality side of smoked salmon should have a bright deep colour and be moist when lightly pressed with the finger tip at the thickest part of the flesh. A perfectly smoked side of salmon will remain in good condition for not more than seven days when stored at a temperature of 18°C (64°F). This versatile food is used for canapés, hors-d'œuvre, sandwiches, and as a fish course for lunch, dinner or supper.

Snails

These edible snails are raised on the foliage of the vine. They are obtainable in boxes which include the tinned snails and the cleaned shells. The snails are replaced in the shells with a mixture of butter, garlic, lemon juice and parsley, then heated in the oven and served in special dishes as a fish course. Snails are now farmed in Britain.

Tomatoes

These are obtainable:

- peeled whole in tins of various sizes;
- as a purée in tins of various sizes and of different strengths;
- in paste form in tubes and tins;
- tomato purée is produced from plum tomatoes.

All types are used a great deal in the preparation of many soups, sauces, egg, fish and farinaceous, meat and poultry dishes.

Truffles

The truffles chiefly used in this country are imported in tins of varying sizes. Truffles are a fungus and many varieties are found in many parts of the world. The black truffle found in the Périgord region of France is the most famous. White truffles are found in Italy.

Because of the jet black colour truffles are used a great deal in the decorating of cold buffet dishes, particularly on chaud-froid work. Slices of truffle are used in the garnishing of many classical dishes such as Sole cubat, Tournedos maréchale, Poulet sauté archiduc. Truffles are considered to be a delicacy and are extremely expensive.

A truffle substitute suitable for cold buffet decorative work is available at a much lower price.

Worcestershire sauce

This is a thin, highly seasoned, strong-flavoured sauce used as an accompaniment and in flavouring certain sauces, meat puddings and pies.

CONFECTIONERY AND BAKERY GOODS

Cake covering

This is produced from hardened vegetable fat with the addition of chocolate flavouring and colour.

Cape gooseberries

A tasty, yellow-berried fruit resembling a large cherry. Cape gooseberries are often dipped into fondant and served as a petit four.

Chocolate vermicelli

A ready-made preparation of small fine chocolate pieces used in the decorating of small and large cakes and some chocolate-flavoured sweets. Chocolate vermicelli is obtainable in 3 kg (7 lb) boxes.

Cocktail cherries

Bright red cherries preserved in a syrup often flavoured with a liqueur known as maraschino. They are obtainable in jars and bottles of various sizes. In addition to being used for cocktails they are also used to give colour to grapefruit and grapefruit cocktails.

Fondant

A soft, white preparation of sugar. It is made by boiling sugar and glucose to a temperature of about 102°C (215°F), allowing it to cool slightly, then working it to a soft cream. Fondant has many uses in pastry and confectionery work, chiefly for coating petit fours, pastries and gâteaux. It may also be obtained as a ready-made preparation.

Gum tragacanth

A soluble gum used for stiffening pastillage; only a very clear white type of gum tragacanth should be used. It is obtained from the shrubs of the genus *Astragalus*.

Honey

A natural sugar produced by bees working upon the nectar of flowers. It is generally used in the form of a preserve and as such it may be offered on breakfast and tea menus. Honey is obtainable in $\frac{1}{2}$ kg (1 lb) jars and 3 kg (7 lb) tins.

Ice-cream

A frozen preparation of a well-flavoured, sweetened mixture which can be made in many ways and in many flavours. Ice-cream may be bought ready prepared, usually in 5 litre (9 pint) cans which are suitable for deep-freeze storage. The storage temperature for ice-cream should not exceed $-19°C$ ($-32°F$). A large number of sweets can be prepared using ice-cream as a base mixed with various fruits, nuts, sauces and cream. Many variations of semi-hot sweets of the baked Alaska type have ice-cream as one of the chief ingredients. Other sweets are made from an enriched ice-cream mixture and frozen in specially shaped moulds which give their names to the sweets (a heart-shaped mould – cœur glacé; a bomb-shaped mould – bombe glacé). All caterers must comply with the Ice-Cream Regulations which govern the production and labelling of ice-cream; if in doubt, contact the local Environmental Health Officer.

Jam

A preserve of fruit and sugar which is obtainable in 28 g (1 oz), $\frac{1}{2}$ kg (1 lb) and 1 kg (2 lb) jars and 3 kg (7 lb) tins. Raspberry and apricot jams are those mostly used in the pastry.

Marmalade

A preserve of citrus fruits and sugar, which is used mainly for breakfast menus and for certain sweets.

Marrons glacés

Peeled and cooked chestnuts preserved in syrup. They are used in certain large and small cakes, sweet dishes and as a variety of petit fours.

Marzipan

A preparation of ground almonds, sugar and egg yolks used in the making of petits fours, pastries and large cakes. Marzipan is freshly made by pastry cooks; it is also obtained as a ready-prepared commodity.

Mincemeat

A mixture of dried fruit, fresh fruit, sugar, spices, nuts, etc., chiefly used for mince-pies. It can also be obtained in $\frac{1}{2}$ kg (1 lb) and 1 kg (2 lb) jars and 3 kg (7 lb) tins.

Pastillage (gum paste)

A mixture of icing sugar and gum tragacanth which may be moulded into shapes for set pieces for cold buffets and also for making baskets, caskets, etc., for the serving of petits fours.

Piping jelly

A thick jelly of piping consistency obtainable in different colours and flavours. It is used for decorating pastries and gâteaux and cold sweets. Piping jelly is obtainable in large tins.

COMMODITIES LIST

PRODUCT	UNIT COST	PRODUCT	UNIT COST	PRODUCT	UNIT COST	PRODUCT	UNIT COST	PRODUCT	UNIT COST
Herbs		*Condiments*		*Cereals*		*Pulses*		*Oils*	
basil		salt:		flour:		aduki beans		olive	
bay leaves		cooking		soft		haricot beans		maize	
borage		table		strong		soissons		groundnut	
chervil		sea		wholemeal		flageolets		margarine	
chive		pepper:		semolina		cannelini		vegetable	
dill		white ground		macaroni		Dutch brown		shortening	
fennel		corns		spaghetti		beans		lard	
lovage		black ground		vermicelli		butter beans			
marjoram		corns		noodles		red kidney beans		*Cheese*	
mint		cayenne		oats:		borlotti beans		British:	
oregano		paprika		rolled		pinto beans		Cheddar	
parsley		mustard:		coarse oatmeal		black-eyed beans		Cheshire	
rosemary		English		medium		broad/fava beans		Double	
sage		vinegar		oatmeal		ful medames		Gloucester	
tarragon		Worcester sauce		fine oatmeal		chick-peas		Leicester	
thyme				pearl barley		split peas:		Derby	
		Gravy		barley flour		green		Caerphilly	
Spices		browning		buckwheat		yellow		Lancashire	
allspice		Bovril		cornflour		lentils:		Wensleydale	
anise		Jardox		custard powder		red		Stilton	
anise pepper				rice:		brown		Caboc	
anise star		*Delicatessen items*		long grain		green		Dunlop	
capsicum		anchovy essence		short grain		dhals		French:	
caraway		aspic		ground		mung beans		Brie	
cardamom		Bombay duck		brown		soya beans		Camembert	
cassia		caviar		rice flour				Port Salut	
celery seed		cèpes		rice paper		*Eggs*		Roquefort	
chillies		chow chow		tapioca		hens		Italian:	
cinnamon		continental		sago		ducks		Bel Paese	
		sausage							

cloves
cumin
coriander
dill seeds
fennel seeds
fenugreek
ginger, ground
ginger, root
juniper berries
nutmeg
mace
poppy seeds
saffron
sesame seeds
turmeric

foie gras
frogs' legs
gelatine:
    leaf
    powdered
olives:
    manzanilla
    Spanish queens
    black
capers
poppadums
potted shrimps
truffles

arrowroot
potato flour
Raising agents
baking powder
yeast:
    fresh
    dried
Sugar
granulated
castor
cube
icing
demerara
Barbados
syrup
treacle
cocoa
couverture
    (sweetened)
couverture
    (unsweetened)
coffee
tea

quails
Milk
pasteurised
UHT
Channel Island
sterilised
homogenised
evaporated
condensed
Milk products
cream:
    double
    whipping
    single
    clotted
    UHT
    (non-dairy
     creams)
yogurt
smetana
butter

Gorgonzola
Mozzarella
Parmesan
Confectionery
colourings
cocktail cherries
chocolate vermicelli
Cape
    gooseberries
fondant
gum tragacanth
honey
jam
lemon curd
marron glacé
marmalade
mincemeat
redcurrant jelly
rennet
wafers

Redcurrant jelly

A clear preserve of redcurrants used as a jam and also in the preparation of savoury sweet sauces such as reforme and Cumberland sauce. Redcurrant jelly is also used as an accompaniment to roast saddle of mutton and jugged hare.

Rennet

A substance originally obtained from the stomach of calves, pigs and lambs, and can now be obtained in synthetic form. Rennet is prepared in powder, extract or essence form and is used in the production of cheese and for making junket (see page 620 of *Practical Cookery*). Vegetable rennet, for vegetarians, is also available.

Vanilla

This is the dried pod of an orchid used for infusing mild sweet flavour into dishes. After use rinse the vanilla stick, dry and store in a sealed jar of castor sugar ready for reuse.

Wafers

Thin crisp biscuits of various shapes and sizes usually served with ice-cream. They are obtainable in large tins of approximately 1000 and half-tins of approximately 500 wafers.

Further information

The Book of Ingredients, Dowell and Bailey, Michael Joseph 1988.

TOPICS FOR DISCUSSION

1. Factors that affect the quality of meat.
2. Fors and againsts of using meat substitute such as TVP, Quorn.
3. Purchasing of meat (by carcass, joints or portion controlled cuts).
4. Much of today's poultry lacks flavour. How can this be remedied?
5. The popularity of fish compared to meat and poultry.
6. The best ways to purchase fish.
7. Buying policy for vegetables and fruit.
8. The importance of vegetables and fruit in the diet.
9. Eggs and the caterer.
10. Compare the uses of butter, margarine or oil in cooking.
11. What is a sensible policy for selling cheese in a restaurant?
12. Is the average caterer sufficiently knowledgeable about the different types of flour and their suitability for specific purposes?
13. Should the caterer be offering a wider range of choice of teas and coffees?
14. The values of using pulses.
15. The values of using herbs and spices.

5

Elementary nutrition, food science and food preservation

—

FOOD AND NUTRIENTS

A food is any substance, liquid or solid, which provides the body with materials:

- for heat and energy;
- for growth and repair;
- for regulating the body processes.

The materials are known as *nutrients*. They are:

- proteins;
- fats;
- carbohydrates;

- vitamins;
- minerals;
- water.

The study of these nutrients is termed nutrition. Only those substances containing nutrients are foods (alcohol is an energy-provider but it also has the effects of a drug, so it is not listed under the nutrients). Most foods contain several nutrients; a few foods contain only one nutrient, such as sugar.

For the body to obtain the maximum benefit from food it is essential that everyone concerned with the buying, storage, cooking and serving of food and the compiling of menus should have some knowledge of nutrition.

Digestion (see Figure 5.1)

This is the breaking down of the food with the help of enzymes. Enzymes are proteins which speed up (catalyse) the break down processes. Digestion takes place

- in the mouth, where food is mixed with saliva, and starch is broken down by the action of an enzyme in saliva;
- in the stomach, where the food is mixed and gastric juices are added, and proteins are broken down;
- in the small intestine, where proteins, fats and carbohydrates are broken down further and additional juices are added.

Absorption

To enable the body to benefit from food it must be absorbed into the bloodstream;

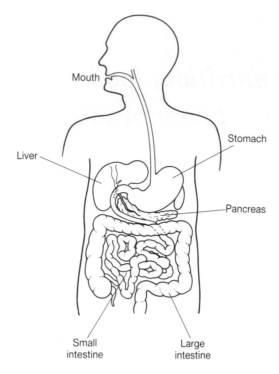

Fig. 5.1 The digestive tract

this absorption occurs after the food has been broken down; the product then passes through the walls of the digestive tract into the bloodstream.

This occurs in:

- the stomach where simple substances, such as alcohol and glucose, are passed through the stomach lining into the bloodstream;
- the small intestine where more of the absorption of nutrients takes place due to a further breakdown of the food;
- the large intestine, where water is reabsorbed from the waste.

Food should smell, look and taste attractive in order to stimulate the flow of saliva and digestive juices. This will help the digestive process and ensure that most food is broken down and absorbed.

If digestion and absorption is not efficient this could lead to a deficiency of one or more nutrients and a state of malnutrition.

THE MAIN FUNCTION OF NUTRIENTS

ENERGY	GROWTH AND REPAIR	REGULATION OF BODY PROCESSES
carbohydrates	proteins	vitamins
fats	minerals	minerals
proteins	water	water

Proteins

Protein is an essential part of all living matter; it is therefore needed for the growth of the body and for the repair of body tissues.

There are two kinds of protein:

* Animal protein, found in meat, game, poultry, fish, eggs, milk, cheese: myosin, collagen (meat, poultry and fish); albumin, ovovitellin (eggs); casein (milk and cheese).
* Vegetable protein, found mainly in the seeds of vegetables. The proportion of protein in green and root vegetables is small. Peas, beans and nuts contain most protein and the grain of cereals, such as wheat, has a useful amount because of the large quantity eaten; for example gliadin and glutenin forming gluten with water (wheat and rye).

Figure 5.2 shows the proportion of protein in some common foods and Figure 5.3 represents the main sources of protein and the contribution made by different protein foods in the typical Western diet. The proportion of animal foods contributing to the total would be very much reduced in developing countries.

It follows that, because protein is needed for growth, growing children and expectant and nursing mothers will need more protein than other adults, whose requirements are mainly for repair. Any spare protein is used for producing heat and

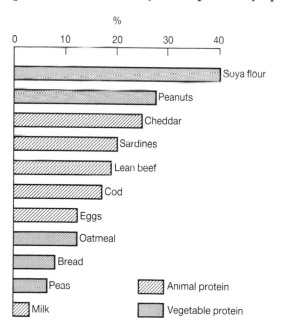

Fig. 5.2 Proportion of protein in some foods

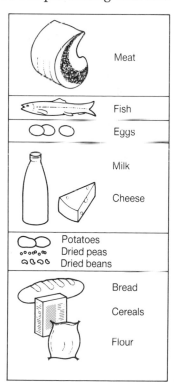

Fig. 5.3 Main sources of protein in the average diet

energy. In diets where the protein intake is minimal, it is important that there is plenty of carbohydrate available so that protein is used for growth and repair, rather than for energy purposes.

THE PROTEIN CONTENT (%) PER 100 g OF SOME ANIMAL AND VEGETABLE FOODS

braised beef	30.0
roast pork	30.0
roast lamb	28.0
roast chicken	25.0
roasted peanuts	24.0
baked cod	20.0
eggs	12.0
white bread	8.0
milk	3.0

WHAT IS PROTEIN?

Protein is composed of different amino acids; so the protein of cheese is different from the protein of meat because the number and arrangement of the acids are not the same. A certain number of these amino acids is essential to the body and must be provided by food. Proteins containing all the essential amino acids in the correct proportion are said to be of high biological value. The human body is capable of converting the other kinds of amino acids to suit its needs.

It is preferable that the body has both animal and vegetable protein, so that a complete variety of the necessary amino acids is available.

During digestion protein is split into amino acids; these are absorbed into the bloodstream and used for building body tissues and to provide some heat and energy.

Fats

There are two main groups of fats: animal and vegetable. The function of fat is to protect vital organs of the body, to provide heat and energy, and certain fats also provide vitamins.

Fats can be divided into:

- solid fat;
- oils (fat which is liquid at room temperature).

Fats are obtained from the following foods (see Figures 5.4 and 5.5).

- animal origin: dripping, butter, suet, lard, cheese, cream, bacon, meat fat, oily fish;
- vegetable origin: margarine, cooking fat, nuts, soya-beans.

Oils are obtained from the following foods:

- animal origin: halibut and cod-liver oil;
- vegetable origin: from seeds or nuts.

PERCENTAGE OF SATURATED* FAT IN AN AVERAGE DIET

milk, cheese, cream	26.0
meat and meat products	25.2
other oils and fats	30.0
other sources	
including eggs, fish, poultry	7.4
biscuits and cakes	11.4
The 25.2% for meat and meat products split down into:	
other meat products	9.1
beef	4.1
lamb	3.5
pork, bacon and ham	5.8
sausage	2.7

* See below under composition of fats.

COMPOSITION OF FATS

Fats are composed of glycerol to which are attached three fatty acids (hence the name triglyceride). Fats differ because of the fatty acids from which they are derived. These may be, for example, butyric acid in butter, stearic acid in solid fat, such as beef suet, oleic acid in most oils. These fatty acids affect the texture and flavour of the fat. The fatty acids found in animal foods (meat and dairy products) are of a different type from those found in other foods (fish, seed and nut oils). The former are termed 'saturated' fatty acids and produce saturated fats whereas the other types of fatty acids are 'unsaturated' and produce unsaturated fats or oils.

To be useful to the body, fats have to be broken down into glycerol and fatty acids so that they can be absorbed; they can then provide heat and energy.

The food value of the various kinds of fat is similar, although some animal fats contain vitamins A and D.

The contribution of animal fat in the Western diet is gradually changing as healthy eating policies encourage a reduction in the total fat intake, particularly animal fats. There has been a swing towards skimmed milk, leaner cuts of meat, cooking with vegetable oils and a reduced market for eggs, high fat cheeses and butter.

Fats should be eaten with other foods such as bread, potatoes, etc., as they can then be more easily digested and utilised in the body.

Certain fish, such as herrings, mackerel, salmon and sardines, contain oil (fat) in the flesh. Other fish, such as cod and halibut, contain the oil in the liver.

Vegetables and fruit contain very little fat, but nuts have a considerable amount.

EFFECTS OF COOKING ON FAT

Cooking has little effect on fat except to make it more digestible.

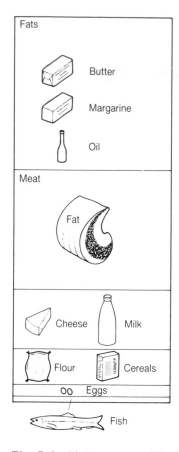

Fig. 5.4 Main sources of fat in the average diet

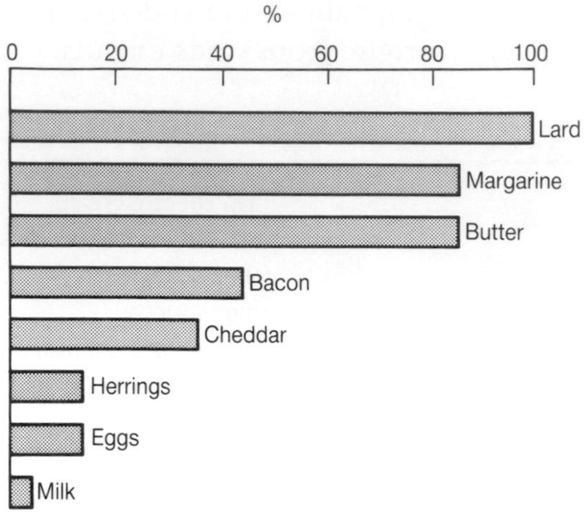

%

Fig. 5.5 Proportion of fat in some foods

Carbohydrates (see Figures 5.6 and 5.7)

There are three main types of carbohydrates:

- sugar (saccharide);
- starch (polysaccharide);
- cellulose.

The function of carbohydrates is to provide the body with most of its energy. Starch is composed of a number of glucose molecules (particles), and during digestion starch is broken down into glucose. It is often now referred to as dietary fibre or NSP (non-starch polysaccharide).

Sugar
There are several kinds of sugar:

- glucose: found in the blood of animals and in fruit and honey;
- fructose: found in fruit, honey and cane sugar;

Fig. 5.6 Main sources of carbohydrate in the average diet

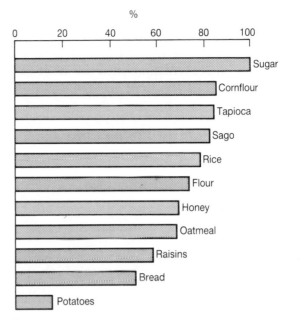

Fig. 5.7 Proportion of carbohydrate in some foods

- sucrose: found in beet and cane sugar;
- lactose: found in milk;
- maltose: produced naturally during the germination of grain.

Sugars are the simplest form of carbohydrate and the end-products of the digestion of carbohydrates. They are absorbed in the form of glucose and simple sugars and used to provide heat and energy.

STARCH
Starch is present in the diet through the following foods:

- whole grains: rice, barley, tapioca;
- powdered grains: flour, cornflour, ground rice, arrowroot;
- vegetables: potatoes, parsnips, peas, beans;
- unripe fruit: bananas, apples, cooking pears;
- cereals: cornflakes, shredded wheat, etc.;
- cooked starch: cakes, biscuits;
- pastas: macaroni, spaghetti, vermicelli, etc.

Cooking effects on starch

Uncooked starch is not digestible. Foods containing starch have cells with starch granules, covered with a cellulose wall which breaks down when heated or made moist. When browned, as with the crust of bread, toast, roast potatoes, skin on rice pudding, etc., the starch forms dextrins and these taste sweeter. On heating with water or milk, starch granules swell and absorb liquid, thus thickening the product, (thickened gravy or cornflour sauce). This thickening process is known as gelatinisation of starch.

CELLULOSE

Cellulose is the coarser structure of vegetables and cereals which is not digested but is used as roughage in the intestine. It is often now referred to as dietary fibre.

Vitamins

Vitamins are chemical substances which are vital for life, and if the diet is deficient in any vitamin, ill-health results. As they are chemical substances they can be produced synthetically.

GENERAL FUNCTION OF VITAMINS

Vitamins assist the regulation of the body processes:

*   to help the growth of children;
*   to protect against disease.

VITAMIN A (see Figure 5.8, page 206)

Function

Vitamin A:

*   assists in children's growth;
*   helps the body to resist infection;
*   enables people to see better in the dark.

Vitamin A is fat soluble; therefore it is to be found in fatty foods. It can be made in the body from carotene, the yellow substance found in many fruits and vegetables.

Dark green vegetables are a good source of vitamin A, the green colour masking the yellow of the carotene. Carotene is gradually destroyed by light (hence the fading of orange coloured spices and vegetables on prolonged storage).

Sources of vitamin A

*   halibut-liver oil
*   cod-liver oil
*   kidney
*   liver
*   butter
*   margarine (to which vitamin A is added)
*   cheese
*   eggs
*   milk
*   herrings
*   carrots
*   spinach
*   watercress
*   tomatoes
*   apricots

Fish-liver oils have the most vitamin A. The amount of vitamin A in dairy produce varies. Because cattle eat fresh grass in summer and stored feeding-stuffs in winter, the dairy produce contains the highest amount of vitamin A in the summer. Kidney and liver are also useful sources of vitamin A.

VITAMIN D

Function

Vitamin D controls the use the body makes of calcium. It is therefore necessary for healthy bones and teeth. Like vitamin A it is fat soluble.

Sources of vitamin D

An important source of vitamin D is from the action of sunlight on the deeper layers of the skin (approximately 75% of our vitamin D comes from this source). Others include:

- fish-liver oils
- oily fish
- egg yolk
- margarine (to which vitamin D is added)
- dairy produce

VITAMIN B

When first discovered vitamin B was thought to be one substance only; it is now known to consist of at least 11 substances, the three main ones being:

- thiamin (B_1);
- riboflavin (B_2);
- nicotinic acid, or niacin.

Others include folic acid and pyridoxine (B_6).

Function

Vitamin B which is water soluble and can be lost during cooking is required to:

- keep the nervous system in good condition;
- enable the body to obtain energy from the carbohydrates;
- encourage the growth of the body.

SOURCES OF VITAMIN B

THIAMIN (B_1)	RIBOFLAVIN (B_2)	NICOTINIC ACID
yeast	yeast	meat extract
bacon	liver	brewers' yeast
oatmeal	meat extract	liver
peas	cheese	kidney
wholemeal bread	egg	beef

VITAMIN C (ASCORBIC ACID)

Function

Vitamin C:

- is necessary for the growth of children;

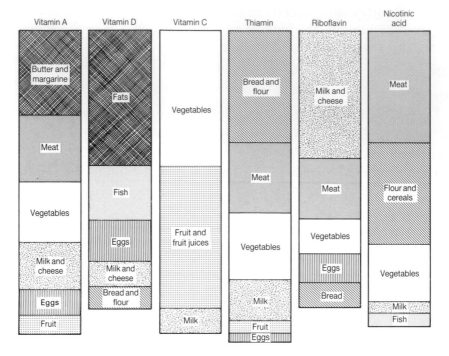

Fig. 5.8   Main sources of vitamins in the average diet

- assists in the healing of cuts and uniting of broken bones;
- prevents gums and mouth infection.

Vitamin C is water soluble and can be lost during cooking or soaking in water. It is also lost by bad storage (keeping foods for too long, bruising, or storing in a badly ventilated place) and by cutting vegetables into small pieces.

Sources of vitamin C

- blackcurrants
- strawberries
- grapefruit
- fruit juices
- potatoes
- lemons
- tomatoes
- Brussels sprouts and other greens
- oranges
- bananas

The major sources in the British diet are potatoes and green vegetables.

Mineral elements

There are 19 mineral elements, most of which are required by the body in very small quantities. The body has at certain times a greater demand for certain mineral elements and there is a danger then of a deficiency in the diet. Calcium, iron and iodine are those most likely to be deficient.

CALCIUM
Calcium is required for:

- building bones and teeth;

- clotting of the blood;
- the working of the muscles.

The use the body makes of calcium is dependent on the presence of vitamin D.

Sources of calcium

Calcium can be found in:

- milk and milk products;
- bones of tinned oily fish;
- wholemeal bread and white bread (to which calcium is added). *Note* It is still the practice to add calcium, iron, thiamin and nicotinic acid to flour despite the DHSS report No. 23 (1981) which recommended that it should be discontinued.
- vegetables (greens);
- drinking water.

Although calcium is present in certain foods (spinach, cereals) the body is unable to make use of it as it is not in a soluble form and therefore cannot be absorbed.

Because of the need for growth of bones and teeth, infants, adolescents, expectant and nursing mothers have a greater demand for calcium.

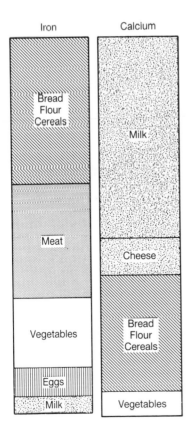

Fig. 5.9 Main source of iron and calcium in the average diet

PHOSPHORUS

Phosphorus is required for:

- building the bones and teeth (in conjunction with calcium and vitamin D);
- the control of the structure of the brain cells.

Sources of phosphorus
- liver
- cheese
- kidney
- bread
- eggs
- fish

IRON

Iron is required for building the haemoglobin in blood and is therefore necessary for transporting oxygen and carbon dioxide round the body.

Sources of iron
- lean meat
- offal
- egg yolk
- wholemeal flour
- green vegetables
- fish

Iron is most easily absorbed from meat and offal, and its absorption is helped by the presence of vitamin C.

Iron may also be present in drinking water and obtained from iron utensils in which food is prepared.

As the haemoglobin in the blood should be maintained at a constant level, the body requires more iron at certain times than others (after loss of blood).

SODIUM

Sodium is required in all body fluids, and is found in salt (sodium chloride). Excess salt is continually lost from the body in urine. The kidneys control this loss. We also lose sodium in sweating, a loss over which we have no control.

Sources of sodium

Many foods are cooked with salt or have salt added (bacon and cheese) or contain salt (meat, eggs, fish).

IODINE

Iodine is required for the functioning of the thyroid gland which regulates basal metabolism (see page 211).

Sources of iodine
- sea foods
- iodised salt
- drinking water obtained near the sea
- vegetables grown near the sea

OTHER MINERALS

Potassium, magnesium, sulphur and copper are some of the other minerals required by the body.

Water

Water is required for:

- regulation of body temperatures by evaporation of perspiration.
- all body fluids
- digestion
- absorption
- metabolism
- excretion
- secretion

SOURCES OF WATER
- drinks of all kinds;
- foods, such as fruits and vegetables, meat, eggs;
- combustion or oxidation: when fats, carbohydrates and protein are used for energy a certain amount of water (metabolic water) is produced within the body.

THE EFFECTS OF COOKING ON NUTRIENTS

Protein

When protein is heated it coagulates and shrinks. Too much cooking can spoil the appearance of the food, such as scrambled eggs, as well as causing destruction of certain vitamins. On being heated, the different proteins in foods set or coagulate at different temperatures; above these temperatures shrinkage occurs, and this is particularly noticeable in grilling or roasting meat. Moderately cooked protein is the most easy to digest: a lightly cooked egg is more easily digested than a raw egg or a hard-boiled egg.

Carbohydrate

Unless starch is thoroughly cooked it cannot be digested properly (insufficiently cooked pastry or bread). When cooked, the starch granules swell, burst and then the starch can be digested. (This is called gelatinisation of starch.)

When sugar is heated it melts and with further heating loses water, gradually turning brown, dark brown and then black. This is known as the caramelisation of sugar.

Fat

The nutritive value of fat is not affected by cooking. During cooking processes a certain amount of fat may be lost from food when the fat melts, such as in the grilling of meat.

Mineral elements

There is a possibility of some minerals being lost in the cooking liquor, so diminishing the amount available in the food. This applies to soluble minerals, such as salt, but not to calcium or iron compounds which do not dissolve in the cooking liquor.

Iron

Iron may be acquired from foods cooked in iron utensils. The iron in foods is not affected by the cooking.

Calcium

Cooking foods in hard water may very slightly increase the amount of calcium in food.

Vitamins

- Vitamins A and D withstand cooking temperatures, and they are not lost in the cooking.
- Vitamin B_1 (thiamin) can be destroyed by high temperatures and by the use of bicarbonate of soda. It is soluble in water and can be lost in the cooking.
- Vitamin B_2 (riboflavin) is not destroyed easily by heat but bright sunlight can break it down.
- Vitamin C is lost by cooking and by keeping food warm in a hot place. It is also soluble in water (the soaking of foods for a long time and bruising are the causes of losing vitamin C). It is unstable and therefore easily destroyed in alkaline conditions (bicarbonate of soda must not be used when cooking green vegetables).

FOOD REQUIREMENTS

Energy is required to enable the heart to beat, for the blood to circulate, the lungs and other organs of the body to function, for every activity such as talking, eating, standing, sitting and for strenuous exercise and muscular activity.

Young and active people require a different amount of food from elderly, inactive people because they expend more energy, and this energy is obtained from food during chemical changes taking place in the body.

The energy value of a food is measured by a term called a kilocalorie or Calorie (this term should be written with a capital C although popularly is often written with a small c). This is the amount of heat required to raise the temperature of 1000 grammes of water from 15 to 16°C.

A new unit is now gradually replacing the Calorie. This is the joule. Since the joule is too small for practical nutrition, the kilojoule (kJ) is used.

1 Calorie = 4.18 kJ

(Both units will be given here and for ease of conversion 1 Calorie will be taken to equal 4.0 kJ.)

Foods contain certain amounts of the various nutrients, which are measured in grammes.

The energy value of nutrients is as follows:

1 g carbohydrate produces 4 Calories (16kJ);
1 g protein produces 4 Calories   (16 kJ);
1 g fat produces 9 Calories   (36 kJ).

The energy value of a food, diet or menu is calculated from the nutrients it contains; 28 g of food containing:

10 g carbohydrate will produce 10 × 4 = 40 Calories (160 kJ)
 2 g protein   will produce 2 × 4 = 8 Calories (32 kJ)
 5 g fat   will produce 5 × 9 = 45 Calories (180 kJ)
      Total   93 Calories (372 kJ)

Foods having a high fat content will have a high energy value; those containing a lot of water, a low energy value. All fats, cheese, bacon and other foods with a high fat content have a high energy value.

Men require more Calories (kJ) than women, big men and women require more than small men and women, and people engaged in energetic work require more Calories (kJ) than those with sedentary occupations.

BASAL METABOLISM

Basal metabolism is the term given to the amount of energy required to maintain the functions of the body and to keep the body warm when it is still and without food. The number of Calories (kJ) required for basal metabolism is affected by the size, sex and general condition of the body. The number of Calories (kJ) required for basal metabolism is approximately 1700 per day.

In addition to the energy required for basal metabolism, energy is also required for everyday activities, such as getting up, dressing, walking, and the amount required will be closely related to a person's occupation.

The approximate energy requirements per day for the following examples are:

Clerk   2000 Calories   (8 000 kJ)
Carpenter   3000 Calories (12 000 kJ)
Labourer   4000 Calories (16 000 kJ)

The tables on page 216 indicate the recommended daily allowance of Calories to provide a healthy diet for the categories of people shown.

VALUE OF FOODS IN THE DIET

Milk and milk products

Cows' milk is almost the perfect food for human beings; it contains protein, carbohydrate, fat, minerals, vitamins and water.

When milk is taken into the body it coagulates in the same way as in the making

RECOMMENDED DAILY INTAKE OF CALORIES

AGE AND SEX	CALORIES	KILOJOULES
Boys and girls		
0–1 year	1000	4 000
2–6 years	1500	6 000
7–10 years	2000	8 000
Boys		
11–14 years	2750	11 000
15–19 years	3500	14 000
Men		
20+ years	3000	12 000
(for average activity)		
Girls		
11–14 years	2750	11 000
15–19 years	2500	10 000
Women		
20+ years	2500	10 000
(for average activity)		

FOR WEIGHT WATCHERS

In lean raw meat the average Calorie and fat content per 100 g is:

	CALORIES (kcal)	FAT (g)
beef	123	4.6
lamb	162	8.8
pork	116	3.7
bacon	116	3.7
beef mince	176	10.6

of junket. This occurs in the stomach when digestive juices (containing the enzyme rennin) are added. Souring of milk is due to the bacteria feeding on the milk sugar (lactose) and producing lactic acid from it, which brings about curdling.

COMPOSITION OF MILK
The approximate composition is as follows:

- 87% water
- 3–4% proteins (mostly casein)
- 3–4% fat
- 4–5% sugar

FOODS CONTAINING THE VARIOUS NUTRIENTS AND THEIR USE IN THE BODY

NUTRIENT	FOOD IN WHICH IT IS FOUND	USE IN BODY
protein	meat, fish, poultry, game, milk, cheese, eggs, pulses, cereals	for building and repairing body tissues; some heat and energy
fat	butter, margarine, cooking-fat, oils, cheese, fat meat, oily fish	provides heat and energy
carbohydrate	flour, flour products and cereals, sugar, syrup, jam, honey, fruit, vegetables	provides heat and energy
vitamin A	oily fish, fish-liver oil, dairy foods, carrots, tomatoes, greens	helps growth; resistance to disease
vitamin B_1 – thiamin	yeast, pulses, liver, whole grain cereals, meat and yeast extracts	helps growth; strengthens nervous system
vitamin B_2 – riboflavin	yeast, liver, meat, meat extracts, whole grain cereals	helps growth, and helps in the production of energy
nicotinic acid (niacin)	yeast, meat, liver, meat extracts, whole grain cereals	helps growth
vitamin C – ascorbic acid	fruits such as strawberries, citrus fruits, green vegetables, root vegetables, salad vegetables, potatoes	helps growth, promotes health
vitamin D (sunshine vitamin)	fish-liver oils, oily fish, dairy foods	helps growth; builds bones and teeth
iron	lean meat, offal, egg yolk, wholemeal flour, green vegetables, fish	building up the blood
calcium (lime)	milk and milk products, bones of fish, wholemeal bread	building bones and teeth, clotting the blood, the working of the muscles
phosphorus	liver and kidney, eggs, cheese, bread	building bones and teeth, regulating body processes
sodium (salt)	meat, eggs, fish, bacon, cheese	prevention of muscular cramp

- 0.7% minerals (particularly calcium)
- Vitamins A, B and D

In Channel Island milk (Jersey and Guernsey) the percentage of fat must be 4%; in all other milk the minimum is 3%.

Milk, therefore, is a body-building food because of its protein, an energy food because of the fat and sugar, and a protective food as it contains vitamins and minerals. Because of its high water content, while it is a suitable food for infants, it is too bulky to be the main source of protein and other nutrients after the first few months of life. It is also deficient in iron and vitamin C.

However, it may be included in everyone's diet as a drink and it can be used in a variety of ways.

Skimmed milk, which has had the cream layer removed, is increasing in popularity. Not only does it provide a lower Calorie intake for those watching their weight, but also the potentially harmful animal fat has been removed.

CREAM

Cream is the fat of milk and the minimum fat content of single cream is approximately 18%, for double cream 48% and clotted cream 60%.

Cream is therefore an energy-producing food which also supplies vitamins A and D. It is easily digested because the fat is in a highly emulsified form (i.e. the fat globules are very small).

BUTTER

Butter is made from the fat of milk and contains vitamins A and D, the amount depending on the season. Like cream it is easily digested.

Composition of butter

The approximate composition is:

- 84% fat
- 15% water
- 1% salt
- vitamins A and D

Butter is also an energy-producing food and a protective food in so far as it provides vitamins A and D.

CHEESE

Cheese is made from milk; its composition varies according to whether the cheese has been made from whole milk, skimmed milk or milk to which extra cream has been added.

The composition of cheddar cheese is approximately:

- 40% fat
- 30% water
- 25% protein
- calcium
- vitamins A and D

The food value of cheese is exceptional because of the concentration of the various nutrients it contains. The minerals in cheese are useful, particularly the calcium and phosphorus. Cheese is also a source of vitamins A and D.

It is a body-building, energy-producing and protective food because of its protein, fat and mineral elements and vitamin content.

Cheese is easily digested, provided it is eaten with starchy foods and eaten in small pieces as when grated.

Margarine

Margarine, which is made from animal and/or vegetable oils, and skimmed milk, has vitamins A and D added to it. The composition and food value of margarine are similar to butter.

Meat, poultry and game

Meat consists of fibres which may be short, as in a fillet of beef, or long, as in the silverside of beef. The shorter the fibre the more tender and easily digested the meat. Meat is carved across the grain to assist mastication and digestion of the fibres.

Hanging the meat helps to make the flesh of meat more tender; this is because acids develop and soften the muscle fibres. Marinading in wine or vinegar prior to cooking also helps to tenderise meat so that it is more digestible. Expensive cuts of meat are not necessarily more nourishing than the cheaper cuts.

Meat contains proteins, variable amounts of fat, water, also iron and thiamin. (Bacon is particularly valuable because of its thiamin, and pork and pork products are especially rich in thiamin.) Tripe, in addition to its protein, is a good source of calcium as it is treated with lime during its preparation. It is also easily digested. Meat of all kinds is therefore important as a body-building food.

Fish

Fish is as useful a source of animal protein as meat.

The amount of fat in different fish varies: oily fish contain 5–18%, white fish less than 2%.

When the bones are eaten, calcium is obtained from fish (tinned sardines or salmon).

Oily fish is not so easily digested as white fish because of the fat; shellfish is not easily digested because of the coarseness of the fibres.

Fish is important for body building, and certain types of fish (oily fish) supply more energy and are protective because of the fat and vitamins A and D contained in the fish.

Eggs

Egg white contains protein known as egg albumin and the amount of white is approximately twice the amount of the yolk.

The yolk is more complex; it contains more protein than the white, also fat, vitamins A and D, thiamin, riboflavin, calcium, iron, sulphur and phosphorus. Lecithin (an emulsifying agent) and cholesterol are also present.

Because of the protein, vitamins, mineral elements and fat, eggs are a body-building, protective and energy-producing food.

COMPOSITION OF EGGS (APPROXIMATE PERCENTAGES)

	WHOLE EGG	WHITE	YOLK
water	73	87	47
protein	12	10	15
fat	11		33
minerals	1	0.5	2
vitamins			

Fruit

The composition of different fruit varies considerably: avocado pears contain about 20% fat, whereas most other fruits contain none. In unripe fruit the carbohydrate is in the form of starch which changes to sugar as the fruit ripens.

The cellulose in fruits acts as a source of dietary fibre.

Fruit is valuable because of the vitamins and minerals it contains. Vitamin C is present in certain fruits, particularly citrus varieties (oranges, grapefruit) and blackcurrants and other summer fruits. Dried fruits such as raisins and sultanas are a useful source of energy because of their sugar content, but they contain no vitamin C.

COMPOSITION OF FRUIT

The approximate composition is:

- water   85%
- carbohydrate   5–10%
- cellulose   2–5%
- minerals   0.5%
- vitamin C   varying amounts

Very small amounts of fat and protein are found in most fruits. Fruit is a protective food because of its minerals and vitamins.

Nuts

Nuts are highly nutritious because of the protein, fat and minerals they contain. Vegetarians may rely on nuts to provide the protein in their diet.

Nuts are not easily digested because of their fat content and cellulose.

Vegetables

GREEN VEGETABLES

Green vegetables are particularly valuable because of their vitamin and mineral content; they are therefore protective foods. The most important minerals they contain are iron and calcium. Green vegetables are rich in carotene, which is made into vitamin A in the body.

The greener the vegetable the greater its nutritional value. Vegetables which are stored for long periods, or are damaged or bruised, quickly lose their vitamin C value, therefore they should be used as quickly as possible.

Green vegetables also act as a source of dietary fibre in the intestines.

ROOT VEGETABLES

Compared with green vegetables most root vegetables contain starch and sugar; they are therefore a source of energy. Swedes and turnips contain a little vitamin C and carrots and other yellow-coloured vegetables contain carotene, which is changed into vitamin A in the body.

POTATOES

Potatoes contain a large amount of starch (approximately 20%) and a small amount of protein just under the skin. Because of the large quantities eaten, the small amount of vitamin C they contain is of value in the diet.

ONIONS
The onion is used extensively and contains some sugar, but its main value is to provide flavour.

PEAS AND BROAD BEANS
These vegetables contain carbohydrate, protein and carotene.

Cereals

Cereals contain from 60 to 80% carbohydrate in the form of starch and are therefore energy foods. They also contain 7–13% protein, depending on the type of cereal, and 1–8% fat.

The vitamin B content is considerable in stoneground and wholemeal flour, and B vitamins are added to other wheat flours, as are calcium and iron salts.

Oats contain good quantities of fat and protein.

Sugar

There are several kinds of sugar, such as those found in fruit (glucose), milk (lactose), cane and beet sugar (sucrose).

Sugar, with fat, provides the most important part of the body's energy requirements.

Saccharin, although sweet, is chemically produced and has no food value.

Liquids

WATER
Certain waters contain mineral salts; hard waters contain soluble salts of calcium. Some spas are known for the mineral salts contained in the local water. Bottled natural mineral waters are sold in many places (particularly supermarkets), and are being used more widely in the catering industry and in the home. Fluoride may be present naturally in some waters, and makes children's teeth more resistant to decay.

FRUIT JUICES
In recent years there has been a tremendous increase in the consumption of fruit juices sold in cartons as a chilled drink or in a 'long-life' form which will keep almost indefinitely before being opened. In addition, freshly squeezed orange juice is a popular alternative drink in many places, including airport and rail terminal restaurants.

BEVERAGES
Tea and coffee have no food value in themselves, but they do act on the nervous system as a stimulant.

Cocoa contains some fat, starch and protein, also some vitamin B and mineral elements.

When tea, coffee and cocoa are served with milk and sugar they do have some food value.

BALANCED DIET AND HEALTHY EATING
(see Plate 96, page 159)

A balanced diet provides adequate amounts of the various nutrients for energy, growth and repair and regulation of body processes.

In order to be healthy the body must have sufficient but not too much of all the nutrients which are present in foods. Provided the diet provides enough food energy to satisfy the demands for basal metabolism and all other activities, and includes a good mixture of foods, all the requirements for the different nutrients will be met.

We all know when we are eating too much food, because we put on weight, and unfortunately this is a very common problem both for the young and for older people. Carrying too much weight not only looks unattractive but is also a health hazard as it puts extra strain on the body. An overweight person should cut down on their intake of high energy foods such as butter, fried food, cakes, pastries, and also be careful to avoid too many purely energy-providing foods such as sweets and fizzy drinks. In this way energy intake will be reduced but not at the expense of the important body-building and protective foods.

Many diseases are linked to poor diet; we know for instance that too little vitamin C will eventually result in scurvy, but also there are many diseases that occur commonly in wealthy countries but which are rare in poorer areas of the world. Many people in developed countries, such as the UK, have a way of life that includes smoking, a relatively high alcohol intake and a diet which is high in fat, low in dietary fibre (especially that from cereals), and contains too much energy. A better diet would contain less fat (particularly dairy fats), less sugar in sweets, chocolate, puddings and beverages, and more bread and potatoes. Wholemeal bread and cereals are particularly beneficial to increase the amount of fibre in our diets.

On the whole people in the West eat plenty of protein and could well look to using some vegetable foods, such as peas, beans, nuts and lentils, for providing protein as a change from animal protein foods.

There is controversy about whether we eat too much salt, and certainly food manufacturers are starting to use less in their tinned products, infant foods, etc.

The importance of healthy eating was highlighted by the Government in the 1980s when two reports were published: NACNE report (National Advisory Committee on Nutrition Education) and the COMA report (Committee on Medical Aspects of Food Policy) on diet and heart disease. Unfortunately the nation's diet has not changed sufficiently yet for benefits to health to be seen and so in 1992 the Government produced its health strategy white paper *The Health of the Nation*. Recommendations for changes in diet have been targeted for action and a programme to achieve these targets was implemented by a Nutrition Task Force (*Eat Well – The Health of the Nation*) in March 1994.

The key targets of importance to caterers are:

- to reduce the food energy derived from fat (particularly saturated fat);
- to reduce the percentage of obese people;

- to reduce the proportions of men and women drinking more alcohol each week than recommended safe levels.

Caterers can help to achieve these targets by providing healthier choices on menus. The importance of adequate nutrition education was also highlighted in the *Eat Well* booklet and this is vital so that caterers have the knowledge and understanding to be able to adapt recipes and menus for healthy eating.

Nutritional guidelines

When compiling menus for institutions, industrial catering, etc., the following guidelines should be considered:

- Spread the calories fairly evenly through the day.
- Provide a dish which is a good source of protein in at least two meals of the day.
- Fruit and vegetables (including potatoes) should be available each day.
- Incorporate high fibre cereals whenever possible, for example, brown rice, a proportion of wholemeal flour in pastry, wholemeal bread or wholemeal pastas.
- Use the minimum of salt in cooking.
- Grill rather than fry.
- Let appetite determine the energy-producing food requirements.

FOOD ADDITIVES

These can be divided into 12 categories, and except for purely 'natural' substances, their use is subject to certain legislation.

- Preservatives: natural ones include salt, sugar, alcohol and vinegar; synthetic ones are also widely used.
- Colouring agents: natural, including cochineal, caramel and saffron, and many synthetic ones.
- Flavouring agents: synthetic chemicals to mimic natural flavours (monosodium glutamate to give a meaty flavour to foods).
- Sweetening: saccharin, sorbitol and aspartame.
- Emulsifying agents (to stop separation of salad creams, ice-cream, etc.); examples are lecithin and glyceryl monostearate (GMS).
- Antioxidants: to delay the onset of rancidity in fats due to exposure to air, such as vitamin E and BHT.
- Flour improvers: to strengthen the gluten in flour, such as vitamin C.
- Thickeners: animal (gelatine); marine (agar-agar); vegetable (gum tragacanth (used for pastillage), pectin); synthetic products.
- Humectants: to prevent food drying out, such as glycerine (used in some icings).
- Polyphosphate: injected into poultry before rigor mortis develops; it binds water to the muscle and thus prevents 'drip', giving a firmer structure to the meat.
- Nutrients: vitamins and minerals added to breakfast cereals, vitamins A and D added to margarine.

- Miscellaneous: anticaking agents added to icing sugar and salt; firming agents (calcium chloride) added to tinned fruit and vegetables to prevent too much softening in the processing; mineral oils added to dried fruit to prevent stickiness.

Further information

Food Safety Directorate, Ministry of Agriculture, Fisheries and Food, Room No 11 Whitehall Place (West Block), London SW1A 2HH.

FOOD SPOILAGE

Unless foods are preserved they deteriorate; therefore, to keep them in an edible condition it is necessary to know what causes food spoilage. In the air there are certain micro-organisms called moulds, yeasts and bacteria which cause foods to go bad.

Moulds

These are simple plants which appear like whiskers on foods, particularly sweet foods, meat and cheese. To grow, they require warmth, air, moisture, darkness and food; they are killed by heat and sunlight. Moulds can grow where there is too little moisture for yeasts and bacteria to grow, and will be found on jams and pickles.

Although not harmful they do cause foods to taste musty and to be wasted – the top layer of a jar of jam should be removed if it has mould on it.

Correct storage in a dry cold store prevents moulds from forming.

Not all moulds are destructive. Some are used to flavour cheese (stilton, roquefort) or to produce antibiotics (penicillin, streptomycin).

Yeasts

These are single-cell plants or organisms larger than bacteria, which grow on foods containing moisture and sugar. Foods containing only a small percentage of sugar and a large percentage of liquid, such as fruit juices and syrups, are liable to ferment because of yeasts. Although they seldom cause disease, yeasts do increase food spoilage; foodstuffs should be kept under refrigeration or they may be spoiled by yeasts. Yeasts are also destroyed by heat. The ability of yeast to feed on sugar and produce alcohol is the basis of the beer and wine-making industry.

Bacteria

Bacteria are minute plants, or organisms, which require moist, warm conditions and a suitable food to multiply. They spoil food by attacking it, leaving waste products, or by producing poisons in the food.

Their growth is checked by refrigeration and they are killed by heat. Certain bacterial forms (spores) are more resistant to heat than others and require higher temperatures to kill them.

Pressure cooking destroys heat-resistant bacterial spores provided the food is cooked for a sufficient length of time, because increased pressure increases the temperature; therefore heat-resistant bacterial spores do not affect canned foods as the foods are cooked under pressure in the cans. Acids are generally capable of destroying bacteria, such as vinegar in pickles.

Dehydrated foods and dry foods do not contain much moisture and, provided they are kept dry, spoilage from bacteria will not occur. If they become moist then bacteria can multiply: if dried peas are soaked and not cooked the bacteria present can begin to multiply.

Other causes

Food spoilage can occur due to other causes, such as by chemical substances called enzymes, which are produced by living cells. Fruits are ripened by the action of enzymes; they do not remain edible indefinitely because other enzymes cause the fruit to become over-ripe and spoil.

When meat and game are hung they become tender; this is caused by the enzymes. To prevent enzyme activity going too far, foods must be refrigerated or heated to a temperature high enough to destroy the enzymes. Acid retards the enzyme action – lemon juice prevents the browning of bananas or apples when they are cut into slices.

The acidity and alkalinity of foods (see Figure 5.10)

The level of acidity or alkalinity of a food is measured by its pH value. The pH can range from 1 to 14, with pH 7 denoting neutral (neither acid nor alkaline).

Most micro-organisms grow best at near neutral pH. Bacteria (particularly harmful ones) are less acid tolerant than fungi, and no bacteria will grow at pH less than 3.5. Spoilage of high acid foods such as fruit is usually caused by yeasts and moulds. Meat and fish are more susceptible to bacterial spoilage, since their pH is nearer neutral.

The pH may be lowered so that the food becomes too acidic (less than pH 1.5) for any micro-organisms to grow, such as the use of vinegar in pickling. In the manufacture of yogurt and cheese, bacteria produce lactic acid; this lowers the pH, and retards the growth of food poisoning and spoilage organisms.

Acid								Alkaline					
1	2	3	4	5	6	7	8	9	10	11	12	13	14
strong acid			**medium acid**		**weak acid**		**weak alkali**		**medium alkali**		**strong alkaline**		
lemons vinegar rhubarb			pear bananas carrots tomatoes				some mineral waters hard water		egg white bicarbonate of soda				

Fig. 5.10   The pH range in some foods

FOOD ALLERGIES

Some people are allergic to some foods which, when handled or eaten, cause an allergic reaction which may prevent employment because they cannot handle the item (tomatoes which may cause a rash), or they become ill and in a small number of cases they die. Only in rare cases is it fatal.

Foods which may cause an allergic reaction to a very small number of people include milk, fish, shellfish, eggs and nuts (particularly peanuts but also cashew, pecan, Brazil and walnuts). Peanuts are often commonly used in Bombay mix, peanut butter, satay sauce, nut-coated cereals, groundnut and arachide oils, salted peanuts, chopped nuts, vegetarian dishes and salads containing nuts etc.

Persons suffering an allergy to nuts need to know if and where they are used.

KEEPING UP TO DATE

Changes are occurring constantly regarding food production and manufacture which may affect the use of foods in the kitchen. Consumers' reaction to reports of changes published in the press or seen or heard on the TV or radio may affect demand. Similarly information about nutritional values can affect customers' preferences and thus cause trends and affect menu selection.

It is therefore essential to be aware of these reports and when necessary to act according to government recommendations. An example of research which has affected kitchen practice has been the use of eggs. Currently the use of beef because of 'mad cow disease' (BSE) and the use of calves' sweetbreads and offal in items such as black pudding are under scrutiny.

Recommendations and contradictions produced by dietetic research can cause trends and affect consumer habits. The use of butter and margarine is such an example.

It is essential to keep up to date through the media and adopt a commonsense attitude to the comments made but to take action when serious recommendations are made by valid research bodies.

METHODS OF PRESERVATION

Foods may be preserved by:

- removing the moisture from the food – drying, dehydration;
- making the food cold – chilling, freezing;
- applying heat – canning, bottling;
- radiation, using X- or gamma-rays;
- chemical means – salting, pickling, crystallising;
- vacuum packing;
- smoking;
- chemical;
- gas storage.

Drying or dehydration

This method of preserving is achieved by extracting the moisture from the food, thus preventing moulds, yeasts and bacteria from growing. In the past this was done by drying foods, such as fruits, in the sun; today many types of equipment are used, and the food is dried by the use of air at a regulated temperature and humidity.

FREEZE DRYING

This is a process of dehydration whereby food requires no preservation or refrigeration yet, when soaked in water, regains its original size and flavour. It can be applied to every kind of food. The food is frozen in a cabinet, the air is pumped out and the ice vaporised. This is called freeze drying and it is the drying of frozen foods by sublimation under conditions of very low pressure. Sublimation is the action of turning from solid to gas without passing through a liquid stage; in this case it is ice to steam without first turning to water.

When processed in this way the food does not lose a great deal of its bulk, but it is very much lighter in weight. When water is added the food gives off its natural smell.

ADVANTAGES OF DRYING

- If kept dry, food keeps indefinitely.
- Food preserved by this method occupies less space than food preserved by other methods. Some dried foods occupy only 10% of the space that would be required when fresh.
- Dried foods are easily transported and stored.
- The cost of drying and the expenses incurred in storing are not as high as other methods of preservation.
- There is no waste after purchase, therefore portion control and costing are simplified.

FOODS PRESERVED BY DRYING

- Vegetables: peas, onions, beetroot, beans, carrots, lentils, cabbage, mixed vegetables, potatoes;
- Herbs; eggs; milk; coffee;
- Fruits: apples, pears, plums (prunes), apricots, figs, grapes (sultanas, raisins, currants);
- Meat; fish.

Vegetables

Many vegetables are dried; those most used are the pulse vegetables (beans, peas and lentils) which are used for soups, vegetable purées and many vegetarian dishes. Usually potatoes are cooked, mashed and then dried. The other dried vegetables are used as a vegetable (cabbage, onions).

Pulse vegetables may be soaked in water before use, then washed before being cooked. Vegetables which are dehydrated (having a lower content of water as more moisture has been extracted) are soaked in water.

Dehydrated potatoes are in powder form and are reconstituted with water, milk, or milk and water. They usually have manufactured vitamin C added as dehydration results in loss of vitamin C.

Herbs

Fresh herbs are tied into bundles and allowed to dry out in a dry place.

Fruits

Sultanas, currants and raisins are dried grapes which have been dried in the sun or by hot air. Figs, plums, apricots, apples and pears are also dried by hot air. Apples are usually peeled and cut in rings or diced and then dried.

All dried fruits must be washed before use, and fruits such as prunes, figs, apricots, apples and pears are cooked in the water in which they are soaked.

Little flavour or food value is lost in the drying of fruits, with the exception of loss of vitamin C.

Milk

Milk is dried either by the roller or spray process. With the roller method the milk is poured onto heated rollers which cause the water to evaporate; the resulting powder is then scraped off. This method is not widely used now as it damages the milk proteins and results in a less soluble dried product, which is more difficult to reconstitute. With the spray process the milk is sent through a fine jet as a spray into hot air, the water evaporates and the powder drops down. The temperature is controlled so that the protein in the milk is not cooked.

Milk powder may be used in place of fresh milk mainly for economic purposes (especially skimmed milk powder) and is used for making custard and white sauce.

Eggs

Eggs are dried in the same way as milk, and although they have a food value similar to fresh eggs, dried eggs do not have the same aerating quality. When reconstituted the eggs should be used at once; if they are left in this state in the warm atmosphere of a kitchen, bacteria can multiply and food poisoning may result; although pasteurised before drying, the mixture may be contaminated in the kitchen and it is a very suitable food for the growth of bacteria. Dried eggs are mainly used in the bakery trade.

Chilling and freezing (see also pages 412 and 460)

Refrigeration is a method of preservation where the micro-organisms in food are not killed; they are only prevented from multiplying. The lower the temperature the longer foods will keep. Refrigerators kept at a temperature between 0–7°C (32–45°F) prevent foods from spoiling for only a short time; most frozen foods can be kept at −17°C (1°F) for a year and at −28°C (−18°F) for two years. Foods must be kept in a deep freeze until required for use.

Cold chilled storage of fresh foods merely retards the decay of the food; it does not prevent it from eventually going bad. The aim of chilling is to slow down the rate of spoilage; the lower the chill temperature within the range −1°C (30°F) and +8°C (46°F) the slower the growth of micro-organisms and the biochemical changes which spoil the flavour, colour, texture and nutritional value of foods. Lowering the temperature to this range also reduces food poisoning hazards although it is important to remember that the food must not be contaminated before chilling.

If food is frozen slowly, large uneven crystals are formed in the cells. The water in each cell contains the minerals which give flavour and goodness to food; if food is frozen slowly, the minerals are separated from the ice crystals which break through the cells; on thawing, the goodness and flavour drain away. Quick-freezing is satisfactory because small ice crystals are formed in the cells of food; on thawing, the goodness and flavour are retained in the cells.

Figure 5.11 shows how only small ice crystals are formed when the temperature falls rapidly through zero, whereas in the second curve, the slower fall results in large ice crystals.

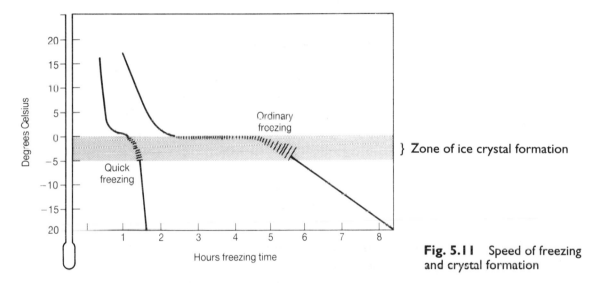

Fig. 5.11   Speed of freezing and crystal formation

MEAT
- Chilling – meat which is chilled is kept at a temperature just above freezing-point and will keep for up to 1 month, if the atmosphere is controlled with carbon dioxide the time can be extended to 10 weeks.
- Freezing – imported lamb carcasses are frozen; beef carcasses are not usually frozen because owing to the size of the carcass it takes a long time to freeze and this causes ice crystals to form which, when thawed, affect the texture of the meat; frozen meat must be thawed before it is cooked.

QUICK-FREEZING OF RAW FOODS AND COOKED FOODS
During the cooking and freezing process, foods undergo physical and/or chemical changes. If it is found that these changes are detrimental to the product, then recipe modification is required. The following products require some modification: sauces, casseroles, stews, cold desserts, batters, vegetables, egg dishes.

Conventional recipes normally use wheat flour for thickening, but in the cook-freeze system this will not give an acceptable final product because separation of the solids from the liquids in the sauce will occur if the product is kept in frozen storage for more than a period of several weeks. To overcome this problem it is necessary to use wheat flour in conjunction with any of a number of classically modified starches, such as tapioca starch, waxy maize starch. Many recipes prove successful with a ratio of 50% wheat flour with 50% modified starch.

Rapid freezing of foodstuffs can be achieved by a variety of methods using different types of equipment, for example:

- plate freezer;
- blast freezer (see Figure 5.12);
- low-temperature immersion freezer;
- still-air cold room;
- spray freezer (using liquid nitrogen or carbon dioxide) – known as cryogenic freezing this is a method of freezing food by very low temperature; it also freezes food more quickly than any other method; the food to be frozen is placed on a conveyor belt and passed into an insulated freezing tunnel; the liquefied nitrogen or carbon dioxide is injected into the tunnel through a spray, and vaporises, resulting in a very rapid freezing process.
- freeze flow – this is a system which freezes food without hardening it.

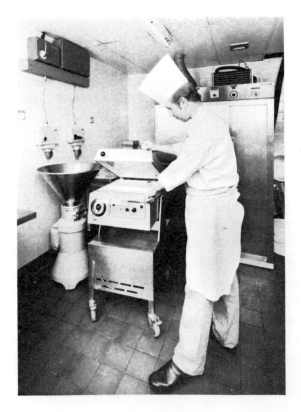

Fig. 5.12   Hotel ready-food kitchen (left to right): high-speed mixer, vacuum packer and blast freezer

FOODS WHICH ARE FROZEN

A very wide variety of foods are frozen, either cooked or in an uncooked state.

- Cooked foods: whole cooked meals; braised meat; vol-au-vents; éclairs; cream sponges; puff pastry items.
- Raw foods: fillets of fish; fish fingers; poultry; peas; French beans; broad beans; spinach; sprouts; broccoli; strawberries; raspberries; blackcurrants.

With most frozen foods, cooking instructions are given; these should be followed to obtain the best results.

Fillets of fish may be thawed out before cooking; vegetables are cooked in their frozen state. Fruit is thawed before use and as it is usually frozen with sugar the fruit is served with the liquor.

ADVANTAGES OF USING FROZEN FOODS

- Frozen foods are ready-prepared, therefore saving time and labour.
- Portion control and costing are easily assessed.
- Foods are always 'in season'.
- Storage is compact.
- Additional stocks are to hand.
- Quality is guaranteed.
- Very little vitamin C is lost from fruits and vegetables even after several months in a deep freeze.

Canning and bottling

Bottled and canned foods are sealed in airtight bottles or tins and heated at a high enough temperature for a sufficient period of time to destroy harmful organisms.

Dented cans which do not leak are safe to use, but blown cans, that is those with bulges at either end, must not be used.

Tinned hams are canned at a low temperature in order to retain their flavour and avoid excessive shrinkage in the can and therefore should be stored in a refrigerator and consumed soon after purchase. Other tinned foods are kept in a dry, cool place and the table below indicates the advised storage time.

STORAGE OF TINNED FOODS

TYPE OF TINNED FOOD	ADVISED STORAGE TIME
fruit	up to 12 months
milk	up to 12 months
vegetables	up to 2 years
meat	up to 5 years
fish in oil	up to 5 years
fish in tomato sauce	up to 1 year

Foods are canned in tins of various sizes (see table below).

TIN SIZES

SIZE	APPROX. WEIGHT	USE
	142 g	baked beans, peas
	227 g	fruits, meats, vegetables
A1	284 g	baked beans, soups, vegetables, meats, pilchards
14Z	397 g	fruits, vegetables
A2	567 g	fruits, vegetables, fruit and vegetable juices
A2$\frac{1}{2}$	794 g	fruits, vegetables
A10	3079 g	fruits, vegetables, tongues

The advantages of canned foods are similar to those of frozen foods, but a disadvantage is that due to the heat processing a proportion of the vitamin C and B_1 (thiamin) may be lost.

Preservation by salting and smoking

SALTING

Micro-organisms cannot grow in high concentrations of salt. This method of preservation is used mainly to preserve meat and fish, and the advantage lies chiefly in the fact that a wider variety of dishes with different flavours can be put on the menu.

The salt added to butter and margarine and also to cheese acts as a preservative.

Meats

Meats which are salted or 'pickled' in a salt solution (brine) are brisket, silverside of beef, ox tongues, legs of pork.

Fish

Fish are usually smoked as well as being salted and include: salmon, trout, haddock, herrings, cods' roes.

The amount of salting varies. Bloaters are salted more than kippers and red herrings more than bloaters.

SMOKING (see Plate 97, page 160)

Smoking of foods has a dual purpose. It preserves and adds desirable flavours to foods such as sides of smoked salmon hung over a smoke pot containing smouldering oak logs or chips. When wood is burnt it releases tannins and it is the acidic nature of the tannins which deter bacteria and preserve the fish. As more tannins are found in the bark and outer wood, using logs gives a better cure than using chippings or sawdust.

The preservative action is partly due to the absorption of chemical substances (tannins) from the smoke and partly due to the drying effect on the surface of the food. Foods to be smoked are usually soaked in brine or salted beforehand.

- Cold smoking – no heat is produced; the lid of the smoke pot is kept sealed so that only smoke and not heat reaches the food; cold smoking is carried out at temperatures between 32°–49°C (89.6–120°F); salmon is cold smoked.
- Hot smoking – temperatures between 100 and 120°C (212–248°F) are used which partially cook the food and produce a drier surface to the product; fish (herring, mackerel, trout, halibut), poultry, meat and sausages are hot smoked; smoking has the advantage of retarding the rancidity which soon develops in storage; added flavours can be injected into the smoking process by the use of sprigs of herbs.

Modern smoking methods inhibit rather than kill micro-organisms in food. Smoked foods must be kept under refrigeration at all times.

Preservation by sugar

A high concentration of sugar prevents the growth of moulds, yeasts and bacteria. This method of preservation is applied to fruits in a variety of forms: jams, marmalades, jellies, candied, glacé and crystallised.

- Jams are prepared by cooking fruit and sugar together in the correct quantities to prevent the jam from spoiling. Too little sugar means the jam will not keep.
- Jellies, such as redcurrant jelly, are prepared by cooking the juice of the fruit with the sugar.
- Marmalade is similar to jam in preparation and preservation, citrus fruits being used in place of other fruits.
- Candied fruit is made when the peel of such fruit as orange, lemon, grapefruit and lime, and also the flesh of pineapple, are covered with hot syrup; the syrup's sugar content is increased each day until the fruit is saturated in a very heavy syrup, then it is allowed to dry slowly.
- Crystallised fruit is made following candying. It is left in fresh syrup for 24 hours and then allowed to dry slowly until crystals form on the fruit. Angelica, ginger, violet and rose petals are prepared in this way.
- Glacé fruit, usually cherries, is first candied, then dipped in fresh syrup to give a clear finish.

Preservation by acids (see page 221 for explanation of pH)

Foods may be preserved in vinegar, which is acetic acid (ethanoic acid) diluted with water. In the UK, malt vinegar is most frequently used, although distilled or white wine vinegar is used for pickling white vegetables such as cocktail onions and also for rollmops (herrings).

Foods usually pickled in vinegar are: gherkins, capers, onions, shallots, walnuts, red cabbage, mixed pickles and chutneys.

Preservation by chemicals

A number of chemicals are permitted by law to be used to preserve certain foods such as sausages, fruit pulp, jam. For domestic fruit bottling, Campden preserving tablets can be used.

Preservation by gas storage

Gas storage is used in conjunction with refrigerators to preserve meat, eggs and fruit. Extra carbon dioxide added to the atmosphere surrounding the foods increases the length of time they can be stored. Without the addition of gas these foods would dry out more quickly.

Preservation by radiation

WHAT IS IRRADIATION?
Foods are exposed to ionising radiation which transfers some of its energy as it passes through the food, killing the pathogenic bacteria, which would otherwise make the food unsafe to eat, or at lower doses the spoilage bacteria, which cause food to rot. Ionising radiation is electromagnetic like radio waves, infrared light or ultraviolet light. It is similar to ultraviolet radiation but has a higher frequency and much greater energy. This is sufficient to protect food effectively, but not enough to make it radioactive.

Irradiation methods have other key advantages over heating, chilling and chemical preservation methods.

- Irradiation works well with frozen or heat-sensitive products, as it does not cause any significant increase in temperature.
- Packaged products can be sterilised in the final pack, thus preventing contamination.
- Irradiation has a minimal impact on the nutritional value of the food. Proteins and carbohydrates are unaffected.
- Irradiation processing is a clean technology. No chemical additives are used or residues left behind in the food and the process does not contaminate or damage the environment.

The chemical changes caused in the food by the ionising radiation are in general much less severe than those arising from other food processing methods such as cooling and heating.

At present 36 countries allow irradiation of about thirty individually specified foods. In 21 of these countries there are active commercial food irradiative plants.

The Food Labelling (Amendment) (Irradiated Food) Regulations 1990 came into force on 1 January 1991 in parallel with those regulations setting out the controls on irradiation. The regulations require all foods which have been irradiated to carry an indication of treatment using the specified words 'irradiated' or 'treated with ionising radiation'.

Preservation by vacuum packing

Sealing cooked food in an airtight package in conditions where air is removed will preserve the food for longer and retain its flavour and colour. The *sous-vide* system of food preservation employs sterile conditions in the vacuum packing and hence the shelf-life of the cooked food is very much prolonged.

Modified atmosphere packaging (MAP) (see table, page 232)

This is a flexible way of extending the shelf-life of many kinds of fresh foods up to two to three times the normal levels. The method involves replacing the normal surrounding or dead space atmosphere within food packages with specific mixtures of gases or single gases. Its objectives are to inhibit the growth of pathogenic bacteria and moulds and to extend the shelf-lives of chilled and certain ambient food products.

Originally the system was known as Controlled Atmosphere Packaging and was used for retail portioning and packaging of red meat. The method was based on what is now known as the date of packaging + 5 days' system using an 80% oxygen/20% carbon dioxide gas mixture. The inert gases used are carbon dioxide, nitrogen and oxygen. They are natural gases like those present in the air but for MAP they are supplied purified and free of bacteria.

- Carbon dioxide (CO_2) inhibits the growth of pathogenic bacteria at temperatures not exceeding 8°C (46.4°F) for a restricted period. CO_2 does not kill the bacteria but will restrict mould growth over long periods.
- Nitrogen has a neutral effect on food stuffs and is used in 100% strength for dried and roasted foods, dairy cakes, cream and milk powders. The gas is also used in conjunction with CO_2 as a support gas.
- Oxygen sustains basic metabolism and prevents spoilage caused by anaerobic bacteria. It is also used in MAP gas mixtures for packaging red meats where it preserves the red colour of the meat.

MAP effectively increases the length of time certain foods can be stored in the refrigerator. The gas mixtures used vary according to the product being packaged. MAP is particularly successful with bakery products where elevated CO_2 content permits high relative humidities with negligible mould growth.

Chefs employed in large food production operations and those employed as development chefs use MAP to aid food preparation and quality. Over the next few years we are likely to see further developments in this area as the catering industry becomes more involved in using gases to aid preservation of ingredients.

FURTHER INFORMATION

McCance and Widdowson, *The Composition of Foods* (HMSO).
Stretch and Southgate, *The Science of Catering* (Edward Arnold, 1986).
Manual of Nutrition (HMSO).
Eating for Health (HMSO).
Kilgour, *Science for Catering Students* (Heinemann).

RECOMMENDED GAS MIXTURE PERCENTAGES (%) FOR MAP
(based on refrigeration storage)

PRODUCT	OXYGEN	NITROGEN	CARBON DIOXIDE	SHELF-LIFE
	(%)	(%)	(%)	
red meat	80	–	20	5–8 days
white fish	30	30	40	5–6 days
fatty fish	–	40	60	5–6 days
salmon	20	20	60	5–6 days
poultry	–	75	25	17–18 days
hard cheese	–	-	100	3 weeks
bacon, cooked meats	–	65–80	20–35	3–4 days
bread	–	30–40	60–70	3 weeks
dairy cakes	–	100	–	3 weeks

Gaman and Sherrington, *Science of Food* (Pergamon).
Guidelines on Pre-cooked Chilled Foods (HMSO).
Food (Control of Irradiation) Regulation 1990 (HMSO).
Education Department, Unilever Ltd, Unilever House, Blackfriars, London EC4.
Health Education Authority, Hamilton House, Mabledon Place, London WC1H 9TX.
Nutrition Society, Grosvenor Gardens House, 35–37 Grosvenor Gardens, London SW1H 0BX.

TOPICS FOR DISCUSSION

1. Why is a balanced diet desirable? What do you consider to be necessary to provide a balanced diet?
2. Why do you think trends, fads and fashions occur in our eating? Discuss how you could encourage a positive approach to having healthy eating habits.
3. How has presentation of foods changed and why have these changes come about?
4. What problems are associated with certain people's diets? What specific considerations are there for the diets of children, the elderly, nursing mothers and teenagers?
5. For what reasons may the nutritional value of foods be affected? Discuss examples of how this may occur and how such effects be prevented.

6

Product development (Chemistry in the kitchen)

Modern day chefs are encouraged to be creative, to use their flair and imagination to create interesting and appetising dishes. An understanding of the basic chemistry of food products will help chefs in their work to produce dishes which are practically feasible. A knowledge of how ingredients perform under different conditions is also valuable in development work.

pH AND WATER (see also page 221)

Pure water has a pH of 7.0. Water is seldom pure. Rain water and distilled water sometimes contain dissolved materials. All water contains dissolved gases from the air. Distilled water has enough dissolved carbon dioxide to make it distinctly acidic. The pH of distilled water is approximately 5.5 and rain water can be even lower when it washes certain industrial pollutants out of the atmosphere. This is known as acid rain.

Dissolved gases contribute to the flavour of water. The nature of water often affects the food we cook in it. For example hard water causes difficulties when cooking pulses since magnesium and calcium interfere with tenderising these foods. Likewise an acidic cooking medium will stop dried beans from absorbing water and soften properly.

Not only is water a component of all foods, but it contributes significantly to the physical differences among foods and to the changes that foods undergo.

PROTEINS

Proteins are an important part of many foods and ingredients that a chef uses. Amino acids are the structural units of proteins. There are some twenty different amino acids found in proteins. The nature of the protein is determined both by the proportions of each amino acid and by the order in which they are arranged. A typical protein may contain 500 amino acids; this means that there can be much variation between different types of protein.

Proteins are the most complex substances known. For example glucose has a simple molecular weight of 180 daltons whereas a simple amino acid such as lactoglobulin has a molecular weight of 4200. Some proteins have a molecular weight of several million.

The structure of an amino acid can affect its chemical properties. The general structure is shown below:

R represents residual
part of molecule

	H	R	O	
	\	|	//	
AMINO GROUP				CARBONYL GROUP
(NH$_2$)	N—C—C			(COOH)
reacts with acid	/	|	\	reactions with alkali
	H	H	OH	

The majority of amino acids have only one carbonyl and amino group. They are termed **neutral**. If more than one amino group is present the amino acid is called **basic**. If more than one carbonyl group is present it is called **acidic**.

Development chefs do not need to know about the proportion or order of the amino acids in a protein. What they should be concerned with is the shape of the protein, and how this shape can be changed.

The amino acids are held together in their long chains by what are called 'strong bonds' which are very hard to break. To split up the proteins into amino acids requires conditions such as heating in the presence of a strong acid or by certain enzymes. The procedures in the kitchen are unlikely to break these strong bonds.

Cooking has a much greater effect on what is known as secondary structure. Since proteins are long chains, they can double back on themselves to form loops. These loops are held in place by 'weak bonds' to give a secondary structure.

Protein shapes

When developing new products it is advisable to understand the shape of the protein molecule. Many of the cooking processes used by chefs will break the weak bonds and thus change the shape of the molecule. The effect of changing the shape of the protein molecule may be useful but in some cases it may be undesirable. There are two main protein shapes: fibrous and globular.

FIBROUS PROTEINS (Figure 6.1)
Fibrous proteins are insoluble, resistant to acids and alkali and are uneffected by moderate heating. They maintain their strand-like shape. They are often coiled like springs and can be elastic or stretchy. Sometimes two or more strands are twisted together and are held together by weak bonding. Fibrous proteins are generally very tough and are found in animal tissue.

GLOBULAR PROTEINS (Figure 6.2)
These are usually water soluble and affected by acid and alkali. They are shaped like tiny balls with weak bonding. These proteins are not usually part of the structure of the plant or animal, but tend to be functional proteins such as enzymes or storage proteins.

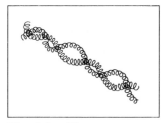

Fig. 6.1 Fibrous protein

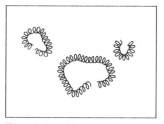

Fig. 6.2 Globular protein

TYPES OF PROTEINS FOUND IN FOOD

TYPE	PROTEIN	WHERE FOUND
fibrous	collagen	connective tissue
fibrous	elastin	connective tissue
fibrous	gluten	wheat flour
fibrous	albumen	egg white, milk
fibrous	casein	milk
fibrous	enzymes	many tissues
fibrous	myosin	muscle

Denaturing protein

It is important to understand what happens to protein when it is cooked, mixed with other ingredients, or treated by different methods such as whipping. The protein is denatured during cooking. Proteins are denatured when their properties are completely altered; the bonds which hold the protein are broken, these bonds are replaced by other weak bonds not normally present and a new shape is formed. Solubility is decreased, visibility increased and it is an irreversible change.

Proteins can be denatured in many different ways:

- Heat: normal cooking methods;
- Salting: by adding salt;
- Mechanical action: whipping egg whites;
- Enzymes: meat tenderisers;
- Acid: by adding acid, yogurt, sour cream.

EFFECT OF HEAT ON GLOBULAR PROTEINS

Making an egg custard is an example. The main ingredients are milk, sugar and eggs. They are beaten together before the cooking process. As it cooks the mixture thickens. The thickening is due to the heat denaturation of the egg proteins. First the egg albumen molecules, in this case the globular proteins, are moved about by the input of heat energy. As this movement becomes more vigorous, the weak bonds that hold the globules in place start to break up. Secondly the protein chains start to unfold and may come into contact with other chains and form new weak bonds. Thirdly a stable three-dimensional mesh of large molecules is formed. This mesh traps many small pockets of water and limits the movement of the water. The effect is a thick smooth texture. If the egg custard is allowed to continue cooking the protein mesh will contract or coagulate and squeeze out the pockets of water. The custard will then curdle and resemble lumps of scrambled egg suspended in milk. This loss of water is known as syneresis. The presence of salt or acid will speed up the process of coagulation. This is evident if vinegar is added to water for poaching eggs.

EFFECT OF HEAT ON FIBROUS PROTEINS

Although fibrous proteins do not dissolve in water they do have capacity to attract and bind water. This is often important in meat cooking particularly when producing chopped meat or minced products that require moisture to be added to them.

When fibrous proteins are heated they contract and squeeze out the associated water. For example when fillet steak is cooked the protein called myosin coagulates at 71°C (160°F). If the temperature continues to increase, the protein contracts, squeezes out much of the water associated with it and thus becomes drier and the eating quality is impaired. For a tender, juicy fillet steak the chef would heat the steak just sufficiently to sear the outside. This will also melt any fat, acting as a lubricant and improving the overall tenderness and eating quality.

Cuts of meat can consist of large amounts of connective tissue, for example collagen and elastin. Collagen is tough and chewy. Elastin is stretchy and heating has little effect on it except helping to produce a tougher product. Meat which contains high proportions is naturally tougher and therefore not usually suitable for prime cooking. Collagen will denature becoming water soluble when heated in water. This then becomes gelatine.

EFFECT OF HEAT ON MATERIALS FOUND IN MEAT

MEAT MATERIAL	WHAT HAPPENS	EFFECT
muscle protein (myosin)	fibres shrink and lose water	meat becomes tougher and drier
connective tissue (collagen)	heat plus water causes collagen to denature	gelatine is formed
fat	fat melts and acts as a lubricant	meat seems more tender

EFFECTS OF ACIDS ON PROTEINS (see page 225 for information on pH)

Acids play an important part in cooking procedures:

- as a component in raising agents in baking powder;
- as a preservative in yogurt;
- as a tenderising agent in meats.

The citric acid in lemon juice will slow down any browning reaction on cut fruit.

Proteins can also be denatured by acids. The albumen in milk is a globular protein.

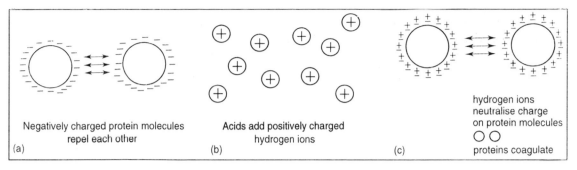

Fig. 6.3   Acid coagulation of milk

In its natural state, each albumen molecule carries a negative electrical charge. Charged particles are similar to north and south poles on magnets, that is like repels like: whenever a negative particle gets near another negative particle they repel each other and remain separate.

If acid is added to milk (see Figure 6.3), then we are adding hydrogen ions which are very small positively charged particles. The hydrogen ions (positively charged) are attracted to the albumen globules (negatively charged) and the two neutralise each other. The albumen is then electrically neutral, and any globules that come in contact stick together or coagulate and form a mass with a gel-like, semisolid consistency. This process is useful in food preparation, for example in cheese making, yogurt and sour cream.

EFFECT OF MECHANICAL ACTION ON PROTEIN

The bonds that maintain the shape of protein molecules are so weak that we are able to break them by agitating the molecules, for example meringues, which are foams (relatively stable masses of air bubbles which are pockets of gas surrounded by a thin film of water). Foams in beer are less stable because there is no stabiliser present.

By whipping egg whites we are adding air and physically agitating the egg white globular proteins. The mechanical stresses resulting from the physical agitation and contact with air act to unfold the globular proteins. The unfolded proteins associate to form a sort of mesh reinforcement of the bubble walls. (This can be considered as the culinary equivalent of quick-setting cement). The egg white foam is relatively stable because it is held together by proteins, while the foam in a head of beer quickly deflates.

Gluten gives bread dough both its elasticity and plasticity. Gluten is formed by two proteins, gliadin and glutenin, coming together in the presence of water; they form a tangled mass of protein molecules. During kneading, the gluten molecules are physically rearranged from a tangled mass to a series of parallel sheets. The molecules in the sheets of gluten are shaped like tiny springs and account for the stretchy nature of bread dough. The sheets of gluten act to trap the gas formed by the yeast growing in the dough and allow the bread to rise.

Enzymes

Enzymes are proteins which are catalysts, meaning that they speed up chemical reactions. Enzymes catalyse a wide range of chemical reactions that take place in all living things. Some enzymes are useful while others lower the quality of foods. An example of one enzyme is rennet added to milk to produce junket.

Each enzyme requires an optimum temperature in which to work. At lower temperatures they will act more slowly and at higher temperatures they will gradually be destroyed. The optimum temperature for an enzyme that comes from a mammal is often close to 37°C (98.6°F) (body temperature). Enzymes are also affected by acidity and can sometimes be controlled by changing the pH. An example of this is using lemon juice to stop the enzyme-catalysed browning of apples.

ENZYME EFFECTS ON FOODS

FOOD	CHANGE	ENZYME SOURCE
Desirable changes		
black tea	oxidation similar to browning of apples	naturally present
beef	tenderising during ageing	naturally present
bananas and apples	conversion of starch to sugar during ripening	naturally present
meat	tenderisers	paw paw, pineapple
Cheddar cheese	conversion of milk to 'curds and whey'	calves' stomach
starch	conversion of starch to glucose syrups	moulds
Undesirable Changes		
fatty meats	development of rancidity	naturally present
fruit jellies	failure to set when using fresh pineapple or paw paw	present in fruit
fruits and vegetables	development of brown colour where exposed to air	naturally present

AGEING OF MEAT – THE ROLE OF ENZYMES

Like cheese and wine, meat benefits from a period of 'ageing' or slow chemical change, before it is consumed. The flavour improves and it becomes more tender. As lactic acid accumulates in the tissue after slaughter, it begins to break down the walls of lysosomes, the cell bodies that store protein-attacking enzymes. As a result, these enzymes will digest proteins indiscriminately. Flavour changes result from the degradation of proteins into individual amino acids, which generally have a strong flavour. It is not clear whether these same enzymes also tenderise the meat by breaking up the actin–myosin complex.

Glycogen, a carbohydrate energy reserve, is stored by the animals. It is glycogen which is converted to the lactic acid required in the ageing process. Glycogen cannot be converted to carbon dioxide and water as it would be in the living animal due to the lack of oxygen, instead it is converted to lactic acid. The lactic acid lowers the pH of the muscle from about 7.0 in the living animal to 5.6 in the dead animal. The lactic acid breaks down the structures in the cells that contain enzymes capable of digesting protein. Protein muscle fibres are partly digested. As a result of these changes the meat is softer and more tender. It has been partially degraded by its own enzymes.

For these changes to occur during ageing it is necessary to have an adequate supply of glycogen in the muscle when the animal is slaughtered. If the animal is not fed or subjected to stress before slaughter the glycogen will have been used up, and the desirable post-mortem changes will not take place. This meat will be darker in colour and tougher in texture.

CARBOHYDRATES

These can be sugars and non-sugars:

TYPES OF CARBOHYDRATES

SUGARS	NON-SUGARS
monosaccharides	polysaccharides (starch)
disaccharides	complex polysaccharides
trisaccharides	(pectin, alginates)
tetrasaccharides	

Carbohydrates are an extremely diverse group of substances. Simple sugars are the first products of the photosynthetic process in plants. Plants trap energy from sunlight using the green pigment called chlorophyll and use it to produce sugars from carbon dioxide and water. In this way plants are the ultimate source of all our food. Sugars may be more or less sweet. Generally the more complex carbohydrates lack a sweet flavour. The number in the chart below under 'sweetness' for simple sugars compares the relative sweetening power of a sugar to sucrose. Values greater than 100 are sweeter and values less than 100 are less sweet than an equal weight of sugar. Some substances are considerably sweeter than sugar. For example saccharin would have a value of 3000. This means that 1 g of saccharin has the sweetening power of 300 g of sucrose.

Fructose and glucose are monosaccharides. Sucrose, maltose and lactose are disaccharides.

Complex carbohydrates are composed of long chains of sugars up to 1000 units in length.

Sugars in cooking

The first concentrated sweetener was honey. Bees produce honey from nectar (a

SIMPLE CARBOHYDRATES FOUND IN FOOD

NAME	SIMPLE SUGARS SWEETNESS	OCCURRENCE IN FOODS
fructose (fruit sugar)	170	fruits, jams, honey
sucrose (table sugar)	100	many foods
glucose (blood sugar)	70	grapes, honeys, jams
lactose (milk sugar)	40	milk, milk products
maltose (malt sugar)	30	malt, glucose syrup

COMPLEX CARBOHYDRATES FOUND IN FOOD

NAME	OCCURRENCE IN FOODS
starch	flours, potatoes, corn
inulin	Jerusalem artichokes
cellulose	vegetables, whole grain cereals
pectin	fruits, jams

weak solution of sucrose produced by flowers). The bees use an enzyme in their saliva to break down the sucrose into fructose and glucose, and concentrate the nectar by evaporating some of the water. Honeys can contain small amounts of other substances found in the nectar from some plants which can be poisonous. Honey is used as a flavouring agent, sweetener and as a humectant (water-holding property). Products which contain honey stay moist longer than those made with sugar.

Sugar is also used for volume as it gives bulk to baked goods, ice-creams, jams and confectionery. It assists in the leavening of some cakes by assisting the incorporation of air. Air is incorporated into cake-making during the creaming process by the physical action of the sugar crystals dragging pockets of air into the fat. The size of crystals affects the properties of the sugar. If the crystals are too large, few pockets of air will be incorporated. If too fine the sugar will dissolve rather than remain in discrete crystals. Sugar is also necessary for the action of pectin for the setting of jams and preserves.

Sugar can contribute to the colour of cooked food products by caramelisation or through the Maillard reaction. Both processes require high temperatures. The Maillard reaction requires the presence of sugar and protein. Both react together at relatively low temperatures, but this is only significant at above 149°C (300°F). The high temperatures required for both these reactions to occur explain why steamed foods are often blander than roasted foods. The Maillard reaction is responsible for colour and flavour in foods such as roasted meats, nuts, coffee beans, bread crusts, etc. Lactose is more likely to participate in the Maillard reaction than some other sugars. Lactose and protein are found in milk. Thus bread brushed with milk before baking will have an attractive brown crust on removal from the oven.

The viscosity of many liquids is affected by sugar.

Complex carbohydrates

These are important in product development because they have a major influence on the texture of foods.

STARCH (Figure 6.4)

Starch is found in foods that come from plants. It consists of long straight or branched chains of glucose molecules. The plant makes starch as a means of storing glucose. Starch is found in seeds, roots and tubers and stored in the form of granules or grains. The starch granules from different sources show characteristic sizes and shapes. Starch molecules in the granules are of two types. One is a long chain of glucose units called *amylose*, accounting for 20–30% of the starch. The rest is a branched molecule shaped rather like a bush called *amylopectin*.

Wheat starch ×125   Oat starch ×125   Potato starch ×125

Fig. 6.4   Types of starches

When starch granules are mixed with cold water, they will only absorb water and swell to a limited extent. The water cannot penetrate between the strongly attached starch chains. As the water is heated, the molecules of water move more rapidly, and thus begin to penetrate the starch grains; the water causes the grain to swell. As swelling occurs the mixture thickens. Some of the starch molecules burst out from the granule and form a tangled mass that contributes to the thickening process known as gelatinisation.

The temperature at which gelatinisation occurs depends upon the type of starch used and generally varies from 60°C (140°F) for potato starch, 83°C (181.4°F) for corn starch. As a rule large starch granules gelatinise at lower temperatures than small starch granules.

Starch grains must be separated before any heat is applied. The chef is able to do this in three ways.

- disperse the starch in cold liquid;
- mix the starch grains with sugar;
- coat the grains with solid or melted fat as in the making of a roux.

The thickening capacity of starches depends on the following facts.

- The type of starch used is important. Arrowroot has a greater thickening capacity than corn or potato starch. High amylose starches have better thickening properties because of the long chain-like molecules which are more likely to become tangled than the compact amylopectin molecules.
- Thickening properties are changed by heat treatment. For example, the browning of flour in the oven has less thickening power because of the chemical changes caused by using this method of heating.
- Sugar decreases the thickness of starch-thickened fillings. The effect of sugar is related to its water-attracting ability; available water is reduced and this allows the starch granules to swell.
- Acid reduces the thickening power of starch. The acid breaks down the starch chains. This breakdown occurs faster if the reaction takes place at high temperature. Therefore any acid required for flavour should be added at the end of gelatinisation to minimise the acid hydrolysis of the starch.

COMPLEX CARBOHYDRATES IN PLANT CELL WALLS

Pectin, cellulose, hemicellulose are found in plants. Cellulose and hemicellulose form the rigid walls around each cell. Pectin is found between the cell walls and acts as a glue-like substance which holds the cells together. All three substances contribute to the fibre in our diets. Rigid cellulose in the cell walls provides much of the crunchiness in vegetables. Cellulose is not water-soluble and is not affected much by cooking. Pectins, however, can be particularly dissolved by hot water. This is exactly what happens when vegetables are cooked and accounts for the softer texture of cooked vegetables and fruit.

Hemicellulose will dissolve in the presence of alkali. Vegetables cooked in the presence of carbonate of soda lose their structure and will become mushy if cooking is continued.

Pectins are used to set jams and jellies and are in flan gel and commercial dessert mixes. Fruits can be divided into high pectin and low pectin types. The low pectin types require the addition of pectin or may be mixed with a high pectin fruit to allow gelling. Pectins are long chains of sugars, which form a network trapping water to form the gel.

A firm gel depends on:

- percentage of pectin;
- molecular weight of the pectin;
- percentage of methyl ester groups;
- amount of sugar;
- pH of the mix.

Most gels are made with about 65% sugar; in excess of this crystallisation will occur on the surface.

Most pectin products will not form gels until the pH is lowered to about 3.5. The firmness of the gelling increases as the pH is lowered. A pH lower than the optimum will cause a weak gel and water separating (syneresis).

TYPES OF PECTIN USED TO DEVELOP FOOD PRODUCTS

- *Rapid-set pectins*: degree of methyl group 70%, forming gels with acid and sugar; optimum pH is 3.5; starts to gel on cooling to 88°C (190.4°F).
- *Slow-set pectins*: degree of methyl groups 50–70%, gels with sugar and acid; pH 2.8–3.2; starts to gel at 54°C (129°F).
- *Low methoxyl pectins*: degree of methyl ester groups <30%; these do not form gels with acid and sugar but will gel in the presence of calcium ions or other polyvalent ions (milk).

Pectin is added to natural juice products to give a permanent cloudiness. Pectin is used as a stabiliser in ice-cream products to prevent large crystals forming. It may also be used in mayonnaise as an emulsifying agent.

LIPIDS

Lipids include fats, oils, cholesterol and certain emulsifying agents known as phospholipids. An example is lecithin found in egg yolk. An important feature of these materials is that they are 'hydrophobic' or repel water.

Lipids are important in food production. They contribute to the eating quality of cakes, pastries, biscuits; they affect the texture of yeast products by separating the gluten layers and, in pastry making, by shortening the gluten strands.

Lipids in culinary work

- Cooking medium – provides heat transfer; used as a lubricant.
- Texture – gives goods a 'shorter texture'; provides smooth mouth feel; aids aeration; aids moistness; provides volume in bread.
- Emulsification – emulsifies sauces, ice-creams, etc.
- Flavour – provides a flavouring agent (butter, olive oil, peanut oil); acts as a solvent for some flavour components of foods.

Lipid structure

In order to use lipids effectively in food production we must know something about their behaviour, or their molecular structure. Fats and oils are triglycerides, meaning they are comprised of three molecules of fatty acids, bonded to one molecule of glycerol.

$$\text{glycerol} \left\{ \begin{array}{l} \text{fatty acid} - 1 \\ \text{fatty acid} - 2 \\ \text{fatty acid} - 3 \end{array} \right.$$

The way fats and oils behave is affected by the nature of the fatty acid. The fatty acids consist of chains of carbon atoms that vary in length from 4 to about 20 carbon atoms. Molecules with short-chain fatty acids will have a lower melting point than those with long-chain fatty acids. These fatty acids may also be divided up into saturated and unsaturated groups. All fats contain a mixture of saturated and unsaturated fatty acids. The difference between a saturated fat and an unsaturated fat is based on their individual chemistry. The chains of carbon atoms that make up fatty acids may be joined together with what is known as a 'single bond' or with a double bond.

$$\cdots - \overset{\displaystyle \overset{H}{|}}{\underset{\displaystyle \underset{H}{|}}{C}} - \overset{\displaystyle \overset{H}{|}}{\underset{\displaystyle \underset{H}{|}}{C}} - \overset{\displaystyle \overset{H}{|}}{\underset{\displaystyle \underset{H}{|}}{C}} - \overset{\displaystyle \overset{H}{|}}{\underset{\displaystyle \underset{H}{|}}{C}} - \cdots$$

Single bond

$$\overset{\displaystyle \overset{H}{|}}{\underset{\displaystyle \underset{H}{|}}{C}} - \overset{\displaystyle \overset{H}{|}}{\underset{\displaystyle \underset{H}{|}}{C}} - \overset{\displaystyle }{\underset{\displaystyle \underset{H}{|}}{C}} = \overset{\displaystyle }{\underset{\displaystyle \underset{H}{|}}{C}} - \overset{\displaystyle \overset{H}{|}}{C}$$

Double bond

If the fatty acid contains no double bonds it is called a saturated fatty acid. If it contains one double bond it is monounsaturated and if there is more than one double bond it is called polyunsaturated.

The saturated fatty acids are found in animal fats and in a few oils from tropical plants such as palm oil and coconut oil. Olive oil is mostly monounsaturated, while sunflower, corn and peanut oils and margarine made from these oils are highly unsaturated.

Types of fatty acids

- Never in fats
  - Formic methanoic
  - Acetic ethanoic
  - Propionic
- Only found in butter
  - Butyric
  - Caproic
  - Caprillic
- Most common
  - Capric
  - Lauric
  - Myristic
  - Palmitic
  - Stearic

SOURCES OF FATTY ACID TYPES

TYPE OF FATTY ACID	NUMBER OF DOUBLE BONDS	WHERE FOUND
saturated	0	palm oil coconut oil butter beef fat mutton fat lard
monounsaturated	I	olive oil peanut oil lard
polyunsaturated	2 or more	corn oil soya bean oil sunflower oil walnut oil

Important facts in the chemistry of fats

- Most fats contain at least five different sorts of fatty acids in their make-up.
- The number of triglycerides is large.
- Oleic acid is the most important of all the fatty acids occurring in fats. Often it is more than 50% of the total fatty acids in a fat and it is always present in a fat.
- If a particular saturated acid is present, then it very often happens that the acids immediately above and below it in the fatty acid series also occur.

Spoilage of fats and oils

Fats require care to maintain quality. They may deteriorate because of:

- odours: many compounds that have a strong aroma can dissolve in fats; if fats are stored in an open container they are able to absorb these odours.
- rancidity (see table, page 246): this is caused by the presence of free fatty acids which have an unpleasant smell; for example, butyric acid accounts for the smell of rancid butter; caproic acid has a very strong smell; rancid fats are able to impart their smell to any foods they are used in or are cooked in.

One way that rancidity develops is when some of the fat molecules are split by a reaction with water that releases fatty acids and glycerol. The action involves an enzyme and is called hydrolysis.

Oxidation will also cause rancidity. This involves the reaction of unsaturated fatty acids with oxygen to release small fatty acids and other molecules that affect the flavour and aroma. The development of rancidity by hydrolysis or oxidation occurs faster under certain conditions.

Other factors can slow down the development of fat oxidation. These are known as antioxidants. They can be naturally occurring or artificial. Examples include vitamin E, ascorbic acid, and certain herbs such as sage and rosemary. Artificial antioxidants include butylated hydroxyanisole (BHA) and butylated hydroxytoluene (BHT). These are added to many commercial fats. Antioxidants only slow the development of rancidity in fats. They cannot prevent it totally.

FACTORS AFFECTING THE DEVELOPMENT OF RANCIDITY IN FATS

FACTOR	EFFECT
water	necessary for development of rancidity by hydrolysis
heat	speeds up most chemical reactions including development of rancidity
lipases (enzymes which split fats)	present in certain foods and can cause rancidity
metal ions (iron)	speeds up development of rancidity in fats, e.g. cast iron pans
light	speeds up oxidation
salt food particles	speeds up development of rancidity

EMULSIONS

The hydrophobic nature of fats and oils presents problems when developing recipes in attempting to make a stable dispersion of an oil and water. Emulsifiers stabilise dispersion of the immiscible liquids. The stable dispersion is called an emulsion. Emulsifiers can be proteins, plant gums or resins, starch, or very small particles such as ground mustard. Thus mustard added to a vinaigrette acts as an emulsifying agent as well as a flavouring agent.

The type of emulsion formed by an oil-water system depends upon a number of factors:

- the composition of the oil and water phases;
- the chemical nature of the emulsifying agent;
- the proportions of the oil and water present.

If the polar group of an emulsifier is more effectively adsorbed than the non-polar group, adsorption by the water is greater than by the oil. The extent of adsorption at a liquid surface depends upon the surface area of liquid available, and increased adsorption of emulsifier by water is favoured by the oil–water interface becoming convex towards the water, thus giving an oil–water emulsion.

The relative proportions of oil and water also help to determine which type of emulsion forms. If more oil than water is present, the water tends to form droplets and a water–oil emulsion is formed. If more water than oil is present an oil–water emulsion is favoured.

Artificial emulsifiers are added during the preparation of many emulsions. An example is GMS (glyceryl monostearate). GMS is a monoglyceride which is formed when one hydroxyl group of glycerol is esterified with stearic acid.

For example:

$$CH_2OH \qquad\qquad CH_2OH$$
$$|\qquad\qquad\qquad\qquad |$$
$$CHOH + CH_3(CH_2)_{16}COOH \rightarrow \quad CHOH + H_2O$$
$$|\qquad\qquad\qquad\qquad |$$
$$CH_2OH \qquad\qquad CH_2O — CO(CH_2)_{16}CH_3$$

hydrophobic portion
of glyceryl monostearate

One part of the GMS molecule is hydrophilic because it contains hydroxyl groups and the rest of the molecule, as indicated, is hydrophobic. When GMS is added to a water–oil emulsion the hydrophilic parts of the molecules are absorbed into the surface of the water droplets and the lipophilic parts are absorbed into the surface of the oil round drops as shown in Figure 6.5, page 252.

Lecithin is the phospholipid emulsifier found in egg yolk and is also extracted from vegetable oils. The structure of lecithin is a triglyceride of two fatty acids and phosphoric acid.

Lecithin

$$CH_2OCOR^1$$
$$|$$
$$CHOCOR^2$$
$$|$$
$$CH_2O\ POR^3$$

R^1 and $R^2 =$ long chain hydrophobic groups
+
$R^3 = CH_2CH_2CH_2H(CH_3)_3$

hydrophilic group

In many recipes, stabilisers are added to products in addition to emulsifiers. Stabilizers are proteins, carbohydrates, starches, gums. Their function is to hold the emulsion together once it has been formed. Such substances improve the stability of emulsions mainly by increasing their viscosity. Viscosity increases, the freedom of movement of the dispersed droplets of the emulsion is reduced, and this lessens the chance of their coming into contact and coalescing.

If you add oil or butter when making hollandaise or mayonnaise, the sauce may curdle because the lecithin has had insufficient time to coat the droplets. This can be rectified by adding the broken sauce to more egg yolks.

The most important characteristic of emulsions is that they require energy for their formation.

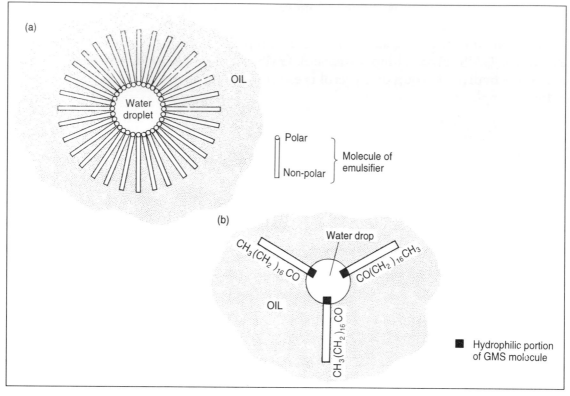

Fig. 6.5 Molecules of emulsifier absorbed at a water–oil interface forming a complete protective film around a water droplet

SENSORY EVALUATION OF FOOD

The most important thing to remember when applying chemistry to food products is that the food must ultimately give pleasure to the consumer. This is dependent on appearance, flavour, smell and texture. These are assessed by our senses. Scientists use complex and expensive equipment to measure the factors in food that determine the taste, aroma or tenderness. The process is based on objective assessment and is vital in product development.

When referring to our senses we are concerned with vision, hearing, smell, touch and taste. Some scientists add three more: temperature, pain and balance. Except for balance, all these senses are used to relay messages about the food.

Taste and smell are the most important chemical receptors and are often used with the most expensive equipment found in food laboratories. Vision and smell operate at a distance, meaning that the individual does not have to come into contact with the food to use these senses.

Examples of the messages that a sense tells us about food.

- Vision
  - colour
  - size

- shape
- freshness
- maturity
- quality
- Smell
  - freshness
  - ripeness
  - character
  - identification
- Hearing
  - sizzling related to temperature
  - texture, crispness, crunchiness
- Touch
  - texture
  - consistency
  - ripeness
  - mouth-feel
- Taste
  - salt
  - sweet
  - sour
  - bitter
- Temperature
  - hot/cold
  - chilled
- Pain
  - chilli pepper

When we eat and enjoy food the messages we receive by our senses are harmonious and from a much more complicated picture than that gained by one sense on its own. Flavour is a combination of smell, taste and mouth-feel. If any one of these components is missing, for example smell when we have a cold, the overall impact is changed.

Cooking and processing food is the use of chemical technology to create a harmonious product using colour, smell, taste, texture and mouth-feel. A knowledge of basic food ingredients and their chemistry will help the chef both develop new recipes, dishes and give him/her a knowledge of how to correct dishes when things go wrong.

Vision

Colour has an effect on the eye appeal, having an overall effect on the presentation of the food. The colour of food is extremely important to our enjoyment of it. People are sensitive to the colour of the food they eat and will reject food that is not considered to have the accepted colour. For example, strawberries that have been preserved in sulphite lose all their natural colour and appear white. If strawberries are to be canned or used in jam, artificial colour must be added before they are considered acceptable to eat. Colour is added to a wide range of food products to enhance attractiveness.

There is a strong link between the colour and the flavour of food. An ability to detect flavour of food is very much connected with its colour and if the colour is unusual our sense of taste is confused. For example, if a fruit jelly is red, it is likely that the flavour detected will be that of a red coloured fruit such as a strawberry even if the true flavour is lemon or banana.

The depth of colour in food also affects our sense of taste. We associate strong colours with strong flavour. For example, if a series of jellies all contain the same amount of given flavour, but are of different shades of the same colour, then those having a stronger colour will appear also to have a stronger flavour.

Smell

Smell is a chemical sense that acts over a distance. Chemicals are detected by their volatile compounds, this means that they must evaporate and become airborne easily. Smell receptors are located in the back of the nasal cavity known as the olfactory area (Figure 6.6, opposite).

The air is able to reach the olfactory area through both the nose and the mouth. Many of the characteristics are associated as flavours actually are related to smell rather than taste. When we eat food, the volatile components evaporate and reach the olfactory area through the back of the throat that connects the mouth and nasal cavity. When we have a cold, the membranes of the nasal cavity swell and prevent access to the area containing the smell receptors. We say we cannot taste when we mean we actually cannot smell the food.

The sense of smell is very sensitive, it may be divided into the following basic types:

- pungent;
- putrid;
- camphoric;
- musky;
- floral;
- peppermint;
- ethereal.

Taste (refer also to page 28)

Taste is another chemical sense, but unlike smell it does not work at a distance. The messages we receive from taste are simpler than those of smell. There are four basic tastes: salt, sweet, sour and bitter; metallic and soapy tastes may also be included.

Taste buds are located on the tongue. Babies and children have more taste buds than adults, the number decreases with age.

For a substance to give a sensation of taste it must be soluble in water. When we eat food, some of it dissolves in saliva which contributes to the taste sensation we experience.

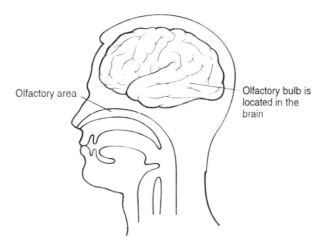

Fig. 6.6   The olfactory area

EXAMPLES OF TYPES OF TASTE

TASTE	EXAMPLE
sweet	sugar, saccharin, aspartame, cyclamates
salt	sodium chloride
bitter	alkaloids (in caffeine)
sour	acids, vinegar, lemon juice
metallic	potassium chloride found in some salt substitutes
soapy	after-taste in baking powder goods

Our reactions to taste differ considerably. Many taste preferences are learnt in childhood. We generally are much more sensitive to bitter than to any other tastes, meaning we are able to taste smaller amounts of bitter substances than of sweet, salty or sour substances.

Taste is affected by several factors. Flavour enhancers, for example MSG (monosodium glutamate), increase the intensity of both salt and bitter tastes and of 'meatiness'.

The temperature of food also affects the way we perceive taste. We are most sensitive to taste when the food is between 22° and 41°C (71.6–105.8°F). Temperatures above and below this range decrease the sensitivity of the taste buds.

EXAMPLES OF TEXTURES ENCOUNTERED IN FOOD

FOOD	TEXTURE	FOOD	TEXTURE
cheese	solid	sauces	thick
	elastic		thin
	crumbly		lumpy
	creamy	vegetables	crisp
	melted		crunchy
	liquid		soft
	viscous	soups	thick
			thin
			lumpy

Touch

Touch referring to sensory evaluation is mouth-feel, the way food feels in the mouth. Mouth-feel is very important when we assess or develop food products, recipes and dishes. Mouth-feel adds to the food acceptability. Texture is a message we receive from mouth-feel. This includes consistency, chewiness, brittleness, crunchiness, astringency, etc. These sensations add greatly to our enjoyment of food.

7

Menu planning

A menu, or bill of fare, is a means of communication, informing the customer what the caterer has to offer. The compiling of a menu is one of the caterer's most important jobs – whether for establishments such as restaurants aiming to make a profit, or for those working to a budget, such as hospitals and schools.

The function of a menu is twofold. It informs:

- the catering staff of what is to be prepared;
- the customer or consumer of what is available.

The staff need to know in advance what is to be ordered, prepared and served; the customer or consumer needs to know what the food is, how it is cooked and, where appropriate, how much it will cost. The information needs to be clearly stated and set out in courses so that the menu is easily understood.

The content of the menu creates an image which reflects the overall style of the restaurant. The printed menu should match the decor of the restaurant and be attractive and well laid-out, as it helps to promote sales, especially if dishes are described in an appetising way. Some caterers see the menu as a means of marketing, particularly when photographs are used of 'specials' or dishes of the day, or to advertise speciality evenings, etc.

Traditional cookery methods and recipes form a sound foundation of knowledge for the craftsman and the caterer. However, it should be remembered that fashions in food change and customers look for new dishes, different combinations of food and fresh ideas on menus. This does not mean that the wide range of popular dishes of the past should be ignored as some of the most successful menus contain a sensible balance of traditional and contemporary dishes.

Students should be both aware of changes in contemporary cooking and prepared to experiment and create new and original recipes so that the caterer can continue to offer the customer fresh interest, variety and pleasure in his or her menus.

It is necessary to make certain that terms are accurately expressed so that the customer receives exactly what is stated on the menu; otherwise it may mean that the *Trade Descriptions Act* is being contravened. In the words of the act: 'Any person who in the course of a trade or business: applies a false trade description to any goods or supplies or offers to supply any goods to which a false trade description is applied shall be guilty of an offence.'

For example, 'Pâté maison' should really be home-made pâté, not factory made. If fried fillets of sole are offered on the menu, then more than one must be offered, and the fish must be sole; and if a 250 g (8 oz) rump steak is given as the portion on the menu, then it must be 250 g (8 oz) raw weight.

If the sole is advertised as 'fried' and the steak as 'grilled' then these processes of cooking should be undertaken; if the soles are named as Dover soles and the steak as rump steak then this is what must be served. Likewise, if the sole is stated to be served with a sauce tartare and the steak with a béarnaise sauce then the sauces should be correctly and accurately made.

The description on the menu should give an indication, as appropriate, of the quality, size, preparation and composition of the dish.

In some types of establishments it may be good practice to offer certain dishes (pasta, steak) in varying sizes of portions.

TYPES OF MENUS

It must be clearly understood that there are several kinds of menus:

- Table d'hôte or set-price menu – a menu forming a meal of two or three courses at a set price. A choice of dishes may be offered at all courses; the choice and number of courses will usually be limited to two, three or four.
- À la carte – a menu with all the dishes individually priced. The customers can therefore compile their own menu, which may be one, two or more courses. A true à la carte dish should be cooked to order and the customer should be prepared to wait for this service.
- Special party or function menus – menus for banquets or functions of all kinds. As all the guests start the meal at the same time it is generally unsuitable to place items such as steak or soufflé on the menu for large numbers. Care needs to be taken with seasonable foods to ensure they will be available if the menu is printed well in advance thus avoiding difficulty and embarrassment.
- Ethnic or speciality menus – these can be set price or dishes individually priced specialising in the food (or religion) of the country or in a specialised food itself: ethnic – Chinese, Indian, kosher, African Caribbean, Greek; speciality – steak, fish, pasta, vegetarian, pancakes. The kitchen staff must know how to obtain and use the ingredients, and important in this respect is the ambience of the restaurant reflecting the menu.
- Hospital menus – these usually take the form of a menu card given to the patient the day before service so that his or her preferences can be ticked. Both National Health Service and private hospitals cater for vegetarians and also for religious requirements. In many cases a dietician is involved with menu compilation to ensure nothing is given to the patients that would be detrimental to their health. Usually hospital meals are of two or three courses.
- Menus for people at work – menus which are served to people at their place of work. Such menus vary in standard and extent from one employer to another due to company policy on the welfare of their staff and work-force. Progressive companies ensure that their employees are well looked after; some may charge for meals and some ask for a token sum and offer meals at a subsidised rate. A

number of staff restaurants charge a price that covers the cost of food and labour with all other charges being subsidised. In most of these places, whether or not it is a factory canteen or head office staff restaurant, the menu often offers at least a two or three course meal with a selection of items – a table d'hôte style menu. There may also be a call-order à la carte selection charged at a higher price. The food will usually be mainly British with some ethnic dishes and vegetarian dishes.

Menus may consist of soup, main course with vegetables, followed by sweets, cheese and yogurts. According to the policy of the management and employee requirements, there will very often be a salad bar and healthy eating dishes included on the menu. When there is a captive clientele who face the same surroundings daily and meet the same people, then no matter how long the menu cycle or how pleasant the people, or how nice the decor, boredom is bound to set in and staff then long for a change of scene. So, a chef or manager needs to vary the menu constantly to encourage customers to patronise the establishment rather than going off the premises to eat. The decor and layout of the staff restaurant plays a very important part in satisfying the customer's needs. The facilities should be relaxing and comfortable so that he or she feels that the restaurant is not a continuation of the work-place. Employees who are happy, well-nourished and know that the company has their interests and welfare at heart will tend to be well-motivated and work better. (See menu examples at the end of this chapter.)

- Menus for children – in schools there is an emphasis on healthy eating and a balanced diet particularly in boarding schools. Those areas with children of various cultural and religious backgrounds have appropriate items available on the menu. Many establishments provide special children's menus which concentrate on favourite foods and offer suitably sized portions. (See Plates 98 and 99, page 257.)

Cyclical menus

These are menus which are compiled to cover a given period of time: one month, three months, etc. They consist of a number of set menus for a particular establishment, such as an industrial catering restaurant, cafeteria, canteen, director's dining-room, hospital or college refectory. At the end of each period the menus can be used again thus overcoming the need to keep compiling new ones. The length of the cycle is determined by management policy, by the time of the year and by different foods available. These menus must be monitored carefully to take account of changes in customer requirements and any variations in weather conditions which are likely to affect demand for certain dishes. If cyclical menus are designed to remain in operation for long periods of time, then they must be carefully compiled so that they do not have to be changed too drastically during operation.

ADVANTAGES OF CYCLICAL MENUS
- They save time by removing the daily or weekly task of compiling menus, although they may require slight alterations for the next period.

- When used in association with cook/freeze operations, it is possible to produce the entire number of portions of each item to last the whole cycle, having determined that the standardised recipes are correct.
- They give greater efficiency in time and labour.
- They can cut down on the number of commodities held in stock, and can assist in planning storage requirements.

DISADVANTAGES
- When used in establishments with a captive clientele, then the cycle has to be long enough so that customers do not get bored with the repetition of dishes.
- The caterer cannot easily take advantage of 'good buys' offered by suppliers on a daily or weekly basis unless such items are required for the cyclical menu.

Preplanned and predesigned menus

ADVANTAGES
- Preplanned or predesigned menus enable the caterer to ensure that good menu planning is practised.
- Before selecting dishes that he or she prefers, the caterer should consider what the customer likes, and the effect of these dishes upon the meal as a whole.
- Menus which are planned and costed in advance allow banqueting managers to quote prices instantly to a customer.
- Menus can be planned taking into account the availability of kitchen and service equipment, without placing unnecessary strain upon such equipment.
- The quality of food is likely to be higher if kitchen staff are preparing dishes that they are familiar with and have prepared a number of times before.

DISADVANTAGES
- Preplanned and predesigned menus may be too limited to appeal to a wide range of customers.
- They may reduce job satisfaction for staff who have to prepare the same menus repetitively.
- They may limit the chef's creativity and originality.

STRUCTURE OF MENUS

- **Length** There is no relationship between the length and quality of a menu. If the menu is too short the customer may be disappointed at having insufficient choice; if the menu is too long it may consist of a large number of dishes of mediocre quality. In general, it is better to offer fewer dishes of a good standard and aim to give the customer what he or she wants (always remembering it is the customer who pays the bill).
- **Design** The design of the printed menu should complement the image, atmosphere and decor of the restaurant or dining room. The management policy on the frequency of menu change determines the design, and can give the appearance of daily change. It must be remembered that design should not

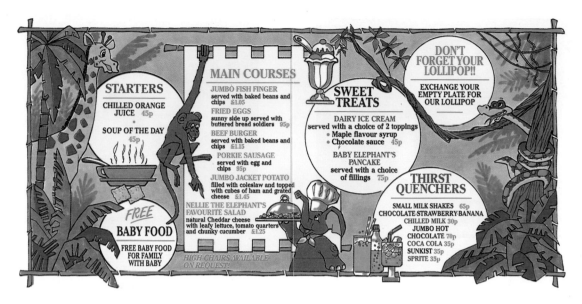

Plate 98   Children's menu

Plate 99   Children's menu

Plate 100   A selection of gâteaux

Plate 101   A selection of pastries

AFTERNOON TEA	MORNING COFFEE	
Served at 3.00 and 4.30 pm daily	Served from 9.00 to 2.30 pm	
Smoked Salmon	Selected Pastries	2.75
Egg Mayonnaise with	Warm Croissant served with	
Mustard and Cress	Selected Preserves	2.75
Cucumber and Anchovy	Homemade Biscuits	1.50
Smoked Turkey and Sweet Mustard		
Cottage Cheese with	Coffee	1.60
Carrot and Hazelnuts	Expresso	1.60
	Capuccino	1.60
Scone with Strawberry Preserve	De-Caffeinated	1.60
and thick Cream		
and	Selected Teas	1.60
A choice of Pastries		
or	Sandwich menu is	
Cream Cake	available during the	
	Luncheon hour	
Indian Tea		
Earl Grey		
Camomile Herbal Tea		
£10.50		

All our prices are inclusive of 15% Service Charge and 15% VAT   01/89

Plate 102   The Ritz Palm Court Menu

Plate 103   Service of scones with clotted cream and jam

Plate 104   A selection of petit fours

dominate practicality. A poor design, however, can be detrimental to the product and the image of the establishment.

- **Language** It is important to be accurate when describing dishes so that the customer can identify the dish. Over-elaboration should be avoided as it may cause disappointment. If we believe that menus are means of communication then we should use the language which is easily understood, that is, English. As the majority of customers are English-speaking then it seems logical that caterers should be encouraged to use the national language. As an example, 'Poulet sauté chasseur' or 'Sautéd chicken Hunter style' is less informative to the customer than 'Chicken pieces fried and served in a white wine, mushroom, tomato and tarragon-flavoured sauce'.

- **Presentation** The way the menu is presented to the customer will often determine initial reaction to it, whether it is on the wall before entering a staff dining room, handed to a patient in a hospital bed or presented by a waiter or waitress. An off-hand, brusque presentation (either written or oral) can be off-putting and can lower expectations of the meal.

ESSENTIAL CONSIDERATIONS PRIOR TO PLANNING THE MENU

- The location of an establishment should allow easy access for both customers and suppliers as and when required. A difficult journey can be off-putting no matter how good the quality of food on offer and can affect repeat business and profitability. If the establishment is in an area noted for regional speciality foods or dishes, the inclusion of a selection of these on the menu can give extra menu appeal.
- You should be aware of any competition in the locality, including their prices and, particularly, their quality. As a result, it may be wiser to produce a menu quite different to those of nearby establishments.
- Make sure your particular establishment is suitable to a particular area – a self-service restaurant situation in an affluent residential district, or a very expensive sea-food restaurant in a run down inner-city area may not be very successful.
- Anticipate and analyse the type of people you are planning to cater for – it may be sensible to create a menu to satisfy, for example, office workers in the city, with a fast lunch service. Also opportunities may exist for outdoor catering.
- The spending power of the customer is a most important consideration. This is particularly important when catering for the needs of nurses in hospitals, children in schools and workers in industry and in offices. Whatever level of catering or type of establishment, a golden rule should be to offer 'value for money'.
- It is the customer not the caterer who selects his or her menu, so analysis of dish popularity is necessary, and those dishes which are not popular should not stay on the menu. Dish sales can be recorded by computer. Customer demand must be considered, and traditional dishes and modern trends in food fashions need to be taken into account.

- It is essential to determine the range of dishes, and whether table d'hôte or à la carte menus are to be offered. Decisions regarding the range of prices have to be made. A table d'hôte menu may be considered with an extra charge or supplement for more expensive dishes, or more than one table d'hôte menu of different prices may be more suitable.
- If space is limited, or there are many customers (and control of the time the customer occupies the seat is needed) then the menu can be adjusted to increase turnover: more self-service items, separate service for coffee, for example.
- Space and equipment in kitchen will influence the composition of the menu and production of dishes. The menu-writer must be aware of any shortcomings or deficiencies in equipment and may be wary of offering dishes that are difficult to produce. Also, certain items of equipment should not be overloaded by the menu requirements (salamander, steamers, fritures).
- The availability and capability of both the preparation and service staff labour must be considered when planning a menu. Enough able and willing staff, both in the kitchen and the restaurant, are necessary to achieve customer satisfaction with any menu.
- Menu planning is dependent on availability of supplies, that is frequency of deliveries of the required amounts. Storage space and seasonal availability of foods need to be taken into account when planning menus.
- Cost factor is a crucial factor when an establishment is run for profit; but, even when working to a budget, the menu is no less crucial. Costing is the crux of the success of compiling any menu. By using computer techniques, costs can be analysed daily.

PLANNING THE MENU

Various factors must be taken into account:

- Type of establishment – there will be considerable variation, for example, in menus for five star hotels and restaurants, school meals, heavy manual workers' canteens or hospitals.
- Type of customer – especially for private parties, for a 21st birthday party, senior citizens' conference, football players after an international, visiting overseas students on a mayor's banquet; all need personal consideration.
- Religious rules if applicable (kosher catering or a Muslim occasion) – lack of knowledge or understanding can easily lead to innocently giving offence.
- Meat or non-meat preferences – the number of non-meat eaters is steadily increasing so this becomes more important.
- Time of the year:
  - the prevailing temperature should be considered as certain dishes suitable for cold weather may not be acceptable in mid-summer;
  - foods in season are usually in good supply and more reasonable in price;
  - special dishes on certain days (Shrove Tuesday, Christmas, Hogmanay).

- Time of day – breakfast, brunch, lunch, tea, high tea, dinner, supper, snack or special function.
- Price range – unless fair prices are charged (so that customers are satisfied that they have received good value for money) repeat business may not occur and the caterer may go out of business.
- Number of courses – varies according to all prior considerations.
- Correct sequence of courses – important if the menu is to achieve a good balance.
- Appropriate language – always use language customers can understand.
- No repetition of wines – if using wine in the cooking of more than one course, ensure that a different type is used.
- Sensible nutritional balance – if a selection of dishes with varying nutritional contents are offered then customers can make their own choices.
- No repetition of commodities – never repeat basic ingredients such as mushrooms, tomatoes, peas, bacon, on one menu; if a basic ingredient is used in one course it should not reappear in any other course on the same menu.
- No repetition of flavours – if using strong seasoning like onion, garlic or herbs such as thyme, sage or bay leaf, do not repeat in more than one course.
- No repetition of colours – colour of food is important to give appetite appeal, but avoid repetition of colour, e.g.:

Celery soup	Tomato soup
Fricassée of chicken	Goulash of veal
Buttered turnips, creamed potatoes	Vichy carrots, Marquise potatoes
Meringue and vanilla ice-cream	Peach Melba

- Texture of courses – ensure variation is given (food should not be all soft or all crisp, but balanced).
- Sauces – if different sauces are served on one menu, the foundation ingredient of each sauce should vary, for example, reduced stock, demi-glace, velouté, cream, butter thickened, yogurt, quark.

Menu policy – summary

- Provide a means of communication.
- Establish the essential and social needs of the customer.
- Accurately predict what the customer is likely to buy and how much he or she is going to spend.
- Purchase and prepare raw materials to preset standards in accordance with predictions and purchasing specifications.
- Skilfully portion and cost the product in order to keep within company profitability policy.
- Effectively control the complete operation from purchase to service on the plate.
- Customer satisfaction is all-important: remember who pays the bill.

MENU COPY

Items or groups of items should bear names people recognise and understand. If a name does not give the right description, additional copy may be necessary. Descriptions can be produced carefully, helping to promote the dish and the menu. However, the description should describe the item realistically and not mislead the customer. Interesting descriptive copy is a skill; a good menu designer is able to illuminate menu terms, specific culinary terms and in doing so is able to draw attention to them. Simplicity creates better understanding and endorses the communication process.

Some menus can be built around a general descriptive copy featuring the history of the establishment or around the local area in which the establishment is located. Descriptive copy can alternatively be based on a speciality dish which has significant cultural importance to the area or the establishment. In doing so the description may wish to feature the person responsible for creating and preparing the dish, especially if the chef is reasonably well known and has appeared on national or local television or radio. The chef may have also had his/her recipes featured in the local press. This too may be included in the menu to further create interest.

Menu copy should be set in a style of print which is easily legible and well spaced. Mixing type face is often done to achieve emphasis; if overdone the overall concept is likely to look a mess and therefore unattractive to the eye.

Emphasis may be easily achieved by using boxes on the menu. Also menu paper and colour of the print can be carefully chosen to make certain dishes stand out.

Some mistakes in menu copy are as follows:

- Descriptive copy is left out when it is required.
- The wrong emphasis is given.
- Emphasis is lost because print size and style are not correctly used.
- The menu lacks creativity.
- The menu is designed for the wrong market.
- Much needed information is omitted.
- Pricing is unclear.
- Menu sequence is wrong.
- Customers do not see valuable copy because added sheets such as 'dish of the day' or 'today's specials' cover up other parts of the menu or cover up essential information.

Menu cover

The cover of the menu should reflect the identity or the decor of the operation and should ideally pick up the theme of the restaurant. A theme can be effective in creating the right image of the restaurant. The cover design must therefore reflect this overall image. The paper chosen must be of good quality, heavy, durable and grease-resistant.

MENU FLEXIBILITY

The flexibility of the menu is something which management may wish to consider. In times of inflation and recession when prices rise or the amount of disposable income decreases and business hospitality budgets diminish, customer demands change and therefore menus become outdated and obsolete.

Some operations use the menu of the day on a wall board or chalk board to provide flexibility in items offered and pricing. This custom started in Paris. A neatly written wall board told customers as they entered the restaurant what was on offer that day. Some establishments change part of their menus, daily or weekly while the main core of the menu remains the same. Changes can be made on paper insert and this added to the hard printed menu. Hors-d'œuvre, side dishes, salads, desserts and beverages do not change frequently. These dishes are printed on the main copy while the speciality dishes, entrées and other dishes which do change more frequently are placed on the paper insert.

Remember that nothing becomes obsolete faster to the regular customer than the same menu. Menu fatigue sets in and you begin to lose customers. Even fast-food establishments which have a basic menu on offer year in year out, still have to create interest by advertising certain new products or new recipes to existing products in order to keep interest alive. Menus should change at least every three months.

GLOSSARY OF FRENCH MENU AND KITCHEN TERMS

Universal respect for French traditions of classical cookery has left a repertoire of French words and terms which are understood and accepted by most professionals. As Italian has been the traditional language for music so French has been the traditional international language for food, drink and writing menus. Current trends however indicate that the vast majority of menus are written in English. Because certain French words and terms remain and are in everyday use in many establishments, the following glossary is included. Some examples are given in brackets.

l'aile (f)	wing of poultry or game birds
à la	in the style of (*à la mode*)
à la française	dishes prepared in the French way
à l'anglaise	in the English style
à la broche	cooked on a spit (chicken)
à la diable	devilled, a highly seasoned dish (kidneys)
à la carte	dishes on a menu prepared to order and individually priced
l'aloyau (m)	sirloin of beef (on the bone)
en aspic (m)	in savoury jelly (breast of chicken)
assorti	an assortment (*fromages assortis*)
au bleu	when applied to meat it means very underdone
au four	cooked in the oven (*pomme au four*)
au gratin	sprinkled with breadcrumbs and/or cheese and browned (cauliflower)
au vin blanc	with white wine

la blanquette	a white stew cooked in stock from which the sauce is made (*blanquette de veau*)
la bordure	a ring, sometimes of rice or potatoes
les bouchées	small puff-pastry cases
bouilli	boiled
le bouquet garni	a faggot or bundle of herbs, usually parsley stalks, thyme and bay leaf, tied inside pieces of celery and leek
braisé	braised
la braisière	braising pan
en branche	a term denoting vegetables, such as spinach, cooked and served as whole leaves
la brioche	a light yeast cake
la broche	a roasting spit
la brochette	a skewer
brouillé	scrambled (*œufs brouillés*)
le buffet	a sideboard of food, or a self-service table
le canapé	a cushion of toasted or fried bread on which are served various hot or cold foods (as a base for savouries); when served cold the base may be toast, biscuit or short or puff-paste with the food on top
la carte du jour	menu, or bill of fare for the day
en casserole	in a fireproof dish
la charlotte	name given to various hot and cold sweet dishes which have a case of biscuits, bread, sponge, etc. (apple charlotte)
le chateaubriand	the head of the fillet of beef
chaud	hot
le chaud-froid	a creamed velouté or demi-glace with gelatine or aspic added, used for masking cold dishes
le civet	a brown stew of game, usually hare (jugged hare)
clair	clear
la cloche	a bell-shaped cover, used for special *à la carte* dishes (*suprême de volaille sous cloche*)
la cocotte	porcelain fireproof dish
la compote	stewed fruit (*compote des poires*)
concassé	coarsely chopped (parsley and tomatoes)
le consommé	basic clear soup
le contrefilet	boned sirloin of beef
le cordon	a thread or thin line of sauce
la côte	rib (*côte de bœuf*)
la côtelette	cutlet (*les côtelettes d'agneau*)
coupe	cut; also dish in which ice-cream is served
le court-bouillon	a cooking liquor for certain foods (oily fish, calf's brains, etc.); it is water containing vinegar, sliced onions, carrots, herbs and seasoning
la crème fouetée	whipped cream
la crème Chantilly	sweetened, whipped vanilla-flavoured cream
la crêpe	pancake (*crêpes à l'orange*) (orange pancakes)
le croquette	cooked foods moulded cylinder shape, egg and crumbed and deep fried (*croquette de volaille* or chicken croquettes)

la croûte	a cushion of fried or toasted bread on which are served various hot foods, (savouries, game stuffing, etc.)
le croûton	cubes of fried bread served with soup, also triangular pieces which may be served with spinach and heart-shaped ones which may be served with certain braised vegetables and entrées
les crustacés (m)	shellfish
la cuisse de poulet	leg of chicken
la darne	a slice of round fish cut through with the bone (*darne de saumon*)
le déjeuner	lunch
le petit-déjeuner	breakfast
le dîner	dinner
du jour (plat du jour)	special dish of the day
duxelles	a basic preparation of finely chopped mushrooms cooked with chopped shallots
émincé	sliced
l'entrecôte (f)	a steak from a boned sirloin
l'escalope (f)	thin slice of meat (*escalope de veau*)
étuvée	cooked in its own juice
la farce	stuffing
farci	stuffed
fécule	a thickening agent made from potato or rice
le feuilletage	puff paste
les fines herbes	chopped parsley, tarragon and chervil
flambé	flamed or lit (*poire flambée*)
le flan	open fruit tart
le fleuron	small crescent pieces of puff paste used for garnishing certain dishes (fish and vegetable)
le foie	liver (*foie de veau lyonnaise* or calves' liver and onions)
le foie gras	fat goose liver
le fondant	a soft icing for cakes
fondu	melted
le four	oven
frappé	chilled (*melon frappé*)
les friandises	petits fours, sweetmeats, etc.
la fricassée	a white stew in which the poultry or meat is cooked in the sauce
frisé	curled (*endive frisée*)
fumé	smoked (*saumon fumé*)
le fumet	a concentrated stock or essence
la garniture	the trimmings on the dish
le gâteau	cake (of a number of portions)
la gelée	jelly (*gelée des fruits*)
le gibier	game (*salmis de gibier*)
la glace	ice or ice-cream
glacé	iced or with ice-cream (*meringue glacé*)
glacer	to glaze under the salamander

gratiner	to colour or gratinate under the salamander or in a hot oven using grated cheese or breadcrumbs
grillé	grilled
hacher	to chop finely or very finely dice; to mince
les herbes (f)	herbs
hors-d'œuvre	preliminary dishes of an appetising nature, served hot or cold
le jambon froid	cold ham
jardinière	cut into batons
julienne	cut into fine strips
le jus-lié	gravy thickened with arrowroot or cornflour or *fécule*
liaison	yolks of eggs and cream when used as a binding or a thickening (soup or sauce)
lier	to thicken (*jus-lié*)
la longe	loin (*longe de veau*)
macédoine	either a mixture of fruit or vegetables (*macédoine de fruits*); or cut into 6 mm (¼ inch) dice
macérer	to steep, to soak, to macerate
la marinade	a richly spiced pickling liquid for enriching the flavour and tenderness of meats before braising
mariné	pickled
la madère	Madeira wine
masquer	to mask or coat (with a sauce)
médaillon	foodstuffs prepared in a round, flat shape (*médaillon de veau*)
le menu	bill of fare
mignonette	coarse ground or crushed pepper
les mille feuilles (f)	'thousand leaves', a puff-pastry cream slice
à la minute	cooked to order
mirepoix	roughly cut onions, carrots, celery and a sprig of thyme and bay leaf
mollet	soft (*œuf mollet* or soft boiled egg)
le moule	mould; also *les moules*, mussels
la mousse	a hot or cold dish of light consistency, sweet or savoury
la moutarde	mustard
moutarder	to smear with mustard, or to add mustard to a sauce
mûr	ripe, mature
natives (f)	a menu term denoting English oysters
navarin	a brown lamb or mutton stew
le nid	nest; imitation nest made from potatoes or sugar, etc.
la noisette or *noisette*	a hazelnut used in confectionery; or small round potatoes cut with a special scoop; or as for noisette butter (nut-brown butter); or a cut of loin of lamb
la noix	nut, also the name given to the cushion piece of the leg of veal (*noix de veau*)
les nouilles (f)	noodles, a flat Italian paste
œuf brouillé	a scrambled egg
œuf en cocotte	egg cooked in an egg cocotte

œuf à la coque	egg boiled and served in its shell
œuf dur	a hard-boiled egg
œuf mollet	a soft-boiled shelled egg
œuf poché	a poached egg
œuf sur le plat	egg cooked in an egg dish
œuf à la poêle	a fried egg
l'oignon (m)	onion
l'orge (f)	barley
oseille (f)	sorrel
les pailles (f)	straws (*pommes pailles* or straw potatoes)
les paillettes de fromage (f)	cheese straws
le pain	bread
panaché	mixed (*salade panaché*)
pané	flour, egg and crumbed
panier	basket
papain	a proteolytic enzyme sometimes called vegetable pepsin, used as a meat tenderiser
papillote	foods cooked *en papillote* are cooked in greased greaseproof paper in their own steam in the oven
la pâte	a dough, paste, batter, pie or pastie
la pâtisserie	a pastry
la paupiette	a strip of fish, meat or poultry stuffed and rolled
paysanne	cut into even thin triangles, round or square pieces
le pilon	the drumstick of a leg of chicken
le piment	pimento
piquant	sharp flavour
piqué	studded (*onion piqué*)
poivre	pepper
poêlé	pot roasted
les pointes d'asperges	asparagus tips
la praline	chopped grilled almonds or hazelnuts or crushed almond toffee
primeurs	early vegetables (*navarin aux primeurs*)
printanière	garnish of spring vegetables
profiteroles	small balls of *choux* paste for garnishing soups or as a sweet course
la purée	a smooth mixture obtained by passing food through a sieve
la quennelle	forcemeat of poultry or fish, pounded, sieved, creamed and shaped, then poached
la râble	the back (*râble de lièvre* or the saddle of a hare)
le ragoût	stew (*ragoût de boeuf*)
le ravioli	an Italian paste, stuffed with various ingredients (meat, spinach, brains, cheese, etc.)
le risotto	Italian rice stewed in stock
le ris	sweetbread (*ris de veau*)
rissolé	fry to a golden brown
rôti	roast

le sabayon	yolks of eggs and a little liquid cooked till creamy
sauté	tossed in fat or turned in fat; also a specific meat dish
soubise	an onion purée
le soufflé	a light dish, sweet or savoury, hot or cold; whites of eggs are added to the hot basic preparation and whipped cream to the cold
le suprême	when applied to poultry it means whole wing and half the breast of the bird (there are two *suprêmes* to a bird); for other foods it is applied to a choice cut
table d'hôte	a fixed price meal of several courses, which may have a limited choice
la terrine	an earthenware utensil with a lid; a terrine also indicates a pâté cooked and served in a terrine
tomaté	preparations to which tomato purée has been added to dominate the flavour and colour
tourné	turned, shaped (barrel or olive shape)
la tranche	a slice
le tronçon	a slice of flat fish cut with the bone (*tronçon de turbot*)
le velouté	basic sauce; or soup of velvet or cream consistency
vert	green (*sauce verte*) sometimes served with cold salmon
voiler	to veil or cover with spun sugar
la volaille	poultry
le vol-au-vent	puff-pastry case

EXAMPLES OF DIFFERENT MENUS

Breakfast menu (Figures 7.1, 7.2, page 270)

A breakfast menu can be compiled from the following foods:

- Fruits: grapefruit, orange, melon, apple, etc.
- Fruit juices: grapefruit, orange, tomato, pineapple, etc.
- Stewed fruit: prunes, figs, apples, pears, etc.
- Yogurt: a selection.
- Cereals: cornflakes, shredded wheat, porridge, etc.
- Eggs: fried, boiled, poached, scrambled; omelets with bacon (streaky, back or gammon) or tomatoes, mushrooms or sauté potatoes.
- Fish: grilled herrings, kippers or bloaters; fried sole, plaice or whiting; fish cakes, smoked haddock, kedgeree.
- Meats (hot): fried or grilled bacon (streaky, back or gammon), sausages, kidneys, calves' liver, with tomatoes, mushrooms or sauté potatoes, potato cakes or bubble and squeak.
- Meats (cold): ham, bacon, pressed beef with sauté potatoes.
- Preserves: marmalade (orange, lemon, grapefruit, ginger), jams, honey.
- Fresh fruits: apple, pear, peach, grapes, etc.
- Beverages: tea, coffee, chocolate.
- Bread: rolls, croissants, brioche, toast, pancakes, waffles.

Fruit Juice — Orange, Grapefruit or Tomato
Fresh Grapefruit or Orange Segments

Stewed Fruits — Prunes, Figs or Apricots

Fresh Fruit Selection, Fresh Fruit Salad

Yogurts

Choice of Cereals, Porridge or Mix your own Muesli

Baker's Selection

Croissant, White and Wholemeal Rolls, Continental Pastry

Your choice of White or Brown Toast

Marmalade, Preserve, Honey, Country Butter or Flora Margarine

Cold Ham and Cheese

English Breakfast Tea with Milk or Lemon

Coffee — Freshly Brewed or Decaffeinated
with Milk or Cream

Hot Chocolate, Cold Milk
Chilled Ashbourne Water

Fig. 7.1 Example of a Continental breakfast

A LA CARTE

FRUITS & JUICES

Fresh Orange or Grapefruit Juice £. . . .Large £. . . .
Pineapple, Tomato or Prune Juice £. . . .Large £. . . .
Chilled Melon £. . . .   Stewed Prunes £. . . .Half Grapefruit £. . . .
Stewed Figs £. . . .   Fresh fruit in Season £. . . .

BREAKFAST FAVOURITES

Porridge or Cereal £. . . .
Eggs, any style: One £. . . .   Two £. . . .
Ham, Bacon, Chipolata Sausages or Grilled Tomato £. . . .
Omelette, Plain £. . . .   with Ham or Cheese £. . . .
Grilled Gammon Ham £. . . .   Breakfast Sirloin Steak £. . . .
A Pair of Kippers £. . . .   Smoked Haddock with a Poached Egg £. . . .
Pancakes with Maple Syrup £. . . .

FROM OUR BAKERY

Croissants or Breakfast Rolls £. . . .   Brioche £. . . .
Assorted Danish Pastries £. . . .   Toast £. . . .

BEVERAGES

Tea, Coffee, Sanka, Chocolate or Milk £. . . .

Service Charge 15%

Fig. 7.2 Example of an English à la carte breakfast menu

Points to consider when compiling a breakfast menu:

- It is usual to offer three of the courses previously mentioned:
  - fruit, yogurt, or cereals;
  - fish, eggs or meat;
  - preserves, bread, coffee or tea.
- As large a menu as possible, should be offered, depending on the size of the establishment, bearing in mind that it is better to offer a smaller number of well-prepared dishes than a large number of hurriedly prepared ones.
- A choice of plain foods such as boiled eggs or poached haddock should be available for the person who may not require a fried breakfast.

Breakfast menus may be table d'hôte or à la carte; a Continental breakfast does not include any cooked dish. A typical Continental breakfast would offer: rolls and butter, croissants, toast, preserves, tea or coffee.

Luncheon menus (see Figure 7.3, page 272)

Customer requirements for lunch vary considerably according to the type of establishment and the preferences of the customer so that menus must be carefully compiled if they are to be successful.

Types of menu
- A set price three-course menu with ideally a choice at each course. The amount of choice will depend on the skills of the caterer in offering what can be afforded within the selling price. In some cases this may be a simple choice between two dishes, in others four or five.
- The above menu with an option for the customer to choose and pay for either one (main course) or two courses.
- A list of well varied dishes each priced individually so that the customer can make up his/her own menu of whatever number of dishes they require.
- Buffet which may be all cold or hot dishes, or a combination of both, either to be served or organised on a self-service basis. Depending on the time of year and location, barbecue dishes can be considered.
- Special party, which may be either:
  - set menu with no choice;
  - set menu with a limited choice such as soup or melon, main course, choice of two sweets;
  - served or self-service buffet.

Only offer the number of courses and number of dishes within each course that can be satisfactorily prepared, cooked and served.

Traditional luncheon menus, both set price and à la carte, can be compiled from the following foods:

- *Fruit cocktails*: melon, grapefruit, orange, Florida, etc.

Autumn Seasonal Suggestions

Salad of Avocado Pear and Prawns
Freshly prepared Soups of the Day
Egg Mayonnaise with Anchovy
Wood Roasted Peppers with Tuna
Pâté with Walnuts Baked in a crust with
Redcurrant and Kumquat
Gazpacho Rojo de Sevilla
Chilled Melon

Swordfish with Garlic
Pan Fried River Trout with Almonds
and Hazelnut Butter
Poached Halibut White Wine and Grapes
Roast Salmon Fillet Lobster Sauce
Vegetarian Trio with Lasagne
Corn Crepe and Rice Peppers
Spatchcock Poussin with baby Onions
Supreme of Chicken Sevillana
Chargrilled Rump Steak Red Wine
and Mushroom Sauce
Gigot Chop Basted with Honey and Herbs
Fresh Vegetables from the morning market

Profiteroles with Melted Chocolate
Salad of Fresh Fruits and Berries
Chocolate Delice
Creme Caramel Passion Fruit Sauce
Basket of Swiss Ice Creams and Sorbets
Cassis Cassis
Dark Chocolate Mousse with Poached Pear
Cheese Board with Grapes and Celery

Fig. 7.3 Luncheon menu

- *Fruits*: melon, grapefruit, avocado pear, mango, paw paw.
- *Fruit juices*: grapefruit, orange, pineapple, tomato, etc.
- *Shellfish, etc.*: potted shrimps, prawns, oysters, caviar, snails, crabmeat.
- *Shellfish cocktails*: lobster, crab, prawn, shrimp.
- *Smoked fish or meat*: salmon, trout, eel, sprats, buckling, mackerel, roe, ham, salami.

- *Hors-d'œuvre*: assorted or simple items, light salads with a vegetable, fish, meat or game content.
- *Soup*: consommé with simple garnish; cold in summer; vegetable soups, cream soup (mushroom); chicken, minestrone, Scotch broth, etc.
- *Pasta*: spaghetti, macaroni, ravioli, canneloni, gnocchi, noodles, risotto, pizza and quiche.
- *Eggs*: when served for a luncheon menu egg dishes are usually garnished: scrambled, poached, soft boiled, en cocotte, sur le plat, omelet.
- *Fish*: nearly all kinds of fish can be served, but without complicated garnishes, they are usually steamed, poached, grilled, deep or shallow fried; mussels, scallops, herrings, skate, whiting, plaice, cod, turbot, brill, sole, scampi, trout, salmon trout, salmon, monkfish, whitebait, kedgeree; dishes to include various fish in light sauces.
- *Main courses*:
  - Brown stews of meat.
  - Braised steaks, braised beef, jugged hare.
  - Goulash, braised oxtail, salmis of game.
  - Hot pot, Irish stew.
  - Meat pies, chicken pies.
  - Meat puddings.
  - Boiled meat (French and English style).
  - Fricassé, blanquette.
  - Calves' head, tripe, sautéed kidneys.
  - Vienna and Hamburg steaks, hamburgers.
  - Sausages, minced meat, chicken à la king.
  - Fried lamb, veal or pork cutlets or fillets.
  - Fried steaks (entrecôte, tournedos, fillets, etc.).
  - Veal escalopes, sweetbreads.
  - Vol-au-vent of chicken or sweetbreads or both.
  - Sauerkraut, pilaff, kebab, chicken cutlets.
  - Vegetarian and ethnic dishes.
- *Roasts*: beef, pork, veal, lamb, mutton, chicken.
- *Grills*:
  - steaks (chateaubriand, fillet, tournedos, point, rump, porterhouse, entrecôte).
  - Cutlets (single, double).
  - Chops (loin, chump).
  - Kidneys, mixed grill, chicken, chicken legs, kebabs.
- *Cold buffet*:
  - Salmon, lobster, crab.
  - Pâté or terrine.
  - Beef, ham, tongue, lamb.
  - Turkey, chicken, chicken pie, raised pies.
  - Vegetarian dishes.
  - Salads, simple or compound; mixed salad leaves tossed in a light oil with

lemon juice or vinegar dressing topped with baked goats cheese, fresh asparagus, fried chicken livers, fried wild or cultivated mushrooms, a poached or soft-boiled egg removed from the shell.

- *Vegetables*: cabbage, cauliflower, French beans, spinach, peas, carrots, tomatoes, asparagus, globe artichoke (hot or cold with suitable sauce) etc.
- *Potatoes*: boiled, steamed, sautéed, fried, roast, creamed, croquette, lyonnaise, etc.
- *Sweets*:
  - Steamed puddings (fruit and sponge).
  - Milk puddings.
  - Fruit (stewed, fools, flans, salad, pies, fritters).
  - Egg custard sweets (baked, bread and butter, cream, caramel, diplomat, cabinet).
  - Bavarois, savarin, baba.
  - Charlottes, profiteroles, gâteaux (see Plate 100, page 258).
  - Pastries (mille-feuille, éclairs, etc.) (see Plate 101, page 258).
  - Various ices and sorbets.
- *Savouries*: simple savouries may also be served; for example Welsh rarebit.
- *Cheese*: a good selection of cheese; biscuits, celery and radishes.
- *Dessert*: Fresh fruit of all kinds and nuts.
- *Coffee or tea.*

A vegetarian lunch menu (Figure 7.4a and b) may be offered as an alternative to or as part of the à la carte or table d'hôte menus.

VEGETARIAN MENU

Iced Cucumber Soup
(Flavoured with mint)

Avocado Waldorf
(Filled with celery & apple bound in mayonnaise, garnished with walnuts)

***

Vegetable Lasagne
(Layers of pasta & vegetables with melted cheese, served with salad)

Mushroom Stroganoff
(Flamed in brandy, simmered in cream with paprika & mustard, served with rice)

Chilli con Elote
(Seasonal fresh vegetables in a chilli & tomato fondue, served with rice)

Poached Eggs Elizabeth
(Set on buttered spinach, coated in a rich cream sauce)

Fig. 7.4a   Vegetarian lunch menu

Friday 24th June

Crostini with Roasted Tomato & Pesto

★★★

Courgette & Coriander Soup

★★★

Red Pepper Plait
Potatoes Dauphinoise & Green Beans

★★★

Strawberry & Rhubarb Compote
or
Vegan "Ice Cream"

★★★

Coffee, Tea or Herbal Tea

Fig. 7.4b   Vegetarian lunch menu

Tea menus (Plate 102, page 258; Figure 7.5, page 276)

These vary considerably, depending on the type of establishment. The high-class hotel will usually offer a dainty menu. For example:

- Sandwiches (smoked salmon, ham, tongue, egg, tomato, cucumber) made with white or brown bread.
- Bread and butter (white, brown, fruit loaf).
- Scones with clotted cream (see Plate 103, page 259).
- Jams, honey, lemon curd.
- Small pastries, assorted gâteaux.
- Fruit salad and cream, ices.
- Tea (Indian, China, Russian, iced, fruit, herb).

The commercial hotels, public restaurants and canteens will offer simple snacks, cooked meals and high teas. For example:

- Assorted sandwiches.
- Buttered buns, scones, tea cakes, Scotch pancakes, waffles, sausage rolls, assorted bread and butter, various jams, toasted tea-cakes, scones, crumpets, buns.
- Eggs (boiled, poached, fried, omelets).
- Fried fish; grilled meats; roast poultry.
- Cold meats and salads.
- Assorted pastries; gâteaux.
- Various ices, coupes, sundaes.
- Tea; orange and lemon squash

HIGH TEA

A very popular meal in Scotland, eaten late afternoon in lieu of dinner.
Often enjoyed by the highland farmer who afterwards
would secure the animals for the night.

☆☆☆☆☆

Fried Haddock in Breadcrumbs
served with Chipped Potatoes

or

Traditional Scottish Mixed Grill
Consisting of
Two Rashers Ayrshire Bacon, 1 slice of Black Pudding,
1 slice of Beef Sausage, Fried Egg, Grilled Liver
served with Chipped Potatoes

☆☆☆☆☆

Brown Bread and Butter

☆☆☆☆☆

Choice of Assorted Scottish Tea Breads
(Girdle Scones, Pancakes, Crumpets)

or

Selection of Scottish Cakes
(Dundee Cake, Gingerbread, Shortbread)

☆☆☆☆☆

Scottish Preserves
(including Wild Bramble Jelly, and Blackcurrant)

☆☆☆☆☆

The Scottish High Tea
is reckoned to be the most pleasant hour of the day

Fig. 7.5   Example of a high tea menu

Dinner menus

A list of some of the foods suitable for dinner menus is given below, and both table d'hôte and à la carte menus should offer a sensible choice, depending upon the size of the establishment, and the capabilities of the staff.

The number of courses on special party menus can be from three upwards. The occasions for special dinner parties are often very important for the guest attending, therefore the compiling of such a menu is extremely important, calling for expert knowledge and wise judgement on the part of the caterer. The following are some traditional and classical dishes which may be used with light contemporary style dishes:

- *Cocktail*: fruit and shellfish.
- *Fruit*: melon, fresh figs, avocado pear, mango, paw paw, etc.
- *Delicacies*: caviar, oysters, snails, potted shrimps, prawns, foie gras.

- *Smoked*: salmon, trout, ham, salami, sausages, sprats, eel.
- *Hors-d'œuvre*.
- *Salads*: small dressed salad served simply, sprinkled with chopped fresh herbs or topped with hot pieces of lightly fried scallops, wild mushrooms or chicken livers; or cold crab, lobster, prawns, crayfish, etc.

- *Soup*: clear and consommé-based, petite marmite, shellfish bisques and cream soups, turtle soup, etc.; cold soups include vichyssoise and consommé.

- *Fish*:
  - poached salmon, turbot, blue trout.
  - shallow poached: sole, turbot, brill, halibut, monkfish, with a classical or contemporary style sauce and garnish.
  - baked: sea bass, mullet, halibut.
  - hot shellfish: scampi, oyster, crab, lobster, crayfish.
  - meunière: sole, fillets of sole, trout.
  - fried: sole, fillets of sole, goujons, scampi.
  - grilled: lobster, sole, salmon.
  - cold: salmon, salmon trout, trout, sole.
  - combinations of several fish in delicately flavoured sauces.

- *Main courses*:
  - light dishes which may be small and garnished.
  - sweetbreads, quail.
  - sauté of chicken, tournedos, noisettes or cutlets of lamb.
  - saddle of hare, filet mignon, vol-au-vent.
  - pot roasted chicken with mushrooms.
  - pheasant in casserole.
  - braised ham, tongue, duck, pheasant, pigeon.

- *Roast*:
  - saddle of lamb or veal, fillet or sirloin of beef.
  - poultry or game such as chicken, turkey, duck, goose, grouse, partridge, pheasant, snipe, woodcock, guinea fowl, wild duck, plover, teal, venison, saddle of hare.

- *Grills*:
  - steaks (chateaubriand, fillet, tournedos, rump, sirloin).
  - lamb (chops, cutlets or kidneys).
  - chicken (kebabs).

- *Vegetable*: French beans, broccoli, asparagus points, peas, broad beans, button Brussels sprouts, aubergine, cauliflower, etc.
- *Potatoes*: parmentier, noisette, olivette, dauphine, nouvelles, rissolées, Mireille, duchesse, Byron, Rösti, etc.

- *Sorbet*: lightly frozen water ice flavoured with fruit, liqueur or champagne sometimes served during a meal of several courses with the intention of refreshing the palate before proceeding with the remainder of the meal; a sorbet or a small assortment of sorbets can also be served as a dessert.

- *Cold dish*: such dishes as chicken in aspic or mousse of foie gras or ham may be served.

- *Vegetarian dishes*: should be a regular feature on menus.

- *Sweet*:
  - light sweets (soufflés, pancakes).
  - cold, iced soufflé, bombes, coupes with fruit such as peaches, strawberries, raspberries, sorbet, posset, syllabub, mousse, bavarois.
  - sweetmeats also known as friandises, mignardises or frivolités (these are different names for very small pastries, sweets, biscuits also known as 'petit fours' (see Plate 104, page 259).

- *Coffee* or *tea*.

- *Savoury*: any hot savouries prepared in neat, small portions may be used on dinner menus.

- *Cheese*: all varieties may be offered.

- *Dessert*: all dessert fruits and nuts may be served.

Banquet menus

When compiling banquet menus, you should consider certain points:

- The food, which will possibly be for a large number of people, must be dressed in such a way that it can be served fairly quickly. Heavily garnished dishes should be avoided.
- If a large number of dishes have to be dressed at the same time, certain foods deteriorate quickly and do not stand storage, even for a short time in a hot plate, such as deep-fried foods.

BANQUET LUNCHEON MENUS
A normal luncheon menu is used, bearing in mind the number of people involved. It is not usual to serve farinaceous dishes, eggs, stews or savouries. A luncheon menu could be drawn from the following and would usually consist of three or more courses.

- *First course*: soup, cocktail (fruit or shellfish), hors-d'œuvre, assorted or single item, a small salad.
- *Second course*: fish, usually poached or steamed fillets with a sauce.
- *Third course*: meat, hot or cold, but not a stew or made-up dish; vegetables and potatoes or a salad would be served.
- *Fourth course*: if the function is being held during the asparagus season, then

---

Avocado filled with cream cheese and two fruit sauces

* * *

Seafood filled fish mousse with crayfish sauce

* * *

*Butter cooked fillet of beef with sliced mushrooms and
tongue in Madeira sauce
A selection of market vegetables
Potatoes garnished with cream cheese*

* * *

Light soft meringue topped with fruit

* * *

Coffee

Sweetmeats

Fig. 7.6
Example of a
banquet
dinner menu

either hot or cold asparagus with a suitable sauce may be served as a course on its
own.
- *Fifth course:* sweet, hot or cold, and/or cheese and biscuits.

BANQUET DINNER MENUS
Here the caterer has the opportunity to excel, as can be seen from the example given
in Figure 7.6.

Functions and banquets

It will be necessary to know the nature of function, as special facilities may be
required. The type of function could be a wedding breakfast, silver or golden
wedding anniversary, coming of age, retirement, presentation, conference, etc.

If there are any special diet requirements of guests, such as vegetarian dishes in
place of meat, then the kitchen should know of them in advance.

The type of meal for functions can vary from a formal sit-down meal to a buffet,
which can be light, hot, fork, or cold. Foods may be served from behind the buffet
or guests may help themselves. Many buffets consist of a selection of hot and cold
foods.

The cost of the menu is agreed with the organiser of the function, and if any of the following are required then they will be charged as extras:

- floral decorations;
- special menu printing;
- orchestra;
- cabaret;
- invitation cards;
- place-name cards;
- table plan;
- toastmaster or MC;
- hire of rooms;
- special decorations.

Light buffets (including cocktail parties)

Light buffets can include:

- Hot savoury pastry patties of lobster, chicken, crab, salmon, mushrooms, ham, etc.
- Hot sausages (chipolatas); various fillings, such as chicken livers, prunes, mushrooms, tomatoes, wrapped in bacon and skewered.
- Bite-sized items: quiche and pizza, hamburgers, meat balls with savoury sauce or dip, scampi, fried fish en goujons, tartare sauce.
- Savoury finger toast to include any of the cold canapés; these may also be prepared on biscuits or shaped pieces of pastry; on the bases the following may be used: salami, ham, tongue, thinly sliced cooked meats, smoked salmon, caviar, mock caviar, sardine, eggs, etc.
- Game chips, gaufrette potatoes, fried fish balls, celery stalks spread with cheese.
- Sandwiches; bridge rolls, open or closed but always small.
- Fresh dates stuffed with cream cheese; crudités with mayonnaise and cardamom dip; tuna and chive Catherine wheels; crab claws with garlic dip; smoked salmon pin wheels; choux puffs with camembert.
- Sweets such as trifles, charlottes, jellies, bavarois, fruit salad, strawberries and raspberries with fresh cream, ice-creams, pastries, gâteaux.
- Beverages: coffee, tea, fruit-cup, punch-bowl, iced coffee.

FORK BUFFETS

For these functions individual pieces of fish, meat and poultry are prepared so that they can be eaten by the guests standing up and balancing a plate in one hand. Salads should also be sensibly prepared so that they can be easily handled by the guest using only a fork; the lettuce should be shredded and kept in short lengths. Chicken or ham mousse, galantine, terrine, pâté, mayonnaise of salmon, lobster and chicken are all suitable dishes.

Fast-food menus

Although some people are scornful of the items on this type of menu, calling them 'junk food', nevertheless their popularity and success is proven by the fact that from the original McDonald's, opened in Chicago in 1955, there are now over 10 000 outlets world-wide. McDonald's offer customers a nutrition guide to their products, and also information for diabetes sufferers.

ALL-DAY BRASSERIE

STARTERS

Soup of the day
Pâtés with toast
King prawns, mussels and smoked salmon
Chilled melon

SALADS

Avocado and prawn on a bed of summer leaves and
served with raspberry vinaigrette
Walnuts and apple with celery, summer leaves and
a light mayonnaise
Mixed side salad with a choice of mayonnaise,
French or raspberry dressings

MAIN COURSES

Coq au vin
Chicken Wellington – supreme of chicken in a
pastry case with lemon butter
Whole roast poussin cooked with rosemary
Cold smoked chicken garnished with seasonal berries
8 oz sirloin served with blue cheese butter
Fresh salmon cold, poached or grilled

DESSERTS AND CHEESE

Three sorbets
Chocolate truffle cake served with whipped cream
Crème brûlée
Seasonal fresh fruits in puff pastry served with cream
Three cheeses served with celery, grapes and biscuits

Fig. 7.7   Menu for an all-day brasserie

TOPICS FOR DISCUSSION

1. A sensible menu policy.
2. The advantages and disadvantages of a cyclical menu.
3. The advantages of using English menus. When would you consider using another language?
4. The essentials of menu design and construction.
5. The various styles of buffet menus.
6. The implications of menu fatigue.
7. How would you promote your menu for a 50 seater high street bistro in the centre of town?

Food purchasing, storage and control

LIAISON WITH FOOD SUPPLIERS

There are certain important factors involved in a successful working relationship with food suppliers. Both parties have responsibilities that must be carried out to ensure proper food safety and quality. Food-borne illness incidents, regardless of the cause, have an impact on the reputation of caterers and suppliers' business will be lost. A good working relationship and knowledge of each other's responsibilities is a major help in avoiding such incidents.

Suppliers must be aware of what is expected of the product. They must also make sure that the caterer is aware of any food safety limitations associated with the product. These are usually stated on all labelling. Such statements may just simply say 'keep refrigerated' or 'keep frozen', others might well include a graph or chart of the projected shelf-life at different storage temperatures. The responsibility for meeting these specifications is an important factor in a successful catering operation.

FOOD PURCHASING

Once a menu is planned, a number of activities must occur to bring it into reality. One of the first and most important stages is to purchase and receive the materials needed to produce the menu items. Skilful purchasing with good receiving can do much to maximise the results of a good menu. There are six important steps to remember:

- know the market;
- determine purchasing needs;
- establish and use specifications;
- design the purchase procedures;
- receive the goods;
- evaluate the purchasing task.

Knowing the market

Since markets vary considerably, to do a good job of purchasing a buyer must know the characteristics of each market.

A market is a place in which ownership of commodity changes from one person to another. This could occur using the telephone, on a street corner, in a retail or wholesale establishment or at an auction.

It is important that a food and beverage purchaser has knowledge of the items to be purchased, such as:

- where they are grown;
- seasons of production;
- approximate costs;
- conditions of supply and demand;
- laws and regulations governing the market and the products;
- marketing agents and their services;
- processing;
- storage requirements;
- commodity and product, class and grade.

The buyer

This is the key person who makes decisions regarding quality, amounts, price, what will satisfy the customers but also make a profit. The wisdom of the buyer's decisions will be reflected in the success or failure of the operation. The buyer must not only be knowledgeable about the products, but must have the necessary skills required in dealing with sales people, suppliers and other market agents. The buyer must be prepared for hard and often aggressive negotiations.

The responsibility for buying varies from company to company according to the size and management policy. Buying may be the responsibility of the chef, manager, storekeeper, buyer or buying department.

A buyer must have knowledge of the internal organisation of the company, especially the operational needs and to be able to obtain the product needs at a competitive price. Buyers must also acquaint themselves with the procedures of production and how these items are going to be used in the production operations, in order that the right item is purchased. For example, the item required may not always have to be of prime quality, for example tomatoes for soups and sauces.

A buyer must also be able to make good use of market conditions. For example, if there is a glut of fresh salmon at low cost, has the organisation the facility to make use of the extra salmon purchases? Is there sufficient freezer space? Can the chef make use of salmon, by creating a demand on the menu?

Buying methods

These depend on the type of market and the kind of operation. Purchasing procedures are usually formal or informal. Both have advantages and disadvantages. Informal methods are suitable for casual buying, where the amount involved is not large and speed and simplicity are desirable. Formal contracts are best for large contracts for commodities purchased over a long period of time. Prices do not vary much during a year, once the basic price has been established. Prices and supply tend to fluctuate with informal methods.

INFORMAL BUYING

This usually involves oral negotiations, talking directly to sales people, face to face or using the telephone. Informal methods vary according to market conditions.

FORMAL BUYING

Known as competitive buying, formal buying involves giving suppliers written specifications and quantity needs. Negotiations are normally written.

Selecting suppliers

Selecting suppliers is important in the purchasing process. Firstly consider how a supplier will be able to meet the needs of your operation. Consider:

- price;
- delivery;
- quality/standards.

Information on suppliers can be obtained from other purchasers. Visits to suppliers' establishments are to be encouraged. When interviewing prospective suppliers, you need to question how reliable a supplier will be under competition and how stable under varying market conditions.

Principles of purchasing

A menu dictates an operation's needs. Based on this the buyer searches for a market that can supply the company. After the right market is located, the various products available that may meet the needs are then investigated. The right product must be obtained to meet the need and give the right quality desired by the establishment. Other factors that might affect production needs include:

- type and image of the establishment;
- style of operation and system of service;
- occasion for which the item is needed;
- amount of storage available (dry, refrigerated or frozen);
- finance available and supply policies of the organisation;
- availability, seasonability, price trends and supply.

The skill of the employees, catering assistants, chefs, must also be taken into account as well as condition and the processing method; the ability of the product to produce the item or dish required; the storage life of the product.

THREE TYPES OF NEEDS

- **Perishable:** fresh fruit and vegetables, dairy products, meat and fish; prices and suppliers may vary; informal needs of buying are frequently used; perishables should be purchased to meet menu needs for a short period only.
- **Staple:** supplies canned, bottled, dehydrated, frozen products; formal or informal purchasing may be used; because items are staple and can be easily stored, bid buying is frequently used to take advantage of quantity price purchasing.
- **Daily use needs:** daily use or contract items are delivered frequently on par stock

basis; stocks are kept up to the desired level and supply is automatic; suppliers may be daily, several times a week, weekly or less often; most items are perishable, therefore supplies must not be excessive but only sufficient to get through to the next delivery.

WHAT QUANTITY AND QUALITY

Determining quantity and quality of items to be purchased is important. This is based on the operational needs. The buyer must be informed by the chef or other members of the production team of the products needed. The chef and his or her team must establish the quality and they should be encouraged to inspect the goods on arrival. The buyer with this information then checks out the market and looks for the best quality and best price. Delivery arrangements and other factors will be handled by the buyer. In smaller establishments the chef may also be the buyer.

When considering the quantity needed, certain factors should be known:

- the number of people to be served in a given period;
- the sales history;
- portion sizes (this is determined from yield testing a standard portion control list drawn up by the chef and management teams).

Buyers need to know production, often to be able to decide how many portions a given size may yield. He or she must also understand the various yields. Cooking shrinkage may vary causing problems in portion control and yield.

The chef must inform the buyer of quantities. The buyer must be aware also of different packaging sizes, such as jars, bottles, cans and the yield from each package. Grades, styles, appearance, composition, varieties, quality factors must be indicated, such as:

- colour;
- texture;
- size;
- absence of defects;
- bruising;
- irregular shape;
- maturity.

Quality standards should be established by the chef and management team when the menu is planned. Menus and recipes may be developed using standardised recipes which directly relate to the buying procedure and standard purchasing specifications.

Buying tips

The following is a list of suggestions to assist the buyer:

- Acquire, and keep up to date, a sound knowledge of all commodities, both fresh and convenience, to be purchased.
- Be aware of the different types and qualities of each commodity that is available.

- When buying fresh commodities, be aware of part-prepared and ready-prepared items available on the market.
- Keep a sharp eye on price variations. Buy at the best price to ensure the required quality and also an economic yield. The cheapest item may prove to be the most expensive if waste is excessive. When possible order by number and weight:

20 kg plaice could be 80 × 250 g (8 oz) plaice

40 × 500 g (1 lb) plaice

20 × 1 kg (2.2 lb) plaice

It could also be 20 kg total weight of various sizes and this makes efficient portion control difficult. Some suppliers (butchers, fishmongers) may offer portion control service by selling the required number of a given weight of certain cuts:

100 × 150 g (6 oz) sirloin steaks

25 kg (50 lb) prepared stewing beef

200 × 100 g (4 oz) pieces of turbot fillet

500 × 100 g (4 oz) plaice fillets.

- Organise an efficient system of ordering with copies of all orders kept for cross checking, whether orders are given in writing, verbally or by telephone.
- Compare purchasing by retail, wholesale and contract procedures to ensure the best method is selected for your own particular organisation.
- Explore all possible suppliers: local or markets, town or country, small or large.
- Keep the number of suppliers to a minimum. At the same time have at least two suppliers for every group of commodities, when possible. The principle of having competition for the caterer's business is sound.
- Issue all orders to suppliers fairly, allowing sufficient time for the order to be implemented efficiently.
- Request price lists as frequently as possible and compare prices continually to make sure that you buy at a good market price.
- Buy perishable goods when they are in full season as this gives the best value at the cheapest price. To help with the purchasing of the correct quantities, it is useful to compile a purchasing chart for 100 covers from which items can be divided or multiplied according to requirement. Indication of quality standards can also be inserted in a chart of this kind.
- Deliveries must all be checked against the orders given for quantity, quality and price. If any goods delivered are below an acceptable standard they must be returned either for replacement or credit.
- Containers can account for large sums of money. Ensure that all the containers are correctly stored, returned to the suppliers and the proper credit given.
- All invoices must be checked for quantities and prices.
- All statements must be checked against invoices and passed swiftly to the office so that payment may be made in time to ensure maximum discount on the purchases.

- Foster good relations with trade representatives because much useful up-to-date information can be gained from them.
- Keep up-to-date trade catalogues, visit trade exhibitions, survey new equipment and continually review the space, services and systems in use in order to explore possible avenues of increased efficiency.
- Organise a testing panel occasionally in order to keep up to date with new commodities and new products coming on to the market.
- Consider whether computer application can assist the operation (see Chapter 14).
- Study the weekly Fresh Food price lists in the *Caterer and Hotelkeeper*.

PORTION CONTROL

Portion control means controlling the size or quantity of food to be served to each customer. The amount of food allowed depends on the three following considerations:

- **The type of customer or establishment**: there will obviously be a difference in the size of portions served, such as to those working in heavy industry or to female clerical workers. In a restaurant offering a three-course table d'hôte menu for £x including salmon, the size of the portion would naturally be smaller than in a luxury restaurant charging £x for the salmon on an à la carte menu.
- **The quality of the food**: better quality food usually yields a greater number of portions than poor quality food: low quality stewing beef often needs so much trimming that it is difficult to get six portions to the kilo, and the time and labour involved also loses money. On the other hand, good quality stewing beef will often give eight portions to the kilogramme with much less time and labour required for preparation.
- **The buying price of the food**: this should correspond to the quality of the food if the person responsible for buying has bought wisely. A good buyer will ensure that the price paid for any item of food is equivalent to the quality – in other words a good price should mean good quality, which should mean a good yield, and so help to establish a sound portion control. If, on the other hand, an inefficient buyer has paid a high price for indifferent quality food then it will be difficult to get a fair number of portions, and the selling price necessary to make the required profit will be too high.

Portion control should be closely linked with the buying of the food; without a good knowledge of the food bought it is difficult to state fairly how many portions should be obtained from it. To evolve a sound system of portion control each establishment (or type of establishment) needs individual consideration. A golden rule should be 'a fair portion for a fair price'.

Convenient portioned items are available, such as individual sachets of sugar, jams, sauce, salt, pepper; individual cartons of milk, cream and individual butter and margarine portions.

Portion control equipment

There are certain items of equipment which can assist in maintaining control of the size of the portions:

- Scoops, for ice-cream or mashed potatoes.
- Ladles, for soups and sauces.
- Butter pat machines, regulating pats from 7 g upwards.
- Fruit juice glasses, 75–150 g.
- Soup plates or bowls, 14, 16, 17, 18 cm.
- Milk dispensers and tea-measuring machines.
- Individual pie dishes, pudding basins, moulds and coupes.

As examples of how portion control can save a great deal of money the following instances are true:

- It was found that 0.007 litre of milk was being lost per cup by spilling it from a jug; 32 000 cups = 224 litres of milk lost daily; this resulted in a loss of hundreds of pounds per year.
- When an extra pennyworth of meat is served on each plate it means a loss of £1000 over the year when 1000 meals are served daily.

Portion amounts

The following list is of the approximate number of portions that are obtainable from various foods:

- Soup: 2–3 portions to the $\frac{1}{2}$ litre.
- Hors-d'œuvre: 120–180 g per portion.
- Smoked salmon: 16–20 portions to the kg when bought by the side; 20–24 portions to the kg when bought sliced.
- Shellfish cocktail: 16–20 portions per kg.
- Melon: 2–8 portions per melon, depending on the type of melon.
- Foie gras: 15–30 g per portion.
- Caviar: 15–30 g per portion.

FISH

Plaice, cod, haddock fillet	8 portions to the kg
Cod and haddock on the bone	6 portions to the kg
Plaice, turbot, brill, halibut, on the bone	4 portions to the kg
Herring and trout	1 per portion (180–250 g fish)
Mackerel and whiting	250–360 g fish
Sole for main dish	300–360 g fish
Sole for filleting	500–750 g best size
Whitebait	8–10 portions to the kg
Salmon (gutted, but including head and bone)	4–6 portions to the kg
Crab or lobster	250–360 g per portion

(A 500 g lobster yields about 150 g meat; a 1 kg lobster yields about 360 g meat).

SAUCES

8–12 portions to ½ litre:
- Hollandaise
- Béarnaise
- Tomato
- Any demi-glace sauce

- Custard
- Apricot
- Jam
- Chocolate

10–14 portions to ½ litre:
- Apple
- Cranberry
- Bread

15–20 portions to ½ litre:
- Tartare
- Vinaigrette
- Mayonnaise

MEATS

Beef
Roast on the bone	4–6 portions per kg
Roast boneless	6–8 portions per kg
Boiled or braised	6–8 portions per kg
Stews, puddings and pies	8–10 portions per kg
Steaks • Rump	120–250 g per one portion
• Sirloin	120–250 g per one portion
• Tournedos	90–120 g per one portion
• Fillet	120–180 g per one portion

Offal
Ox-liver	8 portions to the kg
Sweetbreads	6–8 portions to the kg
Sheep's kidneys	2 per portion
Oxtail	4 portions per kg
Ox-tongue	4–6 portions per kg

Lamb
Leg	6–8 portions to the kg
Shoulder boned and stuffed	6–8 portions to the kg
Loin and best-end	6 portions to the kg
Stewing lamb	4–6 portions to the kg
Cutlet	90–120 g
Chop	120–180 g

Pork
Leg	8 portions to the kg
Shoulder	6–8 portions to the kg
Loin on the bone	6–8 portions to the kg
Pork chop	180–250 g

Ham

• Hot	8–10 portions to the kg
• Cold	10–12 portions to the kg
• Sausages are obtainable 12, 16 or 20 to the kg	
• Chipolatas yield approximately 32 or 48 to the kg	
• Cold meat	16 portions to the kg
• Streaky bacon	32–40 rashers to the kg
• Back bacon	24–32 rashers to the kg

Poultry

• Poussin	1 portion 360 g (1 bird)
	2 portions 750 g (1 bird)
• Ducks and chickens	360 g per portion
• Geese and boiling fowl	360 g per portion
• Turkey	250 g per portion

Vegetables

• New potatoes	8 portions to the kg
• Old potatoes	4–6 portions to the kg
• Cabbage	6–8 portions to the kg
• Turnips	6–8 portions to the kg
• Parsnips	6–8 portions to the kg
• Swedes	6–8 portions to the kg
• Brussels sprouts	6–8 portions to the kg
• Tomatoes	6–8 portions to the kg
• French beans	6–8 portions to the kg
• Cauliflower	6–8 portions to the kg
• Spinach	4 portions to the kg
• Peas	4–6 portions to the kg
• Runner beans	6 portions to the kg

Methods of purchasing

There are three main methods for buying, each depending on the size and volume of the business.

- **The primary market:** raw materials may be purchased at the source of supply, the grower, producer or manufacturer, or from central markets such as Smithfield, Nine Elms or Billingsgate in London. Some establishments or large organisations will have a buyer who will buy directly from the primary markets. Also, a number of smaller establishments may adopt this method for some of their needs (the chef patron may buy his fish, meat and vegetables directly from the market).

- **The secondary market**: goods are bought wholesale from a distributor or middle man; the catering establishment will pay wholesale prices and obtain possible discounts.
- **The tertiary market**: the retail or cash and carry warehouse is a method suitable for smaller companies. A current pass obtained from the warehouse is required in order to gain access. This method also requires the user to have his or her own transport. Some cash and carry organisations require a VAT number before they will issue an authorised card. It is important to remember that there are added costs:

  - running the vehicle and petrol used;
  - the person's time for going to the warehouse.

Cash and carry is often an impersonal way of buying as there are no staff to discuss quality and prices.

Standard purchasing specifications

Standard purchasing specifications are documents which are drawn up for every commodity describing exactly what is required for the establishment. These standard purchasing specifications will assist with the formulation of standardised recipes. A watertight specification is drawn up which, once approved, will be referred to every time the item is delivered. It is a statement of various criteria related to quality, grade, weight, size and method of preparation, if required, such as washed and selected potatoes for baking. Other information given may be variety, maturity, age, colour, shape, etc. A copy of standard specification is often given to the supplier and the storekeeper who are left in no doubt as to what is needed. These specifications assist in the costing and control procedures.

Commodities which can be specified include:

- Grown (primary): butchers meat; fresh fish; fresh fruit and vegetables; milk and eggs.
- Manufactured (secondary): bakery goods; dairy products.
- Processed (tertiary): frozen foods including meat, fish and fruit and vegetables; dried goods; canned goods.

It can be seen that any food product can have a specification attached to it. However, the primary specifications focus on raw materials, ensuring the quality of these commodities. Without quality at this level, a secondary or tertiary specification is useless. For example, to specify a frozen apple pie, this product would use:

- a primary specification for the apple;
- a secondary specification for the pastry;
- a tertiary specification for the process (freezing).

But no matter how good the secondary or tertiary specifications are, if the apples used in the beginning are not of a very high quality, the whole product is not of a good quality.

EXAMPLES OF STANDARD PURCHASING SPECIFICATION

Tomatoes
- Commodity: round tomatoes.
- Size: 50 g (2 oz) 47–57 mm diameter.
- Quality: firm, well formed, good red colour, with stalk attached.
- Origin: Dutch, available March–November.
- Class/grade: super class A.
- Weight: 6 kg (13 lb) net per box.
- Count: 90–100 per box.
- Quote: per box/tray.
- Packaging: loose in wooden tray, covered in plastic.
- Delivery: day following order.
- Storage: temperature 10–13°C (50–55°F) at a relatively humidity of 75–80%.
- Note: avoid storage with cucumbers and aubergines.

Rib of beef (source: Scotch, Aberdeen Angus)
- Cut from a T-bone rib, weighing preferably 17–18 kg (38–40 lb), to measure on the flank no more than 4 cm ($1\frac{1}{2}$ in) from the meat of the main muscle (eye) on the loin end, and no more than 10 cm (4 in) from inside of the chine bone on the chuck end. The rib is cut straight between these points.
- The chine bone is removed squarely to where the meat splits.
- The ribs should not show heavy fat layers on the chuck end or along the flank, nor should the back have heavy fat covering.
- Ribs are aged not less than 10 days and not more than 21 days from date of slaughter.
- The cap (back) is removed from the entire length of the rib and the lean meat trimmed from the cap.
- The back strap, blade bone and blade bone cartilage is removed and the cap securely tied back again to its natural position.
- The fabricated rib will weigh not less than 8 kg (17 lb), nor more than 10 kg (21 lb).
- The rib should not show heavy layers of fat along the flank or on the chuck end, nor should the back have heavy fat covering.
- Ribs with hooks holes and knife cuts are not acceptable.

Quality in ribs is evidenced by meat which looks rich, fine grained and smooth, and is firm but elastic to the touch. The rib has an even distortion of fat all around, while the lean or muscular positions (eye or rib) are ingrained (marbled) with fine dots and streaks of fat.

THE STANDARD RECIPE

Standard recipes are a written formula for producing a food item of a specified quality and quantity for use in a particular establishment. It should show the precise quantities and qualities of the ingredients together with the sequence of preparation and service. It enables the establishment to have a greater control over cost and quantity.

Objective

To predetermine the following:

- the quantities and qualities of ingredients to be used stating the purchase specification;
- the yield obtainable from a recipe;
- the food cost per portion;
- the nutritional value of a particular dish.

To facilitate:

- menu planning;
- purchasing and internal requisitioning;
- food preparation and production;
- portion control.

Also the standard recipe will assist new staff in preparation and production of standard products, which can be facilitated by photographs or drawings illustrating the finished product.

COST CONTROL

It is important to know the exact cost of each process and every item produced, so a system of cost analysis and cost information is essential.

The advantages of an efficient costing system are:

- It discloses the net profit made by each section of the organisation and shows the cost of each meal produced.
- It will reveal possible sources of economy and can result in a more effective use of stores, labour, materials, etc.
- Costing provides information necessary for the formation of a sound price policy.
- Cost records provide and facilitate the speedy quotations for all special functions, such as special parties, wedding receptions, etc.
- It enables the caterer to keep to a budget.

No *one* costing system will automatically suit every catering business, but the following guidelines may be helpful:

- The co-operation of all departments is essential.
- The costing system should be adapted to the business and not vice versa. If the accepted procedure in an establishment is altered to fit a costing system then there is danger of causing resentment among the staff and as a result losing their co-operation.
- Clear instructions in writing must be given to staff who are required to keep records. The system must be made as simple as possible so that the amount of clerical labour required is kept to a minimum. An efficient mechanical calculator or computer should be provided to save time and labour.

To calculate the total cost of any one item or meal provided it is necessary to analyse the total expenditure under several headings. Basically the total cost of each item consists of three main elements:

- **Food or materials costs**: known as variable costs because the level will vary according to the volume of business; in an operation that uses part-time or extra staff for special occasions, the money paid to these staff also comes under variable costs; by comparison, salaries and wages paid regularly to permanent staff are fixed costs.
- All cost of **labour and overheads**: regular charges which come under the heading of fixed costs; labour costs in the majority of operations fall into two categories: **direct labour** cost, which is salaries and wages paid to staff such as chefs, waiters, barstaff, housekeepers, chambermaids and where the cost can be allocated to income from food, drink and accommodation sales; **indirect labour** cost, which would include salaries and wages paid, for example, to managers, office staff and maintenance men who work for all departments (so their labour cost should be charged to all departments). **Overheads** consist of rent, rates, heating, lighting and equipment.

Cleaning materials

An important group of essential items that is often overlooked when costing are cleaning materials. There are over 60 different items that come under this heading, and approximately 24 of these may be required for an average catering establishment. These may include: brooms, brushes, buckets, cloths, drain rods, dusters, mops, sponges, squeegees, scrubbing/polishing machines, suction/vacuum cleaners, wet and wet/dry suction cleaners, scouring pads, detergents, disinfectants, dustbin powder, washing-up liquids, fly sprays, sacks, scourers, steel wool, soap, soda, etc.

It is important to understand the cost of these materials and to ensure that an allowance is made for them under the heading of overheads.

Profit

It is usual to express each element of cost as a percentage of the selling price. This enables the caterer to control his profits.

Gross profit or kitchen profit is the difference between the cost of the food and the net selling price of the food. Net profit is the difference between the selling price of the food (sales) and total cost (cost of food, labour and overheads).

Sales − Food cost = gross profit (kitchen profit)
Sales − total cost = net profit
Food cost + gross profit = sales

Example:			
Food sales for 1 week		=	£8000
Food cost for 1 week		=	£3520
Labour and overheads for 1 week		=	£3440
Total costs for 1 week		=	£6960
Gross profit (kitchen profit)		=	£4480
Net profit		=	£1040

Food sales − food cost   £8000 − £3520 = £4480 (gross profit)
Food sales − net profit   £8000 − £1040 = £6960 (total costs)
Food cost + gross profit   £3520 + £4840 = £8360 (food sales)

Profit is always expressed as a percentage of the selling price.
∴ the percentage profit for the week is:

$$\frac{\text{Net profit}}{\text{Sales}} \times 100 = £\frac{1040 \times 100}{8000} = 13\%$$

A breakdown shows:

		Percentage of sales (%)
Food cost	£3520	44
Labour	£2000	25
Overheads	£1440	18
	£6960	
Net profit	£1040	13
Sales	£8000	

If the restaurant served 1000 meals then the average spent by each customer would be:

$$\frac{\text{Total sales £8000}}{\text{No. of customers 1000}} = £8.00$$

As the percentage composition of sales for a month is now known, the average price of a meal for that period can be further analysed:

Average price of a meal = £8.00 = 100%
8p = 1%

which means that the customer's contribution towards:

$$
\begin{aligned}
\text{Food cost} &= 8\text{p} \times 44 = \text{£3.52} \\
\text{Labour} &= 8\text{p} \times 25 = \text{£2.00} \\
\text{Overheads} &= 8\text{p} \times 18 = \text{£1.44} \\
\text{Net profit} &= 8\text{p} \times 13 = \text{£1.04} \\
\text{Average price of meal} &= \underline{\text{£8.00}}
\end{aligned}
$$

A rule that can be applied to calculate the food cost price of a dish is: let the cost price of the dish equal 40% and *fix the selling price* at 100%.

$$
\text{Cost of dish} = 160\text{p} = 40\%
$$

$$
\therefore \text{Selling price} = \frac{160 \times 100}{40} = \text{£4.00}
$$

Selling the dish at £4, making 60% gross profit above the cost price, would be known as 40% food cost. For example:

Sirloin steak (250 g (8 oz))
250 g (8 oz) entrecote steak at £8.00 a pound = £4.00

$$
\text{To fix the selling price at 40\% food cost} = \frac{4.00 \times 100}{40} = \text{£10.00}
$$

The table below will help you with various food costings:

FOOD COSTINGS

Food cost (%)	To find the selling price multiply the cost price of the food by:	If the cost price of food is £2 the selling price is:	If the cost price is 60p the selling price is:	Gross profit (%)
60	1.66	£3.32	£0.96	40
55	1.75	£3.50	£1.02	45
50	2	£4.00	£1.20	50
45	2.22	£4.44	£1.32	55
40	2.5	£5.00	£1.44	60
$33\frac{1}{3}$	3	£6.00	£1.80	$66\frac{2}{3}$

If food costing is controlled accurately the food cost of particular items on the menu and the total expenditure on food over a given period are worked out. Finding the food costs helps to control costs, prices and profits.

An efficient food cost system will disclose bad buying and inefficient storing and should tend to prevent waste and pilfering. This can help the caterer to run an efficient business and enable him to give the customer adequate value for money.

The caterer who gives the customer value for money together with the desired type of food is well on the way to being successful.

FOOD COST AND OPERATIONAL CONTROL

As food is expensive, efficient stock control levels are essential to help the profitability of the business. The main difficulties of controlling food are as follows:

- Food prices fluctuate frequently because of inflation and falls in the demand and supply, through poor harvests, bad weather conditions, etc.
- Transport costs rise due to wage demands and cost of petrol.
- Fuel costs rise, which affects food companies' and producers' costs.
- Food subsidies are removed to bring the UK into line with the EU.
- Changes occur in the amount demanded by the customer; increased advertising increases demand; changes in taste and fashion influence demand from one product to another.
- Media focus on certain products which are labelled healthy or unhealthy will affect demand; for example butter being high in saturated fats, sunflower margarine being high in polyunsaturates.

Each establishment should devise its own control system to suit the needs of that establishment.

Factors which affect a control system are:

- regular changes in the menu;
- menus with a large number of dishes;
- dishes with a large number of ingredients;
- problems in assessing customer demand;
- difficulties in not adhering to or operating standardised recipes;
- raw materials purchased incorrectly.

Factors assisting a control system include:

- menu remains constant, (McDonald's, Harvester);
- standardised recipes and purchasing specifications used;
- menu has a limited number of dishes.

Stocktaking is therefore easier and costing more accurate.

In order to carry out a control system, food stocks must be secure, refrigerators and deep freezers should be kept locked, portion control must be accurate. A book-keeping system must be developed to monitor the daily operation.

The control cycle of daily operation

PURCHASING

It is important to determine yields from the range of commodities in use which will determine the unit costs. Yield testing indicates the number of items or portions obtained and helps to provide the information required for producing, purchasing and specification. Yield testing should not be confused with product testing which is concerned with the physical properties of the food – texture, flavour, quality. In reality tests are frequently carried out which combine these objectives.

RECEIVING

Goods must be checked on delivery to make sure they meet the purchase specifications.

Before items are delivered, it is necessary to know what has been ordered, both the amount and quality, and when it will be delivered. This is essential so that persons requiring items will know when foods will be available, particularly perishable items and that on arrival they can be checked against the required standard. It is also helpful for the storekeeper to know when to expect the goods so that he or she can plan the working day and also inform staff awaiting arrival of items.

The procedure for accepting deliveries is to ensure that:

1. adequate storage space is available;
2. access to the space is clear;
3. temperature of goods where appropriate is checked;
4. perishable goods are checked immediately;
5. there is no delay in transporting items to cold storage;
6. all other goods are checked for quantity and quality and stored;
7. any damaged items are returned;
8. items past their 'use by' or 'best before' dates are not accepted;
9. receipts or amended delivery notes record returns;
10. one part of the delivery note is retained;
11. the other part is kept by the supplier;
12. a credit note is provided for any goods not delivered;
13. should there be any discrepancies, the person making the delivery and the supplier are informed.

Health and safety requirements

To comply with the regulations it is essential to observe these practices not only because of the legal requirement but for the benefit of all who use the storage areas of the premises.

- Receiving areas must be clean and free from litter.
- Waste bins, empty return boxes, etc. should be kept tidy and safe.
- Waste bins (rubbish and swill) must be kept with lids on and emptied frequently and kept clean.
- All storage areas must be kept clean and tidy.
- Trollies and stacking shelves should be suitable for heavy items.
- The trolley should not be overloaded; accidents can occur due to careless loading such as heavy items on top light items.
- Lifting of heavy items should be done in a manner to prevent injury.
- Cleaning equipment and materials must be available and kept separate from food items.
- All items should be stored safely, shelves not overloaded, heavier items lower than lighter items, with suitable steps to reach higher items.
- Stores should have a wash hand basin, towel, soap and nail brush.

- Unauthorised persons should not have access to the stores or areas where goods are delivered.
- Be prepared for the unexpected, accidents can occur due to:
  - delivery vehicles and trolley movement;
  - breakages of containers, glass jars, etc.;
  - undue waste by delivery or storekeeping staff.
- Know where the first aid box is.
- Know the procedures to follow in the event of an accident.

Temperature of food on delivery
Procedures must be laid down for checking the temperature of foods on arrival at the establishment. Delivery vehicles are subject to legislation and food should be at these temperatures when delivered.

Documentation of deliveries
Goods are ordered from the supplier for the amounts required and when it is to be delivered. The quality and details of the foods will have been specified by the establishment so that when delivered the goods should comply with what is ordered.

STORING AND ISSUING
Raw materials should be stored correctly under the right conditions, temperature, etc. A method of pricing the materials must be decided, and one of the following should be adopted for charging the food to the various departments. The cost of items does not remain fixed over a period of time; over a period of one year a stores item may well have several prices. The establishment must decide which price to use:

- actual purchase price;
- simple average price;
- weighted average price;
- inflated price (price goes up after purchase);
- standard price (fixed price).

Weighted average price example (of beans)

$$= 10 \text{ lb} \times 30\text{p} = \quad 300\text{p}$$
$$20 \text{ lb} \times 40\text{p} = \quad \underline{800\text{p}}$$
$$\text{Total} \quad \underline{1100\text{p}}$$

$\therefore 1100 \div 30 \text{ lb} = 36.6\text{p per lb} = $ weighted average price.

PREPARING
This is an important stage of the control cycle. The cost of the food consumed depends on two factors:

- the number of meals produced;
- the cost per meal.

In order to control food costs we must be able to:

- control the number to be catered for;

- control the food cost per meal in advance of production and service by using a system of precosting, using standardised recipes, indicating portion control.

SALES AND VOLUME FORECASTING

This is a method of predicting the volume of sales for a future period. In order to be of practical value the forecast must:

- predict the total number of covers (customers);
- predict the choice of menu items.

Therefore it is important to:

- keep a record of the numbers of each dish sold from a menu;
- work out the average spent per customer;
- calculate the proportion, expressed as a percentage, of each dish sold in relation to total sales.

Forecasting is in two stages:

- Initial forecasting – this is done once a week in respect of each day of the following week. It is based on sales histories, information related to advance bookings and current trends, and when this has been completed, the predicted sales are converted into the food/ingredients requirements. Purchase orders are then prepared and sent to suppliers.
- The final forecast – this normally takes place the day before the actual preparation and service of the food. This forecast must take into account the latest developments, such as the weather and any food that needs to be used up; if necessary suppliers' orders may need to be adjusted.

Sales forecasting is not a perfect method of prediction, but does help with production planning. Sales forecasting, however, is important when used in conjunction with cyclical menu planning.

Precosting of dishes

This method of costing is associated with standardised recipes which give the total cost of the dish per portion and often with a selling price.

Summary of factors which will affect the profitability of the establishment

These include:

- overcooking food resulting in portion loss;
- inefficient preparation of raw materials;
- poor portion control;
- too much wastage, insufficient use of raw materials; left-over food not being utilised;
- theft;
- inaccurate ordering procedures;
- inadequate checking procedures;

- no reference mark to standardised recipes and yield factors;
- insufficient research into suppliers;
- inaccurate forecasting;
- bad menu planning.

Fig. 8.1   A poorly laid-out store

Fig. 8.2   A well laid-out store

STOREKEEPING (see Figures 8.1, 8.2; page 301)

A clean, orderly food store, run efficiently, is essential in any catering establishment for the following reasons:

- Stocks of food can be kept at a suitable level, so eliminating the risk of running out of any commodity.
- All food entering and leaving the stores can be properly checked; this helps to prevent wastage.
- A check can be kept on the percentage profit of each department of the establishment.

This control may be assisted by computer application, see Chapter 14, page 496. A well-planned store should include the following features:

- It should be cool and face the north so that it does not have the sun shining into it.
- It must be well ventilated, vermin proof and free from dampness (dampness in a dry store makes it musty, and encourages bacteria to grow and tins to rust).
- It should be in a convenient position to receive goods being delivered by suppliers and also in a suitable position to issue goods to the various departments.
- A wash hand basin, soaps, nail brush and hand drier must be provided for staff; also a first-aid box.
- A good standard of hygiene is essential, therefore the walls and ceilings should be free from cracks, and either painted or tiled so as to be easily cleaned. The floor should be free from cracks and easy to wash. The junction between the wall and floor should be rounded to prevent the accumulation of dirt. A cleaning rota should clearly show daily, monthly and weekly cleaning tasks.
- Shelves should be easy to clean.
- Good lighting, both natural and artificial, is very necessary.
- A counter should be provided to keep out unauthorised persons, thus reducing the risk of pilfering.
- The storekeeper should be provided with a suitable desk.
- There should be ample, well-arranged storage space, with shelves of varying depths and separate sections for each type of food (see Plate 105, page 329). These sections may include deep-freeze cabinets, cold rooms, refrigerators, chill rooms, vegetable bins and container stores. Space should also be provided for empty containers.
- Efficient, easy-to-clean weighing machines for large and small-scale work should be supplied.
- Stores staff must wear clean overalls at all times, and suitable shoes to help prevent injury if a heavy item is dropped on the feet.
- Steps to help staff reach goods on high shelves and an appropriate trolley should be provided.

Store containers

Foods delivered in flimsy bags or containers should be transferred to suitable store containers. These should be easy to wash and have tight-fitting lids. Glass or plastic containers are suitable for many foods, such as spices and herbs, as they have the advantage of being transparent; therefore it is easy to see at a glance how much of the commodity is in stock.

Bulk dry goods (pulses, sugar, salt, etc.) should be stored in suitable bins with tight-fitting lids. These bins should have wheels so that they can be easily moved for cleaning. All bins should be clearly labelled or numbered.

Sacks or cases of commodities should not be stored on the floor; they should be raised on duck boards so as to permit a free circulation of air.

Some goods are delivered in containers suitable for storage and these need not be transferred. Heavy cases and jars should be stored at a convenient height to prevent any strain in lifting.

Special storage points

- Always comply with 'best by' or 'use by' dates.
- All old stock should be brought forward with each new delivery.
- Commodities with strong smells or flavours should be stored as far away as possible from those foods which readily absorb flavour; strong-smelling cheese should not be stored near eggs.
- Bread should be kept in a well-ventilated container with a lid. Lack of ventilation causes condensation and encourages moulds. Cakes and biscuits should be stored in airtight tins.
- Stock must be inspected regularly, particularly cereals and cereal products, to check for signs of mice or weevils.
- Tinned goods should be unpacked, inspected and stacked on shelves. When inspecting tins, these points should be looked for:
  - blown tins – this is where the ends of the tins bulge owing to the formation of gases either by bacteria growing on the food or by the food attacking the tin-plate; all blown tins should be thrown away as the contents are dangerous and the use of the contents may cause food-poisoning;
  - dented tins – these should be used as soon as possible, not because the dent is an indication of inferior quality but because dented tins, if left, will rust and a rusty tin will eventually puncture;
  - storage life of tins varies considerably and depends mainly on how the contents attack the internal coating of the tin which may corrode and lay bare the steel.
- Due to fewer preserving additives, many bottled foods now need to be refrigerated once they are opened.
- Cleaning materials often have a strong smell; therefore they should be kept in a separate store. Cleaning powders should never be stored near food.

Storage accommodation

Foods are divided into three groups for the purpose of storage: perishable foods, dry foods and frozen foods.

- Perishable foods include: meat, poultry, game, fish; dairy produce and fats; vegetables and fruit.
- Dry foods include: cereals, pulses, sugar, flour, etc.; bread, cakes; jams, pickles and other bottled foods; canned foods; cleaning materials.
- Frozen foods must be placed immediately into a deep freeze at a temperature of −2°C (28°F).

STORAGE OF PERISHABLE FOODS

Meat and poultry

- Meat joints should be hung on hooks with drip tray to collect any blood.
- Temperature of refrigerator should be between −1°C (30°F) and 1°C (34°F).
- Humidity level should be approximately 90%.
- Meat and poultry should ideally be stored in separate places.
- Cuts of meat may be brushed with oil or wrapped in oiled greaseproof paper.
- Drip trays and other trays used for meat or poultry should be cleaned daily.
- Frozen meat and poultry must be stored at −20°C (21°F).

Fish

- Store in ice in fish refrigerator or fish drainer at between −1°C (30°F) to 1°C (34°F).
- Keep types of fish separated.
- Smoked fish should be separate from fresh fish.
- Frozen fish should be stored at −18°C (0°F).

Vegetables

- Ideally have a cool dry vegetable store with racks.
- As a safety precaution do not stack sacks too high.
- Leave potatoes in sacks.
- Place root vegetables on racks.
- Store green vegetables on racks.
- Store lettuces leave as delivered.
- Remove any vegetables that show decay.
- Leave onions and shallots in nets or racked.
- Place cauliflower and broccoli on racks.
- Leave courgettes, peppers, avocado pears and cucumbers in delivery containers.
- Leave mushrooms in containers.

Fruit

- Soft fruits should be left in punnets and placed in refrigeration.
- Hard fruits and store fruits are stored in cold store.
- Do not refrigerate bananas as they will turn black.

Eggs
- Store refrigerated at 1–4°C (34–40°F).
- Keep away from other foods; their shells are porous and they can absorb strong smells.
- Keep in their delivery boxes; handle as little as possible.
- Use in rotation.

Milk and cream
- Store in the refrigerator below 5°C (41°F).
- Partially used containers should be covered.
- Use in rotation.

Cheese and butter
- Refrigerate at a temperature below 5°C (41°F).
- Cut cheeses should be wrapped.
- Use in rotation.

Bread, etc.
- Use in rotation, first in first out.
- Store in well-ventilated cool store.
- Avoid overstocking.
- Take care that biscuits are stacked carefully to avoid breaking.
- Frozen gâteaux should be kept frozen.
- Cakes containing cream must be refrigerated.

Sandwiches
- All sandwiches must be sold within 4–24 hours of preparation.
- They must be stored at a maximum temperature of 8°C (46°F).
- Sandwiches to be sold within 4 hours are not covered by this legislation.

STORAGE OF DRY GOODS
- Storage must be cool, well lit, ventilated.
- Storage should be off the floor or in bins.
- Issue goods in rotation, last in last out.
- Stack items so that stock rotation is simple to operate.
- Arrange items in such a way that they can easily be checked.

STORAGE OF ICE-CREAM AND FROZEN GOODS
- Store immediately on receipt.
- Storage temperature must be at −20°C (−4°F).
- Use in rotation.
- Keep chest lid closed as much as possible.

Cleanliness and safety of storage areas

High standards of hygiene are essential in the store.

- Personnel must:
  - wear clean clothing;

- be clean in themselves;
- be particular with regard to hand washing;
- have clean hygienic habits.
- Floors must:
  - be kept clear;
  - be cleaned of any spillage at once;
  - be in good repair.
- Shelving must:
  - be kept clean;
  - not be overloaded.
- Cleaning material must be:
  - kept away from foods;
  - stored with care and marked dangerous if they are dangerous chemicals.
- Windows and, where appropriate, doors must be fly- and bird-proof.
- Walls should be clean and where any access by rodents is possible, sealed.
- Equipment such as knives, scales, etc., must be:
  - thoroughly cleaned;
  - stored so that cross-contamination is prevented.
- Cloths for cleaning should be of the disposable type.
- Surfaces should be cleaned with an antibacterial cleaner.
- All bins should have lids and be kept covered.
- All empties should be stacked in a safe area with care.
- Waste and rubbish should not be allowed to accumulate.
- Empty bottles, waste paper, cardboard, etc. should be recycled.

The cold room (see also the section on refrigeration, page 411)

A large catering establishment may have a cold room for meat, with possibly a deep-freeze compartment where supplies can be kept frozen for long periods. The best temperature for storing fresh meat and poultry (short term) is between 4° and 6°C (39–43°F) with a controlled humidity (poultry is stored in a cold room). Fish should have a cold room of its own so that it does not affect other foods. Game, when plucked, is also kept in a cold room.

Chill room

A chill room keeps food cold without freezing, and is particularly suitable for those foods requiring a consistent, not too cold, temperature, such as dessert fruits, salads, cheese. Fresh fruit, salads and vegetables are best stored at a temperature of 4–6°C (39–43°F) with a humidity that will not result in loss of water from the leaves causing them to go limp. Green vegetables should be stored in a dark area to prevent leaves turning yellow. Certain fruits such as peaches and avocados are best stored at 10°C (50°F), while bananas must not be stored below 13°C (55°F) otherwise they will turn black. Dairy products (milk, cream, yogurt and butter) are best stored at

2°C (35°F). Cheese requires differing storage temperatures according to the type of cheese and degree of ripeness. Fats and oils are best stored at 4–7°C (39–45°F) otherwise they are liable to go rancid.

Refrigeration

Because spoilage and food poisoning organisms multiply most rapidly in warm conditions, there is a need for refrigeration through every stage of food delivery, storage, preparation, service and in certain situations onward distribution. Refrigeration does not kill micro-organisms but prevents them multiplying. Many cases of food poisoning can be tracked back to failure to control food temperatures or failure to cool food properly.

Temperature control is so important that statutory measures have been extended by the Food Hygiene Regulations whereby all food must be stored at or below 8°C (46°F) and some foods at lower temperatures. Chilling at 0°–3°C (32–37°F) and freezing at −18° to −22°C (0° to −7.6°F) is the easiest and most natural way of preserving food and maintaining product quality because it:

* cuts down on wastage (reducing operating costs);
* allows a wider variety of food to be stacked;
* gives flexibility in delivering, preparation and use of foods.

To maintain the quality and freshness of food, refrigeration at correct temperatures must be provided:

* at delivery;
* for storage;
* for preparation;
* for onward distribution;
* for holding, display and service.

TYPES OF REFRIGERATION
* Mise en place – these are smaller refrigerators placed near to or under specific working areas. Some types have bain-marie style containers which allow for the storage of the many small prepared food items required in a busy à la carte kitchen.
* Separate cabinets are essential for such foods as pastry; meat and fish; and cold buffets where food is displayed for more than 4 hours.
* Quick chillers – as the slow cooling of cooked food can allow rapid bacterial growth, rapid chillers are available.
* Display cabinets incorporating forced circulation of chilled air.

TEMPERATURE CHECKS (see Plates 106–109, pages 329 and 330)
In addition to the legal requirements for food to be stored at the correct temperature, the maintenance of correct temperature display should be specified on each cabinet and should be monitored regularly, with the use of probes, thermometers, etc. (See also page 411 on 'How refrigeration works'.)

Further information can be obtained from Electricity Association, 30 Millbank, London SW1P 4RD.

Temperatures and storage times are listed in the tables below.

TEMPERATURES AND STORAGE TIMES FOR FREEZERS

SYMBOL	TEMPERATURE MAXIMUM	SAFETY STORAGE TIME
*	−6°C (21°F)	7 days
**	−12°C (10°F)	1 month
***	−18°C (0°F)	3 months
****	−18°C (0°F)	more than 3 months

STORAGE TEMPERATURES FOR FROZEN ITEMS OF FOODS

meat	−20°C to −16°C (−4° to 3°F)
fish	−20°C to −16°C (−4° to 3°F)
frozen foods	−20°C to −16°C (−4° to 3°F)
ice-cream	−22°C to −18°C (−8° to 0°F)

STORAGE TEMPERATURE OF REFRIGERATED FOOD ITEMS

cooked pies, pasties, sausage rolls	7°C (44°F)
pies containing gelatine	5°C (41°F)
other cooked foods	8°C (46°F)
milk and cream	5°C (41°F)
eggs	4°C (40°F)

These are temperatures which must not be exceeded; lower temperatures down to 1°C (34°F) are preferable.

REFRIGERATED PRODUCTS IN THE RIGHT CABINET

TYPE	TEMPERATURE	PRODUCTS
refrigerator	1°–4°C (34°–39°F)	cooked meats (ham, pork, beef, lamb, etc.); cooked poultry and game (chicken, turkey, duck, etc.); dairy products (milk, butter, fats, eggs, cheese); prepared salads, sandwiches
meat cabinet	−2°–0°C (28°–32°F)	fresh lamb, beef, pork, chicken, turkey, duck, etc.
fish cabinet	−2°–0°C (28°–32°F)	fresh fish (cod, plaice, haddock, skate, etc.)
freezer	−18°−−20°C (0°−−4°F)	frozen meat; poultry; vegetables; prepared meals; ice-cream, etc.

POINTS TO NOTE ON REFRIGERATION

- All refrigerators, cold rooms, chill rooms and deep-freeze units should be regularly inspected and maintained by qualified refrigeration engineers.
- Defrosting should take place regularly, according to the instructions issued from the manufacturers. Refrigerators usually need to be defrosted weekly; if this is not done, then the efficiency of the refrigerator is lessened.
- While a cold unit is being defrosted it should be thoroughly cleaned, including all the shelves.
- Hot foods should never be placed in a refrigerator or cold room because the steam given off can affect nearby foods.
- Peeled onions should never be kept in a cold room because the smell can taint other foods.

Vegetable store

This should be designed to store all vegetables in a cool, dry, well-ventilated room with bins for root vegetables and racking for others. Care should be taken to see that old stocks of vegetables are used before the new ones; this is important as fresh vegetables and fruits deteriorate quickly. If it is not convenient to empty root vegetables into bins they should be kept in the sack on racks off the ground.

Ordering of goods within the establishment

In a large catering establishment the stores carry a stock which for variety and quantity often equals a large grocery store. Its operation is similar in many respects, the main difference being that requisitions take the place of cash. The system of internal and external accountancy must be simple but precise.

The storekeeper

The essentials which go to making a good storekeeper are:

- experience
- knowledge of how to handle, care for and organise the stock in his or her charge
- a tidy mind and sense of detail
- a quick grasp of figures
- clear handwriting
- a liking for his or her job
- honesty

There are many departments which draw supplies from these stores – kitchen, still room, restaurant, grill room, banqueting, floor service. A list of these departments should be given to the storekeeper, together with the signatures of the heads of departments or those who have the right to sign the requisition forms.

All requisitions must be handed to the storekeeper in time to allow the ordering and delivery of the goods on the appropriate day. Different coloured requisitions may be used for the various departments if desired.

DUTIES OF A STOREKEEPER
- To keep a good standard of tidiness and cleanliness.
- To arrange proper storage space for all incoming foodstuffs.
- To keep up-to-date price lists of all commodities.
- To ensure that an ample supply of all important foodstuffs is always available.
- To check that all orders are correctly made out, and dispatched in good time.
- To check all incoming stores – quantity, quality and price.
- To keep all delivery notes, invoices, credit notes, receipts and statements efficiently filed.
- To keep a daily stores issue sheet (see Figure 8.3).
- To keep a set of bin cards.
- To issue nothing without receiving a signed chit in exchange.
- To check all stock at frequent intervals.
- To see that all chargeable containers are properly kept, returned and credited, that is all money charged for sacks, boxes, etc. is deducted from the account.
- To obtain the best value at the lowest buying price.
- To know when foods are in or out of season.

TYPES OF RECORDS USED IN STORES CONTROL

Bin card (see Figure 8.3)

There should be an individual bin card for each item held in stock. The following details are found on the bin card:

- name of the commodity
- issuing unit
- date goods are received or issued
- from whom they are received and to whom issued

- maximum stock
- minimum stock
- quantity received
- quantity issued
- balance held in stock

Stores ledger (see Figure 8.5)

This is usually found in the form of a loose-leaf file giving one ledger sheet to each item held in stock. The following details are found on a stores ledger sheet:

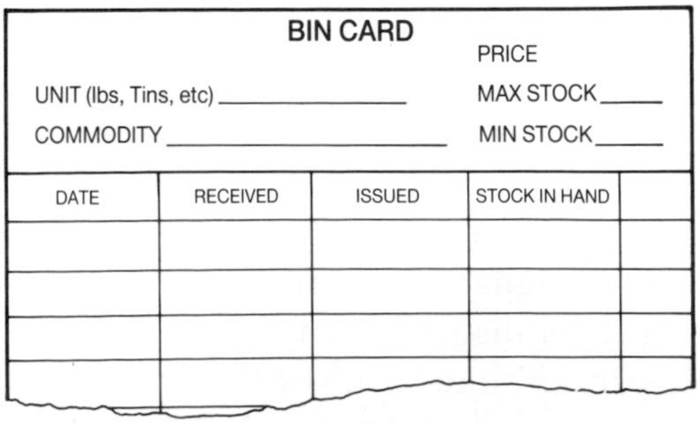

Fig. 8.3 Example of a bin card

Daily Stores Issues Sheet

Commodity	Unit	Stock in hand	Monday		Tuesday		Wednesday		Thursday		Friday		Total pur-chases	Total issues	Total stock
			In	Out	In	Out	In	Out	In	Out	In	Out			
Butter	kg	27		2						3				5	22
Flour	Sacks	2		1			1						1	1	2
Olive oil	Litres	8		1						½				1½	6½
Spices	30g packs	8		4			8						8	4	12
Peas, tin	A10	30		6						3				9	21

.... CANTEEN Week ending .... No. meals served .... Cost per meal ....

Commodity	hand B/F	Stock received during week						Stock used during week							@*	Cost*	in hand C/F
		M.	Tu.	W.	Th	F.	Total	M.	Tu.	W.	Th.	F.	S.	Total			
Apples, canned																	
Apples, dried Apricots, etc – dried																	
Baking powder																	
Baked beans																	

* The cost of stock used can also be checked by using two extra columns

Fig. 8.4   Example of a daily stores issue sheet

- name of commodity
- classification
- unit
- maximum stock
- minimum stock
- date of goods received or issued
- from whom they are received and to whom issued

- invoice or requisition number
- quantity received or issued and the remaining balance held in stock
- unit price
- cash value of goods received and issued and the balancing cash total of goods held in stock

Every time goods are received or issued the appropriate entries should be made on the necessary stores ledger sheets and bin cards. In this way the balance on the bin card should always be the same as the balance shown on the stores ledger sheet.

Departmental requisition book (see Figure 8.6)

One of these books should be issued to each department in the catering establishment which needs to draw goods from the store. These books can either be of different colours or have departmental serial numbers. Every time goods are drawn from the store a requisition must be filled out and signed by the necessary

BIN No   DESCRIPTION   CLASSIFICATION   CODE UNIT MAXIMUM MINIMUM

Date	DETAIL	Invoice or Req No	QUANTITY			UNIT PRICE	VALUE		
			Received	Balance	Issued		Received	Balance	Issued

Fig. 8.5   Example of a stores ledger sheet

DEPARTMENTAL REQUISITION BOOK									267	
Date _____				Class _____						
Description	Quan	Unit	Price per Unit	Issued if Different	Quan	Unit	Price per Unit	Code	£	

Fig. 8.6 Example of a stores requisition sheet

head of department – this applies whether one or 20 items are needed from the store. When the storekeeper issues the goods he or she will check them against the requisition and tick them off; at the same time the cost of each item is filled in. In this way the total expenditure over a period for a certain department can be quickly found. The following details are found on the requisition sheet:

- serial number
- name of department
- date
- description of goods required
- quantity of goods required
- unit;
- price per unit

- issue, if different
- quantity of goods issued
- unit
- price per unit
- cash column
- signature

Order book

This is in duplicate and has to be filled in by the storekeeper every time he or she wishes to have goods delivered. Whenever goods are ordered, an order sheet must be filled in and sent to the supplier, and on receipt of the goods they should be checked against both delivery note and duplicate order sheet. All order sheets must be signed by the storekeeper. Details found on an order sheet are as follows:

- name and address of catering establishment
- name and address of supplier
- serial number of order sheet
- quantity of goods

- description of goods to be ordered
- date
- signature
- date of delivery, if specific day required

Stock sheets

Stock should be taken at regular intervals of either one week or one month. Spot checks are advisable about every three months. The stock check should be taken where possible by an independent person, thus preventing the chance of 'pilfering' and 'fiddling' taking place. The details found on the stock sheets are as follows:

- description of goods
- quantity received and issued, and balance

- price per unit
- cash columns

The stock sheets will normally be printed in alphabetical order.

All fresh foodstuffs such as meat, fish and vegetables, will be entered in the stock sheet in the normal manner, but as they are purchased and used up daily a NIL stock will always be shown on their respective ledger sheets.

COMMERCIAL DOCUMENTS

Essential parts of a control system of any catering establishment are delivery notes, invoices, credit notes and statements.

Delivery notes

These are sent with goods supplied as a means of checking that everything ordered has been delivered. The delivery note should also be checked against the duplicate order sheet.

Invoices

These are bills sent to clients, setting out the cost of goods supplied or services rendered. An invoice should be sent on the day the goods are despatched or the services are rendered or as soon as possible afterwards. At least one copy of each invoice is made and used for posting up the books of accounts, stock records and so on. (See Figure 8.7.)

Invoices contain the following information:

- name, address, telephone numbers (as a printed heading), fax numbers, of the firm supplying the goods or services;
- name and address of the firm to whom the goods or services have been supplied;
- the word *invoice*;
- date on which the goods or services were supplied;
- particulars of the goods or services supplied together with the prices;
- a note concerning the terms of settlement, such as 'Terms 5% per month', which means that if the person receiving the invoice settles his or her account within one month he or she may deduct 5% as discount.

Credit notes

These are advices to clients, setting out allowances made for goods returned or adjustments made through errors of overcharging on invoices. They should also be issued when chargeable containers such as crates, boxes or sacks are returned. Credit notes are exactly the same in form as invoices except that the word *credit note* appears in place of the word *invoice*. To make them more easily distinguishable they are usually printed in red, whereas invoices are always printed in black. A credit note should be sent as soon as it is known that a client is entitled to the credit of a sum with which he or she has been previously charged by invoice.

Statements

These are summaries of all invoices and credit notes sent to clients during the previous accounting period, usually one month. They also show any sums owing or paid from previous accounting periods and the total amount due. A statement is

```
┌─────────────────────────────────────────────────────────────────┐
│ INVOICE                                                           │
├─────────────────────────────────────────────────────────────────┤
│ Phone: 0181 574 1133                      No. 03957              │
│ Fax: 0181 574 1123              Vegetable Suppliers Ltd.,        │
│                                      5 Warwick Road,             │
│                                         Southall,                │
│                                         Middlesex                │
│ Messrs. L. Moriarty & Co.,                                       │
│ 597 High Street,                                                 │
│ Ealing,                                                          │
│ London, W5                       Terms: 5% One month             │
├─────────────────────────────────────────────────────────────────┤
│ Your order No. 67 Dated 3rd September, 19 . . .            £     │
├─────────────────────────────────────────────────────────────────┤
│ Sept 26th   56 lbs Potatoes at 12p per lb               6.72    │
│              7 lbs Sprouts at 15p per lb                1.05    │
│                                                         ─────    │
│                                                         7.77    │
└─────────────────────────────────────────────────────────────────┘
```

```
┌─────────────────────────────────────────────────────────────────┐
│ STATEMENT                                                         │
├─────────────────────────────────────────────────────────────────┤
│ Phone: 0181 574 1133            Vegetable Suppliers Ltd.,        │
│ Fax: 0181 574 1123                   5 Warwick Road,             │
│                                         Southall,                │
│                                         Middlesex                │
│ Messrs. L. Moriarty & Co.,                                       │
│ 597 High Street,                                                 │
│ Ealing,                                                          │
│ London, W5                       Terms: 5% One month             │
├─────────────────────────────────────────────────────────────────┤
│ 19 . . .                                                    £    │
│ Sept 10th      Goods                                      45.90  │
│       17th     Goods                                      32.41  │
│       20th     Goods                                      41.30  │
│       26th     Goods                                      16.15  │
│                                                         ──────   │
│                                                          135.76  │
│       28th     Returns credited                            4.80  │
│                                                         ──────   │
│                                                          130.96  │
└─────────────────────────────────────────────────────────────────┘
```

Fig. 8.7   Example of an invoice and statement

usually a copy of a client's ledger account and does not contain more information than is necessary to check invoices and credit notes.

When a client makes payment he or she usually sends a cheque, together with the statement he or she has received. The cheque is paid into the bank and the statement may be returned to the client duly receipted.

Cash discount

This is a discount allowed in consideration of prompt payment. At the end of any length of time chosen as an accounting period, such as one month, there will be some outstanding debts. In order to encourage customers to pay within a stipulated time, sellers of goods frequently offer a discount. This is called cash discount. By offering cash discount, the seller may induce his or her customer to pay more quickly, so turning debts into ready money. Cash discount varies from $1\frac{1}{4}$ to 10%, depending on the seller and the time: $2\frac{1}{2}$% if paid in 10 days; $1\frac{1}{4}$% if paid in 28 days, for example.

Trade discount

This is discount allowed by one trader to another, a deduction from the catalogue price of goods made before arriving at the invoice price. The amount of trade discount does not therefore appear in the accounts. For example, in a catalogue of kitchen equipment, a machine listed at £250 less 20% trade discount shows:

Catalogue price	£250
Less 20% trade discount	£50
Invoice price	£200

The £200 is the amount entered in the appropriate accounts.

In the case of purchase tax on articles, discount is taken off *after* the tax has been deducted from list price.

Gross price is the price of an article before discount has been deducted.

Net price is the price after discount has been deducted; in some cases a price on which no discount will be allowed.

CASH ACCOUNT

The following are the essentials for the keeping of a simple cash account:

- all entries must be dated;
- all monies received must be clearly named and entered on the left-hand or debit side of the book;
- all monies paid out must also be clearly shown and entered on the right-hand or credit side of the book;
- at the end of a given period - either a day, week or month or at the end of each page - the book must be balanced; that is, both sides are totalled and the difference between the two is known as the balance; if, for example, the debit side (money received) is greater than the credit side (money paid out), then a credit or right-hand side balance is shown, so that the two totals are then equal; a credit balance then means cash in hand;
- a debit balance cannot occur because it is impossible to pay out more than is received.

An example is given in the following table.

CASH ACCOUNT

DR. **FIRST WEEK** **CR.**

Date	Receipts	£	Date	Payment	£
Oct 3	to lunches	222.00	Oct 1	by repairs	54.50
4	„ teas	76.15	2	„ grocer	74.40
5	„ tax rebate	48.92	6	„ butcher	48.64
				„ balance c/fwd	169.53
		347.07			347.07

DR. **SECOND WEEK** **CR.**

Date	Receipts	£	Date	Payment	£
Oct	to balance b/fwd	169.53	Oct 8	by fishmonger	36.30
9	„ sale of pastries	56.45	10	„ fuel	40.00
11	„ goods	175.64	11	„ tax	30.00
			12	„ greengrocer	56.16
				„ balance c/fwd	239.16
		401.62			401.62

DR. **THIRD WEEK** **CR.**

Date	Receipts	£	Date	Payment	£
Oct	to balance b/fwd	239.16	Oct 19	by butcher	38.42
15	„ teas	60.10	21	„ grocer	40.65
17	„ pastries	75.00		„ balance c/fwd	469.11
24	„ goods	57.40			
26	„ goods	64.32			
29	„ goods	52.20			
		548.18			548.18

General rule

Debit – monies coming in.
Credit – monies going out.

Example

Make out a cash account and enter the following transactions:

Oct.	1	Paid for repair to stove	£109.00
	2	Paid to grocer	148.80
	3	Received for lunches	440.00
	4	Received for teas	152.30
	5	Received tax rebate	97.84
	6	Paid to butcher	97.28
Oct.	8	Paid to fishmonger	72.60
	9	Received for sale of pastries	112.90
	10	Paid for fuel	80.00
	11	Paid tax	60.00

	11	Received for goods	351.28
	12	Paid to greengrocer	112.36
Oct.	15	Received for teas	120.20
	17	Received for pastries	150.00
	19	Paid to butcher	76.80
	21	Paid to grocer	81.30
	24	Received for goods	114.80
	26	Received for goods	128.60
	29	Received for goods	104.40

TOPICS FOR DISCUSSION

Food purchasing

1. A food-buying policy.
2. Is there a need for portion control?
3. The relationship between food quality and price.
4. The reasons for using standard purchasing specifications.
5. The use of standardised recipes.
6. How you would implement a cost control system.
7. The advantages of a computerised stockkeeping system.
8. How the role of the storekeeper may change in the future.

Storage and control

1. Why control of goods from receipt (delivery) to final destination (the customer) is essential.
2. What controls are needed regarding goods, staff and the preparation and service of food?
3. The need to be knowledgeable regarding the cost and quality of foods in relation to selling price.
4. The implication of setting the selling price too low and also of setting it too high.

9
Promotion, selling and customer care

ASPECTS OF PROMOTION AND SELLING

Once a catering establishment has been planned, the process has to be generated whereby the buyer and seller come together. Through *promotion*, customers are made aware of the establishment, persuaded to make a visit and encouraged to return. Promotion is concerned with the product. This product constitutes a total package on offer, and includes some of the following concepts:

- the image of the establishment;
- the quality of the product and service;
- the style of management and staff;
- the prices charged;
- the environment, facilities and services.

Promotion should inform the customer of the establishment, make them aware of its existence, persuade them to buy and convince them of the image and quality of the product. This is done through:

- personal selling
- advertising
- sales promotion
- merchandising
- public relations
- agents

Promotion is an activity which must be carefully planned and controlled. Usually, the main objective of the promotional campaign is to stimulate demand by using persuasive messages to attract new customers and past users of the establishment. Such messages must convince prospective customers that the product on offer is good value for money.

Defining the market

The manager or chef should establish the best potential market. This will determine the type of messages to project in order to influence customer behaviour. It will also indicate the best form of media relevant to the age, sex, social class, income level and location of the target customer. It is important for these messages to emphasise the benefits of the product to the customer.

Promotion timing

Promotion timing depends on the objectives and when the decision to purchase is to be made by the customer.

Personal selling (see Plate 110, page 331)

Personal selling is done through contacts with local organisations and committees, for example, or, more directly, through the senior restaurant staff talking to clients. All employees who are in contact with customers must be made aware of the importance of selling the products to increase profits and provide a satisfactory experience for the customer.

All staff must therefore gain a good knowledge of the company's products and services and develop good social skills with an ability to promote and sell. Showing concern for the customers not only makes them feel comfortable but also promotes sales and increases the effectiveness of the establishment.

Advertising

This should convey messages which will influence consumer attitudes and behaviour favourable to the seller. Advertising should:

- increase sales immediately;
- create greater public awareness of the location and existence of the establishment;
- persuade the public that the product and services are good value for money.
- concentrate on the benefits of using the establishment and consuming the product;
- focus on the product differences from those of competitors.

Advertising can be done via the following media:

- posters
- magazines
- newspapers
- radio
- television
- direct mail

The selection depends on finance and the target audience.

DIRECT MAIL

The advantages of direct mail include:

- the ability to select potential customers who are likely to buy the product: target groups can be broken down into geographical location, leisure interest and socio-economic groups, to name a few;
- the ability to express a personal message to each customer;
- the ability to time the promotion;
- the ability to gauge the level of response from various segments of the market and evaluate the cost-effectiveness of the exercise.

Sales promotion

Sales promotion is a day-to-day operation relating to discount offers, price reductions, special offers, such as a free bottle of wine with every meal for two. They are designed to appeal to a certain section of the market: weekend promoting, gastronomic evenings, gastronomic weekends, golfing weekends and food festivals.

Food festivals are held to promote cuisine and beverages of a particular region or country. A themed promotion may help the business and promote sales in the following ways:

- increase sales during off-peak periods by attracting new customers;
- gain publicity in local press and on local radio;
- stimulate and keep the interest of regular customers.

Competing with other establishments and creating a new type of trade, such as conferences, are two other examples of sales promotions activities.

Merchandising

To be a successful caterer a knowledge of merchandising is important. The object of merchandising is to sell more and to reassure customers about the quality of what is being offered: for example, the quality of the cooking, fresh produce being used and persuading customers to return to the establishment.

Merchandising is the art of displaying products attractively to promote sales. This is done to great effect in supermarkets. For example, on the fresh fish counter they display a very small selection of rare or expensive fish and shellfish. This has the effect of making the fish counter interesting, drawing customers' attention and encouraging them to buy, not necessarily the specialist items but more generally the everyday species. An example of merchandising in a fast-food restaurant is the illustrated fascia above the counter showing what is available with the help of coloured photographs. Such a display may also be used in a luxury restaurant where a display of exotic fruits and vegetables helps to promote sales.

In a staff restaurant, tent cards and displays are used at various points on the counter to promote certain dishes. These areas are commonly known as hot spots where the customer is encouraged to buy either an additional item or an item which yields a higher profit margin.

Menus and wine lists are important merchandising tools and should be at the forefront of the merchandising strategy.

THE CUSTOMER

Firstly profile the groups of customers and consider their preferences. Before you decide what you are going to display, first define:

- type of customer (age, background, social class, income groups, gender);
- the people and organisations that use your establishment;
- the frequency of their custom;
- their use of other catering services;
- how they use their time;
- how they use their disposable income.

THE PRODUCT

Consider the product profile, this will define the context of your merchandising policy. You must consider all aspects of the product and products, particularly those aspects which relate to:

- the appearance of food and beverage; for example, preparing dishes in front of the customer such as salads, grilling meat and fish or flambé dishes; this may be suitable in some situations but not others.
- how customers see the service you offer;
- how the product can be further developed with appearance in mind;
- how the product may be promoted using posters, tent cards, illustrated menu cards.

Many of the major supermarkets can give caterers good ideas on how to develop merchandising.

WHAT AND HOW TO DISPLAY
When the marketing context has been established, the next stage is to consider how to show services and products to their best advantage and to develop aspects of them which will provide additional attractions. The caterer may like to focus on:

- the quality and freshness of ingredients;
- the use of fresh flowers and fruits for display;
- using a selection of finished dishes for display; this is done to great effect when displaying a choice of plated sweets on a tray;
- assessing how displayed food on a self-service buffet will look after customers have taken portions from the various dishes;
- how dishes deteriorate in presentation and flavour when they have been standing for too long;
- assessing how the smell of cooking is an advantage or disadvantage; supermarkets encourage the smell of freshly baked bread and this encourages people to buy bread products;
- how the menu is displayed and the language which is used to describe dishes (does the layout and language encourage sales?);
- the provision of essential information about ingredients, sources of wine, vintages and prices in menus and wine lists.

WHERE TO DISPLAY
In any restaurant thought must be given to the space required for merchandising and the strategic points where a display will give maximum effect. Consider:

- customer flow;
- position of check-in and cash desks;
- entrances and exits;
- use of lounges and bar areas;
- use of displays outside restaurants (for example in the street or windows);
- hotel bedrooms for a hotel restaurant;
- the facility of agents of business associates.

WHEN TO DISPLAY
Timing is important both as an opportunity and as a means of getting the best from a merchandising project. Opportunities on many occasions present themselves at short notice and projects need not be long lasting.

Special evening events may be held where key clients or customers are invited to sample food. Major department stores including Marks and Spencers invite store card holders to special evenings, presales events or special Christmas shopping events. These account customers feel special and further encouraged to buy.

If special events are to be held, the caterer must consider:

- the season;
- the weather;
- the event, whether this is to be local or national.

MERCHANDISING ADMINISTRATION

Ideas have to be developed and implemented. All relevant material relating to food and drink must reflect the style and service of the product on offer.

- Descriptive terms used in menus and displays must be appropriate to the aims of the catering establishment. Accuracy and spelling is very important. Remember the menu and wine list are selling tools and should help the customer to understand what you have to offer.
- All themes should be carefully researched; ambition must not exceed capability.
- Point of sale notices should be in keeping with the overall style of the restaurant. Wording must be positive and friendly. Notices should be presented with style and confidence.
- Avoid hand-written notices, these give a very amateur impression of your establishment.
- Items displayed in generous quantities can assist sales. For example, when supermarkets have special offers on, they sometimes stack the product so it gives the impression that it is plentiful; this has the effect of encouraging the customer to buy not one but at least two of the items on special offer.
- Consider combined presentations, port with stilton, dessert wine with the sweet course.
- All display material must be maintained in good order, otherwise it will have the adverse effect of discouraging sales. For example the sweet tray should be replenished. Menus and wine lists should be replaced before they become shabby.

Public relations

Public relations is an exercise concerned with building an 'image' of the establishment in the public's mind. Public relations must create a favourable impression to present and future customers, employees and investors and, therefore, is not usually directly related to a particular product or service.

Evaluation

Evaluation is a necessary part of a promotion campaign. It is achieved by:

- monitoring the enquiries received as a result of a particular advertisement;

- analysing sales figures;
- measuring public awareness of a product and after promotion;
- actual sales in 'test markets'.

SERVICE OF FOOD

The mode of service will depend on the type of establishment, and in some places more than one kind of service will be used, often from one kitchen. The cost of operating these methods varies, but the final objective is the same, that is the food, when presented to the customer, should look attractive, should be of the right temperature, should be as ordered and give value for money.

The kinds of service that are used are:

- waiter or waitress service (Plate 111, page 331);
- cafeteria service (Plate 113, page 331);
- hatch and counter service (Plate 112, page 331);
- snack bar, buffet service, take away.

The kind of service to be provided will depend to some extent upon the type of people to be served, the number of people to be served, the dining accommodation, the number of sittings and the amount of time and money to be spent on the meal.

Waiter/waitress service

This method of service is the most costly to operate; it is used extensively in many kinds of restaurants. The waiter or waitress takes the order from the customer, then the food ordered is collected from the hot plate by the waiting staff and served to the customer.

For the kitchen staff the following points are of importance:

- The food ordered by the waiter should be ready when it is required.
- Food should leave the kitchen at the correct temperature (hot if it should be hot, cold if it is meant to be cold), so that it can be presented correctly to the customer by the waiter.
- Orders received from the waiting staff should be dealt with in strict rotation and must go on a hot plate in the same order. (However, the waiter should not expect food to be on the hot plate before a reasonable period of time.)
- The correct kitchen accompaniment to dishes should be sent from the hot plate with the appropriate dish; the vegetables, as ordered, should be ready to go with the main dishes.

Co-operation between the kitchen and restaurant staff is essential for the successful service of food. The teaching of waiting to young people training to work in the kitchen is invaluable, since they are given an opportunity to see beyond the hot plate and to appreciate the waiters' problems. The need to serve portions of equal size becomes more obvious when a customer complains that the person opposite paying the same money has a portion larger than his or her own. The difficulty of sharing five potatoes between two people or trying to bone an insufficiently cooked sole in front of the customer should cause the kitchen brigade to be careful in the way they prepare and serve the food.

Waiting staff will be used for à la carte and table d'hôte menu service (see Chapter 7), also for banquets, for club service, and for hotel room service (see Figure 9.1).

POINTS TO NOTE

In serving food, the kitchen staff should remember these points:

- It is necessary to dress the dish in such a way that the waiter may effectively transfer the food from the dish to the customer's plate.
- The food must be served on the correct dish, which should be clean and of the right temperature.
- The food should be arranged attractively; this is very important.
- The dish should be clean after the food has been added to it and the correct amount should be placed on the dish.
- Food which is served on a plate should be arranged neatly and the plate rims must be clean.
- Hot foods (except those which are deep fried and would go limp and soft) should be covered with a lid.

Fig.9.1   Room service

Cafeteria service (see Plates 113 and 114; pages 331 and 332)

Cafeteria service developed because of the need to serve large numbers of people quickly and efficiently. Almost any type of food can be displayed: soups, casseroles, roasts, vegetable dishes and warm desserts along with cold dishes, salads, fruits, cold sweets, pastries and beverages.

The menu should be clearly displayed to assist the customer in making his/her choice; each customer takes a tray at the beginning of the counter and proceeds along either taking whatever food is required or being served by a counter assistant. The customers collect their cutlery, napkins and or drinks and proceed to a table to eat. In some situations like company dining rooms, customers are requested on completion of the meal to take their tray and used crockery to a clearing-up point.

Food counters may be:

* small counter-top units for displays of a limited menu;
* refrigerated, ambient and heated display cupboards and back bar cooking equipment;
* a comprehensive combination of units catering for all possible requirements.

Where large numbers of people need to be served over a short period, it may be necessary to concentrate each type of food (snacks, hot foods, salads, beverages) in separate areas or in echelon style with a clearly displayed menu over each unit.

Cafeteria units include:

* hot cupboards, used to warm plates, hold plated foods at a particular temperature or store containers from the oven until counter displays need replenishing;
* bain-marie tops, wet and dry models designed to maintain food in excess of 65°C (149°F);
* overhead gantries, to hold quartz or infrared lamps which help to counteract cross draughts that can cool the food;
* carvery units, free-standing or drop-in units which can incorporate heated tiled areas for dishes of vegetables;
* through units, hot cupboards sited as a pass-through link between the kitchen and service areas;
* cold or heated show cases, fitted with self-service flaps for snacks and plated foods;
* sneeze screens, for hygiene precautions;
* refrigerated units, for displaying cold foods and keeping them at a safe temperature;
* cafeteria counters, fixed or mobile, depending on the situation and requirements of the operation;
* mobile units, versatile and usually made up of a cupboard, counter top and a choice of fittings; mobility is afforded by castors which have brakes for securing the units when in position; they can include: plate dispensers, openings for Gastronorm containers, carvery point, overhead lamps, sneeze screens and display lighting;

- carousel, where kitchen and service areas are linked by a revolving carousel with a number of tiers fitted for cold, hot or ambient temperature food; as the carousel rotates the customer selects and the kitchen replenishes;
- plate dispensers, also known as lowerators, available heated or unheated; these are useful in moving clean crockery from the wash-up to the servery; they are spring-loaded so that as one plate is taken the spring pushes the remainder to the top.
- cash point/s carefully sited so that the customer is able to both pay for his hot food and get it to the table while it is still hot.

HEALTH AND SAFETY

Correct temperature control is essential; as a general rule hot foods are kept above 63°C (145°F) and cold foods depending on the product kept below either 8°C (46°F) or 5°C (41°F). At point of service the food hygiene regulations allow four hours without statutory temperature control although the food should be kept as cold as possible.

Further information can be obtained from Electricity Association, 30 Millbank, London SW1P 4RD.

Hatch service

When high-speed service of meals is required this method may be used. Hatches connect the kitchen and dining-room. These hatches will be numbered and the numbers correspond to items numbered on the menu. The customer makes up his or her mind at the entrance and goes to the appropriate hatch and collects the meal.

Another form of this method of service is to provide the main course at the hatch and a selection of vegetables to be provided. This of course is a slower method of service because, as soon as a choice is provided, service slows down. This type of service is also referred to as counter service.

Snack bars

Snack bars usually provide beverages, sandwiches, salads, fruit, pastries and pies which are suitable for people requiring something quickly or something light. Seating accommodation is provided at the service counter as well as in the room and there may also be provision for take-away food.

Take away

Customer demand for prepared and cooked food to take away has increased over the years (particularly ethnic food) and the enterprising caterer looking for the opportunity to increase his or her turnover would be well advised to explore any potential market demand for his or her products. Suitable greaseproof containers need to be available for the service and carry away of the food.

Buffets

Buffets vary considerably according to the number of people to be served and the type of establishment. All kinds of food, hot or/and cold, may be provided; some (joints of meat or poultry or whole fish) will require carving or skilled service. In some cases the customers may be served only by buffet staff or they may take a plate at the beginning of the buffet and, passing along, serve themselves. There may also be a combination of assisted and self-service such as when joints are carved by a chef and the customers help themselves to vegetables/salads and accompaniments.

Buffets can be simple to include one or two dishes and suitable accompaniments or lavish to include spectacular displays of decorated meats, poultry and game, a number of desserts, fresh fruit and cheese.

Buffets can be provided as a three-course meal with the offer of a choice of items for the first course (soup, simple hors-d'oeuvre or a smoked fish) followed by a choice of cold dishes with salads and one or two hot dishes; finally sweets, fresh fruit, cheese, coffee or tea and sweetmeats, are provided. A selection of breads or/and rolls and butter should always be available.

For further information see *Practical Cookery* (Chapter 5) and *Advanced Practical Cookery* (Chapter 1).

Cocktail parties or receptions

These are events when guests generally stand and circulate. Drinks are offered as the guests enter and the food is prepared in one-bite pieces so that it can easily be consumed whilst conversation is taking place. A wide variety of foods, snacks and canapés may be dressed on large dishes and left on tables for the guests to help themselves, or serving staff may circulate. The snacks are usually cold but often small hot snacks may also be offered usually about half way through the party. The popular time for this kind of event is 6–8 pm but obviously this type of reception may be required at any time of day or night according to the requirements of the customer.

For further information see *Practical Cookery* (Chapter 15).

Automatic Vending (see Figure 9.2, page 328)

This is the process whereby a machine provides consumable products, a service or entertainment by unlimited coin, bank note, credit card or key control, using the minimum of labour to maximise income and profit margins.

Automatic vending has application wherever people gather to work, rest, play or study.

PROVISIONS
Machines can be provided for:

- hot non-alcoholic beverages (soup, tea, coffee, chocolate):
- cold non-alcoholic beverages (post-mix machines providing fruit syrups plus carbonated or non-carbonated water);
- refrigerated food (bottle and can drinks in a cabinet, carton/plastic bottles of fruit juice, milk);
- snacks (crisps, packets of biscuits, confectionery);

Fig. 9.2   Self-service restaurant: general merchandisers vending complete cook-chill dishes for reheating in an adjacent microwave oven, plus hot and cold drinks – all coin- or card-operated

- chilled snacks (for short shelf-life products like sandwiches, butter, ham, cheese);
- refrigerated meals and snacks (sandwiches, plated meals);
- hot meals and snacks (used in conjunction with a microwave oven).

Advantages of vending

- Refreshments are available 24 hours of the day.
- Staff and labour costs are reduced. Loading, cleaning and maintenance are the only requirements.
- Machines can relieve pressure of normal service at peak periods.
- Clearing and washing-up are dispensed with because disposable cartons are used.
- Refreshments are available on the job thus reducing tea breaks.
- Consistency of quality.
- Control of stock, portion, cash and thus cost is easier.
- Operating costs are low.
- The caterer is freed for other productive tasks.
- Space is better utilised.
- Hygiene control is maintained.
- It can work by itself or can be planned to operate in conjunction with other forms of catering service.

Disadvantages of vending

- Vending cannot provide a rapid large scale service.
- There can be a risk of theft and vandalism.
- An electric power failure will stop all the vending equipment.

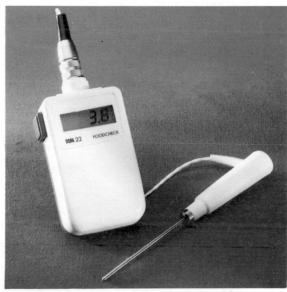

Plate 106   A hand-held thermometer

Plate 107   Testing food with a hand-held thermometer

Plate 108   A delivery temperature recorder which gives a print-out of data

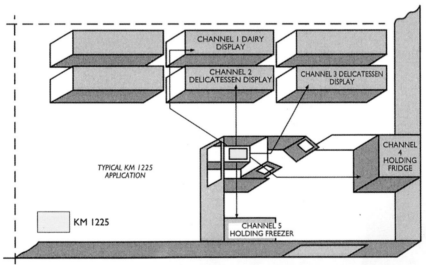

Plate 109 A central monitoring alarm unit and an example of the areas it covers

Plate 110   All staff must be aware of the importance of selling the products

Plate 111
Food service
in a first-class
hotel restaurant

Plate 112   A
refectory serving
counter

Plate 113
Cafeteria service

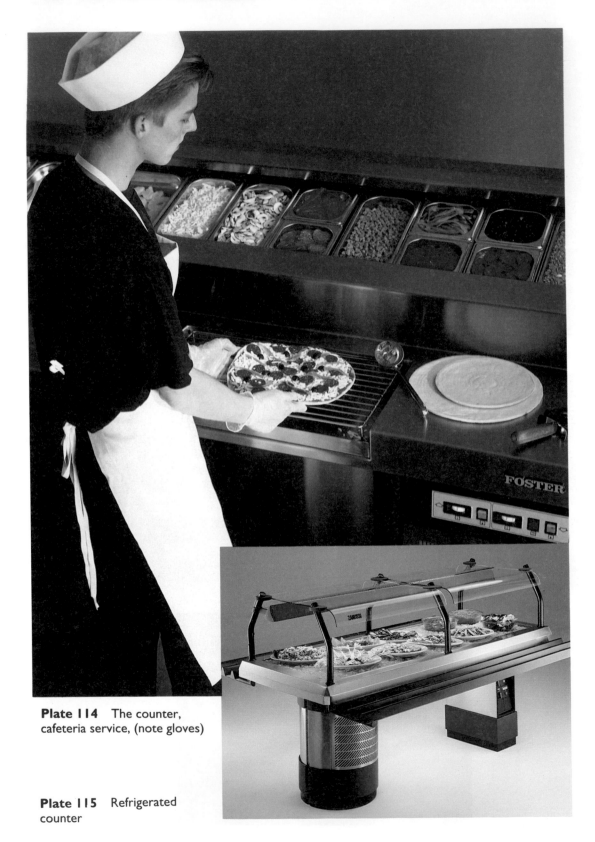

Plate 114 The counter, cafeteria service, (note gloves)

Plate 115 Refrigerated counter

Plate 116   Service counter at a speciality restaurant

MENU			Sausage, Egg & Chips	80p
¼lb Cheeseburger & Chips	£1.	15p	Steak & Kidney Pie	50p
¼lb Hamburger & Chips	£1.	10p	Toast/Bread & Butter	16p
2 oz Burger Egg & Chips		95p	Sausage Rolls	18p
New York Grill	£1.	70p	Cornish Pasties	32p
Three Fish Fingers & Chips		90p	DRINKS	
Cod & Chips	£1.	10p	Tea	15p
Pirates Platter	£1.	60p	Coffee	25p
Sausage, Beans & Chips		75p	Milk	19p

Plate 117   Menu of a speciality restaurant

Plate 118   A basic preparation area

Plate 119 (top right)   Neat working methods are essential

Plate 120 (bottom right)   The kitchen design should ensure an efficient work-flow

VENDING EQUIPMENT

The type of machine will depend upon the environment for which it is required, the density and spread of the customers or work force. This will also determine its location. When purchasing equipment, you should consider:

- cup capacity (industry estimates 1.5 to 3 drinks per person, per day when drinks are charged for; 5 to 6 when they are free);
- ingredient capacity (how often will it need to be restocked?);
- number of selections (industry estimates that a 100 selection food machine will adequately serve 120 people);
- hygiene (is it easy to clean?);
- extraction efficiency (if air extraction is poor, steam will turn any surplus powder in some machines into unhygienic deposits);
- ease of filling (canisters/hoppers should be easily removable so that powder does not spill);
- reliability (the number of moving parts is important; consider solid state or electromechanical control);
- drinks supply rate (how long with continuous use will it take for a hot or cold drink to be dispensed?);
- servicing (how much servicing is the machine likely to require? is it complex? can in-house staff be trained to do it?);
- availability of power and plumbing (where there is no mains water supply, it is possible for machines to be connected to their own separate water tank).

The British Standard BS5071 Kitemark is the national recognised standard which specifies the general requirements and tasks for drink vending machines. It also establishes safety, hygiene and performance standards.

Further information can be obtained from Automatic Vending Association of Great Britain (AVAB), Bassett House, High Street, Banstead, Surrey SM2 2LZ.

Speciality restaurants (see Plates 116, 117; page 333)

Moderately priced speciality eating houses are in great demand and have seen a tremendous growth in recent years. In order to ensure a successful operation it is essential to assess the customers' requirements accurately and to plan a menu that will attract sufficient customers to give adequate profit. A successful caterer is the one who gives customers what they want and not what the caterer thinks the customers want. The most successful catering establishments are those which offer the type of food they *can* sell, which is not necessarily the type of food they would *like* to sell.

Well-cooked fish and chips have always been popular in the UK and probably always will be; and it is interesting to note that one of the most successful speciality restaurant developments in the USA (the home of speciality restaurants) was the English fish and chip shop, complete with the food served in a bag made from an early copy of *The Times*.

The Wimpy House, McDonald's, Texas Pancake House, Pizzaland, the health food restaurant, Kentucky Fried Chicken, the sandwich bar, plus numerous others, are examples of speciality catering houses offering food and drink at moderate prices with menus carefully planned to fit their estimated markets.

Food courts

Food courts originated in the Far East where they can be seen in most major cities and towns. Here the locals meet as families and friends at the food stalls grouped around a central catering area.

Food courts were introduced in to the UK in the 1980s. At first they were not widely accepted; now they have become a regular feature in main shopping centres and railway stations. The interest shown in the concept means that they are beginning to find their way into hotels, hospitals and education centres.

Food courts with a number of independent operators rather than a single one controlling all outlets, makes for the most successful operation. Some food courts will have branded kiosks (Perfect Pizza, Spud 'u' Like).

Franchising

Franchising is where a manager pays a licence fee and makes whatever he/she can above an agreed percentage on the food he/she sells. Various catering concessions and outside contracting arrangements at clubs, leisure centres, colleges and offices are similar to franchising. A form of franchising is also practised in the pub business in addition to other systems like the managed pub.

Many companies who supply caterers with products like soft drinks, ice-cream or coffee distribute their products by means of purchased operators. Some suppliers providing food and drink to caterers have 'brand franchises' sometimes backing their product with appropriate equipment and advertising material to ensure that caterers prepare, present and promote the products in a consistent way.

Operating styles vary considerably from pizza, hamburgers, baked croissants to full menu restaurants, coffee shops and pancake houses. Despite all the differences, all the franchise schemes work on the same basic principle. An established catering company offers a complete package of experience, operating systems and on-going marketing support sufficient to enable outside operators to set up and operate their own units within the chain. The investor makes an initial franchise payment and then pays a continuing royalty or commission which is often expressed as a percentage of gross turnover. All investment in property, buildings and equipment is borne by the franchise; in some cases the franchise might play some part in securing the property.

Franchising has several advantages:
- Firstly it allows for many to be set up nationally and by doing so maximises on economies of scale in purchasing promotional material in the development of the brand image.
- The franchisee gains because the opportunity is shared to invest in a pretested catering concept, backed by advertising, research and development, training and other resources which may otherwise be beyond their finance parameters.

- The banks also show an interest in franchising, in many ways they see it as a reasonably safe investment.

The oldest franchising schemes in the UK are Wimpy, established in the mid 1950s and KFC, which started in the early 1960s. Many of the most active franchise schemes are based on a fast-food style of menu and operating system. Now there is a growing market involving wider menus, medium spend restaurants, mostly licensed. Examples include Pizza Express Chain, and Dutch Pancake Houses.

For many caterers, access to any established name, with the attendant back-up of media, advertising and merchandising material, is a strong argument for franchising.

Ganymede dri-heat

This is a method of keeping foods either hot or cold. It is used in some hospitals as it ensures that the food which reaches the patients is in the same fresh condition as it was when it left the kitchens.

A metal disc or pellet is electrically heated or cooled and placed in a special container under the plate. The container is designed to allow air to circulate round the pellet so that the food is maintained at the correct service temperature.

This is used in conjunction with conveyor belts and special service counters and helps to provide a better and quicker food service.

CUSTOMER CARE

Many food production staff may have the opportunity of direct contact with consumer or customers in most types of establishments. For some it will be a regular aspect of their job, for others it may be for irregular events or special occasions. Waiters and waitresses and food service personnel called upon to serve customers need to be aware of how to provide consumer satisfaction.

Catering staff serving at food service counters directly to customers may be employed in canteens, refectories, dining halls, etc., in schools, hospitals, industrial establishments, offices and other establishments. Other food outlets include fast-food establishments such as crêperies, baked potato houses, McDonalds, fish and chip shops and take-aways; buffets at all kinds of functions including outdoor catering, wedding receptions and carveries. The following information is intended to assist catering employees at all levels not only to provide customer satisfaction but to obtain job satisfaction when caring for customers. The first thing to remember is that a smile puts both the customer and you off to a good start; however it is important to realise that excellent food served from the kitchen is the first essential to satisfy the customer but the finest food produced for a meal can be completely spoiled if served by uncaring staff. Technical skills and technique are very important, but equally or perhaps more important, are sincere caring attitudes and manners, with the food served in an environment which has an atmosphere making the customer feel at ease, wanted and welcome.

Customer care is, therefore, caring for customers. Remember:

- put the customer first;
- make them feel comfortable;
- make them feel good;
- make them feel important;
- make them want to return to your restaurant or establishment;

It is important that you adjust your behaviour to suit certain customers and to treat all customers equally as if they were special. Give them your time and full attention. Use body language to put customers at ease.

Concentrate on:

- your appearance;
- a clean tidy environment;
- answering the phone within three rings;
- achieving positive results;
- using the phone correctly;
- writing to customers;
- finding out what makes customers happy;
- ensuring that what you give is what the customer wants.

The customer needs to be kept informed. You yourself should take responsibility and not pass the buck, and achieve results if people complain. You must show the customer empathy and be able to discuss things from their point of view. They expect good *customer care*.

Customer care is now an important concept: getting customers and keeping them creates revenue (income). All other activities create costs.

Emotional factors surround the products that people buy; these include the after-sales service, speed of delivery and the ambience, especially in a restaurant. Customer satisfaction or dissatisfaction comes more and more from the way people are treated. Customers buy a total package. Customer care gives the caterer the opportunity to be 'special', to stand above the competition, winning customers and keeping them loyal. When a customer comes into contact with you the caterer, your image is being exposed to the customer. The staff of the company are perceived as representing not themselves but the company that they are working for.

Customer perceptions are often emotional, idiosyncratic and sometimes irrational, often based on narrow observations. When a restaurant manager remembers a customer's name, customers are delighted, but if staff treat customers badly, they will be unhappy. Often customers then react making the staff unhappy, thus affecting the business. If staff make the customers happy they will respond in kind:

Happy staff ↔ Happy customers

↓

Good profits

Staff can benefit from good customer-care training. Dealing with people is a highly complex skill; we train people to use complicated machinery but we do not often consider training staff to deal with the most complex machinery of all, the human being.

The caterer must first:

- set standards for customer care;
- set up training schemes;
- measure performance;
- reward accordingly.

Staff must know:

- what the company stands for, what is its mission;
- what behaviour the company values highly;
- that cutting costs is *not* more important than customer care;
- that all guarantees must be honoured;
- that the restaurant or establishment is in business to keep the customer happy;
- that happy customers can lead to repeat business and recommendations to friends and colleagues.

How to win commitment from staff

Staff will be happier and feel more committed by:

- good leadership;
- avoiding unnecessary stress; remove the causes, if they are under your control;
- knowing the fundamental importance of the customer; seek ideas from your staff on how to improve customer care;
- receiving good customer-care training;
- building pride in their work performance;
- having their training reinforced periodically.

Training aspects in customer care

When you are training staff the following can be used as a guide:

- Identify what the staff should know in caring for the customer.
- Know what the customer may ask them.
- Know what's on the menu, the composition of the dishes.
- Know what the special dishes of the day are.
- Know what the chef's specialities are.

Examples of good customer-care phrases you may hear in a restaurant or service area include:

- 'I'll take care of that for you right away.'
- 'I'll go and get it for you myself.'
- 'Is there anything else I can help you with?'
- 'I'll be glad to help you.'
- 'I don't know, but I'll find out now. Please take a seat for a moment.'

- 'I'm sorry to hear about that. Let's find out what went wrong and I'll put it right.'
- 'I'm sorry for the delay. I'll check with the kitchen to see how long your order will be.'

Good communication within the organisation assists in the development of customer care. It is important that the staff are constantly kept informed of what is going on otherwise they will feel that they are not part of the organisation. They must have a sense of 'ownership' or responsibility, since well motivated staff are good for the organisation and they will help in the progressive development of the business, helping to avoid the 'It's not my job attitude'.

If staff are expected to work hygienically and treat the staff well you must likewise treat the staff with respect and care for their well-being. Good staff welfare aids the process of customer care. Staff must have good clean changing rooms, washing or/ and showering facilities, quality facilities for refreshments and medical provision.

Staff too must treat each other with respect, co-operating and supporting each other. A good team spirit will ultimately affect the customer. Remember behaviour begets behaviour so, if one member of staff treats another badly, they in turn may treat the customer badly.

Customer care is a team game: it is about all the staff working to the same aim, getting the customers on their side.

Define standards of performance

The starting point is a clear analysis of what should happen at each of the points of contact that a customer might have with the restaurant and it becomes a check list. For example:

- A customer enters the restaurant or service area.
  - The entrance should be clean and tidy.
  - The doors could be marked 'welcome'
- The customer is then greeted by the head waiter, restaurant manager or receptionist.
  - The reception area is clean, tidy, perhaps decorated with fresh flowers.
  - Menu sample and drinks list on display.
  - All staff smartly dressed and well groomed.
  - Staff smile when greeting customers.
  - If possible head waiter, restaurant manager or receptionist use customer's name.
  - Customer is escorted to the table, assisted into the seating position.
  - If there is any delay, staff apologise and explanation is given to the customer.
  - Waiter introduces him/herself to the customer.
- At the end of the meal, head waiter or restaurant manager escorts customer to the door, smiles and exchanges pleasantries: 'good day'/'good night'.

When defining standards of performance, use numbers: for example, answer the 'phone within three rings; if there is a delay, update the caller every 20 seconds with 'Sorry, the line is still engaged, do you still wish to hold?'

Staff must have a sense of identity with the company or organisation. At McDonalds, there is a 700-page Operations and Training Manual which explains every stage of the cooking process and the correct behaviour to be used when dealing with customers.

Disney gives all new staff an induction programme called 'traditions' which explains about Walt Disney, the characters, what it is like to work in Disneyland and their role. It stresses that all visitors are not 'customers' but 'guests' so they must be treated that way. Although on most days there will be more than half a million of them, they must be dealt with as individuals not as a crowd. These individuals look to the staff to help them enjoy their day, the staff therefore have a crucial role to play. Disney explains to all their staff that they:

- are part of show business;
- are performers in a live show;
- must make sure that nothing spoils the perfect picture the guests see;
- must make a clear distinction between 'on stage' and 'off stage': off stage they are able to relax, on stage they must play the perfect role; they must never be seen with their 'mask off'.

It may be said that caterers are also part of showbusiness, that waiters are performers in a live show. TGI Friday restaurants have further developed this concept where waiters and food service staff are interviewed on the basis of their personality. They become actors as part of a large show. Traditionally waiters that perform flambé dishes 'live' in front of a customer, show off their flair and skill. Such staff develop a sense of importance and pride in their job.

Measure and monitor performance

The defined standards of performance must be monitored and measured. You need to measure success in terms of your premises to customers. Measuring the right thing helps staff understand what is important to customers and how to act accordingly.

Staff who look after customers and provide the service and care they expect, deserve rewarding. Good positive feedback to staff is important; you may:

- just say 'well done' which goes a long way or payment of a bonus;
- make a payment of a bonus;
- give an increment on an annual pay increase;
- give a promotion.

Continuing customer care

Keep in touch with customers through mailshot, advertising, etc. (see page 322).

Customer care skills

ATTITUDE AND BEHAVIOUR

If a customer is rude or aggressive to a waiter (blames a waiter for the chef's mistake), the waiter should not be rude or aggressive in return. If the waiter can remain calm and use his/her skills of patience, the customer will often apologise for their anger. Behaviour is a choice; you should select the behaviour which is appropriate for the customer.

When dealing with customers, behaviour should be:

- professional;
- understanding – customers in a restaurant want a service and are paying for it; learn to understand their needs;
- patient – learn to be patient with all customers.
- enthusiastic – it can be contagious;
- confident – it can increase a potential customer's trust in you;
- welcoming – it can satisfy customer's basic human desire to feel liked and be approved of;
- helpful – customers warm to helpful staff;
- polite – good manners are always welcomed;
- caring – make each customer feel special.

APPEARANCE

Remember you never get a second chance to make a first impression. What you wear and how you look is part of how potential customers judge your organisation. You are part of the company's image.

BODY LANGUAGE

Body language includes:

- how you dress;
- your distance from others;
- posture;
- stance;
- how you sit;
- movements;
- gestures;
- facial expressions;
- eye contact;
- eye movements.

Body language tells us what people really mean. It is the art of seeing what others are thinking. If someone is telling a lie their body language will usually give them away. By focusing on other people's body language you can discover their true feeling towards you and what they think of what you are saying. It has a clear value in business situations and is therefore very important in customer care.

Learn to:

- look for what is important;
- recognise other people so you are able to 'read' them better;
- recognise how to use body language;
- control it and use it to your advantage, so that you give the right positive message to people.

Remember that body language is universal but does mean different things in different cultures.

Signs and meanings

- One gesture: doesn't show how the other person is thinking.
- Arms folded: may mean that:
  - they are being defensive about something;
  - they are cold;
  - they are comfortable.
- Some gestures: are open, expansive, positive.
- Leaning forward with open palms facing upwards: shows interest, acceptance, welcoming attitude.
- Leaning backwards, arms folded, head down: closed defensive and negative, disinterested, rejection.
- Plenty of gestures: warmth, enthusiasm and emotion.
- Using gestures sparsely: cold, reserved logical.

Distance

Each person has around them an area that they regard as a personal space. Beware of intruding into a customer's personal space. Although some customers may regard it as friendliness you may make others feel uncomfortable.

Placing people at a table for a meeting or for lunch or dinner is an art. The way people sit round a table, sends messages.

- Formal meeting – people sit opposite each other.
- Team work – sitting people side by side is stressful.

Eyes

Eye contact should be used as a way of acknowledging customers, making them feel welcome and as a foundation of building a good relationship. Eye contact should be used to show the customer you are listening.

EARS

Really listening is the highest form of courtesy:

- Look at the customer.
- Ignore any negative thoughts you have about them.
- Lean towards them.
- Think at the pace they are talking.
- Listen to every word.
- Try not to interrupt.

- Use facial expressions and body language to show you understand.
- Stick to the subject.
- Use their name wherever possible.

GREETING PEOPLE

If you are already dealing with another customer in the restaurant acknowledge the new customer and reassure them that you will help them as soon as possible. Try to greet people with a smile that's genuine. You may even get one in return, after all smiles are free. Remember that good manners are important.

Use peoples' names, it holds their attention. It demonstrates recognition and respect. Their name is probably the most important word in the world to them. Always use their surname until they give you permission for you to use their first name.

Asking the customer questions will demonstrate

- you have properly understood what the customer wants;
- you have time for them to talk;
- interest on your part;
- you feel the customer is important;
- you are able to find out how they feel;
- you can keep control of the conversation;
- you can understand their needs, their complaints;
- you know how to make customers feel better.

STROKING

This is defined as giving any kind of attention. Humans need stroking. A prolonged absence of it can cause serious adverse effects.

How good a customer feels about your restaurant or catering establishment is directly connected to the amount and types of strokes (attention) they have received.

Stroking can be both positive or negative, it can be physical, verbal and non-verbal.

Some examples of positive stroking include:

- greetings;
- compliments;
- laughing.

Some examples of negative stroking include:

- unpleasant greeting;
- pushing;
- sarcastic remarks;
- absence of praise;
- adverse criticism;
- swearing;
- snatching;
- unpleasant hand gestures.

PACING

Pacing is speaking in a way that is compatible with your customers. Match their speed, tone and volume. Do not talk above their heads.

ASSERTIVENESS

Remember customers are human beings; you may have to handle them when they shout at you, interrupt you, are rude to you, criticise you or blame you for something you have not done. The answer is for you to be assertive, standing up for your rights.

Being assertive means

- stating your views while showing that you understand their views;
- enhancing yourself without diminishing them;
- speaking calmly, sincerely and steadily.

Advantages of assertive behaviour

There are some advantages to be gained:

- It gives you greater self confidence.
- You will be treating others as equals, recognising the ability and limitations of others, rather than regarding them as superiors.
- It gives greater self-responsibility.
- It gives greater self-control; your mind is concentrated on achieving the behaviour you want.
- It can produce a win situation; opinions on both sides are given a fair hearing, so they feel that they have won.

TELEPHONE

A badly handled telephone call can destroy the effect of good advertising. Remember: when using the telephone, give all your attention to the customer; get their name, write it down and use it. Take note of all the other details the customer is wanting. Listen and use your voice correctly. Summarise what you have agreed with the customer at the end of the conversation.

HOW TO HANDLE CUSTOMER COMPLAINTS

Some statistics on complaints:

- 96% of dissatisfied customers do not go back and complain, but they do tell between seven and eleven other people how bad your restaurant or service is;
- 13% will tell at least twenty other people;
- 90% will never return to your restaurant.
- It costs roughly five times as much to attract a new customer as it does to keep an existing one.

Therefore, encourage customers to complain on the spot. If they are unhappy about anything that is served to them, they should be encouraged to inform the member of staff who served them. This will give the establishment the opportunity to rectify the fault immediately. Ask them about their eating experience; this information will be vital for future planning. Treat any customer who complains well; offer them a free drink or a free meal. Make the complainant your ambassadors. Show them empathy, use the appropriate body language, show concern, sympathise. Always apologise. If you handle the complaint well you will make the customer feel important. Remember:

Customer care

↓

Happy customers

↓

Profit

↓

Jobs

TOPICS FOR DISCUSSION

1. Your ideas for promoting a 100-seat industrial catering restaurant in an office block.
2. Examples of advertising.
3. What you understand by good public relations.
4. The advantages of cafeteria service.
5. The popularity of take-aways and what you think the changes will be in take-away services in the future.

Part

3

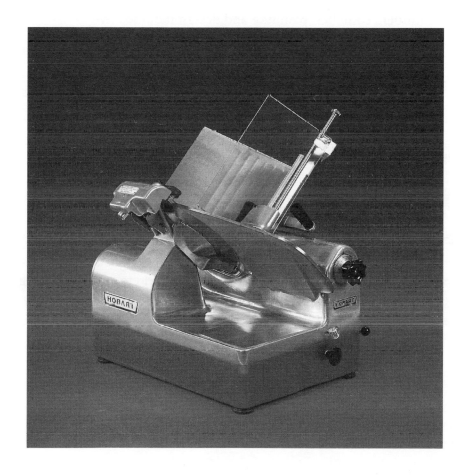

CATERING TECHNOLOGY

10

Kitchen planning, organisation and supervision

—

INFLUENCING FACTORS ON DESIGN

Factors which influence kitchen planning and design include

- the size and extent of the menu and the market it serves;
- services – gas, electricity and water;
- labour, skill level of staff;
- amount of capital expenditure, costs;
- use of prepared convenience foods;
- types of equipment available;
- Hygiene and the Food Safety Act of 1990/91;
- design and decor;
- multi-usage requirements.

The size and extent of the menu

Before a kitchen is planned, the management must know its goals and objectives in relationship to market strategy. In other words what markets are you aiming at and what style of operation are you going to operate? The menu will then determine the type of equipment you will require in order to produce the products that you know from the market research that the customer is going to buy. You also need to know target numbers that you intend to service.

Services

The designer must know where the services are located and how efficient use can be made of them.

Labour and skill level

What kind of people does the company intend to employ? If semi-skilled labour is going to be used in preference to highly skilled labour, this will save on more technological equipment; more prepared food will be used and this will have an effect on the overall kitchen design.

Amount of capital expenditure

Most design has to work with a detailed capital budget. Often it is not always possible to design, then worry about the cost afterwards. Finance will very often determine the overall design and acceptability.

Because space is at a premium, kitchens are generally smaller. Equipment is therefore being designed to cater for this trend, becoming more modular and streamlined and generally able to fit into less space. This is seen as a cost-reduction exercise. Labour is a significant cost factor so equipment is being designed for ease of operation, maintenance and cleaning.

Use of prepared convenience foods

A fast-food menu using prepared convenience food will influence the planning and equipping very differently from à la carte or cook-chill kitchen. Certain factors will have to be determined:

- Will sweets and pastries be made on the premises?
- Will there be a need for larder or butcher?
- Will fresh, frozen or a combination of both be used?

Types of equipment available

The type, amount and size of the equipment will depend on the type of menu being provided. The equipment must be suitably sited. When planning a kitchen, standard symbols are used which can be produced on squared paper to provide a scale design. Computer-aided design (CAD) is now often used.

Hygiene and the Food Safety Act 1990/91

Design and construction of the kitchen must comply with the Hygiene and Food Safety Act 1990/91. The basic layout and construction should enable adequate space to be provided in all food handling and associated areas for equipment as well as working practices and frequent cleaning to be carried out.

Design and decor

The trend towards provision of more attractive eating places, carried to its utmost perhaps by the chain and franchise operators, has not been without its effect on kitchen planning and design. One trend has been that of bringing the kitchen area totally or partially into view, with the development of back bar type of equipment; for example, where grills or griddles are in full public view and food is prepared on them to order.

While there will be a continuing demand for the traditional heavy duty type of equipment found in larger hotels and restaurant kitchens, the constant need to change and update the design and decor of modern restaurants means that the equipment life is generally shorter, reduced perhaps from ten years to seven or five or even less, to cope with the demand for change and redevelopment.

This has resulted in the generally improved design of catering equipment with the introduction of modular units.

Multi-usage requirements

Round the clock requirements such as in hospitals, factories doing shift work, the police and armed forces, have also forced kitchen planners to consider design of kitchens with a view to their partial use outside peak times. To this end kitchen equipment is being made more adaptable and flexible, so that whole sections can be closed down when not in use, in order to maximise savings on heating, lighting and maintenance.

KITCHEN DESIGN

Kitchens must be designed so that they can be easily managed. The management must have easy access to the areas under their control and have good visibility in the areas which have to be supervised. Large operations should work on separate work floors, for reasons of efficiency and hygiene:

- Product – raw materials to finished product.
- Personnel – how people move within the kitchen; for example, staff working in dirty areas (areas of contamination) should not enter areas of finished product, or where blast chilling is taking place.
- Containers/Equipment/Utensils – equipment should, where possible, be separated out, into specific process areas.
- Refuse – refuse should be kept separated and should not pass into other areas in order to get to its storage destination.

Product flows

This section should be subdivided into high risk and contaminated sections. High risk food is that which during the process is likely to be easily contaminated.

Contaminated food is that which is contaminated on arrival before processing: unprepared vegetables, raw meat.

Back tracking or cross-over of materials and product must be avoided.

Work flow

Food preparation rooms should be planned to allow a 'work flow' whereby food is processed through the premises from the point of delivery to the point of sale or service with the minimum of obstruction. The various processes should be separated as far as possible and food intended for sales should not cross paths with waste food or refuse. Staff time is valuable and a design which reduces wasteful journeys is both efficient and cost-effective.

The overall sequence of receiving, storing, preparing, holding, serving and clearing is achieved by:

- minimum movement;
- minimal back tracking;
- maximum use of space;
- maximum use of equipment with minimum expenditure or time and effort.

Work space

Approximately 4.2 m (15 sq. ft) is required per person; too little space can cause staff to work in close proximity to stoves, steamers, cutting blades, mixers, etc., thus causing accidents. A space of 1.37 m ($4\frac{1}{2}$ ft) from equipment is desirable and aisles must be adequate to enable staff to move safely. The working area must be suitably lit and ventilated with extractor fans to remove heat, fumes and smells.

Working sections

The size and style of the menu and the ability of the staff will determine the number of sections and layout that is necessary. A straight line layout would be suitable for a snack bar whilst an island layout would be more suitable for a hotel restaurant.

Access to ancillary areas

A good receiving area needs to be designed for easy receipt of supplies with nearby storage facilities suitably sited for distribution of foods to preparation and production areas.

Hygiene must be considered so that kitchen equipment can be cleaned and all used equipment from the dining area can be cleared, cleaned and stored. Still room facilities may also be required.

Equipment

The type, amount and size of equipment will depend on the type of menu being provided. Not only should the equipment be suitably situated but the working weight is very important to enable the equipment to be used without excess fatigue. When a kitchen is being planned, standard symbols are used which can be produced on squared paper to provide a scale design. Wash hand facilities and storage of cleaning equipment should not be omitted.

Kitchen equipment manufacturers and gas and electricity suppliers can provide details of equipment relating to output and size.

The various preparation processes require different areas depending on what food is involved. A vegetable preparation area means that water from the sinks and dirt from the vegetables are going to accumulate and therefore adequate facilities for drainage should be provided. Pastry preparation on the other hand entails mainly dry processes.

Whatever the processes, there are certain basic rules that can be applied which not only make for easier working conditions but which help to ensure that the food hygiene regulations are complied with.

Food preparation areas

Proper design and layout of the preparation area can make a major contribution to good food hygiene. Staff generally respond to good working conditions by taking more of a pride in themselves, in their work and in their working environment.

Adequate work space must be provided for each process and every effort must be made to separate dirty and clean processes. Vegetable preparation and wash up areas should be separate from the actual food preparation and service areas. The layout must ensure a continuous work flow in one direction in order that cross-over of foods and any cross-contamination is avoided. The staff should not hamper each other by having to cross each others' paths more than is absolutely necessary.

Actual work-top areas should be adequate in size for the preparation process and should be so designed that the food handler has all equipment and utensils close to hand.

Accommodation must be based on operational need. The layout of the kitchen must focus on the working and stores area, and the equipment to be employed. These areas must be designed and based on the specification of the operation.

Kitchens can be divided into sections; these must be based on the process:

- Dry areas: for storage.
- Wet areas: for fish preparation, vegetable preparation, butchery, cold preparation.
- Hot wet areas: for boiling, poaching, steaming; equipment needed will include:
    - atmospheric steamers,
    - pressure steamers,
    - combination oven,
    - bratt pans,
    - steam jacketed boilers.
- Hot dry areas: for frying, roasting, grilling; equipment needed will include:
    - cool zone fryers,
    - pressure fryers,
    - bratt pans,
    - roasting ovens,
    - charcoal grills,
    - salamanders,
    - induction cookers,
    - halogen cookers,
    - microwave,
    - cook and hold ovens.
- Dirty areas: for refuse, pot wash areas, plate wash; equipment needed will include:
    - compactors,

- refuse storage units,
- pot wash machines,
- dishwashers,
- glass washers.

Size of kitchen and food preparation areas

Size is determined also by purpose and function.

- The operation is based on the menu and the market it is to service.
- The design and equipment is based on the market.
- Consideration must be given to the management policy on buying raw materials. Choice will determine kitchen plans on handling raw materials.

Prepared food will require different types of equipment and labour requirements compared to part-prepared food or raw state ingredients.

Prepared food examples are sous vide products, cook/chill, cook/freeze, prepared sweets. Part-prepared food examples are peeled and cut vegetables, convenience sauces and soups, portioned fish/meat. Raw state food examples are unprepared vegetables, meat which requires butchering, fish requiring filleting and portioning.

Consideration must also be given to the service policy on using all plate service or a mixture of plate and silver service or self-service, and how all this will affect the volume and type of dishwashing.

Planning and layout of the cooking area

Because 'raw materials' enter the cooking section from the main preparation areas (vegetables, meat and fish, dry goods), this section will be designed with a view to continuing the flow movement through to the servery. To this end, roasting ovens for example, are best sited close to the meat preparation area, the steamers adjacent to the vegetable preparation area.

Layout is not, however, just a question of equipment siting and selection, much depends on the type of management policy on the use of prepared foods and the operating cycle. Clearly the cooking section should contain no through traffic lanes, used by other staff to travel from one section to another. The layout should be so planned that raw foodstuffs arrive at one point, are processed in the cooking section and are then despatched to the servery. There should be a distinctive progression in one direction.

As with other areas, the cooking section should be designed with a view to making maximum use of the available area and to provide economy of effort in use.

ISLAND GROUPINGS

In an island arrangement, equipment is placed back-to-back in the centre of the cooking area. There will need to be sufficient space to allow for this, including adequate gangways around the equipment and space to place other items along the walls.

Wall siting

An alternative arrangement involves siting equipment along walls. This arrangement is possible where travel distances are reduced and normally occurs in smaller premises (or sections thereof).

L- or U-shaped layouts

L- or U-shaped arrangements create self-contained sections that discourage entry by non-authorised staff and can promote efficient working, with distances reduced between work centres.

When planning the layout of the cooking section the need to allow sufficient space for access to equipment such as ovens should be borne in mind. Opening doors creates an arc that cannot be reduced and the operator must have sufficient room for comfortable and safe access. It is likely also that trolleys will be used for loading and unloading ovens, or rolling tables drawn into position in front of the oven.

The choice of layout

A selection of equipment will be made after detailed consideration of the functions that will be carried out within the cooking area of the kitchen. The amount of equipment will depend upon the complexity of the menus offered, the quantity of meals served, and the policy of use of materials, from the traditional kitchen organisation using only fresh vegetables and totally unprepared items, to the use of prepared foods, chilled items, frozen foods, where the kitchen consists of a regeneration unit only.

Given, however, that a certain amount of equipment is required, the planner has the choice of a number of possible layouts, within the constraints of the building shape and size, and the location of services. The most common are the island groupings, wall siting and the use of an L- or U-shaped layout and variations upon these basic themes.

Siting of equipment

The kitchen operation must work as a system. It is advisable to site items of equipment used for specific functions together. This will help increase efficiency and avoid shortcuts.

Wash hand basins must be sited strategically to encourage frequent hand washing in all food preparation areas. One should be in evidence at each work station.

The kitchen environment

Space

The Office, Shop and Railway Premises Act 1963, stipulates 11.32 cu metres (400 cu ft) per person, discounting height in excess of 3 m (10 ft).

Humidity

A humid atmosphere creates side effects such as food deterioration, infestation risk, condensation on walls and slippery floors. Anything higher than 60% humidity lowers productivity. Provision for replacement of extracted air with fresh air is essential.

TEMPERATURE
No higher than 20–26°C (68–79°F) is desirable for maximum working efficiency and comfort with 16–18°C (61–64°F) in preparation areas.

NOISE
Conversation should be possible within 4 m (13 ft).

LIGHT
Minimum legal level in preparation areas is 20 lumens per sq ft with up to 38 lumens preferable in all areas.

VENTILATION
Air change of a minimum of 30 times an hour for the cooking environment, 50 where there is a low ceiling, and 60 for specialised cooking creating intense heat and smoke, such as tandoori.

MAINTENANCE
Planning and equipping a kitchen is an expensive investment, therefore to avoid any action by the Environmental Health Officer, efficient, regular cleaning and maintenance is essential. (The Dorchester kitchens are swept during the day, given soap/detergent and water treatment after service and any spillages cleaned up immediately. At night, contractors clean the ceilings, floors and walls.) (See also the section on Kitchen hygiene, page 534.)

Kitchen design industry trends

In most cases throughout the industry, companies are looking to reduce labour costs while maintaining or enhancing the meal experience for the customer. Trends in various situations are given below:

- Hotels: greater use of buffet and self-assisted service units.
- Banqueting: move towards plated service, less traditional silver service.
- Fast food: new concepts coming onto the market, more specialised chicken and seafood courts, more choices in ethnic food.
- Roadside provision: increase in number of operations, partnerships with oil companies, basic grill menus now enhanced via factory-produced à la carte items.
- Food courts: development has slowed down; minor changes all the time; most food courts offer an 'all day' menu.
- Restaurants/hotels: less emphasis on luxury end, 5-star experience.
- Theme restaurants: will continue to improve and multiply.
- Hospitals: greater emphasis on bought-in freezer and chilled foods; reduced amount of on-site preparation and cooking.
- Industrial: more zero-subsidy staff restaurants, increased self-service for all items; introduction of cashless systems will enable multi-tenant office buildings to offer varying subsidy levels.

- Prisons, institutions: little if any change; may follow hospitals by buying in more preprepared food; may receive foods from multi-outlet central production units, tied in with schools, meals on wheels provision, etc.
- University/colleges: greater move towards providing food courts; more snack bars and coffee shops.

Kitchen equipment trends

- Refrigeration: more concentration on providing CFC-free equipment.
- Environmental: with an environmentally conscious society, energy conservation will feature higher in the development agenda; these will include heat recovery systems, recirculated air systems, improved working conditions and lighting systems.
- Cooking: more use of induction units, combination ovens, microwave and tunnel ovens.
- Servery counters: more decorative units being used.
- Dishwasher/potwash: greater economy of water, more mechanised and automated use of combination machines.
- Ventilation: moves towards integrated wash systems, recirculated air systems, integral air supply, integral fire suppression.

General trend will be towards self-diagnostic equipment and automated service call out. With the use of replacement components, there is less emphasis on repairs.

Consultants

There are a number of specialist consultants involved in kitchen design. Consultants are often used by companies to provide independent advice and specialist knowledge. Their expertise should cover:

- equipment;
- food service systems and methods;
- architectural elements;
- mechanical and electrical services;
- drainage;
- ventilation/air conditioning;
- statutory legislation (Food Act, Health and Safety Act, fire regulations);
- green issues/legislation (waste management);
- refrigeration;
- energy conservation;
- recycling.

Consultants should provide the client with unbiased opinions and expertise not available in their company. Their aim should be to raise the standards of provision, equipment installation, while providing an efficient and effective food production operation which also takes into account staff welfare.

EQUIPMENT DESIGN

There is no UK standard for equipment design, but the Environmental Health Officers, The Food Manufacturer's Foundation and Process Plant Association have drafted the following principles of design.

- Construction materials must be non-toxic, non-flaking, corrosion-resistant, durable, resistant to heat and resistant to acids.
- Food contact surfaces should be easy to clean, smooth and continuous without breaks, cracks, open seams, chips or pitting. It is extremely difficult to clean internal corners and crevices. Unless designed for cleaning in place, all food contact surfaces must be accessible for cleaning and inspection by easy methods of dismantling.

Equipment must be so designed and constructed and finished in such a way that it can be cleaned and disinfected easily, safely, thoroughly and rapidly without the need for skilled fitters or specialised tools.

Recommendations for equipment

Equipment is preferable with:

- tubular machinery frames;
- stainless steel table legs;
- drain cocks and holes instead of pockets and crevices which could trap liquid;
- dials fitted to machines having adequate clearance to facilitate cleaning.

Preparation surfaces

The choice of surfaces on which food is to be prepared is vitally important. Failure to ensure a suitable material may provide a dangerous breeding ground for bacteria. Stainless steel tables are the best as they do not rust and their welded seams eliminate unwanted cracks and open joints. Sealed tubular legs are preferable to angular ones because again they eliminate corners in which dirt collects. Tubular legs have often been found to provide a harbourage for pests.

Preparation surfaces should be jointless, durable, impervious, correct height and firm based.

Surfaces must withstand repeated cleaning at the required temperature without premature deterioration through pitting and corrosion.

Choosing cutting boards

Look at the following aspects when choosing cutting boards:

- Water absorbency: soft woods draw fluids into them and with the fluids, bacteria is also drawn in.

- Wooden cutting boards made of hard wood if cleaned and sterilised are perfectly acceptable in catering premises.
- Resistance to stains, cleaning chemicals, heat and food acids.
- Toxicity: the cutting board must not give off toxic substances.
- Durability: the cutting board must withstand wear and tear.
- Cutting boards must not split or warp.

Appearance can be deceptive. Dean Cliver and Afese AK, two researchers at the University of Wisconsin, Madison, USA set out ways of decontaminating wooden kitchen surfaces and ended up finding that such surfaces are pretty good at decontaminating themselves.

When working with wood from nine different species of tree, four sorts of plastic, the results were always the same. They spread salmonella, listeria and *Escherichia coli* over the various samples and left them there for three minutes. The level of bacteria on the plastic remained the same, while the level on the wood plummeted often by as much as 99.9%. Left overnight at room temperature the bacteria on the plastic actually multiplied, while the wooden surfaces cleaned themselves so thoroughly that De Cliver and Ms AK could not record anything from them.

This is because the porous structure of the wood, previously thought to be a disadvantage in soaking up the fluid with the bacteria in it. Once inside the bacteria sticks to the wood's fibres and they are 'strangled' by one of the many noxious anti-microbial chemicals with which living trees protect themselves.

Colour coding

To avoid cross contamination, it is important that the same equipment is not used for handling raw and high risk products without being disinfected. To prevent the inadvertent use of equipment for raw and high risk foods, it is recommended that where possible, different colours and shapes are used to identify products or raw materials used:

- Red for raw meat;
- Blue for raw fish;
- Brown for cooked meats;
- Green for vegetables;
- White for general purpose;
- Yellow for sandwiches.

Fixing and siting of equipment

Where practicable, equipment should be mobile to facilitate its removal for cleaning, that is castor mounted with brakes on all the wheels.

A guide for stationary equipment

To allow for the cleaning of wall and floor surfaces stationary equipment must be:

- 500 mm from the walls;
- 250 mm clearance between the floor and underside of the equipment.

KITCHEN ORGANISATION

The purpose of kitchen organisation is to produce the right quantity of food of the highest standard, for the required number of people, on time, by the most effective use of staff, equipment and materials. Regardless of whether the organisation is simple or complex, the factors which have the greatest effect on the organisation will be the menu and the system used to prepare and present the menu items. For example, a very extensive menu can be offered if much of the *mise-en-place* (preparation prior to service) is prepared throughout the day and kept refrigerated until required at service time. If an establishment has a finishing kitchen for the final preparation and presentation by a small number of skilled cooks, then, with adequate *mise-en-place*, fish, meat, vegetables, potatoes, pastas and eggs, cooked by sautéing, grilling, deep frying and so on, can be completed quickly and efficiently to the benefit of the customer. This system, which has been operated very effectively in some establishments for many years, means that all staff are fully used. The design of the finishing kitchen is important here and needs to include refrigerated cabinets for holding perishable foods, adequate cooking facilities and bain-marie space for holding sauces, etc.

Restaurants which provide a limited menu, such as steak houses, are able to organise very few staff to cope with large numbers of customers to quite a high degree of skill. The required standard can be produced because few skills are needed. Nevertheless an employee producing grilled steaks, pancakes or whatever has to be organised in a systematic way and the flow of the work should be smooth.

Other kinds of establishments which are required to produce large amounts of food to be served at the same time include schools, hospitals, industrial establishments, airlines and departmental stores. Staff have to be well organised and supplied with large-scale preparation and production equipment and the means of finishing dishes quickly. To enable this to happen satisfactorily the preparation-production-freezing or chilling-reheat cycle has been developed, enabling staff to be involved in simply reheating or finishing the foods. It is essential that very high standards of hygiene must be practised in situations using a system of deep freezing or chilling and reheating.

As costs of space, equipment, fuel, maintenance and labour are continually increasing, considerable time, thought and planning have had to be given to the organisation and layout systems of kitchens. The requirements of the kitchen have to be clearly identified with regard to the type of food that is to be prepared, cooked and served. All areas of space and the different types of equipment available must be fully justified and the organisation of the kitchen personnel must also be planned at the same time.

In the late nineteenth century, when labour was relatively cheap, skilled and plentiful, public demand was for elaborate and extensive menus; and in response to this, Auguste Escoffier, one of the most respected chefs of the past era, devised what is known as the *partie* system. The number of parties required and the number of staff in each will depend on the size of the establishment. Figure 10.1 (page 362) is an example of a large hotel's traditional kitchen brigade.

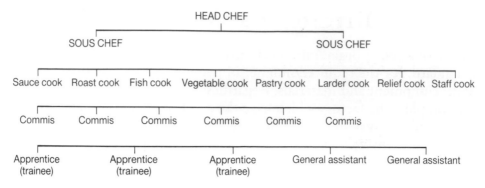

Fig. 10.1 Example of a traditional kitchen brigade in a large hotel

With a sound knowledge of fresh, part-prepared and ready prepared foods, together with an understanding of kitchen equipment and planning (see Figure 10.2, page 364), the organisation of a kitchen can be economically and efficiently implemented. Even with two similar kitchens the internal organisation is liable to vary as each person in charge will have their own way of running the kitchen. However, everyone working in the system should know what he or she has to do, and how and when to do it.

The kitchen organisation will vary mainly due to the size and type of establishment. Obviously where a kitchen has 100 chefs preparing banquets for up to 1000 people, a lunch and dinner service for 300 customers with an à la carte menu, and floor service, the organisation will be quite different to a small restaurant serving 30 table d'hôte lunches, or a full-view coffee shop, a speciality restaurant with a busy turnover, or a hospital kitchen.

WORKING METHODS

A skilled craftsman or craftswoman is one who, among other things, completes the skill in the minimal time, to the highest standard and with the *least* effort. Effort requires expenditure of energy, and energy is the commodity which needs to be conserved, not wasted, in the kitchen. Any person working in a hot environment, with the stress of working against the clock, needs to get into the habit of working in such a way that energy is not wasted. To achieve this it is necessary to use commonsense and to know how to save energy so that the habit of working methodically and economically becomes second nature (Figure 10.3). This state of mind can be developed by students producing 12 items even though the real effects will only be evident when producing, say, 100 or 500 items.

Simplifying an operation

The objective is to make work easier and this can be achieved by simplifying the operation, eliminating unnecessary movements, combining two operations into one or improving old methods. For example, if you are peeling potatoes and you allow

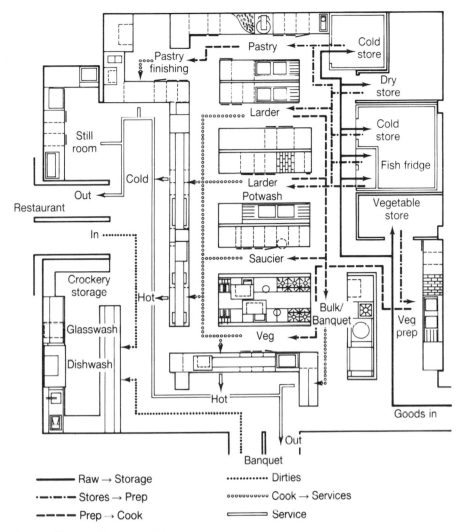

Fig. 10.2 Design for a well-planned kitchen

the peelings to drop into the container in the first place, the action of moving the peelings into the bowl and the need to clean the table could have been eliminated. This operation is simplified if, instead of a blunt knife, a good hand potato peeler is used, because it is simple and safe to use, requires less effort, can be used more quickly and requires less skill to produce a better result. If the quantity of potatoes is sufficient, then a mechanical peeler could be used, but it would be necessary to remember that the electricity used would add to the cost and that the time needed to

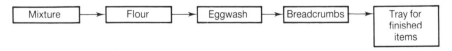

Fig. 10.3 Example of correct sequence for working methods

clean a mechanical aid may lessen its work-saving value. If it takes 25 minutes to clean a potato mashing machine which has been used to mash potatoes for 500 meals, it could be time well spent in view of the time and energy saved mashing the potatoes. It may not be considered worthwhile using the machine to mash potatoes for 20 meals. Factors such as this need to be taken into account.

Overcoming fatigue

Working methods may be observed in catering at many different levels, from the experienced methodical chef wiping the knife after cutting a lemon, to the complexity of the Ganymede system in a large hospital or the carefully planned call-order unit in a fast-food operation where, because of careful thought and study, wastage of time, money and materials is reduced to a minimum. But even with the aid of mechanical devices, labour-saving equipment and the extensive use of foods which have been partially or totally prepared, people at work still become fatigued. It is most important to stand correctly, well balanced with the weight of the body divided on to both legs with the feet sensibly spaced and the back reasonably straight when working for long periods in one place. Particular care is needed when lifting: stand with legs apart and bend the knees (not the back) and use the leg muscles to assist lifting. The object to be raised should be held close to the body.

It is possible to cultivate the right attitude to work as well as good working habits. Certain jobs are repetitive, some require considerable concentration, while others cause physical strain; not all work provides equal job satisfaction. If 500 fish cakes have to be shaped it is worthwhile setting targets to complete a certain number in a certain time. Such simple things as not counting the completed items but counting those still to be done motivates some people to greater effort. Some circumstances do not lend themselves to overcoming the physical pressures: for example if 150 people require 150 omelets then, provided the eggs are broken and seasoned and kept in bulk with the correct size ladle for portioning, the attitude to adopt may be to try to do each omelet better and quicker than the last. If careful thought and study are given to all practical jobs wastage of time, labour and materials can often be eliminated.

Equipment and layout (Figure 10.4)

Properly planned layouts with adequate equipment, tools and materials to do the job are essential if practical work is to be carried out efficiently. If equipment is correctly placed then work will proceed smoothly in proper sequence without backtracking or criss-crossing. Work tables, sinks and stores and refrigerators should be within easy reach in order to eliminate unnecessary walking. Equipment should be easily available during all working times.

The storage, handling of foods, tools and utensils and the movement of food in various stages of production needs careful study. Many people carry out practical work by instinct and often evolve the most efficient method instinctively (Figures 10.5 and 10.6, pages 366 and 367). Nevertheless careful observation of numerous

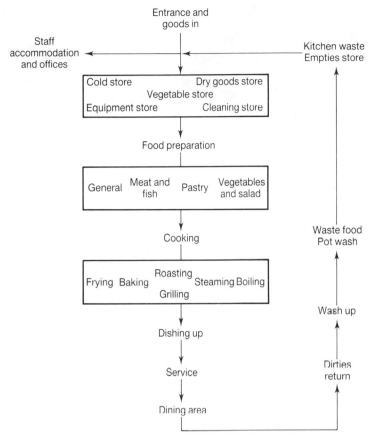

Fig. 10.4 Work flow, incorporating delivery, storage, preparation, cooking and service

practical workers will show a great deal of time and effort wasted through bad working methods. It is necessary to arrange work so that the shortest possible distance exists between storage and the place where the items are to be used.

When arranging storage see that the most frequently used items are nearest to hand. Place heavy items where the minimum of body strain is required to move them. Keep all items in established places so that time is not lost in hunting and searching. Adjustable shelving can be a help in organising different storage requirements. Only after all the preplanning of the job is complete comes the actual work itself.

Careful preparation of foods and equipment (a good mise-en-place) is essential if a busy service is to follow and is to be operated efficiently so that orders move out methodically without confusion (Figure 10.7, page 367, Plates 118–120 pages 334 and 335).

The work to be done must be carefully planned so that the items requiring long preparation or cooking are started first. Where a fast production is required lining up will assist efficiency. Work carried out haphazardly, without plan or organisation, obviously takes longer to do than work done according to plan. There is a sequence

Fig. 10.5   Organised food preparation

to work that leads to high productivity and an efficient worker should learn this sequence quickly.

When French beans are prepared they should all be topped and tailed, then cut – not topping, tailing then cutting each bean separately. When food is cut, articles to be cut should be on the left of the chopping board (for right-handed people), drawn with the left hand to the centre of the board, cut and pushed to the right. This should be a continuous, smoothly flowing process.

Food is often wasted by the use of bad working methods. For example, when spinach is prepared, to tip a whole box of spinach into the sink of water, then pick off the stalks so that they drop back on to the unpicked spinach will always result in waste. This is a bad practice used by careless cooks because three-quarters of the way through the job the contents of the sink (including an amount of good spinach) are thrown away. This can happen in the preparation of other vegetable such as sprouts, potatoes, carrots.

These are just a few examples of how planning and working methodically can save time, energy and materials.

Fig. 10.6   Disorganised food preparation

Fig. 10.7   Working in a well-organised kitchen

Service	7.00	8.00	9.00	10.00	11.00	12.00	1.00	2.00	3.00	4.00
		Breakfast				Lunch				
Catering manager		Job allocation – bookwork				Supervision			Admin	
Asst manager		Bookwork				Supervisor and assistant			Cash-up Bookwork	
Head chef		Main meal prep				Kitchen back-up			Admin	
Second chef	Main meal prep					Kitchen back-up				
Grill/veg chef	B'fast prep	Cooked b'fast to order grill bar prep		Veg/salad prep		Call order grill bar				
Cashier/vending (1)		Cash		Vending machines		Cash				
Cashier/vending (2)	Fill, clean and replenish vending machines					Cash/salad bar replenish				
Food service assistant (1)			Sandwich prep	Counter prep		Counter				
Food service assistant (2)			Sandwich prep	Counter prep		Counter				
Food service assistant (3)			Kitchen assistant Cold sweets			Counter			Clean down	
Storeman/porter			Goods issue Pot wash			Wash-up			Clean down	
Kitchen porter			Lay tables Wash-up			Wash-up			Clean down	
Kitchen porter			Cleaner			Pot wash				

(Vertical labels between 11.00 and 12.00: "Prepare for service"; between 2.00 and 3.00: "Staff lunch")

Fig. 10.8 Example of staff hours in an industrial kitchen

Plate 121   Gas convection/microwave oven

Plate 122 The robot coupe

Plate 123 Automatic slicer

Plate 124   Gastronorm counter

Plate 125   Automatic pastry roller

Plate 126   Copper pans

Plate 127   Drywipes

DEPARTMENT OF HEALTH
ASSURED SAFE CATERING · CRITICAL CONTROL POINTS

Step	Hazard	Action
1 **Purchase**	High-risk* (ready-to-eat) foods contaminated with food-poisoning bacteria or toxins (Poisons produced by bacteria).	Buy from reputable supplier only. Specify maximum temperature at delivery.
2 **Receipt of food**	High-risk* (ready-to-eat) foods contaminated with food-poisoning bacteria or toxins.	Check it looks, smells and feels right. Check the temperature is right.
3 **Storage**	Growth of food poisoning bacteria, toxins on high-risk* (ready-to-eat) foods. Further contamination.	High-risk* foods stored at safe temperatures. Store them wrapped. Label high-risk foods with the correct 'sell by' date. Rotate stock and use by recommended date.
4 **Preparation**	Contamination of High-risk* (ready-to-eat) foods. Growth of food-poisoning bacteria.	Wash your hands before handling food. Limit any exposure to room temperatures during preparation. Prepare with clean equipment, and use this for high-risk* (ready-to-eat) food only. Separate cooked foods from raw foods.
5 **Cooking**	Survival of food-poisoning bacteria.	Cook rolled joints, chicken, and re-formed meats eg. burgers, so that the thickest part reaches at least 75°C. Sear the outside of other, solid meat cuts (eg. joints of beef, steaks) before cooking.
6 **Cooling**	Growth of any surviving spores or food poisoning bacteria. Production of poisons by bacteria. Contamination with food-poisoning bacteria.	Cool foods as quickly as possible. Don't leave out at room temperatures to cool, unless the cooling period is short, eg place any stews or rice, etc, in shallow trays and cool to chill temperatures quickly.
7 **Hot-holding**	Growth of food-poisoning bacteria. Production of poisons by bacteria.	Keep food hot, above 63°C.
8 **Reheating**	Survival of food-poisoning bacteria.	Reheat to above 75°C.
9 **Chilled storage**	Growth of food-poisoning bacteria.	Keep temperature at right level. Label high-risk ready-to-eat foods with correct date code.
10 **Serving**	Growth of disease-causing bacteria. Production of poisons by bacteria. Contamination.	COLD SERVICE FOODS - serve high-risk foods as soon as possible after removing from refrigerated storage to avoid them getting warm. HOT FOODS - serve high-risk foods quickly to avoid them cooling down.

A. *High-risk foods are those which may easily support the growth of food poisoning organisms and won't be cooked any further before you serve them, for example; cooked fish, meat patés, cooked egg dishes, pre-prepared dairy products that may only be re-heated.
B. Some food-poisoning bacteria can form spores which may survive cooking.

If cooling is delayed or takes a long time, these spores may grow or produce toxins (poisons). After cooking, food should be cooled quickly to prevent or reduce this. The list above is not exhaustive but shows some of the hazards likely to be present in any operation. In your catering operation you may be able to identify other hazards not listed above. If you do so make sure you control these as well.

Plate 128   Control of hygiene in food preparation (courtesy of Department of Health)

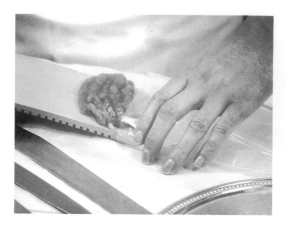
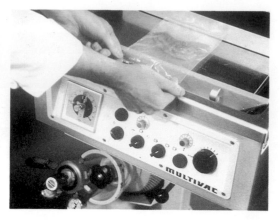

Plate 129 The sous-vide process

ROLE AND FUNCTION OF PERSONNEL IN A TRADITIONAL KITCHEN

(as implemented by Escoffier (1846–1935) a highly respected chef)

In many establishments it is necessary for staff to be working to provide meals throughout the day and, in some cases, split shifts. The split-shift system is operated

Plate 130   A Boeing 747 with 40 150 essential items for every flight

so that most staff are available for both lunch and dinner. With this system the working hours will be, for example, from 9.30 am to 2.30 pm and 6 pm to 10 pm. Some establishments operate two shifts to cover the lunch and dinner service, with one shift working from 8 am to 4 pm and the other from 4 pm to 11 pm (Figure 10.8, page 368).

Under the two-shift system each section will have a chef de partie in charge of one shift and a demi chef de partie responsible for the other shift.

Head chef

In large establishments the duties of the executive chef, chef de cuisine, head chef or person in charge, are mainly administrative; only in small establishments would it be necessary for the chef to be engaged in handling the food. The chef should:

- organise the kitchen;
- compile the menus;
- order the foodstuffs;
- show the required profit;
- engage the staff;
- supervise the kitchen (particularly at service time).

a For a 30 seater restaurant

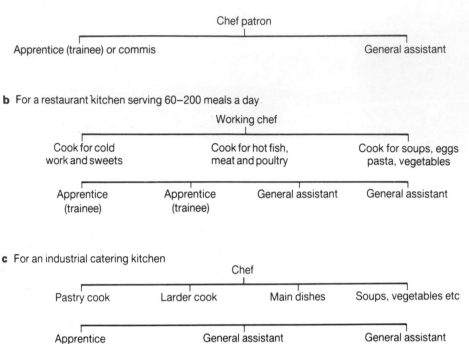

b For a restaurant kitchen serving 60–200 meals a day

c For an industrial catering kitchen

d For the kitchen of a commercial hotel or restaurant

Fig. 10.9   Example of some types of kitchen organisation

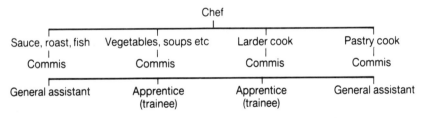

Fig. 10.10   Subsidiary departments under the control of the chef

- advise on purchase of equipment;
- be responsible, in many cases, either wholly or partially, for the stores, still room and the washing-up of silver, crockery, etc.

Second chef (le sous-chef)

The second chef relieves the head chef when the latter is off duty and is the chef's 'right hand', whose main function is to supervise the work in the kitchen so that it runs smoothly and according to the chef's wishes. In large kitchens there may be several sous-chefs with specific responsibility for separate services such as banquets and grill room.

Chef de partie (section chef)

The chefs de partie are each in charge of a section of the work in the kitchen. This is the job of the specialist. The chefs de partie organise their own sections, delegate the work to assistants and are, in fact, the 'backbone' of the kitchen.

Assistant cooks (les commis chefs)

The chefs de partie are assisted by commis or assistants, the number varying with the amount of work done by the party. For example the vegetable party is larger than the fish party, due to the quantity of work to be prepared, so there are more assistants on that party. The first commis is usually capable of taking over a great deal of the responsibility, and in some cases will take charge of the party when the chef is off duty.

Apprentice

The apprentice is learning the trade and is moved to each of the parties to gain knowledge of all the sections in the kitchen.

The work of the chefs and their parties is discussed below. (See also Figures 10.9 and 10.10, page 376.)

Sauce section

The sauce cook prepares the entrées (all the meat, poultry and game dishes which are not roasted or grilled). This includes all made-up dishes, such as vol-au-vents, stews, and braised, boiled, poêled and sautéed dishes. The sauce cook will prepare certain garnishes for these dishes and make the meat, poultry and game sauces.

Roast section

All roasted and grilled meat, poultry and game are cooked by the roast cooks. All grilled and deep-fried fish and other deep-fried foods, including potatoes, are also cooked by this party, as well as many savouries. The only deep-fried foods which may not be cooked by the roast party are those cooked in pastry. The work of the rôtisseur includes the garnishing of the grills and roasts; the roast cook grills the mushrooms and tomatoes and makes the Yorkshire pudding and roast gravy.

Fish section

Except for grilled and deep-fried fish, all the fish dishes and fish sauces and garnishes are cooked by this party, as well as béchamel, sauce hollandaise and melted butter. The preparation of the fish is usually done by a fishmonger in the larder.

Vegetable section

All the vegetables and potatoes, other than those which are deep fried, and the egg and farinaceous dishes are the responsibility of the vegetable party as well as the vegetable garnishes to the main dishes. Such things as soups, savoury soufflés and, in some places, pancakes will be cooked by this party.

Soup section

In large establishments there may be a separate party to make the soups and their garnishes. In some brigades, the eggs and pasta dishes may also be the responsibility of this party.

Larder section

The larder is mainly concerned with the preparation of food which is cooked by the other parties. This includes the preparation of poultry and game and, in smaller establishments, the preparation of meat. The fish is prepared by a fishmonger in the larder by cleaning, filleting and portioning, although most establishments now order ready prepared fillets of fish.

All the cold soup, egg, fish, meat, poultry and game dishes are decorated and served by this party. Cold sauces, sandwiches and certain work for cocktail parties, such as canapés and the filling to bouchées, are done here.

The hors-d'œuvre and salads are made up by the *hors-d'œuvrier* in his or her own place, which is near to the larder.

The oysters, cheeses and dessert fruits may also be served from the larder.

Butcher

Usually the butcher works under the direct control of the chef or sous-chef and dissects the carcasses and prepares all the joints and cuts ready for cooking. Many establishments now order meat prejointed or precut.

Pastry section

All the sweets and pastries are made by the pastry cooks, as well as items required by other parties, such as vol-au-vents, bouchées, noodles, etc and also the covering for meat and poultry dishes.

Ice-cream and petits fours are made here. Formerly, a *glacier* was employed to make all the ice-creams, but most ice-cream is now produced in factories.

The bakery goods, such as croissants and brioche, may be made by the pastry cook when there is no separate bakery.

Baker

A baker used to make all the bread, rolls, croissants, etc., but few hotels today employ their own bakers.

Relief cook

The chef tournant usually relieves the chefs of the sauce, roast, fish, and vegetable parties on their day off. The first commis in the larder and pastry usually relieves his own chef. In some places a commis tournant will also be employed.

Duty cook

The duty cook is employed where split duty is involved. This chef is on guard to do any orders in the kitchen during that time when most of the staff are off duty and also for the late period when the other staff have gone home. Split duty hours involve a break from approximately 2.30 to 5.30 pm. Usually a commis is on guard in the larder and pastry.

Night cook

A night cook is employed to be on duty part of the night and all night if necessary to provide late meals.

Breakfast cook

The breakfast cook will prepare all the breakfasts and in smaller establishments will often do additional duties, sometimes working until after lunch.

Staff cook

The staff cook provides the meals for the employees who use the staff room; these are the wage-earning staff and include uniformed and maintenance staff, room maids, etc. This applies in large hotels.

Grill cook and carver

In places where there is a call for a large number of grills and roast joints a grill cook and a carver will be employed, in many cases operating in front of the customers in the dining room or grill room.

Kitchen clerk

The kitchen clerk is responsible for much of the chef's routine clerical work and is, in fact, secretary to the chef. During service time the clerk will often call out the orders from the hot plate. Today, in some establishments, computers are used for ordering dishes.

Kitchen porters

Kitchen porters are responsible for general cleaning duties.
    Larger parties such as the pastry, larder and vegetable parties may have one or

more porters to assist the chefs. They may prepare breadcrumbs, chop parsley, peel vegetables and carry food from one section to another.

When several porters are employed one is usually appointed head porter and he may be responsible for extra duties, such as changing laundry.

Scullery

The sculleryman or 'plongeur' is responsible for collecting and washing all the pots and pans and then returning them to the appropriate place in the kitchen.

In many establishments the work of the kitchen porter and the sculleryman is combined.

Stillroom

The stillroom is used for the preparation and service for all the beverages (tea, coffee, chocolate) as well as the bread and butter, rolls and toast. Simple afternoon teas are also served from the stillroom.

Plate room/silver

All silver dishes and cutlery are cleaned and polished in the plate room. The kitchen is supplied from here with clean silver ready for service.

China pantry

Here the used crockery and glass are returned, washed and stored ready for service.

Food-lift men

Where food is served to customers in their rooms, lift men are employed to send it to the floors by a food lift.

Stores

The storekeeper is in charge of the stores and is responsible for checking all inward delivery of goods. In some places the storekeeper will not be responsible for checking perishable foodstuffs; these will go direct to the kitchen and be checked by the chef or sous-chef.

The storekeeper will be responsible for the issuing of food to the separate parties.

More details of the stores and the duties of the storekeepers will be found in Chapter 8.

The party system is gradually being replaced by a process approach. As managers and chefs seek to establish more efficient ways of organising professional kitchens, the process approach banks together equipment designed for special functions; for example:

- hot dry cooking: ovens, fryers, grills;
- hot wet cooking: steamers, boilers.

The party system divides the work according to dish requirements. The process approach divides the work according to different processes for the dishes required to be produced.

KITCHEN SUPERVISION

The organisation within different industries varies according to their specific requirements and the names given to people doing similar jobs may also vary. Some firms will require operatives, technicians, technologists; others need craftsmen, supervisors, managers. The supervisory function of the charge hand, foreman, chef de partie or supervisor may be similar.

The catering industry is made up of: people with craft skills, the craftsmen who are involved with production; the supervisors, such as chefs de partie; those who use managerial skills and determine policy. It is those who have a supervisory function that we are concerned with here.

A useful definition of good supervision is that it is the effective deployment of money, material and manpower.

Supervisory function

Certain leadership qualities are needed to enable the supervisor to carry out his or her role effectively. These qualities include the ability to:

- communicate;
- co-ordinate;
- motivate;
- initiate;
- mediate;
- inspire;
- make decisions;
- organise.

Those under supervision should expect from the supervisor:

- consideration;
- respect;
- understanding;
- consistency;

and in return the supervisor can expect:

- loyalty;
- respect;
- co-operation.

The good supervisor is able to obtain the best from those for whom he or she has responsibility and can also completely satisfy the management of the establishment that a good job is being done.

The job of the supervisor is essentially to be an overseer. In the catering industry the name given to the supervisor may vary – sous-chef, chef de partie, kitchen supervisor or corner chef. In hospital catering the name would be sous-chef, chef de partie or kitchen supervisor. The kitchen supervisor will be responsible to the catering manager, while in hotels and restaurants the chef de parties will be responsible to the head chef, while in hotels and restaurants the chef de parties will be responsible to the chef de cuisine. The exact details of the job will vary according to the different areas of the industry and the size of the various units, but generally the supervisory role involves three functions: technical; administrative; social.

TECHNICAL FUNCTION

Culinary skills and the ability to use kitchen equipment are essential for the kitchen supervisor. Most kitchen supervisors will have worked their way up through the section or sections before reaching supervisory responsibility. The supervisor needs to be able 'to do' as well as knowing 'what to do' and 'how to do it'. It is also necessary to be able to do it well and to be able to impart some of these skills to others.

ADMINISTRATIVE FUNCTION

The supervisor or chef de partie will, in many kitchens, be involved with the menu planning, sometimes with complete responsibility for the whole menu but more usually for part of the menu, as happens with the larder chef and pastry chef. This includes the ordering of foodstuffs (which is an important aspect of the supervisor's job in a catering establishment) and, of course, accounting for and recording materials used. The administrative function includes the allocation of duties and, in all instances, basic work-study knowledge is needed to enable the supervisor to operate effectively. The supervisor's job may also include the writing of reports, particularly in situations where it is necessary to make comparisons and when new developments are being tried.

SOCIAL FUNCTION

The role of the supervisor is perhaps most clearly seen in staff relationships because the supervisor has to motivate the staff under his or her responsibility. 'To motivate' could be described as the initiation of movement and action; and having got the staff moving the supervisor needs to exert control. Then in order to achieve the required result the staff need to be organised.

Thus the supervisor has a threefold function regarding the handling of staff, namely: to organise, to motivate, to control; this is the essence of staff supervision.

Elements of supervision

The accepted areas of supervision include:

- forecasting and planning;
- organising;
- commanding;
- co-ordinating;
- controlling.

Each of these will be considered within the sphere of catering.

FORECASTING

Before making plans it is necessary to look ahead, to foresee possible and probable outcomes and to allow for them. For example, the chef de partie knows that the following day is his assistant's day off, he looks ahead and plans accordingly; when the catering supervisor in the hospital knows that there is a 'flu epidemic and two of his cooks are feeling below par he plans for their possible absence; if there is a spell of fine hot weather and the cook in charge of the larder foresees a continued demand for cold foods, or when an end to the hot spell is anticipated, then the plans are modified. For the supervisor forecasting is the good use of judgement acquired from previous knowledge and experience. For example, because many people are on holiday in August fewer meals will be needed in the office restaurant; no students are in residence at the college hostel, but a conference is being held and 60 meals are required. The Motor Show, bank holidays, the effects of a rail strike or a wet day, as well as less predictable situations, such as the number of customers anticipated on the opening day of a new restaurant, all need to be anticipated and planned for.

PLANNING

From the forecasting comes the planning: how many meals to prepare; how much to have in stock (should the forecast not have been completely accurate); how many staff will be needed; which staff and when. Are the staff capable of what is required of them? If not, the supervisor needs to plan some training. This, of course, is particularly important if new equipment is installed. Imagine an expensive item, such as a new type of oven, ruined on the day it is installed because the staff have not been instructed in its proper use; or, more likely, equipment lying idle because the supervisor may not like it, may consider it is sited wrongly, does not train staff to use it, or for some similar reason.

As can be seen from these examples it is necessary for forecasting to precede planning, and from planning we now move to organising.

ORGANISING

In the catering industry organisational skills are applied to food, to equipment and to staff. Organising in this context consists of ensuring that what is wanted is where it is wanted, when it is wanted, in the right amount and at the right time.

Such organisation involves the supervisor in the production of duty rotas, maybe training programmes and also cleaning schedules. Consider the supervisor's part in organising an outdoor function where a wedding reception is to be held in a church hall: 250 guests require a hot meal to be served at 2 pm and in the evening a dance will be held for the guests, during which a buffet will be provided at 9 pm. The supervisor would need to organise the staff to be available when required, to have their own meals and maybe to see that they have got their transport home. Calor gas stoves may be needed, and the supervisor would have to arrange for the stoves to be serviced and for the equipment used to be cleaned after the function. The food would need to be ordered so that it arrived in time to be prepared. If decorated hams were to be used on the buffet then they would need to be ordered in time so that they could be prepared, cooked and decorated over the required period of time. If the staff have never carved hams before, instruction would need to be given; this entails organising training. Needless to say, the correct quantities of food, equipment and cleaning materials would also have to be at the right place when wanted; and if all the details of the situation were not organised properly problems could occur.

COMMANDING

The supervisor has to give instructions to staff on how, what, when and where; this means that orders have to be given and a certain degree of order and discipline maintained. The successful supervisor is able to do this effectively, having made certain decisions and, usually, having established the basic priorities. Explanations of why a food is prepared in a certain manner, why this amount of time is needed to dress up food, say for a buffet, why this decision is taken and not that decision, and how these explanations and orders are given, determine the effectiveness of the supervisor.

CO-ORDINATING

Co-ordinating is the skill required to get staff to co-operate and work together. To achieve this, the supervisor has to be interested in the staff, to deal with their queries, to listen to their problems and to be helpful. Particular attention should be paid to new staff, easing them into the work situation so that they quickly become part of the team or *partie*. The other area of co-ordination for which the supervisor has particular responsibility is in maintaining good relations with other departments. However, the important persons to consider will always be the customers, the patients, the school children, who are to receive the service, and good service is dependent on co-operation between waiters and cooks, nurses and catering staff, stores staff, caretakers, teachers, suppliers and so on. The supervisor has a crucial role to play here.

CONTROLLING

This includes the controlling of people and products, preventing pilfering as well as improving performance; checking that staff arrive on time, do not leave before time and do not misuse time in between; checking that the product, in this case the food, is of the right standard, that is to say, the correct quantity and quality; checking to prevent waste, and also to ensure that staff operate the portion control system correctly.

This aspect of the supervisor's function involves inspecting and requires tact; controlling may include the inspecting of the swill-bin to observe the amount of waste, checking the disappearance of a quantity of food, supervising the cooking of the meat so that shrinkage is minimised and reprimanding an unpunctual member of the team.

The standards of any catering establishment are dependent on the supervisor doing his or her job efficiently, and standards are set and maintained by effective control, which is the function of the supervisor.

Responsibilities of the supervisor

DELEGATION

It is recognised that delegation is the root of successful supervision; in other words, by giving a certain amount of responsibility to others the supervisor can be more effective.

The supervisor needs to be able to judge the person capable of responsibility before any delegation can take place. But then, having recognised the abilities of an employee, the supervisor who wants to develop the potential of those under his or her control must allow the person entrusted with the job to get on with it.

MOTIVATION

Since not everyone is capable of, or wants, responsibility, the supervisor still needs to motivate those who are less ambitious. Most people are prepared to work so as to improve their standard of living, but there is also another very important motivating factor: most people desire to get *satisfaction* from the work they do. The supervisor must be aware of why people work and how different people achieve job satisfaction and then be able to act upon this knowledge.

WELFARE

People always work best in good working conditions and these include freedom from fear: fear of becoming unemployed, fear of failure at work, fear of discrimination. Job security and incentives, such as opportunities for promotion, bonuses, profit sharing and time for further study, encourage a good attitude to work; but as well as these tangible factors people need to feel wanted and to feel that what they do is important. The supervisor is in an excellent position to ensure that this happens. Personal worries affect individuals' performance and can have a very strong influence on how well or how badly they work. The physical environment will naturally cause problems if, for example, the atmosphere is humid, the working situation ill-lit, too hot or too noisy, and there is constant rush and tear, and frequent major problems to be overcome. In these circumstances staff are more liable to be quick-tempered, angry and aggressive, and the supervisor needs to consider how these factors might be dealt with.

UNDERSTANDING

The supervisor needs to try to understand both men and women (and to deal with both sexes fairly), to anticipate problems and build up a team spirit so as to overcome the problems. This entails always being fair when dealing with staff and giving them encouragement. It also means that work needs to be allocated according to each individual's ability; everyone should be kept fully occupied and the working environment must be conducive to producing their best work.

COMMUNICATION

Finally, and most important of all, the supervisor must be able to communicate effectively. To convey orders, instructions, information and manual skills requires the supervisor to possess the right attitude to those with whom he or she needs to communicate. The ability to convey orders and instructions in a manner which is acceptable to the one receiving the orders is dependent not only on the words but on the emphasis given to the words, the tone of voice, the time selected to give them and on who is present when they are given. This is a skill which supervisors need to develop. Instructions and orders can be given with authority *without* being authoritative.

Thus the supervisor needs technical knowledge and the ability to direct staff and to carry responsibility so as to achieve the specified targets and standards required by the organisation; this he or she is able to do by organising, co-ordinating, controlling and planning but, most of all, through effective communication.

TOPICS FOR DISCUSSION

1. Who should be responsible for planning a kitchen?
2. Discuss the worst organised kitchen that you have seen and how it could be improved.
3. Give good and bad examples of working methods.
4. Discuss advantages and disadvantages of the straight shift and split-shift systems from the point of view of the staff and the employer.
5. Compile a list of all the factors which affect the good design of a kitchen. Discuss why they are necessary to enable efficiency.
6. Poor design may cause accidents in the kitchen. Discuss the ways in which accidents can be prevented.
7. Discuss the reasons why organisation of staff needs to be considered in relation to a specific menu and the factors which influence the composition of the menu.
8. Discuss the qualities which go towards being a good a) chef; b) chef de partie.
9. Organising ability is a quality which is often quoted as an essential element to being successful in the kitchen. Discuss, with examples if possible, of your understanding of organising ability regarding a) the resources; b) staff; c) yourself.
10. Discuss the difference in planning a kitchen based on process rather than the product.

11

Catering equipment

Kitchen equipment is expensive so initial selection is important, and the following points should be considered before each item is purchased or hired:

- Overall dimensions (in relation to available space).
- Weight – can the floor support the weight?
- Fuel supply – is the existing fuel supply sufficient to take the increase?
- Drainage – where necessary, are there adequate facilities?
- Water – where necessary, is it to hand?
- Use – does the food to be produced justify good use?
- Capacity – can it cook the quantities of food required efficiently?
- Time – can it cook the given quantities of food in the time available?
- Ease – is it easy for staff to handle, control and use properly?
- Maintenance – is it easy for staff to clean and maintain?
- Attachments – is it necessary to use additional equipment or attachments?
- Extraction – does it require extraction facilities for fumes or steam?
- Noise – does it have an acceptable noise level?
- Construction – is it well made, safe, hygienic and energy efficient, and are all handles, knobs and switches sturdy and heat resistant?
- Appearance – if equipment is to be on view to customers does it look good and fit in with the overall design?
- Spare parts – are they and replacement parts easily obtainable?

Kitchen equipment may be divided into three categories:

- Large equipment – ranges, steamers, boiling pans, fish-fryers, sinks, tables.
- Mechanical equipment – peelers, mincers, mixers, refrigerators, dish-washers.
- Utensils and small equipment – pots, pans, whisks, bowls, spoons.

Manufacturers of large and mechanical kitchen equipment issue instructions on how to keep their apparatus in efficient working order, and it is the responsibility of everyone using the equipment to follow these instructions (which should be displayed in a prominent place near the machines).

Arrangements should be made with the local gas board for regular checks and servicing of gas-operated equipment; similar arrangements should be made with the electricity supplier. It is a good plan to keep a log-book of all equipment, showing where each item is located when servicing takes place, noting any defects that arise, and instructing the fitter to sign the log-book and to indicate exactly what has been done.

LARGE EQUIPMENT

Ranges and ovens

A large variety of ranges is available operated by gas, electricity, solid fuel, oil, microwave or microwave plus convection.

Solid tops should be washed or wiped clean with a pad of sacking. When cool the range tops can be more thoroughly cleaned by washing and using an abrasive. After any kind of cleaning a solid top should always be lightly greased.

On the open type of range all the bars and racks should be removed, immersed in hot water with a detergent, scrubbed clean, dried and put back in place. The gas jets should then be lit to check that none are blocked. All enamel parts of ranges should be cleaned while warm with hot detergent water, rinsed and dried.

The insides of ovens and oven racks should be cleaned while slightly warm, using detergent water and a mild abrasive if necessary. In cases of extreme dirt or grease being baked on to the range or oven a caustic jelly may be used, but thorough rinsing must take place afterwards.

Oven doors should not be slammed as this is liable to cause damage.

The unnecessary or premature lighting of ovens can cause wastage of fuel, which is needless expense. This is a bad habit common in many kitchens.

When a solid-top gas range is lit, the centre ring should be removed, but it should be replaced after approximately five minutes, otherwise unnecessary heat is lost.

CONVECTION OVENS (Figures 11.1, 11.2)

These are ovens in which a circulating current of hot air is rapidly forced around the inside of the oven by a motorised fan or blower. As a result, a more even and constant temperature is created which allows food to be cooked successfully in any part of the oven. This means that the heat is used more efficiently, cooking temperatures can be lower, cooking times shortened and overall fuel economy achieved.

Forced air convection can be described as fast conventional cooking; conventional in that heat is applied to the surface of the food, but fast since moving air transfers its heat more rapidly than does static air. In a sealed oven, fast hot air circulation reduces evaporation loss, keeping shrinkage to a minimum, and gives the rapid change of surface texture and colour which are traditionally associated with certain cooking processes.

There are four types of convection oven.

- Where forced air circulation within the oven is accomplished by means of a motor-driven fan, the rapid air circulation ensures even temperature distribution to all parts of the oven.
- Where low velocity, high volume air movement is provided by a power blower and duct system.
- A combination of a standard oven and a forced convection oven designed to operate as either by the flick of a switch.

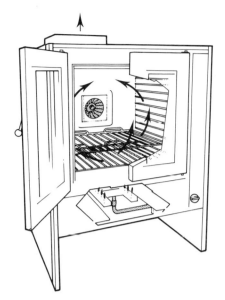

• A single roll-in rack convection oven with heating element and fan housed outside the cooking area. An 18-shelf mobile oven rack makes it possible to roll the filled rack directly from the preparation area into the oven.

Fig. 11.1 Forced air convection oven

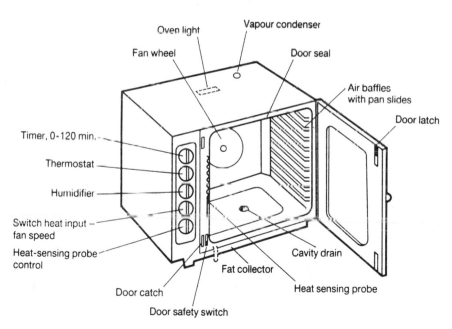

Fig. 11.2 Hot air convection oven

Further information can be obtained from Forced Air Convection Ovens (Cornwell, Greene, Belfield, Smith & Co.), 20 Kingsway, London WC1.

CONVECTION AND STEAMING OVEN (Figure 11.3, page 390)
This combination oven can be used for cooking by convection, steam or a combination of both. It can be used for roasting, braising, poaching, fast steaming, baking, grilling, toasting, defrosting and regenerating frozen and cook-chill foods.

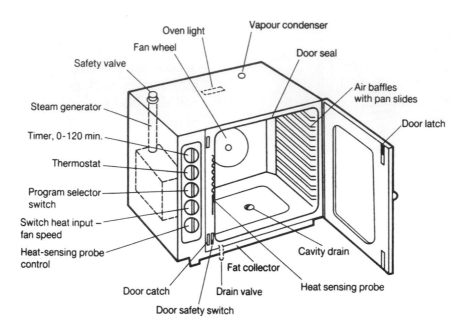

Fig. 11.3 Hot air steamer oven

COOK AND HOLD OVENS

Food can be placed in these ovens and set to switch on during off-peak periods (when energy cost may be cheaper). The ovens can then cook at a low temperature, reducing shrinkage and evaporation loss until the required internal temperature is reached after which the oven continues to hold the food at the required state. Cook and hold ovens are often used in busy carvery operations.

SMOKING OVENS

Smoking certain foods is a means of cooking, injecting different flavours and preserving. Smoking ovens or cabinets are well insulated with controlled heating elements on which wood chips are placed (different types of wood chips give differing flavours). As the wood chips burn, the heated smoke permeates the food (fish, chicken, sausages, etc.), which is suspended in the cabinet.

MICROWAVE OVENS (Plate 121, page 369; see also *Practical Cookery*, pages 106–108)

Microwave is a method of cooking and heating food by using high frequency power. The energy used is the same as that which carries television from the transmitter to the receiver, but is at a higher frequency.

The waves disturb the molecules or particles of food and agitate them, thus causing friction which has the effect of cooking the whole of the food. In the conventional method of cooking, heat penetrates the food only by conduction from the outside. Food being cooked by microwave needs no fat or water, and is placed in a glass, earthenware, plastic or paper container before being put in the oven (Figure 11.4). Metal is not used as the microwaves are reflected by it.

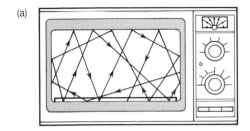

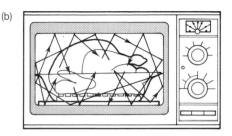

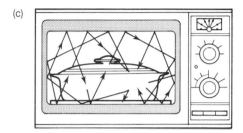

Fig. 11.4(a) Microwave energy being reflected off cooking cavity walls; (b) microwave energy being absorbed by food; (c) microwave energy passing through cooking container material

All microwave ovens consist of a basic unit of various sizes with varying levels of power. Some feature additions to the standard model, such as automatic defrosting systems, browning elements, 'stay-hot' controls and revolving turntables.

The oven cavity has metallic walls, ceiling and floor which reflect the microwaves. The oven door is fitted with special seals to ensure that there is minimum microwave leakage. A cut-out device automatically switches off the microwave energy when the door is opened.

When cleaning, do not allow the cleaning agent to soil or accumulate around the door seal as this could prevent a tight seal when the door is closed. Never use an abrasive cleaner to clean the interior of the oven as it can scratch the metallic walls; do not use aerosols either as they may penetrate the internal parts of the oven. Follow the manufacturer's instructions carefully for cleaning.

Further information can be obtained from The Microwave Association, 115 Sugden Road, London SW11 5ED and Merrychef Ltd, Station Road West, Ash Vale, Aldershot, Hampshire GU12 5XA.

Combination convection and microwave cooker (Figure 11.5, page 392)
This cooker combines forced air convection and microwave, either of which can be used separately but which are normally used simultaneously, thereby giving the advantages of both systems: speed, coloration and texture of food. Traditional metal cooking pans may also be used without fear of damage to the cooker.

INDUCTION COOKERS (Figure 11.6, page 393)
These are solid top plates made of vitroceramic material which provide heat only when pans are put on them and which stop the heat immediately the pans are removed.

A generator creates a two-way magnetic field at the top level. When a utensil with

Fig. 11.5 Convection microwave oven

a magnetic base is placed on the top a current passes directly to the pan, meaning that a far more efficient use is made of the energy than with conventional cooking equipment. Since the ceramic top is not magnetic but merely a tray to stand the pots and pans on, it never heats up. Tests indicate more than 50% energy saving. If a pan of water is to be brought to the boil there is no delay waiting for the top to heat up; the transmission of energy through the pan is immediate. When shallow frying, cold oil and the food can be put into the pan together without affecting the quality of the food as the speed of heating is so rapid.

Induction tops have a number of advantages over ranges using conventional sources:

- energy saving;
- flexible;
- faster cooking time;
- easy maintenance;
- hygienic;
- safe;
- improved working environment (less heat in the kitchen).

However, induction tops are expensive and special cooking utensils are required. Any non-magnetic material does not work and aluminium and copper are unsuitable. Stainless steel, steel enamelled ware, iron and specially adapted copper pans are suitable.

HALOGEN HOB

This runs on electricity, and comprises five individually controlled heat zones, each of which has four tungsten halogen lamps located under a smooth ceramic glass

Fig. 11.7   Halogen hob

Fig. 11.6   Induction hob

surface. The heat source glows red, when switched on, getting brighter as the temperature increases.

When the hob is switched on, 70% of the heat is transmitted as infrared light directly into the base of the cooking pan, the rest is from conducted heat via the ceramic glass. Ordinary pots and pans may be used on the halogen hob, but those with a flat, dark or black base absorb the heat most efficiently.

The halogen range includes a convection oven, and the halogen hob unit is also available mounted on a stand.

STEAMERS

There are basically three types of steaming ovens:

- atmospheric (see Figure 11.8, pages 394–5);
- pressure;
- pressureless (see Figure 11.9, page 395).

There are also combination steaming ovens: pressure/convection steam; pressureless/ fully pressurised; steaming/hot air cooking; combination of hot air and steam; combination of hot air and steam with two settings (Figure 11.10, page 395).

In addition, dual pressure steamers, switchable between low pressure and high pressure, and two pressure settings plus zero are available. Steaming ovens continue to develop, improve and become more versatile. The modern combination steamers which can be used for steaming, stewing, poaching, braising, roasting, baking,

Fig. 11.8a Atmospheric steamer

vacuum cooking, gratinating, reconstituting, blanching and defrosting, have electronic controls for easier setting and more precise time/temperature control. The advantage of the electronic controls is that they assist in fuel efficiency. They are available in several sizes and there are many examples of their efficiency. For example, one large hotel quotes: 'using five electrically heated combi-steamers we served 500 English breakfasts straight from the oven – no messing about with hot plates and cupboards'.

With such a wide range of models available it is increasingly important to consider carefully which model is best suited to a particular kitchen's requirements.

Cleanliness of steamers is essential, and trays and runners should be washed in hot detergent water and then rinsed. Any water-generating chamber should be drained, cleaned and refilled and the inside of the steamer cleaned. Grease door controls occasionally, and when the steamer is not in use, leave the door slightly open to let air circulate inside the steamer.

Further information can be obtained from Catering Equipment Manufacturers Association of Great Britain (CEMA), Carlyle House, 235–237 Vauxhall Bridge Road, London SW1V 1EJ.

Large pans, boilers and fryers

BRATT PAN (Figure 11.11, page 396)
The bratt pan is one of the most versatile pieces of cooking equipment in the kitchen because it is possible to use it for shallow frying, deep frying, stewing, braising and boiling. A bratt pan can cook many items of food at one time because of its large surface area. A further advantage is that it can be tilted so that the contents can be quickly and efficiently poured out on completion of the cooking process. Bratt pans are heated by gas or electricity and several models are available incorporating various features to meet differing catering requirements.

BOILING PANS (Figure 11.12, page 396)
Many types are available in different metals – aluminium, stainless steel, etc – in various sizes (10, 15, 20, 30 and 40 litre capacity) and they may be heated by gas or electricity. As they are used for boiling or stewing large quantities of food, it is important that they do not allow the food to burn; for this reason the steam-jacket

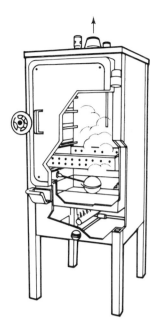

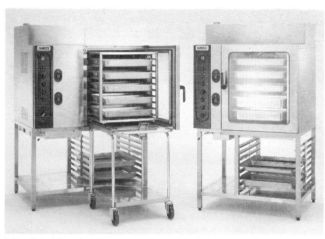

Fig. 11.9   Pressureless steamer

Fig. 11.8b   Atmospheric steamers

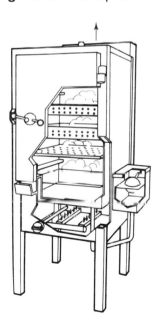

Fig. 11.10   Combination steamers

type boiler is the most suitable. Many of these are fitted with a tilting device to facilitate the emptying of the contents.

After usc, the boiling pan and lid should be thoroughly washed with mild detergent solution and then well rinsed. The tilting apparatus should be greased occasionally and checked to see that it tilts easily. If gas fired, the gas jets and pilot should be inspected to ensure correct working. If a pressure gauge and safety valve are fitted these should also be checked.

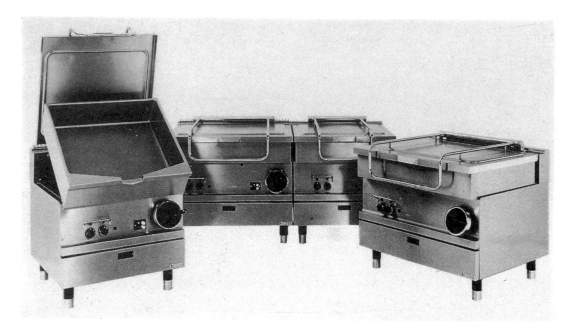

Fig. 11.11   Selection of bratt pans

Fig. 11.12   Tilting boiling bans (below) and tilting kettle (right)

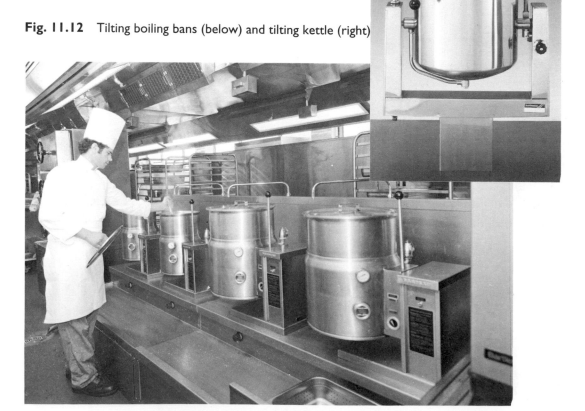

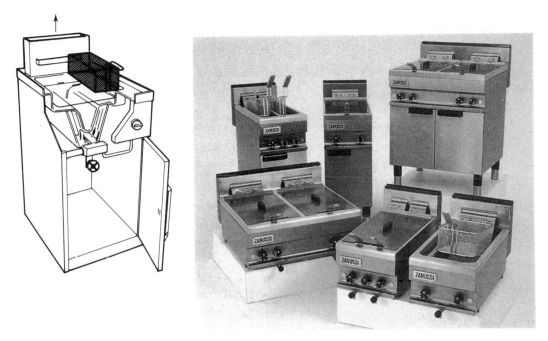

Fig. 11.13 Examples of deep fat-fryers: gas heated (above) and electrically heated (right)

DEEP FAT-FRYERS

A deep fat-fryer is one of the most extensively used items of equipment in many catering establishments. The careless worker who misuses a deep fat-fryer and spills food or fat can waste money.

Fryers are heated by gas or electricity and incorporate a thermostatic control in order to save fuel and prevent overheating. There is a cool zone below the source of heat into which food particles can sink without burning, thus preventing spoiling of other foods being cooked. This form of heating also saves fat.

PRESSURE FRYERS

Food is cooked in an air-tight frying vat thus enabling food to be fried a lot faster and at a lower oil temperature.

HOT AIR ROTARY FRYERS

These are designed to cook batches of frozen blanched chips or battered foods without any oil in 4–6 minutes.

Computerised fryers are available which may be programmed to control automatically cooking temperatures and times, on and off switches, basket lifting and product holding times. Operational information is fed from a super-sensitive probe, which is immersed in the frying medium and passes information about temperature and rates of temperature change which may be caused by: the initial fat temperature, amount of food being fried, fryer efficiency and capacity, fryer recovery rate, quantity and condition of fat, product temperature and water content.

With all the above information the fryer computes exact cooking times and an automatic signalling device indicates the end of a cooking period.

Deep fat-fryers should be cleaned daily after use by:

* turning off the heat and allow the fat or oil to cool;
* draining off and straining the fat or oil;
* closing the stopcock, filling the fryer with hot water containing detergent and boiling for 10–15 minutes;
* draining off the detergent water, refilling with clean water plus $\frac{1}{8}$ litre of vinegar per 5 litres of water and reboiling for 10–15 minutes;
* draining off the water, drying the fryer, closing the stopcock and refilling with clean fat or oil.

HOT-CUPBOARDS (commonly referred to in the trade as the hotplate) (Figure 11.14)

Hot-cupboards are used for heating plates and serving dishes and for keeping food hot. Care should be taken to see that the amount of heat fed into the hot-cupboard is controlled at a reasonable temperature. This is important, otherwise the plates and food will either be too hot or too cold and this could obviously affect the efficiency of the service. A temperature of 60–76°C (140–169°F) is suitable for hot-cupboards and a thermostat is a help in maintaining this.

Hot-cupboards may be heated by steam, gas or electricity. The doors should slide easily, and occasional greasing may be necessary. The tops of most hot-cupboards are used as serving counters and should be heated to a higher temperature than the inside. These tops are usually made of stainless steel and should be cleaned thoroughly after each service.

Fig. 11.14 Hotplate area of a central kitchen

BAINS-MARIE

Bains-marie are open wells of water used for keeping foods hot, and are available in many designs, some of which are incorporated into hot-cupboards, some in serving counters, and there is a type which is fitted at the end of a cooking range. They may be heated by steam, gas or electricity and sufficient heat to boil the water in the bain-marie should be available. Care should be taken to see that a bain-marie is never allowed to burn dry when the heat is turned on. After use the heat should be turned off, the water drained and the bain-marie cleaned inside and outside with hot detergent water, rinsed and dried. Any drain-off tap should then be closed.

Grills and salamanders

The salamander or grill heated from above by gas or electricity probably causes more wastage of fuel than any other item of kitchen equipment through being allowed to burn unnecessarily for long unused periods. Most salamanders have more than one set of heating elements or jets and it is not always necessary to have them all turned on full.

Salamander bars and draining trays should be cleaned regularly with hot water containing a grease solvent such as soda. After rinsing they should be replaced and the salamander lit for a few minutes to dry the bars.

For under-fired grills (Figure 11.15) to work efficiently they must be capable of cooking food quickly and should reach a high temperature 15–20 minutes after lighting, and the heat should be turned off immediately after use. When the bars are cool they should be removed and washed in hot water containing a grease solvent, rinsed, dried and replaced on the grill. Care should be taken with the fire bricks if they are used for lining the grill as they are easily broken.

Fig. 11.15   An under-fired grill

Fig. 11.16   Griddle

CONTACT GRILLS
These are sometimes referred to as double-sided or infragrills and have two heating surfaces arranged facing each other. The food to be cooked is placed on one surface and is then covered by the second. These grills are electrically heated and are capable of cooking certain foods very quickly, so extra care is needed, particularly when cooks are using this type of grill for the first time.

FRY PLATES, GRIDDLE PLATES (Figure 11.16)
These are solid metal plates heated from below, and are used for cooking individual portions of meat, hamburgers, eggs, bacon, etc. They can be heated quickly to a high temperature and are suitable for rapid and continuous cooking. Before cooking on griddle plates a light film of oil should be applied to the food and the griddle plate to

prevent sticking. To clean griddle plates, warm them and scrape off loose food particles; rub the metal with pumice stone or griddle stone, following the grain of the metal; clean with hot detergent water, rinse with clean hot water and wipe dry. Finally reseason (prove) the surface by lightly oiling with vegetable oil.

Griddles with zone heating are useful when demand varies during the day. These reduce energy consumption in quiet periods while still allowing the service to be maintained.

Mirror chromed griddles have a polished surface which gives off less radiated heat which saves energy and makes for a more pleasant working environment.

Barbecues

Barbecues are becoming increasingly popular because it is easy to cook and serve quick tasty food on them and the outdoor location, smell and sizzle develop an atmosphere which many customers enjoy.

There are three main types of barbecue: traditional charcoal, gas (propane or butane) and electric. Remember that the charcoal-fired type takes about an hour before the surface is ready. With gas and electricity the barbecue is ready to cook almost immediately.

Gas is the more flexible and controllable. Propane gas is recommended because it can be used at any time of the year. Butane, does not work when it is cold. Propane is, however, highly flammable and safety precautions are essential. Anyone connecting the gas container must be competent in the use of bottle gas. The supply pipe must be guarded to avoid accidental interference, and the cylinder must be placed away from the barbecue. The cylinder must be upright and stable with the valve uppermost and securely held in position. Connections must be checked for leaks.

Sinks

Different materials are used for sinks according to the purpose for which they are intended:

- heavy galvanised iron for heavy pot wash;
- stainless steel for general purposes.

Tables

- Formica or stainless steel topped tables should be washed with hot detergent water then rinsed with hot water containing a sterilising agent – alternatively, some modern chemicals act as both detergent and sterilising agents. Wooden tables should not be used.
- Marble slabs should be scrubbed with hot water and rinsed. All excess moisture should be removed with a clean, dry cloth.

No cutting or chopping should be allowed on table tops; cutting boards should be used.

Hot pans should not be put on tables; triangles must be used to protect the table surface.

The legs and racks or shelves of tables are cleaned with hot detergent water and then dried. Wooden table legs require scrubbing.

BUTCHER'S OR CHOPPING BLOCK

A scraper should be used to keep the block clean. After scraping, the block should be sprinkled with a few handfuls of common salt in order to absorb any moisture which may have penetrated during the day.

Do not use water or liquids for cleaning unless absolutely necessary as water will be absorbed into the wood and cause swelling.

Storage racks

All type of racks should be emptied and scrubbed or washed periodically.

MECHANICAL EQUIPMENT

The Health and Safety Executive have two publications on catering machinery, both obtainable from HMSO. If a piece of mechanical equipment can save time and physical effort and still produce a good end result then it should be considered for purchase or hire. The performance of most machines can be closely controlled and is not subject to human variations, so it should be easier to obtain uniformity of production over a period of time.

The caterer is faced with two considerations:

- the cost of the machine: installation, maintenance, depreciation and running cost;
- the possibility of increased production and a saving of labour cost.

The mechanical performance must be carefully assessed and all the manufacturer's claims as to the machine's efficiency thoroughly checked. The design should be fool-proof, easy to clean and operated with minimum effort.

When a new item of equipment is installed it should be tested by a qualified fitter before being used by catering staff. The manufacturer's instructions must be displayed in a prominent place near the machine. The manufacturer's advice regarding servicing should be followed and a record book kept showing what kind of maintenance the machine is receiving, and when. The following list includes machines typically found in catering premises which are classified as dangerous under the Prescribed Dangerous Machines Order, 1964.

Warning: before cleaning, all machines should be switched off and the plug removed from the socket.

- Power-driven machines
  - Worm-type mincing machines.
  - Rotary knife bowl-type chopping machines.
  - Dough mixers.

- Food mixing machines when used with attachments for mincing, slicing, chipping and any other cutting operation, or for crumbling.
  - Pie and tart making machines.
  - Vegetable slicing machines.
- Potato-peelers
  - Potatoes should be free of earth and stones before loading into the machine.
  - Before any potatoes are loaded the water spray should be turned on and the abrasive plate set in motion.
  - The interior should be cleaned out daily and the abrasive plate removed to ensure that small particles are not lodged below.
  - The peel trap should be emptied as frequently as required.
  - The waste outlet should be kept free from obstruction.
- Machines whether power-driven or not
  - Circular knife slicing machines used for cutting bacon and other foods (whether similar to bacon or not).
  - Potato chipping machines.

FOOD PROCESSING EQUIPMENT

Food mixer

This is an important labour-saving, electrically operated piece of equipment used for many purposes: mixing pastry, cakes, mashing potatoes, beating egg whites, mayonnaise, cream, mincing or chopping meat and vegetables.

- It should be lubricated frequently in accordance with manufacturer's instructions.
- The motor should not be overloaded, which can be caused by obstruction to the rotary components. For example, if dried bread is being passed through the mincer attachment without sufficient care the rotary cog can become so clogged with bread that it is unable to move. If the motor is allowed to run, damage can be caused to the machine.
- All components as well as the main machine should be thoroughly washed and dried. Care should be taken to see that no rust occurs on any part. The mincer attachment knife and plates will rust if not given sufficient care.

Fig. 11.17 High-speed food processor (left); food processor with attachments (above) and blender machine (below)

Vertical, high-speed cutter mixer or bowl cutter

These are fast, versatile, labour-saving machines which can deal with a great amount of the repetitive time-consuming work which takes place in some kitchen operations.

They are used mainly for cutting and mixing and some models have attachments for kneading dough and other mixes or for mincing meat.

Fig. 11.18 Vertical, variable speed mixers

Food processing machines (see Plate 122, page 370; Figures 11.19, 11.20)

Food processors are generally similar to vertical, high-speed cutters except that they tend to be smaller and to have a larger range of attachments. They can be used for a large number of mixing and chopping jobs but they cannot whisk or incorporate air to mixes.

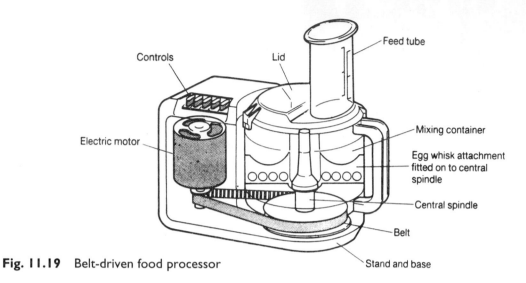

Controls   Lid   Feed tube

Electric motor

Mixing container

Egg whisk attachment fitted on to central spindle

Central spindle

Belt

Stand and base

Fig. 11.19   Belt-driven food processor

Fig. 11.20   High speed food processor

LIQUIDISER OR BLENDER

This is a versatile, labour-saving piece of kitchen machinery which uses a high-speed motor to drive specially designed stainless steel blades to chop, purée or blend foods efficiently and very quickly. They are also useful for making breadcrumbs. As a safety precaution food must be cooled before being liquidised.

FOOD-SLICERS (see Plate 123, page 370)

Food-slicers are obtainable both manually and electrically operated. They are labour-saving devices, but can be dangerous if not used with care so working instructions should be placed in a prominent position near the machine.

- Care should be taken that no material likely to damage the blades is included in the food to be sliced. It is easy for a careless worker to overlook a piece of bone which, if allowed to come into contact with the cutting blade, could cause severe damage.
- Each section in contact with food should be cleaned and carefully dried after use.
- The blade or blades should be sharpened regularly.
- Moving parts should be lubricated, but oil must not come into contact with the food.
- Extra care must be taken when blades are exposed.

CHIPPER (HAND OR ELECTRIC)

The manual type should be washed and dried after use. Care should be taken with the interior of the blades, and they should be cleaned with a folded cloth. When chipping potatoes, pressure should be applied gradually to prevent damage to the cutting blades which can be caused by violent jerking.

The electric chipper should be thoroughly cleaned and dried after use, particular attention being paid to those parts which come into contact with food. Care should be taken that no obstruction prevents the motor from operating at its normal speed. Moving parts should be lubricated according to the maker's instructions.

MASHER (HAND OR ELECTRIC)

The hand type should be washed immediately after use, then rinsed and dried.

The electric masher should have the removable sections and the main machine washed and dried after use, extra care being taken over those parts which come into contact with food. The same care should be taken as with electric chippers regarding obstruction and lubrication.

ICE-CREAM MAKERS, JUICERS AND MIXERS

Ice-cream and sorbet machines are available from 1 litre capacity and enable establishments to produce home made ice-cream and sorbets using fresh fruit in season or frozen and canned fruits at all times of the year.

Juicers and mixers can provide freshly made fruit and vegetable juices, milk shakes and cocktails.

BOILERS

Water boiling appliances for tea- and coffee-making

There are two main groups of water boilers: bulk boilers from which boiling water can only be drawn when all the contents have boiled, and automatic boilers which provide a continuous flow of boiling water.

BULK BOILERS

These are generally used when large quantities of boiling water are required at a given time. They should be kept scrupulously clean, covered with the correct lid to prevent anything falling in, and when not used for some time they should be left filled with clean cold water.

AUTOMATIC BOILERS

These boilers have automatic waterfeeds and can give freshly boiled water at intervals. It is important that the water supply is efficiently maintained, otherwise there is a danger of the boiler burning dry and being damaged.

Pressure boilers

This is the type that operates many still sets, consisting of steam heating milk boilers and a pressure boiler providing boiling water. Care should be taken with the pilot light to see that it is working efficiently. As with all gas-fired equipment it is essential that regular inspection and maintenance is carried out by gas company fitters.

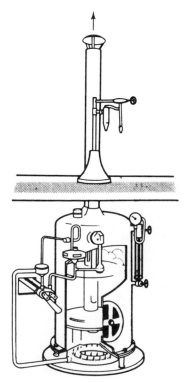

Fig. 11.21   A pressure boiler

Coffee and milk heaters

Water-jacket boilers are made for the storage of hot coffee and hot milk with draw-off taps from the storage chamber. Inner linings may be of glazed earthenware, stainless steel or heat-resistant glass. It is very important that the storage chambers are thoroughly cleaned with hot water after each use and then left full of clean cold water. The draw-off taps should be cleaned regularly with a special brush.

REFRIGERATORS

How refrigeration works

Cold is the absence of heat and to make things cold it is necessary to remove the heat that items have absorbed. This is the function of a refrigerator. Heat must be added to raise water from tap temperature of say 10°C (50°F) to its boiling point of 100°C (212°F). The addition of further heat to boiling water causes it to change its state into steam.

A substance such as ammonia which boils at minus 33°C (minus 28°F) would absorb heat at even lower temperatures. Ammonia is one of a number of liquids called 'refrigerants' which are used to absorb heat from the interior of well insulated containers or cabinets known as refrigerators. Water, from which heat is removed, cools down and forms ice. Ice blocks can be used to cool a refrigerator interior. The heat from the food stored in the refrigerator is absorbed by the ice and turned back into water as the interior cools down. Further ice blocks are then required to prolong the cooling process.

With the use of a refrigerant like liquid ammonia circulating through the pipes in

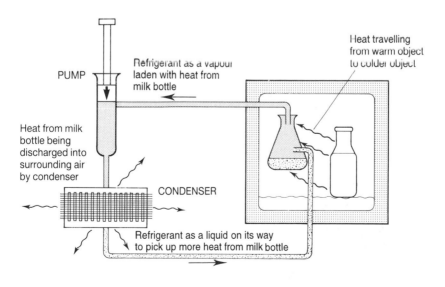

Fig. 11.22   How refrigeration works

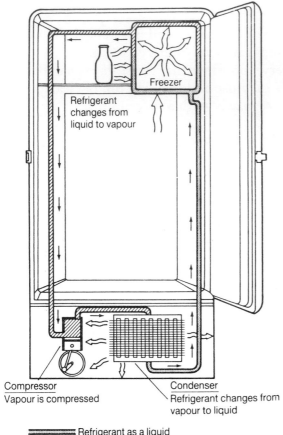

Refrigerant changes from liquid to vapour

Freezer

Compressor
Vapour is compressed

Condenser
Refrigerant changes from
vapour to liquid

══════ Refrigerant as a liquid

▨▨▨▨ Refrigerant as a vapour

∿∿⇒ Heat flow

Fig. 11.23   How compression-type refrigeration works

the refrigerated compartment, heat is taken out of the food and the liquid ammonia boils, becoming a vapour or 'gas'. When this vapour is removed or sucked out and replaced with more liquid, the cooling process can be maintained as long as required. In practice the vapour is not lost but is first compressed and then by giving up its heat to the air outside the refrigerant is condensed back to a liquid. It then returns to the refrigerator cooling unit for re-use.

Compression type refrigerator

- The evaporator inside the cabinet where the liquid refrigerant absorbs heat and boils into a vapour.
- The compressor adds pressure to the refrigerator vapour. The compressor will be driven by an electric motor.
- The condenser is where high pressure vapour loses heat to the outside air and condenses into a liquid.

LOCATION

Adequate ventilation is vital as the condenser of the refrigeration system gives off heat equal to the amount of cooling performed plus the power taken by the compressor motor. In high temperature refrigeration, the total can be as much as three to four times the motor power. Therefore refrigeration equipment should always be located in a well ventilated room.

Foods should be outside refrigerators for the minimum possible period during loading or unloading. Foods need to be kept at a steady cold temperature for maximum storage life.

Absorption-type refrigerator

This type of refrigerator does not have any moving parts as no compressor is used. A solution of ammonia gas in water is the refrigerant, and the gas is given off from the solution when it is heated by an electrical element or gas flame. The ammonia gas passes to the condenser where it is liquefied; the liquefied ammonia then passes to the evaporator with some nitrogen, where it boils and draws the heat from the cabinet. The gases produced pass to the absorber, where they mix with water and become a solution again. The solution returns to be heated again while the nitrogen returns to the evaporator.

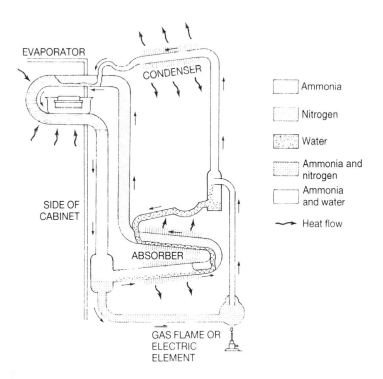

Fig. 11.24 How absorption-type refrigeration works

Refrigerants

A refrigerant must have a boiling point below the temperature at which ice forms and it should be non-corrosive.

The cabinet

This must be well insulated to minimise entry of heat from outside. In modern refrigerators, insulations such as expanded polystyrene and foamed polyurethane are used extensively.

Cold rooms, chill rooms, deep-freeze cabinets and compartments

In large establishments it is necessary to have refrigerated space at different temperatures. The cold rooms may be divided into separate rooms: one at a chill temperature for storing salads, fruits, certain cheeses; one for meats, poultry, game and tinned food which have to be refrigerated; one for deep-frozen foods. Frequently, the cold room storage is designed so that the chill room, the cold room and the deep-freeze compartment lead on from each other. Refrigerated cabinets, thermostatically controlled to various desired temperatures, are also used in large larders. Deep-freeze cabinets are used where a walk-in, deep-freeze section is not required and they maintain a temperature of $-18°C$ ($-0°F$). Chest-type deep-freeze cabinets require defrosting twice a year. It is important to close all refrigerator doors as a matter of course to contain the cold air.

Hygiene precautions

Refrigeration cannot improve the quality of foodstuffs and can only retard the natural process of deterioration.

For maximum storage of food and minimum health risk:

- Select the appropriate refrigerator equipment for the temperature requirement of the food.
- Always ensure refrigerators maintain correct temperature for food stored.
- Keep unwrapped foods, vulnerable to contamination and flavour and odour transfer, in separate refrigerators or in airtight containers and away from products such as cream, other dairy products, partly cooked pastry, cooked meat and delicatessen foods.
- Do not store foods for long periods in a good, general-purpose refrigerator because a single temperature is not suitable for keeping all types of food safely and at peak condition.
- Never keep uncooked meat, poultry or fish in the same refrigerator, or any other food which is not in its own sealed, airtight container.
- Never refreeze foods that have been thawed out from frozen.
- Always rotate stock in refrigerator space.
- Clean equipment regularly and thoroughly, inside and out.

Location

As adequate ventilation is vital, locate refrigeration equipment in a well-ventilated room away from:

- sources of intense heat – cookers, ovens, radiators, boilers, etc.;
- direct sunlight – from window or sky lights;
- barriers to adequate air circulation.

Loading

- Ensure there is adequate capacity for maximum stock.
- Check that perishable goods are delivered in a refrigerated vehicle.
- Only fill frozen food storage cabinets with prefrozen food.
- Never put hot or warm food in a refrigerator unless it is specially designed for rapid chilling.
- Ensure no damage is caused to inner linings and insulation by staples or nails, in packaging.
- Air must be allowed to circulate within a refrigerator to maintain the cooling effect – do not obstruct any airways.

Cleaning

Clean thoroughly inside and out at least every two months as blocked drain lines, drip trays and air ducts will eventually lead to a breakdown.

- Switch off power.
- If possible transfer stock to available alternative storage.
- Clean interior surfaces with lukewarm water and a mild detergent. Do not use abrasives or strongly scented cleaning agents.
- Clean exterior and dry all surfaces inside and out.
- Clear away any external dirt, dust or rubbish which might restrict the circulation of air around the condenser.
- Switch on power, check when the correct working temperature is reached, refill with stock.

Defrosting

This is important as it helps equipment perform efficiently and prevents a potentially damaging build up of ice. Presence of ice on the evaporator or internal surfaces indicates the need for urgent defrosting; if the equipment is designed to defrost automatically this also indicates a fault.

Automatic defrosting may lead to a temporary rise in air temperature; this is normal and will not put food at risk.

For manual defrosting of chest freezers always follow suppliers' instructions to obtain optimum performance. Never use a hammer or any sharp instrument which could perforate cabinet linings – a plastic spatula can be used to remove stubborn ice.

Emergency measures

Signs of imminent breakdown include: unusual noises, fluctuating temperatures, frequent stopping and starting of the compressor, excessive frost build up, absence of normal frost.

Prepare to call a competent refrigeration service engineer, but first check that:

- the power supply has not been accidentally switched off;
- the electrical circuit has not been broken by a blown fuse or the triggering of an automatic circuit breaker;
- there has been no unauthorised tampering with the user temperature control device;
- any temperature higher than recommended is not due solely to routine automatic defrosting, to the refrigerator door being left open, or to overloading the equipment or to any blockage of internal passage of air;
- there is no blockage of air to the condenser by rubbish, crates, cartons, etc. If you still suspect a fault, call the engineer and be prepared to give brief details of the equipment and the fault. Keep the door of the defective cold cabinet closed as much as possible to retain cold air. Destroy any spoilt food.

Monitoring refrigeration efficiency

All types of refrigerators, walk-in, cabinet with or without forced air circulation should be fitted with display thermometers or chart recorders that will enable daily monitoring to check that the equipment is working correctly. Sensors which can set off available alarms must be placed in the warmest part of the cabinet.

Chilled display units include:

- multi-deck cabinets with closed doors used for dispensing sandwiches, drinks and other foods, used if food needs to be displayed for more than four hours;
- open and semi-open display cabinets where food is presented on the base of the unit and cooled by circulating cooled air;
- Gastronorm counters (see Plate 124, page 371).

Because of surrounding conditions it is unsafe to assume that refrigerated display cabinets will maintain the temperature of the food below 5°C (41°F) which is why these units should never be used to store food other than for display periods of not more than four hours.

Maintenance and servicing should be carried out regularly by qualified personnel.

Further information can be obtained from Refrigeration and Unit Air-Conditioning Group, 34 Palace Court, London W2 4JG.

DISHWASHING MACHINES

For hygienic washing up the generally recognised requirements are a good supply of hot water at a temperature of 60°C (140°F) for general cleansing followed by a sterilising rinse at a temperature of 82°C (180°F) for at least one minute. Alternatively low-temperature equipment is available which sterilises by means of a chemical, sodium hypochlorite (bleach). Further information can be obtained from Lever Industrial, Lever House, St James Road, Kingston-upon-Thames, Surrey KT1 2BA.

Dishwashing machines take over an arduous job and save a lot of time and labour, ensuring that a good supply of clean, sterilised crockery is available.

There are three main types:

- Spray types – the dishes are placed in racks which slide into the machines where they are subjected to a spray of hot detergent water at 48–60°C (118–140°F) from above and below. The racks move on to the next section where they are rinsed by a fresh hot shower at 82°C (180°F). At this temperature they are sterilised, and on passing out into the air they dry off quickly.
- Brush-type machines – use revolving brushes for the scrubbing of each article in hot detergent water; the articles are then rinsed and sterilised in another compartment.
- Agitator water machines – baskets of dishes are immersed in deep tanks and the cleaning is performed by the mechanical agitation of the hot detergent water. The loaded baskets are then given a sterilising rinse in another compartment.

Dishwashing machines are costly and it is essential that the manufacturer's instructions with regard to use and maintenance are followed at all times.

MISCELLANEOUS EQUIPMENT

Food waste disposers

Food waste disposers are operated by electricity and take all manner of rubbish, including bones, fat, scraps and vegetable refuse. Almost every type of rubbish and swill, with the exception of rags and tins, are finely ground, then rinsed down the drain. It is the most modern and hygienic method of waste disposal. Care should be taken by handlers not to push waste into the machine with a metal object as this can cause damage.

Other equipment which may be found in a busy kitchen include an automatic pastry roller (see Plate 125, page 371) and toasters (Figure 11.25).

SMALL EQUIPMENT AND UTENSILS

Small equipment and utensils are made from a variety of materials such as non-stick coated metal, iron, steel, copper, aluminium, wood.

Iron

Items of equipment used for frying, such as movable fritures and frying-pans of all types, are usually made of heavy, black wrought iron.

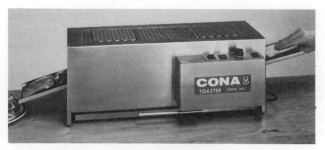

Fig. 11.25 A selection of continuous output roller toasters

Fritures should be washed in a strong, grease-solvent solution, then thoroughly rinsed and dried; or they can be thoroughly cleaned with a clean cloth.

Frying-pans when new should be 'proved'; they are coated with a layer of oil and placed on a hot stove or in a hot oven for 15–20 minutes, then wiped firmly with a clean cloth. A little fat or oil is added and they are wiped with another clean cloth. If an abrasive is necessary to clean the pan, salt may be used; if not, a good firm rub with dry cloth or paper and a final light greasing are sufficient. Always keep lightly oiled.

Frying-pans are available in several shapes and many sizes, eg:

- omelet pans;
- oval fish frying-pans;
- frying-pans;
- pancake pans.

Baking sheets are made in various sizes of black wrought steel. The less they are washed the less likely they are to cause food to stick. New baking sheets should be well heated in a hot oven, thoroughly wiped with a clean cloth and then lightly oiled. Before being used baking trays should be lightly greased with a pure fat or oil. Immediately after use and while still warm they should be cleaned by scraping and dry-wiping. Hot soda or detergent water should be used for washing.

Tartlet and barquette moulds and cake tins should be cared for in the same way as for baking sheets.

Tinned steel

A number of items are made from this metal:

Fig. 11.26   Examples of equipment which is hard to clean: 1. jelly bag; 2. Mouli; 3. and 4. Mouli attachments; 5. muslin; 6. sieve; 7. colander; 8. conical strainer – coarse; 9. conical strainer – fine; 10. potato slicer; 11. 12-inch ruler

- conical strainer (*chinois*), used for passing sauces and gravies;
- fine conical strainer, used for passing sauces and gravies;
- colander, used for draining vegetables;
- vegetable reheating container;
- soup machine and mouli strainer, used for passing thick soups, sauces and potatoes for mash;
- sieves.

All the above items should be thoroughly washed immediately after each use and dried; if this is done, washing is simple and quick. If the food or liquid clogs and dries in the mesh it is difficult to clean (see Figure 11.26, page 420). The easiest way to wash a sieve is to hold it upside down under running water and tap vigorously with the bristles of a stiff scrubbing brush. If the sieve is moved up and down quickly in water, clogged food will be loosened.

Care should be taken when using sieves: they should be the right way up when food is passed through; the food should be stroked through with a wooden mushroom, not banged, as this can damage the mesh. Only foodstuffs such as flour should be passed through the sieve upside down.

Copper (Plate 126, page 372; Figure 11.27, page 416)

Pans of copper, lined with tin, are made in various shapes, sizes and capacities and are used to cook practically every kind of food:

Fig. 11.27   Examples of copper equipment: 1. salmon kettle; 2. saucepan; 3. sauteuse; 4. sauté pan; 5. sugar boiler; 6. pomme Anna mould; 7. bowl; 8. braising pan; 9. dariole mould; 10. savarin mould; 11. 12-inch ruler

- shallow saucepan with sloping sides (*sauteuse*);
- shallow, flat, round pan with vertical sides (*sauté pan*);
- saucepan;
- stockpot;
- large, round, deep pan;
- rectangular braising-pan;
- roasting tray;
- turbot kettle;
- salmon kettle;
- gravy, soup, sauce storage pans (*bain-marie*);
- moulds of various sizes and shapes (*dariole, charlotte, savarin, bombe, timbale*).

Copper equipment is expensive, but it is first-class for cooking as copper is a good conductor of heat; also, food burns less easily in copper pans than in pans of many other metals.

The disadvantages of copper are that it tarnishes easily and looks dirty. The tin lining of copper pans can be damaged by misuse, such as excessive dry heat which can soften the tin and spoil the lining. Putting a pan on a fierce fire without liquid or fat is bad practice and can damage the tin lining. Retinning is expensive.

Copper equipment should be inspected periodically to see if the tin is being worn away; if so, it should be collected by a tinsmith and retinned.

Certain items of copper equipment (large vegetable boilers, sugar boilers, mixing bowls and egg white bowls) are not lined with tin but made wholly of copper.

THE CLEANING OF COPPER EQUIPMENT

To keep large quantities of copper equipment clean the following points should be observed:

- Two large sinks, into which the pots may be completely immersed, should be available. The water in one sink should be capable of being raised to boiling point.

- All dirty pans should be well soaked for a few minutes in boiling water to which a little soda has been added.
- They should be well scoured, using either a brush or wire wool or similar agent with a scouring powder.
- The pans are then rinsed in clean hot water and placed upside down to try.
- The copper surfaces, if tarnished, may be cleaned with a paste made from equal quantities of silver sand, salt and flour mixed with vinegar; the pans are then thoroughly rinsed and dried. Alternatively, a commercial cleaner may be used.

Aluminium

Note: Minimum use of aluminium is recommended: stainless steel is to be preferred.

Saucepans, stockpots, sauteuses, sauté pans, braising pans, fish kettles and large, round deep pans and dishes of all sizes are made in cast aluminium. They are expensive, but one advantage is that the pans do not tarnish; also because of their strong, heavy construction they are suitable for many cooking processes.

A disadvantage is that in the manufacture of aluminium, which is a soft metal, other metals are added to make pans stronger. As a result certain foods can become discoloured (care should be taken when mixing white sauces and white soups). A wooden spoon should be used for mixing, then there should be no discoloration. The use of metal whisks or spoons must be avoided.

Water boiled in aluminium pans is unsuitable for tea-making as it gives the tea an unpleasant colour. Red cabbage and artichokes should not be cooked in aluminium pans as they will take on a dark colour, caused by chemical reaction.

CLEANING OF CAST ALUMINIUM PANS

- All pans should be well soaked in hot detergent water; soda should not be used.
- After a good soaking, pans should be scoured with a hard bristle brush or rough cloth with an abrasive powder if necessary. Harsh abrasives should be avoided if possible.
- After scouring, the pans are rinsed in clean hot water and thoroughly dried.

Stainless steel (Figure 11.28)

Specially manufactured stainless steel pots and pans are now being extensively used in place of copper. Copper is considered inappropriate in terms of initial cost, retinning and cleanliness. The vast majority of new establishments buy stainless steel.

Stainless steel is also used for many small items of equipment.

Non-stick metal

An ever-increasing variety of kitchen utensils (saucepans, frying pans, baking and roasting tins) are available and are suitable for certain types of kitchen operation, such as small scale or à la carte. Particular attention should be paid to the following points, otherwise the non-stick properties of the equipment will be affected:

Fig. 11.28 Examples of stainless steel equipment: 1. Saucepan; 2. Mixing bowl; 3. Tray; 4. Stockpot; 5. Bowl; 6. Basin; 7. Mandolin; 8. Twelve-inch ruler

- excessive heat should be avoided;
- use plastic or wooden spatulas or spoons when using non-stick pans so that contact is not made to the surface with metal;
- extra care is needed when cleaning non-stick surfaces; the use of cloth or paper is most suitable.

There are many small pieces of equipment made from metal of all types (see Figures 11.29, 11.30).

Fig. 11.29 Examples of metal equipment: 1. frying basket; 2. friture and draining wire; 3. baking tray; 4. double grill wires; 5. cooling wire; 6. raised pie mould; 7. frying pan; 8. omelet pan; 9. grater; 10. pancake pan; 11. flan ring; 12. deep tartlet mould; 13. shallow tartlet ring; 14. boat-shaped mould; 15. twelve-inch ruler

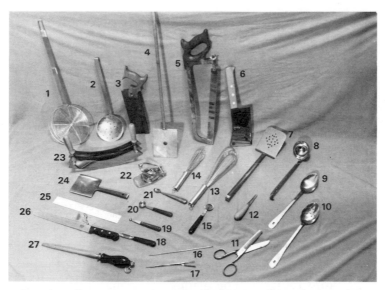

Fig. 11.30 Examples of small equipment: 1. spider; 2. skimmer; 3. tenon saw; 4. iron spatula; 5. butcher's saw; 6. chopper; 7. fish slice; 8. ladle; 9. metal spoon; 10. perforated spoon; 11. fish scissors; 12. oyster knife; 13. balloon whisk; 14. small whisk; 15. ravioli wheel; 16. trussing needle; 17. larding needle; 18. vegetable peeler; 19. solferino cutter; 20. parisienne cutter; 21. olivette cutter; 22. egg slicer; 23. four-bladed chopper; 24. meat bat; 25. 12-inch ruler; 26. carving knife; 27. steel

Wood and compound materials

CUTTING BOARDS
These are an important item of kitchen equipment which should be kept in use on all table surfaces to protect the table and the edges of cutting knives.

Wooden chopping boards (see page 359)
To comply with current regulations, wooden boards should not splinter or leak preservatives. They should be of close-grained hard wood either in a thick, solid slab or separate pieces with close-fitting joints.

- Before using a new board, wash to remove wood dust.
- After use scrub with hot detergent water, rinse with clean water, dry as much as possible and stand on its longest end to prevent warping.
- Do not use for heavy chopping; use a chopping block instead.

Cutting boards of compound materials
There are several types available. When selecting compound cutting boards it is essential to purchase those with a non-slip surface.

- Polyethylene: six boards can be obtained marked in different colours along one edge. These can be kept in a special rack after washing and when not in use. This system is designed to cut down on cross-contamination by using one board exclusively for one type of food (see page 360).
- Rubber: cutting boards are also made of hard rubber and rubber compounds

(rubber, polystyrene and clay). These are hygienic because they are solid, in one piece and should not warp, crack or absorb flavours. They are cleaned by scrubbing with hot water and then drying or passing through a dishwasher.

ROLLING PINS, WOODEN SPOONS AND SPATULAS

These items should be scrubbed in hot detergent water, rinsed in clean water and dried. Rolling pins should not be scraped with a knife as this can cause the wood to splinter. Adhering paste can be removed with a cloth. Wooden spoons and spatulas will soon be replaced by a high-density plastic capable of withstanding very high temperatures. Wooden spoons/spatulas are considered unhygienic unless washed in a suitable sterilising solution such as sodium hypochloride solution (bleach) or a solution of Milton. Metal piping tubes are being replaced by plastic. These can be boiled and do not rust.

WOODEN SIEVES AND MANDOLINS

When these are being cleaned, care of the wooden frame should be considered taking into account the previous remarks. The blades of the mandolin should be kept lightly greased to prevent rust (stainless steel mandolins are available).

China and earthenware (Figure 11.31)

Bowls and dishes in china and earthenware are useful for serving and for microwaved dishes. They should be cleaned in a dishwasher with mild detergent and rinse aid, or by hand using the appropriate detergent for hand washing.

Materials

All materials should be washed immediately after use in hot detergent water, rinsed in hot, clean water and then dried. Tammy cloths, muslins and linen piping bags must be boiled periodically in detergent water. Kitchen cloths should be washed or changed frequently, otherwise accumulating dirt and food stains may cause cross-contamination of harmful bacteria/germs on to clean food.

Fig. 11.31 Examples of china and other earthenware: 1. casserole; 2. oval dish; 3. ravier; 4. bowl; 5. soufflé dish; 6. dish; 7. 12-inch ruler; 8. pie dish; 9. sole dish; 10. and 11. egg dishes; 12. basin

- Muslin and tammy cloth, made from calico, are used for straining soups and sauces.
- Jelly bags are made from thick flannel or nylon for straining jellies.
- Piping bags are made from linen, nylon or plastic and are used for piping preparations of all kinds.
- Kitchen cloths
    - General purpose – for washing up and cleaning surfaces.
    - Tea towel (teacloth) – for drying up and general-purpose hand cloths.
    - Bactericide wiping cloths – impregnated with bactericide to disinfect work surfaces. The cloths have a coloured pattern which fades and disappears when the bactericide is no longer effective; the cloth should then be discarded.
    - Oven cloths – thick cloths designed to protect the hands when removing hot items from the oven. Oven cloths must only be used dry, never damp or wet, otherwise the user is likely to be burned.

Papers

- Greaseproof or silicone – for lining cake-tins, making piping bags and wrapping greasy items of food.
- Kitchen – white absorbent paper for absorbing grease from deep-fried foods and for lining trays on which cold foods are kept (see Plate 127, page 372).
- General purpose – thick, absorbent paper for wiping and drying equipment, surfaces, food, etc.
- Towels – disposable, for drying of hands.

Foils

- Clingwrap – a thin, transparent material for wrapping sandwiches, snacks, hot and cold foods. Clingwrap has the advantage of being very flexible and easy to handle and seal. Due to risk of contamination, it is advisable to use a clingwrap that does not contain PVC, or is plasticiser-free.
- Metal foil – a thin, pliable, silver-coloured material for wrapping and covering foods and for protecting oven roasted joints during cooking.

TOPICS FOR DISCUSSION

1. List the essential requirements of kitchen equipment.
2. Discuss the respective advantages of a conventional oven, convection oven and a combination convection/steaming oven.
3. Compare induction cooking plates, halogen hobs or the conventional cooking tops.
4. Compare copper pans or stainless steel pans.
5. What are the benefits of the bratt pan?
6. What essential items of mechanical equipment are needed?
7. Discuss the importance of sufficient refrigeration.

422 THE THEORY OF CATERING

8.   What are the benefits of the food waste disposer or the advantages of a food computer.
9.   What is the argument for maintaining wooden chopping boards.
10. Discuss the design of equipment in relation to maintaining high standards of hygiene.

12

Catering services

—

Gas, electricity and water are technical subjects, but a simple study will help the student in understanding the important part all three play in the catering industry.

Heat transfer

This is carried out by one of three methods illustrated in Figures 12.1–3: radiation, conduction and convection.

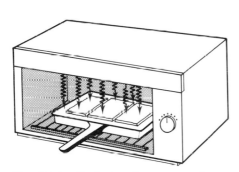

Fig. 12.1 Radiation: heat passes from the salamander directly on to the food being grilled

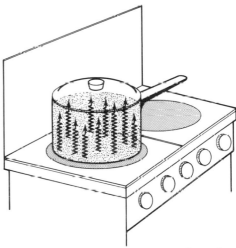

Fig. 12.2 Conduction: heat is conducted from the range top through the solid base of the pan

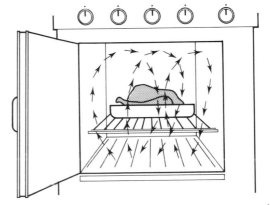

Fig. 12.3 Convection: heated air is convected around the oven

GAS

Most gas used today is natural gas. It comes from underground sources in the seas around the British Isles. Natural gas is non-toxic and odourless. When it is brought ashore a smell is added to it. This gives it the characteristic smell so it can easily be detected. There are a few areas of the country which are not connected to the natural gas pipeline network. In these areas gas can be supplied in liquid form, liquid petroleum gas (LPG) such as Calor. The gas is either delivered in bottles or stored in large tanks.

Different gases have different calorific or energy values.

For example:

- natural gas 950–1200 Btu/ft^3 (35.4–45.6 MJ/m^3);
- propane 2530 Btu/ft^3 (96 MJ/m^3);
- methane 995 Btu/ft^3 (37.8 MJ/m^3).

Gas safety

Gas is a safe fuel, but like all fuels, it must be used with respect.

WHAT TO DO IF YOU SMELL GAS
- Open the doors and windows to get rid of the gas.
- Check to see if the gas has been left on, or if a pilot light has gone out. If so, turn the appliance off.
- If this is not the case, there is probably a gas escape. Turn the gas supply off at the meter and phone the emergency service immediately.

DO NOT ATTEMPT THE FOLLOWING
- Do not turn any electrical switches on or off. You can use the phone to call the emergency services.
- Do not smoke.
- Do not use matches or naked flames.

Service supply pipes

In the kitchen there will be many service supply pipes. They are usually colour coded for easy identification:
- Gas   Yellow
- Air   Light Blue
- Electricity   Orange
- Water   Green
- Steam   Silver Grey

Measuring consumption

Gas travels along the 'main' and into the service pipe which supplies gas into houses and other buildings. Before the gas is used it passes through a meter which measures how much gas is used.

The meter measures gas in hundreds of cubic feet. British Gas converts this figure into metric, so the bill shows how much gas has been used in cubic metres. The customer is then charged in kiloWatt hours (see Figure 12.4).

A standing charge is added to the bill. This is a basic amount which is to cover the cost of providing the supply.

HOW TO WORK OUT THE COST

(Note gas is measured by volume (hundreds of cubic feet) but charged for in therms.)

For an accurate calculation YOU WILL NEED TO KNOW	HOW TO FIND OUT
	Note the present meter reading and deduct the previous reading (as shown on the gas bill).
The volume of gas used	e.g. 2112 (present) − 2034 (previous) ——— 78
	As a rough guide to the cost of gas used, multiply this figure by the price per therm as stated on the gas bill. Remember to add the standing charge to obtain the total amount of your gas bill.
The calorific value of the gas supplied	This is a measure of the heating power of gas and is stated on every gas bill in two ways: e.g.

37.9 MJ/m^3	1016 Btu/ft^3
(Megajoules per cubic metre)	(British Thermal Units per cubic foot)

(Under existing laws, Btu/ft^3 is used to calculate gas bills – MJ/m^3 is also given to accommodate possible future changes in legislation

Fig. 12.4 How to work out the cost

How to read the meter

There are two different types of meters, they have either dials or numbers (see Figure 12.5).

READING A DIAL METER

You only need to read the four bottom dials with the black pointers. Write down the reading shown on each dial, beginning with the one on the left. If the pointer is between two numbers, write down the lower one. If the pointer is between 9 and 0, write down 9.

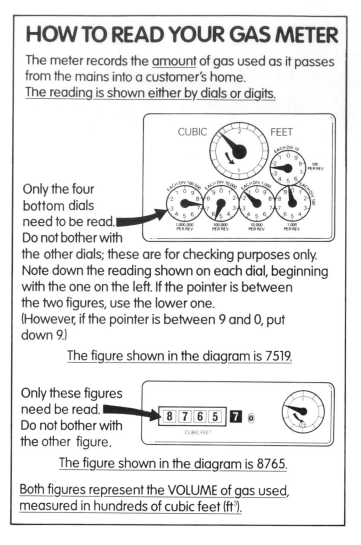

HOW TO READ YOUR GAS METER

The meter records the <u>amount</u> of gas used as it passes from the mains into a customer's home.
<u>The reading is shown either by dials or digits.</u>

Only the four bottom dials need to be read. Do not bother with the other dials; these are for checking purposes only.
Note down the reading shown on each dial, beginning with the one on the left. If the pointer is between the two figures, use the lower one.
(However, if the pointer is between 9 and 0, put down 9.)

<u>The figure shown in the diagram is 7519.</u>

Only these figures need be read. Do not bother with the other figure.

<u>The figure shown in the diagram is 8765.</u>

<u>Both figures represent the VOLUME of gas used, measured in hundreds of cubic feet (ft^3).</u>

Fig. 12.5
How to read your gas meter

For example the number shown is 7519.

READING A DIGIT METER

If you have a digit meter, you only need to write down the four numbers in the black area, the others are for checking purposes.

Care and servicing of gas appliances

In order to be sure of getting the best performance from catering equipment it should be regularly serviced, but the general efficiency of appliances can be sustained by careful use plus regular cleaning and checks. Every local branch of British Gas can arrange to service all gas catering, water heating and space heating equipment, either as a 'one-off' or on a regular basis.

When having gas equipment serviced or installed you should use a **CORGI** (Council for Registered Gas Installers) installer. British Gas is a **CORGI** registered installer.

British standards and gas catering equipment

Standard specifications are laid down for the manufacture of gas catering equipment. Quality assurance is covered by ISO 9000 and the Catering Equipment Manufacturers' Associations' (CEMA) guarantee.

Under their 'Tested for Safety' scheme, British Gas lists all gas catering appliances which have met the safety requirements of BS 5314 and/or EN 203. The scheme itself has been developed in order to be in line with European and international safety standards. It has been adopted by CEMA and by the National Association of Restaurant Engineers in their continuing efforts to upgrade and improve the quality of their products.

Controls

THERMOSTATS

A thermostat keeps the oven at a set temperature. It works by controlling the heat output of the burner. There are two types:

- A rod type, different metals are joined together and when heated they bend and expand at different rates;
- Mercury vapour or liquid type, the liquid expands when it gets hot.

PRESSURE GOVERNORS

These are fitted to appliances to compensate for any variance in the pressure of the gas supply. They are usually set at a pressure that will provide the best performance from the appliance.

FLAME SUPERVISION DEVICES

A flame supervision device is a safety device. The main gas burner is lit from a pilot light. If for any reason the pilot light goes out, the flame supervision device will prevent the gas from coming out of the main burner.

Flame supervision devices vary from simple bi-metal strips, with two pieces of metal joined together, to thermodynamic or electronic controls which include ignition as part of the operation.

Gas catering equipment

OPEN TOP RANGE

The open top range (see Figure 12.6, page 428) can be either medium or heavy-duty but is more frequently the former. It can have either four or six rings on the hob. The one illustrated has a directly fired oven which gives a heat gradient, being hotter at the top. This allows different dishes to be cooked at the same time.

SOLID TOP RANGE

Usually heavy-duty rather than medium-duty, this range will have either a directly or semi-externally heated oven. It is frequently the most important piece of equipment in a large conventional kitchen (see Figure 12.7, page 428).

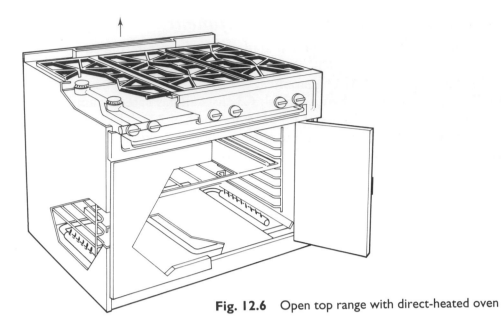

Fig. 12.6   Open top range with direct-heated oven

Convection oven

Convection ovens may be externally or semi-externally heated; the one illustrated in Figure 12.8 is externally heated. They are suitable for all normal roasting and baking. Because of the built-in circulation fan and the even temperature distribution, the full oven capacity may be used and cooking time reduced. This type of oven is extremely suitable for the rapid reheating and end-cooking of frozen foods.

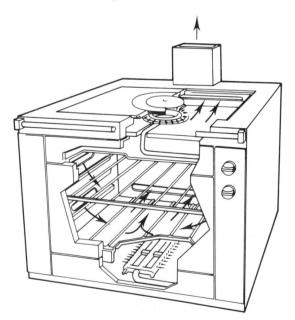

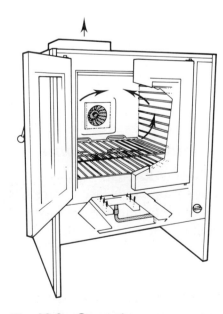

Fig. 12.7   Solid top range with semi-externally heated oven

Fig. 12.8   Convection oven

COMBINATION OVEN

This is a combined steaming oven and convection oven, which cooks in three modes – hot air convection, forced steam circulation or a combination of both. It is suitable for baking, roasting or steaming and can be used for the regeneration of chilled foods.

ATMOSPHERIC STEAMING OVEN

The atmospheric steaming oven is suitable for cooking all root vegetables, sweet and savoury puddings and some fish dishes. (See Figure 11.8, pages 394 and 395.)

BRATT PAN

This is capable of handling up to 200 average portions an hour. The bratt pan is mainly used as a multi-purpose appliance for shallow and deep frying and boiling. (See Figure 11.11, page 396.)

DEEP FAT-FRYER

There are two main types of deep fat-fryer: the 'V' pan type, where the heating burners are external, and models with immersion tube heaters. In both types there is a zone of relatively cool oil below the source of heat into which food particles can sink without charring. They can be used for cooking all fried foods that are immersed in a heating medium. (See Figure 11.13, page 397.)

OVER-FIRED GRILL (SALAMANDER)

The source of heat, either from refractory bricks or a metal fret, is above the food. The salamander is used to cook food by radiant heat, eg chops, steak, toast and for the quick heating of dishes before service.

Fig. 12.9 Over-fired grill (salamander)

EXPANSION WATER BOILER

Operating on the principle that water expands when heated, expansion water boilers can cater for boiling water demands in excess of 170 litres (300 pints) an hour.

Further information

Commercial Gas Centre, 139 Tottenham Court Road, London W1P 9LN; Tel: 0171-242 0789.

At these premises there is a comprehensive display of gas catering, heating and hot water appliances, at which student visits are welcome.

CALOR GAS

Calor gas is liquefied petroleum gas, often abbreviated to LPG. The particular gas used by the catering industry is propane, which is as powerful and efficient as mains gas. Calor gas is used by thousands of establishments of varying sizes that are situated beyond the reach of mains gas. It is supplied by being piped into storage tanks or in cylinders, depending on the number of appliances required to be operated.

Leading equipment manufacturers make all types of equipment using Calor gas for cooking, water heating and central heating. The gas is also invaluable in outdoor catering, where it is used extensively.

CHARCOAL

This is the black, porous residue of burnt wood. Traditionally, charcoal was the fuel used most often for grilling and was considered the best because of the flavour it gave to the meat being grilled. The most popular alternative is a gas-fired grill (see Figure 12.10). From the economic point of view the following considerations have to be borne in mind:

- comparative costs of charcoal and gas;
- lack of flexibility in use of charcoal;

Fig. 12.10 Charcoal flavour grill. Gas heated with refractory stones, fitted with a flame-failure device and pilot assembly, it produces the same taste effect as charcoal and is suitable for all types of gas

- ease of flexibility in use of gas;
- labour requirements for charcoal grill (lighting, refuelling, cleaning);
- no labour requirement for gas grill;
- comparison of flavour of meats grilled by charcoal and gas;
- customer likes and dislikes.

ELECTRICITY

Electricity cannot be seen, heard, tasted or smelt. Installed and used correctly, it is a very safe source of energy, but misused can kill or cause serious injury. It is therefore essential that any electrical installation is undertaken by qualified engineers in accordance with BS 7671:1992 *Requirements for Electrical Installations, IEE Wiring Regulations*, 16th edition. All installations should be carried out by registered contractors of the National Inspection Council for Electrical Installation Contracting (NICEIC).

As electricity cannot be stored other than in batteries, it is produced by power stations as required by the consumers. Recent figures show that 66% of electricity in the UK is produced from coal, 7% from oil, 3% from gas and 22% from nuclear energy. The remainder is produced from hydroelectric schemes and other renewable sources. These figures are, however, still changing as the proportion of gas being used rises, largely at the expense of coal.

The broad principle of generation is that a turbine drives a generator to produce electricity. That turbine may be steam driven, with the steam being raised by fossil fuel or nuclear energy; gas driven; or in the case of hydroelectricity, water driven. Once generated, electricity is distributed to consumers via the National Grid. All electricity supplied to the UK is alternating current (AC).

To be used, electricity must pass through a complete circuit from the source of supply, through the load (an appliance) and back to the source. Substances can be classed according to their ability to pass electricity. Those which pass electricity easily are known as conductors: metal, water, damp earth and the human body. Those which resist are known as insulators: porcelain, wood, rubber, most plastics.

Electrical terms

Volts are a measure of the electric 'pressure'. Comparing electricity to water, 'voltage' corresponds to pounds per square inch of water pressure. For electricity to flow through a wire, the electric pressure at one end must be greater than at the other, that is a 'voltage difference'. Domestic supplies are commonly at 240 volts.

Amperes are a measure of the rate of flow of electric current.

Watts are a measure of power, that is the rate at which an electric appliance is passing electric current for a given voltage. For example, an appliance passing 10 amps at 240 volts has a power rating of $10 \times 240 = 2400$ Watts or 2.4 kiloWatts (kW). Conversely, the current in amps can be found by dividing the power in Watts by the voltage, for example, a 3 kW (3000 Watt) appliance at 240 volts will draw a current of 3000 ÷ 240 = 12.5 amps. This calculation allows the rating of a circuit or fuse for an appliance to be determined.

Ohms are a measure of the resistance of the wires to the passage of electricity. This can be compared to the resistance offered by a pipe to water flowing through it. Ohm's Law states that the current flowing through a wire of a particular resistance is proportional to the voltage across it. This can be stated as:

$$ \text{Amps} = \frac{\text{Volts}}{\text{Ohms}} \quad \text{or} \quad \text{Volts} = \text{Amps} \times \text{Ohms} \quad \text{or} \quad \text{Ohms} = \frac{\text{Volts}}{\text{Amps}} $$

Electrical installation

As stated earlier, all electrical installations must meet the requirements of the current IEE Regulations, and these will be met if members of the NICEIC are used for such work.

It is essential that the installation should be maintained in a safe condition. Any worn or frayed wiring, damaged plugs or sockets or other defects should be reported for attention from a qualified person.

A **consumer unit** or fuse box may contain fuses or miniature circuit breakers (mcb), main switches and residual current devices (rcd).

Fuses and **mcbs** act to break the circuit if too much current is passing, which would lead to overheating, damage to the insulation, and possibly fire. A fuse contains a fine wire which melts to break the circuit, whereas an mcb switches off the circuit when a certain current is exceeded. An mcb can be manually reset once the fault has been identified and cured. Modern installations more frequently use mcbs instead of fuses.

An **rcd** detects a faulty current passing to earth and switches off the supply in microseconds. They can be fitted to cover whole areas or individual equipment and are particularly recommended for appliances used outdoors. Rcds are not a replacement for fuses or mcbs, but they do provide additional protection from the risk of electric shock. It is important that they are regularly checked and there are circumstances where they do not provide complete protection, so they should never be abused or considered a substitute for sound wiring practices and maintenance.

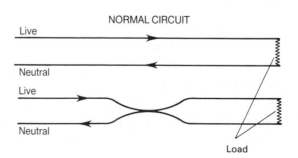

Fig. 12.11   Short circuit

CAUSES OF A BLOWN FUSE
Some causes include:

- too many appliances plugged into a circuit;
- connecting a power appliance to a lighting circuit;
- short circuit due to insulation failure: live and neutral wires touch and cause a very high current to pass; often due to wear of the insulation (see Figure 12.11);
- fault inside an appliance causing a short circuit.

Replacement of fuses (Figure 12.12)

Remember: always switch off before changing fuses.

First note which circuit has failed. If it is obvious what has caused the fault (a failed appliance), disconnect that item and seek qualified assistance to repair it. The fuse box should have the circuits identified under the lid or adjacent to it. If this is not the case, remove the fuses in turn and look for wire breaks or scorch marks.

REWIRABLE FUSES
Fuse wire is obtainable in varying thicknesses, usually rated for 5, 10, 15 or 30 amperes, and for general purposes should be used as follows:

- lighting circuits maximum of 5 amps;
- radial circuits maximum of 15 or 20 amps;
- cookers or ring circuits 30 amps.

Always fit fuses of the correct rating for the circuit. Never use a thicker wire in a rewirable fuse or a larger cartridge fuse, even as a temporary measure. Do not just rely on the blown fuse as a guide, it may not be the correct one in the first place.

Wire fuses

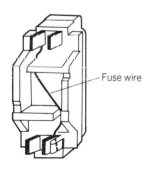
Fuse wire

Fig. 12.12   Wire fuses

Loosen the retaining screws and remove the old wire. Wind the new wire of the correct rating clockwise round one screw. Tighten the screw. Thread the wire through the fuse carrier to the other screw and wind it round clockwise, leaving a little slack. Tighten the screw and cut off the surplus wire. Replace the fuse carrier, refit the fuse box cover and switch on the main switch.

CARTRIDGE FUSES

Main fuses may be of the cartridge type, as shown in Figure 12.13, which also shows the ratings and colours commonly found. Cartridge fuses are often mounted in a fuse carrier which is in two halves. Unscrew the fuse carrier, fit a new cartridge of the correct rating, re-assemble the carrier and screw tight. Replace the carrier, refit the fuse box cover and switch on the main switch.

Small cartridge fuses are also used in British 13-amp 3-pin plugs, as shown in Figure 12.14, which also shows the ratings and colours.

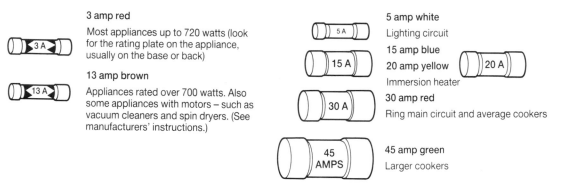

3 amp red

Most appliances up to 720 watts (look for the rating plate on the appliance, usually on the base or back)

13 amp brown

Appliances rated over 700 watts. Also some appliances with motors – such as vacuum cleaners and spin dryers. (See manufacturers' instructions.)

5 amp white

Lighting circuit

15 amp blue

20 amp yellow

Immersion heater

30 amp red

Ring main circuit and average cookers

45 amp green

Larger cookers

Fig. 12.13   Main fuses

Fig. 12.14   Plug fuses (usually two sizes as shown)

CIRCUIT BREAKERS

If circuit breakers are fitted, look for the circuit breaker that has operated and switch off the main switch. After correcting the cause of failure, reclose the circuit breaker, replace the cover and switch on the main switch.

Remember: Always seek professional help with any repair outside your level of knowledge or training.

Wiring of plugs (see Figure 12.15)

All 13-amp flat-pin plugs now sold are required by law to conform to BS 1363 and have internal fuses and sleeved pins.

1. Unscrew the plug cover. Loosen one cord grip screw and remove the other. (Some plugs have sprung plastic cord grips instead.)
2. Remove the fuse and loosen the terminal screws.
3. Carefully cut away the outer sheath of the flex for about 4–5 cm (1½–2 in), leaving the coloured inner wires exposed.
4. Position the flex in the plug so that the outer sheath will be held by the cord grip, and cut the wires to reach about 13 mm (½ in) beyond the appropriate terminal.

Remember: Green/yellow wire to earth terminal (marked E or ⏚); Blue wire to Neutral terminal (marked N); Brown wire to Live terminal (marked L).

5. Carefully strip enough insulation to expose about 6 mm ($2\frac{1}{2}$ in) of wire for screwhole terminals, or about 13 mm ($\frac{1}{2}$ in) for clamp type terminals. Twist the strands of wire together.
6. Fasten the outer sheath firmly in the cord grip.
7. Wrap each uncovered wire clockwise round the appropriate pillar, or insert it in the terminal; tighten the screw. Ensure there are no 'whiskers' of bare wire.
8. Check everything, insert the correct fuse and replace the plug cover.

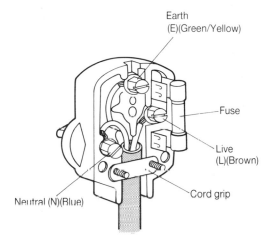

Fig. 12.15   Three-pin cartridge fused plug

Industrial plugs and sockets

Electric catering equipment may be installed using plug and socket connections (see Figure 12.16). This allows it to be disconnected easily for cleaning and servicing, which is especially important in maintaining hygiene standards.

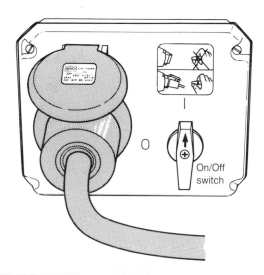

Fig. 12.16   Plug and socket connection

Modern commercial catering installations frequently use industrial plugs and sockets made to international standard IEC 309, British Standard BS EN 60309-1/2: 1992. They are marked for their rated duty and may also be recognised by the colour coding for both the plug and socket or socket lid.

- Yellow is for use between 100 and 130 volts (not usually seen in a kitchen but common on building sites, etc.)
- Blue is for 200–250 volts, used for single phase equipment.
- Red is for 380–480 volts, used for three-phase equipment.

The sockets when marked 'IPX4' are 'splashproof' and when marked 'IPX7' are 'watertight' (either with the plug fitted or less plug and with the socket lid closed). There are various sizes from 16A to 125A, configured so that a plug will fit only its equivalent socket.

Light switches

Where light switches are located in a kitchen or storeroom, waterproof types should be selected. This will enable washing of walls, ducting etc. to be carried out safely.

Electricity meters

The Electricity Association Services publish a leaflet on *How to read your meter* (obtainable from 30 Millbank, London SW1P 4RD (see Figure 12.17).

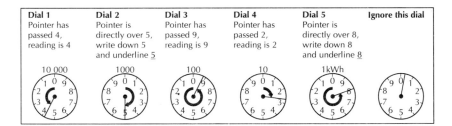

Dial 1	Dial 2	Dial 3	Dial 4	Dial 5	Ignore this dial
Pointer has passed 4, reading is 4	Pointer is directly over 5, write down 5 and underline 5	Pointer has passed 9, reading is 9	Pointer has passed 2, reading is 2	Pointer is directly over 8, write down 8 and underline 8	
10 000	1000	100	10	1kWh	

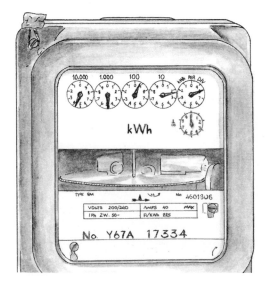

Fig. 12.17   How to read your meter

COMPARISON OF FUELS

The two fuels most generally used in catering are electricity and mains gas. Bottled gas is also used in some kitchens. Before deciding on the fuel to use (if there is a choice) the following factors should be considered:

- safety;
- cost;
- efficiency;
- storage requirements;
- constancy of supply;
- cleanliness and need for ventilation;
- cost of equipment, installation and maintenance.

COMPARISON OF ELECTRICITY AND GAS

ADVANTAGES	DISADVANTAGES
Electricity	
• Clean to use. Low maintenance	• Time taken to heat up in a few instances
• Easily controlled and labour saving	• Particular utensils are required for induction hobs
• Good working atmosphere – no oxygen is required and no carbon dioxide or water vapour is produced	
• Little heat loss	
• No storage space required	
• Low ventilation requirements	
Gas	
• Convenient, labour saving	• Some heat is lost into kitchen
• No smoke or dirt	• Regular cleaning required for efficient working
• Easily controllable with immediate full heat and the flames are visible	• For gas to produce heat it must burn; this requires oxygen which is contained in the air and, as a result carbon dioxide and water are produced.
• Special utensils not required	• As a result of the above, adequate ventilation must be provided for combustion and to ensure a satisfactory working environment.
• No fuel storage required	

ENERGY CONSERVATION

The Energy Efficiency Office estimates that the total energy consumption of the British catering industry is in excess of 77 770 million MJ (21 600 million kWh) per year. As a whole, the catering industry accounts for over 1.3% of the total energy used in the United Kingdom.

With moderate improvements in efficiency, and some rationalisation in the use of equipment, savings in excess of 20% are achievable which, overall, could save the industry millions of pounds per year; this would also assist the national interest by reducing energy consumption by over 16 000 million MJ per year.

Around 40% of energy is expended in preparing, cooking and serving food. The greatest proportion of this energy is used in the cooking equipment and much of it is wasted by excess use and poor utilisation of equipment such as salamanders, and all stoves and ovens being turned fully on as soon as chefs appear in the kitchen, regardless of whether they are required immediately or not. This type of practice inevitably causes maximum heat to be expended in a short space of time which requires further energy to be expended for mechanical ventilation.

Saving energy

In the interest of energy conservation be aware of the following:

- Cookers, ranges, grills: keep clean and regularly maintained; check thermostats and heating controls regularly; turn off after use.
- Hot cabinets and bains-marie: keep clean, especially door runners; check temperature controls; switch off after use; do not use for reheating food, maintain lower temperature in plate-warming cabinets.
- Refrigeration equipment: keep doors closed; check door seals and temperatures; defrost regularly; do not overload but utilise space sensibly; do not place hot food in refrigerator.
- Dishwashers: maintain in good working order; de-scale regularly; check water and rinse temperatures; consider water softening.
- Ventilation extracts: maintain regularly; check fan efficiency and suitability; clean filters, ducting, fan blades, and fan motors regularly to free them from grease and dust; check air openings are not obstructed.

Energy-saving equipment

- Hot cupboards: with a double skin of metal, the space between is filled with an insulating material.
- Microwave ovens: require a low degree of energy compared with traditional cooking methods.
- High-pressure steamers: can be used in place of boiling pans and steaming ovens.
- Induction hobs: on average use 49% less energy than a traditional electric hob; à la carte kitchens can save up to 64%. Further savings can be made because little or no ventilation and extraction are needed.
- Steamers: steaming foods is an energy-efficient process and has the added advantage of retaining a larger proportion of nutrients in food than boiling.
- Combination ovens: forced-air/convection, steaming/convection, microwave/convection can result in savings of energy when used correctly.
- Bratt pans: used for all wet products; improve energy use over pans on boiling tops.
- Timers/controls: allow energy to be used only when needed.

Further information can be obtained from Enquiries Bureau, Energy Technology Support Unit, Building 156, Harwell Laboratory, Didcot, Oxon OX11 0RA, and the Energy Efficiency Office, Department of the Environment.

WATER

Water undertakers (authorities) are required, by law, to provide a supply of clean, wholesome water; water free from suspended matter, odour and taste; all bacteria which are likely to cause disease; and mineral matter injurious to health.

Water is obtained from the residue of rainfall and is collected from a number of sources, dependent on the geography of the country. The collection points may include natural lakes, rivers, springs, artificial reservoirs, underground water-bearing strata, lakes and wells. The source may affect the nature and quality of the water. Water is normally collected and held in storage reservoirs in order to provide a constant supply of water and is passed through a number of cleansing processes prior to distribution to the consumer.

Treatment

PRIMARY FILTRATION
Water collected from open sources such as rivers will be passed through a mesh screen in order to remove large solid matter such as twigs and leaves.

The water is stored in reservoirs where suspended matter settles to the bottom.

SECONDARY FILTRATION
The water is drawn from the reservoir as required and passed through a sand or micromesh filter to remove any particles still in suspension.

CHLORINATION
Water is treated with chlorine to kill any bacteria remaining in the water. (In some parts of the country fluoride may be added.)

TESTING
The water is regularly tested to ensure that it is fit for consumption.

Distribution and consumption

Water is pumped into the distribution system of trunk and street mains for delivery to the consumer.

The consumer is required to comply with the local water by-laws made by the local water authority. These are designed to prevent waste, undue consumption, misuse or contamination of the water supply provided by the water authority. Any persons contravening any of these by-laws may be liable for fines. The by-laws state the materials, methods of jointing and the types of installations which may be used, and also state that all new systems or alterations or additions to existing systems must conform.

Consumer's cold water supply

The water undertaker will provide a supply to the boundary of the premises and at this point a stopcock will be fitted. The consumer is responsible for the supply from the boundary onwards and a stopcock should be fitted just inside the premises to enable the consumer to turn off the water in an emergency.

WATER COSTS

Commercial premises will normally have a meter and will be charged for the amount of water used. Domestic premises may have a meter or, more commonly, are charged a water rate related to the general building rate.

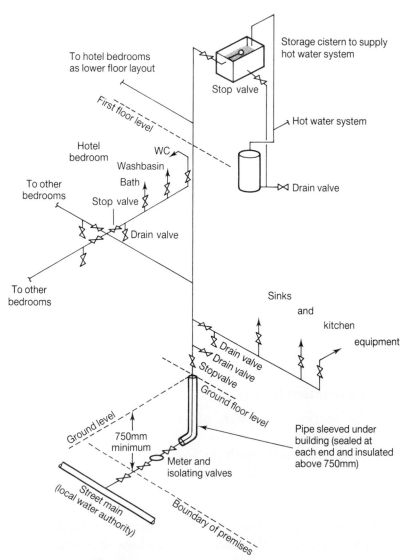

Fig. 12.18 Direct cold water supply to a small hotel

TYPES OF SYSTEMS OF SUPPLY

On entering the building the water supply should be fitted with a stopcock and a facility for draining down for maintenance. There will normally be other stopcocks throughout the premises enabling water supplies to be cut off at different points.

New and existing systems fall in two categories:

- Direct system of cold water supply: this type of system provides water to all taps and items of equipment at mains pressure (see Figure 12.18). Water for the hot water system may be stored in a cistern.
- Indirect system of cold water supply: most modern systems are of this type, especially in commercial premises. The indirect system uses a cistern for storage of water which means that in the event of failure or heavy usage of the mains

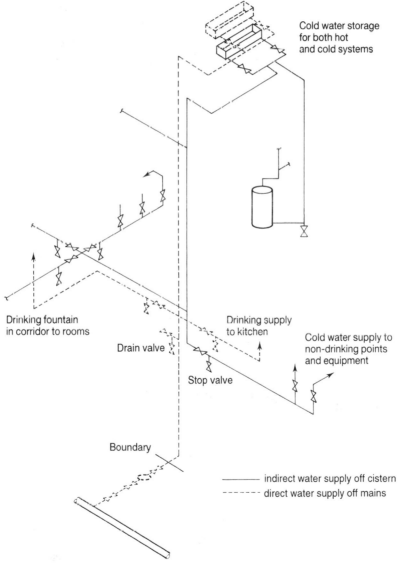

Fig. 12.19   Indirect cold water supply to a small hotel

supply there is still a supply of water available until the mains supply is restored. Water for the hot and cold water systems will normally be supplied from this storage (see Figure 12.19). The indirect system will always have drinking water, or water used in food preparation, taken directly from the mains supply to ensure that it is uncontaminated. In large buildings, such as multi-storey blocks, the mains pressure may be insufficient to supply all drinking water direct from the main, in this case special drinking water cisterns are installed and the water is circulated after pumping.

TYPES OF EQUIPMENT IN COLD WATER SYSTEMS

Stopcock

This is a valve installed in a pipe to control the flow of water to a system or item of equipment (see Figure 12.20).

The valve should be turned off and on during routine maintenance to ensure that it will operate in an emergency.

The washer may require replacing during maintenance, as may the packing gland or 'O' ring around the spindle connected to the handwheel.

Gate valve

This is an alternative type of valve used to control the flow of water in a pipe where the pressure is low or the water is at high temperature (see Figure 12.21).

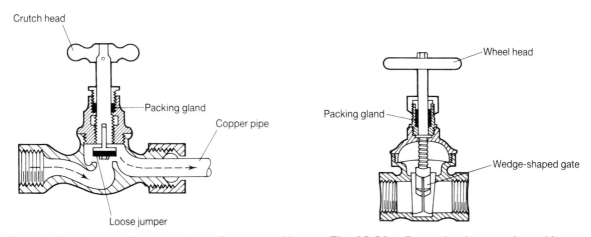

Fig. 12.20   Stop valve (section through a stopcock)   **Fig. 12.21**   Gate valve (section through)

The valve should be turned off and on during routine maintenance to ensure that it will operate in an emergency. The packing gland may require repacking during maintenance.

Ball-valve

Ball-valves are float-operated valves used to control the flow of water into cisterns (see Figure 12.22). The latest type of ball-valve is designed to prevent any possible contamination of the water supply in the cistern.

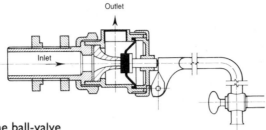

Fig. 12.22 Operation of the ball-valve

The ball-valve should be adjusted to make it close at the required water level in the cistern and should be fixed securely to the cistern.

The ball-valve should undergo regular maintenance because, like taps, it will be in constant use. The washer or diaphragm may require replacing; the float should be checked for buoyancy and the point at which it closes should correspond with the water level in the cistern.

COMPARISONS OF TYPES OF SYSTEMS OF COLD WATER SUPPLY

Direct
Advantages include:

- The direct or non-storage system contains less pipework, has no cistern (or only a small one for the hot water system), and is therefore easier and cheaper to install and maintain.
- As all the water passes direct to the taps, all taps will have drinking water which has not been subjected to possible risk of contamination during storage.

Disadvantages include:

- In the event of damage to the mains supply, or during major maintenance, the premises may be completely without water. In many towns and cities the mains supply is subject to fluctuation of pressure at peak times due to the demand, and the pressure and efficiency of the supply will be affected.
- Catering and other items of equipment may cause contamination of the water supply, both in the building and to the mains water supply, if incorrectly installed or unprotected by suitable devices. Items of equipment such as food and vegetable processors, bottle-washing and dishwashing machines, some water softeners, water-cooled refrigerators and certain types of drink vending or dispensing machines, may cause this type of contamination, and they must be connected in accordance with the local water by-laws.

Indirect
Advantages include:

- The indirect or storage system is provided with a large capacity cistern which will ensure that water is still available if the main supply is interrupted. Because the system is largely supplied from the cistern, the demand on the water main is reduced.

- Equipment supplied from the cistern will not contaminate the drinking water supply.
- Equipment which requires hot and cold supplies will be supplied with water at the same pressure.
- The system will have a lower pressure and will be quieter in operation and this minimises wear on taps.

Disadvantages include:

- All stored water should be considered potentially contaminated, even though the cistern should have a tight-fitting lid, because the water will have come into contact with the air.
- The system requires a storage cistern and has more and larger pipes than a direct system. This means it will be more expensive to install and may require more maintenance.

Physical characteristics of water

SOFT WATER

Generally, water is soft; a practical test is that it will produce lather easily when soap is dissolved in the water. Soft water is mildly acidic and can dissolve salt, sugar and other substances used in catering processes.

The nature of water may be affected by the ground it has filtered through before collection and treatment by the water undertaker. Soft water which has passed through ground containing organic material will have had its acidity increased; this will not harm anyone who drinks the water but it may lead to some dissolving of utensils if they contain materials such as lead or copper or lead-based solder. The dissolved material may then contaminate the water to a state of toxicity above safe health levels.

HARD WATER

Water which has passed through ground containing limestone (chalk) is known as hard water. There are two types of hardness – temporary and permanent – and hard water will normally contain a percentage of both.

- Temporary hardness is due to the natural presence of calcium or magnesium bicarbonates dissolved in the water. The hardness can be removed by heating, or boiling the water, but in a kettle or water boiler it can produce fur or scale which will coat the internal surface. Although this scale is harmless it can cause discoloured water and reduce the efficiency of heaters and, in extreme cases, it may cause complete blockages in pipes, resulting in steam generation and the explosion of tea or coffee makers.
- Permanent hardness is created by carbonates and sulphates of calcium and magnesium dissolved in the water and is much more difficult to remove.

ON-SITE TREATMENTS
In catering establishments a number of on-site processes are used to treat water.

Manual method
For general cleansing the most common types of treatment to soften water are:

- Soap added to water: the first amount softens the water and any more added will form a lather. But there are disadvantages: it is uneconomical; and scum forms, making it unsuitable for washing.
- Soda; which is cheap and quite effective; the correct amounts should be added: London water with 16 degrees of hardness requires 28.39 g (1 oz) soda to 45.4 litres (26 pints) of water. When using soda and soap together the soda should be added first and allowed to dissolve so that it softens the water before the addition of soap.
- Ammonia solution. This works in the same way as soda.

These methods will remove temporary hardness as well as permanent hardness.

Automatic methods
- Water softeners: many establishments use an automatic water softening plant which will remove both temporary and permanent hardness. The size of softener is dependent on the volume of water to be passed through it. Manufacturers will give guidance on the choice of the correct unit. Drinking water should not be softened as hard water is more 'healthy' and so the drinking supplies should be drawn off the system before being connected to a water softener. Water softeners use a base exchange method. They remove the hardness by a chemical action but, dependent on the quality of the water, and the size of water softener, the chemical action with the agent slows as it becomes clogged and will need cleaning with a brine solution. This cleaning is carried out automatically in many modern machines but the salt tank must be kept topped up.

  Where it is uneconomical or undesirable to soften water, for example when water is fed to a single tea or coffee maker, ion magnetic units may be used. In these situations, in hard water areas, the unit may 'fur' up quickly due to the removal of temporary hardness. The fitting of an ion magnetic unit on the supply to the coffee maker will reduce the amount of descaling required and lengthen the efficient operational life of the machine. Owing to the small diameter of the water supplies of some tea and coffee making machines, the manufacturers may recommend the fitting of a filter on the supply to the unit. This is done to ensure the quality and, when used in conjunction with the scale reducer, will increase the working life.
- Descaling: where hard water has created scale in pipes or catering equipment the efficiency and useful lifetime will be reduced unless descaling is done. Descaling and flushing is carried out using a strong acid which is pumped through the equipment and then thoroughly flushed out. This work should be carried out by a plumber or specialist. Small amounts of scale can be removed from utensils and

kettles by commercial products or by boiling vinegar in the utensil and then boiling with clean water.

Freezing of pipes

All pipes and equipment installed inside or outside a building should be protected against frost and the risk of freezing.

EXTERNAL

Pipes below ground should be installed at a depth below the normal effect of frost, not less than 750 mm (29½ in) below the ground. Where pipes rise above this level then suitable insulation material should be applied.

A modern addition to insulation is the use of trace heating where a strip containing an electric element is spirally wrapped around the pipe and is controlled automatically by a thermostat to prevent the pipe from freezing.

INTERNAL

The water pipes should be located to prevent heat loss such as may occur in roof spaces and under ground floors. A suitable insulation material should be applied to pipes and storage cisterns.

Drinking water supplies are also subject to heat gain and condensation in hot places such as kitchens and centrally heated buildings; insulation should be used to prevent this.

PRECAUTIONS

- Lag all pipes.
- Keep temperatures above 0°C (32°F).

METHODS OF THAWING PIPES

1. Start from an unfrozen portion or free outlet.
2. Wrap a cloth around the part, and pour hot water over it.
3. A blow lamp should only be used by a plumber or experienced person.
4. Place a heater near the frozen part to raise the temperature of the air.
5. If a waste pipe is frozen, pour hot water down it. (See Figure 12.23.)

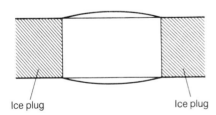

Ice plug   Ice plug

Fig. 12.23 Effect of water freezing in pipe causes bulge

FOR BURST PIPES

1. Turn off the main tap.
2. Turn off the stopcock between cistern and main pipe.
3. Open all taps, allow the water to escape.
4. Send for a plumber.

Drainage of water

TRAPS

Traps should be provided at the outlet from each item of sanitaryware or equipment to prevent the penetration of foul smells and air-borne bacteria in the sanitation system into the room in which the equipment is placed.

The trap will contain a quantity of water (seal), which should be contained at all times in sufficient volume to prevent loss whilst the system is in operation or at rest.

The types of traps and depth of seal will vary (see Figure 12.24), but most modern systems will have a trap seal of 75 mm (3 in) except in the case of WCs where, because of the volume of water the seal would be more difficult to lose, it measures 50 mm (2 in).

Traps are normally fitted to the outlet of a fitting or item of equipment and will be no smaller in diameter than the outlet size of the fitting. The pipe connected should also be no smaller than the outlet size.

Tubular traps are the best design for hotel and catering establishments as they are less liable to blockages and scaling up. Traps made of plastic are smooth and are generally not affected by effluent from these types of establishments.

All traps in hotel and catering establishments should either include a cleaning eye or be of the sectional type which allows for disconnection for cleaning.

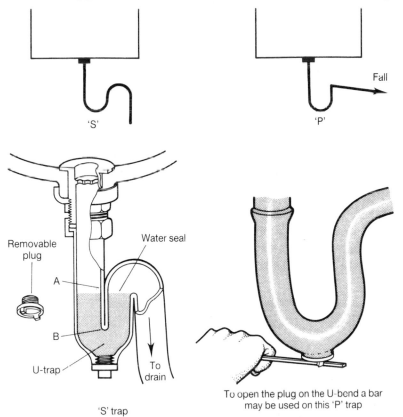

Fig. 12.24 'P' and 'S' traps

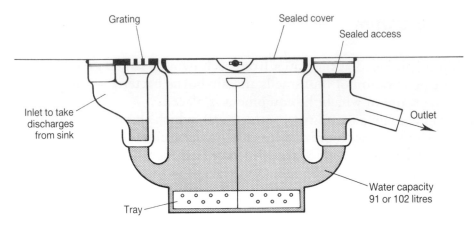

Dimensions: 600mm × 450mm × 135mm and 915mm × 450mm × 135mm

Fig. 12.25   Detail of grease trap

Minor blockages will be obviated by regular maintenance and may often be cleared by the use of a rubber plunger or a kinetic gun. (Care must be taken if water contains bleach or similar substances and protective gloves, clothing and eye protection should be worn.)

GREASE TRAP

During the preparation of many foods and the cleaning of cooking utensils, grease and fat of different types may be discharged into the sanitation system. The grease will, in many cases, be in an emulsion state (hot liquid) and will adhere to the sides of the pipes, causing a build-up to which solid particles may adhere and cause a blockage.

Grease traps may be used to prevent this by providing a large volume of water within a trap to act as a cooling and solidifying agent (see Figure 12.24). The grease will float to the top of the trap and is regularly skimmed from the top and disposed of as solid waste.

The frequency of cleaning will relate to the size of kitchen and the type of food preparation undertaken. It is important that regular maintenance is carried out as grease traps may easily cause blockages and unhygienic spillage into the food preparation area.

Some local authorities discourage the use of grease traps because they are often poorly maintained.

INSPECTION CHAMBERS (Figure 12.26, page 449)

All drainage systems include inspection chambers at junctions of pipes, changes in direction or size, and in long drain runs so that in the event of a blockage no section is more than 45 m (49 yards) from the access point provided by the inspection chamber. This dimension is used as it would be physically difficult to use drain rods longer than 45 m to clear a blockage.

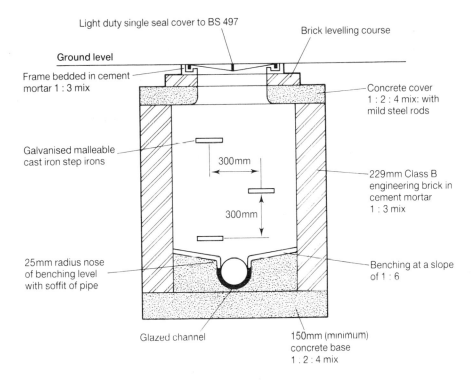

Fig. 12.26   Section through shallow brick inspection chamber

Inspection chambers will differ in design according to the material used for the drain pipes but may include brick, cast iron and plastic. Minimum sizes of inspection chambers are indicated in the building regulations related to the position, type of material and depth.

Clearing obstructions

Regular maintenance will assist in the efficient operation of sanitation systems but obstructions may still occur, normally due to misuse.

Preventative maintenance

Preventative maintenance of the sanitation systems in hotel and catering establishments is important in the hygienic and efficient running of the establishment. Many plumbing companies offer maintenance facilities as well as commercial cleaning specialists.

Registered plumbers will have a wide knowledge of the operation of the sanitation system whilst specialist cleaners may only have a limited knowledge of systems although a detailed knowledge of the cleaning process.

Descaling

Waste pipes which may be subject to heavy usage and scaling-up, such as urinal wastes, should be regularly treated with a suitable commercial descaling agent.

DRAIN AND WASTE PIPE RODDING

This is the traditional method of clearing a blockage and preventing the build-up of solids during maintenance.

On waste pipes a thin, spirally bound wire rod is used, whilst in larger drainpipes modern polyethylene rods, scrapers and augers may be used. Each method may use manual power or, more commonly, power-driven rods are used.

Some specialist equipment uses a mix of rods and water jetting.

WATER JETTING

Drains which receive large volumes of catering discharge containing grease which has not passed through a grease trap will be subject to possible blockage. Water jetting is a common method of clearing obstructions and preventing build-up of solids in the system.

In each of the above processes protective clothing should be worn and care taken to clear and wash any areas where food is prepared on completion. Food processing should cease in any area where one of these processes has to occur as bacteria may escape into the atmosphere during the clearing process.

Further information can be obtained from your local water company.

TOPICS FOR DISCUSSION

1. The advantages of gas or electricity for kitchen equipment.
2. How to effect economy in the consumption of energy by catering equipment.
3. Why maintenance of all services is essential.
4. How water conservation can be achieved.
5. Why hot water is more costly than cold water and how these costs can be reduced.

13

Catering systems

QUALITY ASSURANCE

BS 5750 on quality assurance lays down a standard of carrying out operations by which all materials and components are subjected to comprehensive regular checks at critical points throughout the food production process. Complying with BS 5750 is a guarantee of a quality product because it attempts to ensure that the manufacturing management system is subjected to regular independent checks and rigorous scrutiny. The accreditation certificate can be withdrawn if the company fails to adhere to the specification at any time.

Large food production companies and major catering companies are becoming accredited for BS 5750 in order to supply a guaranteed quality product which enables them to use the 'due diligence' defence under the Food Safety Act.

PROBLEMS

Food production systems, such as cook-chill, cook-freeze and sous-vide, have been introduced into certain areas of catering in order to increase efficiency and productivity; changes have been made to maximise utilisation of equipment and to maintain high levels of output and viability.

The problems of the catering industry are as follows:

- Staff
    - unattractive work conditions;
    - limited skilled staff;
    - mobility of labour.
- Food
    - high cost;
    - wastage.
- Equipment
    - high cost of replacement and maintenance;
    - under-usage.
- Energy
    - wasteful high-cost traditional systems;
    - availability.
- Overheads
    - wage increases;
    - payments to National Insurance.
- Space
    - most kitchens and services are too large in relation to output;
    - space is very costly.

The solution to these problems comes in the form of centralisation of production, using the skilled staff available to prepare and cook in bulk and then to distribute to finishing kitchens, which are smaller in size, employing semi-skilled and unskilled labour.

Cook-freeze and cook-chill systems have been developed to meet these requirements, each system having advantages over the other depending on the size and nature of the overall operation. For example, cook-freeze is not adaptable to very small units or to haute cuisine. Cook-chill can be adapted to any type of unit but cannot take advantage of seasonal, cheaper commodities.

Sous-vide, which is a method of working under vacuum-sealing, ice-water bath chilling and chilled storage, has also been developed as a production system.

Many catering operations face problems because of the growing shortage of skilled catering staff and the ever-increasing turnover of employees. Therefore:

- It is essential that skilled staff are more fully utilised and given improved working conditions.
- Certain catering tasks require deskilling so as to be carried out by a greater proportion of unskilled staff.
- Better benefits and conditions of employment must be provided for fewer key staff in order to reduce levels of staff turnover and enhance job satisfaction.

Assured Safe Catering

This is a system developed for and with caterers to control food safety problems. It is based upon some of the principles of HACCP (see below).

It involves looking at the catering operation step by step from the selection of ingredients right through to the service of food to the customer. With careful analysis or each step of the catering operation anything that may affect the safety of the food is identified. The caterer can then determine when and how to control that hazard. Assured Safe Catering helps prevent safety problems by careful planning in easy steps.

HYGIENE OF FOOD PRODUCTION SYSTEMS

(Figures 13.1 and 13.2; pages 453 and 454)

Hygiene committees

It is generally recognised that one of the principal concerns of food production for caterers is to ensure that the food is safe when consumed. The need for special attention to be given to food hygiene is now well recognised. This involves everyone, whether directly or indirectly involved with food handling. In order for both to focus attention on the subject it is advisable for large caterers to set up hygiene committees. These should comprise those with an immediate responsibility for maintaining hygiene standards, quality control and training personnel, and also include representatives from all sections of the food production line, including the Food Service Personnel.

It is advisable that staff be seconded on to the committee for a set period of time, maximum two years, to encourage others in the organisation to show an interest. The objective is to set the pace in food hygiene standards. It can be useful from time to time to invite specialist speakers to talk on hygiene subjects relating to the industry on cleaning, equipment or transportation.

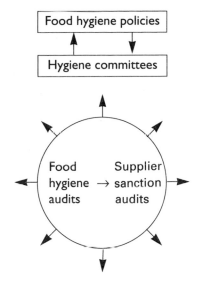

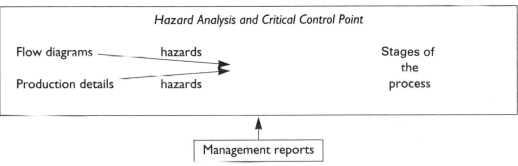

Fig. 13.1 The process of food hygiene management for production

Hazard Analysis and Critical Control Point (HACCP)

Developed in the USA in the mid 1970s HACCP is already used extensively in food manufacturing and processing. HACCP is a process which critically examines each stage of the process and where these may appear vulnerable in terms of producing a hazard into the food, then particular attention is given at that point. The process therefore critically examines the food production flow until the food is consumed. Once potential hazards in the food's journey are identified, whether it be in the kitchen or before, then particular attention can be given to eliminate or minimise the hazard. One of the advantages of HACCP is that a multi-disciplinary team is involved because it covers the entire range of activities associated with the product. The system does require the food preparation staff to be trained and committed to be effective.

For any caterer wishing to introduce HACCP the following need to be identified:

• a flow diagram showing the path of the food throughout its manufacture (Figure 13.3, page 454);

- product details so that any special characteristics that could cause a problem are noted;
- where in each stage there is the likelihood of a hazard occurring; the risks should then be assessed as high, medium or low and then monitoring and control procedures can be implemented.

Food	Preparation	Cooking	Holding	Regeneration	Presentation
fresh	weigh/measure	blanche	chill	regithermic	bain marie
fresh cooked	clear/open	warm	sous vide	microwave	service flats
fresh prepared	chop/cut	simmer	freeze	convection	plates
canned	combine/mix	boil	tray	traditional	trays
frozen	blend	steam	hot cupboard		vending
chilled	shape/coat	grill	cold cupboard		buffet
vacuum	form	sauté			trolley
dehydrated		brown			dishes
smoked		bake			
salted		roast			
crystallized		broil			
acidified		fry			
pasteurized		microwave			
bottled					
UHT					

Foods in ←——————————— Process ———————————→ Ouput

Fig. 13.2   Elements of production

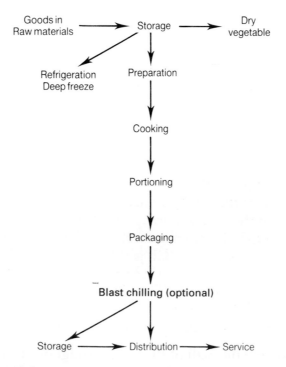

Fig. 13.3   Work flow model

Food sampling and bacterial swabs are generally used to complement the HACCP programme.

HACCP must not be seen as a sophisticated and thus complicated programme intended only for the larger operators. Every food has its critical point to some extent; this is why food production is so vulnerable. Those involved in food production must be aware of these stages where hazards occur and make every effort to eradicate or minimise them by paying extra attention to hygiene at the crucial stages in the production cycle. A programme of periodic monitoring will ensure that these parts of the food production chain will be properly monitored and safe.

EXAMPLES OF CRITICAL CONTROL POINTS
- Inspection (including temperature checks) of goods on delivery and before use.
- Separate storage and handling of ingredients and the finished product.
- Correct temperature ranges of refrigerated and frozen goods.
- Cleaning procedures for equipment and utensils.
- Cross-contamination with other menu items in process.
- Personal hygiene and health standards.
- Proficiency in use and cleaning of equipment.

Food hygiene audits

Food hygiene audits are intended to scrutinise the food production operation with a view to recording deficiencies and areas for improvement, or simply to monitor performance at a certain point. These may be linked to any quality assurance criteria.

The approach to the audit may vary but it generally involves a suitably qualified person carrying out an in depth inspection of both premises, plant and the food production practices. There should be a report back procedure to management with both observations where necessary and any recommendations.

Caterers can change their techniques of operation for various reasons, without being aware of any hazards that are introduced and it is very easy for staff who are familiar with the production plant to fail to see problem areas that are emerging. It may be that staff are beginning to be lax in connection with a certain task. It could be that maintenance is required to parts of the building. Similarly, equipment may need attention. Day-to-day familiarity with the work and the operation often means that those closest to it simply do not notice problems and therefore a hygiene audit is one way of bringing in someone who can look critically, to the extent of picking up any problem areas or practices.

The frequence of these audits will vary. High intensity production will justify more frequent audits. It is important that whatever emerges from the in-depth inspections must be properly recorded and brought to the attention of the appropriate people, either the management or individual food handlers or both. Management must in turn ensure that the hygiene audit is acted upon, otherwise there is little value in the exercise.

Standards of hygiene

To ensure safe hygienic standards in any system the following points are crucial.

REFRIGERATION

Efficient refrigeration and temperature control are essential otherwise there is the danger of deterioration in structure, quality, appearance and nutritional value. Any rise in temperature will encourage the growth of micro-organisms and lead to poor quality food which may need to be destroyed.

It is vital that accurate temperature control and monitoring are carried out throughout the cook-freeze, blast-freeze, storage and regeneration process to ensure that food is always held at acceptable and safe temperatures.

Fig. 13.4   Wheel-in refrigeration

Devices used to measure temperature (see Plates 106–109 on pages 329–330, and Figure 13.5) include:

- hand-held probes, which provide a digital read-out for random checking at all stages;
- audible alarms, fitted inside cold stores to warn of rises in temperature;
- temperature gauges, which give a visible reading of the temperature.

PRODUCTION

In order to ensure that high quality, palatable food is produced at all times it is essential that working conditions are maintained to the highest possible standards, as laid down in the HMSO publication *Clean Catering*, such as:

- stringent personal hygiene precautions against infection of the food;
- all working surfaces and utensils thoroughly cleaned to minimise spread of bacteria;
- clean equipment and utensils separated from used items awaiting cleaning;
- separation of raw and cooked foods at all times;
- strict control of cooking times and temperatures;

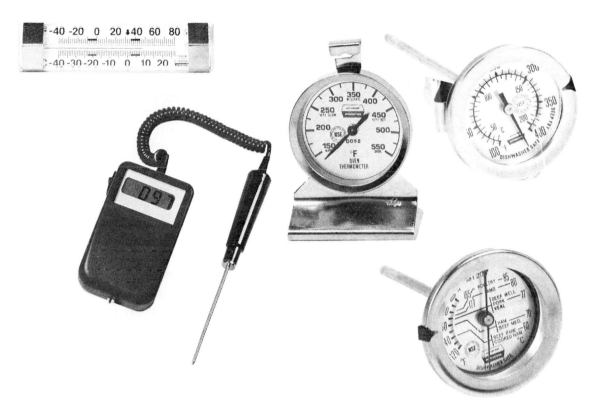

Fig. 13.5   A selection of temperature measuring devices (clockwise from top left): refrigerator/ freezer thermometer; oven thermometer; confectionery/deep fat fry thermometer; meat thermometer; digital thermometer (general kitchen thermometer)

- staff training in food hygiene;
- consultation with medical and Public Health Officers when planning food production systems

Fig. 13.6   Preparing the food

Fig. 13.7   The food technologist and chef working together

EQUIPMENT

The equipment used will vary according to the size of the operation but if food is batch-cooked then convection ovens, steaming ovens, bratt pans, jacketed boiling pans, tilting kettles, etc. may be used. Certain oven models are available in which a set of racks can be assembled with food and wheeled in for cooking.

The main difference between cook-freeze and cook-chill is the degree of refrigeration and the length of storage life. Other than these differences the information given in this chapter relates to both systems. (For details of cook-freeze, see page 467.)

COOK-CHILL

Cook-chill is a catering system based on normal preparation and cooking of food followed by rapid chilling storage in controlled low-temperature conditions above freezing point, 0–3°C (32–37°F) and subsequently reheating immediately before consumption (Figure 13.8). The chilled food is regenerated in finishing kitchens which require low capital investment and minimum staff. Almost any food can be cook-chilled provided that the correct methods are used during the preparation.

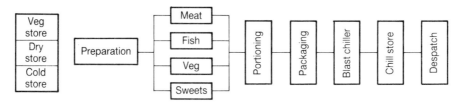

Fig. 13.8　Production unit: planning for cook-chill

The cook-chill system is used in volume catering, in hospitals, schools and in social services. It is also used for banquets, in conference and exhibition catering, in vending machines where meals are dispensed to the customer, in factories, hospitals and services outside of main meal times.

Foods suitable for the cook-chill process

MEATS

All meat, poultry, game and offal can be cook-chilled. Meat dishes that need to be sliced, such as striploin of beef, is cooked, rapidly chilled, sliced and packaged for storage. The regeneration temperature must reach 70°C (158°F) in the centre of the produce for 2 minutes. Therefore, it is not possible to serve undercooked meats.

FISH

All precooked fish dishes are suitable for cook-chilling.

EGG DISHES

Omelets and scrambled eggs are now commonly used in this process especially on airlines. Omelets are now manufactured by companies who are able to supply the airline with the chilled product. The quality of the end product has greatly improved and continues to do so as more and more money is invested in product development.

SOUPS AND SAUCES
Most soups and sauces can now be successfully chilled. Those with a high-fat or egg-yolk content do need a certain amount of recipe modification to prevent separation on regeneration.

DESSERTS
There are a large number of desserts which chill well, especially the cold variety. Developments continue with hot sweets especially those which require a hot base and a separate topping.

Recipe modification

Successful production of chilled food does require a certain amount of recipe modification. These modifications may have to be introduced during the preparation or cooking or both.

BATTERED FISH
The batter should be made thicker, using a mixture with a higher fat content. This type of batter does not easily break away from the fish and will give a crisper end product.

STEWED/BRAISED ITEMS
Cut meat into smaller portions to avoid undue thickness. Flour-based sauces must be thoroughly cooked otherwise they will continue to thicken during regeneration.

SCRAMBLED EGGS
Cook until the egg begins to scramble, remove from heat and allow the product to continue to cook to a soft consistency. Chill immediately in shallow dishes, stir during chilling.

CREAMED AND MASHED POTATOES
More liquid is added than normal giving a loose and less dense product. This assists the chilling and regeneration stages as the potato absorbs more liquid when chilled.

The purpose of chilling food

The purpose of chilling food is to prolong its storage life. Under normal temperature conditions, food deteriorates rapidly through the action of micro-organisms and enzymic and chemical reactions. Reduction in the storage temperature inhibits the multiplication of bacteria and other micro-organisms and slows down the chemical and enzymic reactions. At normal refrigeration temperatures reactions are still taking place but at a much slower rate, and at frozen food storage temperatures, $-20°C$ ($-4°F$) approximately, all reactions nearly cease. A temperature of $0–3°C$ ($32–37°F$) does not give a storage life comparable to frozen food but it does produce a good product.

It is generally accepted that, even where high standards of fast chilling practice are used and consistent refrigerated storage is maintained, product quality may be acceptable for only a few days (including day of production and consumption). The storage temperature of 0–3°C (32–37°F) is of extreme importance to ensure both full protection of the food from microbiological growth and the maintenance of maximum nutritional values in the food. It is generally accepted that a temperature of 10°C (50°F) should be regarded as the critical safety limit for the storage of refrigerated food. Above that temperature, growth of micro-organisms may render the food dangerous to health.

In a properly designed and operated cook-chill system, cooked and prepared food will be rapidly cooled down to 0–3°C (32–37°F) as soon as possible after cooking and portioning and then stored between these temperatures throughout storage and distribution until required for reheating and service. Food prepared through the cook-chill system should be portioned and transferred to a blast chiller unit within 30 minutes. This will reduce the risk of the food remaining at warm incubation temperatures and prevent the risk of contamination and loss of food quality.

The cook-chill process

- The food should be cooked sufficiently to ensure destruction of any pathogenic micro-organisms.
- The chilling process must begin as soon as possible after completion of the cooking and portioning processes, within 30 minutes of leaving the cooker. The food should be chilled to 3°C (37°F) within a period of $1\frac{1}{2}$ hours. Most pathogenic organisms will not grow below 7°C (45°F), while a temperature below 3°C (37°F) is required to reduce growth of spoilage organisms and to achieve the required storage life. However, slow growth of spoilage organisms does take place at these temperatures and for this reason storage life cannot be greater than five days.
- The food should be stored at a temperature between 0–3°C (32–37°F).
- The chilled food should be distributed under such controlled conditions that any rise in temperature of the food during distribution is kept to a minimum.
- For both safety and palatability the reheating (regeneration) of the food should follow immediately upon the removal of the food from chilled conditions and should raise the temperature to a level of at least 70°C (158°F).
- The food should be consumed as soon as possible and not more than 2 hours after reheating. Food not intended for reheating should be consumed as soon as convenient and within 2 hours of removal from storage. It is essential that unconsumed reheated food is discarded.
- A temperature of 10°C (50°F) should be regarded as the critical safety limit for chilled food. Should the temperature of the chilled food rise above this level during storage or distribution the food concerned should be discarded.

Cook-chill is generally planned within a purpose-designed, comprehensive, new central production unit to give small, medium or large-scale production along predefined flow lines, incorporating traditional catering/chilling/post-chilling packaging and storage for delivery to finishing kitchens. Within an existing kitchen, where existing equipment is retained with possible minor additions and modifications, chilling/post-chilling packaging and additional storage for cooked chilled food are added.

Finishing kitchens

These can consist of purpose-built regeneration equipment plus refrigerated storage. Additional equipment, such as a chip fryer, boiling table and pressure steamer for chips, sauces, custard, vegetables, etc., can be added if required to give greater flexibility.

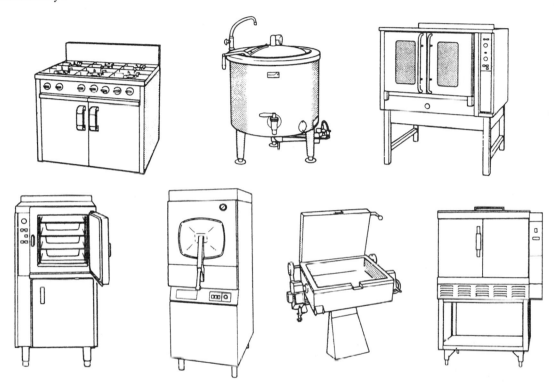

Fig. 13.9   Cook-chill equipment (source: British Gas)

Where chilled food is produced to supply a service on the same premises, it is recommended that the meals should be supplied, stored and regenerated by exactly the same method as used for operations where the production unit and finishing kitchens are separated by some distance. Failure to adhere to just one procedure could result in disorganised production and reduced productivity. Once a decision is taken to sever production from service this method should be followed throughout the system.

Distribution of cook-chill

Distribution of the chilled food is an important part of the cook-chill operation. Fluctuations in storage temperature can affect the palatability and texture of food and lead to microbiological dangers requiring the food to be discarded. The distribution method chosen must ensure that the required temperature of below 3°C (37°F) is maintained throughout the period of transport. Should the temperature of the food exceed 5°C (41°F) during distribution the food ought to be consumed within 12 hours; if the temperature exceeds 10°C (50°F) it should be discarded (Department of Health guidelines). Because of this, refrigeration during distribution is to be encouraged in many circumstances.

In some cases the cook-chill production unit can also act as a centralised kitchen and distribution point. Food is regenerated in an area adjacent to the cook-chill production area and heat retention or insulated boxes are used for distribution. During transportation and service the food must not be allowed to fall below 62.8°C (145°F).

Know the legal requirements

Contravention of the Food Safety Act 1990 and lack of due diligence can be very costly if legal action is taken and proved against the caterer or food manufacturer. The labelling of food products, recording of temperatures, maintenance of hygiene standards and promotion of staff training is essential in defence of due diligence. For this defence to be successful, the caterer must convince the court that all the requirements under the law have been complied with and that the accepted customs and practices of the profession have been carried out. It is also of paramount importance that a caterer records that these systems have been adhered to by the submission of documentary evidence.

Avoiding the dangers of cook-chill

It is essential to:

- maintain and record the correct temperatures;
- maintain high standards of hygiene;
- use fresh, high-quality ingredients avoiding raw materials which may contain excessive numbers of micro-organisms.

DELIVERIES
All food purchased must be of prime quality and stored correctly under the required temperatures.

PREPARATION
All food must be prepared quickly under the appropriate conditions avoiding any possible cross-contamination and at the correct temperature.

INITIAL COOKING AND PROCESSING
During the cooking process the centre of the food must reach a temperature of at least 70°C (158°F); preferably this temperature should reach 75°F or even 80°C (167–177°F) to achieve a greater safety margin.

PORTIONING
This should take place under appropriate conditions in a controlled environment,

which is maintained to the highest hygiene standards. The depth of the food should be no more than approximately 5 cm (2 inch). The containers must be labelled with date of cooking, number of portions and reheating instructions.

CHILLING

All food must be chilled within 30 minutes of cooking and reduced to a temperature of 0–3°C (32–37°F) within 90 minutes.

PORTIONING AFTER CHILLING

In some cook-chill systems the food is chilled in multiportion containers, then plated before reheating. The portioning process should be carried out in a controlled environment within 30 minutes of the food leaving the chilled store and before reheating commences at a temperature of 10°C (50°F). It is then transported under chilled conditions to the desired location, for example the hospital ward where it is reheated to at least 70°C (158°F) but preferably 80°C (177°F) on the plate on which it is to be served.

STORAGE (SEE BELOW)

All chilled cooked food must be stored in its own special refrigeration area. Never store cooked chilled food under the same conditions as fresh products. Always monitor the temperature of the product regularly.

REHEATING

All cook-chill food must be reheated as quickly as possible to a minimum temperature of 70°C (158°F), ideally 75°C (167°F) but preferably 80°C (177°F).

Storage and quality of cook-chill foods

It has been found that during the storage period before reheating and consumption, certain products deteriorate in quality.

- The flavour of certain meat dishes, in particular white meats, veal and poultry, deteriorates after three days.
- Chilled meats without sauces can develop acidic tastes.
- Fatty foods tend to develop off flavours due to the fat oxidising.
- Fish dishes deteriorate more rapidly than meat dishes.
- Dishes containing meat tend to develop a flat taste and if spices have been used these can dominate the flavour of the meat by the end of the chilled storage period.
- Vegetables in general may discolour and develop a strong flavour.
- Dishes which contain large amounts of starch may taste stale after the chilled storage time.

CONTAINERS

The choice of containers must protect and in some cases enhance the quality of the product at all stages, it must assist in the rapid chilling, safe storage and effective reheating. Therefore the container must be:

- *sturdy:* to withstand chilling, handling and reheating;

- *safe:* not made of a substance that will cause harmful substances to develop in the food, nor react with the food to cause discolouring or spoilage;
- *have an easy-to-remove lid:* without damaging contents or causing spillage;
- *attractive:* to enhance the appearance of the product;
- *airtight and watertight:* so that moisture, flavours or odours do not penetrate the food or escape during storage and transportation.

There are various types of containers.

Single-portion containers

These can be of cardboard laminated with plastic; aluminium foil (unsuitable for microwave heating); plastic compounds; stainless steel and ceramic which are durable and reusable (stainless steel is, however, unsuitable for microwave ovens).

Multiportion containers

These can be of strong plastic compounds, stainless steel, ceramic or aluminium foil. Gastronorm containers are shown in Figure 13.10

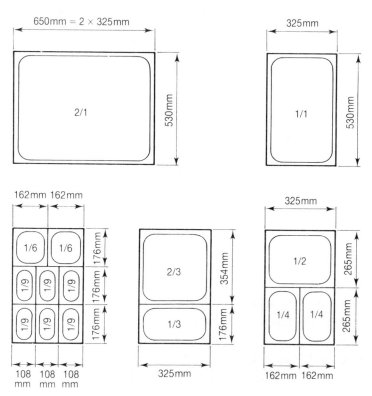

Fig. 13.10 Module sizes for gastronorm containers

LABELLING

Labels must stick securely to the containers and be easy to apply, clearly identifying the product. Colour coding is sometimes used to help identify the different days of product for example.

- *Sunday* – white
- *Monday* – red
- *Tuesday* – yellow
- *Wednesday* – blue
- *Thursday* – orange
- *Friday* – green
- *Saturday* – purple

Chilling equipment

Only specially purpose built and designed equipment can take the temperature of cooked food down to safe levels fast enough.

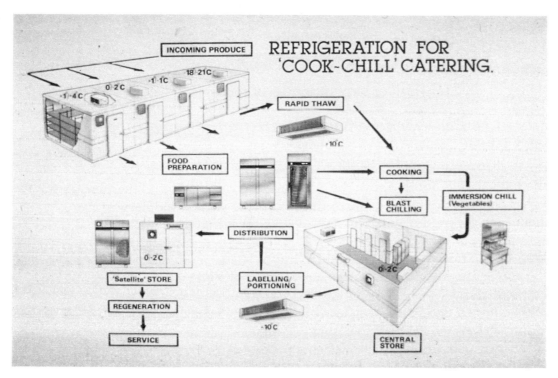

Fig. 13.11   Refrigeration for cook-chill catering

BLAST CHILLERS OR AIR BLAST CHILLERS

These use rapidly moving cold air to chill the food evenly and rapidly. Some models have temperature probes so that the temperature of the food being chilled can be checked without opening the door.

CRYOGENIC BATCH CHILLERS

These use liquid nitrogen at a temperature of $-196°C$ ($-321°F$); this is sprayed into the chilling cabinet containing the warm food. In the warmer temperature of the cabinet, the liquid nitrogen turns to super cold gas absorbing the heat from the food as it does so. Fans move the cold gas over and around the food, once the gas has become warm it is removed from the cabinet. Some equipment uses carbon dioxide instead of nitrogen.

Reheating equipment

The caterer has the following choice of equipment for regenerating cook-chill products.

COMBINATION OVENS
These are ideally suited for bulk production, which can be used with steam which is very effective in producing quality products.

STEAMERS
These may be used for certain foods, especially vegetables.

MICROWAVE OVENS
These are used for small amounts of food.

INFRARED OVENS
These may be used for small or large quantities of food.

Points to remember to ensure a satisfactory product

- Time and temperature are crucial.
- The food should not wait longer than 30 minutes to be chilled.
- The food should not be above 3°C (38°F) at the end of the chilling time. A higher temperature may be due to the food being packed too deep in the containers; the food may have been covered; there may be a malfunction in the equipment.
- Food should not be stored beyond its 'use-by' date.
- The temperature of the food rising above 3°C (38°F) during transportation this may be due to:
  - the journey taking too long using unrefrigerated transport;
  - the refrigerated van not operating correctly;
  - the insulated box (if used) not being precooled, or the lid not properly fitted. Whatever the cause, it must be recorded and the appropriate persons informed. If the temperature has not risen above 10°C (50°F) and the food is going to be served within 12 hours, the food may be allowed through. This will obviously depend on the type of food. Outside of these limits it should be discarded. If in doubt, throw it out.
- Food should not be overcooked after reheating. This may be due to the food being heated too long or the temperature too high or faulty equipment being used.
- Avoid food not reaching 70°C (158°F) within the 30 minutes allowed for reheating. This may be due to:
  - the label information not being followed correctly;
  - the label information not being correct;
  - the lid being taken off when it should have been left on;

- faulty equipment.
  If the food temperature is unsafe, throw it away.
- Avoid damaged containers. This may be due to:
  - mishandling during transportation;
  - badly stacked storage containers.
- Observe high standards of personal hygiene and kitchen hygiene, to avoid product contamination or cross-contamination.
- Portions must be controlled when filling packages in order to:
  - ensure efficient stock control;
  - control costs;
  - ensure that sufficient food is delivered to regenerating/finishing kitchens. Check that the standard regeneration procedures are safe to use.
- Food containers must be sealed correctly before storage in order to:
  - protect the food from airborne contamination;
  - enhance the presentation of dishes;
  - prevent the evaporation of moisture when heated;
  - reduce the dehydration effects chilling has on food;
  - avoid finishing products being tampered with.
- All food products must be labelled correctly before storage to:
  - identify the product and the day of production by the colour coding and 'eat by' date;
  - facilitate stock control;
  - maintain stock rotation;
  - enable visitors such as Environmental Health Officers to check that the food safety laws have and are being complied with;
  - ensure that quality tracking can be carried out.
- Ensure that older stock is consumed before the new.
- Ensure the security of storage areas against unauthorised access in order to:
  - prevent pilferage or damage by unauthorised persons;
  - prevent unnecessary opening of store doors which could destabilise storage temperature and thus may affect the temperature of the product rendering it unsafe.

Comparison of cook-chill and fast-food systems

The characteristics of each system are listed in the table below.

COOK-FREEZE

Cook-freeze is a specialised food production and distribution system that allows caterers to take advantage of the longer life through blast freezing at -18 to $-20°C$ ($0°$ to $-32°F$) and stored at that temperature until required for resale or consumption for up to 3–6 months. Blast freezers have increasingly been introduced with success into catering operations. The ability to freeze cooked dishes and

CHARACTERISTICS OF COOK-CHILL AND FAST-FOOD SYSTEMS

	COOK-CHILL	FAST-FOOD
Types of equipment	Flexible, general purpose	Single purpose Single function
Design of process	Functional	Product flow
Set-up time	Variable	Long
Workers	Variously skilled, partie system, limited flexibility	Low skill Flexible
Inventories for start of process	Vary, depending on 'foods in' required Limited by preplanning and forecasting	High to meet potential demand. Limited in time by planning and forecasting
Holding inventory	Five days max. Level forecasted	Ten mins max. Level controlled
Lot sizes	Small to large (multiples of ten)	Individual
Production time	Variable depending on menu requirements	Short or constant
Product range	Fairly wide but within constraints of three or four course meals, lunch or dinner.	Very restricted
System structure	Stock/Customer/Operation	Stock/Queue/Operation
Capacity	Variable	Highly variable
Scheduling	Externally orientated	Externally orientated

prepared foods, as distinct from the storage of chilled foods in a refrigerator or already frozen commodities in a deep-freeze, allows a caterer to make more productive use of kitchen staff. It also enables economies to be introduced into the staffing of dining rooms and restaurants.

The cook-freeze process

Cook-freeze uses a production system similar to that used in cook-chill. The recipes used have to be modified, enabling products to be freezer-stable, and modified starches are used in sauces so that on reheating and regeneration the sauce does not separate. Blast freezers are used in place of blast chillers. The freezing must be carried out very rapidly to retain freshness and to accelerate temperature loss through the latent heat barrier, thus preventing the formation of large ice crystals and rupturing of the cells.

Blast freezing takes place when low temperature air is passed over food at high speed, reducing food in batches to a temperature of at least $-20°C$ ($-4°F$) within 90 minutes. Blast freezers can hold from 20 to 400 kg (40–800 lb) per batch, the larger models being designed for trolley operation.

Preparation of food

The production menu for a month is drawn up and the total quantities of different foods required calculated. Supplies are then ordered, with special attention given to their being:

- of high quality;
- delivered so that they can immediately be prepared and cooked without any possibility of deteriorating during an enforced period of storage before being processed.

The dishes included in the menu must be cooked to the highest standards with rigid attention to quality control and to hygiene. Deep-freeze temperatures prevent the multiplication of micro-organisms but do not destroy them. If, therefore, a dish were contaminated before being frozen, consumers would be put at risk months later when the food was prepared for consumption. The exact adjustment of recipes to produce the best result when the food is subsequently thawed and reheated is still in process of being worked out by chefs, using numerous variations of the basic system. The single change needed in cookery recipes involving sauces is the selection of an appropriate type of starch capable of resisting the effect of freezing. Normal starches will produce a curdled effect when subsequently thawed and reheated.

In order to achieve rapid freezing with a quick reduction of temperature to $-18°C$ ($0°F$) or below, the cooked food must be carefully portioned (close attention being paid to the attainment of uniform portion size). Portions, each placed into a disposable aluminium foil container, may conveniently be placed into aluminium foil trays holding from 6 to 10 portions each, sealed and carefully labelled with their description and date of preparation.

Freezing

The food thus divided into portions and arranged in trays is immediately frozen. An effective procedure is to place the trays on racks in a blast-freezing tunnel and expose them to a vigorous flow of cold air until the cooked items are frozen solid and the temperature reduced to at least $-5°C$ ($23°F$). The quality of the final product is to a significant degree dependent on the rapidity with which the temperature of hot cooked food at say $80°C$ ($176°F$) is reduced to below freezing. The capacity of the blast freezer should be designed to achieve this reduction in temperature within a period of 1 to $1\frac{1}{4}$ hours.

Storage of frozen items

Once the food items are frozen they must at once be put into a deep-freeze store maintained at $-18°C$ ($0°F$). For a catering operation involving several dining rooms and cafeterias, some of which may be situated at some distance from the kitchen and frozen store, a 4 weeks' supply of cooked dishes held at low temperature allows full use to be made of the facilities.

Transport of frozen items to the point of service

If satisfactory quality is to be maintained, it is important to keep food, frozen in the cooked state, frozen until immediately prior to its being served. It should therefore be transported in insulated containers to *peripheral* or finishing kitchens, if such are to be used, where it will be reheated.

If frozen dishes are to be used in outside catering, provision should be available for transporting them in refrigerated transport and, if necessary, a subsidiary deep-freeze store should be provided for them on arrival.

THE REHEATING OF FROZEN COOKED PORTIONS

In any catering system in which a blast-freezing tunnel has been installed to freeze precooked food, previously portioned and packed in metal foil or other individual containers, it is obviously rational to install equipment that is particularly designed for the purpose of reheating the items ready to be served. The blast freezing system is effective because it is, in design, a specially powerful form of forced convection heat exchanger arranged to extract heat. It follows that an equally appropriate system for replacing heat is the use of a forced convection oven, specially for the reception of the trays of frozen portions. Where such an oven is equipped with an efficient thermostat and adequate control of the air circulation system, standardised setting times for the controls can be laid down for the regeneration of the various types of dishes that need to be reheated.

Quality control

Adequate control of bacterial contamination and growth, which are hazards in any kitchen, can be achieved by a survey of the initial installation by a qualified analyst, and regular checks taken on every batch of food cooked. Very large kitchens employ a full-time food technologist/bacteriologist. In smaller operations the occasional services of a microbiologist from the public health authority should be used.

How freezing affects different foods

MEAT, POULTRY AND FISH

The tendency for the fat in meat to oxidise and go rancid even in frozen storage, means that lean meat is better than fatty meat for freezing. Chicken fat contains a natural antioxidant (vitamin E), therefore it will react to prevent rancidity occurring.

Fresh meat must always be used for cook-freeze dishes. Never use meat that has been previously frozen. This is because each time meat is thawed, even in cool conditions there is a chance for food poisoning bacteria to multiply.

Some loss of flavour in fish is unavoidable and any surfaces left exposed can suffer from oxidation thus producing a rancid taste. Deep-fried fish in batter has to be modified so that the batter does not peel off as a result of the freezing process. The batter should be made thicker or with a higher fat content.

Freezing does not stop the enzyme activity in the meat, poultry or fish that makes the fat present in the flesh go rancid. This particularly affects the unsaturated fats which are present in pork, poultry and fish. These items should therefore not be stored frozen for longer than 2 to 3 months. It is advisable therefore to trim all fat before processing these items.

FRUIT AND VEGETABLES

When fruit and vegetables turn brown, it is because of the action of enzymes present. These enzymes cause discoloration and gradually destroy the nutritive value of the fruit. Refrigeration slows this process down and freezing will further slow it down but not stop it completely. Therefore, fruit and vegetables should be blanched or completely cooked which will stop the enzymic processes.

The freezing process also has a softening effect on the texture of fruit and vegetables. This is accepted for hard fruits such as apples, unripened pears, etc. It is not suitable for soft fruits such as strawberries. Fruits like strawberries are only suitable for freezing if they are to be later used as a filling or in a sauce, but not for decorative purposes.

Only exceptionally fresh vegetables should be used for freezing. Avoid bruised vegetables which may produce the development of 'off' flavours. Blanch the vegetables to inactivate the enzymes, but avoid overblanching, otherwise vegetables will be overcooked. Blanch if possible in high pressure steamers as this will help reduce vitamin C loss.

Recipe modification

Generally, recipes have to be modified for the cook-freeze process.

Sauces, batters, thickened soups, stews and gravies will break down and separate unless the flour used in the recipes has an addition of waxy starch. Colflo and Purity 69 are two commercially manufactured starches which are used in cook-freeze recipes.

Jellies and other products containing gelatine are unsuitable because they develop a granular structure in the cook freeze process, unless the recipe is modified with stabilisers.

Packaging

Packaging is a very important consideration as this affects the storage and regeneration of the product. Containers must protect the food against oxidation during storage and allow for freezing and reheating. The containers must be:

- watertight;
- non-tainting;
- disposable or reusable;
- equipped with tight-fitting lids.

PACKAGING MATERIALS

There are a number of packaging materials available which include plastic compounds, aluminium foil and cardboard plastic laminates. These are available as single portion packs, complete meal packs and bulk packs.

CHOOSING THE CONTAINER

Various things affect your choice of container:

- Menu choice: single packs provide the greatest flexibility.
- Food value: the overheating of complete meal packs or the edges of bulk packs, will damage the nutritional value.
- Storage space: large bulk packs make the best use of space.
- Handling time: after cooking, bulk packs are the quickest and easiest to fill whereas complete packs are the more difficult to fill. Bulk packs do, however, have to be portioned at the time of service and are therefore more time-consuming than if single packs are used.
- Quality of the food.

Freezing time is obviously affected by the depth of the food; therefore, bulk packs, where the food is relatively deep, may not survive the freezing process as well as single portion packs. Bulk packs also rely on trained service staff to present the food attractively and portion it accurately.

Regeneration instructions can be complex if complete meal packs contain different food components which in theory may require different lengths of reheating time.

Freezing equipment

Specialist equipment is required in order to reduce the temperature of the food to the required storage temperature of $-18°C$ ($0°F$).

AIR BLAST FREEZERS OR BLAST FREEZERS
These take approximately 75–90 minutes to freeze food depending on how it is packaged. Extremely cold air between $-32°C$ and $-40°C$ ($-26°F$ and $-40°F$) is blown by fans over the cooked food. The warm air is constantly removed and recirculated through the heat exchange unit to lower its temperature. In the larger cook-freeze units the food is pushed in on a trolley at one end and then wheeled out at the other end frozen.

CRYOGENIC FREEZERS
These use liquid nitrogen with the freezing time taking on average 25 minutes, dependent on the food being frozen, provided the food is left uncovered. Liquid nitrogen at $-196°C$ ($-321°F$) is sprayed into the freezing chamber. Fans circulate the nitrogen so that the foods freeze evenly. The warm gas is pumped out of the cabinet as more cold nitrogen is pumped in. Some freezers used liquid carbon dioxide.

PLATE FREEZERS AND TUNNEL FREEZERS
These are used in food manufacturing and are less likely to be used in catering.

Transportation and distribution

Cook-freeze meals have to be delivered to finishing kitchens at the same temperature as they were held in storage. For short distances insulated containers are used. These are cooled down before being used. However, it is safer and more efficient to use refrigerated vans.

Finishing kitchen equipment

Thawing cabinets are similar to a forced air convection oven, but use a temperature of 10°C (50°F).

RAPID THAWING CABINET

This is used to defrost containers of frozen meals before they are placed in the oven; this has the effect of halving the reheating time. The temperature of the food is brought from −20°C to 3°C (−4°F to 37°F) in approximately 4 hours, under safe conditions. Warming is kept at a steady controlled rate by a process of alternating low volume heat with refrigeration.

COMBINATION OVENS

These are suitable for large quantities of food.

MICROWAVE OVENS

These are only suitable for small amounts of food.

DUAL PURPOSE OVENS

These are microwave ovens which have a second heat source, for example an infrared grill, and a defrost control which switches the microwave power on and off.

FORCED AIR CONVECTION OVENS

These are suitable for large quantities of food.

Points to remember to ensure a satisfactory product

PREPARATION

- Make sure that all preparation and cooking areas are clean and that the equipment is in working order.
- Never use previously frozen food.
- Avoid any delay between preparation and cooking.

COOKING

- Check on the cooking process for the food that this process takes account of the overall effect on flavour, texture and nutritional value.
- Always use temperature probes to check that the centre of the food has reached a safe temperature before the final cooking is complete.

PORTIONING AND PACKAGING

- Make sure all areas are clean and hygienically safe.
- Ensure that all packaging is ready and that it is of the correct size and material.
- All reusable containers must be cleaned and thoroughly sterilised.
- Make sure that all assistants who portion and package wear food-handling gloves.
- Make sure that all general equipment used in this area is sterilised.
- Accurately portion the food according to the recipe.
- Do not pack the food to a depth greater than 5 cm (2 inches). For food which is to be microwaved the depth should be less.

- Portions must be controlled when filling to:
  - standardise costs;
  - control costs;
  - facilitate stores control;
  - assist in food service;
  - standardise the thawing and reheating process;
  - allow the sealing to be properly completed.
- Food containers must be sealed correctly before storage in order to:
  - prevent spoilage due to contact with the cold air;
  - prevent spillage prior to freezing;
  - allow for safe stacking, helping to prevent damage to containers.
- Cover the food before blast freezing.
- Check and record the temperature of the food.

LABELLING
- Label all food correctly.
- Ensure labels have the right information which should include:
  - production date;
  - use-by date;
  - name of dish;
  - description of contents;
  - storage life;
  - number of portions;
  - instructions for reheating/regenerating with type of oven, temperature, time, and whether lid should be on or off.
- Correct labelling will:
  - accurately identify the contents of the container;
  - enable quick and efficient stock-taking;
  - indicate important information regarding the packaging, date and the use-by date;
  - give information on the number of portions contained in the package.

FREEZING
- Check all fast freezers are ready for use.
- Freezing should be done immediately after cooking.
- The foods must be frozen below $-5°C$ ($23°F$) within 90 minutes.
- There must be at least 2 cm ($\frac{3}{4}$ inch) air space between layers of containers in the freezer.
- Immediately after freezing the food must be transported to the deep-freeze storage.

STORING
- Store the food at the correct deep-freeze storage temperature of $-20°C$ to $-30°C$ ($-4°F$ to $-22°F$) and at least below $-18°C$ ($0°F$).
- Monitor deep freezer temperatures at all times, keep accurate records.
- Maintain the stock control rotation, keep all stock record systems up to date.

- Store the food in the accepted manner on shelves and racks above the floor away from the door and with enough space around to allow the cold air to circulate.
- Always wear protective clothing when entering the deep freeze store.
- Destroy any foods that have passed their use-by date.
- It is important to monitor and record food temperatures regularly in order to:
  - prevent contamination from incorrect storage conditions;
  - ensure flavour and texture is maintained.
- Stock rotation procedures must be followed in order to:
  - prevent damage or decay to stock;
  - ensure that older stock is used before new stock.
- Storage areas must be secured from unauthorised access in order to:
  - prevent pilferage or damage by unauthorised persons;
  - prevent injury to unauthorised persons;
  - prevent unnecessary opening of store doors, which would destabilise the temperature.

DISTRIBUTION

- Maintain freezer temperatures during distribution.
- DHSS guidelines state that if the food is going to be regenerated within 24 hours, the permissible temperature range is between 0° and −18°C (32° and 0°F). Otherwise the temperature must be kept below −18°C (0°F).
- All documentation and control systems for checking delivery should be carefully followed and implemented.

REGENERATION

- Check that the work area is ready for operation.
- Remove products from deep freeze for regeneration, check the labels.
- Make sure equipment is at the correct temperature and in working order.
- Follow the regeneration instructions on the label.
- The foods must be reheated to at least 70°C (158°F) but to 75–80°C (167–177°F) immediately before service. Check temperature has been reached by using a sterilised temperature probe.
- Serve the food as soon as possible after regeneration.
- Food that has not been eaten within 2 hours should be thrown away. Food which has been allowed to cool must never be reheated.

GENERAL

- To avoid separated sauces, the recipe must be modified correctly using the appropriate starches.
- Meat and fish will taste rancid with badly prepared food or too long a storage period.
- Soggy coated food will occur if the lid is not removed when regenerating.
- A back log of food for freezing will occur with poor production planning.
- Freezer burns are due to badly packaged food or when food is stored too long.
- Standards of personnel hygiene and kitchen temperature are of paramount importance to maintain a clean and safe product.

OVERALL BENEFITS OF COOK-CHILL/COOK-FREEZE

To the employer:

- Portion control and reduced waste.
- No over-production.
- Central purchasing with bulk buying discounts.
- Full utilisation of equipment.
- Full utilisation of staff time.
- Overall savings in staff.
- Savings on equipment, space and fuel.
- Fewer staff with better conditions – no unsociable hours, no weekend work, no overtime.
- Simplified less frequent delivery to units.
- Solves problem of moving hot foods. (EC regulations forbid the movement of hot foods unless the temperature is maintained over 65°C (149°F). Maintaining 65°C is regarded as very difficult to achieve and high temperatures inevitably will be harmful to foods.)

To the customer:

- Increased variety and selection.
- Improved quality, with standards maintained.
- More nutritious foods.
- Services can be maintained at all times, regardless of staff absences.

Advantages of cook-freeze over cook-chill

- Seasonal purchasing provides considerable savings.
- Delivery to units will be far less frequent.
- Long-term planning of production and menus becomes possible.
- Less dependence on price fluctuations.
- More suitable for vending machines incorporating microwave.

Advantages of cook-chill over cook-freeze

- Regeneration systems are simpler – infrared and steam convection ovens are mostly used and only 12 minutes is required to reheat all foods perfectly.
- Thawing time is eliminated.
- Smaller capacity storage is required: 3 to 4 days supply as opposed to up to 120 days.
- Chiller storage is cheaper to install and run than freezer storage.
- Blast chillers are cheaper to install and run that blast freezers.
- Cooking techniques are unaltered (additives and revised recipes are needed for freezing).
- All foods can be chilled so the range of dishes is wider (some foods cannot be

frozen). Cooked eggs, steaks and sauces such as Hollandaise can be chilled (after some recipe modification where necessary).
- No system is too small to adapt to cook-chill.

Further information can be obtained from the Electricity Association, 30 Millbank, London SW1P 4RD and the Department of Health.

VACUUM COOKING (SOUS-VIDE) (Plate 129, page 374)

This is a form of cook-chill, using a combination of vacuum sealing in plastic pouches, cooking by steam and then rapidly chilling in an ice-water bath, as this most effective way of chilling. The objective is to rationalise kitchen procedures without having a detrimental effect on the quality of the individual dishes.

The process is as follows:

- Individual portions of prepared food are first placed in special plastic pouches. The food can be fish, poultry, meats, vegetables, etc., to which seasoning, a garnish, sauce, stock, wine, flavouring, vegetables, herbs and/or spices can be added.
- The pouches of food are then placed in a vacuum-packaging machine which evacuates all the air and tightly seals the pouch.
- The pouches are next cooked by steam. This is usually in a special oven equipped with a steam control programme, which controls the injection of steam into the oven, to give steam cooking at an oven temperature below 100°C (212°F). Each food item has its own ideal cooking time and temperature.
- When cooked, the pouches are rapidly cooled down to 3°C (37°F), usually in an iced water chiller or an air blast chiller for larger operations.
- The pouches are then labelled and stored in a holding refrigerator at an optimum temperature of 3°C (37°F).
- When required for service the pouches are regenerated in boiling water or a steam combination oven until the required temperature is reached, cut open and the food presented.

Vacuum pressures are as important as the cooking temperatures with regard to weight loss and heat absorption. The highest temperature used in *sous-vide* cooking is 100°C (212°F) and 1000 millibars is the minimum amount of vacuum pressure used.

As there is no oxidation or discoloration it is ideal for conserving fruits, such as apples and pears (pears in red wine, fruits in syrup). When preparing meats in sauces the meat is preblanched then added to the completed sauce.

Sous-vide is a combination of vacuum sealing, tightly controlled *en papillotte* cooking and rapid chilling. Potential users are brasseries, wine bars, airlines, private hospitals and function caterers seeking to provide top quality with portion convenience.

Advantages

- Long shelf-life, up to 21 days, refrigerated.
- Ability to produce meals in advance means better deployment of staff and skills.
- Vacuum-packed foods can be mixed in cold store without the risk of cross-contamination.
- Reduced labour costs at point of service.
- Beneficial cooking effects on certain foods, especially moulded items and pâtés. Reduces weight loss on meat joints.
- Full flavour and texture is retained as food cooks in its own juices.
- Economises on ingredients (less butter, marinades, etc.).
- Makes precooking a possibility for à la carte menus.
- Inexpensive regeneration.
- Allows a small operation to set up bulk production.
- Facilitates portion control and uniformity of standard.
- Has a tenderising effect on tougher cuts of meat and matures game without dehydration.

Disadvantages

- Extra cost of vacuum pouches and vacuum-packing machine.
- Unsuitable for meats (fillet steak) and vegetables which absorb colour.
- All portions in a batch must be identically sized to ensure even results.
- Most dishes require twice the conventional cooking time.
- Unsuitable for large joints as chilling time exceeds 90 minutes.
- Complete meals (meat and two vegetables) not feasible; meat component needs to be cooked and stored in separate bags.
- Extremely tight management and hygienic controls are imperative.
- Potentially adverse customer reaction ('boil-in-the-bag' syndrome).

Points to remember

- High standards of kitchen hygiene and personnel hygiene must be employed.
- Prime quality ingredients should be used.
- All aspects of the Food Safety Act must be adhered to.
- Where possible *sous-vide* should operate under a temperature controlled environment.
- All the basic principles of cook-chill apply to *sous-vide*.

CENTRALISED PRODUCTION

Why centralise?

Reasons for considering centralised production units are as follows:

- labour: reduction of kitchen preparation staff in end units;

- food cost: greater control over waste and portion sizes; competitive purchasing through bulk buying;
- equipment: intensive central use of heavy equipment reduces commitment in individual units;
- product: more control on product quality;
- labour strategy: staff are employed at regular times (9 am to 5 pm) which can eliminate or lessen the difficulty of obtaining staff who will work shifts.

When considering a centralised production system it is essential that a detailed financial appraisal is produced and then looked at carefully, as each establishment has its own considerations. No general rule can be given as the profitability depends on the product, the size of each unit, the number of units and the method of preserving food.

Design

Centralised production systems can be designed in two ways:

- using existing catering (operations) unit and modifying, etc.;
- purpose-built.

Type of units

Centralised production units are grouped into four types:

- units preparing fresh cooked foods which are then despatched;
- cook-freeze: food is partly prepared or cooked, then frozen and regenerated when required;
- cook-chill: food is cooked, then chilled and regenerated when required;
- sous-vide: food is sealed in a special casing, vacuum-sealed, cooked and chilled.

Food production and preparation

The profitability of the production system depends largely upon contents of the end-unit menus.

MEAT

Careful purchasing is essential and the menu must be planned carefully:

- The cut of meat required must be clearly specified in order to produce the exact dishes.
- Strict portion control must be adhered to.
- Trimmings/by-products must be fully utilised: meat trimming for cottage/shepherd's pie, bones for stock.

VEGETABLE PREPARATION

Because of increasing labour costs and difficulty in obtaining staff, a number of establishments now purchase: prepared potatoes, that are washed, peeled and in some

METHODS OF PRODUCTION

1.	Conventional	Term used to describe production utilising mainly fresh foods and traditional cooking methods.
2.	Convenience	Method of production utilising mainly convenience foods.
3.	Call order	Method where food is cooked to order either from customer (as in cafeterias) or from waiter. Production area often open to customer area.
4.	Continuous flow	Method involving production line approach where different parts of the production process may be separated (e.g. fast food).
5.	Commissary/ centralised	Production not directly linked to service. Foods are 'held' and distributed to separate service areas.
6.	Cook-chill	Food production, storage and regeneration method utilising principle of low temperature control to preserve qualities of processed foods.
7.	Cook-freeze	Production, storage and regeneration method utilising principle of freezing to control and preserve qualities of processed foods. Requires special processes to assist freezing.
8.	*Sous-vide*	Method of production, storage and regeneration utilising principle of sealed vacuum to control and preserve the quality of processed foods.

cases shaped; prepared root vegetables; topped and tailed French beans; and ready prepared salads.

Reception and delivery

It is desirable to have two loading bays, one for receiving and one for delivery. They should be adjacent to the relevant store to facilitate loading. The receiving bay should be adjacent to the prime goods store for purchased meat, vegetables, etc., and the delivery bay near to the finished goods stores which contain items ready to go out to their end units.

Staff

Apart from a butcher some of the staff may not be highly skilled. The various processes involved in meat production can be divided as follows and staff trained for each procedure:

- machine operators: staff operating dicing machines, mincing machines, hamburger machines, to a strict procedure;
- trimmers: staff who are taught to trim carcasses and prime cuts;
- packers: who pack goods into foil cans, operate vacuum-packing machines, and label or pack finished goods into containers; caterers will have to consider if it is economically viable to have a butchery or whether to buy in prepared meats (this very much depends upon the range of menu).

Frequently, staff who are employed to carry out specific functions within a centralised kitchen may not have catering qualifications but will be trained by the organisation.

Method of operation

There are two types of operations:

- weekly production;
- daily total run.

Forecasts obtained from the end unit determine the quantity of the production run. This prepares items of a particular type on one occasion only. As soon as the run is completed the next run is then scheduled. The main advantage of this type of production is in the comparative ease with which a control system may be installed and operated.

A disadvantage is that, in the event of an error in production scheduling, it is wasteful and costly to organise a further production run of small volume. Another disadvantage is that the method leads to the building-up of stocks, both finished and unfinished, thereby affecting the profitability of the operation.

A daily total run is based upon the needs of items required by the end-unit. A disadvantage is that the forecast gap is shorter, so the end units are not able to provide accurate requisitions.

Purchasing

Any organisation depending for its existence on the economics of bulk purchasing must pay particular attention to the process of buying.

The following are the main objectives of the buyer:

- Quality and price of goods must be equalled with the size of purchase order.
- All purchase specifications must be met.
- Buying practice must supplement a policy of minimum stock holding.

Transport

The distribution of goods, routing and the maintenance of vehicles are very important to a centralised production operation. The usual practice is for transport to be under the control of a senior manager, who also has the complicated job of batching-up deliveries (normally weekly or bi-weekly). It is important that the senior manager has considerable administrative skill in order to prevent errors occurring.

Centralised production very often means that production is separated from the food service by distance, time or both. An example is in hospital wards; here there are satellite kitchens or regeneration kitchens. Other examples exist in aircraft catering and banqueting. Banqueting houses that use cook-chill either purchase from their own production unit or an independent company (see page 462).

Fast food

Fast food is characterised by a smooth operation. The principal control adopted is 'door time': 3.5 minutes is the control average, $1\frac{1}{2}$ minutes queuing and 1 minute serving. Capital costs are high for production equipment. The menu range is narrow with the equipment often being specially developed to do one job. This is essentially one cell or family of related parts of one product.

Increases in volume required is met by increasing the speed of foods through the system. This is achieved by increasing labour and by duplicating the same cell. Workers are multi-functional but often of low skill. Staffing can be applied to a number of parts depending on volume of throughput. This type of staffing can give high job satisfaction (although short-term) similar to the rotation of chefs through the partie system.

This operation comes nearer to the continuous flow ideal and is often quoted as a classic just-in-time system.

The principles of manufacturing exist in both fast food and cook-chill systems. Other systems such as cook-freeze and *sous-vide* will take on a variety of cells relating to different parts of the meal. The fast-food system is primarily based upon one-cell systems. All systems use variations in the number of workers to control costs.

Small centralised operations

There are some very good examples of smaller centralised operations to be seen now in the catering industry. The purpose of installation is to provide ready-prepared goods which may be served to banquets or supplied to grills/coffee shops.

The preparation of the food takes place during the kitchen 'slack' period, principally after the luncheon service. The made-up items are put into polythene bags which contain from one to six portions. The packed items are marked with the date of packing, and the name of the item, and then blast frozen preparatory to storage. They are kept in store from 3 to 6 months and moved to a first-in, first-out basis. Some items have limited storage time so careful checking of dates is an important factor to consider. Refrigerators in the outlets are stocked up daily from the central code store.

When an item is ordered it is reheated by a simple boiling process which is operated by a timer. The cooked items are placed on the plate, with the garnish and vegetables being added separately. There are also, of course, many other refinements: carefully calculated production schedules and coloured photographs of the dishes to guide presentation, for example.

IN-FLIGHT CATERING

In-flight catering is one of the most extensive food production operations within the catering industry (see Plate 130, page 375). Some in-flight caterers may produce up to 36 000 meals a day during the peak season. This section describes a typical system that would be used by many in-flight caterers throughout the world. Caterers involved in large scale production are able to learn from the in-flight production system, in particular the production planning process, production scheduling and the production systems.

Basic principles of the design of in-flight food production kitchens

Factors which will influence the design are similar to designing other food production systems (see pages 451–477):

- the size and extent of the operations in terms of the maximum number of flight meals to be produced;
- amounts of capital expenditure costs;
- policy on the use of preprepared products;
- the use of latest technology;
- hygiene, food safety legislation.

The flow process (Figure 13.12, page 484)

Each kitchen should have a flow process chart detailing the materials (food) and labour, the chart will show the main parts of the process, demonstrating the flow of materials and labour, the transportation of products, storage and chilling. The chart will also clearly identify when the operator should temperature test and for how long.

Production planning

Good production planning for in-flight caterers involves a similar principle to JIT (just-in-time production techniques), meaning 'producing the necessary units, in the necessary quantities, at the necessary time'. This concept has in some way been used by large-scale caterers for some time, the difference being they have never referred to it as JIT, just good business practice. The principles of JIT are:

- stock levels kept down to the level as and when required; order in as and when needed (stockless production);
- elimination of waste;
- enforced problem solving;
- continuous flow manufacturing.

There is and has to be a strong emphasis on continual improvement rather than accepting the *status quo*.

BALANCING RESOURCES AND PASSENGER NEEDS IN A PRODUCTION PLAN
To achieve the tight balance between passenger needs and resources, the following need to be considered:

- **Orders**
  - from the airline;
  - for stock;
  - broken down into details.

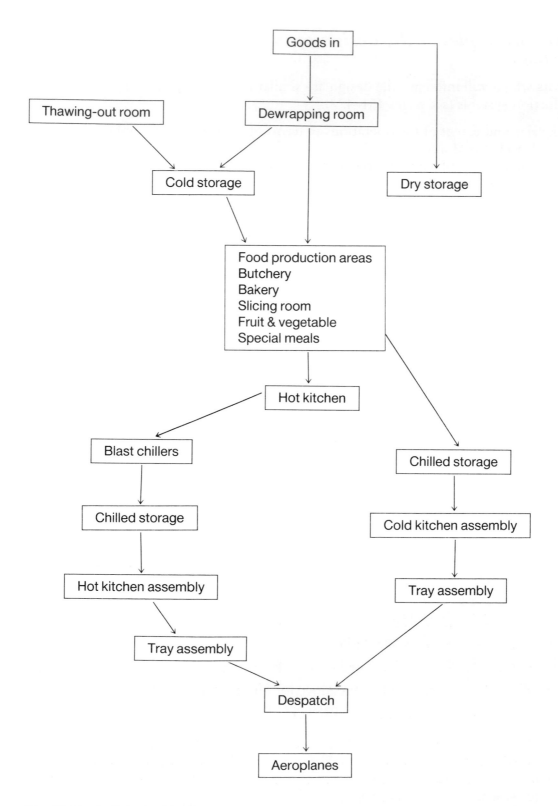

Fig. 13.12   In-flight food production flow chart

- **Priority**
  - sequenced into date, time aircraft is due to take off;
  - special meal requirements identified;
  - evenly balanced work load where appropriate.
- **Availability**
  - labour;
  - equipment;
  - if overload, work can be subcontracted if necessary (in peak periods some caterers may subcontract some of their work).
- **Cost**
  - balance of high/low margin orders;
  - down-time costs from excessive change-overs;
  - cost of subcontracting.

OVERALL PRODUCTION CONTROL

A production plan is rarely, if ever, carried out in all its details. Equipment breaks down, staff can be off sick, suppliers fail to deliver, skilled people leave the company, etc.

The function of production control is to ensure that production is maintained in line with the production plan wherever possible and secondly, to respond to the things which do go wrong and rework the plan in to get back on schedule.

The food production managers monitor the supply and production process to ensure that there is always up-to-date information on what has been achieved and what further actions may be necessary to maintain the production flow. Where deviations from the production plan are spotted, corrective action is then taken to overcome any shortfalls in the production.

Regular checks must be made on food availability and alternative suppliers must be identified in cases of emergency where a designated supplier fails to deliver on time or the exact quantity.

All food production managers and supervisors must be aware of what labour hours are available and how the operation is performing in terms of quality and productivity.

Examples of catering menus and menu specifications
(Figures 13.13–13.16, pages 486–489)

The following illustrations give some idea of the current menus to be experienced on board, and typical volumes used at a catering centre during one year.

The production system

A large scale operation producing approximately 30 000 meals a day supplying 200 fully catered flights could well be dealing with over 300 food suppliers. In a typical system all stock would be on a 48-hour holding cycle, raw materials being held for no longer than 24 hours before being used in production.

The meal requirements are given to the food production manager and despatch

Product	Quantity
Smoked salmon roulade with mackerel mousse (slice – 2 × 15 gm)	30 gm
Cucumber batons	×2
Assorted lettuce leaf	×1
Lemon slice	×1
Parsley sprig	×1
Braised blade eye of beef in red wine sauce	110 gm 40 gm
Button onions	×3
Button mushrooms	×3
Carrot batons	25 gm
Broccoli	25 gm
Cocotte potatoes	×3
Lemon & sultana cheesecake	×1
Lemon coulis	10 gm
Lemon zest	6 gm
Cheesepack with red Leicester & oak smoked Cheddar cheese	×1

Airline		
Effective date		
Class Club		
Meal Hot meal – CAT 1		
Code HM2C A		**Cycle** A
Special Instruction China equipment		
Issue no. 2	**Meal no.** 36A	**Plu. no.** 331

Butter portion	×1
UHT milk portions	×1
Thorntons chocolate	×1

Fig. 13.13 Menu specification

control department. There is often a computer link which relays all flight details and eating requirements on each flight. The manager (usually the head chef of executive chef) gives the orders to the stores department. All orders to each supplier are on computer print-outs ready to be checked against a receipt of delivery.

The delivery should be systematically enrolled to avoid cross-contamination, segregating the delivery of each high risk food, for example poultry, meat and fish. The deliveries must be checked against the production requirements on the computer print-out, if there is any discrepancy the order should be refused.

The dry goods should be brought to the dry storage area. Any cold and frozen goods should be dealt with in a separate area where they can be unwrapped. This is to prevent any cardboard boxes or external wrappings entering into the food production or cold storage areas. These goods should be transferred to colour-coded plastic boxes. Computer-printed tags can be used to identify each plastic box. The tag attached to the box will normally have the day and date contents of each box.

Bar Service

APERITIFS
Sherry · Campari
Vermouth, sweet or dry

— ★ —

SPIRITS
Scotch, American and Canadian Whiskies
Gin · Rum · Vodka

— ★ —

WINES
Fine still and sparkling wines from
the vineyards of the world

— ★ —

LIQUEURS
Cognac · Drambuie · Cointreau
Tia Maria · Port · Baileys
Southern Comfort

— ★ —

BEERS
English beers · Lager
Low alcohol lager

— ★ —

SOFT DRINKS
Coca-Cola
Gini
Schweppes: Tonic Water · Bitter Lemon
Lemonade · Soda Water · Mineral Water
Canada Dry Ginger Ale
Juices: Orange · Apple · Tomato

— ★ —

DIET DRINKS
Diet Coca-Cola
Schweppes Slimline Tonic

— ★ —

Champagne is also available at
current bar tariff rate

☐ Our Well-being in the Air menu offers you
an alternative dining style.
Light easily digested dishes made from
the freshest ingredients.

Menu

☐ Feta cheese and herb tortellini salad

— ★ —

Escalope of turkey with provençale sauce
Stir fried vegetables and new potatoes

or

☐ Fillet of lemon sole filled with mushroom and prawn
Served with white wine sauce, spinach and
saffron rice with lentils

— ★ —

Strawberry and rhubarb mousse

— ★ —

Cheese and crackers with butter

— ★ —

Coffee, decaffeinated coffee or tea

We apologise if, owing to previous passenger
selection, your choice is not available

Refreshments

☐ Fresh melon with citrus fruit

— ★ —

Selection of sandwiches including tuna with celery,
egg with anchovy mayonnaise and Ploughman's
cheese with pickle

— ★ —

Sweet pastry

— ★ —

Tea or coffee

Fig. 13.14 An in-flight menu

Frozen goods then pass into purpose-built thawing rooms. Chilled products are transferred to the cold storage areas. All storage rooms must be controlled and monitored 24 hours a day. When required these items are removed into the production areas where skilled operatives continue the production process.

Lunch

Our Club World menu today offers you the choice of a leisurely four course meal or a light alternative of hors d'oeuvre accompanied by salad and hot rolls, followed if you wish, by dessert, cheese and biscuits, and fresh fruit.

This light meal will be served within an hour of the start of today's meal service, allowing you the maximum rest, work, or sleeping time.

Appetizers

Lobster, fennel and green bean salad

or

Vegetable, lentil and grain terrine

Seasonal Salad

Mixed salad with lemon vinaigrette or Thousand Islands dressing

Hot Breads

Bakery selection of multi-grain, crusty and wholemeal rolls
Butter or sunflower margarine

Entrées

Grilled lamb cutlet and fillet steak with thyme and rosemary butter

or

Stir fried chicken with shiitake mushrooms and waterchestnuts

or

Polenta and aubergine gâteau with tomato and hazelnut

Cheese

Mature Cheddar and goat cheese with crackers and butter

Fresh Fruit

Dessert

Summer fruit jelly

Coffee and Chocolates

Coffee, decaffeinated coffee or tea
Chocolates

Afternoon Tea

In order that we may maximize your time for work or relaxation on today's flight we invite you to enjoy your afternoon tea at any time after lunch. Please make your selection from the buffet menu below and advise a member of the cabin crew when you wish to be served. Alternatively, the crew will serve you from the trolley approximately one and a half hours before landing.

Selection of sandwiches including crab salad, turkey and farmhouse Cheddar with cream cheese

or

Tortellini and vegetable salad with mustard vinaigrette

Sultana or muesli scone
Clotted cream and strawberry preserve

or

Fresh fruit tartlet

Coffee or tea

Fig. 13.15 In-flight menu

Sausages (Assorted)	33.5 tonnes	*Milk*	602,250 pints
Fresh Salmon	67.25 tonnes	*Double Cream*	46,397 pints
Fillet Steaks 4.5oz	9.75 tonnes	*Chocolate Boxes (Club)*	557,507 boxes of 2 chocs
Bacon	15 tonnes	*Bread Loaves*	20,930 leaves
New Zealand Lamb	125 tonnes	*Lettuce*	182,736 lettuce
Chicken Breasts	40.5 tonnes	*Melons*	38,950 melons
Carrots	75 tonnes	*Tomato Sauce*	9,552 bottles
Cream Cheese	3.5 tonnes	*Cornflakes*	77,150 pkts small
Live Lobsters	39 tonnes	*Tea*	1,983,240 bags
Frozen Lobster Meat	30 tonnes	*Fresh Eggs*	2,700,000 eggs
Prawns	31 tonnes	*Hard Boiled Eggs*	1,421,550 eggs
Caviar	6 tonnes	*Biscuits*	50,154 tins
Flour	65.5 tonnes	*Strawberry Jam*	274,464 portions
Sugar	10.5 tonnes	*Lemonade*	1,204,752 cans
Smoked Salmon	22 tonnes	*Coca Cola*	2,868,728 cans
Fresh Strawberries	44.5 tonnes	*Orange Juice*	1,101,400 cups
Fresh Tomatoes	126.5 tonnes	*Orange Juice*	170,000 litres

Fig. 13.16   Volumes of product used per year at a British Airways catering centre

Over the last few years there has been a move towards purchasing prepared and preprepared items; this is likely to accelerate in the future. A whole manufacturing industry has grown up around the supply of such products to other caterers. The advantage of using such products is that they provide greater cost control, reduce labour and processing costs, reduce hygiene costs and often give better standardisation, while giving the caterer greater flexibility in operations and purchasing power.

Some caterers still have their own bakery and pastry departments. Most buy in bread and bread rolls and therefore concentrate on sweets and pastries. Again the tendency is now towards purchasing preprepared sweets.

BASIC PREPARATION AREAS
Traditionally all fruit and vegetables were prepared on site. This is now not normally the practice as suppliers will produce high quality prepared cut vegetables and fruit for the airlines. Cut vegetables are available fresh vacuum-packed. Many caterers now purchase fruit baskets direct, cut fruit and freshly portioned cheese. There are a small number of specialist suppliers who manufacturer specially for in-flight caterers.

HOT PRODUCTION AREA
Food which has to be processed into hot dishes is produced in the hot kitchen area. This system is a variation of the traditional cook-chill system. This system is a catering system based on normal preparation and cooking of food with some modifications to assist in product stability and presentation. This is followed by rapid chilling, storage in controlled low temperature conditions above freezing point 0–3°C (32–37°F) and subsequently reheated on board the aircraft before consumption.

The purpose of chilling food is to prolong its storage life. Under normal temperature conditions, food deteriorates rapidly through the action of micro-organisms and enzymic and chemical reactions. Reduction in the storage temperature inhibits the multiplication of bacteria and slows down the chemical and enzymic reactions. It is generally accepted that even when high standards of fast chilling practice are used and consistently refrigerated storage is maintained, product quality may be acceptable for only a few days (including the day of production and consumption). The storage temperature is of extreme importance to ensure both full protection of food from microbiological growth and the maintenance of maximum nutritional values in the food.

The food once cooked and portioned will be rapidly cooled down to 0–3°C (32–37°F) and is stored between these temperatures throughout storage and distribution on to the aircraft. Food once cooked must be transferred to the blast chiller within 30 minutes. This reduces the risk of the food remaining at warm incubation temperatures and prevents the risk of contamination and loss of food quality.

Date code/colour code

This is a system by which the receiving, production, thawing, cooking or other significant date is encoded on potentially hazardous food supplies or meal components. The coding is primarily for the control of the growth of psychrophilic bacteria (bacteria that multiply in refrigeration) under refrigerated conditions. Either an open date code consisting of the day and month, or the standard In-flight Caterers' Association (IFCA) colour code should be used whenever a critical control point still exists for the food product.

The standard IFCA colour code is as follows:

- *Monday* – dark green
- *Tuesday* – brown
- *Wednesday* – yellow
- *Thursday* – orange
- *Friday* – light green
- *Saturday* – blue
- *Sunday* – red

FUTURE DEVELOPMENTS

The kitchen

The kitchen is a centre of creativity but it also creates much cost. The question is, how does the food and beverage manager get the cost of food preparation down to a level, or a percentage, which allows the profitable exploitation of the kitchen and the accompanying restaurant?

The answer is that the manager should know what it means to prepare traditional food in a modern, cost-saving way, making use of:

- modern cooking and regeneration equipment;
- new generations of high quality convenience-orientated, partly prepared food components;
- new working methods in the kitchen.

In a traditional kitchen, whole products are prepared from scratch. This means that:

- large storage rooms are needed for raw materials;
- storage rooms are needed for peeled/cooked preparations;
- numerous preparation rooms are needed for:
  - meat;
  - fish;
  - vegetables;
- various preparation tools are needed:
  - meat saw;
  - chopper;
  - vegetable peeler;
  - cutter;
- traditional cooking equipment is needed:
  - fry pan;
  - grill;
  - cooking pots;
  - deep fryer;
  - braising pan;
- large stove top is needed for a large team.

The chef

The food and beverage manager's biggest challenge will certainly be to convince the tradition-orientated chef that the time has come to adopt new economical ways of preparing food.

The chef will no longer mainly excel in preparing food, but he will spend more time on:

- selection of most suitable ingredients and meal components;
- menu development, recipes;
- controlling the correct cooking and regeneration procedures;
- organising the kitchen staff.

The chef/pastry chef thus becomes the production manager who:

- plans;
- organises;
- supervises;
- personalises.

Key questions

Will future employers be able to rely on their managers' know-how to organise or reorganise food and beverage systems which will contribute to the improved economical results needed and guarantee the quality level required?

For a regeneration-on-the-plate recipe, we have to answer the following questions:

- *Who* makes the recipe?
- *Which* recipe?
- *Where* – work area?
- *When* – 1, 2, 3 days ahead or the same day, in the morning, evening?
- *How* – with what type of products?
  with what type of equipment?
  with what type of technique?

Important points to follow:

- only regenerate what is needed;
- strictly follow recipes (measuring);
- produce at the right time;
- train the young chefs in this type of food preparation.

The assembly kitchen concept

Research – quality – production – tradition – innovation. This is a system based on accepting and incorporating latest technological development in manufacturing and conservation of food products. In the modern assembly kitchen, the chef does not automatically buy his ingredients. On the contrary, he will carefully choose from the 'five product types' (see page 494) what is best for him by asking himself:

- Which fresh produce will I use?
- Which semi-prepared food bases will I use?
- Which finished products will I use?

In their excellent book *Une Expérience : Le Piano à 5 Gammes*, Lionel Saunier and Pierre Labalette explain that by working in this way they manage 'to be innovative whilst respecting tradition'. Between *Escalope de saumon à l'oseille* served in the 'Restaurant de Frères Troisgros' and the *Escalope de saumon à l'oseille* 'ready-to-serve', there is the version assembly kitchen. It is the version *neo-traditionnelle*. It is a modern way of preparing food by chefs who believe in traditional quality but realise that this should be done by full exploitation of any technological progress made. It is here where culinary skills and organisational talent are married with new generations of food ingredients and kitchen equipment.

The assembly kitchen still relies on skilled personnel. For it requires a thorough understanding of how to switch over from the traditional labour-intensive

---

Saunier, L. and Labalette, P. Une expérience: le piano à 5 gammes.

production method to a more industrial type of production, with some of the principles of the cook-chill, cook-freeze or *sous-vide* production systems taken on board. It realises the existence and availability of modern kitchen equipment and new generations of high quality convenience orientated food bases.

Thus, the concept includes:

- preparing the food component in an appropriate kitchen, respecting the legislation;
- arranging everything cold (even raw) onto the plate;
- regenerating (even cooking) on the same plate as served;
- if necessary, serving the sauce.

Success requires:

- appropriate material and equipment;
- very precise preliminary preparations (mise en place);
- support by well trained team (kitchen + service staff).

Advantages include:

- less staff needed for arranging;
- the regeneration can be done near the consumer;
- different types of plates can be regenerated at the same time;
- hygiene and consequently safety is guaranteed;
- storage rooms only needed for 5 types of products (see page 494);
- large preparation areas disappear;
- smaller equipment is needed.

Inconveniences include:

- very hot plates;
- some additional investments (trolleys, etc.);
- some products cannot be prepared (French fries, etc.).

A planning schedule would envisage:

- 2 days
  - cooking and chilling;
  - storing at +3°C (37°F) in labelled, dated gastronorm containers.
- 12 hours
  - arrange food onto plates;
  - storage at +3°C (37°F) on trolley.
- 30 min
  - taking the trolley out of storage;
  - setting of regeneration equipment;
  - regeneration.
- 2 min
  - taking out and finishing of plates;
  - sauce, garnish;
  - serving;
  - cleaning of equipment.

The principal investments will be for:

- multi-purpose equipment which are covering most of the cooking methods;
- storage for dry, chilled, frozen products;
- equipment to chill or freeze;
- equipment to regenerate:
  - on plates;
  - gastronorm pans.

The new generation equipment must be:

- easy to handle;
- easy to clean;
- gastronorm;
- good service (maintenance).

The five types of products are:

1. FRESH (raw product):
   - meat with bones;
   - whole fish;
   - vegetables, potatoes, fruits, unpeeled;
   - milk.
2. SHELF-STABLE:
   - sterilised, pasteurised:
     - vegetables, potatoes, fruits;
     - dairy products, meat products.
   - dehydrated products, partly elaborated:
     - stocks, sauces;
     - bouillons, soups, purées;
     - mousses, creams, custards;
     - culinary aids.
3. FROZEN:
   - meat, fish, vegetables, potatoes, fruits;
   - pastry products, ice cream.
4. CHILLED ('Fresh' products, partly elaborated:)
   - meat or fish, boned, cut into pieces or portioned;
   - washed, peeled and cut vegetables, potatoes, fruits, etc.
5. CHILLED (products, normally cooked and packed or sous-vide):
   - meat, fish, vegetables, desserts (with or without sauce).

TOPICS FOR DISCUSSION

1. The advantages and disadvantages of cook-chill and cook-freeze system.
2. Essential hygiene and food safety requirements for cook-chill and cook-freeze systems.

3. The reason for quality control, temperature control, microbiological control when producing cook-chill and cook-freeze foods.
4. Types of operation suitable for using cook-chill and cook-freeze foods.
5. For and against a centralised production system with examples.
6. The ohmic food production system and its main advantages.
7. The principles of in-flight catering.
8. Catering on board the trains travelling through the Channel Tunnel.

14

Computers in catering

—

WHY USE COMPUTERS?

It is true to say that the majority of the general public do not associate the use of computers (applied information technology) with the provision of food and beverages. Nevertheless, like any other well-run business caterers cannot afford to ignore the many advantages which the developments in information technology has made possible in the efficient and effective operation of their business. This chapter gives an overview of just some of the areas where information technology can help the caterer.

Before looking at how information technology can help caterers we should be aware of some of the developments which have brought us to the current situation. Today it is generally forgotten that a catering company, J. Lyons & Co., were the first commercial users of computing in the United Kingdom when they developed Lyons Electronic Office (or LEO). This was used to help in the administration of their large hotel and catering business in 1954. Since those days there has been a major technical revolution which has seen the size and price of computers fall as dramatically as the available computing power, reliability and ease of use has risen.

Today cheap and powerful computers are within the reach of even the smallest business. Complete computer packages designed especially for the caterer are readily available over a wide price range and general-purpose systems are now much easier to use and set up. These systems allow the caterer to solve a range of business problems and assist in planning and forecasting developments.

It should be noted that the most valuable commodity for any business is reliable up-to-date information, hence the need for computers and their information storage and manipulation.

A computer system consists of hardware and software. Hardware is the name given to the physical equipment which is used to enter, record and process data and to extract information. Software is the name given to the instructions (or programs) which carry out the tasks we wish the system to perform.

SOFTWARE

Software is simply a set of instructions written in a language which the computer understands. There are two principal types of software: system software and application software.

System software

Operating systems together with the type of processor fitted give compatibility from computer to computer. The operating system must be compatible with the technical design of the computer and the application software you wish to use. Modern operating systems require powerful computers and large memories but are relatively easy to use and have a great range of facilities.

The most popular type of operating system found in the catering industry at the present time is called MS/DOS; this may also be fitted with a graphical user interface (for use with a mouse as an input device) known as Windows. Another operating system coming into more widespread use is called UNIX. This requires more power than either MS/DOS by itself or MS/DOS with Windows but is more powerful for large intensive applications.

Generally when you first switch on the computer you are presented with the operating system and from here you will launch the desired application.

Application software

This is the software which performs the task(s) we want the computer to undertake, for example a stock control or payroll system. System software is the software which controls the way in which the system performs the tasks required of it. The most common type of system software with which the end-user comes into contact is the Operating System. Both types of software must be present in the computer before you can carry out applications.

Computers can carry out almost any task requiring the processing of data, but through good programming they can be an effective source of operating and management information. The range of applications available is very large but some of the most common applications found in catering are as follows.

ELECTRONIC POINT OF SALE SYSTEMS (EPOS)
These are systems which take the place of the traditional cash register. At the

Fig. 14.1   Using EPOS in a bar of a large conference centre

simplest level they take the form of a single cash register with a CPU and memory; these offer greatly enhanced facilities over a traditional cash register.

Typical facilities offered include multiple total storing to enable sales to be analysed as required by the end-user: price look-up, which enables the user to press a key labelled with the name of a dish or a drink and the correct price will be added to the transaction, and multi-level pricing, to cope with special offers or 'happy hour' arrangements.

More sophisticated systems offer a large range of features and usually feature a number of machines linked together in restaurants and bars and also to a central computer. These large systems offer an extremely sophisticated control process which reduces work for the staff and supplies detailed information about the business to the management. For example, orders keyed in by the bar staff when a guest arrives in a restaurant may be transferred to the restaurant account giving the guest one consolidated account at the end of the meal. Waiting staff entering the guest's order, possibly via a touch screen terminal, into the system will find that it will automatically print out in the correct department, saving a great deal of time and work. As this process proceeds, the guest account is automatically prepared ready for presentation at the end of the meal.

With this type of system all orders to kitchen and bars are printed and show the time the order was processed, thus ensuring that errors and arguments between staff due to badly hand-written checks and excessive delay are avoided. Because the account is developed by the system as the meal progresses, there is no danger that items will be omitted from the bill or items will be incorrectly charged which not infrequently happens with a manual system.

Management reports are very comprehensive giving such details as sales of analysis of each dish or drink item and sales made by each member of staff. Sales breakdown by each outlet, by each member of staff and for each session are also easy to obtain. Most systems will also give the profit on each item sold and may be linked to stock control systems. When waiting staff are responsible for their own guest bills then the system will not allow them to log off until all accounts are cleared and the cash paid into a central point.

Information of this type, intelligently used, can assist the management to ensure that the business operates to maximum effectiveness.

STOCK CONTROL SYSTEMS

At the simplest level these systems allow the user to enter stock received and issued, extract details of consumption and calculate the value of stock in hand. More sophisticated systems provide these basic facilities plus a considerable range of other features such as details of suppliers, automatic issue of orders when stocks drop to a predefined level, detailed records of issues and current prices of all stock items.

Stock control is relatively easy to operate on bar stock but dealing with food items, especially fresh foods is far more complex as food items are rarely used in the quantities in which they are supplied, and there is a wide range of measurements in use which require accurate conversion tables. There is also the need to deal effectively with wastage.

If we take the relatively simple stock item of fresh eggs, these may be supplied by the dozen, or a multiple of a dozen, or by the case, or multiple or fraction of a case, or in some cases by the tray, or multiple of a tray. They may be used in recipes as single eggs or by weight in ounces, or grams, or by volume, by the fluid ounce, or by the pint, or litre. This may be further compounded by recipes calling for just egg yolk or egg white or by different quantities of each. Further complications may be made by the use of pasteurised egg and dried egg in certain recipes.

FOOD AND BEVERAGE MANAGEMENT SYSTEMS

Food and beverage management systems take the concept of stock control one stage further. They add a control framework which, when correctly implemented, gives greatly improved levels of management control. With this type of system a database is created of all recipes in use in the business, together with a further database containing the ingredients used to support those dishes.

Typical information stored about each ingredient is:

- Ingredient code
- Ingredient name
- Ingredient description
- Category
- Purchase unit
- Unit of use
- Unit of measure

- Content Weight
- Price
- Supplier
- Tax rate
- Shelf life
- Re-order level
- Percentage usable

Typical information stored about each recipe is:

- Recipe code
- Quantity of production
- Selling Unit
- Tax Code
- Reorder level

- For each ingredient in recipe:
  - Ingredient code
  - Ingredient amount
  - Ingredient unit of measure
- Profit required (%)

Many systems also allow for some descriptive narrative for each recipe.

With this information as a base it is possible for kitchen staff to order goods from the stores by recipe and to automatically scale for the quantity required and effectively cost those dishes. The system will then give the required selling price to achieve the required profit.

Food and beverage management systems, because of their cost and complexity, still tend to be used by large-scale users, particularly where tight control of costs and adherence to preset budgets is important, for example large production cook-chill units and hospitals. Add-on modules allow for cyclic menus and nutritional analysis; one supplier even has a module for controlling the costs in the training kitchens of catering colleges!

Comprehensive reporting is offered which give a high level of management information and thus control. For example it is easy to check purchase levels and to track high-cost ingredients. These systems are frequently being linked to point-of-sale systems to take the control process one stage further.

MENU ENGINEERING

This is a technique, originally developed in the USA, which takes data about sales volume, costs and profits of each dish on the menu. By changing the ratio of the areas it is possible, in theory, to create a menu offering the optimum balance between popularity and maximum profit. The technique can be carried out with pencil and paper but it is far more effective when the data is entered into a computer system. Over a period of time it is then possible to develop a 'computer model' of all dishes on the menu which can be referred to time after time simply by updating the variable details in light of known facts.

DIETARY ANALYSIS

This is another requirement which can be carried out without the support of a computer but is very much more effective with computer support. As we become more selective about what we eat, customers require more dietary information about the dishes on our menus. Dietary analysis works from large databases of dietary information and will give details of the composition of foods or dishes at the touch of a button. Again there is a range of systems available, from systems which give a relatively crude breakdown, to systems which are linked to government food tables and give extremely accurate and comprehensive data.

Dietary analysis systems may be 'stand-alone' or integrated to food and beverage management systems.

Generic software

This is the term we give to software which we use to support the operation of a business but which does not have a specific purpose. The most common types found in the catering industry are: word processing, spreadsheets and databases. When buying business PCs these systems are often supplied with the computer as added-value items. When they are purchased separately, a wide range of price and facilities is available. Most modern packages operate within a Windows graphic environment.

WORD PROCESSING

At the most basic level this package replaces the traditional typewriter for the production of printed material. It is probably the most widely used type of computer software within a business environment. In addition to the production of business letters, memos and reports, today's word processors, which offer a wide range of typestyles and sizes of type, are ideal for the production of menus. For this purpose the business will require a high quality printer but the costs will soon be recovered when set against the traditional costs of printing. Prior to the introduction of the word processor, the caterer was faced with the problem of ordering large quantities of printed menu cards, which were necessary to obtain an effective price, but which created problems with pricing or menu changes; prices were often written in by hand or altered as the costs of ingredients changed.

SPREADSHEETS

A spreadsheet package is used primarily to deal with numerical data. A typical system available today will also allow the user to sort information and present the information contained in the system in a graphic format. Unlike a word processor which is ready for immediate use when loaded, the spreadsheet requires the user to first design a worksheet to hold the data.

At the most basic level a spreadsheet worksheet consists of a table of columns (which are vertical) and rows (which are horizontal). Where each column and row intersect a cell is formed. A cell may contain a number (value), or a label (text) to identify the number, or a calculation (formula) which is based on the contents of the value cells. A typical worksheet will contain in excess of 2 million cells, usually only a fraction of which are used, the screen acting as a window on just a small portion of the worksheet at any given time.

Prior to use a blank worksheet is designed to hold labels, values and formulae in the required places. Variable data may then be entered as they are collected from information provided by the business. This enables very efficient models to be built up over a period of time. If the current worksheet is changed, many different tasks may be carried out. The range of uses is endless and the systems are extremely flexible. For example, it is relatively easy for a novice user to design a worksheet to deal with the costing of recipes or projected cash flow (which may of course be compared with actual cash flow in due course).

DATABASE MANAGEMENT SYSTEMS

A computer will hold any data which the user wishes to place into it; however, without an easy means of manipulation the process is time-consuming and unfriendly. It is perhaps easier to think of a database file as a computerised filing cabinet; the management software will then allow us to structure the way in which the data is stored and makes it relatively easy to retrieve exactly the information required.

When you use a database for the first time, it is necessary to design the structure in which to place the required data. A few years ago this was restricted in almost all systems to text, but many systems available today will allow the storage of graphics, digitised photographs, video images and sound. Once we have constructed the structure of the database file, it is simply a matter of entering the data. By loading different database files we can use a database management system for many different applications.

Most commercial applications such as food and beverage management systems are built around the database concept. Simple databases, which an end-user may wish to design and use, could be stock control, especially for dry goods, and inventory use and personnel systems.

CHOOSING A COMPUTER

As already discussed computers are less expensive and more powerful than ever before; however, they are still relatively expensive pieces of equipment and if we choose incorrectly a great deal of time and effort will be wasted. In fact the costs involved in setting up and running the computer will be far more expensive than the purchase price.

Many people have produced complete books on the topic of choosing a business computer. This small section relates only to IBM-compatible PCs and only attempts to alert you to some of the issues involved.

The first task is to identify the areas of the business which could potentially benefit from computerisation. Remember that computers are good at repetitious tasks with large volumes of data to process. They can provide information to help you make effective decisions but they cannot in themselves take decisions for you.

At this stage it will be necessary to undertake a feasibility study of the existing task(s) involved to identify exactly what happens and what volume of activity takes place. On reviewing this process it may prove that you only need to revise the existing system and that a computer is not strictly necessary.

If the decision is to go ahead then you must identify what information the system must provide. From this it is fairly easy to identify what data must go into the system to give that information as output. Once you have identified these features together with volume and critical operational constraints such as speed, types of printer and methods of output, you are ready to go shopping.

Software

As it is the software which will actually carry out the task required it is best to look at this area first. Apart from a detailed check list drawn up from the above information a purchaser will need to consider the following issues:

- Does the software cover all the major requirements of the specification?
- What hardware configuration is required?
- Is special supporting equipment or software required?
- How well does it meet the detailed requirements of the specification?
- What arethe performance standards?
- What level of customisation is possible?
- Is the product supported by regular updates? What are the costs of this?
- How easy is it to use?
- What level of support is available?
- Are you satisfied with the supplier?
- Financial arrangements available?

Hardware

Whilst the hardware must at minimum be capable of running the required software, you should spend as much as possible on the processor both and internal (RAM) and external (hard disk) memory. Memory especially is reasonably cheap if specified at the time of purchase. Software is becoming more hungry for space with every upgrade or development and a system running at capacity is generally unhappy and will give problems in operation.

The following gives some of the areas a prospective purchaser will need to consider:

- Speed of performance
- Capacity
- Physical size and space requirements
- Expandability
- Compatibility
- Reliability
- Ease of use/ergonomics
- Operating costs
- Maintenance Support

Sources of supply

If you simply need a system for general office using generic business software, then it may appear cost-effective to purchase from the direct mail suppliers who advertise in most computing magazines or from one of the large warehouses or high street shops. Through large buying capacity, they are often able to offer attractive deals. Some caution is required, however, as generally a level of preknowledge is expected, if not implied, and levels of user-support may be more in line with the needs of a home-user than that of a business relying on the systems.

In most cases a specialist dealer/distributor will offer a higher level of support but, of course, at a cost. If you are a new user it is often much more cost-effective in the long term to build up a relationship with a good local dealer who will get to know your needs and can offer good, although not impartial, advice.

Most catering information technology (IT) systems are supplied by specialist companies. Again although not offering impartial advice they will be only too happy to discuss your specification and advise accordingly. Most suppliers provide a complete service including hardware, software, installation and training. Prices, facilities and range of services provided vary widely and it is essential to shop around. In most cases with these large systems once the decision is made, you are committed to the company for the life of the system, so it is important that all factors are taken into account.

For impartial advice it is possible to use the services of a consultant. Consultants will investigate possible solutions for a specific problem or task, then will offer a number of systems for the establishment to choose. It is important to bear two things in mind when dealing with consultants:

- they must be impartial, that is not taking commission from hardware or software suppliers;
- the final choice of system will be left to the establishment.

Consultants can be extremely useful but do not make up for a lack of knowledge of information technology and of its application to a business.

USING COMPUTERS

Much of this chapter has looked at the types of computer systems available to the caterer and also at issues which need to be considered prior to selection and purchase. Once the systems have been selected and purchased, however, the business will need to ensure the maximum effectiveness from its investment. A computer system must give a competitive edge; no matter how well chosen, this will only happen if the systems are correctly implemented and operated.

Many of the concerns of operating computers will of course rest with the management of the business but it is also important that operatives of all grades understand their contribution to the effective operation of the system. For example, a stock control system will not give the correct information in reports if the storekeeper is careless when entering delivery notes and invoices. The management will therefore ensure that members of staff using the systems or preparing data for entry to the systems are correctly trained, that working conditions are comfortable and comply with legislation and that regular monitoring of system performance takes place.

Organisational structure

In large catering businesses, especially large hotels, there may be a member of the management team, usually known as the Systems Manager, with responsibility for the operation of all IT systems within the business. The Systems Manager will probably report to the General Manager or Chief Accountant so this role is usually at head of department level. The Manager must understand the operation of the business very thoroughly and have a good all round knowledge of applied IT. In addition to being responsible for the smooth operation of the IT systems on a day-to-day basis, the Systems Manager will also be responsible for updating of systems,

Fig. 14.2   The back office computer system of a large hotel

the IT training of new and existing staff and compliance with all relevant legislation. In smaller businesses these responsibilities will usually be taken over by the manager or owner of the business or by an assistant manager or department head.

Legislation

This is an area which is rapidly expanding reflecting the increase in use of IT and the need to offer legal protection to suppliers, users and people on whom data is held in computers.

There are two principal pieces of legislation which have a major impact on the way that information technology is used in businesses:

Firstly the **Data Protection Act** of 1984 defines eight basic principles which must be followed if anyone wishes to store data about living identifiable individuals on a computer system. It gives the person whose data is stored right of access to that data and lays down principles for secure storage of that data.

The other major concern for caterers is the **Screen Display (VDU) Regulations** of 1992; these regulations lay down very strict guidelines about the way computers are operated and the environment in which they are operated. For example, there should not be glare from windows or artificial light and the working environment must be ergonomically correct to ensure that there are no long-term health hazards for staff using the systems. The legislation also covers the actual design of the appearance of the software on the screen and states that training must take place on a regular basis. It also covers issues in respect of extended use by an operative.

There is also legislation in force to protect the copyright of the software supplier, the **Copyright Design and Patent Act** of 1989; amongst its provisions this law makes it an offence to buy a piece of software and load it on more than one machine without additional payment. There is also the **Computer Misuse Act** of 1990. This act makes it a criminal offence to access a computer without permission or to corrupt data stored in a computer.

SUMMARY

In this chapter we have seen how computers have a long tradition of use within catering and how the reducing costs and increasing power and reliability of computers is seeing a massive uptake of use within catering businesses. We have also seen how it is necessary to ensure that applied information technology is used correctly to ensure that the maximum benefit is derived by the business.

Computing is a fast advancing area of technology and it is perhaps unwise to look too far into the future where these developments may take us. It seems certain that the increasing tendency to integrate computer systems will lead to a single point of data capture and more effective use of data. The increasing use of computers as communication links, for example to external suppliers using electronic data exchange, will also have a significant impact over the next few years.

Whatever the future holds it is vital that caterers, whatever the size of their business, make use of applied information technology if they wish to remain effective and gain a lead over their competitors.

TOPICS FOR DISCUSSION

1. Identify the basic elements of a computing system. What purpose does each of the elements serve?
2. A hospitality establishment has need for printed output from its computer system. What type of printer should it select for:
    *   high quality menu printing;
    *   order printing in the kitchen;
    *   order printing in the restaurant.
    Why are these needs different?
3. There are many ways of entering information into a computer. Identify three methods of input which would be suitable for use in different types of catering computing system and give examples of their use.
4. Word processing, spreadsheet and database are three types of standard business software packages which are frequently used within the hospitality industry. Give one use of each software package within a catering business.
5. Identify three software packages which are unique to the hospitality industry. Discuss how the use of one of these packages could give a caterer an advantage over a competitor without access to a similar system.

Part

4

LEGISLATION AND THE CATERER

15

Health and safety at work

—

The dual responsibility of employers and employees at work is to ensure that the premises and equipment are safe and that they are kept safe so as to prevent accidents. Employers need to assess any hazards or risks and organise procedures to deal with any accidents. Employees, full-time, part-time or temporary, need to be trained to prevent accidents, to report hazards and to comply with instructions intended to reduce risks.

Safety signs are used to inform all persons using an establishment in order to prevent accidents or what to do in the event of an accident.

CONTROL OF SUBSTANCES HAZARDOUS TO HEALTH (COSHH)

Substances dangerous to health are labelled **very toxic, toxic harmful, irritant** or **corrosive.** Whilst only a small number of such chemicals are used in catering for cleaning, it is necessary to be aware of the regulations introduced in 1989 and to know of the symbols used on products.

Principles

Those persons using such substances must be made aware of their correct use and proper dilution where appropriate, and must wear protection: goggles, gloves and face masks as appropriate. Eye goggles should be worn when using oven cleaners, gloves when hands may come into contact with any chemical cleaner and face masks when using grease cutting and oven degreasers.

It is essential that staff are trained to take precautions and not to take risks. What does COSHH require? The basic principles of occupational hygiene underlie the COSHH Regulations:

- Assess the risk to health arising from work and what precautions are needed.
- Introduce appropriate measures to prevent or control the risk.
- Ensure that control measures are used and that equipment is properly maintained and procedures observed.
- Where necessary, monitor the exposure of the workers and carry out an appropriate form of surveillance of their health.
- Inform, instruct and train employees about the risks and the precautions to be taken.

Rules of using chemicals

- Always follow makers' instructions.
- Always store in original containers. Decanting a chemical means you may lose its name and classification.
- Keep lids tightly closed.
- Do not store in direct sunlight, near heat or naked flames.
- Read the labels. Know the product and its risk.
- Never mix chemicals.
- Know the first-aid procedure.
- Always add product to water, not water to product.
- Dispose of empty drums immediately.
- Dispose of waste chemical solutions safely.
- Wear the correct safety equipment.

LEGISLATION

Every year in the UK a thousand people are killed at work; a million people suffer injuries; and 23 million working days are lost annually because of industrial injury and disease. As catering is one of the largest employers of labour the catering industry is substantially affected by accidents at work.

In 1974 the *Health and Safety at Work Act* was passed with two main aims:

- to extend the coverage and protection of the law to all employers and employees;
- to increase awareness of safety amongst those at work, both employers and employees.

The law imposes a general duty on an employer 'to ensure so far as is reasonably practicable, the health, safety and welfare at work of all his employees'. The law also imposes a duty on every employee while at work to:

- take reasonable care for the health and safety of himself or herself and of other persons who may be affected by his or her acts or omissions at work;
- co-operate with his or her employer so far as is necessary to meet or comply with any requirement concerning health and safety;
- not interfere with, or misuse, anything provided in the interests of health, safety or welfare.

It can be clearly seen that both health and safety at work is everybody's responsibility.

Furthermore the Act protects the members of the public who may be affected by the activities of those at work.

Penalties are provided by the Act which include improvement notices, prohibition notices and criminal prosecution. The Health and Safety Executive has been set up to enforce the law and the Health and Safety Commission will issue codes of conduct and act as advisers.

Responsibilities of the employer

The employer's responsibilities are to:

- provide and maintain premises and equipment that are safe and without risk to health;
- provide supervision, information and training;
- issue a written statement of 'safety policy' to employees to include:
  - general policy with respect to health and safety at work of employees;
  - the organisation, to ensure the policy is carried out;
  - how the policy will be made effective.
- consult with the employees' safety representative and to establish a Safety Committee.

SAFETY REGULATIONS

As from 1993 six health and safety at work regulations have come into force.

- *Management of Health and Safety at Work Regulations 1992*
  - risk assessment;
  - control of hazardous substances;
  - training.
- *Work Place (Health, Safety and Welfare) Regulations 1992*
  - floors to be of suitable construction;
  - floors free from hazardous articles or substances;
  - steps taken to avoid slips, trips and falls.
- *Manual Handling Operation Regulations 1992*
  - reducing incorrect handling of loads;
  - preventing hazardous handling.
- *Fire Precautions in Places of Work*
  - means of fire fighting;
  - evacuation procedures;
  - raising the alarm.
- *Provision and Use of Work Equipment*
  - ensure correct usage;
  - properly maintained;
  - training given.
- *Health and Safety (Display Screen Equipment)*
  - to see that staff using visual display units have suitable work place and take regular breaks.

Risk assessment and reduction

Prevention of accidents and preventing food poisoning in catering establishments is essential, therefore it is necessary to assess the situation and decide what action is to be taken. Risk assessment can be divided into four areas:

- Minimal risk – safe conditions with safety measures in place.
- Some risk – acceptable risk, however attention must be given to ensure safety measures operate.
- Significant risk – where safety measures are not fully in operation (also includes food most likely to cause food poisoning). Requires immediate action.
- Dangerous risk – operations of process or equipment to stop immediately. The system of equipment to be completely checked and recommended after clearance.

To operate and assessment of risks the following points should be considered:

- Assess the risks.
- Determine preventative measures.
- Decide who carries our safety inspections.
- Decide frequency of inspection.
- Determine methods of reporting back and to whom.
- Detail how to ensure inspections are effective.
- See that on the job training in safety is related to the job.

The purpose of the exercise of assessing the possibility of risks and hazards is to prevent accidents. Firstly it is necessary to monitor the situations, to have regular and spasmodic checks to see that standards set are being complied with. However, should an incident or incidences occur, it is essential that an investigation is made as to the cause or causes and any defects in the system remedied at once. Immediate action is required to prevent further accidents. All personnel need to be trained to be actively aware of the possible hazards and risks and to take positive action to prevent accidents occurring.

The work place

The highest number of accidents occurring in catering premises are due to persons falling, slipping or tripping. Therefore, floor surfaces must be of a suitable construction to reduce this risk. A major reason for the high incidence of this kind of accident is that water and grease are likely to be spilt and the combination of these substances is treacherous and makes the floor surface slippery. For this reason any spillage must be cleaned immediately and warning notices put in place, where appropriate, stating the danger of slippery surface. Ideally a member of staff should stand guard until the hazard is cleared.

Another cause of falls is the placing of articles on the floor in corridors, passageways or between stoves and tables. Persons carry trays and containers have their vision obstructed and items on the floor may not be visible; the fall may occur onto a hot stove and the item being carried may be hot. These falls can have very bad consequences.

The solution is to ensure that nothing is left on the floor which may cause a hazard. If it is necessary to have articles temporarily on the floor, then it is desirable that they are guarded so as to prevent accidents.

Kitchen personnel should be trained to think and act in a safe manner so as to avoid this kind of accident.

Manual handling

The incorrect handling of heavy and awkward loads causes accidents and staff can be off work for some time. How to lift heavy items the correct way is illustrated in Figure 15.1. The safer way to lift items is to bend at the knees rather than bend the back. Strain and damage can be reduced if two people do the lifting rather that one person.

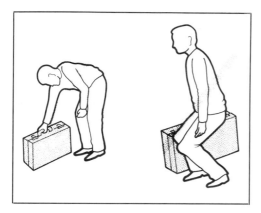

Fig. 15.1   How to lift correctly

When goods are moved on trolleys, trucks or any wheeled vehicles, they should be loaded carefully (not overloaded) and in a manner which enables the handler to see where they are going.

It is essential that heavy items are stacked at the bottom and that steps are used with care.

Particular care is needed when large pots are moved containing liquid, especially hot liquid. They should not be filled to the brim.

Warning that equipment handles, lids etc., can be hot, should be indicated by a small sprinkle of flour or something similar.

Extra care is needed when taking trays from ovens or salamanders so that the tray does not burn someone else.

Provision and use of work equipment

Equipment selected for use must be suitable for what it is intended. It should be of the right capacity and be sited conveniently and safely. All equipment must be properly maintained and staff using it must receive training with regards to correct usage and the safety measures which need to be taken.

Equipment must conform to EU safety directive. Since 1 January 1995, British Standards have been combined with European Standards and equipment must carry the CE mark indicating that the required safety standards are met.

PERSONAL PROTECTIVE EQUIPMENT

Due to the hazardous nature of some of the work in the kitchens, it is necessary to assess the risks to employees. Provision of protective clothing and footwear, properly maintained, is essential to safety. Suitable storage, such as lockers, needs to be available for the storage of personal clothing.

Items such as oven cloths and heat-proof gloves need to be provided and maintained or replaced so that they are safe to use.

First-aid equipment must be readily available and replenished when necessary. There must be one trained first-aider for every 50 employees.

KITCHEN EQUIPMENT

All equipment should be safe and used correctly, properly maintained and not misused.

- Tables must be strong, easily cleaned for hygiene reasons and never sat on.
- Bratt pans and tilting pans should not be able to be accidently tilted.
- Fat fryers must not have thermostats tampered with and must never be overfilled.
- Step ladders should only be used for reaching items stored on high shelves, not for standing on boxes or a chair.
- Electrical equipment must have special attention particularly those listed under Dangerous Machines Order 1964:
  - worm type mincing machines
  - rotary bowl choppers;
  - mixing machines;
  - slicing, shredding machines;
  - chipping, chopping machines.

  Only trained and over 18-year-olds are allowed to use and clean such machines and warning signs and instruction in their use must be sited by the machine.
- Gas equipment must have instructions for igniting any piece of gas equipment and these should be followed. In the event of a gas leak or problems with pilot lights, maintenance personnel or the gas equipment suppliers should be contacted immediately.
- Maintenance should be regular to ensure correct function and safety of all gas and electrical equipment. This includes checking seals on microwave ovens.
- Extraction system should function correctly and particular care is needed to see that it is regularly cleaned as fat is liable to accumulate.
- Walk in refrigerators and deep freezers must have a door operable from the inside.
- Records of staff trained in the use of equipment and records of maintenance need to be kept.

DISPLAY SCREEN EQUIPMENT

Persons using VDU (Visual Display Units) must operate in suitable conditions so as to reduce strain. Such units should be situated so that the working conditions are good, well ventilated, comfortable with good seating. Regular breaks are essential so as to reduce eye strain, and eye tests given and spectacles should be provided if needed.

Staff facilities and welfare

The welfare of all employees at a place of work is the responsibility of the employee. Facilities should be provided that are both safe and beneficial and include:

- sufficient working space (minimum 11 cubic metres (14.4 cubic yards) per person);
- easy evacuation in an emergency;
- floors and exit routes non-slip and in good repair;
- proper ventilation;
- temperature comfortable (normally 16°C (61°F) never below 13°C (55°F) except when foods are to be kept cold); kitchen temperature will be above normal;
- system of maintenance put into practice;
- system of cleaning in operation;
- quick disposal of waste, so that is does not accumulate;
- safe and non-obstructed, loading and unloading bays;
- provision of adequate toilets, working facilities, drinking water;
- changing facilities and accommodation for outdoor clothes, separate for men and women;
- provision of a rest room, to include a non-smoking area.

Enforcement of legislation

Health and safety inspectors and local authority inspectors (Environmental Health Officers) have the authority to enforce legal requirements. They are empowered to:

- issue a prohibition notice which immediately prevents further business until remedial action has been taken;
- issue an improvement notice whereby action must be taken within a stated time, to an employee, employer or supplier;
- prosecute any person breaking the Act; this can be instead of or in addition to serving a notice and may lead to a substantial fine or prison;
- seize, render harmless or destroy anything that the inspector considers to be the cause of imminent danger.

ENVIRONMENTAL HEALTH OFFICERS

The Environmental Health Officer has two main functions: one is to enforce the law; the other aspect of the job is to act as an adviser and educator in the areas of food hygiene and catering premises. Here his or her function is to improve the existing standard of hygiene and to advise how this may be achieved. Frequently health education programmes are organised by Environmental Health Officers which may include talks and free literature. If in doubt about any matter concerning food hygiene, pests, premises or legal aspects the Environmental Health Officer is there to be consulted.

ACCIDENTS

It is essential that people working in the kitchen are capable of using the tools and equipment in a manner which will neither harm themselves nor those with whom they work. Moreover, they should be aware of the causes of accidents and be able to deal with any which occur.

Accidents may be caused in various ways:

- excessive haste – the golden rule of the kitchen is 'never run'; This may be difficult to observe during a very busy service but excessive haste causes people to take chances which inevitably lead to mishaps;
- distraction – accidents may be caused by not concentrating on the job in hand, through lack of interest, personal worry or distraction by someone else; the mind must always be kept on the work so as to reduce the number of accidents;
- failure to apply safety rules.

Reporting accidents

Any accident occurring on the premises where the employee works must be reported to the employer and a record of the accident must be entered in the Accident Book.

Any accident causing death or major injury to an employee or member of the public must be reported by the employer to the Environmental Health Department. Accidents involving dangerous equipment must also be reported even if no one is injured (Figure 15.2).

Accident prevention

It is the responsibility of everyone to observe the safety rules; in this way a great deal of pain and loss of time can be avoided.

PREVENTION OF CUTS AND SCRATCHES

Knives

These should never be misused and the following rules should always be observed:

- The correct knife should be used for the appropriate job.
- Knives must always be sharp and clean; a blunt knife is more likely to cause a cut because excessive pressure has to be used.
- Handles should be free from grease.
- The points must be held downwards.
- Knives should be placed flat on the board or table so that the blade is not exposed upwards.
- Knives should be wiped clean with the edge away from the hands.
- Do not put knives in a washing-up sink.

Choppers

These should be kept sharp and clean. Care should be taken that no other knives, saws, hooks etc., can be struck by the chopper, which could cause them to fly into the air. This also applies when using a large knife for chopping.

Cutting blades on machines

Guards should always be in place when the machine is in use; they should not be

Full name of injured person:			
Occupation:		Supervisor:	
Time of accident:	Date of accident:	Time of report:	Date of report:
Nature of injury or condition:			
Details of hospitalisation:			
Extent of injury (after medical attention):			
Place of accident or dangerous occurrence:			
Injured person's evidence of what happened (include equipment/items/or other persons): Use separate sheets if necessary			
Witness evidence (1):		Witness evidence (2):	
Supervisor's recommendations:			
Date:	Supervisor's signature: This form must be sent to the company health and safety officer		

Fig. 15.2   Sample in-house record of accidents and dangerous occurrences

tampered with nor should hands or fingers be inserted past the guards. Before the guards are removed for cleaning, the blade or blades must have stopped revolving.

When the guard is removed for cleaning, the blade should not be left unattended in case someone should put a hand on it by accident. If the machine is electrically operated the plug should, when possible, be removed.

Cuts from meat and fish bones
Jagged bones can cause cuts which may turn septic, particularly fish bones and the bones of a calf's head which has been opened to remove the brain. Cuts of this nature, however slight, should never be neglected. Frozen meat should not be boned out until it is completely thawed out because it is difficult to handle, the hands become very cold and the knife slips easily.

PREVENTION OF BURNS AND SCALDS
A burn is caused by dry heat and a scald by wet heat. Both burns and scalds can be

Fig. 15.3 Heat- and flame-resistant kitchen apparel

very painful and have serious effects, so certain precautions should be taken to prevent them:

- Sleeves of jackets and overalls should be rolled down and aprons worn at a sensible length so as to give adequate protection.
- A good, thick dry cloth or gloves are most important for handling hot utensils (Figure 15.3). It should never be used wet on hot objects and is best folded to give greater protection. It should not be used if thin, torn or with holes.
- Trays containing hot liquid, such as roast gravy, should be handled carefully, one hand on the side and the other on the end of the tray so as to balance it.
- Hot pans brought out of the oven should have something white, such as a little flour, placed on the handle and lid as a warning that it is hot. This should be done as soon as the pan is taken out of the oven.
- Handles of pans should not protrude over the edge of the stove as the pan may be knocked off the stove.
- Large full pans should be carried correctly: when there is only one handle the forearm should run along the full length of the handle and the other hand should be used to balance the pan where the handle joins the pan. This should prevent the contents from spilling.

- Certain foods require extra care when heat is applied to them, as for example when a cold liquid is added to a hot roux or when adding cold water to boiling sugar for making caramel. Extra care should always be taken when boiling sugar.
- Frying, especially deep frying, needs careful attention. When shallow or deep frying fish, for example, put the fish into the pan away from the person so that any splashes will do no harm. With deep frying, fritures should be moved with care and if possible only when the fat is cool. Fritures should not be more than two-thirds full. Wet foods should be drained and dried before being placed in the fat, and when foods are tipped out of the frying basket a spider should be at hand. Should the fat in the friture bubble over on to a gas stove then the gas taps should be turned off immediately. Fire blankets and fire extinguishers should be provided in every kitchen, conveniently sited ready for use.
- Steam causes scalds just as hot liquids do. It is important to be certain that before steamers are opened the steam is turned off and that when the steamer door is opened no one is in the way of the escaping steam. The steamer should be in proper working condition; the drain hole should always be clear. The door should not be opened immediately the steam is turned off; it is better to wait for about half a minute before doing so.
- Scalds can also be caused by splashing when passing liquids through conical strainers; it is wise to keep the face well back so as to avoid getting splashed. This also applies when hot liquids are poured into containers.

MACHINERY

Accidents are easily caused by misuse of machines. The following rules should always be put into practice:

- The machine should be in correct running order before use.
- The controls of the machine should be operated by the person using the machine. If two people are involved there is the danger that a misunderstanding can occur and the machine be switched on when the other person does not expect it.
- Machine attachments should be correctly assembled and only the correct tools used to force food through mincers.
- When mixing machines are being used the hands should not be placed inside the bowl until the blades, whisk or hook have stopped revolving. Failure to observe this rule may result in a broken arm or severe cut.
- Plugs should be removed from electric machines when they are being cleaned so they cannot be accidentally switched on.

GAS EXPLOSIONS

The risk of explosion from gas is considerable. To avoid this occurring it is necessary to ensure that the gas is properly lit. On ranges with a pilot on the oven it is important to see that the main jet has ignited from the pilot. If the regulo is low, sometimes the gas does not light at once; the gas collects and an explosion occurs. When lighting the tops of solid-top ranges it is wise to place the centre ring back for a few minutes after the stove is lit because the gas may go out; gas then collects and an explosion can occur.

KITCHEN EQUIPMENT

On 1st January 1996 a significant European Union directive concerning the design and installation of **gas-fuelled catering equipment** becomes mandatory. All gas appliances sold after that date, new or secondhand, must be fitted with a fuel cut-out mechanism should the main pilot light be extinguished. Equipment will be withdrawn from the market place if it does not comply. This gas directive joins other European laws which will either come into effect before 1996 or are already in the process of becoming strict guidelines or explicit instructions. These rules set out safe practice on topics as diverse as electromagnetic compatibility, pressure in systems and the surface temperature of oven doors. They accompany the six sets of UK Health and Safety at Work Regulations (1992) which came into force in 1993, the legislation which implements European Union directives on Health and Safety at Work. These regulations have developed changes in the manufacture of existing equipment.

Electrical equipment is mostly covered by a non-binding European Union directive, The Low Voltage directive. This was approved by the European Union's members in February 1973, which was passed into UK Health and Safety law in 1989, in the form of the Low Voltage Electrical Equipment Safety Regulations.

FLOORS

Accidents are also caused by grease and water being spilled on floors and not being cleaned up. It is most important that floors are always kept clean and clear; pots and pans etc., should never be left on the floor, nor should oven doors be left open, because anyone carrying something large may not see the door or anything on the floor, and trip over.

Many people strain themselves by incorrectly lifting or attempting to lift items which are too heavy. Large stock pots, rondeau, forequarters and hindquarters of beef, for example, should be lifted with care. Particular attention should be paid to the hooks in the meat so that they do not injure anyone.

On no account should liquids be placed in containers on shelves above eye-level, especially when hot. They may be pulled down by someone else.

Safe kitchens are those which are well lit and well ventilated and where the staff take precautions to prevent accidents happening. But when accidents do happen it is necessary to know something of first-aid.

Further information can be obtained from the Royal Society for the Prevention of Accidents, Cannon House, Priory Queensway, Birmingham B4 6BS, or the Health and Safety Executive, Broad Lane, Sheffield, South Yorkshire S3 7HQ.

FIRST AID

As the term implies this is the immediate treatment on the spot to a person who has been injured or is ill. Since 1982 it has been a legal requirement that adequate first-aid equipment, facilities and personnel to give first aid are provided at work. If the injury is serious the injured person should be treated by a doctor or nurse as soon as possible.

First-aid equipment

A first-aid box, as a minimum, should contain:

- a card giving general first aid guidance;
- 20 individually wrapped, sterile, adhesive, waterproof dressings of various sizes;
- 4 × 25 g (1 oz) cotton wool packs;
- 1 dozen safety pins;
- 2 triangular bandages;
- 2 sterile eye pads, with attachment;
- 4 medium-sized sterile unmedicated dressings;
- 2 large sterile unmedicated dressings;
- 2 extra large sterile unmedicated dressings;
- tweezers;
- scissors;
- report book to record all injuries.

First aid boxes must be easily identifiable (see Figure 15.4) and accessible in the work area. They should be in the charge of a responsible person, checked regularly and refilled when necessary.

All establishments must have first-aid equipment and employees qualified in first-aid. Large establishments usually have medical staff such as a nurse and a first-aid

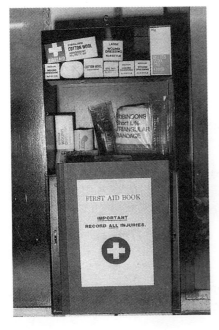

Fig. 15.4 First aid kit and book

room. The room should include a bed or couch, blankets, chairs, a table, sink with hot and cold water, towels, tissues and a first-aid box. Hooks for clothing and a mirror should be provided. Small establishments should have members of staff trained in first aid and in possession of a certificate. After a period of three years trained first-aid staff must update their training to remain certificated.

All catering workers and students are recommended to attend a first-aid course run by the St John Ambulance, St Andrew's Ambulance Association or British Red Cross Society.

Shock

The signs of shock are faintness, sickness, clammy skin and a pale face. Shock should be treated by keeping the person comfortable, lying down and warm. Cover the person with a blanket or clothing, but do not apply hot water bottles.

Fainting

Fainting may occur after a long period of standing in a hot, badly ventilated kitchen. The signs of an impending faint are whiteness, giddiness and sweating. A faint should be treated by raising the legs slightly above the level of the head and, when the person recovers consciousness, putting the person in the fresh air for a while and making sure that the person has not incurred any injury in fainting.

Cuts

All cuts should be covered immediately with a waterproof dressing, after the skin round the cut has been washed. When there is considerable bleeding it should be stopped as soon as possible. Bleeding may be controlled by direct pressure, by bandaging firmly on the cut. It may be possible to stop bleeding from a cut artery by pressing the artery with the thumb against the underlying bone; such pressure may be applied while a dressing or bandage is being prepared for application but not for more than 15 minutes.

Nose bleeds

Sit the person down with the head forward, and loosen clothing round the neck and chest. Ask them to breathe through the mouth and to pinch the soft part of the nose. After 10 minutes release the pressure. Warn the person not to blow the nose for several hours. If the bleeding has not stopped continue for a further 10 minutes. If the bleeding has not stopped them, or recurs in 30 minutes, obtain medical assistance.

Fractures

A person suffering from broken bones should not be moved until the injured part has been secured so that it cannot move. Medical assistance should be obtained.

Burns and scalds

Place the injured part gently under slowly running water or immerse in cool water, keeping it there for at least 10 minutes or until the pain ceases. If serious, the burn or scald should then be covered with a clean cloth or dressing (preferably sterile) and the person sent immediately to hospital.

Do **not** use adhesive dressings, apply lotions or ointments or break blisters.

Electric shock

Switch off the current. If this is not possible, free the person by using a dry insulating material such as cloth, wood or rubber, taking care not to use the bare hands otherwise the electric shock may be transmitted. If breathing has stopped, give artificial respiration and send for a doctor. Treat any burns as above.

Gassing

Do not let the gassed person walk, but carry them into the fresh air. If breathing has stopped apply artificial respiration and send for a doctor.

Artificial respiration

There are several methods of artificial respiration. The most effective is mouth-to-mouth (mouth-to-nose) and this method can be used by almost all age groups and in almost all circumstances.

Again it is stressed that we would recommend all students to complete a first-aid course.

Further information can be obtained from the St John Ambulance Association, 1 Grosvenor Crescent, London SW1X 7EF.

FIRE PRECAUTIONS

Fires in hotel and catering establishments are fairly common and can result in injury or loss of life to employees and customers.

Fire prevention

A basic knowledge regarding fire should assist in preventing fires and handling them if they do occur. Three components are necessary for a fire to start, if one of the three is not present, or is removed, then the fire does not happen or it is extinguished. The three parts are:

- fuel – something to burn;
- air – oxygen to sustain combustion (to keep the fire going);
- heat – gas, electricity, etc.

Methods of extinguishing a fire

(see Plates 131 and 132; page 537)

To extinguish a fire the three principal methods are:

- starving – removing the fuel;
- smothering – removing the air (oxygen);
- cooling – removing the heat.

Therefore, one of the sides of the 'fire triangle' (see Figure 15.5) is removed.

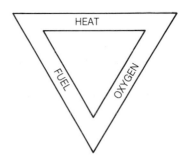

Fig. 15.5   The fire triangle

The fuel is that which burns, heat is that which sets the fuel alight and oxygen is needed for fire to burn. Eliminate one of these and the fire is put out. Oxygen is present in air, so if air is excluded from the fuel and the heat then the fire goes out. For example, should the clothes of someone working in the kitchen catch alight, then the action to be taken is quickly to wrap a fire blanket round the person and place them on the floor. In so doing the flames have been cut off from the source of air. (The oxygen has been taken from the triangle.) In the event of a fire, windows and doors should be closed so as to restrict the amount of air getting to the fire.

Foam extinguishers work on the principle that the foam forms a 'blanket' thus excluding air from coming into contact with the fuel.

Should fat or oil in a pan ignite (see Figure 15.6), then the pan should be quickly covered with a lid, fire blanket or other item so as to exclude air. It is also essential to turn off the source of heat (gas or electricity) so that the heat is taken from the triangle.

Water extinguishes by dousing the flames, thus taking the heat out of the triangle provided the fuel is material such as wood and paper. If fat or oil is alight water must **not** be used as it causes the ignited fat to spread, thus increasing the heat.

Local hotel owner fined after fire

The owner of the Country Square Hotel has been fined under the Fire Prevention Act for 20 offences following investigations into a fire at the hotel in April last year.

He was prosecuted by the Fire Brigade and fined £3,550 after pleading guilty to all offences before magistrates.

The fire spread throughout the hotel following a chip-pan blaze in the basement kitchen.

The Fire Brigade told the court it had discovered obstructions in four exit routes while it was attempting to douse the flames at the five-storey hotel.

The court heard that doors protecting the staircase and exits had been left propped open or were missing. The same applied to doors at basement level and on upper floors, allowing the whole premises to become saturated with smoke, the court was told.

Corridors and exits in the basement were obstructed by builders' materials and gas cylinders and the door from the kitchen had been left open, allowing flames to travel unimpeded into the corridor to both staircases of the hotel, said the Fire Brigade report.

A nightly security check had not been carried out the night of the fire, while the overall effect of the 20 offences committed was "to place all the means of escape in jeopardy", the court heard.

A man was rescued from a second-floor window and a woman from an internal staircase.

Fig. 15.6   Newspaper report of a fire at a hotel

Water extinguishers must **not** be used on live electrical equipment because water is a conductor of electricity and the person holding the extinguisher could be electrocuted.

In the event of a small fire in a store it may be possible to remove items in the store to prevent the fire from spreading; windows and doors are to be closed, if it is safe to do so. Evacuation should not be delayed if the fire is already well developed. Fighting a small fire in a store should normally take priority over removing items from it unless the store is large enough for both activities to be carried out.

Fire doors are installed for the purpose of restricting an area so that, in the event of a fire, the fuel is limited.

Procedures in the event of a fire

* Raise the alarm – break glass of fire alarm point or shout fire!!
* Call the fire brigade.
* Turn off heat and fans.
* Attempt to smother the fire, if small, with a fire blanket or wet cloth.
* Attempt to fight the fire with appropriate extinguisher, if it is safe to do so. Do not extinguish gas burners *before* turning off the gas.
* If the fire is too large or cannot be extinguished, close doors and windows if possible and leave the building.
* Do not panic.
* Do not jeopardise your own safety or that of others.
* Do not wait for the fire to get out of control before calling the fire brigade.

It is important that in all catering establishments exits and passageways are kept clear and that doors open outwards. Fire doors and windows should be clearly marked and fire-fighting equipment must be readily available and in working order. Periodic **fire drills should be held at least once a year and be taken seriously since lives may be endangered if a fire should start.** Fire alarm bells must be tested at least four times a year and staff should be instructed in the use of fire-fighting equipment. All extinguishers should be refilled immediately after use.

All fire extinguishers should be manufactured in accordance with British Standard specifications; they should be coloured, with a code to indicate the type and with operating instructions on them.

* Red – water;
* Cream – foam;
* Black – carbon dioxide;
* Blue – dry powder;
* Green – halon (vapourising liquid).

Fire blankets must also conform to British Standard specifications.

Use of portable fire extinguishers

WATER (RED)

Water is used for fire in solid combustible materials such as wood, plastic and paper. Water has better cooling properties than most other agents, therefore it is especially suitable for fires that may re-ignite if they are not cooled sufficiently. Most water extinguishers contain carbon dioxide gas which expels the water.

Disadvantages

- Because water is a conductor of electricity it must never be used on live electrical equipment.
- Water jets and sprays should not be used on fat fires because they may cause ignited fat to spread.

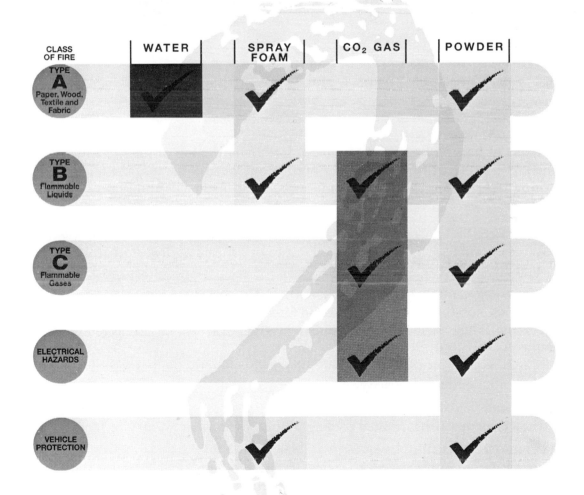

15.7 Choice of fire extinguisher

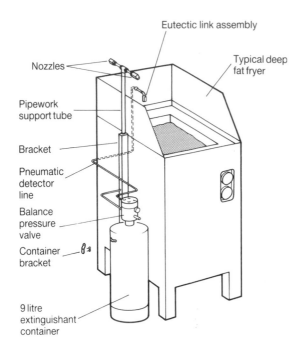

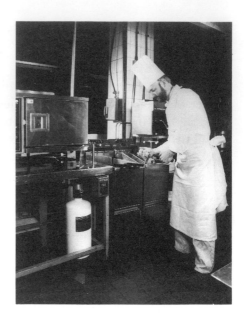

Fig. 15.8   Foam fire extinguishing systems for deep fat fryers

FOAM (CREAM)

Foam puts out fires by forming a blanket of foam over the top of the fire and smothering it. It is particularly good for putting out fat fires because the foam stays in position and so stops the fire re-igniting. Foam can also be used on fires on solid materials.

Disadvantages

* Foam is a conductor of electricity and must not be used on live electrical equipment.

CARBON DIOXIDE OR HALON EXTINGUISHING SYSTEMS (BLACK)

Partial or total flooding systems are used in kitchens to smother fires and prevent fire spreading. They must allow staff time to evacuate and will be connected to an automatic gas shut-off.

Carbon dioxide gas is used on fires of inflammable liquids and has the advantage that it does not conduct electricity.

Disadvantage

* Carbon dioxide gas has limited cooling properties and hot fat may re-ignite.

DRY POWDER (BLUE)

Dry powder is commonly used for fat fires. It does not conduct electricity and some all-purpose powders can be used on solid fuel fires.

Disadvantage

* Dry powders have limited cooling properties and hot fat may re-ignite.

Halon (green)

The halon used is known at BCF which is short for bromochlorodifluoromethane. This is a gas which does not conduct electricity.

Disadvantage

• If used in an enclosed situation halon gives off a thick cloud which can irritate the user's throat and it should not be inhaled.

Each extinguisher should be fixed on a suitable bracket, be properly maintained and always available for use, and immediately refilled after use. It is important that staff learn how to use them.

Other extinguishers

Fire hoses

Fire hoses are used for similar fires to those classified under water fire extinguishers. It is necessary to be familiar with the instructions displayed by the fire hose before using it.

Water sprinkler systems

A sprinkler system consists of an array of sprinkler heads at ceiling level connected to a mains water supply. The distances between sprinkler heads and the water pressure required is laid down for each occupancy in the *Rules of the Fire Officer's Committee for Automatic Sprinkler Installations*, (29th edition). In the event of a fire the nearest sprinkler head above the fire operates when the temperature at ceiling level rises above a preset level, such as 68°C (154°F) and sprays an area of 12 to 20 sq m (39 to 66 sq ft). Additional heads operate later if necessary to control the fire.

Research and development by the manufacturers of fire-fighting equipment inevitably leads to changes and increased efficiency in the various appliances; as it is important that the best fire extinguishers are always available, always consult the Fire Prevention Branch of the Fire Brigade, and for a list of approved extinguishers apply to the Fire Officers' Committee.

Further information can be obtained from the Fire Protection Association, 140 Aldersgate Street, London EC1A 4HX.

Topics for discussion

1. Discuss the causes of accidents and how they may be prevented. Are some people accident prone, others naturally clumsy and others lacking in common sense? If so how can they be 'educated' to be safe workers?
2. Do notices regarding safety have any effect? How best may people employed in the kitchen be made aware of hazards, thus making a potentially dangerous environment much safer?
3. Attendance at a first-aid course could be made obligatory for every catering

employee. Do you think this would be sensible and if you do, or do not, explain why?

4. Discuss what training and the procedures following training, should be provided for every person being employed in catering establishment. Does training reduce accidents, fires etc.?

5. What provision should be made for the welfare of catering staff? Discuss this, bearing in mind costs and the fact that in the industry many employees are casual or part-time.

6. How can premises be made secure and stealing be prevented?

7. Discuss the hazards that should be prevented in the kitchen.

8. Discuss the relationship between the caterer and the Environmental Health Officer.

9. Discuss accident prevention and the responsibilities of the worker and the employer.

10. Is ample provision made for first aid?

11. What fire precautions and appropriate systems are in place for fire prevention?

12. If you find temperatures and food hygiene legislation complex, discuss how could it be simplified.

13. Discuss the relationship between knowing the law and implementing it.

16

Hygiene

Hygiene is the science and practice of preserving health and is one of the most important subjects for all persons working in the Hotel and Catering Industry to study, understand and practise in their everyday working lives. The subject is broken down into three areas : personal, food and kitchen hygiene, all of which are of equal importance.

PERSONAL HYGIENE

Germs or bacteria are to be found in and on the body and they can be transferred onto anything with which the body comes in contact. Personal cleanliness is essential to prevent germs getting onto food.

Personal cleanliness

Self-respect is necessary in every food-handler because a pride in one's appearance promotes a high standard of cleanliness and physical fitness. Persons suffering from ill-health or who are not clean about themselves should not handle food.

BATHING
It is essential to take a bath or a shower every day (or at least two or three times a week), otherwise germs can be transferred onto clothes and so onto food, particularly in warm weather.

HANDS
Hands must be washed thoroughly and frequently, particularly after using the toilet, before commencing work and during the handling of food.

Fig. 16.1 Poisoned any good customers lately?

They should be washed in hot water, with the aid of a nail brush and bactericidal soap. This can be dispensed from a fixed container in a liquid or gel form and is preferable to bar soap, which can accumulate germs when passed from hand to hand. After washing, hands should be rinsed and dried on a *clean* towel, suitable paper towel or by hand hot-air drier (Figure 16.2). Hands and fingernails can be a great source of danger if not kept clean, as they can so easily transfer harmful bacteria on to the food.

Fig. 16.2   Air-flow hand dryer

Rings (except for a plain wedding band), watches and jewellery should not be worn where food is handled. Particles of food may be caught under the ring, and germs could multiply there until they are transferred onto food.

Watches should not be worn because some foodstuffs have to be plunged into plenty of water. Apart from this, the steam in a kitchen will ruin watches that are not waterproofed anyway.

Jewellery should not be worn, since it may fall off into food, unknown to the wearer; small sleepers for pierced ears are, however, permissible.

FINGERNAILS

These should always be kept clean and short as dirt can easily lodge under the nails and be dislodged when, for example, making pastry, so introducing bacteria into food. Nails should be cleaned with a nail brush and nail varnish should not be worn.

HAIR

Hair should be washed regularly and kept covered where food is being handled. Hair that is not cared for is likely to come out or shed dandruff which may fall into food. Men's hair should be kept short as it is easier to keep clean; it also looks neater. Women's hair should be covered as much as possible. Both men's and women's hair can be kept in place using hair lacquer or a hair net. The hair should never be scratched, combed or touched in the kitchen, as germs could be transferred via the hands to the food.

NOSE

The nose should not be touched when food is being handled. If a handkerchief is used, the hands should be washed afterwards. Ideally, paper handkerchiefs should be used and then destroyed, and the hands washed afterwards. The nose is an area where there are vast numbers of harmful bacteria; it is therefore very important that neither food, people nor working surfaces are sneezed over, so spreading germs.

MOUTH

There are many germs in the area of the mouth, therefore the mouth or lips should not be touched by the hands or utensils which may come into contact with food. No cooking utensils should be used for tasting food, nor should fingers be used for this purpose as germs may be transferred to food. A clean teaspoon should be used for tasting, and washed well afterwards.

Coughing over foods and working areas should be avoided as germs are spread long distances if not trapped in a handkerchief.

EARS

The ear-holes should not be touched while in the kitchen as, again, germs can be transferred.

TEETH

Sound teeth are essential to good health. They should be kept clean and visits to the dentist should be regular so that teeth can be kept in good repair.

FEET

As food-handlers are standing for many hours, care of the feet is important. They should be washed regularly and the toenails kept short and clean. Tired feet can cause general fatigue which leads to carelessness, and this results in a lowering of the standards of hygiene.

CUTS, BURNS AND SORES

It is particularly important to keep all cuts, burns scratches and similar openings of the skin covered with a waterproof dressing. Where the skin is septic (as with certain cuts, spots, sores and carbuncles) there are vast numbers of harmful bacteria which must not be permitted to get on food; in most cases people suffering in this way should not handle food.

COSMETICS

Cosmetics, if used by food-handlers, should be used in moderation, but ideally their use should be discouraged. Cosmetics should not be put on in the kitchen and the hands should be washed well afterwards; they should be put on a clean skin, not used to cover up dirt.

SMOKING (Figure 16.3)

Smoking must never take place where there is food, because when a cigarette is taken from the mouth, germs from the mouth can be transferred to the fingers and so on to food. When the cigarette is put down the end which has been in the mouth can transfer germs on to working surfaces. Ash on food is most objectionable and it should be remembered that smoking where there is food is an offence against the law.

Smoking chef fined after health check

A chef carried on smoking as he cut up meat in front of a health investigator, a court heard this week.

The senior environmental officer said that a cat was allowed to walk around while food was being prepared and that staff were wearing dirty overalls.

On a later visit he found the chef smoking a cigarette as he chopped up chicken.

TV pub 'revolting'

A picturesque pub featured in a BBC programme was fined a total of £6,750 yesterday for food hygiene breaches. The magistrate hearing the case described the kitchen as 'absolutely revolting'.

Fig. 16.3   Newspaper reports of hygiene breaches

SPITTING

Spitting should never occur, because germs can be spread by this objectionable habit.

CLOTHING AND CLOTHS

Clean whites (protective clothing) and clean underclothes should be worn at all times. Dirty clothes enable germs to multiply and if dirty clothing comes into contact with food the food may be contaminated. Cloths used for holding hot dishes should also be kept clean as the cloths are used in many ways such as wiping knives, wiping dishes and pans. All these uses could convey germs on to food.

Outdoor clothing, and other clothing which has been taken off before wearing whites, should be kept in a locker, away from the kitchen.

General health and fitness

The maintenance of good health is essential to prevent the introduction of germs into the kitchen. To keep physically fit, adequate rest, exercise, fresh air and a wholesome diet are essential.

SLEEP AND RELAXATION

Persons employed in the kitchen required adequate sleep and relaxation as they are on the move all the time, often in a hot atmosphere where the tempo of work may be very fast. Frequently, the hours are long or extended over a long period of time, as with split duty, or they may be extended into the night. In off-duty periods it may be wise to obtain some relaxation and rest rather than spend all the time energetically. The amount of sleep and rest required depends on each person's needs and the variation between one person and the next is considerable.

EXERCISE AND FRESH AIR

People working in conditions of nervous tension, rush, heat and odd hours need a change of environment and particularly fresh air. Swimming, walking or cycling in the country may be suitable ways of obtaining both exercise and fresh air.

WHOLESOME FOOD AND PURE WATER

A well-balanced diet, correctly cooked, and pure water will assist in keeping kitchen personnel fit. The habit of 'picking' (eating small pieces of food while working) is bad; it spoils the appetite and does not allow the stomach to rest.

Meals should be taken regularly; long periods without food are also bad for the stomach. Pure water is ideal for replacing liquid lost in perspiring in a hot kitchen, or soft drinks may be taken to replace some of the salt as well as the fluid lost in sweating.

Kitchen clothing

It is most important that people working in the kitchen should wear suitable clothing and footwear. Suitable clothing must be:

1. protective;
2. washable;
3. of a suitable colour;
4. light in weight and comfortable;
5. strong;
6. absorbent.

PROTECTIVE
Clothes worn in the kitchen must protect the body from excessive heat. For this reason chef's jackets are double-breasted and have long sleeves (see Plate 133, page 538); they are to protect the chest and arms from the heat of the stove and to prevent hot foods or liquids burning or scalding the body.

Aprons
These are designed to protect the body from being scalded or burned and particularly to protect the legs from any liquids which may be spilled; for this reason the apron should be of sufficient length to protect the legs.

Chef's hat
This is designed to enable air to circulate on top of the head and thus keep the head cooler. The main purpose of the hat is to prevent loose hairs from dropping into food and to absorb perspiration on the forehead. The use of lightweight disposable hats is both acceptable and suitable.

Fig. 16.4 Footwear

Footwear
This should be stout and kept in good repair so as to protect and support the feet. As the kitchen staff are on their feet for many hours, boots (for men) and clogs (for men and women) give added support and will be found most satisfactory.

Modern industrial safety shoes with steel toecaps are to be encouraged. Sandals, training shoes etc., are insufficient protection from spillage of hot liquids.

WASHABLE

The clothing should be of an easily washable material as many changes of clothing are required.

COLOUR

White clothing is readily seen to be soiled when it needs to be changed and there is a tendency to work more cleanly when wearing 'whites'. Chefs' trousers of blue and white check are a practical colour but also require frequent changing.

LIGHT AND COMFORTABLE

Clothing must be light in weight and comfortable, not tight. Heavy clothing would be uncomfortable and a heavy hat in the heat of the kitchen would cause headaches.

STRONG

Clothes worn in the kitchen must be strong to withstand hard wear and frequent washing.

ABSORBENT

Working over a hot stove causes people to perspire; the perspiration will not evaporate in an inadequately ventilated atmosphere and so underclothes made from absorbent material, such as cotton, should be worn. The hat absorbs perspiration and the neckerchief is used to prevent perspiration from running down the body, for wiping the face and also to protect the neck, which is easily affected by draughts.

Summary of personal hygiene

The practice of clean habits in the kitchen is the only way to achieve a satisfactory standard of hygiene. These habits are as follows:

- Hands must be washed frequently and always after using the toilet. Food should be handled as little as possible.
- Bathing must occur frequently.
- Hair must be kept clean and covered in the kitchen; it should not be combed or handled near food.
- Nose and mouth should not be touched with the hands.
- Cough and sneeze in a handkerchief, not over food; people with colds should not be in contact with food.
- Jewellery, rings and watches should not be worn.
- Smoking and spitting must not occur where there is food.
- Cuts and burns should be covered with a waterproof dressing.
- Clean clothing should be worn at all times and only clean cloths used.
- Foods should be tasted with a clean teaspoon.
- Tables should not be sat on.
- Only healthy people should handle food.

KITCHEN HYGIENE

Neglect in the care and cleaning of any part of the premises and equipment could lead to a risk of food infection. Kitchen hygiene is of very great importance to:

- those who work in the kitchen, because clean working conditions are more agreeable to work in than dirty conditions;
- the owners, because custom should increase when the public know the kitchen is clean;
- the customer – no one should want to eat food prepared in a dirty kitchen.

Cleaning materials and equipment

To maintain a hygienic working environment a wide range of materials and equipment is needed. These are some of the items which need to budgeted for, ordered, stored and issued:

- brooms
- brushes
- buckets
- cloths
- dusters
- dustbins
- mops
- sponges
- squeegee
- scrubbing machine
- wet suction cleaner
- dry suction cleaner
- ammonia
- disinfectant
- dustbin powder
- floor cleaner
- flyspray
- oven cleaner
- plastic sacks
- scouring powder
- soap
- steel wool
- washing powder

Kitchen premises

VENTILATION

Adequate ventilation must be provided so that fumes from stoves are taken out of the kitchen, and stale air in the stores, larder and still-room is extracted. This is usually effected by erecting hoods over stoves and using extractor fans.

Hoods and fans must be kept clean; grease and dirt are drawn up by the fan and, if they accumulate, can drop onto food. Windows used for ventilation should be

Health risk at one in 10 food outlets

POOR standards of hygiene pose a serious health risk to consumers in more than one in 10 businesses where food is handled, a government-funded investigation will reveal this week.

Fast-food shops, restaurants and food manufacturers are the worst offenders, according to a survey by environmental health officers who visited 5,000 establishments in England and Wales. The investigation was ordered by the Audit Commission, which monitors the efficiency of local government services.

Results to be published on Tuesday will give a relatively clean bill of health to hospitals, schools, colleges and residential homes for the elderly or disabled. Most food shops, butchers, hotels and public houses present a moderate degree of danger, says the study.

The investigation, which led to prosecutions and closure orders, is intended to provide the first detailed comparison of standards of food-handling in different areas of the country.

Fig. 16.5   Newspaper report highlighting poor standards of hygiene

screened to prevent the entry of dust, insects and birds. Good ventilation facilitates the evaporation of sweat from the body, which keeps one cool.

LIGHTING

Good lighting is necessary so that people working in the kitchen do not strain their eyes. Natural lighting is preferable to artificial lighting. Good lighting is also necessary to enable staff to see into corners so the kitchen can be properly cleaned.

PLUMBING

Adequate supplies of hot and cold water must be available for keeping the kitchen clean, for cleaning equipment and for staff use. For certain cleaning hot water is essential, and the means of heating water must be capable of meeting the requirements of the establishment.

There must be hand-washing and drying facilities and suitable provision of toilets, which must not be in direct contact with any rooms in which food is prepared or stored.

Hand-washing facilities (separate from food preparation sinks) must also be available in the kitchen with a suitable means of drying the hands (hot air or paper towels).

CLEANING OF TOILETS AND SINKS

Toilets must never be cleaned by food-handlers. Sinks and hand basins should be cleaned and thoroughly rinsed.

FLOORS

Kitchen floors have to withstand a considerable amount of wear and tear, therefore they must be:

- capable of being easily cleaned;
- smooth, but not slippery;
- even;
- without cracks or open joints;
- impervious (non-absorbent).

Quarry tile floors or vinyl sheet or epoxy resin floors, properly laid, are suitable for kitchens, since they fulfil the above requirements.

Thorough cleaning is essential: floors are swept, washed with hot detergent water and then dried. This can be done by machine or by hand, and should be carried out at least once a day. As a safety precaution, suitable warning signs should be used to alert staff if the floor is wet.

WALLS

Walls should be strong, smooth, impervious, washable and light in colour. The joint between the wall and floor should be rounded for ease of cleaning. Suitable wall surfaces include ceramic tiles, heat resistant plastic sheeting, stainless steel sheeting, and resin bonded fibreglass.

Clean with hot detergent water and dry. This will probably be done monthly, but frequency will depend on circumstances.

Plate 131   Fire blanket

Plate 132   Types of fire extinguishers

Plate 133 Suitable clothing must be worn in the kitchen

CEILINGS
Ceilings must be free from cracks and flaking. They should not be able to harbour dirt.

DOORS AND WINDOWS
Doors and windows should fit correctly and be clean. The glass should be clean inside and out so as to admit maximum light.

FOOD LIFTS
Lifts should be kept very clean and no particles of food should be allowed to accumulate as lift shafts are ideal places for rats, mice and insects to gain access into kitchens.

Hygiene of kitchen equipment (see also Chapter 11)

Kitchen equipment should be so designed that it can be:

* cleaned easily;
* readily inspected to see that it is clean.

Failure to maintain equipment and utensils hygienically and in good repair may cause food poisoning.

Material used in the construction of equipment must be:

* hard so that it does not absorb food particles;
* smooth so as to be easily cleaned;
* resistant to rust;
* resistant to chipping.

Containers, pipes and equipment made from toxic materials, such as lead and zinc, should not be in direct contact with food or drink or be allowed to wear excessively;

copper pans that need retinning on the inside will expose harmful copper to food. Food must be protected from lubricants.

Easily cleaned equipment is free from unnecessary ridges, screws, ornamentation, dents, crevices or inside square corners, and has large, smooth areas. Articles of equipment which are difficult to clean (mincers, sieves and strainers) are items where particles of food can lodge so allowing germs to multiply and contaminate food when the utensil is next used.

NORMAL CLEANING MATERIALS

- *Metals*: as a rule all metal equipment should be cleaned immediately after use.
- *Portable items*: remove food particles and grease. Wash by immersion in hot detergent water. Thoroughly clean with a hard bristle brush or soak until this is possible. Rinse in water at 77°C (171°F), by immersing in the water in wire racks.
- *Fixed items*: remove all food and grease with a stiff brush or soak with a wet cloth, using hot detergent water. Thoroughly clean with hot detergent water. Rinse with clean water. Dry with a clean cloth.
- *Abrasives*: should only be used in moderation as their constant scratching of the surface makes it more difficult to clean the article next time.
- *Marble*: scrub with a bristle brush and hot water and then dry.
- *Wood*: scrub with a bristle brush and hot detergent water, rinse and dry.
- *Plastic*: wash in reasonably hot water.
- *China, earthenware*: avoid extremes of heat and do not clean with an abrasive. Wash in hot water and rinse in very hot water.
- *Copper*: remove as much food as possible. Soak. Wash in hot detergent water with the aid of a brush. Clean the outside with a paste made of sand, vinegar and flour. Wash well. Rinse and dry. Alternatively, a proprietary copper cleaner may be used. Copper pans are gradually being replaced in commercial kitchens, mainly due to the expense involved in retinning.
- *Aluminium*: do not wash in water containing soda as the protective film which prevents corrosion may be damaged. To clean, remove food particles. Soak. Wash in hot detergent water. Clean with steel wool or abrasive. Rinse and dry.
- *Stainless steel*: stainless steel is easy to clean. Soak in hot detergent water. Clean with a brush. Rinse and dry.
- *Tin*: tin which is used to line pots and pans should be soaked, washed in detergent water, rinsed and dried. Tinned utensils, where thin sheet steel has a thin coating of tin, must be thoroughly dried, otherwise they are likely to rust.
- *Zinc*: This is used to coat storage bins of galvanised iron and it should not be cleaned with a hard abrasive.
- *Vitreous enamel*: clean with a damp cloth and dry. Avoid using abrasives.
- *Equipment requiring particular care in cleaning* (sieves, conical strainers, mincers graters). Extra attention must be paid to these items, because food particles clog the holes. The holes can be cleaned by using the force of the water from the tap, by using a bristle brush and by moving the article, particularly a sieve, up and down in the sink, so causing water to pass through the mesh. Whisks must be

Fig. 16.6   Pot and pan washer, specially designed for the proper cleansing of large equipment

thoroughly cleaned where the wires cross at the end opposite the handle as food can lodge between the wires. The handle of the whisk must also be kept clean.

- *Saws and choppers, mandolins*: these items should be cleaned in hot detergent water, dried and greased slightly.
- *Tammy cloths, muslins and piping bags*: after use they should be emptied, food particles scraped out, scrubbed carefully and boiled. They should then be rinsed and allowed to dry. Certain piping bags made of plastic should be washed in very hot water and dried. Nylon piping bags should not be boiled.

CLEANING OF LARGE ELECTRICAL EQUIPMENT (OVENS, MINCERS, MIXERS, CHOPPERS, SLICERS) (Figure 16.6)

1. Switch off the machine and remove the electric plug.
2. Remove particles of food with a cloth, palette knife, needle or brush as appropriate.
3. Thoroughly clean with hand-hot detergent water all removable and fixed parts. Pay particular attention to threads and plates with holes in mincers.

Fig. 16.7 Hygienic storage of equipment

4. Rinse thoroughly.
5. Dry and reassemble.
6. While cleaning see that exposed blades are not left uncovered or unguarded and that the guards are replaced when cleaning is complete.
7. Any specific maker's instructions should be observed.
8. Test that the machine is properly assembled by plugging in and switching on.

All equipment once cleaned should be stored properly (Figure 16.7).

Kitchen energy distribution systems

A system of this type operates from stainless steel housings (known as 'raceways') which are fastened to walls, floors ceilings or may be island mounted. Inside the raceways are runs of electrical bus-bars or bus-wires and plumbing pipes. At intervals, appropriate for the kitchen equipment served, are switch or valve sockets, electrical, gas, water, steam, etc.

Connecting flexible cords and pipes from the kitchen equipment plug into the sockets and are designed to hang clear of the floor and are smooth plastic coated for easy cleaning.

For maximum advantage from this idea, the hygiene, safety, flexibility, ease of cleaning and maintenance, most of the kitchen equipment is mounted on castors.

Periodic cleaning is carried out by pulling the equipment out from the wall or island, unplugging all the services then moving the equipment away on its castors giving free access to all wall and floor surfaces as well as backs and sides of equipment.

Further information can be obtained from Eurocaddy Systems Ltd, Powder Mill Lane, Dartford, Kent DA1 1NN.

FOOD HYGIENE

The Food Safety Act 1990 includes:

- increased powers for the Environmental Health Officers;
- provision of training for food operatives;
- registration of food premises with the local authority;
- the defence of 'due diligence'. If the person in charge of a catering operation can show that he or she took all reasonable precautions to avoid committing an offence then this can be used in defending any presentation under the Food Safety Act 1990.

Fig. 16.8   Identify the faults

Provision of safe food

This is a management responsibility. In order to provide safe food a safety control system should be implemented. The HACCP approach provides a means of ensuring the provision of safe food for the customers. HACCP stands for Hygiene Analysis and Critical Control Point.

Hazard analysis (Figure 16.8) identifies all the factors that could lead to hazards for the consumer: all ingredients, stages in the processing of foods, environmental features and human factors that could lead to unsafe food being served.

Critical Control Points (CCPs) are the points at which control is essential to ensure that potential hazards do not actually become hazardous:

- Is the food delivered at the correct temperature?
- Is the food stored and displayed at the correct temperature?
- Is cross-contamination prevented as far as possible (see Figure 16.9, page 546)?
- Are cleaning schedules in place for equipment?
- Are personnel correctly trained and hygienic in their work practices?

In small catering units the main principles should still apply but a modified form of HACCP is more appropriate. This is Assured Safe Catering (ASC). ASC emphasise the importance of safety precautions in the preparation, handling and temperature control of food. It is vital that catering staff are properly trained if an ASC system is to work effectively and that record sheets are kept of controls which are in place. (See defence of 'due diligence' above).

The most succulent, mouth-watering dish into which has gone all the skill and art of the world's best chefs, using the finest possible ingredients, may look, taste and smell superb, yet be unsafe, even dangerous to eat because of harmful bacteria.

It is of the utmost importance that everyone who handles food, or who works in a place where food is handled, should know that food must be both clean and safe. Hygiene is the study of health and the prevention of disease, and because of the dangers of food poisoning, hygiene requires particular attention from everyone in the catering industry.

There are germs everywhere, particularly in and on our bodies; some of these germs if transferred to food can cause illness and in some cases death. These germs are so small they cannot be seen by the naked eye, and so food which looks clean and does not smell or taste bad may be dangerous to eat if harmful germs have contaminated it and multiplied.

The duty of every person concerned with food is to prevent contamination of food by germs and to prevent these germs or bacteria from multiplying.

Food-handlers must know the Food Hygiene Regulations, but no matter how much is written or read about food hygiene the practice of hygiene habits by people who handle food is the only way to safe food.

Food poisoning

Over fifty thousand people each year have been found by doctors to be suffering

60 workers hit by food bug in City

Bank and finance house workers from the City overwhelmed Bart's Hospital's casualty department yesterday after a food poisoning out-break. The London ambulance service carried 26 victims to hospital and many others staggered in by themselves after lunch.

50 casualties with sickness, dizziness and diarrhoea were treated and another nine were at a neighbouring hospital.

City of London police said the source of the outbreak was be-lieved to be a high-class mobile food firm which delivers to businesses.

A spokesman said: "It appears that all the workers had lunches from the same firm. We are not disclosing the firm's name at the moment, although we have been given it."

A spokesman said: "We are hoping to get most of the casual-ties out tonight.

"We are rushed off our feet and have had to call in back-up staff."

None was reported as being seriously ill.

CASES of food poisoning may be up to 30 times higher than official records show, a new report claims.

More than two million people fell ill last year after eating contaminated foodstuffs.

And the problem is costing the country millions of pounds in time off work and medical bills.

Bowled out by mayonnaise

One of the most expensive food poisoning cases, lasting three years, was resolved recently. One hundred and fifty eight people, including members of two cricket teams, one consisting of solicitors and the other of accountants, suffered a variety of food poisoning related complaints, after eating sandwiches containing mayonnaise made from fresh eggs. The legal case lasted three years and the final pay-out to 76 people is expected to be over £100,000. Legal fees alone were estimated at £25,000.

Diners complained of "severe stomach pains" after eating steak and kidney puddings at the City event.

Warning as food bug cases rocket

FOOD poisoning cases are soaring in Britian and the official figures represent only the 'tip of the iceberg' it was claimed yesterday.

There were 30,000 reported cases in 1987, over 50,000 in 1992 up from 11,000 in 1978. To make matters worse, as many as 90 per cent of cases go unreported, said the director of food hygiene with the Public Health Laboratory Ser-vice.

"In most cases the problem lies in the kitchen and the immediate cause is the failure to observe sim-ple rules of food hygiene," he told a seminar in London organised by the Food and Drink Federation.

He added: "There is an urgent need for more education on food hygiene issues, but bacterial food poisoning could be eliminated altogether if a few key points were followed."

He said people should keep the kitchen clean, wash their hands before preparing food, avoid cross-contamination between cooked and uncooked foods, al-ways thaw, cook and reheat food adequately, and store food prop-erly.

Most people did not realise stor-ing food at room temperature could allow micro-organisms to grow, he said. And only half those questioned in a nationwide survey were aware of the possibility of one high-risk food dripping on to and contaminating another in the fridge.

Salmonella is present in about 60 per cent of raw and frozen chickens.

Thorough cooking destroys the bacteria. But if the bird has not been thawed properly in the fridge before cooking, the salmonella can survive and multiply, causing food poisoning.

And pre-cooked meals should not be stored beyond their recom-mended date.

The head of food science with the Ministry of Agriculture said that a Ministry survey of 2,000 households showed a widespread unawareness of basic rules of hygiene in the kitchen.

The Ministry of Agriculture is recommending that the Education Department introduces food hygeiene into the school science curriculum, so that boys and girls learn the basics at the beginning.

Fig. 16.9   Extracts from newspaper reports on food poisoning

from food poisoning. This represents the average number of notified cases over the last few years, and there are thousands more who have not notified their doctor, but have suffered from food poisoning. This appalling amount of ill-health could largely be prevented. Failure to prevent it may be due to:

- ignorance of the rules of hygiene;
- carelessness, thoughtlessness or neglect;
- poor standards of equipment or facilities to maintain hygienic standards;
- accident.

Food poisoning can be prevented by:

- high standards of personal hygiene;
- attention to physical fitness;
- maintaining good working conditions
- maintaining equipment in good repair and in clean condition;
- adequate provision of cleaning facilities and cleaning equipment;
- correct storage of foodstuffs at the right temperature;
- correct reheating of food;
- quick cooling of foods prior to storage;
- protection of food from vermin and insects;
- hygienic washing-up procedure;
- food-handlers knowing how food poisoning is caused;
- food-handlers carrying out correct procedures to prevent food poisoning.

WHAT IS FOOD POISONING?
Food poisoning can be defined as an illness characterised by stomach pains and diarrhoea and sometimes vomiting, developing within one to 36 hours after eating the affected food.

CAUSES OF FOOD POISONING
Food poisoning results when harmful foods are eaten, contaminated by:

- chemicals which entered foods accidentally during the growth, preparation or cooking of the food;
- germs (harmful bacteria) which have entered the food from humans, animals or other sources and the bacteria themselves, or the toxins (poisons) produced in the food by certain bacteria, have caused the foods to be harmful. By far the greatest number of cases of food poisoning is caused by harmful bacteria.

CHEMICAL FOOD POISONING
Certain chemicals may accidentally enter food and cause food poisoning.

- Arsenic is used to spray fruit during growth, and occasionally fruit has been affected by this poison.
- Lead poisoning can occur from using water that has been in contact with lead pipes and then drunk or used in cooking.

- Antimony or zinc poisoning from acid foods stored or cooked in poor quality enamelled or galvanised containers can occur.
- Copper pans should be correctly tinned and never used for storing foods, particularly acid foods, as the food could dissolve harmful amounts of copper.
- Certain *plants* are poisonous such as some fungi, rhubarb leaves and the parts of potatoes which are exposed to the sun above the surface of the soil.
- Rat poison may accidentally contaminate food.

Prevention of chemical food poisoning

Chemical food poisoning can be prevented by:

- using correctly maintained and suitable kitchen utensils;
- obtaining foodstuffs from reliable sources;
- care in the use of rat poison, etc.

BACTERIAL FOOD POISONING

Food contaminated by bacteria (germs) is by far the most common cause of food poisoning. Cross-contamination is when bacteria are transferred from contaminated to uncontaminated foods via hands, boards, knives, surfaces, etc.

To prevent the transfer of bacteria by cross-contamination, these points should be observed:

- Ensure food is obtained from reliable sources.
- Handle foods as little as possible; when practicable use tongs, palette knives, plastic gloves, etc.

Fig. 16.10   Food plated when handler wears plastic gloves

- Ensure utensils and work surfaces are clean and sanitised.
- Use cloths impregnated with a bactericide which fades in colour when no longer effective.
- Pay particular attention when handling raw poultry, meat and fish.
- Wash raw fruits and vegetables.
- Clean methodically and as frequently as necessary; clean as you go.
- Keep foods covered as much as possible.
- Have boards and knives coloured for particular foods, for example red for meat, blue for fish, yellow for poultry (Figure 16.11).
- Take particular care in thorough reheating of made up dishes.

Bacteria are minute, single-celled organism which can only be seen under a microscope. They are everywhere in our surroundings, and as most bacteria cannot move by themselves they are transferred to something by coming into direct contact with it.

Some bacteria become spores which can withstand high temperatures for long periods of time (even six hours) and on return to favourable conditions revert to normal bacteria again which then multiply.

Some bacteria produce toxins outside their cells so that they mix with the food; the food itself is then poisonous and symptoms of food poisoning follow within a few hours (Figure 16.12, page 548).

Other bacteria cause food poisoning by virtue of large numbers of bacteria in food entering the digestive system, multiplying further and setting up an infection.

Certain bacteria produce toxins which are resistant to heat; foods in which this toxin has been produced may still cause illness, even though the food is heated to

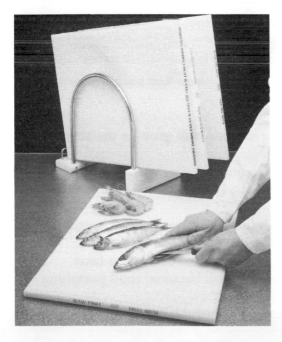

Fig. 16.11 Separate chopping boards for different foods will help to prevent cross-contamination

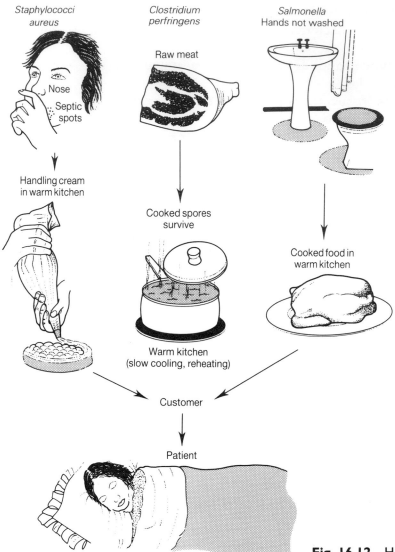

Staphylococci
aureus

Nose

Septic
spots

Handling cream
in warm kitchen

Clostridium
perfringens

Raw meat

Cooked spores
survive

Warm kitchen
(slow cooling, reheating)

Salmonella
Hands not washed

Cooked food in
warm kitchen

Customer

Patient

Fig. 16.12   How food poisoning may be caused

boiling-point and boiled for half an hour. Some bacteria will grow in the absence of air (anaerobes), others need it (aerobes).

Bacteria multiplying by dividing in two, under suitable conditions, once every 20 minutes. Therefore one bacterium could multiply in 10 to 12 hours to between 500 million and 1000 million bacteria.

Not all bacteria are harmful. Some are useful, such as those used in cheese production; some cause food spoilage, such as souring of milk.

Some bacteria which are conveyed by food cause diseases other than food poisoning, diseases known as food-borne diseases. With bacterial food poisoning the bacteria multiply in the food.

Typhoid and paratyphoid are diseases caused by harmful bacteria carried in food or water. Scarlet fever, tuberculosis and dysentery may be caused by drinking milk which has not been pasteurised.

The time between eating the contaminated food (ingestion) to the beginning of the symptoms of the illness (onset) depends on the type of bacteria which have caused the illness.

For the multiplication of bacteria certain conditions are necessary:

- food must be the right kind;
- temperature must be suitable;
- moisture must be adequate;
- time must pass.

Food

Most foods are easily contaminated; those less likely to cause food poisoning have a high concentration of vinegar, sugar or salt, or are preserved in some special way (see Chapter 5).

The following foods are particularly susceptible to the growth of bacteria because of their composition. Extra care must be taken to prevent them from being contaminated.

- stock, sauces, gravies, soups;
- meat and milk products (sausages, pies cold meats);
- milk and milk products;
- eggs and egg products;
- all foods which are handled;
- all foods which are reheated.

The bacterium *Campylobacter* causes symptoms similar to salmonella food poisoning and can be present in unpasteurised milk and undercooked chicken.

To prevent diseases being spread by food and water the following measures should be taken:

- Water supplies must be purified.
- Milk and milk products should be pasteurised.
- Carriers should be excluded from food preparation rooms.

Temperature

Food poisoning bacteria multiply rapidly at body temperature, 37°C (98.6°F). They grow between temperatures of 10°C (50°F) and 63°C (145°F). This is a similar heat to a badly ventilated kitchen and for this reason foods should not be kept in the kitchen. They should be kept in the larder or refrigerator. Lukewarm water is an ideal heat for bacteria to grow in. Washing-up must not take place in warm water as bacteria are not killed and the conditions are ideal for their growth, therefore pots and pans, crockery and cutlery may become contaminated. Hot water must be used for washing up.

Boiling water will kill bacteria in a few seconds, but to destroy toxins boiling for a half-hour is necessary. To kill the most heat-resistant spores, 4 to 5 hours' boiling is required. It is important to remember that it is necessary not only to heat foods to a sufficiently high temperature but also for a sufficient length of time to be sure of safe food. Extra care should be taken in warm weather to store foods at low temperatures and to reheat thoroughly foods which cannot be boiled.

Bacteria are not killed by cold although they do not multiply at very low temperatures; in a deep freeze they lie dormant for long periods (Figure 16.13). If foods have been contaminated before being made cold, on raising the temperature the bacteria will multiply. Foods which have been taken out of the refrigerator, kept in a warm kitchen and returned to the refrigerator for use later on may well be contaminated.

Moisture

Bacteria require moisture for growth – they cannot multiply on dry food. Ideal foods for their growth are jellies with meats, custards, creams, sauces, etc.

Time (Figures 16.14, 16.15)

Under ideal conditions one bacterium divides into two every 20 minutes; in six to seven hours millions of bacteria will have been produced. Small numbers of bacteria may have little effect, but in a comparatively short time sufficient numbers can be produced to cause food poisoning. Particular care therefore is required with foods stored overnight, especially if adequate refrigerated space is not available.

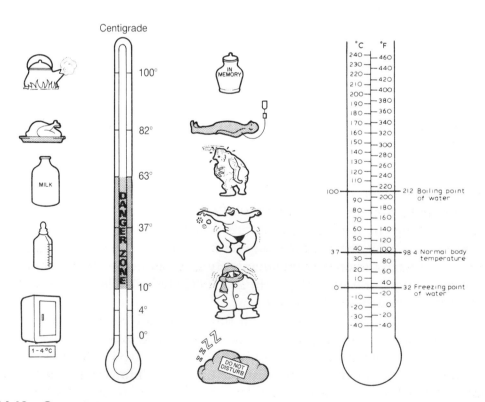

Fig. 16.13 Germometer

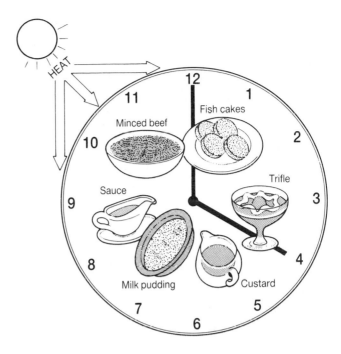

Fig. 16.14 Germs multiplying on moist foods in warm temperature over time

Types of food poisoning bacteria
The commonest food poisoning bacteria are:

- the salmonella group (causing food poisoning because of large numbers of bacteria in the food);
- *taphylococcus aureus* (causing food poisoning due to poison (toxin) production in the food);
- *Clostridium perfringens* (causing food poisoning due to large numbers of bacteria producing toxins in the intestines).

Salmonella group (Figures 16.16, 16.17)
These bacteria can be present in the intestines of animals or human beings; they are excreted and anything coming into contact directly or indirectly with the excreta may be contaminated (raw meat at the slaughter house or the unwashed hands of an infected person). Infected excreta from human beings or animals may contaminate rivers and water to be used for drinking purposes, although chlorination of water is very effective in killing harmful bacteria.

Salmonella infection is the result of human being or animals eating food contaminated by salmonella-infected excreta originating from human beings or animals, so completing a chain of infection. For example, when flies land on the excreta of a dog which has eaten infected dog-meat and the flies then go on to food, if that food is then left out in warm conditions for a time, the people who eat the contaminated food could well suffer from food poisoning.

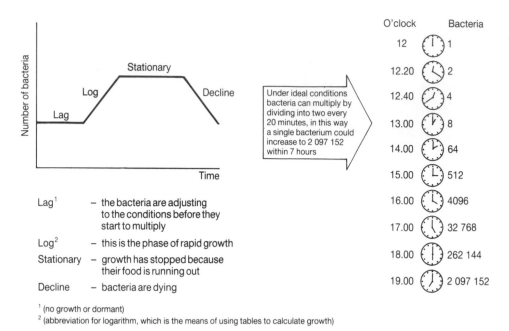

Lag¹   – the bacteria are adjusting
             to the conditions before they
             start to multiply

Log²   – this is the phase of rapid growth

Stationary – growth has stopped because
             their food is running out

Decline   – bacteria are dying

¹ (no growth or dormant)
² (abbreviation for logarithm, which is the means of using tables to calculate growth)

Fig. 16.15   Danger temperature at which germs can multiply

Food poisoning hits conference

Doctors attending a conference on diabetes at the weekend were struck down with food poisoning, believed to be salmonella.

Four hundred clinicians, nurses and health specialists had eaten cold meats, meat pies, seafood and salad at Friday lunchtime.

That evening two of the delegates were admitted to the casualty department with severe vomiting and diarrhoea. The next day a further 23 people with suspected salmonella poisoning were admitted to the hospital.

By Saturday evening 35 people had been seen, some at neighbouring hospitals and 80 people had reported symptoms of food poisoning.

VIPs food poison alert

More than 150 VIPs at two banquets in the city of London are suspected victims of food poisoning.

Salmonella is believed to be the cause and suspicion has centred on a cheese and egg savoury – Canape Roquefort – which was on both menus.

Fig. 16.16   Reports on *Salmonella* food poisoning

Foods most affected by the salmonella group are poultry, meat and eggs (rarely processed egg products or duck eggs, although some hens' eggs have been found to be infected with salmonellae). Contamination can be caused by:

* insects and vermin, because salmonellae are spread by droppings, feet, hairs, etc.;

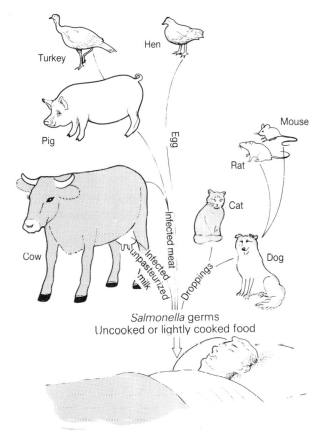

Fig. 16.17 Foods contaminated by Salmonella organisms if uncooked or lightly cooked may result In food poisoning

- the food itself (as, very occasionally, with duck eggs);
- cross-contamination (if a chicken is eviscerated on a board and the board is not properly cleaned before another food (such as cold meat) is cut on the board;
- the food infected by a human being who has the disease or who is a carrier (a person who does not suffer from food poisoning but who carries and passes on the germs to others).

Preparation of mayonnaise using raw eggs is a common practice but one which is fraught with danger. The problem is that raw eggs often contain salmonellae. To avoid the consequential high risk of food poisoning, the Department of Health (DoH) issued guidelines stating that unpasteurised eggs should not be used for preparing mayonnaise. Using raw egg products can be both unwise and costly. It is *not* illegal to use raw eggs to prepare mayonnaise, but the chances of food poisoning are high. In view of the DoH guidelines, a commercial kitchen using unpasteurised raw eggs would need to be able to show a sophisticated checking system to avoid the use of contaminated eggs and/or the use of some other factor (such as acidity) to control any food poisoning bacteria. Without being able to show these matters, it is

554 THE THEORY OF CATERING

difficult, if not impossible to rely upon a due diligence defence. The usual catering kitchen is very unlikely to have the equipment, skills and controls available to make these checks in order to satisfy the defence. The message for caterers is either to use bought-in commercially prepared mayonnaise, or to use pasteurised eggs. The alternatives are probably too expensive to contemplate.

Staphylococcus aureus

These germs are present on human hands and other parts of the skin, or sores, spots etc., and in the nose and throat.

Foods affected by *Staphylococcus aureus* include foods which have been handled because the hands have been infected from the nose or throat, cuts etc. Brawn, pressed beef, pies and custards are foods frequently contaminated (either by food-handlers or air-borne infection) because they are ideal for foods for the multiplication of the bacterium.

Clostridium perfringens

These bacteria are distributed from the intestines of humans and animals and are found in the soil.

Foods affected by *Clostridium perfringens* include raw meat which is the main source of these bacteria, the spores of which survive light cooking.

Clostridium botulinum is another type of bacterium which causes food poisoning, but it is rare in the UK.

Campylobacter bacteria are a common cause of diarrhoea in the UK. Large numbers are not required to cause illness (see page 549); poultry and meats are the main foods infected but adequate cooking will kill the bacteria.

Bacillus cereus is found in soil where vegetables and cereals, like rice, may grow. Long, moist storage of warm cooked food, especially rice, allows the spores to revert to bacteria which multiply and produce toxin.

Listeria bacteria are aerobic, non-sporing organisms which can cause serious food-borne disease, particularly in the elderly, the chronically sick or babies. These bacteria are found in soil, vegetables and animal feed. They are killed by correct cooking but grow at refrigeration temperatures and in mildly acidic conditions such as that found in soft cheeses where lactic acid is present.

There is particular concern over contamination of prepacked salads and chilled raw chicken. Although it is unlikely that a small number of organisms would cause any harm to healthy people, the bacteria can cause illness in vulnerable groups, infecting babies in the womb, elderly people and the sick.

Sources of infection

Food-poisoning bacteria live in:

- the soil;
- humans – intestines, nose, throat, skin, cuts, sores, spots etc.;
- animals, insects and birds – intestines and skin etc.

Prevention of food poisoning from bacteria

To prevent food poisoning everyone concerned with food must:

- prevent bacteria from multiplying;
- prevent bacteria from spreading from place to place.

This means harmful bacteria must be isolated, the chain of infection must be broken and conditions favourable to their growth eliminated. (The conditions favourable to their growth – heat, time, moisture and a suitable food on which to grow – are explained on pages 549–550). It is also necessary to prevent harmful bacteria being brought into premises or getting on to food. This is achieved by a high standard of hygiene of personnel, premises, equipment and food-handling.

KITCHEN HYGIENE

Infection can be spread by:

- humans: coughing, sneezing, by the hands;
- animals, insects, birds: droppings, hair etc;
- inanimate objects: towels, dishcloths, knives, boards.

Human

People who are feeling ill, suffering from vomiting, diarrhoea, sore throat or head cold must not handle food.

As soon as a person becomes aware that he or she is suffering from, or is a carrier, of typhoid or paratyphoid fever, or salmonella or staphylococcal infection likely to cause food poisoning or dysentery, the person responsible for the premises must be informed. He or she must then inform the Medical Officer for Health.

Standards of personal hygiene should be high at all times (see Personal cleanliness, page 534).

Animal (Figure 16.18)

Vermin, insects, domestic animals and birds can bring infection into food premises.

RATS AND MICE

Rats and mice are a dangerous source of food infection because they carry harmful bacteria on themselves and in their droppings. Rats infest sewers and drains and, since excreta is a main source of food-poisoning bacteria, it is therefore possible for any surface touched by rats to be contaminated.

Rats and mice frequent warm dark corners and are found in lift shafts, meter cupboards, lofts, opening in walls where pipes enter, under low shelves and on high shelves. They enter premises through any holes, defective drains, open doorways and in sacks of food-stuffs.

Signs to look for are droppings, smears, holes, runways, gnawing marks, grease marks on skirting boards and above pipes, clawmarks, damage to stock and also rat odour.

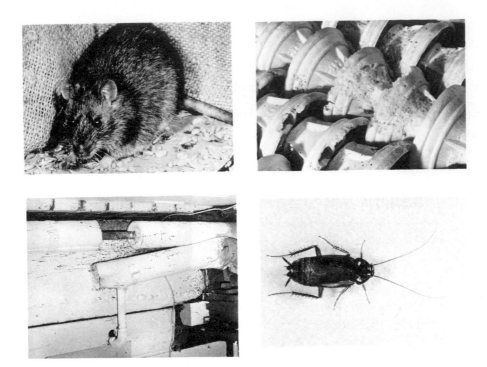

Fig. 16.18 Pests and the damage they cause

Rats spoil ten times as much food as they eat and there are at least as many rats as human beings. They are very prolific, averaging ten babies per litter and six litters per year, so that under ideal conditions it is theoretically possible for one pair of rats to increase to 350 million in three years. To prevent infestation from rats and mice the following measures should be taken:

- Food stocks should be moved and examined to see that no rats or mice have entered the store-room.
- No scraps of food should be left lying about.
- Dustbins and swill-bins should be covered with tight-fitting lids.
- No rubbish should be allowed to accumulate outside the building.
- Buildings must be kept in good repair.
- Premises must be kept clean.

If premises become infested with rats or mice the environmental health inspector or a pest control contractor should be contacted.

INSECT INFECTION
House flies (Figure 16.19) are the foremost of the insects which spread infection. Flies alight on filth and contaminate their legs, wings and bodies with harmful bacteria, and deposit these on the next object on which they settle; this may well be food. They also contaminate food with their excreta and saliva.

This is what happens when a fly lands on your food.

Flies can't eat solid food, so to soften it up they vomit on it.

Then they stamp the vomit in until it's a liquid, usually stamping in a few germs for good measure.

Then when it's good and runny they suck it all back again, probably dropping some excrement at the same time.

And then, when they've finished eating, it's your turn.

Fig. 16.19 Risk of food poisoning from flies

To control flies, the best way is to eliminate their breeding place, As they breed in rubbish and in warm, moist places, dustbins in summer are ideal breeding grounds; correct control and disposal of waste is paramount.

Waste material is a potential threat to food safety because it is a source of contamination which can provide food for the variety of pests (Figure 16.20, page 558).

Waste can be divided into five groups.

- **Dry non-food waste**. This comes mainly from packaging wood, cardboard, plastic some of which can be sorted for resale. Cardboard and paper can be compacted by a waste compactor machine.
- **Dry food waste**. This can either be a) disposed of at source in a waste disposal unit which grinds the waste into small particles, mixed with water and flushed into the drainage system or b) stored in galvanised steel bins with close fitting lids for disposal to swill collectors. The Disease of Animals (Waste Food) Order 1973 requires all swill collectors to be licensed by the local authority. The operator will arrange for cleaned and sterile bins to be delivered and collected on a regular basis.
- Unsavoury or offensive food waste. This should be disposed of immediately where possible using a waste disposal unit.
- Waste cooking oils and fats. Large quantities have a resale value, small quantities can be absorbed into dry food waste.
- Bulky waste. This can be disposed of by either a) incineration (only by using specific equipment or in isolated areas) or b) by compaction (Figure 16.21, page 559) the advantages of compaction are:
  - small, compact bulks easier to handle;
  - less accessibility to pests;
  - saving in refuse collection charges which are often charged by volume.

The refuse site should be a clean, easy to clean area with a water supply for washing down and adequate drainage. The site should be well lit and ventilated.

Fig. 16.20(a) Hygienic waste disposal   **(b)**   Unhygienic waste disposal

For general internal rubbish, plastic or paper lined bins which can be destroyed with the rubbish are preferable to other types of bin.

Other ways to control flies are to:

* screen windows to keep flies out of kitchens;
* install ultra-violet electrical fly-killers (Figure 16.22, page 560);
* use sprays to kill flies (only where there is no food);
* employ a pest control contractor.

Cockroaches like warm, moist, dark places. They leave their droppings and a liquid which gives off a nauseating odour. They can carry harmful bacteria on their bodies and deposit them on anything with which they come into contact.

Silverfish are small silver-coloured insects which feed on starchy foods (among other things) and are found on moist surfaces. They thrive in badly ventilated areas and improving ventilation will help to control them.

Fig. 16.21   A waste compactor will minimise the volume of rubbish

Beetles are found in warm places and can also carry harmful germs from place to place.

Insects are destroyed by using an insecticide, and it is usual to employ people familiar with this work. The British Pest Control Association has a list of member companies.

Cats and dogs

Domestic pets should not be permitted in kitchens or on food premises as they carry harmful bacteria on their coats and are not always clean in their habits. Cats also introduce fleas and should not be allowed to go in places where food is prepared.

Birds

Entry of birds through windows should be prevented as food and surfaces on which food is prepared may be contaminated by droppings.

Dust

Dust contains bacteria, therefore it should not be allowed to settle on food or surfaces used for food. Kitchen premises should be kept clean so that no dust can accumulate. Hands should be cleaned after handling dirty vegetables.

Washing up

The correct cleaning of all equipment used for the serving and cooking of food is of vital importance to prevent multiplication of bacteria. This cleaning may be divided into the pan wash (plonge) or scullery and the china wash-up.

Fig. 16.22   Electrical equipment to attract, kill and collect winged insects

SCULLERY

For the effective washing up of pots and pans and other kitchen equipment the following method of work should be observed:

- Pans should be scraped and all food particles placed in a bin.
- Hot pans should be allowed to cool before being plunged into water.
- Pans which have food stuck to them should be allowed to soak (pans used for starchy foods, such as porridge and potatoes, are best soaked in cold water).
- Frying-pans should be thoroughly wiped with a clean cloth; they should not be washed unless absolutely necessary.
- Trays and tins used for pastry work should be thoroughly cleaned with a clean dry cloth, while warm.
- Pots, pans and other equipment should be washed and cleaned with a stiff brush, steel wool or similar article, in hot detergent water.
- Pan scrubbers are electrically driven with a hydraulic or flexible drive transmission. Brush type heads can be varied to suit differing surfaces or types of soiling. Pan scrubbers can either be wall mounted near the pot wash or free standing mounted on mobile dollies to assist with equipment cleaning.
- The washing-up water must be changed frequently; it must be kept both clean and hot.
- The cleaned items should be rinsed in very hot clean water to sterilise.
- Pans which have been sterilised (minimum temperature 77°C (171°F)) dry quickly; if it has not been possible to rinse in very hot water they should be dried with a clean cloth.
- Equipment should be stored on clean racks, pans should be stacked upside down.

CHINA WASH-UP

The washing up of crockery and cutlery may be by hand or machine.

Handwashing

- Remove scraps from plates with a scraper or by hand.
- Wash in water containing a detergent as hot as the hands can bear (whether gloves are worn or not).
- Place utensils in wire baskets and immerse them into water thermostatically controlled at 77–82°C (171–180°F) for at least two minutes.
- The hot utensils will air-dry without the use of a drying cloth.
- Both the washing and sterilising water must be kept clean and at the correct temperature.

Machine washing-up

There are several types of machines which wash and sterilise crockery. In the more modern machines the detergent is automatically fed into the machine, which has continuous operation. To be effective the temperature of the water must be high enough to kill any harmful bacteria and the articles passing through the machine must be subjected to the water for sufficient time to enable the detergent water to cleanse all the items thoroughly. The detergent used must be of the correct amount and strength to be effective. Alternatively low temperature equipment is available which sterilises by means of a chemical, sodium hypochlorite (bleach).

Where brushes are used they must be kept free from food particles.

Further information can be obtained from Lever Industrial, Lever House, St James's Road, Kingston-upon-Thames, Surrey KT1 2BA.

Hygienic storage of foods

One of the most important ways to prevent contamination of food is the correct storage of food (see also Chapter 8). Foodstuffs of all kinds should be kept covered as much as possible to prevent infection from dust and flies. Foods should be kept in a refrigerated cold room or refrigerator where possible.

Hot foods which have to go into a refrigerator must be cooled quickly. This can be done in several ways: by dividing large quantities of food into smaller containers; by cooling in a draught of air using fans or by raising the container and placing an article underneath, for example, a triangle or weight, so that air can circulate; or by placing the container in a sink with running cold water. If large quantities of food, such as minced beef, are left in one container the outside cools but the centre is still warm. When reheated the time taken to bring such a large quantity to the boil is sufficient to allow the bacteria to continue to multiply. If the food is not boiled long enough food poisoning can occur (see the section on Temperature, page 549).

Particular care must be taken to store foods correctly in the warmer months; food not refrigerated in hot weather does not cool completely and, furthermore, flies and bluebottles are numerous in the summer. It is not by chance that the vast majority of food poisoning cases occur in the summer months in the UK.

Following consultations in 1993, the Government has announced proposals which will considerably simplify food storage temperature. The main features of the new proposals are:

- a general requirement to keep foods at temperatures which will not result in a risk to health;
- to store such foods at or below 8°C (46°F); there will be exemptions for foods where chill control is not necessary;
- flexibility for certain food businesses to store at higher temperatures where this can be justified by a safety assessment;
- a hot holding requirement of at least 63°C (145°F) for foods which could provide a risk to health;
- tolerances for limited periods outside the chill and hot holding controls.

The main differences from the existing regulations are the removal of the detailed list of foods subject to control. The current two-tiered chill controls of 5°C (41°F) and 8°C (46°F) will be replaced by the single 8°C (46°F) control. These relaxations will place much more responsibility on food businesses to be able to conduct effective risk analysis – proof of 'due diligence' will become even more important.

These proposals are likely to come into effect in July 1995, so anyone considering changing their refrigeration equipment should bear these proposals in mind. The relevant Code of Practice should be issued in October.

Foods requiring special attention (See also Food Hygiene Regulations 1990, page 564)

MEAT
- All made-up dishes, such as cottage pie, need extra care. They must be very thoroughly cooked.
- Reheated meat dishes must be thoroughly reheated.
- Pork must be well cooked (this is because pork may be affected by trichinosis, which is a disease caused by a minute roundworm).
- Poultry which is drawn in the kitchen should be cleaned carefully; boards, tables and knives must be thoroughly cleaned afterwards, otherwise there is a danger of contamination from excreta.
- Meat should be handled as little as possible. Minced and cut-up meats are more likely to become contaminated because of infection from the food-handler. Boned and rolled joints require extra care in cooking as inside surfaces may have been contaminated.
- Sausages should be cooked right through.
- Tinned hams are lightly cooked, therefore they must be stored in a refrigerator.

FISH
Fish is usually washed, cooked and eaten fresh and is not often a cause of food poisoning, except in reheated fish dishes. Care must be taken to reheat thoroughly such dishes as fish cakes, fish pie, coquilles de poisson, etc.

Some shellfish, such as oysters and mussels, have caused food poisoning because they have been bred in water which has been polluted by sewage. They are today purified before being sold. All shellfish should be used fresh. If you buy them alive, there is no doubt as to their freshness.

EGGS

Both hens' eggs and ducks' eggs have been implicated in causing food poisoning, and Department of Health guidelines now suggest that it would be prudent to avoid eating raw eggs or uncooked foods made from them, such as home-made mayonnaise, home-made mousses, etc. If dried eggs are used they should be reconstituted and used right away, not left in this condition in a warm kitchen as they may have been contaminated in or after processing. Bulk liquid egg undergoes pasteurisation but may be contaminated after the container is opened. Hollandaise sauce which is made with eggs is an example of a food which should not be kept in a warm kitchen for long. If not used in the morning it should not be used in the evening.

MILK DISHES

When used in custards, trifles and puddings unless eaten soon after preparation, milk should be treated with care. If required for the following day these dishes must be refrigerated.

WATERCRESS AND OTHER GREEN SALAD

Watercress must be thoroughly washed as it grows in water which could be contaminated by animals. All green salads and other foods eaten raw should be well washed.

SYNTHETIC CREAM

Synthetic cream can be a cause of food poisoning if allowed to remain in warm conditions for long periods. It is easily contaminated by handling and from the air. Particular care is required in the handling and holding at the correct temperature of soups, sauces and gravies because bacteria multiply rapidly in these foods.

REHEATED FOODS

In the interests of economy a sound knowledge of handling left-over food is necessary. Many tasty dishes can be prepared, but care must always be taken to see that the food is thoroughly and carefully reheated. If care is not taken then food poisoning can result (see page 548). Only sound food should be used ('if in doubt, throw it out').

After each meal service all unserved food should be cleared away in clean dishes, cooled quickly in the larder and placed in a cold room or refrigerator.

Interesting dishes can be made out of left-over meats, poultry, fish and certain vegetables by mixing them with foods such as rice, gherkins, tomatoes, chives, parsley, and a well-seasoned dressing such as mayonnaise or vinaigrette.

Trimmings and bones of meat, game and poultry can be used for stock. Trimmings of meat fat cooked or uncooked may by minced and rendered down for dripping.

- *Fish*: cooked kippers and haddock may be turned into savouries if freed from skin and bone, finely minced or pounded with anchovy essence and a little butter and used as a spread on toast.

  Cold fish may be used in many interesting dishes. For example:
  - curried fish
  - fish cakes
  - fish cutlets or croquettes
  - fish pie
  - fish kedgeree
  - fish salad
- *Vegetables*: cold left-over cooked vegetables, such as peas, cauliflower, haricot beans, potatoes, may be mixed with vinaigrette or mayonnaise and used for salads. Cold boiled potatoes can be used for potato salad or for sauté potatoes. Cold mashed potatoes may be used for fish cakes or potato cakes.
- *Meat*: left-over cooked items, such as bacon, ham, tongue, kidneys or liver, may be mixed with mince of any meat and used to give extra flavour to croquettes and rissoles.

  Cold meats can be used for a number of dishes. For example:
  - minced beef for cottage pie
  - minced lamb or mutton
  - Cornish pasties
  - salad
  - miroton of beef

  Left-over poultry, such as chicken, if cut into joints can be reheated carefully in a curry sauce.

  If the skin and bone are removed the poultry can be used for:
  - salad
  - mayonnaise
  - cutlets or croquettes
  - vol-au-vent or bouchées
- *Rice, spaghetti, macaroni* can be turned into mixtures for hors-d'œuvre with items such as chopped onion, chives, tomatoes, beetroot, cooked meat, haricot or French beans and a dressing of vinaigrette or mayonnaise.
- *Bread*: trimmings of crusts should be kept until dry, lightly browned in the oven, then passed through a mincer to make browned breadcrumbs (chapelure) which may be used for crumbling cutlets, croquettes of fish, etc.

  Stale bread can also be used for bread pudding. Stale sponge cake can be used for:
  - trifles
  - cabinet puddings
  - queen of puddings
- *Cheese*: left-overs of cheddar cheese can be grated or chopped and used for Welsh rarebit.

FOOD HYGIENE REGULATIONS

These regulations should be known and complied with by all people involved in the handling of food. A copy of the full regulations can be obtained from HMSO and an abstract can be obtained which gives the main points of the full regulations.

These points are as follows:

Equipment

This must be kept clean and in good condition.

Personal requirements

- All parts of the person liable to come into contact with food must be kept as clean as possible.
- All clothing must be kept as clean as possible.
- All cuts and abrasions must be covered with a waterproof dressing.
- Spitting is forbidden.
- Smoking is forbidden in a food room or where there is food.
- As soon as a person is aware that he is suffering from or is a carrier of such infections as typhoid, paratyphoid, dysentery, salmonella or staphylococcal infection he must notify his employer, who must notify the Medical Office of Health.

Requirements for food premises

TOILETS

- These must be clean, well lighted and ventilated.
- No food room shall contain or directly communicate with a toilet.
- A notice requesting people to wash their hands after using the toilet must be displayed in a prominent place.
- The ventilation of the soil drainage must not be in a food room.
- The water supply to a food room and toilet is only permitted through an efficient flushing cistern.

WASHING FACILITIES

- Hand basins and an adequate supply of hot water must be provided.
- Supplies of soap, nail-brushes and clean towels or warm air machines must be available by the hand basins.

OTHER FACILITIES

- *First Aid*: bandages and waterproof dressings must be provided in a readily accessible position.
- *Lockers*: enough lockers must be available for outdoor clothes.
- *Lighting and ventilation*: food rooms must be suitably lit and ventilated.
- *Sleeping room*: rooms in which food is prepared must not be slept in. Sleeping rooms must not be adjacent to a food room.
- *Refuse*: refuse must not be allowed to accumulate in a food room.
- *Buildings*: the structure of food rooms must be kept in good repair to enable them to be cleaned and to prevent entry of rats, mice, etc.
- *Food storage temperatures*: see pages 561–562.
- *Storage*: foods should not be placed in a yard lower than 0.5 m (18 in) unless properly protected.

PENALTIES

Any person guilty of an offence shall be liable to a heavy fine and/or a term of imprisonment. Under the latest Food Safety Act, unhygienic premises can be closed down by a local authority immediately, on the advice of the Environmental Health Officer.

The Environmental Health Officer when visiting premises will probably check for:

- grease in ventilation ducts and on canopies;
- long-standing dirt in less accessible areas;
- cracked or chipped equipment;
- provision for staff toilets and clothing;
- 'now wash your hands' notice;
- adequate and correct storage of food (cooked food stored above raw food if there is not separate refrigerated provision);
- correct storage temperature of foodstuffs;
- signs of pests and how they are prevented;
- any hazards;
- cleaning, training records and proper supervision.

CHECKLIST FOR CATERING ESTABLISHMENTS

- Entrances and exits unobstructed.
- Fire doors undamaged and in operating position.
- Escape routes clearly indicated.
- Fire-fighting equipment visible and accessible.
- Lighting good.
- Suitable supply of hot and cold water.
- Good ventilation.
- Separate hand-washing basin.
- Soap, nail-brush and towels by basin.
- Floors in good repair, clean and dry.
- Equipment operating correctly.
- Guards on machines.
- All surfaces undamaged and clean.
- Staff trained to use machines.
- Notice concerning use of machine close to it.
- Suitable protective clothing worn.
- Food, equipment and cleaning materials stored properly.
- Rubbish bins covered and emptied regularly.
- Staff work in accordance with safety guidelines.

FOOD HYGIENE (AMENDMENTS) REGULATION 1990/1991

These amendments specify the temperature controls for certain foods. They also apply to foods in transit and catering operations using mobile facilities.

- Certain foods should be kept at 8°C (46°F) or under.
- Certain foods should be kept at 5°C (41°F) or under.
- All hot food must be kept at above 63°C (115°F).
- Although chilling extends shelf-life of foods, high standards of hygiene and control of storage life is essential.
- Storage temperature of below 5°C (41°F) for all perishables should be achieved as quickly as possible.
- The regulations relate to the temperature of the food not to the air temperature of the chiller units or hot cupboards.
- To comply with the regulations regular and frequent checks must be made to monitor temperatures.

Practical implications

- On receipt of deliveries goods should be cooled to the proper temperature as soon as possible.
- To account for defrost cycle or breakdown of refrigeration an allowance of 2°C (3°F) is permitted.
- A maximum time of two hours for cold food preparation in the kitchen is tolerated provided there is no more than 2°C (3°F) rise above the 5°C (41°F) or 8°C (46°F) specified temperature.
- Food intended to be served hot at 63°C (115°F) or above can be held at a temperature below 63°C (115°F) but for no more than two hours.
- Exception is made for foods served warm (hollandaise sauce). They may be kept for no more than two hours and any remaining must be discarded.
- Foods intended to be served cold 5°C (41°F) or 8°C (46°F) may be held at a higher temperature but for no longer than four hours; it must then be brought back to 5°C (41°F) or 8°C (46°F).
- Displayed foods (sweet trolley, cheese board, self-service display, 'counter display with assisted service') need not be maintained at the required temperature provided displayed food is kept to a minimum and does not exceed four hours.

Exceptions for certain foods from temperature controls

- Sterilised canned foods are exempt, but cans that have only been pasteurised, such as large hams and some pâtés, should be kept below 5°C (41°F) and the label should specify chilled storage.
- Sandwiches kept for less than four hours require no temperature control. Sandwiches containing sirloin, salad, meat, eggs etc., are subject to relevant

control of 5°C (41°F) may be held at 8°C (46°F) or below so long as they are intended for sale within 24 hours.

- Cooked pies and pasties encased in pastry and having nothing added after cooking, such as gelatine, should be sold on day of production or day after, sausage rolls are exempt.
- Uncut egg, milk and pastry products (custard tarts) should be sold within 24 hours.
- Freshly baked cream cakes, quiches and similar flans may be damaged if put into chiller or directly after baking as moisture could affect the pastry. These items can be cooled slowly up to two hours before chilling then cooled quickly.

Foods to be kept at 5°C (41°F) or under

- Cut segments of ripened soft cheese.
- Hard and soft cheese in a cooked product to be eaten without further heating.
- Cooked products containing meat, fish, eggs (or their substitutes, cheese, cereals, pulses, vegetables)
  - intended to be eaten without further heating (canned meats and poultry once removed from can, cooked vegetable and cereal salads, meat and fish pâté, Scotch eggs, pork pies with gelatine added quiche, sandwich fillings);
  - smoked and cured fish;
  - smoked and cured meat;
  - salads containing items subject to 5°C (41°F) such as rice salad;
  - sandwiches and rolls containing ripe soft cheese, smoked or cured fish and meat and cooked products.

Foods to be kept at 8°C (46°F) or under

- Uncut whole ripe soft cheese (Brie, Danish blue, Stilton, Roquefort, Camembert, Dolcelatte) and the remaining part of the whole portion from which a segment has been cut.
- Hard and soft cheese included in a cooked item intended to be eaten without further heating.
- Cooked products where manufacturers instructions require reheating (pizzas, ready-made meals).
- Dairy-based desserts, including milk substitutes (fromage frais, mousses, cream caramels, whipped cream desserts with a pH value of 4.5 or more).
- Vegetable salads that are prepared (lettuce leaves, coleslaws, cut tomatoes and those containing fruit).
- Uncooked or partly cooked pastry and dough products containing meat or fish or their substitutes (fresh pasta with meat or fish filling).
- Sandwiches or rolls containing soft ripe cheese, smoked or canned fish or meat to be sold within 24 hours.
- Cream cakes containing both dairy or non-dairy cream.

An awareness of these regulations is essential, however due to their complexity; if in doubt, err on the side of safety and store at 5°C (41°F).

SUMMARY OF FOOD HYGIENE

Dangers to food

- Chemical (copper, lead, etc.).
- Plant (toadstools).
- Bacteria (cause of most cases of food poisoning).

Bacteria

- Almost everywhere; not all are harmful.
- Must be magnified 500–1000 times to be seen.
- Under ideal conditions, they multiply by dividing in two every 20 minutes.

Sources of food-poisoning bacteria.

- Human – nose, throat, excreta, spots, cuts, etc.
- Animal – excreta.
- Foodstuffs – meat, eggs, milk, from animal carriers.

Method of spread of bacteria

- Human – coughs, sneezes, hands.
- Animals – excreta (rats, mice, cows, pets, etc.), infected carcasses.
- Other means – equipment, china, towels.

Factors essential for bacterial growth

- Suitable temperature.
- Time.
- Enough moisture.
- Suitable food.

Methods of control of bacterial growth

- Heat – sterilisation, using high temperatures to kill all micro-organisms;
         – pasteurisation using lower temperatures to kill harmful bacteria only;
         – cooking.
- Cold – refrigeration at 3–5°C (37–41°F) stops growth of food poisoning bacteria and retards growth of other micro-organisms;
        – deep freeze at −18°C (0°F) stops growth of all micro-organisms.

Foods commonly causing food poisoning

- Poultry.
- Made-up meat dishes.

- Trifles, custards, synthetic cream.
- Sauces.
- Left-over foods.

Common causes of food poisoning

- Food prepared too far in advance.
- Storage at ambient temperature.
- Inadequate cooling.
- Inadequate reheating.
- Contamination processed food.
- Undercooking.
- Inadequate thawing.
- Cross-contamination.
- Improper warm holding.
- Infected food handlers.

Food poisoning prevention

- Comply with the rules of hygiene.
- Take care and thought.
- Ensure that high standards of cleanliness are applied to premises and equipment.
- Prevent accidents.

Specific points to be applied:

- High standards of personal hygiene.
- Attention to physical fitness.
- Maintaining good working conditions.
- Maintaining equipment in good repair and clean.
- Use separate equipment and knives for cooked and uncooked foods.
- Ample provision of cleaning facilities and equipment.
- Correct storage of foods at the right temperature.
- Safe reheating of foods.
- Quick cooking of foods prior to storage.
- Protection of foods from vermin and insects.
- Hygienic washing up procedure.
- Food handlers knowing how food poisoning is caused.

DEFINITION OF TERMS

Antibiotic	Drug used to destroy pathogenic bacteria within human or animals bodies.
Antiseptic	Substance that prevents the growth of bacteria and moulds, specifically on or in the human body.
Bactericide	Substance which destroys bacteria.

Carrier	Person who harbours, and may transmit, pathogenic organisms without showing signs of illness.
Cleaning	Removal of soil, food residues, dirt, grease and other objectionable matter.
Contamination	Occurrence of any objectionable matter in food.
Danger zone of bacterial growth	Temperature range within which multiplication of pathogenic bacteria is possible (from 10–63°C (50–145°F)).
First-aid materials	Suitable and sufficient bandages and dressings, including waterproof dressings and antiseptic. All dressings to be individually wrapped.
Food handling	Any operation in the production, preparation, processing, packaging, storage, transport, distribution and sale of food.
Gastroenteritis	Inflammation of the stomach and intestinal tract that normally results in diarrhoea.
Germicide	Agent used for killing micro-organisms.
Incubation period	Period between infection and the first signs of illness.
Mildew	Type of fungus similar to mould.
Moulds	Microscopic plants (fungi) that may appear as woolly patches on food.
Optimum	Best.
Pathogen	Disease-producing organism.
Pesticide	Chemical used to kill pests.
Residual insecticide	Long-lasting insecticide applied in such a way that it remains active for a considerable period of time.
Sanitiser	Chemical agent used for cleansing and disinfecting surfaces and equipment.
Spores	Resistant resting-phase of bacteria protecting them against adverse conditions, such as high temperatures.
Sterile	Free from all living organisms.
Sterilisation	Process that destroys all living organisms.
Steriliser	Chemical used to destroy all living organisms.
Toxins	Poisons produced by pathogens.
Viruses	Microscopic pathogens that multiply in living cells of their host.
Wholesome food	Sound food, fit for human consumption.

Further information

The Royal Society for the Promotion of Health, 13 Grosvenor Place, London SW1X 7EN.

Royal Institute of Public Health and Hygiene, 28 Portland Place, London W1N 4DE.

The Institution of Environmental Health Officers, Chadwick House, Rushworth Street, London SE1 0QT.

Local Environmental Health Departments.

Health and Safety Executive, Broad Lane, Sheffield, South Yorkshire S3 7HQ.

Health Education Authority, Hamilton House, Mabledon Place, London WC1H 9TX.

Health and Safety Executive, Regina House, Old Marylebone Road, London NW1.

Royal Society of Health, 38A St George's Drive, London SW1V 4BH.

Food Hygiene Bureau Ltd, Long Hanborough, Oxford OX8 8LH.

TOPICS FOR DISCUSSION

1. Discuss why hygiene is important and why it is necessary to have legislation and Environmental Health Officers to obtain safe hygiene in catering establishments.
2. Construct a list of any instances in your experience, or you have heard of, of unhygienic practices. Explain how you would control such happenings and prevent their reoccurrence.
3. Discuss where and by whom should hygiene be taught. Can you suggest ways to make the topic more relevant and interesting?
4. Why do you think food poisoning outbreaks occur? Discuss how do you think they could be prevented.
5. Kitchens are frequently and often constantly in use thus preventing problems of maintaining high standards of hygiene. Explain how you think this can be remedied.

17

Industrial relations

—

Effective relationships in industry depend upon:

* co-operation between employee and employer;
* knowing the laws passed by Parliament (legislation);
* having the right attitude towards those laws.

This brief introduction to industrial relations is intended to produce just such an attitude so that students and employees will work harmoniously and efficiently and thus obtain job satisfaction. Good industrial relations are created when employees and employers know both their responsibilities and their rights and use this knowledge to their mutual benefit and to the advantage of those they serve in the catering industry.

However, the nature of the catering industry means that good industrial relationships are not easy to create for the following reasons:

* labour turnover is often high;
* a vast majority of establishments are small;
* many employers take pride in the relationship they have with their employees and do not favour unions;
* few employees are union-minded;
* no one union is solely concerned with the industry;
* many employees are foreign and do not speak English;
* many establishments are seasonal and operate for only part of the year;
* many part-time workers are employed;
* unsocial hours are worked;
* the industry has a history of poor conditions, poor wages and low status.

LEGAL ASPECTS

A range of legislation since 1970, affecting employers and employees, has gradually been helping to improve the situation in the industry. This legislation includes:

* Equal Pay Act 1970;
* Trade Union & Labour Relations Act 1974;
* Sex Discrimination Act 1975;
* Employment Protection Act 1975;
* Race Relations Act 1976;
* Health and Safety at Work Act 1974.

Industrial tribunals

In order to administer and enforce the implementation of the Acts, industrial tribunals have been set up to settle disputes over unfair dismissal, redundancy and cases of alleged discrimination. The intention has been to protect the individual employee and to strengthen and encourage good relationships between employers and the trade unions.

Communications

In effect, communication channels between staff and management should exist with opportunities and facilities for trade union meetings so that employees have greater participation in the establishment's organisation. To be effective, communication often needs to be written and, by law, staff working 16 hours a week or more are entitled to a written statement of terms and conditions of employment. An example of such a statement can be seen in Figure 17.2.

Trade unions and the catering industry

Those employed in the catering industry who join trade unions mainly belong to the Transport and General Workers Union or the General and Municipal Workers Union. The primary aim of the unions is to look after the interests of their members

Fig. 17.1   Co-operation

```
Name of establishment
Address
Employee's name ........................... Address .........................................
Job title ...................................... .........................................
                                              .........................................
Date of commencement ................... Remuneration .................................
Terms & conditions of holidays and holiday pay
Sick pay arrangements
Pensions & pension schemes
Disciplinary rules
Grievance procedure
Previous service
Length of notice to terminate contract
Other specific conditions
```

Fig. 17.2 Example of written statement of terms and conditions of employment

at work, in particular, hours of work, conditions and pay. Their function is to negotiate on behalf of their members with the employers through their local officials. In the event of disagreement between the unions and the employers the Advisory Conciliation and Arbitration Service (ACAS) could be used.

For example, a shop steward in a kitchen should listen to any employee who is a member of the union if he or she has a grievance which seems justified. On their behalf the shop steward could approach the chef or catering manager to resolve the issue. The shop steward may obtain the advice of the branch or district union officer before taking up the case. The role of the trade union is to look after members' interests and this includes the smooth running of a hygienic and safe kitchen.

Women in employment

A female employee who is pregnant and who has been working for a stated period of time for the same employer may not be dismissed because of her pregnancy unless her condition makes it impossible to work competently. An employee who leaves work to have a baby is entitled to her job back after the baby is born, provided she has the required minimum service, has continued to work up to the specified time before confinement and, before her absence, informs her employer of her intention to return. Maternity pay is paid to employees complying with the stated conditions.

Details are obtainable from the Department of Social Security and Citizens Advice Bureaux.

Equal Pay Act 1970

This Act specifies that pay must be the same for men and for women doing like work or work that is graded as similar. For example, a man or a woman employed to wash-up are both, by law, entitled to the same pay. This would also apply if a female chef de partie for the pastry was employed; the pay would be the same as for a male chef de partie of equal competence and experience.

Sex Discrimination Act 1975

Within the terms of this Act it is unlawful to discriminate on the grounds of a person being male or female, or being married when selection, appointment, transfer, dismissal or promotion are being considered. This means that both men and women should be assessed and decisions made according to their ability, competence, reliability, and not according to gender. For example, if a kitchen supervisor and a storekeeper are required, both positions should be available to men and women; it is against the law to restrict the posts to male or to female applicants.

Race Relations Act 1976

This Act makes it illegal to discriminate against a person because of their race. However, factors which could affect employment issues relate, for example, to language and religion. The potential waiter, unable to make himself understood or to understand the language of the customers, or the cook whose religion restricts the handling of certain foods, may well jeopardise the opportunity for obtaining and keeping employment, but a person cannot be discriminated against solely because of their race.

Employment Protection Act 1975

The purpose of this Act is to prevent the unfair dismissal of a member of staff. It is essential to know what are considered to be fair reasons for dismissal of staff as well as some reasons considered to be unfair.

Fair reasons for dismissal could include:

- incompetence – lack of skill, lack of technical or academic qualifications;
- misconduct – stealing or flagrant breach of hygiene rules;
- illegality – a foreign worker without a work permit;
- genuine redundancy.

Unfair dismissal would include:

- for being a member of, or proposing to join, a trade union;
- unfair selection for redundancy.

GLOSSARY

The following is a list of some of the terms used in negotiations and committees:

Abstain	Voting neither for nor against, effectively not voting.
Abstention	This is a vote which is cast neither for nor against.
Address the Chair	When speaking at a meeting members must speak to the Chair and not to other members.
Ad hoc committee	A committee formed to do a specific job which ceases to exist when this special work is complete.
Adjourn	When the meeting or part of the business is delayed until later.
Against	A vote in disagreement with the motion.
Agenda	The list of items to be discussed by the committee.
AGM	Annual General Meeting
Amendment	This is a proposition to change the wording of a motion. The

amendment needs a proposer and a seconder; it is then put to the vote and if carried (has a majority vote for it), the motion as amended replaces its original form. If the amendment is defeated then the original motion stands. More than one amendment can be put forward; each is discussed separately and then voted on in the order received.

AOB	Any other business. Usually the last item on the agenda for the matters not included on the agenda. Should be used as little as possible since matters need to be considered before discussion.
Arbitration	When, in a dispute, agreement cannot be reached and the decision of an independent person or persons is accepted.
Chair, Chairman or Madam Chairman	The person conducting the meeting.
Check-off	Union dues deducted by the employer who then pays the dues to the union.
Closed shop	This is the situation where individuals must be a member of the same union to which the other workers belong, or when new employees must join the union. The agreement of both the employer and the trade union is required to operate a closed shop.
Collective agreement	Agreements made between several trade unions and several employers or employer's associations.
Collective bargaining	Negotiations to result in collective agreement regarding conditions of work, allocation of work, discipline, facilities for trade union officials and procedures for consultation.
Consensus	The general feeling of the meeting.
Conciliation	A process whereby an outside party brings opposing parties in dispute together to settle the dispute.
Constitution	A formal document which states the aims of the organisation, its membership and how it should be managed.
Co-opted member	A person invited to join a committee by its members because of special assistance he or she can bring to the committee.
Correction of minutes	When minutes of the previous meeting are due to be signed as a correct record it is sometimes found necessary to correct them if the meeting agrees to the correction.
Defeated	Said of a motion which has been voted on and decided against.
Delegate	A person authorised by a committee or organisation to represent it on its behalf.
Ex officio	Means 'because of his or her office' for example the Chair of an organisation is usually a member (ex officio) of all its committees because of being the Chair.
For	A vote in favour of the motion.
Job evaluation	A term used to determine the value of jobs in a way acceptable to those in the job.
Joint consultation	When employees and employers discuss before decisions are taken.
Legislation	The law, having legal authority.
Lobby	Recognised way of persuading people to support an idea.
Lost	Said of a motion when it has been voted and decided against.
Minutes	The written record of a committee's decisions. All resolutions, amendments, and decisions, including votes, must be recorded. Discussions may be summarised.

Motion	A statement which will be discussed and then may be put to the vote.
Move	The proposer of a motion is said 'to move it' when he or she asks that it be put to the vote.
Nem con	'No one against'. A motion is passed 'nem con' when some vote for, none against, but some abstain.
Nomination	The giving of the name of a person for office or to be a member of a committee.
Out of order	Not conforming to the rules of procedure or the proper conduct of the meeting.
Point of order	When a member requests the Chair to correct or bring the running of the meeting to comply with the Rules of Procedure.
Proposer	The principal speaker for the motion.
Proxy	A person given authority to exercise a member's vote, to vote instead of that member.
Quorum	The minimum number of members required to be present for business. The number should be stated in the Rules of Procedure. If insufficient members attend then the situation is described as inquorate.
Resolution	The actual wording of a motion.
Ruling	The Chair's decision on a matter of procedure which must be followed without discussion.
Shop steward	The trade union member elected by the department or section he or she represents. He or she communicates management proposals to his or her colleagues and represents their views to management.
Status quo	If a change causes a dispute then the original situation is reverted to until agreement is reached.
Seconder	The next person to support a motion following the proposer.
Substantive agreement	An agreement which determines, for example, rates of pay, hours of work, holiday arrangements.
Trade dispute	A dispute between employers and employees or between employees and employees.
Unanimous	When all members present vote for the motion.

TOPICS FOR DISCUSSION

1. Discuss why persons employed in the catering industry may need to know about legislation.
2. Why are good relations between employer and employee important? Who benefits from this?
3. Discuss what legislation you think would improve the industry. Explain why.

18

Guide to study and employment

To be successful today in the catering industry, it is best to obtain qualifications. These qualifications indicate a level of achievement which may be reached at the place of work or in an educational establishment. A variety of ways are used to measure ability and competence. However, it should be remembered that in the catering industry successful people are those who not only achieve the required techniques and knowledge but those who have the right attitude to others. Such qualities as reliability, conscientiousness, willingness, co-operativeness, integrity, loyalty, punctuality and courtesy should be developed. A good employee can in time become supervisor and then employer.

Most people enter the catering industry because of its appeal, practical aspects and/or involvement with people. A successful career in catering demands a responsibility to oneself, hard work and consistent study. It is necessary, however, to know how to cope with the various assessment techniques used. Therefore, some suggestions follow which may give guidance to students and other persons entering or already employed in the industry.

SUCCESSFUL STUDYING

Catering is a very practical occupation; nevertheless there is a considerable amount of study needed for the learning of the theoretical aspects of catering courses and the following comments may be of assistance:

- Learning requires effort and hard work, but thorough preparation gives confidence.
- Studying in a quiet place, such as the local library's reading room, is effective for most people and can give the best results.
- Studying is more efficient when students are not tired.
- The careful rewriting of lesson notes aids learning.
- Do not leave revision until too near the examination but revise throughout the course, because spaced-out learning is more effective than 'cramming'.
- Study consistently throughout the course.
- Organise regular times for both study and revision.
- Practice in answering previous examination questions can be useful at appropriate stages of the course.

Most students and candidates need to know how they are progressing on the course of study, both in relation to other members of the course and the standards required of the course. This information is obtained from teachers and various methods of evaluating students and candidates are used. It is essential that students and candidates are made aware that they are working in the best manner to reach the required standard. Guidance is needed so this is achieved.

What to study

The syllabus of most catering courses is written in objective competence terms, which enables the student to know precisely what should be known and what they should be able to do at the end of the course. An advantage of having the course content expressed in this way means that the student and the teacher are both aware of the depth and breadth to which the course will be examined. Towards the end of the course students should check the syllabus for any omissions in their knowledge; the sensible student then accepts responsibility to remedy any gaps by further study and revision. NVQs and other assessment procedures are programmes specifying what should be done and known.

EVALUATION PROCEDURES

Students or candidates are subjected to various techniques designed to assess what has been learned and therefore it is helpful to consider those methods in which catering students will be involved, although all students will not necessarily use all the methods. They include the evaluation of theoretical aspects by written or oral methods:

- subjective-type examination (brief answer and essay type);
- objective-type examination;
- continuous assessment;
- oral questioning.

It is essential for students to understand that, although the theoretical and practical aspects of the course may be assessed separately, theory and practice cannot be separated, because the understanding of the theory is necessary for achieving good results in the practical situation.

Continuous assessment

One purpose of continuous assessment is to enable students to know how they are progressing during the course; this is achieved by periodic evaluations or assessments. The advantage of this system is that a person does not fail on one particular occasion as could occur with a single examination. Furthermore the student and the teacher can become aware of weaknesses early in the course and steps can be taken to remedy them.

Continuous assessment of theory work

Some students or candidates may be expected to present work throughout the course in place of, or as well as, an examination. This work may include homework, work completed in the class or projects and the marks awarded for these can be used in place of an examination mark. Again the student or candidate benefits from this system: if the student is away or unwell on the day of an examination, for example, this can cause a problem, but with work spread over the course this problem does not occur. The NVQ system uses this method.

Oral questioning

To assess a candidate's knowledge and understanding of the practical applications, questions may be asked and answered by word of mouth. The student or candidate must be able to hear the question clearly, be allowed a sensible amount of time to produce an answer and the question must not be ambiguous. If the question is not clear to the candidate, the candidate should courteously say that the question has not been understood. It should then be rephrased in a different way.

Difficulties may arise due to dialect, foreign pronunciation, language difficulties, such as speech or hearing defects.

The candidate is advised not to 'waffle', to answer the question to the point and where appropriate, to use technical words and terms correctly.

Theory examinations

The object of a theory examination is to find out if the candidate knows the answers. The students have to convey to the examiner the required answers and this may be done by objective-type questions (short answer) or subjective-type questions, which may range from a brief answer to a short essay or the use of both.

OBJECTIVE-TYPE QUESTIONS

When objective-type questions are asked it cannot be too strongly emphasised that students or candidates read the question *carefully*, decide which is correct, then mark the paper accordingly. If the student is not sure of the answer it is wise to proceed to the next question. Having considered all the questions in this way, the student can then carefully re-read the questions which have not been answered and mark the paper in the appropriate box.

For most students or candidates it will be unwise to review the questions they have answered straightaway (provided the question has been carefully read); this is because with multiple-choice questions the distractors should be plausible and doubts might come into the student's mind.

Finally, more than adequate time is allowed for objective-type examinations; since time is not a limiting factor there is no urgency to complete the paper quickly – accuracy is the key to success.

Examples of objective-type questions can be found in *NVQ/SVQ Workbooks (Levels 2 and 3): Food Preparation and Cooking* and *Questions and Answers on Theory of Catering* (all published by Hodder & Stoughton Educational).

SUBJECTIVE-TYPE QUESTIONS

As with objective-type questions it is essential that care is taken when reading the question. With essay-type questions it is also necessary to take care in producing the answer and the following points should be considered.

- **Writing** must be readable. The easier it is to read, the more favourable is the impression given of the student's paper.
- **Spelling:** the facts are what the examiner wants, but if there are many words spelt wrongly an unfavourable impression is given. French words should be correct. It is better to use correctly spelt English words than mis-spelt French words. Extra care must be taken not to mis-spell words which are similar in French and English, (filet and fillet, carotte and carrot). Simple words are often spelt wrongly, such as gravy, plaice, gherkin, lettuce etc.
- **Answering questions:**
  - The meaning of the answer must be clear to the examiner.
  - The question should be understood and answered to the point.
  - The answer should be precise, with no padding.
  - No essential facts should be omitted from the answer.
  - All parts of a question should be answered.
  - Avoid using first person singular ('Braising is a nice method of cooking, but I like fried steak').
  - Avoid slang expressions and terms, which are not good English.
  - Avoid vagueness and inaccurate phrases ('spot of water').
  - Use correct terms and words (sugar is not *diluted*, but dissolved); gelignite does not go into bavarois!
  - Use accepted abbreviations for weight and measures, but avoid marge, veg, fridge.
  - Answer only the number of questions asked for. No extra marks will be gained if more are answered, but be certain to answer the required number of questions.
  - Answer questions in any order, but number them clearly.
  - Re-read the answers carefully when the paper is completed.
- **Layout:** a paper laid out clearly creates a favourable impression. The following points may be helpful:
  - Leave a generous margin.
  - Tabulate answer where suitable.
  - If an essay form answer is necessary give an introduction and have a good concluding paragraph.
  - Name the recipe, underline the heading.
  - Where diagrams can be used these should be drawn carefully.
- **Summary:** it is necessary to know the facts and to present them clearly. The writing must be legible, the English and spelling correct, the layout neat and the information to the point.

Projects and portfolios of evidence

Projects are usually devised to assess the candidate's ability to obtain information through research into written material and/or through persons having experience and knowledge in the appropriate area, or by observation of a situation so as to produce a worthwhile project. It is necessary to know clearly what is required and an indication of how it will be evaluated. Therefore, if a recommendation or conclusion is expected this should be made clear at the outset. Guidance must be given on how and what is to be included in the presentation of the project and how aspects of the projects will be assessed. It is important that the completed work is of sufficient length to cover the topic competently but not extended beyond the scope required.

Candidates or students must know if diagrams, photographs or examples are required and the format of presentation. If this information is not clear then candidates or students should obtain clarification before commencing the project.

If requests for information are made to people in the industry, always enclose a stamped addressed envelope and remember that it must be courteously written, the information required is brief and to the point and if in the form of a questionnaire, that it is clear, concise and not long.

If you are dealing with interviewing people at work, bear in mind that they are busy people; therefore, be prepared to be as brief as reasonably possible, be courteous and make certain that their help is appreciated.

National Vocational Qualifications

This system of assessment known as NVQ, or as SVQ in Scotland, is intended to appraise the candidate's or student's competence in a practical situation and his or her knowledge and understanding of the work being done, known as underpinning knowledge. There are four levels of qualification

- Level 1   Operative
- Level 2   Craft
- Level 3   Supervisory/advanced craft
- Level 4   Junior/mid-management

These levels are constructed in units which are divided into elements. A unit covers an area of work. For example, in cook and prepare fish dishes, the elements for this unit are: Prepare fish dishes and cook fish dishes. This unit is part of level 2. Each unit and each element has a number. Prepare and cook fish dishes is unit 2D2. Element 2D2.1 is Prepare fish for cooking and element 2D2.2 is Cook fish dishes.

The Assessor evaluates the candidate's performance in a practical situation, where possible in a working environment, and supplements the assessment by oral and/or written questions to assess the candidate's knowledge and understanding of each element.

In most cases the Assessor will be the lecturer in the college or supervisor at the place of work. The assessment is made according to the standards defined in the Units and may take into account a candidate's previous experience and achievement. This is known as Accreditation of Prior Learning (APL).

A record of all aspects of the assessment is kept, thus providing proof or evidence of achievement. This record is known as the Evidence Diary. It is essential that this record is kept so that candidates and assessors have in writing an accurate record of activities and achievement.

Progression is possible through the levels; having satisfactorily completed one level the candidate can proceed to the next if desired.

Examination advice

Hints on examinations

A problem which has to be faced by many people is nerves: these may only be controlled to a certain degree according to each individual. Confidence in one's own ability helps, and this confidence comes from knowledge; provided candidates have done their utmost to learn, there need be no excessive nervousness.

Preparation for examinations
- Revise throughout the course, but in addition revise the whole course prior to the examination.
- Determine when revision is most effective for you; some people prefer early morning, others late evening.
- Near the examination, practise answering past examination questions in the same time allowed as in the actual examination.
- Do not rely only on past examination questions.

Examination day prior to the examination
- Allow plenty of time so as to arrive punctually.
- Have an adequate number of pens.
- If you wish to chew sweets, select those without wrappings so that you do not disturb others.
- Most examinations occur in the summer, therefore wear suitable clothes.

The examination

If there is a choice of questions then take extra care reading them so that you fully understand the question; you can then select those you can answer best.

Most candidates' nerves disappear as soon as they start writing in the theory examinations. Some people, however, find their minds go blank; in this case it may help to concentrate on one small part of the question, particularly questions on practical cookery. The student who may not have learnt a particular recipe by heart can often, by thinking hard of the practical preparation, arrive at a sufficiently sound answer to satisfy the examiner.

Obtaining employment and building a career

With the decision made to come into catering, it is to be hoped that prior to or during the course students will have worked in the industry and have seen the different types of work available. If possible, try to obtain experience in a variety of different establishments (hotels, hospitals, industrial, restaurants). You may find that you wish to specialise in the pastry, for instance, or that to work in a hospital appeals to you. People do best that which interests them most, so try to find out what appeals to you.

Points to consider prior to obtaining employment

- Keep an accurate record of all employment, including part-time and college-sponsored work.
- Keep all certificates together in a safe place.
- Maintain an accurate record of all education received.
- Prepare a curriculum vitae (CV) (a comprehensive and correct account of yourself and your achievements) to include:
  - date of birth;
  - address;
  - educational establishments attended, both school and college, full-time and part-time, with dates;
  - educational achievements, not only academic but also sporting, musical etc.;
  - employment, stating period of time worked, and how employed;
  - interests, youth clubs, Scouts, Guides, boys' or girls' brigades etc., first aid, sports, community work, travel, music, reading; any awards, such as Duke of Edinburgh's, Queen's Guide or Queen's Scout, first-aid certificates, should be mentioned.
- Ask two people to act as referees for you and to be prepared to provide references if required by potential employers. These referees are not to be relatives, but two people who know you from different situations (minister of religion, youth leader, former employer, as well as college tutor). Not all employers require or take up references but it is courteous to inform anyone who is prepared to give a reference that you have applied for a job, in case the reference is requested. This is particularly important as your career progresses.
- Keep up to date with job vacancy advertisements; use libraries for journals and periodicals containing this information.
- Attend student careers conventions.
- Write to companies for details of their career and employment information.
- Discuss your interests with teaching staff and obtain their advice.
- Develop the attitudes and qualities required to make you a good prospect for an employer ('employable'); for example, that you are willing to:
  - work and learn, and to improve and progress;
  - accept constructive criticism;
  - work with others (porters as well as the chef de partie);
  - be co-operative, courteous, reliable, punctual, loyal, honest, hardworking and cheerful;
  - be confident and flexible.

How to obtain employment

- Direct contact:
  - many colleges receive requests for staff from employers (jobs may be

displayed on a noticeboard);
- some college staff have personal contact with catering establishments and vacancies;
- through part-time employment and/or college placements in industry;
- through friends and relatives, and former students who have contacts in the industry.

- Answering advertisements: vacancies are advertised in national and local newspapers and in magazines and periodicals. Use public and college libraries to obtain access to these publications.
- Using agencies: Jobcentres and private employment agencies are important sources of job vacancies. The Services have their own recruitment offices.

Preparing for an interview

First read the advertisement carefully and if it seems a suitable job then find out about the establishment before applying for the job. If possible speak to someone employed there, but remember that their comments will be subjective.

Consider the following points:

- When writing for an application form, use handwriting.
- Complete the application form accurately and neatly, and have it typed if possible.
- On no account give any false information.
- If names of referees are required, inform the referees that you have applied for the job, having previously obtained their permission.
- If a photo is required, send a recent head and shoulders passport-type photo.
- If your CV is required send a photocopy of it.

Going for an interview

- Prepare in advance any questions you may wish to ask.
- Have any certificates available in case they are required.
- Make certain you know where the interview is taking place, how to get there and how long it takes.
- Leave extra time so that should there be delays because of traffic or transport problems you arrive on time.
- Take with you the letter stating the address and phone number of where the interview is to be held, so that if you are delayed then you can phone and explain the situation.
- Dress neatly and cleanly.
- Avoid excessive jewellery and make up.
- Remember that clean hands and finger nails are essential.

At the interview

- Be reasonably confident but not overconfident.
- You may be nervous, but this is to be expected. (It may not show.)

- When seated, sit up and do not lounge.
- If you normally smoke – *don't*.
- A natural smile, not a grin, is helpful.
- Speak up when answering questions and keep to the point.
- You should be given the opportunity to ask questions at the end of the interview; if this has not happened then say you wish to ask a question(s).
- Do not be surprised if you are asked about what you hope to do in the future – you need to have thought this out before the interview and have some idea of what to say.

After the interview

- If you get the job: congratulations!
- If you do not, then consider how the experience was worthwhile.
- Evaluate why you did not get the job:
  - were other applicants more suitable?
  - did your interview go badly, for example, because you were too nervous, did not know the answers, felt unwell, did not like the interviewer;
  - perhaps you did not suit the employer's needs, etc.?
- Remedy any shortcomings you discover in yourself.
- Apply again for other jobs until you succeed.

Building a career

Having got on the ladder, you need to consider the following points when trying to get up it:

- Do not get off one ladder until you have got onto another one; in other words make certain you have a job to go to before leaving present employment.
- It is generally advisable to stay with your first employer for at least one year, and to spend at least a year in subsequent jobs.
- It is desirable to keep in continuous employment; gaps do not present employers with a view of a stable employee.
- Advancement is more likely if you keep within one area of catering (contract, hospital, restaurants) so that experience gained can be of benefit to employers.
- However, some careers, such as teaching, need people experienced in several aspects of the industry.
- Know where you are going and have attainable goals. However, if a real mistake has been made and a move has been wrong then a change may be for the best.

In evaluating the need to progress, these factors need to be considered apart from the money: value of new experience, establishment's reputation, conditions and hours of work, opportunities for advancing in existing establishment, facilities offered for self-development, such as further courses, overseas experience, etc.

If possible, when leaving college or any employment, endeavour to leave in such a way that you can return at any time. The catering industry needs people who are prepared to work hard, to enjoy their work and to work together as a team.

COMPETITIONS

The nature and composition of the catering industry is such that it lends itself to a variety of competitions in which participation can be interesting, stimulating and rewarding.

Potential benefits include:

- useful experience:
- opportunity to show one's capabilities;
- opportunities to see other people's work and by making comparisons possibly improve one's own standards;
- opportunity to learn;
- improvement of self-confidence;
- opportunity to gain awards which can make a useful addition to a CV.

Preparation

1. Once a decision is made to enter a competition, then develop an attitude of mind and effort to win.
2. Read the rules carefully, noting any queries, after 24 hours re-read and again a third time at least. Many competitors fail or spoil entries by not having carefully read, understood and abided by the rules. If in doubt consult the competition organisers.
3. Practise and rehearse as much as possible and endeavour to find someone knowledgable to give critical comment and advise.

Examples of competitions

COOKERY: SINGLE DISHES

Practice is essential if you are to be successful until you are satisfied with your results. On the day, your appearance, attitude and a neat, clean and orderly method of work will be noted favourably by the judges. Present your dish on time, hot (if required); check seasonings carefully and ensure that the dish is clean and has eye appeal. Concentrate on balancing the ingredients; avoid excessive use of overpowering flavours. Portion control must be skilfully executed. After the competition endeavour to get a critique from the judges.

MANAGEMENT

Competitions which require management thinking and proposed action can be most stimulating and helpful. Examples range from fairly elementary management problems to producing business plans for specific operations, such as setting up a wine bar, a fast-food operation, a restaurant or a hotel.

QUIZZES

These are a versatile form of competition as they can be set at any level and can be simple or complex. Preparing to participate in a quiz is a good incentive to study; quizzes can make popular and interesting events for spectators and they can help develop team spirit within groups.

COOKERY: MENU

Choose your menu carefully taking into account all the points of pages 261–262. Ideally the menu should be prepared, cooked and served on more than one occasion (prior to the competition) to a critical number of guests who will offer their opinion. Rehearsing will also help to get the timing right on the day.

COOKERY AND WINE

These competitions require skill and knowledge of balancing food with suitable wines. Either a menu can be produced and wines chosen to accompany, or, the wines selected and a suitable menu chosen so that a happy marriage of wine and food results. This type of competition is usually offered to a partnership of chef/wine waiter and it is essential in the preparation that both partners are satisfied with the combination of food and wine, not only at each course but overall. The serving of the meal with the wines to a critical panel in advance of the competition can be very helpful. Assessment by the judges who will usually be sat at table and served, will usually include not only the quality of the food and how it has been complemented with the wines, but also the quality of both the food and wine service. Always endeavour to obtain a critique from the judges.

WINE

Wine competitions vary and can include:

* displaying a knowledge of wines both theoretically and by tasting;
* skill in preparing various bottles of wine for service opening, decanting, tasting etc.;
* suggesting certain foods that complement certain wines.

PLANNING

These can include, for example, planning of kitchens, for differing operations of various sizes; planning lay-outs for various types of restaurants and food service outlets; planning of various types of catering facilities.

This type of competition may be offered to individuals or teams but in either case it is advisable to engage in theoretical and practical research and gain as much information as possible before drafting any plans. Then a preliminary plan can be drawn and criticism and comment sought from suitable experienced people before the final planning draft for the competition, is completed.

Index

Italicised numbers denote figures and plates

woodpigeon *59*, 91
Worcester Pearmain apples 126
Worcestershire sauce 46, 192
work flow 365
work place 29, 33
Work Place (Health, Safety and
    Welfare) Regulations (1992)
    510
working methods 362–7
wort 175
wrasse *70*, 103

yakitori 53
yams 51, 111–12
yeast 162–3, 175, 205, 213, 220
    beer making 174
    dried foods 223
    ethnic influences 46, 48
    malt vinegar 184
    and sugar 163
    and wine making 173–4
yellow colouring 185
yellow courgette *81*

yellow pepper *81*
yin yang 53
yogurt 137, 141
yolks, egg 130, 134, 205, 208, 213,
    215, 234
York ham 70
Yorkshire pudding 46, 65

zinc deficiency 29